Consumer Perception of Product Risks and Benefits

Gerard Emilien • Rolf Weitkunat • Frank Lüdicke
Editors

Consumer Perception of Product Risks and Benefits

 Springer

Editors
Gerard Emilien
Clinique du Nord
Port Louis, Mauritius

Rolf Weitkunat
Philip Morris Products S.A
Neuchâtel, Switzerland

Frank Lüdicke
Philip Morris Products S.A
Neuchâtel, Switzerland

ISBN 978-3-319-50528-2   ISBN 978-3-319-50530-5   (eBook)
DOI 10.1007/978-3-319-50530-5

Library of Congress Control Number: 2017934508

Printed on acid-free paper

This Springer imprint is published by Springer Nature
The registered company is Springer International Publishing AG
The registered company address is: Gewerbestrasse 11, 6330 Cham, Switzerland

Foreword

Consumer products are extraordinarily diverse, as are the consumers who might accept or reject, use or misuse them. As a result, ensuring informed consumer decision-making requires the full range of expertise assembled in this encompassing volume. In the language of decision science,[1] that expertise includes capabilities in *analysis*, of the risks and benefits that products might bring; *descriptive* research, regarding consumers' intuitive understanding of those outcomes; and *interventions*, designed to inform those intuitions, so that consumers can make sound choices and producers can meet their needs.

Consumer Perception of Product Risks and Benefits summarizes analytical research relevant to premarketing evaluation of expected product performance, epidemiological tracking of actual consumer experiences, and weighing of those risks and benefits. It summarizes descriptive research regarding the cognitive, affective, social, economic, and political factors affecting consumers' decisions about acquiring and using consumer products. It summarizes intervention options and experiences, in the context set by its analytical and descriptive contributions, as well as the legal and ethical obligations imposed by the societies in which these transactions occur. Its coverage is open and eclectic, with authors drawn from varied disciplines and employment settings and contributions that provide access to varied approaches. A reader who knew nothing about these burgeoning fields before starting the book would have a good feeling for its sweep, excitement, and controversies upon finishing.

That reader would also realize the needless perils of designing and marketing products without incorporating the research summarized here. As reflected in the

---

[1]Fischhoff, B. (2013). The sciences of science communication. *Proceedings of the National Academy of Sciences, 110*(Supplement 3), 14033–14039. doi:10.1073/pnas.1213273110; Fischhoff, B., & Kadvany, J. (2011). *Risk: A very short introduction.* Oxford: Oxford University Press; Fischhoff, B., Brewer, N., & Downs, J. S. (Eds.). (2011). *Communicating risks and benefits: An evidence-based user's guide.* Washington, DC: Food and Drug Administration. http://www.fda.gov/AboutFDA/ReportsManualsForms/Reports/ucm268078.htm

case studies scattered throughout the volume, some firms and agencies have long employed behavioral scientists to conduct descriptive research attuned to technical analyses of consumer products and the social context for interventions. Other organizations, though, may be too small to bring the requisite expertise on staff. They may also lack the absorptive capacity to secure it from internal sources. Overcoming those barriers is a strategic responsibility for their senior leadership. The editors and authors are to be commended for making that case so clear.

Department of Engineering and Public   Baruch Fischhoff
Policy, Institute for Politics and
Strategy, Carnegie Mellon University
Pittsburgh, PA, USA
http://www.cmu.edu/epp/people/faculty/baruch-fischhoff.html

Preface

Books on consumer behavior often focus on undergraduate students. This book looks at a wider audience that also includes professionals in industry, research scientists, regulators, R&D and risk managers, policy makers, public health administrators, and advanced students. It covers topics ranging from consumer psychology to research methodology. It addresses regulatory aspects of marketing new products in the EU, the USA, and Asia. The book responds to the growing need for methodological guidance in consumer research and related areas. The field is rapidly growing and existing approaches often do not fully apply or not fully cover what is required. The general intention is to contribute to the discussion around establishing sound conceptual and methodological standards in the field.

The starting point of this journey is that most, if not all, consumer products present some combination of benefits and costs, the balance of which may vary considerably for different product types. Also, there is always the possibility that a product will not deliver the intended benefits and/or bring about unexpected risks. This can be so for a large array of reasons and applies to all types of services and products, including convenience products, preference products (e.g., beer, soft drinks, and toothpaste), shopping products, and high-involvement products. While such categories can help to organize the topics and questions, it must be realized that each product type is unique and requires individual consideration.

The idea that consumption can be conceived as risk-taking and at the same time risk-reducing behavior was formulated in the 1960s. The perception of risk has been characterized as a multifaceted construct, each different risk facet being related to a potential loss that a consumer may face. There are financial, performance, health, psychological, social, and time risks. The specific mix of risks is highly product specific and also depends on the individual consumer and the context. The study of product risk perception is at the heart of important societal discourses going beyond issues related to traditional risk analysis and marketing strategy development.

Theories of risk perception have often assumed that risks are being understood rationally and have focused on quantifying probabilities of outcomes, costs, and benefits. It has been argued that the relationship between perceived risk and perceived benefits may, in a simple way, depend on the individual's general affective evaluation of the product and its expected utility. In many studies, risk perception is still measured by asking respondents to provide simple ratings of some sort. It becomes clear from the contributions of this book that simple approaches of this sort require updating, given the level of progress that has been made in many relevant scientific areas.

Consumer concerns, for example regarding food safety, have steadily increased since around the 1970s, yet only recently have risk perceptions been systematically studied. Product safety has since then received close attention from regulatory authorities, media, industry, and the general public. This attention is still intensifying due also to very novel types of products, like probiotic microorganisms added to food.

Risk communication presents a related formidable challenge. A general problem for all risk and hazard communications is that the modern world is already full of them, especially in the form of warnings. Warnings and disclosures are ubiquitous and have become part of everyday life. Research has shown that warnings can communicate benefits and risks to consumers successfully, but only if they are appropriately designed for the target audience, accounting for initial beliefs, message content, message modality, and source and receiver effects. Understanding how individuals interpret, process, and respond to risk and risk information is crucial to create effective messaging that will be understood and accepted.

These and other subjects on "Consumer Perception of Product Risks and Benefits" are critically reviewed and discussed in this book by a selection of excellent scholars. The book consists of 30 contributions organized into four parts that focus on Product Risks, Perception of Product Risks and Benefits, Consumer Behavior, and Regulation and Responsibility.

The first contribution of part I (Product Risks) on "Types of Consumer Products" by Ilene Zackowitz and collaborators describes which consumer factors impact purchase decisions and explores several categories of consumer products. In the second contribution, John Kozup discusses the "Risks of Consumer Products." An overview of the various product risks and their effects on consumers is presented. Dominique Deplanque discusses "Non-Clinical research-based product assessment" as a large number of guidelines and rules governing the market access process have been introduced, including the requirement for non-clinical evaluations prior to human use. Drugs and other medicines probably undergo the strictest non-clinical assessments, using not only animal models but also in vitro and in silico approaches. Rolf Weitkunat presents "Clinical Research-based Product Assessment" methodologies, describing how clinical trials, most developed in pharmacotherapy research, must be carefully adapted for meaningfully assessing consumer products. Olivier Ethgen and Olivier Bruyere discuss the field of "Epidemiological Product Assessment," reviewing major epidemiological concepts and methods employed to assess potential causal relationships between exposures and the occurrences of diseases, injuries, or other adverse outcomes. Viviane Kovess-Masfety reviews the "Individual and Population Risks." The contribution begins with a definition of risk in epidemiology. The consequences of the precautionary principle are presented and the author concludes on the importance of addressing individual-level effects and mental health when evaluating and managing risks. Kim Hye Kyung introduces key principles and theoretical frameworks of "Risk Communication." Given the highly interdisciplinary nature of risk communication, practitioners should be able to understand the complex dynamics of risk communication from numerous vantage points, at both the individual and societal level.

The first contribution of part II (Perception of Product Risks and Benefits) on "Comprehension of Products and Messages" by Christopher Cummings reviews distinct historical approaches to understanding and investigating product and message comprehension and the details of how comprehension has been conceptualized and measured across disciplines. "Perception of Product Risks" by Arnout Fischer addresses the psychological mechanisms of risk perception. Specific product dimensions trigger cognitive processes like dread and uncertainty that increase, or reduce, risk perception. Stefan Cano and Thomas Salzberger discuss the methodological challenges of "Measuring Risk Perception," psychometrically a most complex concept. Salzberger and Cano then present "The Perception Risk Instrument (PRI)" capturing the domains of Perceived Health Risk and Perceived Addiction Risk and providing measures that are directly comparable across different tobacco and nicotine-containing products and subpopulations. Gerrod Parrott reviews "The Role of Emotions in Risk Perception." The ways in which emotions affect the perception of risk are grounded in a conception of emotion involving appraisals, feelings, and the preparation of behavioral and cognitive action, considering biological, individual, and social levels of analysis. In "Rational Choice and Bounded Rationality," Ronald Goldsmith presents an overview of consumer decision-making, emphasizing two major forces that frame consumer decisions, namely, the goals humans strive to attain and the resources they have. In "Temporal Discounting of Future Risks," Chengyan Yue and Jingjing Wang discuss how temporal discounting can lead consumers to choose smaller, more immediate rewards over larger but more delayed ones. In the contribution on "Cognitive Styles and Personality in Risk Perception," Eric Ping Hung Li describes current conceptualizations of risk perception in consumer behavior research, providing a review of the literature on personality traits, cognitive styles, risk perception, and cultural dimension frameworks. In "Consumer Values and Product Perception," Katrin Horn explores the role of consumer values in the perception of product risks and benefits.

The first contribution of part III (Consumer Behavior) on "Perception, Attitudes, Intentions, Decision and Actual Behavior" by Arnout Fischer discusses how linear models that assume a causal link from perception over attitude, intention, and decisions to finally behavior have long dominated consumer behavior research, examples being the theory of planned behavior, the technology acceptance model, and the norm activation model. In the contribution on "Consumer Products and Consumer Behavior," Antony Davies argues that in many markets, consumers face a choice problem in which the marginal costs of obtaining additional information necessary to improve a purchase decision exceed the marginal benefits of the improved decision. Consumer then often attempts to mitigate the lack of information through the use of heuristics. The contribution on "Consumer Resistance" by Yany Gregoire and collaborators offers a review of consumer resistance. Two facets are consumer anti-consumption and revenge. The contribution on "Motivation" by Gregory Bonn shows that the scientific focus is often on cognitive or conscious deliberation. "Marketing and Market Research" are discussed by Burak Tunca, highlighting the contemporary developments that influence the current thinking in these areas. "Consumer Behavior Research Methods," authored by Polymeros Chrysochou, distinguishes consumer behavior research methods based on the type of data used. The contribution describes important qualitative and quantitative methods, concluding with an evaluation of how to improve research quality in the field. In the contribution on "Use, Misuse and Abuse" of consumer products, the authors Michel Bourin and Abdeslam Chagroui argue that the nonmedical use and abuse of medicines is a serious public health problem due to a variety of adverse health effects and addiction risks. Qing Wang and Naina Narain, in "Consumer Behavior in Special and Subpopulations," provide an overview of research on consumer behavior in particular groups and summarize how the netnography approach can be applied for communicating with special populations.

In the first contribution of part IV (Regulation and Responsibility) on "Regulatory Prospective for Medicinal Products," Louis Morris argues that more obviously than for other product types, the benefits of medical products are counterbalanced by their risks, rendering adequate risk communication essential to assure that people can weigh product risks and benefits to make informed decision. "Regulations of Consumer Products," by Zahra Meghani, outlines that consumer product regulations in the USA, the European Union, and Japan vary significantly, depending on the product category. In "Manufacturer Responsibilities," Elizabeth Goldsmith describes how manufacturers actually make products. It is their responsibility to make consistent, technologically advanced, high-quality products useful and safe for consumers and society, upholding ethics and industry standards and protecting the environment. In "Consumer Responsibilities," Sue McGregor argues that there are no consumer rights without human rights and that we cannot be responsible consumers unless we are responsible humans. The contribution on "Society and Policy Maker's Responsibilities" by Jennifer Kuzma focuses on the responsibilities of the public sector in consumer-product governance. The contribution on "Consumer Perception of Responsibility" by Sue McGregor is an inaugural attempt to conceptualize consumer perceptions of responsibility by consumers. The author makes the case for the emergent but under-researched phenomenon of consumers' self-ascribed sense of social responsibility.

We hope that this book will stimulate the search for answers to the many important and difficult questions on consumer perception of product risks and benefits. This book would not have been possible without the support of many people, in particular the authors. The latter have devoted a large amount of time and effort to contribute to this edition. We therefore express our gratitude to all authors and are glad to say that for us the many interactions and discussions have been a most pleasurable and instructive experience. Being collaborators for Research & Development within Philip Morris Products S.A (part of Philip Morris International group of companies) in Switzerland, we are grateful that our employer has provided us generously with the liberty to devote part of our time to this edition. This book is sponsored by Philip Morris International (PMI). The authors received an honorarium for contributing to this edition. The contributions reflect the views of the individual authors and not necessarily those of PMI or the editors.

Neuchatel, Switzerland   Gerard Emilien
October 2016   Rolf Weitkunat
                                                                                        Frank Lüdicke

Contents

Contributors

Meriel Bench Vredenburgh & Associates, Inc., Carlsbad, CA, USA

Gregory Bonn, Ph.D. Department of General Studies, King Fahd University of Petroleum and Minerals, Dhahran, Saudi Arabia

Japan Society for the Promotion of Science, Nagoya University, School of Education and Human Development, Nagoya, Japan

Michel Bourin, M.D., Pharm.D. Nantes University, Nantes, France

Olivier Bruyère, M.D., Ph.D. Department of Public Health, Epidemiology and Health Economics, University of Liège, Liège, Belgium

Bone and Cartilage Metabolism Unit, Faculty of Medicine, University of Liège, Liège, Belgium

Stefan Cano, Ph.D., C.Psychol., A.F.B.Ps.S. Modus Outcomes, Letchworth Garden City, UK

Abdeslam Chagraoui, Ph.D., Pharm.D. Faculty of Medicine, University of Rouen, Rouen Cedex 1, France

Polymeros Chrysochou, Ph.D. Department of Business Administration, Aarhus School of Business and Social Sciences, Aarhus, Denmark

Ehrenberg-Bass Institute for Marketing Science, School of Marketing, University of South Australia, Adelaide, SA, Australia

Christopher L. Cummings, Ph.D. Wee Kim Wee School of Communication and Information, Nanyang Technological University, Singapore, Singapore

Antony Davies, Ph.D. Duquesne University, Greenberg, PA, USA

Dominique Deplanque, M.D., Ph.D. Faculty of Medicine, Department of Medical Pharmacology, Lille, France

Gerard Emilien, M.D., Ph.D., F.R.C.P. Clinique du Nord, Port Louis, Mauritius

Olivier Ethgen, Ph.D. SERFAN Innovation S.P.R.L, Namur, Belgium

Faculty of Medicine, Department of Public Health, Epidemiology and Health Economics, University of Liège, Liège, Belgium

Arnout R. H. Fischer, Ph.D. Marketing and Consumer Group, Wageningen University, Wageningen, The Netherlands

Ronald E. Goldsmith, Ph.D. Marketing Department, College of Business, Florida State University, Tallahassee, FL, USA

Elizabeth Beard Goldsmith, Ph.D. Department of Retail, Merchandising and Product Development, College of Human Sciences, Florida State University, Tallahassee, FL, USA

Yany Gregoire, Ph.D. Department of Marketing, HEC Montréal, Montréal, QC, Canada

Katrin Horn, Ph.D. The Semiotic Alliance, London, UK

Viviane Kovess-Masfety, M.D., Ph.D. Department of Epidemiology and Biostatistics, Ecole des Hautes Etudes en Sante Publique (EHESP), Universite Paris V (Rene Descartes), Paris Cedex, France

John Kozup, Ph.D. Center for Marketing and Public Policy Research, Villanova School of Business, Villanova, PA, USA

Jennifer Kuzma, Ph.D. School of Public and International Affairs, North Carolina State University, Raleigh, NC, USA

Hye Kyung Kim, Ph.D. Division of Communication Research, Wee Kim Wee School of Communications and Information, Nanyang Technological University, Singapore, Singapore

Eric Ping Hung Li, Ph.D. The University of British Columbia, Okanagan, Kelowna, BC, Canada

Frank Lüdicke, M.D. Philip Morris Products SA, Neuchatel, Switzerland

Sue L. T. McGregor, Ph.D. Mount Saint Vincent University, Seabright, NS, Canada

Zahra Meghani, Ph.D. Philosophy Department, University of Rhode Island, Kingston, RI, USA

Louis A. Morris, Ph.D. Louis A Morris & Associates, Inc., Dix Hills, NY, USA

Naina Narain, B.Sc. (Hons) University of Warwick, Coventry, UK

Marcelo Vinhal Nepomuceno, Ph.D. Department of Marketing, HEC Montréal, Montréal, QC, Canada

W. Gerrod Parrott, Ph.D. Department of Psychology, Georgetown University, Washington, DC, USA

Mina Rohani, Ph.D. Department of Marketing, HEC Montréal, Montréal, QC, Canada

Thomas Salzberger, Ph.D. Institute for Statistics and Mathematics, and the Institute for Marketing Management, Vienna University of Economics and Business, Wien, Austria

Burak Tunca, Ph.D. University of Agder, School of Business and Law (Bygg 19), Kristiansand, Norway

Alison G. Vredenburgh, Ph.D., C.P.E. Vredenburgh & Associates, Inc., Carlsbad, CA, USA

Michael J. Vredenburgh Vredenburgh & Associates, Inc., Carlsbad, CA, USA

Qing Wang, Ph.D., D.Sc. Warwick Business School, The University of Warwick, Coventry, UK

Jingjing Wang Department of Applied Economics, University of Minnesota, St Paul, MN, USA

Rolf Weitkunat, Ph.D. Philip Morris Products SA, Neuchatel, Switzerland

Chengyan Yue, Ph.D. Department of Horticultural Science, University of Minnesota, St Paul, MN USA

Ilene B. Zackowitz, Ph.D., C.P.E. Vredenburgh & Associates, Inc., Carlsbad, CA, USA

List of Abbreviations

Apps	Applications
ADHD	Attention deficit hyperactivity disorder
ADI	Acceptable daily intake
ADME	Absorption, distribution, metabolism and elimination
ANOVA	Analysis of variance
APHIS	Animal and Plant Health Inspection Service
API	Application programming interface
AR	Attributable risk
BBB	Better Business Bureau
BPA	Bisphenol A
CAA	Consumer Affairs Agency
CAPI	Computer-assisted personal interviews
CATI	Computer-assisted telephone interviews
CBD	Compulsive buying disorder
CC	Calcium-collagen chelate
CDC	Center for Disease Control
CDIs	Cognitive debriefing interviews
CEV	Consciousness-emotion-value
CHDS	Christchurch Health and Development Study
CI	Consumers International, confidence interval
CFRB	Coordinated Framework on the Regulation of Biotechnology
CPSC	Consumer product safety commission
CSR	Corporate social responsibility
CTT	Classical test theory
CWB	Consumer well-being
dACC	Dorsal anterior cingulate cortex
DALY	Disability-adjusted life years
DAWN	Drug abuse warning network
DIY	Do-it-yourself
dLPFC	Dorsal lateral prefrontal cortex
DHS	Department of Homeland Security

DSM	Diagnostic and Statistical Manual of Mental Disorders
DSM-5	Diagnostic and Statistical Manual of Mental Disorders, 5th edition
ED	Emergency department
ED 50	Median effective dose
EEG	Electroencephalography
EFSA	European Food Safety System
EMA	European Medicines Agency
EMR	Electromagnetic radiation
EPA	Environmental Protection Agency
EPPM	Extended parallel process model
ERG	Existence, relatedness, and growth
FDA	Food and Drug Administration
FFDCA	Federal Food, Drug and Cosmetic Act
fMRI	Functional magnetic resonance imaging
FS	Former smokers
FSBL	Food safety basic law
FTC	Federal Trade Commission
GEO	Genetically engineered organisms
GMO	Genetically modified organisms
GPSD	General Product Safety Directive
HIV	Human immunodeficiency virus
HSM	Heuristic systematic model
HTS	High-throughput screening
ICD	International classification of diseases
ICH	International Council for Harmonization
I_E	Incidence of the disease in exposed individuals
IGD	Internet gaming disorder
I_{NE}	Incidence of the disease in nonexposed individuals
iPSCs	Induced pluripotent stem cells
IRT	Item response theory
ISN	Informational subjective norms
I_T	Incidence of the disease in the total population (i.e., those who are exposed plus those who are not exposed)
ITT	Intention-to-treat
LA-25 NS	Never smokers from legal age of smoking to 25 years of age
LD 50	Median lethal dose
LOAELS	Lowest observed adverse effect levels
LOV	List of values
MAFF	Ministry of Agriculture, Forestry and Fisheries
MEC	Means-end chain
MGCFA	Multigroup confirmatory factor analysis
MHLW	Ministry of Health, Labor and Welfare
MMWR	Morbidity and Mortality Weekly Report
MRC	Medical Research Council in the UK

MRTP	Modified risk tobacco products
MSDS	Material safety data sheets
MTurk	Mechanical Turk
NAc	Nucleus accumbens
NHST	Null hypothesis significance testing
NMR	Nicotine metabolite ratio
N_{NC}	Number of new cases of the disease over a given period of time
NOAELS	No observed adverse effect levels
NRT	Nicotine replacement therapy
NS	Never smokers
N_T	Total number of individuals initially free of the disease in the group followed over that given period of time
NTSB	National Transportation Safety Board
OR	Odds ratio
OSTP	Office of Science and Technology Policy
P	Prevalence of exposure to the risks factor in the population
PAR	Population-attributable risk
PCC	Posterior cingulate cortex
PCE	Perceived consumer effectiveness
PIGC	Perceived information gathering capacity
PMA	Premarket approval
PMDA	Pharmaceuticals and Medical Devices Agency
PRI	Perception risk instrument
PRI-P	Perceived risk instrument for personal risk
PRI-G	Perceived risk instrument for general risk
QSARs	Quantitative structure–activity relationship
RCB	Relevant channel beliefs
RCT	Randomized Clinical Trials
RISP	Risk information seeking and processing model
RR	Relative risk
RVS	Rokeach Value Survey
SAMHSA	Substance Abuse and Mental Health Services Administration
SARF	Social amplification of risk framework
SASH	Society for the Advancement of Sexual Health
SCQ	Smoking Consequences Questionnaire
SCQ-A	Smoking Consequences Questionnaire—adult version
SCT	Social cognitive theory
SCUBA	Self-contained underwater breathing apparatus
SDT	Self-determination theory
SES	Socioeconomic status
SEU	Subjective expected utility
S-ITQ	Smokers with intention to quit
SmPC	Summary of product characteristics
S-NITQ	Smokers with no intention to quit

SUD	Substance use disorder
SUTV	Stable unit treatment value
SVS	Schwartz Value Survey
TAM	Technology acceptance model
THC	Delta 9-tetrahydrocannabinol
THS	Tobacco heating system
TPB	Theory of planned behavior
UNCPG	United Nations Guidelines for Consumer Protection
USDA	US Department of Agriculture
VALS	Values and lifestyles
VAS	Visual analogue scales
vLPFC	Ventral lateral prefrontal cortex
vmPFC	Ventromedial prefrontal cortex
VS	Ventral regions of Striatum
VTA	Ventral tegmental area
YLD	Years lived with disability
YLL	Years of life lost

Part I
Product Risks

Types of Consumer Products

Ilene B. Zackowitz, Michael J. Vredenburgh, Meriel Bench, and Alison G. Vredenburgh

1 Characteristics of Consumers and Products

This introductory contribution considers the extensive range of consumers, consumer products and the categories within which they can be considered. Consumer products are those, which are used by the customer for personal consumption or for household use. No longer does the simple paradigm of storefronts and tangible products dominate today's consumer marketplace. Instead, intangibles, like digital goods, are becoming more common consumer products. Whether the item is baby food, a cosmetic like lipstick, or even a cosmetic for a character in a video game, there is one underlying similarity: they are purchased. This contribution describes how consumer factors, such as age, education and socio-economic status influence purchase decisions and examines both the obvious and not so obvious categories of products available to global consumers. Marketing considerations discussed include customer buying behavior, distribution and effective promotional efforts for the different categories of products.

1.1 What Is a Consumer?

A consumer is a person who pays to consume the goods and services produced by a seller (Boundless 2016). A Consumer does not purchase items for use in manufacturing or for resale. They make the decision about whether to purchase an item and are personally influenced by marketing and advertisement campaigns. Consumers participate in a global marketplace through purchasing goods. Outside

I.B. Zackowitz (✉) • M.J. Vredenburgh • M. Bench • A.G. Vredenburgh
Vredenburgh & Associates, Inc., 2588 El Camino Real, F353, Carlsbad, CA 92008, USA
e-mail: ilenez@me.com

© Springer International Publishing AG 2017
G. Emilien et al. (eds.), *Consumer Perception of Product Risks and Benefits*,
DOI 10.1007/978-3-319-50530-5_1

of a few personally independent subsistence farmers, all human societies use products, whether they are tribe members in New Guinea or executives in Beijing. Even some of the most remote regions of the world participate in global consumerism; for example, the Inuit people of Canada have replaced many of their dog sleds with factory-produced snowmobiles (Muse 2009). Starting from the beginning of mankind, we as a people have innovated, created, and developed visionary items that now play crucial roles in our daily lives. When developing a product for consumer use, it is important to consider the diverse characteristics of the potential user population, user interface, and the environment in which products are anticipated to be used.

While we are all consumers, there are many important categorizations to consider. While some products are only intended for a very small subset of consumers, other products are almost universal. Factors such as age, socio-economic status (SES), education, language, disability, and gender are demographic characteristics and attributes that best determine which product types will meet their individual needs as consumers.

Age plays an important role when it comes to product selection. For example, seniors are more likely to require health care products than younger people. Popular adolescent products include skateboards, clothing, and cellphones and their applications (apps). Products for infants are purchased and used by parents and caretakers, while products marketed to preschoolers are often tailored towards creativity or learning. For each age group, designers must consider how products can affect their users. For example, infant products are made to be safe to touch and ingest. Items made for older adults may enhance safety and aid in activities of daily living, such as hearing aids, reading glasses, and shopping carts.

Socio-economic status (SES) not only influences the types of products people can purchase, but also what products they are exposed to through peers, colleagues, travel and work. Wealth has played a critical role in global consumerism since early trade. Product designers consider SES when targeting market segments to buy their product. For example, the grocery store "Food for Less" locates its outlets in low SES regions across the United States while Whole Foods Markets are in locations where there are wealthier consumers. People with lower SES are more likely to play the lottery and purchase more processed foods. On the other hand, wineries often target affluent communities.

The education level of consumers affects income and as a result, the types of products that are preferred. People with less education may be more influenced by short term costs, and give quality lower priority in product selection. People with more education have different expectations about products, experiences and user environments. More educated individuals may be more likely to purchase educational books, magazines, and other learning devices. In a broader sense, more education is often correlated with wealth, which in turn affects purchase decisions.

There are approximately 6909 distinct languages spoken worldwide (Anderson 2010) and almost 200 countries (World Atlas 2015) inhabit our seven continents. Even with such a demographically rich population, we all require the same basic products. It is interesting to consider how goods around the world are translated through many different cultures and ways of life. For example, language becomes important when addressing product safety. Literacy affects whether consumers can read and understand instructions and warnings. This can become a major issue when it comes to prescriptions and over-the-counter medications, as well as other potentially hazardous products such as cleaners and electric tools.

People with disabilities require specialized products to increase the accessibility of environments and products. Individuals with cognitive deficits such as autism, Down syndrome and brain damage may benefit from technology products. For example, there are apps that help people with language impairment to speak. There are many products for people with physical limitations including wheelchairs, and other mobility devices, prosthetics, grabbing and reaching devices, bathing aids, remote controls and visual alarms.

1.2 What Is a Consumer Product?

What do an iPhone, a baby stroller, and a table saw have in common? They are all physical objects that can be held, broken and generally have a resale value. They must be manufactured, and transported to consumers. The economic principles of supply and demand are largely applicable to any of these goods. Whether a product is this book you are reading or the shirt on your back, a global economy flourishes with eclectic sourcing. While the details of your shirt's construction may differ, the same principle generally applies: the shirt's cotton may be from Egypt, its dyes from India, and it may be assembled in Vietnam. Clearly, manufacturing both simple and more sophisticated products can involve many parts of the world. Table 1 is an overview of the categories of consumer products that are discussed in detail within the contribution.

1.2.1 Variety of Products

There is a difference between mass, special interest and tailored products. For example, computer binary representations of a song differ drastically from a pet Dalmatian, yet both the dog and digital media are considered consumer goods. A hundred years ago, classifying products was simpler; now intangible goods, such as computer data or a service agreement, diverge greatly from many traditional products. The very fabric of "supply and demand" is unraveled with a nearly infinite supply of digital goods. Thus, we must adopt a broad approach to understanding consumer products, due to their diverse nature. Though intangible products (i.e. service agreements, insurance policies, etc.) existed a century ago, they were slow and costly to draft. These intangible goods of the last century still behaved like tangible goods regarding supply and demand, as the documents were limited in supply. In contrast, downloading a media file often costs less than a cent of electricity. Thus, creating copies of a computer file, and therefore supply of that

Table 1 Types of consumer products

Marketing considerations	Convenience	Staples	Luxury	Specialty	Unsought	Emergency
Buying behavior	Purchased often, little planning, brand loyalty	Purchased often, viewed as necessary, based on availability	Requires deliberation, comparison	Requires product-specific interest	Unplanned, response to persuasive promotion	Unplanned, response to unexpected event
Price	Inexpensive	Inexpensive	Expensive	Moderate to expensive	Inexpensive to moderate	Inexpensive to expensive
Distribution	Wide, large market	Virtually all households, mass appeal	Smaller target market	Limited target market	Limited target market	Large target market
Promotion	Value focused	Low profit, rarely on sale	Specialized and exclusive outlets, status focus	Specialized outlets	Persuasive ads, sales, salespeople	Focused on availability
Examples	Prepared foods, soap, toilet paper	Rice, milk, bread	Designer clothing, electronics	Athletic gear, pet supplies	Door-to-door sales, in-store promotions	Drain cleaner, cold medicines, coffins

good, is nearly free, and can model the quantity of many digital goods by assuming infinite supply.

Eating is a biological imperative so almost all consumers purchase at least some food. As every person reading this book has consumed food, cuisine is used to differentiate different product categories. Rice is a food that is regularly purchased by most people of the world. Staple foods, such as rice, are examples of products with mass appeal, which tend to be competitively priced and are sold in large volumes relative to special interest or tailored products. Consequently, the largest sectors of the food production market are dedicated to the production of staple foods. Truffles and saffron, on the other hand, are luxury foods that are sold much less frequently, are difficult to acquire, and are purchased by a much smaller subset of consumers. Luxury foods are one type of special-interest products, but food does not need to be a luxury to be special-interest. Niche foods (i.e. kosher or halal foods, gluten free, mock meat for vegan diets) are not widely consumed, but are not necessarily expensive. Consequently, niche foods are also a subset of special-interest products.

There are several categories of products that are discussed in this contribution: Convenience products are designed to save consumers' time; staple products do not require much customer effort or forethought and have mass appeal; comparison shopping products require thought and deliberation; luxury and specialty products require significant thought or effort and may be tailored to the consumer; reactionary and emergency products are items that customers are not aware of or do not think about until they need them; intangible products such as digital goods and services; non-consumer, industrial products; and self-service and do-it-yourself consumer choices.

2 Convenience Products

A convenience product is a product that consumers purchase with little planning, is routinely purchased and appeals to a large target market, and the consumer purchases it with little planning (Lombardo 2015). Such products typically appeal to a large market segment (Product Decisions Tutorial 2015a). Consumers' purchasing considerations differ depending on how much thoughtfulness played a role in buying. Spontaneously adding a pack of gum to a purchase at the check-out line is an example of a convenience product. The consumer uses little forethought or comparison to alternatives and these products are widely available at outlets such as gas stations, supermarkets and corner stores.

2.1   Products to Save Consumer's Time

There are millions of products currently on the market that are designed to save consumer's time. Consumers often use convenience products with the justification that time is money. The necessity to decrease time spent on essential daily activities, such as cooking, cleaning and running errands applies to most consumers, and products designed specifically for those purposes increasingly meet this need.

In order to understand this movement towards convenience, we can recall the classic American lifestyle as portrayed in the media of the 1950s as an example. In that era, women were typically stay-at-home mothers, who had time to cook, clean, and care for children as their primary responsibility. Clearly, that style of running a household is outdated with the majority of women worldwide now participating in the workforce (United Nations 2010), which reduces the time they have to manage household tasks. The development of prepared foods stemmed from the need to reduce food preparation time. One interesting note is that product developers actually had to scale back their efforts to economize all cooking, especially for baked goods. Women still felt the need to contribute at least some amount of effort to baking goods, rather than just mixing powder and water that results in brownies or a cake. They felt they needed the process of baking to remain intact, while reducing the preparation time, which is why most baking mixes require adding eggs or oil, yet still much more convenient than baking from scratch (Shapiro 2004).

Disposable travel goods are a convenience product and are the result of different circumstantial influences. Most travelers do not have the luggage space for full-sized toiletries, especially for short trips. Airline restrictions severely limit the amount of liquids that individuals are allowed to bring in their carry-on bag. Widely available disposable travel goods provide a solution to both of these issues. Airports, convenience stores, and grocery stores stock these, providing consumers with a quick and easy way to accomplish their hygiene needs while traveling.

Smart phone applications (apps) are another product that many may consider convenience products but do not comport with the typical description (purchased often), since apps are generally purchased only once. Those who make use of smart phone apps would be the first to agree that convenience these products provide is life enhancing. Various apps are available to make numerous tasks more convenient; for example, users can quickly and conveniently complete tasks that used to be time-consuming such as banking. Consumers can use apps to quickly and conveniently perform many tasks from their cell phones like staying current on news, doing research, translating languages, monitoring fitness, connecting with friends, and reading books and magazines.

These technologies are slowly replacing various consumer products. Although print and paper magazines and newspapers are still being produced, movement towards a fully technological world is occurring. Garnering information about the world has never been easier, and is instantaneous for many consumers. Another enormous draw to these apps is that they are usually free or priced low, sometimes eliminating the cost of subscriptions and decreasing the amount of paper waste as a byproduct.

2.2   Widely Available and Inexpensive

In order for convenience products to reach their target market, they must have widespread availability. These products include many household items that can be purchased from a wide variety of retail outlets including department stores, supermarkets, convenience stores, drug stores, warehouse clubs, discount stores and even vending machines. Consumers typically have sufficient knowledge about the convenience products they wish to purchase such that there is little need for research or comparison-shopping. Therefore, convenience products do not require complicated information-based ads; promotions are focused on value and reminding the consumer the product is available (Lombardo 2015).

Because of the high manufacturing volume of convenience products such as food, personal care and cleaning products, pricing per item tends to be relatively low. Consumers often see little value in shopping around for these items since additional effort yields minimal savings (Product Decisions Tutorial 2015a). Therefore, consumers do not need to spend a lot of time contemplating such purchases and comparing similar items. Examples of widely available convenience products include disposable diapers, fast food and toilet paper.

Although convenience products typically do not require comparison-shopping, these items often exhibit brand loyalty by their consumers (Lombardo 2015). For example, if consumers crave a drink and snack, they can acquire these items at virtually any convenience store. Most consumers demonstrate brand loyalty because they have a favorite kind of soft drink and snack chip. There will always be a market for convenience products, because people have the need to divert their energy into activities that matter to them more than everyday perfunctory rituals like cleaning, personal hygiene and food preparation.

3   Staple Products

There are some products that do not require much customer effort or forethought and are used by virtually every type of household. Products purchased regularly and out of necessity are considered staple goods. Like convenience products, these items have lower profit margins and because they are generally priced low, rarely go on sale (Hudson 2015). These products are usually restocked as they run out since they are viewed as necessary. Therefore, demand for staple goods rarely changes even when the price changes.

Food is an important category of staple products. There are more than 50,000 edible plants in the world, but just 15 of them provide 90% of the world's energy intake. Rice, corn and wheat make up two-thirds of this. Other staple foods include millet, tubers and dairy products (Dunn 1993). Food staples traditionally depend on what plants are native to a region. However, with improvements in agriculture, food storage and transportation, some food staples are changing. For example, in the South Pacific Islands, tubers such as taro are a traditional food staple whose consumption has fallen while consumption of cereal grains not native to the islands has increased by about 40% (Dunn 1993).

Staple goods differ depending on where the consumer lives. While most Americans stocking their households consider milk, eggs and bread to be staples, other countries consider rice and corn to be necessary food staples. Whether people live in China, the United States or a country in South America, they will probably use toilet paper and eat some form of rice. Not a lot of thought will typically go into the decision of whether to buy these products and selection is based on availability, price, or feature (such as brown, white, or jasmine rice, etc.).

Other products are not quite staples, but have mass appeal. They have more variation in product types than staple goods. Examples include flatware, dishes, pens, bed linens, off the rack clothing and other household items. Some of these items also have luxury versions. For example, kitchen knives are found in virtually every household (see Fig. 1) and in a wide variety of stores. However, there are also high-end specialty knives for professional chefs as discussed below.

Fig. 1 Some products are used by virtually all households, such as kitchen knives (Photo by Alison Vredenburgh)

4 Comparison Shopping Products

The next two categories, comparison shopping products and luxury goods, include products that require consideration and comparison. These are products consumers purchase less frequently than convenience and staple products. Shoppers are willing to spend more time selecting these items that are generally more expensive (Product Decisions Tutorial 2015a). Comparison-shopping products may also possess additional psychological benefits to the purchaser, such as raising their perceived status within the social group. Since shoppers are willing to expend time and energy to locate these products, the target market is much smaller than that of convenience goods. Consequently, marketers are typically more selective when choosing distribution outlets to sell these products (Product Decisions Tutorial 2015a). Examples of comparison-shopping products include many clothing brands, electronics and household furniture.

4.1 Products that Require Comparison and Deliberation

When products are more expensive or have a variety of potential features, people may put more thought and deliberation into their purchase. For example, when buying a new refrigerator, consumers may deliberate about the desired size, whether they want the freezer on the top bottom or side, whether they want an icemaker in the door, the energy use, and the finish. Similarly, mattresses can be very expensive and come in a variety of sizes, levels of firmness and type of construction such that consumers will physically compare the comfort level each provides before making a purchase. When purchasing a laptop, analysis may include the size, storage, operating system, comfort of keyboard, and compatibility with other electronics (see Fig. 2). Other examples of such products include bicycles and automobiles. Consequently, shopping products can be categorized into two groups: homogenous and heterogeneous.

4.2 Homogeneous and Heterogeneous Shopping Products

Homogeneous products are perceived by consumers to be very similar in nature; the final purchase is usually determined by the lowest price. Oftentimes these products cannot be distinguished from competing products from another supplier (Michael 2015). When shopping for a homogeneous product, all versions of the product serve the same purpose and consumers are unlikely to care which is available. Fruits and vegetables are prime examples of homogeneous substances: many suppliers offer fruits and vegetables for sale, but regardless of supplier, all brands offer the same

Fig. 2 When purchasing a laptop size, storage, and compatibility are important considerations (Photo by Alison Vredenburgh)

end-product. Most homogeneous products are very similar in physical composition, as well as quality, and the only real difference among suppliers is price.

In contrast to homogeneous products, heterogeneous products are items that cannot be easily substituted or replaced by others. Heterogeneous products have distinct features that make them unique to certain brands and suppliers (Michael 2015). These items might vary in physical appearance, as well as quality and price. Heterogeneous products are often designed to attract different segments of the population, and cater to people of varying geographical locations and socioeconomic status. Books and magazines are examples of heterogeneous products, as are electronic goods, such as computers. For example, it is not easy to substitute a PC for a Mac since the computer platforms are different (Grimsley 2015a).

5 Luxury and Specialty Products

Generally, consumers put the most thought into purchasing luxury goods (i.e. a sports car) and specialty products (such as sporting gear) than into staple and convenience goods (i.e. a bag of rice or cleaning supplies), and they are much more selective when purchasing these products. Unlike comparison shopping products, oftentimes, consumers know in advance what brand, make or model they prefer and so do not need to spend time researching their options. Target markets for luxury products are generally very small and retailers selling such products are often considered exclusive (Product Decisions Tutorial 2015a). Specialty products are goods that would be of interest to a specific population with specific interests. Unlike luxury products, specialty products are not necessarily expensive, but they fail to appeal to a large segment of the population.

5.1 Special Interest Products

While most luxury goods have a non-luxury counterpart, what distinguishes these products is the significant thought, effort, or money required in these purchase decisions. Advertising or sales presentation is of the utmost importance, as there is generally more anticipation and consideration before purchase. Even though luxury products tend to be more expensive up front, many tend to have good perceived value. Luxury chocolates' high price often reflects the high quality ingredients and manufacturing, whereas an electric Tesla car can have value placed on its low operating cost, craftsmanship, and performance. Regularly, luxury goods find commercial success by providing the best value to dollar, even when the absolute price is higher. While commercial products are generally not considered "luxury," they help demonstrate the same value proposition. For example, a commercial blender will be overbuilt with the intention of providing a relatively large number of operation hours. Whereas, a less expensive home blender is made with cheaper plastic components, and will last significantly few hours before it fails. Consequently, industrial kitchen supplies and kitchen luxury goods have overlap, as both product types are optimized towards perceived value.

Special interest products are sought by a limited target market and thus do not have mass appeal. Specialty sporting equipment, such as SCUBA gear, would be considered a special interest product since only the approximately 1.2 million SCUBA divers worldwide (Thrackrey 2015) would consider purchasing the necessary gear including dive computers, tanks, regulators, buoyancy compensators and weight belts. Other sporting and recreation equipment would be classified as special interest products such as surf and cycling gear.

The wide array of specialty products available in some markets can be quite surprising. Many people have pets and buy specialty products for their animals. Just like people, pets require healthcare and food. Most people with vet bills understand how expensive maintaining a pet's health can be. Veterinarians use many products similar to doctors, but there are differences to consider as well. Vets use harnesses, special leash racks, dog carrier pads for ultrasounds, cages, and even puppy printed gauze for wounds. Moreover, consumers may purchase specialty pet products such as clothing, toys, costumes and even safety gear (see Fig. 3).

It is sometimes difficult to determine if some specialty products are about the pet or the owner. An example of this is pet treats that are produced to look like bacon or with grill marks, characteristics that are appealing to the human purchaser and likely irrelevant to the pet.

Some products can be classified into more than one category. Above, we discussed kitchen knives as having mass appeal and being an item that could be found in most, if not all homes. However, there are professional chef's knives that would be classified as a special interest product. Knives have many different materials and components, many of which would be of little interest to the average cook. However, to professional and some domestic chefs, the different components are an important consideration.

Fig. 3 Consumers
purchase many specialty pet
products like costumes and
safety gear (Photo by Ilene
Zackowitz)

5.2 Products Tailored to the Consumer

Custom products are made to the consumer's exact specifications. A wide range of products can be tailored to the consumer, such as a custom frame for a work of art and a personally tailored suit. Custom products tend to require much more time and labor than their mass-produced counterparts and so, consequently, tend to come at a premium. The relatively high price often reduces the subset of consumers interested in buying the more expensive custom product. Thus, consumers that seek a custom product are more likely to employ comparison-shopping and give serious consideration to the content of the customization. Jewelry is one product category that is frequently tailored to the consumer. For example, wedding bands are often specially designed for the couple. The rings depicted in Fig. 4 are customized with the spouses' fingerprints on one another's rings.

Luxury cars are another product category that can be tailored to the consumer. For example, car buyers can order cars to their exact specifications, including, exterior and interior color, built-in GPS and tech interface systems, back-up cameras, self-parking systems, sound and video options, heated seats and steering wheel, special wheels and high-end trim packages; all available to consumers who are willing to pay a premium for their preferences.

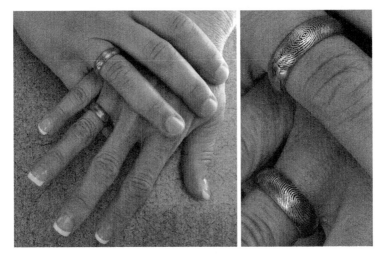

Fig. 4 Wedding bands can be customized with the spouses' fingerprints (Photos by Ilene Zackowitz)

6   Reactionary Products: Unsought and Emergency Goods

Not all consumer product purchases are intended; they are purchased out of obligation, necessity or persuasion. Unsought goods are products whose purchase is unplanned by the consumer but occurs as a result of a marketer's actions. Purchase decisions are made when the customer is exposed to persuasive promotional activity, such as an effective salesperson or incentives like special discounts (Product Decisions Tutorial 2015a). A high degree of marketing is often necessary since consumers may be unaware of the product or have no desire to purchase it (Grimsley 2015b). Examples of unsought goods include life insurance and items sold door-to-door, such as magazine subscriptions and Girl Scout cookies.

Emergency goods are a category of products that customers purchase due to sudden events and which often involve little pre-purchase planning; they are purchased in response to the unexpected (Product Decisions Tutorial 2015a). For example, drain cleaner is commonly purchased in response to a clogged drain. These products are generally acquired quickly; forethought and anticipation are not applicable to these purchases, since they are purchased to remedy a specific event.

An unexpected death can cause those responsible for the funeral to be influenced by emotion. Consequently, some will take the path of least resistance and purchase the most readily available coffin, even if a purchase of that size would normally warrant more comparison-shopping. While it is easy to empathize with these individuals, their hasty coffin purchase reflects emotion and fatigue when the buyer does not have the luxury of making a more calculated purchase. Luckily, many other reactionary products are not so morbid; cold medicine has a similar time sensitivity factor. Many consumers wait until they have a cold before reacting to it

Fig. 5 When selecting cold medicine, patience and discernment of the consumer can be compromised by their ailment (Photo by Alison Vredenburgh)

by purchasing cold medicine, a time when their patience and selectivity can be compromised due to their ailment (see Fig. 5).

7   Intangibles and Services

Intangible products include all goods sold to customers that cannot be seen, touched, smelled or otherwise handled by the consumer. Examples of intangible products include insurance, tax preparation, cell phone service and transportation services. A service is an action that a person does for someone else such as haircuts, medical check-ups, mail delivery, car repair, and teaching.

Some consumer products have both tangible and service components. Goods are normally structural and can be transferred in an instant while services are delivered over a period of time; goods can be returned, while a service, once delivered, cannot. You may purchase a new air conditioning system along with a service contract. The air conditioning hardware is considered a good while future repair and maintenance work that will be done to the system is a service.

7.1 Digital Goods

Intangible goods, such as a downloaded song, have nearly infinite supply, as the costs to download and distribute the song are negligible. Unbounded supply is turning many technology companies on their heads. While the dust in the wild west of the tech boom is starting to settle, novel and seemingly backward business models are proving the most successful. Video games have overtaken film to become one of the most profitable forms of media with a global video game market valued at over $93 billion USD (van der Meulen 2014). Riot Games made approximately $1.3 billion USD by only selling cosmetic items to characters in their otherwise free-to-play game. Tech giant Google helped pioneer "free" services to consumers as an extremely successful business model. Google's profits came from selling advertisement space, as well as selling mined user data. This free-to-consumer business model seems to be unique to digital goods and services, largely resulting from the relatively low cost to provide a mass digital product or service.

While the line between software and service is hard to define, it becomes even more muddled when considering the SaaS (Software as a Service) business model, which is also emerging as a successful model. SaaS allows software to be displayed on a consumer's device, but the actual computation is being done remotely via servers. Customers will often pay for a subscription to the service. Though, from the consumer's perspective, the SaaS software may act and function more like traditionally purchased and installed software. This network-based model has some unique advantages that give it an edge for some applications. For example, the data associated with the product can be accessed by a wide variety of devices that can be transported anywhere there is a network connection. Free-to-play games, such as the above example, tend to follow the SaaS model. Players of the game can use their same account from nearly any computer with an internet connection.

Digital goods are far more diverse than just software or apps. Digital media has begun to replace most forms of media. Whether it is a digital song, or the digital schematics to 3D print, there is an initial cost to record or create the file, but distribution and replication are often negligible costs. 3D printing is poised to bring many of the benefits of digital replication to tangible items. Already, large libraries of items to fabricate are freely available (thinigiverse.com). If these printers were to be as similarly distributed as household document printers, many companies and products may become obsolete. Obsolescence is a common phenomenon that ripples behind technological ingenuity. For example, pagers are small digital devices that could send a user a short message, wirelessly. Even though their adoption became large scale, they became obsolete with the popularity and wide spread availability of cell phones.

7.2 Services

Something is considered a service when consumers obtain it through the labor of others (Product Decisions Tutorial 2015b). Services can result in the creation of a tangible good (a photographer sells photographic prints or an album at the end of the job) but the main item being purchased is the service itself. Unlike tangible goods, services are not stored and are only available at the time of use. Many products have both a goods and services aspect.

Medical care is an example of a service that may have some tangible components but the main product being purchased is the care itself. For example, optometrists may sell glasses, but their main function is to provide eye examinations. Restaurants are another type of business that provide both a physical good (prepared food) as well as service in the form of ambiance and the physical aspects of being served food. Hair stylists also provide intangible services, while the salon may sell hair care products. Massage therapists provide principally an intangible service to their customers (see Fig. 6).

8 Industrial Products Available to Consumers

With the popularity of home improvement stores, products previously considered to be industrial are now often available to consumers. At times complications may arise when consumers use products traditionally designed for industrial use. When these products are used in employment-related endeavors, employers have the

Fig. 6 Massage therapists provide an intangible service to customers (Photo by Ilene Zackowitz)

responsibility to train employees in their proper and safe use to ensure employees and customers are not injured. The training component is missing when the lay consumer uses such products. Industrial products that are available to consumers for purchase and rent include ladders, mowers, paint stripper chemicals, solvents, power tools, generators and compressors.

With more home-based businesses and do-it-yourselfers, the line delineating what constitutes a product for professionals is becoming blurred. For example, if a person decides to build a 3D printer, and use that printer to start a small business, than the printer is both being used as a do-it-yourself project as well as in a professional capacity. The parts and tools to build the printer would be purchased from consumer venders, like any other consumer product. But, because the printer is now part of a small business, the printer's related parts and tools can also be seen as industrial products. The duality of being both an industrial product and consumer product only exists for small businesses and lay people who choose to do certain tasks themselves. Larger businesses tend to purchase from business to business venders. Thus, both small businesses and lay people rely on consumer products.

9 Self-Service and the Do-It-Yourself Economy

In decades past, gas station attendants pumped your gas, sales people measured your feet when buying new shoes and you always had to wait in line for the grocery clerk to ring up and bag your groceries. Not so in today's growing do-it-yourself industry (Consumer Reports 2014). You can now bank without a teller, buy groceries without a cashier and in some restaurants, even order and pay for a meal without ever speaking to a server. The rapid expansion of self-service options can be credited to the inexpensive and improved technologies that are readily embraced by younger generations who are comfortable interacting with touchscreens. Another branch of the self-service economy, do-it-yourself, known as DIY, is an increasingly popular consumer behavior. DIY involves building, modifying, or repairing something without the direct assistance of experts or professionals. DIY involves behaviors where individuals engage raw and semi-raw materials and component parts to produce, transform, or reconstruct material possessions (Wolf and McQuitty 2011).

A distinction that can be made between self-service and DIY is that speed and convenience are at the heart of the move toward self-service (Consumer Reports 2014) whereas there is typically nothing convenient about most DIY projects (Wolf and McQuitty 2011). Unlike self-service banking and gas stations, DIY home remodeling (Fig. 7) and appliance installation are typically labor intensive and inconvenient.

Both the DIY and self-service consumer markets are growing steadily. In 2013, the value of the global DIY market was approximately $31.9 billion US and is forecasted to reach $43.7 billion US by 2018 (Statista 2015). Similarly, new

Fig. 7 Many people prefer to do construction projects themselves (Photo by Ilene Zackowitz)

technologies will lead to more self-service options that will become increasingly effortless. For example, once the price of radio-frequency-identification (RFID) technology drops, tracking tags now used for high-end items can be incorporated into low-cost items such as groceries. When that occurs, the self-checkout process may become obsolete, because customers could complete the process by wheeling their carts nonstop through a barrier that automatically totals all of the items and bills them electronically (Consumer Reports 2014). In the increasingly advanced technological landscape of today's consumer markets, we can expect to see advances in both the development of products designed to simplify consumers' lives as well as the ease at which consumers can purchase goods. The advancement of consumer products and how they reach the buyer will be an interesting journey to witness.

References

Anderson, S. R. (2010). *How many languages are there in the world?* Linguistic Society of America. Accessed December 15, 2015, from http://www.linguisticsociety.org/sites/default/files/how-many-languages.pdf

Boundless. (2016, May 26). *Defining consumers*. Boundless Marketing Boundless. Accessed January 9, 2017 from https://www.boundless.com/marketing/textbooks/boundless-marketing-textbook/consumer-marketing-4/introduction-to-consumers-33/definingconsumers-173-1278/

Consumer Reports. (2014, July). *When customer service becomes self-service*. Accessed December 15, 2015, from http://www.consumerreports.org/cro/magazine/2014/09/when-customer-service-becomes-self-service/index.htm

Digital Design. (2015). thinigiverse.com. Accessed December 12, 2015, from https://www.thingiverse.com

Dunn, M. G. (1993). *Exploring your world: The adventure of geography*. Washington, DC: National Geographic Society.

Grimsley, S. (2015a). *Heterogeneous products: Definition & overview*. Study.com. Accessed December 2, 2015, from http://study.com/academy/lesson/heterogeneous-products-definition-lesson-quiz.html

Grimsley, S. (2015b). *Unsought products: Definition & examples*. Study.com. Accessed December 2, 2015, from http://study.com/academy/lesson/unsought-products-definition-examples-quiz.html

Hudson, M. (2015). *What are staple goods?* About.com. Accessed December 2, 2015, from http://retail.about.com/od/glossary/g/staple_goods.htm

Lombardo, J. (2015). *Consumer products: Convenience, shopping, specialty & unsought products*. Study.com. Accessed December 1, 2015, from http://study.com/academy/lesson/consumer-products-convenience-shopping-specialty-unsought-products.html

Michael, R. (2015). *Homogeneous products: Definition & overview*. Study.com. Accessed December 2, 2015, from http://study.com/academy/lesson/homogeneous-products-definition-lesson-quiz.html

Muse, B. (2009). *Sled Dogs to Snowmobiles*. Accessed December 2, 2015 from http://benmuse.typepad.com/ben_muse/2009/03/sled-dogs-tosnowmobiles.Html

Product Decisions Tutorial. (2015a). *Categories of consumer products*. Accessed December 1, 2015, from http://www.knowthis.com/productdecisions/categories-of-consumer-products KnowThis

Product Decisions Tutorial. (2015b). *What is a product?* Retrieved and Accessed December 1, 2015, from Knowthis.com. Retrieved December 2, 2015, from http://www.knowthis.com/product-decisions/what-is-a-product

Shapiro, L. (2004). *Something from the oven: Reinventing dinner in 1950s america*. New York: Viking.

Statista. (2015). *Value of the DIY market worldwide from 2012 to 2018 (in billion U.S. dollars)*. Statista.com. Retrieved December 3, 2015, from http://www.statista.com/statistics/374093/global-diy-market-value/.

Thrackrey, W. (2015). *How many recreational scuba divers in the world?* Answers.com. Accessed December 3, 2015, from http://www.answers.com/Q/How_many_recreational_scuba_divers_in_the_world?#slide=1

United Nations. (2010). *The world's women 2010, trends & statistics.* Department of Economic Affairs. United Nations Publication. Accessed December 12, 2015, from http://unstats.un.org/unsd/default.htm

van der Meulen, R. (2014). *Gartner says worldwide video game market to total $93 billion in 2013.* Gartner.com. Accessed December 12, 2015, from http://www.gartner.com/newsroom/id/2614915

Wolf, M., & McQuitty, S. (2011). Understanding the do-it-yourself consumer: DIY motivations and outcomes. *Academy of Marketing Science, 1*(3), 154–170.

World Atlas. (2015). *How many countries are in the world?* World Atlas.com. Accessed December 15, 2015, from http://www.worldatlas.com/nations.htm

Risks of Consumer Products

John Kozup

1 Consumer Risk

Consumers face a number of risks throughout the course of their daily lives. For example, a quick glance at a recent report released by the Center for Disease Control identifying the leading causes of death in the United States highlights the many health risks faced by consumers. The leading cause of death is heart disease, followed by cancer, chronic lower respiratory diseases and of particular import to this contribution, accidents, or unintentional injuries, which can have a variety of causes (including those emanating from consumer product risk). There are, of course, numerous types of accidents that can cause serious injury and death—many directly tied to the use (or misuse) of a product. For example, over 30,000 people are typically killed in car accidents each year. Additionally, there are many other types of accidents associated with product use that range from the unsurprising (e.g., ladders, All-Terrain-Vehicles) to the tragic (e.g., toys). Yet health risk is only one type of risk faced by consumers. There are monetary risks, functional risks, social risks, and psychological risks associated with product purchase and use that consumers must consider.

Taking a historic perspective on consumer risk, Bauer (1960) proposed that consumer behavior could be viewed as an instance of risk taking. Subsequently this notion of risk has been incorporated into a number of consumer behavior theories (e.g., Engel et al. 1973; Howard and Sheth 1969). Bauer argued that, "Consumer behavior involves risk in the sense that any action of a consumer will produce consequences which he cannot anticipate with anything approximating certainty, and some of which at least are likely to be unpleasant" (1960, p. 24). This is

J. Kozup (✉)
Villanova School of Business, Department of Marketing, 800 Lancaster Avenue, Villanova, PA 19085, USA
e-mail: john.kozup@villanova.edu

© Springer International Publishing AG 2017   23
G. Emilien et al. (eds.), *Consumer Perception of Product Risks and Benefits*,
DOI 10.1007/978-3-319-50530-5_2

because, as others have noted, the central problem of consumer behavior is choice (Taylor 1974).

Taylor (1974) noted that when consumers are in the processes of deciding among products, two types of risk are apparent. First there is uncertainty about the outcome. Second, there is uncertainty about the consequences that are associated with product use. Risk can be viewed as a loss or as one's expectation of loss that is associated with an exchange. Interestingly this loss can be considered in psycho-social terms or in functional/economic terms. Under some conditions, the consumer may experience both types of loss. Stone and Winter (1985) extend this early discussion of the concept of risk to a broader context. They note that according to Bauer's (1960) original conceptualization of risk, consumer researchers focused on two aspects of risk—objective risk and perceived risk. Objective risk refers to specific risks that are quantifiable such as morbidity and mortality measures. For example, consumers engaging in risky surgical procedures, smoking cigarettes, eating raw meat or skydiving subject themselves to real objective risk. Perceived risk is a psychological construct, also quantifiable and inherent in consumer product evaluations and decisions. Some researchers, such as Stone and Winter (1985) argue that the distinction between objective and perceived risk is meaningless. More specifically, they state, "During information processing, concepts are not only dealt with to the degree perceived, but also most probably only 'exist' to this degree, as well...this holds true not only for positive valued concepts such as price, beauty, power, and believability, but also for the negatively valued concept of risk" (p. 12). In other words, they argue that the distinction between perceived risk and objective, or real world risk, is meaningless. For example consider psychological risk, social risk, or time risk. To imagine a legitimate, real world aspect of time risk is challenging. Stone and Winter (1985) ask, "could someone conceive of an 'objective' time risk? This hardly seems possible" (p. 3). The same holds true for social and psychological risk, for it would not seem reasonable for consumers to conceive of some "real world" psychological risk that exists beyond that which would be perceived" (p. 3). The most important consideration is to view risk from the perspective of the consumer. That is, when considering product risk, risk should represent the importance of the consequences associated with the use of the product, not the importance of the product to the consumer.

Bettman (1973) developed a model of the components of risk. He differentiated between inherent risk and handled risk. Inherent risk refers to the latent risk a product class holds for a consumer. That is, it is the "innate degree" of conflict the product class is able to arouse. On the other hand, handled risk is the amount of conflict the product class is able to arouse when the buyer chooses a brand from a product class in his usual buying situation. "That is, handled risk to a first approximation represents the end results of the action of information and risk reduction processes on inherent risk" (Bettman 1973, p. 184). Bettman uses the product class of aspirin to demonstrate the difference. "For example, a consumer may feel there is a great deal of risk associated with the product class aspirin. However, she has a favorite brand which she buys with confidence. In such a case, inherent risk is high, but handled risk may be low for aspirin" (p. 184).

Cunningham (1964, 1966, 1967a, b, c) measured the uncertainty and danger (consequences) consumers considered in different product categories. He was concerned with two issues uncertainty (i.e. would an untried brand work as well) and consequences (i.e., how much danger would the consumer experience trying a new brand).

Early conceptualizations of risk in the literature include Cox (1967). He proposed the risk associated with product purchase is related to "financial" or" social-psychological" risk. Woodside (1968) considered risk along the following three dimensions: "social", "functional" and "economic"; then (1971) indicated that consumer risk includes time loss, hazard loss, ego loss and money loss. Jacoby and Kaplan (1972) reinforced the concept of financial risk and added physical risk, and thus proposed the following five types of risks: financial risk; functional or performance risk; physical or health risk; psychological risk; and social risk.

To summarize the types of risks faced by consumers, a segmentation analysis combined with a purchase typology is warranted. The first type of risk, monetary risk is evidenced most acutely in consumers with little income, discretionary money or property. From a purchase typology standpoint, high-ticket items requiring significant expenditures are most susceptible to monetary risk. Common examples of monetary or financial risk include: credit risk, foreign exchange risk and interest rate risk. Practical consumers are most susceptible to the second form of risk, functional risk, which is defined as performance-related risk. If alternative means of performing the function are available, risk is enhanced both from a purchase and use standpoint. For example, technological products (e.g. cellphones, computers) and automobiles present functional risk for consumers. Health risk, while amenable to the entire population, is particularly salient to those vulnerable populations such as the elderly, frail or in ill health. Food and drug purchases are the most sensitive to health risk along with mechanical, electrical or chemical goods. Social risk arises from threats to self-esteem and self-confidence. Consumers lacking in such traits are most susceptible to social risk. Symbolic goods (e.g. clothing, jewelry, cars, homes) are most vulnerable to purchase-related social risk. Lastly, psychological risk cuts through a broad swath of traits including affiliations and status concern. Consumers lacking such traits are most sensitive. Purchase-related psychological risk is highest among personal luxury categories.

2 Risks to the Environment and Society

Sustainability Concerns and Stakeholder Response
Environmental risk and sustainability continues to be an issue of considerable interest to manufacturers, non-profit organizations, government agencies, and consumers. It is becoming increasingly evident that current patterns of consumption are not sustainable in the long-term; the world's natural resources are being rapidly depleted while environmental risks are pervasive. This is especially true with

respect to the United States. Although only accounting for 4.6% of the world's population, the United States consumes over 33% of the world's resources (EarthTrends 2007).

Environmental risk has been identified as a component of sustainable policy for decades. In 1987 the United States World Commission on the Environment and Development defined sustainability as, "Meeting the needs of the present without compromising the needs of future generations". The triple bottom line of sustainability (e.g. good for business/good for the environment/good for society) has become a benchmark norm for corporate, governmental and consumer organizations. Through the adoption of best practices there is an emerging opportunity for manufacturers to secure an integral role in driving the consumer demand for sustainable business practices, integrating CSR and sustainability into the consumer perception of value, promoting the visibility of triple bottom line efforts and thus mitigating consumer product risks. Environmental risk became a salient consumer characteristic with the *Exxon Valdez* oil spill and manufacturers and marketers subsequent response to said consumer concerns (Mayer et al. 2001).

Several key findings from the academic literature illuminate the concept of sustainability as it relates to product risk. First, many consumers have difficulty when asked to describe the concept of *product* sustainability (Dobson 2000; Sonneveld et al. 2005). Second, if a product's environmental risk is considered at all during evaluative and choice processes, it is generally not the primary attribute that influences consumers' product evaluations (e.g., Sammer and Wüstenhagen 2006; Vermeir and Verbeke 2006). For example, when purchasing food products, taste, price, and convenience are important considerations (Glanz et al. 1998). Similarly, safety, performance, and style are key product features when consumers evaluate automobiles (Roberts and Urban 1988). However, sustainability and environmental risk play a key role in certain consumer evaluative processes. For example, within the household cleaners and laundry detergent product categories, product risk and sustainability are of greater consumer concern (Schuhwerk and Lefkoff-Hagius 1995). Also consumers have indicated willingness to give up convenience for environmentally safer products or packaging (Hume and Strnad 1989). Consumers' willingness to pay higher taxes for government support of environmental initiatives and the growth of "green" retailers and manufacturers that adhere to rigorous environmental standards (beyond those mandated at the regulatory level) have also risen in importance (Rapert et al. 2010).

The EU has long recognized the importance of sustainability to the future of business and society by outlining general frameworks by which companies' environmental risk and sustainability efforts can be assessed. In 2001, the Sustainable Development Strategy for Europe stated that, "in the long term, economic growth, social cohesion and environmental protection must go hand in hand" (European Commission 2001). Additionally, the European Commission identified Corporate Social Responsibility as "a concept whereby companies integrate social and environmental concerns in their business operations and in their interaction with their stakeholders on a voluntary basis" (European Commission, p. 8). This definition of CSR makes note of the social and environmental risk components of the triple bottom line integral to sustainability. Thus, from definitions established by the EU, the concepts of environmental risk and sustainability are closely linked. Moreover, steps continue to be taken to improve sustainability efforts as evidenced by the EU Sustainable Development Strategy (European Commission 2001). The strategy focuses specifically on addressing the following seven global challenges in an attempt to effectively manage environmental risk, establish sustainable communities, and improve quality of life: (1) climate change and clean energy, (2) sustainable transport, (3) sustainable consumption and production processes, (4) conservation and management of natural resources, (5) public health, (6) social inclusion, demography/migration and (7) global poverty. The International Standards Organization (ISO) provides guidance on both environmental manufacturing and product risk compliance as well as on first- and third- party environmental claims (Hedblom 1998). Specifically, in addition to environmentally compliant good manufacturing practices, ISO provides guidelines on direct environmental impact of a company's manufacturing practices on brand attributes and third party seal of approval legitimacy.

From a U.S. standpoint both the Environmental Protection Agency (EPA) and Federal Trade Commission (FTC) provide "safe harbor" guidelines for mitigating and communicating environmental risk to consumers.

3 An Evidence-Based Approach to Risk Assessment: Measuring Risk Throughout the Product Life Cycle

3.1 Defining Product Risk Assessment Throughout the Product Life Cycle

Product risk assessment is the systematic use of available information to identify products, or features of products, which may cause or contribute to physical injury or death. From an ISO perspective, Risk assessment is comprised of both the identification of risks followed by their evaluation or ranking (IRM 2010). Specifically, risk assessment is an interdisciplinary evaluation process based on information derived from data such as exposure rates (OECD 2016). Standard practice includes comprising different data sources to inform regulatory options thus aiding in the selection of the appropriate response to a potential product hazard. Consequently, risk assessment provides valuable guidance to the formulation and conduct of sound risk management policy. Product risk assessments evolve in the scope of products being assessed based on different factors. For example, a range of products covered in a risk assessment may vary during the course of the analysis as more information about the hazards become available. This may lead to a single manufacturer's product becoming a class-wide recall based on competing product risks. Thus, risk assessment data has important implications for brand managers concerned with reputation as well as product liability litigators. Risk assessments are typically comprised of four core goals: (1) hazard identification, (2) injury scenarios, (3) threat severity and (4) likelihood estimation as well as reconciliation with societal laws and norms. Regulatory agencies use product risk assessment to determine which products require government action to reduce or manage stakeholder risk. The product life cycle stages of introduction (product development), growth (product refinement), maturity (backward innovation/low cost competitors) and decline (product withdrawal) all have implications both for consumer product use and misuse therefore product risk assessment is warranted throughout the life cycle.

3.2   Common Components of Consumer Product Risk Assessment

In addition to the common goals mentioned above, typical components of a consumer product risk assessment include: (1) product identification, (2) product use, (3) scenario estimation, (4) estimation of threat severity, (5) probability of occurrence, (6) risk estimation and (7) risk evaluation (OECD 2016). Safety goals incorporate the measurable performance of safety processes from the design process through manufacture, distribution and sales with subsequent accident analysis (Morgan 2001). Methodological factors common to consumer product risk assessment consist of proper sample selection including vulnerable (e.g. children) and affected populations; the frequency of product use and in what risk contexts the product is being used (DeBruin et al. 2007). Scenario development must be comprehensive to yield relevant safety data. Thorough recording and elucidation of all events in a scenario, including where and how they could occur achieves the goal of optimal consumer product safety data. Human factors such as consumers' attention or lack of attention to risk communication including warnings and instructions are also important in scenario development. In addition to perceptual issues, behavioral aspects such as compliance to safety instructions must also be considered. Properly framed warnings and usage information are important risk mitigation mechanisms as misuse and abuse (noncompliance) can result in regulatory scrutiny and liability for manufacturers.

Scenario development is a complex and idiosyncratic process. From a goal-based perspective, an optimal use scenario demonstrates the interaction between the product, its use environment and the affected population to create potentially unsafe situations. Subsequently, every scenario yields a typology of potential injuries indexed for severity of harm. Such an injury severity scale must comprise the full domain impact of an injury. This allows for proper regulatory guidance and response (Mann 2003).

ISO 10377 (and ISO/IEC Guide 51) includes risk analysis guidelines for manufacturers and suppliers as well as guidance for risk evaluation. Product risk assessments performed by manufacturers and suppliers are a key source of consumer product risk information. Specifically, the ISO guideline describes how to: (1) identify, assess, reduce or eliminate hazards, (2) manage risks by reducing them to tolerable levels and (3) provide consumers with hazard warnings or instructions essential to the safe use or disposal of consumer products (ISO 2013). Factors considered in the guidelines include hazard identification, exposure analysis, scenario estimation, and the probability of injury. Pre-purchase analysis, ongoing data assessment through the supply chain and consumer-level testing are components of the standard.

ISO 10377 is comprised of several core components that must be fully integrated into the product life cycle including: (1) general principles, (2) safety in design, (3) safety in production and (4) safety at the retail level (ISO 2013, 2014). General principles include a human resource/organizational behavior component; that is, promoting a safety culture within an organization. Such a culture is comprised of several elements including (1) continuous process improvement processes, (2) monitoring of production activities with an emphasis on safety and (3) recording incidents and procedures for data analysis (ISO 2013). Safety in design, another component of the ISO standard is crucial to the product life cycle stage of product introduction and growth. Specifically, this component includes what constitutes an *acceptable* level of product risk through the process of hazard identification, risk assessment and risk reduction/elimination. Product launches may be delayed to unacceptable hazards or product modifications may be made during the growth phase of a product. Human factors also play a role here as product warnings, disclosures and instructions provide a communication of any residual risks to the consumer as well as proper usage guidelines. Safety in production touches all four stages of the product life cycle as it emphasizes essential supply chain processes including manufacturing, product specification and sample testing. Standards must be adhered to as product modifications are made to (a) cater to customer needs or (b) facilitate cost savings (as in the case of reverse innovation for cost modification); hence the need to monitor throughout the PLC. Lastly, safety in the retail environment must be adhered to as it has a direct impact on consumers throughout the PLC. Therefore, the safety responsibilities of channel members including wholesalers, distributors, and retailers in product handling, service and consumer communication are of key importance.

Throughout the supply chain, risk assessments are performed by channel members. Assuming a stepwise approach, risk assessment begins at the design stage. An individual channel member's risk assessment of their product may not be relevant to competing products, because of differences in product design, production, intended users, and risk tolerance. Risk assessments are also conducted at the component part/assembly stage by suppliers as well as the manufacturing stage. Additionally, brand owners, importers and retailers may perform a risk assessment. Standards vary from voluntary to mandatory dependent on the specific product or product class. Third parties may be contracted to perform product risk assessments with agreements ranging from outsourcing for specialist knowledge to contracting with a confirmatory assessment or certification group.

A risk assessment takes on particular importance throughout the product life cycle as it determines whether steps should be taken by manufacturers or regulators to reduce consumer risk. Risk acceptability is a moving target. Differing product safety contexts produce differing responses (and scrutiny) from regulatory authorities. Several factors account for differing evaluations of risk including (1) whether vulnerable populations such as young children, the infirm or the elderly are affected and (2) one can reasonably foreseeable use or misuse of a product. An additional consideration is consumers' potential for hazard recognition. While consumers may recognize the inherent risk in some products such as firearms, they may be unable to recognize risks inherent in chemical products (DeBruin et al. 2007). Product age is also often a germane factor in the risk assessment. Second-hand goods or older supplied goods supplied may develop defects due to product lifespan limits.

At the macro-supplier level, product risk assessments performed by regulators typically share a core set of characteristics. First, risks are assessed by product category and are supplied by a range of suppliers across a broad set of situations. Second, many product risk assessments occur post-market (vs. pre-market). Third, regulators tend to place safety issues at the forefront of a risk assessment (termed "risk prioritization"). This is a stakeholder-based approach where regulators assess safety concerns from consumers, industry, and affected constituencies with the most serious potential safety hazards given priority and resource allocation for thorough risk assessment. Fourth, regulatory risk assessment is typically utilized in the following ways: the evaluation of existing pre-market requirements, the establishment of new pre-market requirements or whether intervention is necessary to reduce product risks to consumers.

3.3   Types of Risk Assessment

Both quantitative and qualitative approaches to risk assessment are utilized in different consumer risk contexts (Eliasson et al. 2015). Quantitative risk analysis is the more exhaustive, costly and time consuming risk assessment method. Quantitative risk analysis entails calculating the likelihood of occurrence of particular threats and the risks related to these particular threats are then estimated according to predetermined measurement scales. Qualitative risk analysis is more common than quantitative due to the time and cost involved. Qualitative analysis entails a broader approach, is more subjective and less costly for the business involved. For example, in one method, consumer product risks are reviewed for known vulnerabilities against a database of potential vulnerabilities by expert analysts. The risk is then indexed against relative scales to determine threat probability.

When deciding on the appropriate consumer product risk assessment technique, one must have an understanding of exposure assessment and analysis. Exposure assessment is a risk assessment technique used to establish the level of exposure under a particular use or exposure situation (Bruinen de Bruin et al. 2007). Typical to any exposure assessment are several key questions which can be illustrated with an example. First, when assessing for chemical risk (exposure to hazardous chemicals), during the product life cycle and through the supply chain could consumers be exposed to potential risks? Several possible answers exist including during manufacturing, during distribution, during end-use or (if plausible) outside the supply chain. Second, what are the possible routes for exposure? Routes include industrial sources, within-product sources or distributed environmental sources. Third, what is the magnitude of exposure through these key routes? Fourth, how does this exposure compare to relevant hazards? Fifth, What actions regarding chemical risk need to be taken?

A specific type of exposure assessment commonly used to assess consumer product risk is epidemiological investigation. This technique provides estimates of risk magnitude related to a particular level of exposure in a population (Blumenthal et al. 2001). In addition to quantifying probabilities of occurrence, epidemiological methods, have the potential to control for alternative explanations or other risk factors of the consumer risk outcome under observation. Epidemiological studies are often used in the establishment of guidelines and safety standards. The basic elements of an epidemiological study can be characterized as follows: (1) formulation of a research question, (2) sample selection, (3) selection of exposure indicators, (4) exposure measurement, (5) data analysis, (6) evaluation of alternative explanations (e.g. bias, chance) in data conclusions (Blumenthal et al. 2001; OECD 2013).

Additional epidemiological studies utilize observational techniques (e.g. case control studies) including standard cross-sectional studies, ecological studies, longitudinal and cohort studies. While the obvious limitation of observational studies is the lack of experimental controls and internal validity provided by a randomized experimental design, these observational studies give valuable insights to harm occurrence and incidence within a population; thereby informing supply chain members as well as regulators. Let it be noted that studies can be either descriptive or causal in nature. Properly designed epidemiological studies yield data that is generalizable to the affected population. These studies require that the product or service has been used for a sufficient number of consumers over a sufficient period of time.

Indexing is another commonly used technique in risk assessment. By definition, indexing is a systematic approach to identify, classify, and order sources of risk and to examine differences in risk perception (Birkmann 2007; Quinn 2001). Indexing has several important functions from a risk assessment standpoint including: risk identification and severity, identifying and prioritizing risks by population segment, identifying affected populations by location and discerning need for additional action. Risk indexing also aids in the identification of the nature and variation of within-population risks, risk variation based on independent variables such as exposure or individual difference variables such as demographic or economic variables. Risk indices are used by regulatory authorities as a baseline for policy formulation via the classification methodology.

Overall, risk assessment is a crucial factor in effective product life cycle management. Throughout each phase of the supply chain, risk assessments must be conducted to for the protection of all participants. Manufacturers and suppliers, from both a brand management and a liability protection standpoint, must have risk assessment frameworks in place to: (1) protect consumers from any potential product risk, (2) inform consumers of risks that can be mitigated with proper handling (behavioral compliance) and (3) comply with regulatory guidelines. Utilizing recognized and accepted risk assessment techniques in one's sector yields *actionable data* that informs proper risk management policies.

4 Managing Risk: The Role of Proper Compliance

4.1 Global Regulatory Standards

As previously discussed, typical risk management frameworks includes evaluation, risk confrontation, intervention, risk communication, and subsequent risk management components. There are numerous industrywide, national and international standards that exist for proper risk management. While there are different jurisdictions and guidelines, commonalities due exist that rise to the level of best practice in risk management. This contribution will highlight certain important regulatory standards while highlighting common principles that guide proper management for consumer product risk.

Compliance with mandatory safety standards is important for some products and jurisdictions. A regulator's assessment for a product that breaches a product safety prohibition or mandatory safety standard is likely to include legal aspects of non-compliance rather than rely on risk analysis considerations alone. Some jurisdictions emphasize compliance with relevant voluntary safety standards as an important consideration that influences their risk evaluation. Voluntary standards often specify safety requirements for the product.

While one specific ISO standard concerning supply chain assessment was discussed, ISO 31000 provides proper guidance for effective risk management and is recognized internationally (Purdy 2010; ISO 2009a). Specifically, ISO 31000 is an international standard that provides principles and guidelines for effective risk management. The standard is not industry specific, amenable to any type of risk, can be applied cross-sector and can be tailored to meet specific organizational needs (ISO 2009a). In addition, the standard contains risk management terminology, principles for guiding effective risk management, and guidance in forging an effective risk management framework.

ISO 31000 provides for the proper implementation of a risk management process. Board mandate and organizational dissemination is the primary component of ISO 31000 guidelines extremely pertinent to consumer product risk mitigation. Four key components are provided by the standard and present a common risk approach for organizations. The first set of guidelines concerns the design of a framework which includes the formation of a risk management policy.

Implementing the risk management policy including the risk management process constitutes the second set of guidelines. Assessing the framework is the next step followed lastly by modification and improvement of risk management processes and procedures. International consumer product risk and hazard recognition and mitigation regulations consistently refer to ISO guidelines as a baseline for proper risk management formulation.

4.2   U.S. Standards

The U.S. has taken a more activist stance on consumer product risk management in the past decade. Precipitating factors include negative public response to environmental disasters such as Hurricane Katrina and financial crises such as the subprime mortgage crisis. Common elements exist for risk assessment across the various regulatory agencies. From the Consumer Product Safety Commission, Food and Drug Administration and Federal Trade Commission, to the Environmental Protection Agency and USDA, a shared commonality of consumer safety and product risk mitigation.

4.3   Consumer Product Safety Commission (CPSC)

The CPSC is tasked with ensuring safety in the design, manufacture and distribution of consumer products throughout the product life cycle. In addition to regulatory oversight, the CPSC recommends best practices for supply chain actors including: (1) making safety a priority at the design stage through the safety hierarchy of risk (i.e. eliminating the risk, guarding against the risk and warning users of the risk), (2) how to build safety within the supply chain, (3) monitoring the business and regulatory environment for risk regulations and (4) risk preparedness processes and procedures (CPSC 2016).

4.4   Food and Drug Administration (FDA)

Residing within the Department of Health and Human Services (DHS), FDA is comprised of seven centers and offices. The FDA assures the safety, efficacy, and security of the U.S. food supply, human and veterinary drugs, biological products, medical devices, cosmetics, tobacco products and products that emit radiation (FDA 2016). From a consumer product risk standpoint, FDA approves medications, medical devices and other medical products for public use, and then, through a continuous risk assessment (post-market risk surveillance), evaluates the products' risks and benefits after they have been made publicly available.

4.5 Department of Homeland Security (DHS)

Consumers' experiences in the travel and tourism sector are at the core of DHS's mission. Terror threats present a number of risks to critical infrastructure. DHS has three agencies (U.S. Coast Guard, the Office for Domestic Preparedness and the Information Analysis and Infrastructure Protection (IAIP) Directorate) accountable for critical infrastructure security (DHS 2016).

4.6 National Transportation Safety Board (NTSB)

Consumer product safety practices in the railroad, highway, air and marine sectors are regulated by the NTSB. All significant safety incidents and accidents within these sectors are investigated by the NTSB with the agency issuing safety recommendations aimed at preventing future accidents.

4.6.1 Canadian Standards

The objective of *Canadian risk management policy* is to safeguard the government's property, interests, and certain interests of employees during the conduct of government operations. Departments within the Public Service of Canada are required to identify, minimize, and contain risks and to compensate for, restore and recover from risk events. The Canadian risk management process includes the following phases: identifying issues, assessing key risk areas, measuring likelihood and impact, indexing, milestoning, strategy selection and implementation, follow-up monitoring and continuous process adjustment (Hardy 2010).

4.6.2 British Standards

In addition to following ISO 31000 protocols, the *British Risk Management Code of Practice* emphasizes the future business operations from a risk-based perspective. This includes strategic implementation through program, project and change management. Additionally, ongoing operations are emphasized including people, processes, and information security (BSI British Standard 2016).

4.6.3 European Union Standards

EU risk assessment principles for consumer products are based around: (1) hazard identification, (2) exposure assessment and (3) risk characterization. In addition to adhering to ISO protocols the European Union established the Community Rapid

Information System (i.e. RAPEX) as a means of communication concerning consumer product risks between member states and the Commission. The RAPEX risk assessment guidelines describe a three-step process of risk assessment and communication. First, there is the development of an injury scenario that establishes a link between the product and an estimated severity of injury. Second, probability estimation of the likelihood of occurrence is undertaken. Lastly, the risk estimation is produced by combining the estimated severity and probability (OECD 2013).

4.6.4 Best Practices

When discussing best practices for consumer product risk mitigation, certain core principles should be identified. Specifically, a risk management initiative must comply with applicable internal and regulatory governance requirements; thus assuring all stakeholders risk is minimized while improving decision making and operational efficiency throughout the supply chain (Lalonde and Boiral 2012; International Organization for Standardization 2009a, b). Best practice principles also include proportionality (the risk management initiative should fit the size, nature and complexity of the supply chain member), alignment (with corporate mission and function), scope and embeddedness into corporate activities (RIMS 2011). Any consumer product risk management initiative must be adaptable to changing environmental circumstances. Lastly, risk management must be a Board-level priority thus integrated into organizational culture.

As previously discussed, best practices can be conveyed through various frameworks. Standard risk management frameworks convey antecedent conditions, a stepwise approach to problem formulation and hazard identification, a detailed risk assessment that comprises elements of exposure assessment, risk estimation and consequence analysis. Lastly, a risk evaluation is made that leads to proper risk management measures (RMM's) in accordance with regulatory and industry standards (Leitch 2010). Common responses to risk recognition follow a "4T" typology: tolerate the risk, treat the risk, transfer it or terminate the risk (ISO 2009b).

5 Conclusion

Consumers face numerous risks in their daily lives. From a normative standpoint, consumers depend on a sound risk management ecosystem to reduce and eliminate risks in their respective environments. Organizations throughout supply chain and in various phases of the product life cycle must maintain rigorous safety standards to (1) mitigate risk and maintain reputational equity, (2) comply with regulatory standards and (3) reduce their own liability and risk of litigation. With the increased risk of litigation and class actions surrounding consumer product risk in certain jurisdictions such as the U.S., continuous risk assessment and risk management measures are likely to grow in both sophistication and frequency.

References

Association of Insurance and Risk Managers, Alarm and the Institute for Risk Management. A structured approach to enterprise risk management. (2010). pp. 1–18.

Bauer, R. A. (1960). Consumer behavior as risk-taking. In R. S. Hancock (Ed.), *Dynamic marketing for a changing world* (pp. 389–398). Chicago: American Marketing Association.

Bettman, J. R. (1973). Perceived risk and its components: A model and empirical test. *Journal of Marketing Research, 10*, 184–189.

Birkmann, J. (2007). Risk and vulnerability indicators at different scales: Applicability, usefulness and policy implications. *Environmental Hazards, 7*(1), 20–31.

Blumenthal, U. J., Fleisher, J. M., Esrey, S. A., & Peasey, A. (2001). Epidemiology: A tool for the assessment of risk. In L. Fewtrell (Ed.), *Water quality: Guidelines, standards and health* (pp. 135–160). London: IWA Publishing.

British Standards Institution. (2016). *Information about standards.* Accessed June 1, 2016, from http://www.bsigroup.com/en-GB/standards/Information-about-standards/

Consumer Product Safety Commission. (2016). Accessed July 1, 2016, from https://www.cpsc.gov/Regulations-Laws--Standards/Statutes/

Cox, D. F. (1967). *Risk-taking and information-handling in consumer behavior.* Boston: Harvard University.

Cunningham, S. M. (1964). Perceived risk as a factor in product-oriented word-of-mouth behavior: A first step. In L. G. Smith (Ed.), *Reflections on progress in marketing* (pp. 229–238). Chicago: American Marketing Association.

Cunningham, S. M. (1966). Perceived risk as a factor in the diffusion of new product information. In R. M. Hass (Ed.), *Science, technology. and marketing* (pp. 698–721). Chicago: American Marketing Association.

Cunningham, S. M. (1967a). The major dimensions of perceived risk. In D. F. Cox (Ed.), *Risk-taking and information-handling in consumer behavior* (pp. 82–108). Boston: Harvard University.

Cunningham, S. M. (1967b). Perceived risk as a factor in informal consumer communications. In D. F. Cox (Ed.), *Risk-taking and information-handling in consumer behavior* (pp. 265–288). Boston: Harvard University.

Cunningham, S. M. (1967c). Perceived risk and brand loyalty. In D. F. Cox (Ed.), *Risk-taking and information-handling in consumer behavior* (pp. 507–523). Boston: Harvard University.

De Bruin, Y. B., Lahaniatis, M., Papameletiou, D., Del Pozo, C., Reina, V., Van Engelen, J., & Jantunen, M. (2007). Risk management measures for chemicals in consumer products: documentation, assessment, and communication across the supply chain. *Journal of Exposure Science and Environmental Epidemiology, 17*, S55–S66.

Department of Homeland Security. (2016). Accessed August 1, 2016. https://www.dhs.gov/about-dhs

Dobson, A. (2000). *Green political thought.* London: Psychology Press.

Earthtrends. (2007). *EarthTrends update July 2007: Vulnerability and adaptation to climate change.* Accessed August 1, 2016, from http://armspark.msem.univ-montp2.fr/bfpvolta/admin/biblio/EarthTrends%20Update%20July%202007.pdf

Eliasson, K., Nyman, T., & Forsman, M. (2015). Usability of six observational risk assessment methods. In Proceedings 19th Triennial Congress of the IEA, Melbourne 9–14, pp. 1–2.

Engel, J. F., Kollat, D. T., & Blackwell, R. D. (1973). *Consumer behavior* (2nd ed.). New York: Holt, Rinehart, & Winston.

European Commission. (2001). *Promoting a European framework for corporate social responsibility.* Accessed June 1, 2016, fromhttp://ec.europa.eu/employment_social/soc-dial/csr/pdf/044-compnetnat_bitc_uk_011218_en.ht

Food and Drug Administration. (2016). *What does FDA do?* Accessed August 1, 2016, from http://www.fda.gov/AboutFDA/Transparency/Basics/ucm194877.htm

Glanz, K., Basil, M., Maibach, E., Goldberg, J., & Snyder, D. (1998). Why Americans eat what they do: Taste, nutrition, cost, convenience, and weight control concerns as influences on food consumption. *Journal of the American Diabetic Association, 98*(10), 1118–1126.

Hardy, K. (2010). *Managing risk in government; An introduction to enterprise risk management* (pp. 1–50). Washington, DC: IBM Center for Business and Government.

Hedblom, M. O. (1998). Environment, for better or worse (Part 3). *Ericsson Review, 1*, 1–15.

Howard, J. A., & Sheth, J. N. (1969). *The theory of buyer behavior.* New York: Wiles.

Hume, S., & Strnad, P. (1989, September 25). Consumers go green. *Advertising Age, 3*, 92.

International Organization for Standardization. (2009a). ISO 31000: 2009(a). Risk management: Principles and guidelines.

International Organization for Standardization. (2009b). ISO Guide 73(b): Risk vocabulary.

International Organization for Standardization. (2013). ISO 10377. Consumer product safety. Guidelines for suppliers.

International Organization for Standardization/International Electrotechnical Commission. (2014). ISO/IEC Guide 51: Safety aspects—Guidelines for their inclusion in standards.

Jacoby, J., & Kaplan, L. (1972). The components of perceived risk. In M. Venkatesan (Ed.), *Proceedings, third annual convention of the association for consumer research* (pp. 382–393). Chicago: Association for Consumer Research.

Lalonde, C., & Boiral, O. (2012). Managing risks through ISO 31000: A critical analysis. *Risk management, 14*(4), 272–300.

Leitch, M. (2010). ISO 31000: 2009. The new international standard on risk management. *Risk Analysis, 30*(6), 887–892.

Mann, C. J. (2003). Observational research methods. Research design II: Cohort, cross sectional, and case-control studies. *Emergency Medicine Journal, 20*(1), 54–60.

Mayer, R. N., Lewis, L. A., & Scammon, D. L. (2001). The effectiveness of environmental marketing claims. In P. Bloom & G. Gundlach (Eds.), *Handbook of marketing and society* (pp. 399–420). Thousand Oaks, CA: Sage.

Morgan, F. (2001). The effectiveness of product safety regulation and litigation. In P. Bloom & G. Gundlach (Eds.), *Handbook of marketing and society* (pp. 436–461). Thousand Oaks, CA: Sage.

Organization for Economic Co-operation and Development. (2013). Summary of The OECD Workshop on Product Risk Assessment, *www.oecd.org/officialdocuments/ publicdisplaydocumentpdf/?cote=dsti/cp/cps%282012%2916/final&doclanguage=en.* Accessed 1 June 2016

Organization for Economic Co-operation and Development. (2016). Product risk assessment practices of regulatory agencies. pp. 1–19

Purdy, G. (2010). ISO 31000: 2009—Setting a new standard for risk management. *Risk analysis, 30*(6), 881–886.

Quinn, C. (2001). Risk mapping in semi-arid Tanzania: Review of common pool resource management in Tanzania. Report prepared for NRSP Project R7857 (DRAFT). Accessed July 1, 2016, from http://www.york.ac.uk/res/celp/webpages/projects/cpr/tanzania/pdf/Annex7.pdf

Rapert, M. I., Newman, C., Park, S. Y., & Lee, E. M. (2010). Seeking a better place: Sustainability in the CPG industry. *Journal of Global Academy of Marketing Science, 20*(2), 199–207.

Risk and Insurance Management Society. (2011). An overview of widely used risk management standards and guidelines, pp. 1–24.

Roberts, J. H., & Urban, G. L. (1988). Modeling multiattribute utility, risk, and belief dynamics for new consumer durable brand choice. *Management Science, 34*(2), 167–185.

Sammer, K., & Wüstenhagen, R. (2006). The influence of eco-labelling on consumer behavior— results of a discrete choice analysis. *Business Strategy and the Environment, 15*(3), 185–199.

Schuhwerk, M. E., & Lefkoff-Hagius, R. (1995). Green or non-green? Does type of appeal matter when advertising a green product? *Journal of Advertising, 24*(2), 21–31.

Sonneveld, K., James, K., Fitzpatrick, L., & Lewis, H. (2005). Sustainable packaging: How do we define and measure it? Proceedings of the 22nd IAPRI Symposium.

Stone, R.N., & Winter, F. (1985). Risk in buyer behavior contexts: A clarification. BEBR faculty working paper No. 1216, pp. 20–22.

Taylor, J. W. (1974). The role of risk in consumer behavior. *Journal of Marketing, 38*, 54–60.

Vermeir, L., & Verbeke, W. (2006). Sustainable food consumption: Exploring the consumer attitude-behavioral intention gap. *Journal of Agricultural and Environmental Ethics, 19*(2), 169–194.

Woodside, A. (1968). Social character, product use and advertising appeals. *Journal of Advertising Research, 8*, 31–35.

Woodside, A. (1971, October). Product advertising and price perceptions of the small business customer. *Journal of Small Business Management, 9*, 15–20.

Non-Clinical Research-Based Product Assessment

Dominique Deplanque

1 An Approach That Has Become Essential

The US Food and Drug Administration (founded in 1848, along with the Patent Office) is probably one of the world's oldest consumer protection agencies (history of the FDA at www.fda.gov). An important change occurred on June 30th, 1906, when President Roosevelt signed the Food and Drugs Act (prohibiting the interstate transport of unlawful food and drugs). This fell under the remit of the Division and Bureau of Chemistry, although the latter dealt with the regulation of product labeling more than pre-market approval. The Bureau progressively devoted more effort to drug regulation, with some emphasis on so-called "patent medicines" following a series of incidents caused by products such as Lash-Lure®, an eyelash dye that caused eye injuries in a number of women. The next major change came on June 25th, 1938, with the introduction of the Food, Drug, and Cosmetic Act, following the "Elixir Sulfanilamide" scandal (history of the FDA at www.fda. gov). In 1937, a Tennessee drug company had marketed this new drug formulation for pediatric patients. However, the solvent in this untested product was a highly toxic chemical analogue of antifreeze, and over 100 people (including many children) died. The Food, Drug, and Cosmetic Act brought cosmetics and medical devices under control, and required that drugs be labeled with adequate directions for safe use. Moreover, it mandated pre-market approval of all new drugs, such that a manufacturer would have to prove to FDA that a drug was safe before it could be sold. From this time onwards, several other national or international agencies (such as the European Medicines Agency, EMA) have been created. A large number of guidelines and rules governing the market access process have been introduced,

D. Deplanque (✉)
Department of Medical Pharmacology, Faculty of Medicine, University Lille-North of France,
1 Place Verdun, 59045 Lille, France
e-mail: Dominique.deplanque@univ-lille2.fr

© Springer International Publishing AG 2017
G. Emilien et al. (eds.), *Consumer Perception of Product Risks and Benefits*,
DOI 10.1007/978-3-319-50530-5_3

including the requirement for non-clinical evaluations before human use. Drugs and other medicines undergo the strictest non-clinical assessments, in which both pharmacodynamic and pharmacokinetic issues should be examined. Moreover, it is not possible today to bring a new molecule to the market without testing its acute and chronic toxicity, mutagenesis, carcinogenesis, teratogenicity and effects on the reproductive system in several pertinent *in vitro* and *in vivo* models (Blomme 2016). These approaches and methods have sometimes also been used to assess non-drug products, such as foodstuffs, cosmetics and consumer products containing chemicals. However, these non-clinical approaches do not always guarantee the future users' safety. For example, some products (such as medical devices) cause serious accidents not only through device dysfunction but also occasionally due to human error in the use of a badly designed device. Accordingly, the latest regulations require human factors and usability engineering to be taken into account in the development of medical devices (FDA Center for Devices and Radiological Health Office of Device Evaluation 2016). It is essential to anticipate future developments in pertinent non-clinical models because we lack knowledge of the acute and chronic toxicities of a number of chemicals (such as endocrine disruptors) and nanotechnologies. In addition to new biotechnological approaches (such as induced pluripotent stem cells, iPSCs) and organs-on-chips), the development of Phase 0 clinical trials may be a key element in product testing and approval. In fact, the human is probably the best model for future human use, provided that the main issues are accurately forecast and addressed.

2   The Non-Clinical Evaluation of Drugs: A Major, Restrictive Model

Drug development is a long, complex and expensive process that results in more failures than successes; less than 10% of candidate molecules enter Phase I clinical trials. While several thousand novel molecules are discovered or synthesized each year, non-clinical safety testing represents a major issue—especially during the compound optimization stages of drug discovery and in the early stages of clinical development. Toxicity assessment is then a crucial issue for companies whose future business activity will depend on tests performed early in the development of a future drug candidate. A decade ago, it was assumed that stopping ineffective or unsafe molecules as early as possible in discovery process would result in substantial productivity gains. Nevertheless, the latest evidence suggests that the non-clinical safety-related attrition rate has not changed and that the drug development process has not been streamlined (Blomme 2016). In the development of a new drug, it is important to rapidly determine the compound's true toxicity profile and the expected safety margin. To this end, it is essential to use a variety of models that are able to accurately predict the compound's behavior in humans (including the drug candidate's physicochemical properties and putative targets). However, the use of a variety of assays and models generates huge volumes of data that should be analyzed with caution when deciding whether to continue the evaluation process or not. From a public health point of view, drug regulatory authorities seek to reduce the health risk to individuals and population as much as possible.

2.1 Pharmacodynamic Properties: How Does the Drug Work?

One of the first steps in the toxicity assessment process is to precisely evaluate the compounds pharmacodynamic properties (drug targets and effects) and pharmaco-kinetic properties (drug metabolism). Some pharmacodynamic parameters are sometimes already partially described, thanks to the way in which the molecule has been discovered. Indeed, high-throughput screening (HTS) methods are mainly based on selective ligand-receptor interactions in genetically modified cells or in other specific bioassays (Walters and Namchuk 2003; Fraietta and Gasparri 2016). This type of approach enables one to (i) establish whether or not a compound is able to bind and activate/inactivate a target, and (ii) determine the intensities of the binding and the biological response. The use of HTS can thus help to define the target or biological system that a new compound activates or inhibits most selec-tively and strongly. Studies of *in vitro* models can also help to predict drug interactions. However, whenever possible, these *in vitro* studies should be complemented by *in vivo* studies—ideally in an animal model of the human disease that might be treated with the drug candidate. Using chemical, surgical or genetic approaches, it is now possible to reproduce a number of human diseases in small or large animals. For example, neurological diseases (such as stroke, Alzheimer's disease and Parkinson's disease) can be reproduced in rats and mice. Type 1 or 2 diabetes can also be easily developed in various animals. Likewise, some cardio-vascular diseases (such as heart failure) can be induced in various species, including pigs (Milani-Nejad and Janssen 2014). More recently, progress in biotechnology (such as genomic approaches involving CRISPR/Cas9 technology) has opened up almost unlimited possibilities (Dow 2015; Fraietta and Gasparri 2016). Neverthe-less, the ability of animal models to accurately predict human diseases is subject to debate, and there are ethical limitations on animal experiments. Despite a number of shortcomings, these pharmacodynamic approaches are crucial for better defining a compound's pharmacological profile, potential targets and certain safety features (notably its effects on the heart, lung and brain). Pharmacodynamic studies probe some other crucial parameters, including dose-effect relationships, time-effect relationships and the median effective dose (ED 50, the dose that is effective in 50% of test organisms or treated individuals). These parameters will be of great importance for further toxicological studies and for definition of the dose to be used in clinical trials.

2.2 Pharmacokinetic Properties: Where and How Do a Drug and Its Metabolites Distribute?

Drug pharmacokinetics are often more difficult to study than drug pharmacodynamics. Indeed, pharmacokinetics concerns all the processes to which a drug is subjected (i.e. absorption, distribution, metabolism and elimination, ADME; Fig. 1). Pharmacokinetics is a very complex process, with many interactions and the involvement of key organs such as the liver and the kidney. The distribution of a drug or other type of compound across tissues and organs depends not only on its physicochemical characteristics but also on the presence or absence of selective transporters in these tissues. Although drug metabolism (which predominantly takes place in the liver) generally yields inactive compounds, the production of a metabolite with greater activity or toxicity may have harmful consequences. Lastly, drug elimination will also depend on many different factors. Overall, it is still difficult to predict pharmacokinetic properties by using only *in vitro* models, and sometimes even animal models are not fully predictive. Usually, *in vivo* studies are performed in three different animal species and an administration route as similar as

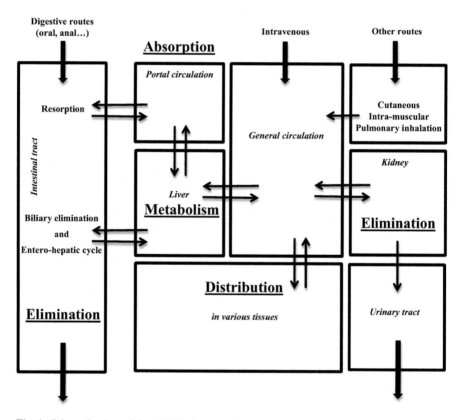

Fig. 1 Schematic view of the ADME pharmacokinetic process

possible to that planned for clinical use. Novel, physiologically-based pharmacokinetic models have also been developed (Rowland et al. 2011). These models predict the processes of drug clearance, distribution, absorption, quantitative drug-drug interactions, and the impact of age, genetics, disease, and formulation. The FDA first validated this type of approach in the 1990s for the approval of tretinoin, a highly teratogenic active ingredient of a topical anti-wrinkle cream. Ever since a workshop held in 2002, the FDA has encouraged study sponsors to use physiologically-based pharmacokinetic modeling and simulation to determine the best dosing strategy (Rowland et al. 2011). In order to validate the results of animal experiments and modeling studies, data from early-phase clinical trials remain crucial and, ultimately, constitute the only way of determine a new drug's true pharmacokinetic profile.

2.3 Evaluation of Acute and Chronic Toxicity

The acute and chronic toxicities of a new pharmacological compound are evaluated in a range of tests. The goal is to identify any toxic or undesirable effects that may occur during the proposed conditions of use in humans and in the context of the targeted disease. The different tests also contribute to better qualitative and quantitative understanding of the compound's pharmacological properties in humans. The evaluation of acute toxicity takes account not only of qualitative and quantitative effect but also of the latter's time dependency (Table 1). The calculation of the median lethal dose (LD 50) is no longer compulsory; determination of the maximum non-lethal dose and the "no-observable-adverse-effect level" (NOAEL) is preferred. These parameters are very important for choosing the dose given in subsequent clinical trials. In acute toxicity studies, at least two species of mammal are used (usually rats and mice). Animals are typically observed for at least 2 weeks. Toxic signs (including the time and date of onset, severity, duration, and outcome) are noted for each animal. All animals are then necropsied, and a histopathological examination is performed—particularly on organs in which a macroscopic abnormality is observed.

Chronic toxicity is studied using the same principles, although the dosage is repeated for between 2 weeks and several months. The duration of the exposure to the drug is directly proportional to the planned duration of treatment in humans (2 weeks of exposure in the animal for treatments of up to 2 weeks in humans, 1 month of exposure for treatments of up to 1 month, etc.). Exposure for 6 months is required for use in clinical trials for more than 6 months. As specified in Table 1, the animal experiments are performed in at least two mammal species (including a non-rodent species). The planned clinical administration route must be used in the animal experiments, and both males and females must be included. The animals are closely observed during the toxicity tests. The body weight, food intake and behavior are scrupulously analyzed, and a range of biological assays is performed. Lastly, the animals are necropsied and the organs are carefully examined.

Table 1 In vivo preclinical testing of acute and chronic drug toxicity

Type of toxicity and treatment duration	Objectives	Animals	Dose(s)	Administration
Acute (single dose)	• To establish a dose-effect relationship • To determine the minimum non-lethal dose and the NOAEL[a] • To determine the nature of acute toxic effects • To provide some indication of the effects that will possibly be observed in humans • To take samples for the kinetic study of toxicological effects	• ≥ 2 mammal species • Usually the rat and mouse • 5 males and 5 females from each species	• A single administration for each dose tested • Defined according to the dose previously used in pharmacodynamic studies • Estimation of the lethal dose and the dose-response curve	• Drugs in suspension or solution • At least two distinct administration routes • Administered via the route planned in humans and one other systemic route
Subacute (0–1 month) Subchronic (1–3 months) Chronic (>3 months)	• To determine toxic effects after repeated administration • To observe cumulative or delayed effects • To determine whether or not the toxic effects are reversible • To identify target organs • To define a dose lacking an effect and (perhaps) a dose-response curve • To choose the dosage level for long-term studies	• ≥ 2 mammal species • Including a non-rodent model (e.g. the dog) • Number: 10 males and 10 females in each group (rodents) and 6 males and 6 females in each group (non-rodents) • The choice of species should take account of the metabolism expected in humans	• Defined according to the doses already evaluated in single-dose acute studies or short-term repeated-dose studies • Three treatment groups and a control group should be used • Different levels should be tested: a low dose (with a pharmacodynamic effect but no toxicity), an intermediate dose and a high dose (a multiple of the planned dose, and which should reveal toxic effects)	• Administered via the route planned in humans • The drug formulation should not modify eating behavior • The animals' drug exposure should be demonstrated (plasma level).

[a]Determination of the median lethal dose has not been compulsory since 1991

Toxicokinetic data are also acquired during this stage of development by determining the degree of exposure to the molecule as a function of the duration and the administered dose. Changes of blood, plasma and serum levels of both the investigational compound and its metabolites are closely monitored. Hence, the studies' objective is not only to observe and characterize toxic effects but also to precisely define the dose that will be used for future clinical trials.

2.4 Mutagenesis and Carcinogenesis

Screening for both mutagenic and carcinogenic effects is another important step in development. Mutagenesis is defined as a sudden, permanent modification of hereditary characteristics through changes in the number and nature of genes. The goals of mutagenesis and carcinogenesis testing are to (i) demonstrate any drug-induced changes in the genetic material, (ii) evaluate the likelihood of transmission of any abnormalities to future generations, and (iii) assess the risk of cancer development in the present generation of cells or animals (depending on the model used). Several batteries of *in vitro* and *in vivo* tests can be used. One of the most famous is the Ames test, performed in bacteria (Ames et al. 1975). The results of this simple, cheap, rapid test can predict a drug's potential mutagenic effects. Another important *in vitro* test consists of measuring chromosomal aberrations in murine lymphoma cells or other mammalian cells. Chromosomal aberrations can also be analyzed *in vivo* in rodent hematopoietic cells. Taken as a whole, the results of these tests will provide important information on a drug candidate's potential mutagenic activity. Carcinogenesis tests in animals are designed to establish whether life-long treatment of a drug might favor the development of tumors. The proof of the drug exposure should be also clearly demonstrated (namely by measuring plasma drug concentrations). Animals such as rats and mice are usually treated from weaning to at least 24 to 30 months of age, which that represents a large proportion of the lifespan for these small rodents. Here again, the planned clinical administration route must be used, and three different doses are usually tested.

2.5 Reproductive Functions

The term "reproductive functions" covers the whole cycle of reproduction, fertility, embryo/fetal toxicity, teratogenicity, and the toxic consequences in offspring with regard to survival, physical and mental development, and reproductive capacity (Table 2). The primary goal of these reproductive toxicity studies is therefore to characterize the compound's profile with respect to toxic effects on three different segments: fertility and early embryonic development, embryonic/fetal

Table 2 Preclinical evaluation of drug effects on reproductive functions

Segment	Objectives	Animals	Dose and administration	Estimated parameters
Segment I Fertility and embryogenesis	To highlight: • Effects on mating behavior • The maintenance or loss of the fetus • The appearance of fetal anomalies • Possible impairments in the progeny	• Both males and females before mating • Pregnant females • ≥2 mammal species, including a non-rodent • The choice of species should take account of the metabolism expected in humans	• Dose escalation • Administered via the route planned in humans	• Maternal toxicity • Implantation rate • Number of fetuses (dead or alive) • Fetus weight • Sex ratio
Segment II Embryonic/ fetal toxicity and teratogenicity	To highlight any effect on: • The maintenance or loss of the fetus • The appearance of fetal anomalies • Possible impairments in the progeny	• Pregnant females • ≥2 mammal species including a non-rodent • The choice of species should take account of the metabolism expected in humans	• Dose escalation • Administered via the route planned in humans	• Implantation rate • Sampling of the uterus before birth • Weight and sex of the fetus • Organ histopathology
Segment III Pre- and post-natal studies	To highlight any effect on: • Fetal growth • Breast-feeding • Development of progeny	• Late pregnancy or breast-feeding females • ≥2 mammal species including a non-rodent • The choice of species should take account of the metabolism expected in humans	• Dose escalation • Administered via the route planned in humans	• Weight and sex of the fetus • Organ histopathology

development, and pre- and postnatal development (including maternal functions). Indeed, fertility can be affected in males and females, and the effects can range from a slight decrease in reproductive capability to complete sterility. Embryonic/ fetal toxicity will influence the ability to survive to term, whereas teratogenicity produces irreversible, adverse effects in the developing embryo and fetus and thus harms the offspring's physical status.

Following to the thalidomide disaster in the 1960s (in which more than 10,000 children suffered from a teratogenic limb defect that was only later demonstrated in a rabbit model), better determination of the teratogenic risk in appropriate models has become an important concern. Different batches of pregnant females from at least two mammalian species (including a non-rodent species) should now be used. The choice of the most appropriate species is based on knowledge of the compound's supposed metabolism. Moreover, the metabolism in the animal should be as similar as possible to the predictable metabolism in humans. The discovery of teratogenicity in animal experiments is a bad sign for the drug's chances of clinical development, although the absence of any harmful effects should not be simply interpreted as a guarantee of total safety. Only human studies and the drug's subsequent use under "real-life" conditions can provide high-quality data in this respect.

2.6 Integration of Preclinical Study Results in Clinical Development

All the above-described studies do not always have been completed before the first-in-human study. Indeed, the choice of the testing strategy depends on the available safety data (derived from previous non-clinical or clinical tests), which can be used to define the future drug's benefit-risk ratio. The timing of non-clinical safety studies (with regard to clinical development) must also be considered. In the International Council for Harmonisation (ICH)'s Guideline M3, the type and duration of non-clinical safety studies are correlated with the clinical development schedule (ICH 2009). In most cases, the following non-clinical safety studies should be conducted before the first-in-human study: single-dose and repeated-dose studies (minimum duration: 2 weeks); two *in vitro* genotoxicity studies; safety pharmacology studies, and initial characterization of the pharmacokinetic profile. For other clinical phases, and as part of the preparation of a new drug application for the authorities, the results of the long-term repeated-dose studies, the full mutagenesis battery, the carcinogenesis tests, and the evaluation of reproductive functions should be provided. In addition to these toxicological approaches, the pharmaceutical formulation should be specifically designed before human use. This includes synthesizing the drug in sufficient quantities with optimal quality and purity—which sometimes raises the problem of stability. A relevant, specifically packaged and labeled pharmaceutical formulation of the compound should also be developed. All these stages must comply with good manufacturing practice, as explicitly defined by the ICH Q7 guideline (ICH 2000).

3 The Development of New Approaches

As discussed above, toxicity tests are intended to identify harmful effects caused by acute or chronic exposure to a substance. Given that several factors determine toxicity (such as the administration route, dose, frequency of exposure, and ADME/ biochemical properties), it is imperative to use the best models in this evaluation. Animal models have been used for a long time, and the development of genetic technologies is opening up new perspectives. However, *in vivo* models remain particularly constrained by ethical and financial issues. Hence, *in vitro* and *in silico* toxicity testing is becoming increasingly plausible. Indeed, recent advances in HTS, the use of a broad variety of cell-based models, and the development of computational methods may help us to evaluate a chemical's toxicity and shorten the time between discovery and first-in-human studies.

3.1 What Role Do in silico Approaches Have?

In silico toxicology assessments use computational resources to analyze, model and predict the toxicity of chemical substances (Raies and Bajic 2016). Along with *in vitro* and *in vivo* models, *in silico* assessments may minimize the need for animal testing, reduce the duration of toxicity testing and improve safety. As long as the model is relevant, an important advantage of these methods is the ability to forecast a compound's toxicity even before it has been synthetized. A wide variety of tools are necessary for developing relevant *in silico* models: databases on known toxicity and properties of chemicals, software for generating molecular descriptors, simulation tools for systems biology and molecular dynamics, modeling methods and tools for generating toxicity prediction models, adequate computing resources and, lastly, appropriate statistical tools. These prerequisites emphasize some of the limitations of *in silico* models. In fact, most computational toxicology models are not efficient enough to justify their use in drug discovery. The reasons include the complexity and variety of toxicity mechanisms for any given tissue, and the extremely broad range of chemical structures associated with similar toxic endpoints. Another limitation of computational toxicology models is related to the quality and quantity of the data used as training set; most available datasets do not provide the necessary level of robustness and chemical diversity. Lastly, published models are often not sufficiently validated *ex silico* (Blomme 2016). Nevertheless, some computational approaches are of major value in drug discovery and development. *In silico* methods can provide a better understanding of a drug's pharmacodynamic profile, quantitative structure-activity relationships (QSARs), genetic toxicity and interactions with drug transporters. Importantly, the recent increase in public-sector, private-sector and in-house databases and their combination with appropriate information technology infrastructures can only improve knowledge about toxicity if these various expert systems can interact. Recent regulatory changes in the industrial chemicals and cosmetics sectors have prompted a significant number of advances in the development, application, and assessment of non-animal testing approaches (Patlewicz and Fitzpatrick 2016). In light of advances in HTS approaches and constructs, *in silico* approaches will probably become of great importance in drug discovery.

3.2 From Cell-Based Models to Organs-On-Chips

High-content screening involves a multitude of cellular approaches. In all cases, complex information is extracted from single cells at medium to high throughputs. Any analytical approach that produces multiparameter, phenotypic information from cells (either cultured *in vitro* or within multicellular organisms) can be defined as a "high-content" assay. Appropriate staining (fluorescent dyes, molecular probes, antibodies, etc.), automated microscopy and quantitative image analysis enables the detection of phenotypic changes occurring under specific pharmacological conditions (Fraietta and Gasparri 2016). The potential of such HTS has been drastically expanded by recent advances in cell-based assay technologies, such as the introduction of three-dimensional cell culture, iPSCs and genome-editing technologies (e.g., CRISPR/Cas9). The great majority of high-content assays are based on cancer cell lines, such as HeLa and U-2 osteosarcoma cells. One of the main limitations of these cells is that they have defects in DNA repair pathways, which predisposes them to the accumulation of additional mutations. Hence, over-passaged cell lines are likely to have a different phenotype or to respond differently to external stimuli, relative to the original cells. This may be a major problem in the pre-clinical evaluation of the toxicological effects of a new drug or other chemical. Interestingly, new cell-based models have been developed, such as primary cell cultures derived from normal tissues grown *in vitro* (specialized hepatocytes or neurons, for example). Under these conditions, tissue-specific toxicological effects in normal cells can be analyzed. Nevertheless, major limitations to use in *in vitro* assays include a lack of inter-preparation reproducibility and difficult maintenance in culture. In this context, the use of stem cells (which are able to undergo numerous divisions while maintaining their differentiation capability) has been extensively studied (Fraietta and Gasparri 2016). Gordon and Yamanaka's discovery that mature cells could be reprogrammed to become pluripotent (Nobel Prize 2012) facilitates the use of human cells and also solves a potential ethical issue, since access to human embryonic stem cells is limited in many countries. These iPSCs enable the effects of new drugs or chemicals to be assessed in differentiated, tissue-specific human cells. Cells have also been engineered in an attempt to produce more relevant disease models (Benam et al. 2015). Use of the latest genome-editing techniques (such as the CRISPR/Cas 9 system) may lead to the generation of different types of engineered cells. Two- and three-dimensional (2D and 3D) cell cultures have also been developed, such as tumor spheroids and cells embedded in a 3D matrix (Fraietta and Gasparri 2016). The combination of iPSCs, genome editing, and 2D or 3D structuration enables the development of normal or pathological *in vitro* models for better evaluation of new drugs and chemicals (Benam et al. 2015). With a view to evaluating cell-cell communication and tissue-tissue interactions in a more relevant organ context, recent advances have led to the creation of what have been called organs-on-chips (Ingber 2016). Organs-on-chips are microfluidic cell culture devices created with computer microchip manufacturing techniques. They contain hollow microchannels lined with living cells and tissues cultured within an organ-relevant physical context. The channels are continuously perfused with life-sustaining culture medium. A range of physiological or pathological conditions can be mimicked and thus improve the validity of these models. The combination of these technologies with the human iPSCs, high-resolution, real-time imaging, and *in vitro* analysis of biochemical, genetic, and metabolic responses opens up potentially unlimited possibilities (Ingber 2016).

3.3   Phase 0 trials: The Human as a Possible "Non-Clinical" Model

Before to performing a conventional first-in-human (Phase I) study, there is a growing body of evidence to suggest that new drugs could also be tested in a "human model"—in parallel with pre-clinical development. These alternative approaches, variously referred to as exploratory investigational new drug applications, Phase 0 trials and exploratory clinical trials, were set up by the regulatory authorities with a view to reducing the risks to humans and limiting drug exposure during first-in human trials (ICH 2009; Burt et al. 2016). In this context, Phase 0 trials are first-in-humans trials in which drug exposure is lower than in Phase I studies (i.e. less than the maximum tolerated dose). They are not intended to assess efficacy or tolerability. This "*in humano*" approach is situated in the spectrum ranging from human *in vitro* cell-based studies, animal studies, and studies in isolated human organs or tissues to systemic, therapeutic exposure in humans (Burt et al. 2016). Various modalities are possible, such as a single micro-dose or multiple doses repeated for no more than 14 days. In the single micro-dose trial, a dose of between 100 µg and 1/100th of the NOAEL is administered, and only an extended single-dose toxicity study in rodents is need. In the repeated-dose trial, a starting dose of less than 1/50th of the NOAEL is used; a 14-day, repeated-dose toxicity test in both rodents and non-rodents is needed, along with the results of an Ames test and a chromosomal aberration assay (Burt et al. 2016). Of course, the limited systemic exposure of Phase 0 studies requires more sensitive assays than conventional analytical tools. The three most commonly used techniques are liquid chromatography-tandem mass spectrometry, positron emission tomography and accelerator mass spectrometry. The availability of these tools is probably one of the main limiting factors in this field. Like conventional first-in-human studies, Phase 0/exploratory clinical trials probe key properties that are relevant for "go/no-

Table 3 Comparison between Phase 0/micro-dosing trials and Phase I trials (adapted from Burt et al. 2016)

	Phase 0/micro-dosing	Phase I
Possible associated aims		
• Assessment of systemic tolerability	No	No
• Assessment of efficacy	No	Possible
• Proof of mechanism	Possible with specific markers	Possible
Preclinical requirements		
• *In vitro* models	Full requirements	Full requirements
• Toxicology	Limited requirements	Full requirements
• Genotoxicology	None or limited requirements	Full requirements
Requirement for good manufacturing practice	Flexible, depends on the pre-clinical information	Full requirements
Main study characteristics		
• Number of participants	4–10	6–30
• Duration	1–14 days (may be longer, depending on the half-life)	6–60 days (may be longer, depending on the half-life)
• Maximum dose	< Maximum tolerated dose	Maximum tolerated dose
• Drug exposure	Limited	Multiple and repeated doses allowed
• Population	Healthy volunteers or patient/ vulnerable populations	Healthy volunteers (except in oncology studies)

go" decision-making and improvement of the drug development process (Table 3). These studies provide early information about drug pharmacokinetics in humans, drug-drug interactions, pharmacodynamic mechanisms, and specific cellular adverse reactions (mitochondrial toxicity, for example), and can also guide the development of new biomarkers (Burt et al. 2016). Given that animal models are notoriously poor predictors of human pathophysiology and treatment responses, the human is probably the best model of the human! In addition to exploratory clinical trials and conventional Phase I studies in healthy subjects, pharmaceutical companies are also developing early-stage evaluations in small numbers of patients, with a view to rapidly validating their drug candidates' mechanisms of action and safety profile.

4 Issues Related to the Evaluation of Products Other than Drugs or Medicines

4.1 Medical Devices: When a Non-Clinical Assessment Needs a Clinical Approach

Medical devices constitute a broad group of products that ranges from relatively simple devices (like bandages and surgical gloves) to complex equipment (like pacemakers, angioplasty catheters, MRI scanners and medical software). Bringing a new device to the market is subject to authorization. It is not clear that either the US or the European system particularly leads to the marketing of safer medical devices. Both authorization systems are based on the classification of medical devices (Table 4). The severity of the assessments required to obtain marketing authorization depends on the device's designated class (van Drongelen et al. 2015).

In the USA, the government via the FDA carries out all marketing authorization procedures. Once a new product has been classified, the corresponding marketing authorization application can be initiated. The FDA has two main procedures for market authorization: pre-market notification (also referred to as a 510(k), principally for Class II medical devices) and pre-market approval (PMA) for the majority of Class III medical devices. The PMA procedure is most stringent; the manufacturer has to submit an extensive set of documents to the FDA, including clinical data (study protocols, safety and effectiveness data, adverse reactions and complications, patient information, and results) for Class III medical devices. In the 510 (k) procedure, the manufacturer has to show that its device is substantially equivalent to currently marketed device (van Drongelen et al. 2015). The European system is more complex, since devices are evaluated by third party companies (referred to as notified bodies) designated and supervised by the European Union. The conformity assessment procedures and level of stringency depend on the class of the medical device. Stringency is higher for class III and implantable devices, although the equivalence principle has also been used for a long time. The US and Europe systems for establishing the safety and efficacy of new medical devices have both been criticized for their predominant focus on equivalence with existing devices. Following the occurrence of unexpected adverse effects with devices approved for sale on the basis of equivalence data (such as metal-on-metal hip implants), the European Commission issued its Implementing Regulation 920/2013 on the designation and the supervision of notified bodies in 2013. The goal was is to achieve a higher and more uniform level of competence among notified bodies across Europe (EC 920/2013).

Table 4 Medical device classifications

FDA	Regulations	Risk level	Examples	EMA
Class I (About 55% of devices)	General regulations	Very low	Bandages, culture media	Class I
		Low	Contact lenses, epidural catheter, surgical gloves	Class IIa
Class II (About 40% of devices)	General and special regulations	Moderate	Orthopedic implants, glucose monitors, dental implants, hemodialysis systems	Class IIb
Class III (About 5% of devices)	General and special regulations Premarket notifications	High	Pacemakers, angioplasty catheters	Class III

There are many other differences between the US and Europe systems, notably in terms of the technical requirements. In the USA, the documentation for a PMA must include separate sections on non-clinical laboratory studies and on clinical investigations involving human subjects. Nevertheless, FDA has only defined specific requirements for a small group of devices. For example, title 21 of the Code of Federal Regulations describes performance standards for electronic, ionizing-radiation-emitting, microwave- and radio-frequency-emitting, light-emitting and sonic, infrasonic and ultrasonic-radiation-emitting products. These standards are mandatory, and mainly cover limits on emissions and exposure (van Drongelen et al. 2015). In Europe, the law provides only general requirements regarding the safety, performance, design and construction of medical devices. These "essential requirements" are applicable to all types of medical devices. In addition to these general requirements for the safety and performance of a device during its life time, several specific items are mentioned: chemical, physical and biological properties, infection and microbial contamination, construction and environmental properties, protection against radiation, requirements for medical devices connected to or equipped with an energy source, and user information to be supplied with the device (van Drongelen et al. 2015). These requirements apply not only to medical devices but also to many everyday products that must also obtain European marketing authorization.

Besides these numerous requirements, the real debate is about whether clinical data (including the results of randomized clinical trials) should be required for Class III medical devices. In fact, it is currently not possible to gain market authorization without providing clinical data of some sort. Given the rapidly increasing number of medical devices that use information technology and software, new guidelines on usability engineering have been developed. In this respect, usability means complying with the need to ensure patient and user health and safety by preventing user errors (Bras Da Costa et al. 2015). This was first proposed in a European directive (EC/47/2007) and more recently in new FDA guidelines (FDA 2016). These approaches obviously require the application of expertise in human factors and ergonomics for the correct identification and prevention of user errors but also require expertise in risk analysis, risk management and related methods (Bras Da Costa et al. 2015). In this context, the evaluation of medical devices is becoming ever more complex; the convergence of science and digital technology has resulted in the rapid development of innovative devices that allow the easy and accurate characterization of certain parameters in health and in disease. These devices include smartphone-connected diagnostic instruments, handheld/mobile ECG and ultrasound devices, lab-on-a-chip technologies and telemedicine tools. Current and future progress will require a regulatory framework that promotes the most effective, robust technologies for clinical use (Bhavnani et al. 2016). With regard to the status of new technologies, there are again many differences between the USA and Europe. Several connected health technologies are considered to be medical devices in USA but not in Europe. Most recently, electronic cigarettes and other borderline products (i.e. products that can satisfy the legal definition of medicinal products, medical devices or consumer products) have also been considered differently in USA, in Great Britain and in France. In this context, besides specific rules, the International Medical Device Regulators Forum is preparing guidelines for the worldwide harmonization of legislative requirements (van Drongelen et al. 2015). Although these guidelines will only be advisory, they may help to streamline the market authorization process for various devices (and not just medical devices).

4.2   Cosmetics and Personal Care Products

Risk assessment for cosmetics and personal care products currently requires the use of alternative methods because animal testing has been banned since March 2013. As described above, alternative *in vitro* and *in silico* approaches have been proposed. Some of these methods are effective and have been validated by the European Union Reference Laboratory for Alternatives to Animal Testing as tests for irritation, corrosion and phototoxicity (Quantin et al. 2015). One of the models that is ready for use is the *ex vivo* human skin model of percutaneous absorption. Dermal toxicity (such as irritation and corrosion) could also be tested with a reconstructed human epidermis or a membrane-sealing test. The need to evaluate skin sensitization has led to the development of tests based on the correlation between epidermis protein reactivity and skin sensitization; one of these tests is based on the postulate that if a substance is able to bind proteins, then it can potentially act as a contact allergen. Many other recently developed tests take into account the involvement of different immune cell types and mechanisms, although integrated testing is now needed (Quantin et al. 2015). Toxicokinetic evaluations should also be considered. Hence, animal-free, systemic toxicity testing could potentially include the development of integrated test strategies, collaboration and data sharing between different industrial sectors. All the accumulated information will be fed into system biology models that perform a probabilistic risk assessment as a function of exposure scenarios and individual risk levels (Leist et al. 2014). Among these approaches, quantitative *in vitro—in vivo* extrapolation is of great importance. The starting point is the determination of the "real" toxicant concentration to which a cell is exposed. Next, one calculates the corresponding human plasma concentration by using a physiologically-based pharmacokinetic model and *in vitro* data on metabolic conversion, human physiology and metabolic parameters. Despite some encouraging results, these approaches (which are very well advanced for drug assessments) requite further development for all other products that contain chemicals (Leist et al. 2014).

4.3   The Global Burden of Endocrine Disruptors and Their Possible Life-Long Toxicity

Over the last 20 years or so, a large number of studies have suggested that exposure to low doses of certain chemicals may disrupt the body's endocrine system. Bisphenol A (BPA, one of the most widely used and widely dispersed industrial chemicals, found primarily in polycarbonate plastics) is a typical but controversial example of an endocrine disruptor. BPA is known to mimic the female hormone estrogen and has been found to leach from plastic materials. As with other hormones and other potent endocrine disruptors, it appears that the effects are often not observed until much later in the life cycle. This makes it extremely difficult to link exposure to effects in humans (Gies and Soto 2013). It is noteworthy that despite the development of both governmental and industry programs for risk identification or risk assessment of hormonally active substances in Europe since 1982, the harmful effect of BPA was probably discovered accidentally in 1993 by a group of endocrinologists at Stanford University. The researchers identified BPA as an estrogenic contaminant in the polycarbonate cell culture dishes after autoclaving (Krishnan et al. 1993). BPA also challenged our beliefs that (i) high doses produce more serious effects than low doses, and (ii) that if a high dose of a chemical does not cause harm, then neither will a low dose. The usual toxicological approaches (including the evaluation of the dose-response relationship) may not be applicable to the endocrine-disrupting effect of many substances. Both the stage at which the chemical acts and the duration of exposure may be particularly important. Indeed, an organism is most sensitive to endocrine disruptors during its development, whereas while the total duration of the exposure (rather the dose level) is also an important determinant. The complexity of the exposure assessment and the BPA's toxicological profile may have contributed to the differences of many orders of magnitude in the acceptable doses for humans determined by a number of scientific and regulatory bodies and committees (Gies and Soto 2013). These controversial results emphasize the difficulty of this type of evaluation and the need for more relevant approaches and models. The challenge for the coming years is to balance the principle of precaution on one hand against the risk of widespread use of a chemical whose health implications are not understood on the other. The European Chemicals Agency (established by the European Union's Registration, Evaluation, Authorization and Restriction of Chemical Substances legislation) relies on the industry for most risk assessments and toxicity test data (EC 1907/2006). The challenge is thus to increase both research quality and research independence, in order to avoid both public health issues and economic impacts. Recent controversies over the toxicological evaluation of pesticides and genetically modified foods have also contributed to this debate (Resnik 2015).

4.4   The Evaluation of Food Toxicity: From Traditional Ingredients to Novel Foods

Foods and food ingredients include a broad spectrum of materials, ranging from simple chemical compounds to complex whole foods and ingredients. Food additives and flavorings are usually chemically defined substances that lend themselves to conventional toxicological testing. Food additives and flavorings are governed by legislation that notably requires a demonstration of safety. Other ingredients used for technological purposes (such as solvents and enzymes) have their own sets of regulations and internationally agreed standards. If a safe history of traditional use is absent, foods or ingredients are considered to be "new" and are subject to the novel foods legislation in place in a growing number of countries. These regulations are managed by the FDA in the USA and the European Food Safety Authority in the European Union (Blaauboer et al. 2016). Most of these novel foods (including genetically modified organisms) are used as ingredients. In the risk assessment of foods, it is necessary to (i) identify possible toxic compounds on the basis of their chemical structure and mechanism of action, (ii) describe concentration-dependent effects and long-term low-concentration exposure effects, and (iii) perform a proper risk-benefit analysis. Although the characterization and detailed chemical and nutritional analysis of the food is probably the first step, animal toxicology studies may also be of value in the absence of other relevant models or methods (Blaauboer et al. 2016). Nevertheless, the application of these approaches to food ingredients (including genetically modified organisms) is much more challenging than for non-food substances (i.e. drugs) because of the complexity of the food' composition; the more complex the food, the more challenging the assessment. The conventional toxicological approach of setting an acceptable daily intake (which typically includes a 100-fold safety margin relative to the NOAEL seen in toxicology studies) is possible for chemical nutrients but not for the majority of novel foods (Blaauboer et al. 2016). Based on these considerations, a roadmap for safety assessment of food and ingredients has been developed. The first step is to define the type of food (i.e. as a chemically simple or complex food ingredient) and to define the intended target population and use. Next, information on the material's physicochemical properties and composition (including changes occurring during to production process) should be provided. Beyond this, computational approaches may be used to predict the presence of impurities (QSAR approaches), bio-accessibility, bioavailability, and metabolic aspects, and virtual tissue/organ models can be applied to safety/efficacy assessments. Taking into account all these previous evaluations, the daily exposure can be estimated. Nevertheless, further testing will be needed if *in silico* models generated one or more alerts or if the exposure is forecast to exceed a threshold of toxicological concern. In this context, an integrated testing strategy should include appropriate assays for the better identification of the mode of action, the determination of dose-response relationships and the measurement of parameters that can translate to humans. *In vitro* assays (preferably HTS methods), bioinformatics tools and systems biology will be of assistance. As extensively described above, data on true exposure and ADME in humans or from physiologically-grounded, pharmacokinetic models should also be used. The last option is to perform studies in human volunteers, in order to confirm safety and demonstrate nutritional suitability in the general population and/or subgroups (Blaauboer et al. 2016). Although these early-stage clinical evaluations (typically performed on small numbers of participants) will also help to evaluate the allergenic potential and certain non-toxic effects (such as tasting, palatability and acceptability) further reassurance may have to be provided by post-marketing monitoring plans.

4.5   Issues Concerning Nanomaterials

The unique chemical and biological properties of nanomaterials make them useful in many products for human use, including those used in industry, agriculture, medicine, clothing, cosmetics and foods (Piperigkou et al. 2016). The unusual physicochemical properties of engineered nanoscale materials are attributable to their small size, chemical composition, surface structure, solubility, shape and aggregation. In October 2011, the European Commission published a guideline in which a nanomaterial is defined as "a natural, incidental or manufactured material containing particles, in an unbound state or as an aggregate or as an agglomerate and where, for 50% or more of the particles in the number size distribution, one or more external dimensions is in the size range 1 nm-100 nm" (2011/696/EU). When nanoparticles enter the body, they encounter the immune system and may induce desirable or undesirable immune effects. Given the small size and unusual physicochemical properties of nanomaterials, toxicological adverse events may affect the lung, liver or brain. The current consensus is that each product must undergo its own safety evaluation, with a need for particular investigations on a case-by-case basis. The standard battery of preclinical toxicology tests performed for all novel drugs should be sufficient to catch any tissue- specific adverse outcomes related to nanoparticles. However, it should be recognized that additional product-specific preclinical testing might be required. This issue has led to the development of specific pharmacokinetic approaches that take account of the role of blood proteins in the clearance of nanomaterials, the impact of surface curvature versus surface chemistry, and the role of surface architecture and other geometric considerations (Moghimi et al. 2012). Nanomedicines or nanoparticles containing drugs are not faced with the same issues; maintaining the substance in the body is the main challenge. In contrast, the challenge for nanoparticles used in foods or agriculture may be to reduce their presence in the human body (Moghimi et al. 2012; Desai 2012). In this context, assessment of the safety of nanoparticles as a whole is of great importance. International standard-setting bodies have recognized this issue and have agreed that as a minimum set of measurements—size, zeta potential (surface charge) and solubility of nanomaterials should be used as predictors of their toxicity (FDA Nanotechnology Task Force 2007). Besides these pharmacokinetic and basic toxicological considerations, the issue of immunogenicity is also tremendously important. Indeed, over the past decade, significant progress has been made in understanding the immunogenicity of nanoparticles, the immune cell response to nanoparticles, the consequences of nanoparticle-specific antibody formation and the impact of these factors on drug delivery with nanoparticles. In the future, research should focus on methods for better characterizing undesirable nanoparticle contaminants and their undesirable immune and antigenic effects (Ilinskaya and Dobrovolskaia 2016). Improving the mechanistic understanding of nanoparticle effects in biological systems is also an important challenge, namely for designing safer nanomedicines and safer nanomaterials for use in various other fields (Piperigkou et al. 2016).

5   Rethinking the Future

For medical technology and many other everyday products, standards and regulations are needed to ensure safety, protect the public, and guarantee that products are fit for purpose. These obligations require the development of alternative methods that limit or avoid animal use. Furthermore, data-sharing remains an important challenge. Moreover, in the context of novel personal health technologies, the current regulatory approach is not only unfeasible and difficult to enforce but may also suppress innovation (Vincent et al. 2015). Given that many technological products (other than drugs and standard medical devices *per se*) will be used to support and deliver health care or will have an impact on medical practices, regulators need to rethink their approaches. The field of healthcare is not the only one to be affected by new technologies. For example, there are issues with the use of touch-screen tablets in the office environment. Although office work and office equipment are regulated, the health and safety regulations are unlikely to apply to tablet computers if it is not possible to easily check how or where they are being used (Stawarz and Benedyk 2013). Rather than trying to regulate these issues, more flexible approaches are needed—such as shifting the focus away from the introduction of technology towards user education (Vincent et al. 2015). Although it is difficult to predict the lack of long-term safety for certain chemicals, novel foods or nanotechnologies, we should also try to develop integrated approaches that take account of the potential risks to the individual and to the environment as a whole. Here again, consumer education is probably one of the main challenges for the coming years.

References

Ames, B. N., McCann, J., & Yamasaki, E. (1975). Methods for detecting carcinogens and mutagens with the Salmonella/mammalian-microsome mutagenicity test. *Mutation Research, 31*, 347–364.

Benam, K. H., Dauth, S., Hassell, B., Herland, A., Jain, A., Jang, K. J., et al. (2015). Engineered in vitro disease models. *Annual Review of Pathology Mechanisms of Disease, 10*, 195–262.

Bhavnani, S. P., Narula, J., & Sengupta, P. P. (2016). Mobile technology and the digitization of healthcare. *European Heart Journal, 37*, 1428–1438.

Blaauboer, B. J., Boobis, A. R., Bradford, B., Cockburn, A., Constable, A., Daneshian, M., et al. (2016). Considering new methodologies in strategies for safety assessment of foods and food ingredients. *Food and Chemical Toxicology, 91*, 19–35.

Blomme, O. A. G. (2016). Toxicology strategies for drug discovery: Present and future. *Chemical Research in Toxicology, 29*, 473–504.

Bras Da Costa, S., Beuscart-Zéphir, M. C., Bastien, J. M. C., & Pelayo, S. (2015). Usability and safety of software medical devices: Need for multidisciplinary expertise to apply the IEC 62366: 2007. *Studies in Health Technology Informatics, 216*, 353–357.

Burt, T., Yoshida, K., Lappin, G., Vuong, L., John, C., de Wildt, S. N., et al. (2016). Microdosing and other phase 0 clinical trials: Facilitating translation in drug development. *Clinical and Translational Science, 9*, 74–88.

Desai, N. (2012). Challenges in development of nanoparticle-based therapeutics. *American Association of Pharmaceutical Scientists Journal, 14*, 282–295.

Dow, L. E. (2015). Modeling disease in vivo with CRISPR/Cas9. *Trends in Molecular Medicine, 21*, 609–621.

EC 1907/2006. (2006). Regulation of the European Parliament and the Council of 18 December 2006 concerning the Registration, Evaluation, Authorization and Restriction of Chemicals (REACH). *Official Journal of the European Union.* Accessed November 26, 2016, from http://eur-lex.europa.eu/legal-content/EN/TXT/PDF/?uri=CELEX:02006R1907-20140410

EC 47/2007. (2007). Council Directive 2007/47/CE. *Official Journal of the European Union.* Accessed November 26, 2016, from http://eur-lex.europa.eu/legal-content/EN/TXT/PDF/?uri=CELEX:22007D0047&

EC 920/2013. (2013). Commission implementing regulation of 24 September 2013 on the designation and the supervision of notified bodies under Council Directive 90/385/EEC on active implantable medical devices and Council Directive 93/42/EEC on medical devices. *Official Journal of The European Union.* Accessed November 26, 2016, from http://eur-lex.europa.eu/legal-content/EN/TXT/PDF/?uri=CELEX:32013R0920&

EU 2011/696. (2011). Commission Recommendation of 18 October 2011 on the definition of nanomaterial. *Official Journal of the European Union.* Accessed November 26, 2016, from http://eur-lex.europa.eu/legal-content/EN/TXT/PDF/?uri=CELEX:32011H0696&

FDA Center for Devices and Radiological Health Office of Device Evaluation (2016, February 3). *Applying human factors and usability engineering to medical devices.* Accessed November 26, 2016, from http://www.fda.gov/downloads/MedicalDevices/.../UCM259760.pdf

FDA History. (2016). http://www.fda.gov/AboutFDA/WhatWeDo/History/Origin/default.htm. Accessed 26 November 2016.

FDA Nanotechnology Task Force. (2007). Nanotechnology task force report. Accessed November 26, 2016, from http://www.fda.gov/downloads/ScienceResearch/SpecialTopics/Nanotechnology/ucm110856.pdf

Fraietta, I., & Gasparri, F. (2016). The development of high-content screening technology and its importance to drug discovery. *Expert Opinion on Drug Discovery, 11*, 501–514.

Gies, A., & Soto, A. M.. (2013). Bisphenol A: Contested science, divergent safety evaluations. In European Environment Agency—Report n° 1/2013. *Late lessons from early warnings: Science, precaution, innovation* (Part A, pp. 215–239).

ICH. (2000). Good manufacturing practice guide for active pharmaceutical ingredients Q7. ICH Harmonised Tripartite Guideline. Accessed November 26, 2016, from http://www.ich.org/fileadmin/Public_Web_Site/ICH_Products/Guidelines/Quality/Q7/Step4/Q7_Guideline.pdf

ICH. (2009). Guidance on nonclinical safety studies for the conduct of human clinical trials and marketing authorization for pharmaceuticals M3 (R2). In International conference on harmonization of technical requirements for registration of pharmaceuticals for human use 8–16. ICH Secretariat, Geneve. Accessed November 26, 2016, from http://www.ich.org/fileadmin/Public_Web_Site/ICH_Products/Guidelines/Multidisciplinary/M3_R2/Step4/M3_R2__Guideline.pdf

Ilinskaya, A. N., & Dobrovolskaia, M. A. (2016). Understanding the immunogenicity and antigenicity of nanomaterials: Past, present and future. *Toxicology and Applied Pharmacology, 299*, 70–77.

Ingber, D. E. (2016). Reverse engineering human pathophysiology with organs-on-chips. *Cell, 164*, 1105–1109.

Krishnan, A. V., Stathis, P., Permuth, S. F., Tokes, L., & Feldman, D. (1993). Bisphenol-A: An oestrogenic substance is released from polycarbonate flasks during autoclaving. *Endocrinology, 132*, 2279–2286.

Leist, M., Hasiwa, N., Rovida, C., Daneshian, M., Basketter, D., Kimber, I., et al. (2014). Consensus report on the future of animal-free systemic toxicity testing. *ALTEX, 31*, 341–356.

Milani-Nejad, N., & Janssen, P. M. (2014). Small and large animal models in cardiac contraction research: Advantages and disadvantages. *Pharmacology & Therapeutics, 141*, 235–249.

Moghimi, S. M., Hunter, A. C., & Andresen, T. L. (2012). Factors controlling nanoparticle pharmacokinetics: An integrated analysis and perspective. *Annual Review of Pharmacology and Toxicology, 52*, 481–503.

Patlewicz, G., & Fitzpatrick, J. M. (2016). Current and future perspectives on the development, Evaluation, and application of in Silico approaches for predicting toxicity. *Chemical Research in Toxicology, 29*, 438–451.

Piperigkou, Z., Karamanou, K., Engin, A. B., Gialeli, C., Docea, A. O., Vynios, D. H., et al. (2016). Emerging aspects of nanotoxicology in health and disease: From agriculture and food sector to cancer therapeutics. *Food and Chemical Toxicology, 91*, 42–57.

Quantin, P., Thélu, A., Catoire, S., & Ficheux, H. (2015). Perspectives and strategies of alternative methods used in the risk assessment of personal care products. *Annales Pharmaceutiques Françaises, 73*, 422–435.

Raies, A. B., & Bajic, V. B. (2016). *In silico* toxicology: Computational methods for the prediction of chemical toxicity. *WIREs Computational Molecular Science, 6*, 147–172.

Resnik, D. B. (2015). Retracting inconclusive research: Lessons from the Séralini GM maize feeding study. *Journal of Agricultural and Environmental Ethics, 28*, 621–633.

Rowland, M., Peck, C., & Tucker, G. (2011). Physiologically-based pharmacokinetics in drug development and regulatory science. *Annual Review of Pharmacology and Toxicology, 51*, 45–73.

Stawarz, K., Benedyk, R. (2013, September 9–13). Bent necks and twisted wrists: Exploring the impact of touch-screen tablets on the posture of office workers. In *Proceedings of the 27th International BCS human computer interaction conference*. British Computer Society, 2013. Presented at BCS HCI 2013, London, UK.

van Drongelen, A., Hessels, J., Geertsma, R. (2015). Comparison of market authorization systems of medical devices in USA and Europe. In *RIVM Letter report 2015-0001*. National Institute for Public Health and the Environment, The Netherlands.

Vincent, C. J., Niezen, G., O' Kane, A. A., & Stawarz, K. (2015). Can standards and regulations keep up with health technology? *JMIR mHealth and uHealth, 3*, e64.

Walters, W. P., & Namchuk, M. (2003). Designing screens: How to make your hits a hit. *Nature Review Drug Discovery, 2*, 259–266.

Clinical Research-Based Product Assessment

Rolf Weitkunat

1 Introduction

Clinical trials are conducted in many areas, including therapy, prognosis, and prevention research, where they provide a well developed and powerful research methodology. In order to apply this methodology in consumer product research, its properties must be well understood and carefully adopted, and sometimes modified. This contribution provides an overview of the historical developments and methodological properties of clinical trials and points out aspects that require special attention in the context of consumer product research.

2 Trying Conjectures

When a consumer product or service is assumed to lead to a specific effect, it can be attempted to substantiate a claim by conducting an experimental study. The methodology of conducting experiments in humans is most developed in drug therapy research and is referred to as clinical research; *clinical trial* being the term to denote a specific experimental clinical study—irrespective of whether or not the participants are healthy or diseased, as the "clinical" refers to "human", not to "disease". Also, the "clinical" separates research conducted in humans clearly from pre-clinical research (both *in-vitro* and *in-vivo*). The element "trial" points at something being tried in some formal empirical investigation, which is already the essence of clinical trials. Trying something means, in general, raising a conjecture-based question to the world, let her speak, and then (through *modus*

R. Weitkunat (✉)
Philip Morris Products SA, Quai Jeanrenaud 5, 2000 Neuchatel, Switzerland
e-mail: Rolf.Weitkunat@pmi.com

© Springer International Publishing AG 2017
G. Emilien et al. (eds.), *Consumer Perception of Product Risks and Benefits*,
DOI 10.1007/978-3-319-50530-5_4

tollens) conclude whether what was conjectured is not the case or might be the case. How we come to a conjecture in the first place is a fascinating but metaphysical question, and this author agrees with intuitionistic views of the critical rationalistic philosophy of science on the matter (Popper 1935, p. 208, simply speaks of "idea" and "unjustified anticipation"), although this will not be further addressed in this contribution.

How now do we try things? By flicking a switch, we can indeed turn the lamp on; there being light. We have confirmed the conjecture empirically. This is straightforward, as the relationship between action and reaction is essentially deterministic, and in case of doubt we can simply retry. If we want to know whether switching the automatic transmission of our car from S (sporty) to E (economy) actually leads to a reduced gasoline consumption, things are already getting a bit more complicated; as the effect is not instantaneously visible (albeit possibly audible, but sound is not a direct measure of fuel consumption but merely, at best, an indicator or proxy variable) and it is also quite likely more confounded. Confounders might be our driving style, the outdoor temperature, and the route we take. Due to the more complicated, causally interwoven factors influencing our car's fuel consumption, which we might choose to view as being at least partially, but more likely mostly, probabilistic by their nature and mode of action, and due to the gradual rather than all-or-nothing effect (as with the lamp), we are this time quite unlikely to get away with only one trial. We will need to retry, and finally, after a few weeks, to aggregate the consumption data that we obtain from test driving periods with and without the transmission set to E, using some statistics maybe. The good news is that we do not really have to worry much about a complicated study design and about sequence effects, or about the need to use a brand new car for every driving period. A car is a car after all, and it should largely respond as any machine does, in accordance to the parameters set, essentially irrespective of its mileage differing or not by a few thousand.

With respect to generalizing the findings of our trials so far, we do not have much of a problem either. Switching light switches and setting automatic transmissions to energy saving will, in the vast majority of cases, lighten up rooms and reduce fuel consumptions respectively. Things get tougher though when what we try does not relate to objects but to subjects, i.e., to human beings. As mentioned above, the methodology of clinical trials has been, and still is, most developed in therapy research, which is why this is where we will start, before moving on to research on consumer products.

Trying something in humans is much more difficult than trying a light or a transmission. Take a fictitious novel migraine pill for example. Based on the 2003 National Health Interview Survey, US migraine prevalence was 8.6% in males and twice as high in females (17.5%), with prevalence peaking in the late teens and 20s and around 50 years of age (Victor et al. 2010). A lot of research has been conducted on biological, psychological, and environmental risk factors and mechanisms. For example, there is evidence that in about one out of ten migraine patients the headache is associated with weather conditions (Hoffmann et al. 2015). Could we simply pick, for example, a female 60-years old weather-sensitive migraine patient and try the pill with her? What might happen is that the pill would relieve the headache on the first migraine day while on the subsequent episode, even four pills would have no effect. In addition consider that, had we picked another patient, one pill could have worked on both occasions—or on neither of them. Now, does the pill work or not? This is impossible to say from the data obtained by our trial so far, as obviously how humans respond to the same exposure can widely differ, both across individuals and occasions. The epidemiology of migraine already points at different subgroups and possibly different subtypes of migraine, related to sex, age, and possibly weather sensitivity. Thus, if we want to know whether in general say two of the novel pills relieve migraine headache, we can obviously not restrict ourselves to a particular patient (or two), as even for our one patient the pills might not work the same all the time. Rather, in order to be able to recommend the pill to all adult migraine patients (i.e., to generalize our findings to the whole target population of adult migraine patients), we need to investigate a whole sample of them, making sure that not all of our study sample is female and/or older than 30 years of age, as this would imply missing out on men and/or younger patients.

There are other questions we have to address when we plan our trial. How do we find the patients to participate in the trial? Sometimes there are attractive methods that allow to conveniently fill the sample. For example, one could contact the members of an online migraine support group that discusses their sensitivity to weather conditions. While those patients might be quite motivated to participate, this particular way of recruitment might select migraine patients that are not representative of the whole population of migraine patients—as their migraines are likely to be related to weather conditions whereas the majority of migraine patients' headaches are not. Also, the particular way of recruitment can lead to other differences, both known and unknown, between the study participants and the whole population of migraine patients. Also, should we provide pills on some migraine days but not on others, and then compare the headache levels between the two types of days? We could, but what if pills *per se* (i.e., irrespective of their contents) would have an effect on migraine? One never knows. The problem is indeed ubiquitous and referred to as placebo effect. If in our weather-sensitive study sample the placebo effect of two white pills would be particularly strong, we might conclude that the presumably active compound that is contained in the pills would generally be efficacious, where it in fact is not. Could we mitigate this problem by sometimes using a second set of identical pills that do not contain the compound, and keep very careful track of which kind of pills were taken, when, and by whom? We could. We could also split the total study sample upfront into two halves and provide the active pills to one half and the placebo pills to the other. Of course, we then would have to take precautions that the severity of migraine would be equally distributed across the two groups, as well as other factors that could potentially influence the response to the pills. Such factors include, but are not restricted to, the duration of the disease, weather sensitivity, and age of the patients. Also, we would be better not to tell our sample what kind of pills they take, as otherwise we could introduce a differential placebo effect, most likely stronger in the active pill group. Thus, we should keep the patients blind with regard to what kind of pills they receive, and even better also the study personnel, to avoid any sort of unforeseeable influence (bias). Such a double-blind strategy can be implemented by randomly allocating the type of pill (active vs. placebo) to each patient, and to make sure that the groups are of equal size, we can deploy block randomization. Randomization also reduces the chances of having, for example, migraine severity or some unknown pill response predisposition differentially distributed across the sub-groups. For these advantages, most clinical trials are actually designed as random-ized clinical trials.

What this illustrates is that trialing something (i.e., some external intervention of interest, as the pill in this example) with respect to some outcome (relieve of migraine headaches) in some specified group of people (defined by inclusion- and exclusion criteria, as adult patients with migraine but not with other types of headaches in our example) is quite a bit more challenging than testing whether a light bulb can be switched on or gasoline can be saved by changing the transmission settings. Some careful thoughts are needed with respect to the target population and how the study sample can be recruited from it in an unbiased manner, and how the intervention of interest is planned and administered, so that the study results even have a chance of being conclusive with respect to the research question. Clinical trials thus require meticulous design, planning, and execution, and the devil is definitely in the details. And there are many more details to consider than those we have just lightly touched. For the taste of it: How, by the way, do we measure levels of migraine headache and its reduction in a reliable manner? Pain is a private event, and there is no direct and objective access to it, like for example to body temper-ature through a thermometer. This being so: could we simply switch to body temperature as our effect measure? We could. But it would not be meaningful. Temperature is not a valid surrogate endpoint for migraine pain, even if it can be measured at a high level of precision; in fact, it is a meaningless biomarker in this context, and measuring it would tell us absolutely nothing about the efficacy of the pill for relieving migraine headache. Some further thoughts must be given to even more details of the study, like study duration: We could, for each patient, only treat and record one migraine episode. However, it would probably be more relevant for assessing the value of the pill if we would extend the treatment over a few months and then look at the overall results—which of course raises the issue as to how to integrate the findings from each individual episode. But then, would it be ethical and/or scientifically smart to compare the novel pill to a placebo, or would it not be a more reasonable approach to compare it with some existing therapy? If so, should we attempt to demonstrate that the new pill is indeed better (superior) to the existing one (the active comparator, in clinical research parlance) or would we be satisfied with showing non-inferiority? We also must plan the statistical analysis of the study data and, related to this, decide on the expected size and variability of the treatment effect(s), considering of what magnitude such effects would need to be for them being of any clinical relevance, and how many patients we should consequently include in our study to make it sufficiently likely to find the expected effect when it actually exists. And so on.

As this short outline clarifies, designing good (i.e., conclusive) clinical trials is cumbersome and requires profound knowledge, specific skills, experience and diligence, let alone the huge amount of logistical planning and operative work for the execution of the study, its documentation and quality control. Also, studies conducted in humans require a lot of prerequisites, including the demonstration that the product, or pill in our example, we want to assess is produced against well-defined quality standards, evidence that the new drug is safe to take and that the dose is reasonably chosen, approval of the study protocol by an ethics committee and of course informed consent of the study participants.

3 Historical Developments

The current conceptualization, design, conduct and analysis of clinical experiments, as implemented in medicine, public health, psychology, research in education, consumer research, and many other areas, is largely based on the twentieth century works of the English geneticist and statistician Sir Ronald Aylmer Fisher and his compatriot, the epidemiologist Sir Austin Bradford Hill. Fisher conducted agricultural field research and considered rigorous experimental design as the basis for drawing valid inference on probabilistic hypotheses regarding the causal impact of the deliberate variation of experimental exposures/factors (like fertilization) on experimental units (plots of land; Fisher 1925) in terms of measured effects (crop yield). Fisher deemed randomization the cornerstone of experiments, to warrant the unbiased allocation of units to experimental groups (conditions, treatments, factor levels), so rendering all residual error in the data unsystematic noise, achieved through asymptotically balancing all background variables across the comparison groups, irrespective of whether or not these individual (baseline) covariates are even known or measured. Potential confounders so prevented from being systematically associated with the experimental manipulation renders the latter the only possible explanation of the observed effects. Aside from considering the distributional properties of the individual variables for the choice of the appropriate statistical calculations, no further prior assumption or multidimensional statistical model is needed. Rather, the "likelihood" (Fisher's "p-value" of the statistical "test of significance") of observing in the "dependent variable" (Tolman 1932) an effect of at least the measured magnitude under the assumption of the experimental factor ("independent variable") having no effect ("null hypothesis") can directly be calculated. From an epistemological point of view, Fisher had proposed a probabilistic inductive inference method for concluding on a causal effect of the experimental manipulation, by rejecting the opposing null hypothesis with a quantified likelihood of this conclusion being erroneous. Even though it is not of particular importance for the issues here addressed, it should be noted that the current practice of frequentist statistical testing largely reflects a range of variants of inconsistent amalgams of Fisher's significance test logic and the method of hypothesis testing proposed by Neyman and Pearson (1933), and that neither party had ever intended to merge the two methods.

The institution of the experimental design and analysis method in therapy research is generally attributed to Austin Bradford Hill, who planned the first modern blinded and properly randomized controlled trial (RCT) on the effects of streptomycin in patients with pulmonary tuberculosis (launched in 1947 by the Medical Research Council in the UK; MRC 1948). Probably less well-known, it was also Hill who, seemingly in 1955, coined the expression "intention-to-treat" (Lewis and Machin 1993), which will be addressed in more detail below. As not all research questions on matters of human health relate to therapy effects and thus often cannot be addressed through experiments (which are in many circumstances impractical, irrelevant, unreliable, unethical, or a mixture thereof, coupled with the notorious issue of the questionable generalizability of experimental findings to the real world), Hill was strongly engaged in observational research and methods development. Based on a case-control study in patients from 20 hospitals in London, conducted together with Richard Doll, Hill concluded that smoking was an important risk factor for lung cancer (Doll and Hill 1950), a finding subsequently confirmed by the seminal prospective British Doctor's cohort study which started in 1951 (Doll and Hill 1964). This etiologic endeavor, which included more than 40,000 physicians and measured chronic disease risk factors and long-term health outcomes, was indeed far beyond the scope of an experimental design. Hill was well aware of the methodological challenges of observational studies related to bias and confounding. In 1965 he proposed "viewpoints" (sometimes denoted as "Hill's criteria for causation") to consider in order to facilitate drawing inductive causal inferences based on observational data. While John Stuart Mill, 1843 in his System of Logic, had previously suggested methods of induction in the context of experimental data, no such an attempt had yet been made for observational data (Morabia 2013).

With the Nuremberg Code, written in 1947, and the Declaration of Helsinki, established in 1964, the framework for conducting clinical trials was defined, with a focus on protecting the rights and wellbeing of study participants by voluntary participation, and setting standards like mandatory informed consent and the ability to withdraw at any time from the study. In spite of the watershed amendments to the American Food, Drug and Cosmetics Act in 1962, which made RCTs a requirement for marketing authorization of novel drugs and providing the Food and Drug Administration with regulatory authority, acceptance of the experimental therapy research approach increased only gradually after the Second World War. Opposition towards RCTs by clinicians was driven by traditions of viewing medicine as mainly experience-based and largely grounded in clinical judgment, a widespread lack of statistical understanding, and ethical concerns against placebo arms. In his memoires, Hill (1990) pointed out that he carefully avoided using the word "randomization" in the streptomycin-trial study protocol, in order not to raise opposition from collaborating physicians. The increasing acceptance of experimental studies on treatment benefits, up to the present where the method has gained the status of a "gold standard" (cf. Cartwright 2010), occurred in the 1970s, promoted by the formation of the evidence-based medicine-movement, materially pioneered by David Sackett, who co-initiated the Cochrane-Collaboration. The collaboration was named after the Scottish epidemiologist Archibald Cochrane, whose preoccupation with closing the gap between what is known versus what is actually done in clinical medicine and his lifelong call for RCT-based substantiation of any medical intervention's benefit outweighing its harm was thereby acknowledged. As was the case with RCTs, evidence-based medicine was initially not easily accepted by all parts of the medical establishment (e.g., Grahame-Smith 1995).

To help clinicians critically appraise the accumulating published evidence on the benefits of therapies, Sackett (1989) had developed a first design-focused hierarchy of evidence with "large randomized trials with clear-cut results (and low risk of error)" on top of the hierarchy (p. 38). This and subsequent study-design evidence hierarchies led to some confusion, as the logic originally proposed for therapy studies was not infrequently simply generalized to other domains, including diagnostic and prognostic research, even though RCTs can, for example (as briefly indicated above), contribute little or nothing to etiological research on chronic disease risks. This has been clearly pointed out early on by Sackett and others, but has not always been considered carefully. Sackett and Wennberg (1997) wrote (p. 1536): "Evidence based medicine is not restricted to randomized trials and meta-analyses. It involves tracking down the best external evidence with which to answer our clinical questions. To find out about the accuracy of a diagnostic test, we need to find proper cross sectional studies of patients clinically suspected of harboring the relevant disorder, not a randomized trial. For a question about prognosis, we need proper follow up studies of patients assembled at a uniform, early point in the clinical course of their disease." The widely believed misconception that RCTs carry some special scientific weight in *any* context and would be necessary for true ("hard") science-based conclusions (cf. Worrall 2007) has recently been addressed in a series of high-profile publications in medical journals (e.g. Ho et al. 2008), and the message seems to be gradually reaching all clinical areas. For example, DeVries and Berlet (2010), while pointing out the importance of high-quality RCTs in therapeutic research, state that prognostic studies follow different criteria, as the exposure variable being studied would not be researcher-controlled, cannot be randomly assigned, and a RCT "is inherently not possible" (p. 207).

4 Epistemological Aspects

An underlying reason for the sometimes unclear weighing of RCT-based evidence is possibly a lack of discriminating between the concepts of internal and external validity (Campbell and Stanley 1963). Internal validity depends on the tightness of built-in controls and essentially refers to the degree of certainty at which effects observed in a particular study can be causally attributed unequivocally to the experimental manipulation. This notion is reflected in Tolman's dichotomy of dependent and independent variables, reflecting the concepts of effects of causes and of causes of effects, respectively. It is clear from the rationale underlying Fisher's experimental method that for all non-deterministic cause-effect relationships, well-controlled randomized experiments provide the highest level of internally valid evidence—at least as long as the analysis does not deviate from the original study design, as for example in subgroup comparisons, where randomization-based protection from baseline covariate imbalance is typically lost. Obviously, high levels of experimental control are well in-line with deductivism, rigorous hypothesis testing, and concerns about internal validity.

External validity is, in contrast, a very different concept, and tends to be "at odds" with internal validity, although the latter is often considered the *sine qua non* of the former (Campbell and Stanley 1963, p. 5; Steckler and McLeroy 2008). External validity addresses the question as to whether research results can be generalized to other, typically real-life contexts and populations. Due to the strict and largely canonical error-prevention controls and restrictions that are applied to maximize internal validity, external validity is the notorious Achilles heel of experiments, including RCTs, in particular when research findings are to be transported to conditions of usual clinical care practices. Many typical RCT features aiming at maximizing internal validity and often referred to bluntly as "rigorous" contribute to the problem of generalizability of study results. These include highly selected patient samples free of comorbidities and concomitant medications, high compliance levels, short study durations and more or less artificial and highly restricted settings and tight procedural controls. Even the best (i.e., most "rigorous") RCT in the world, however, does not ensure infallibility nor does it generate external validity without a strong set of assumptions regarding the generalizability of the research to the real world. Thus utmost "rigor" (in terms of maximized internal validity) and complete irrelevance (in terms of absence of external validity) can easily coexist. Unless translated into specific hypotheses for subsequent empirical testing (further research), other than with internal validity, external validity cannot be achieved by rigorous adherence to methodological standards built on deductive logic within a given experiment. As Gadenne (2013, p. 5) has clearly pointed out, "the problem of external validity is the problem of induction". The complexity around the concepts of internal and external validity points at the challenges related to assigning weights to sets of evidence provided by different studies. It is obvious, however, that extrapolating study design-based evidence hierarchies mindlessly beyond their contexts (e.g. clinical randomized experiments to proof therapeutic concepts) and assuming their universal applicability is careless and can result in fallacious inferences and misguided policy decisions (cf. Rothman 2014).

Somewhat along the same lines as internal and external validity, the distinction of the two therapy research aspects of efficacy (i.e., whether a treatment can in principle work under ideal circumstances) and effectiveness (i.e., whether it will work under realistic circumstances) was popularized by Cochrane (1972). In line with the above considerations regarding internal validity, RCTs can, when certain assumptions hold, be the ideal approach for assessing the efficacy of drugs (Gupta 2011), and they can then be analyzed through a simple comparison of average outcomes between groups, not further adjusted for covariates, to draw causal conclusions on the efficacy of the experimental variation. As usual, the devil is in the detail or, more specifically, in the assumptions that are needed to draw valid conclusions from experimental results, in addition to more general requirements (related to the Duhem-Quine problem of required auxiliary assumptions) that need to be fulfilled (e.g. construct validity, measurement accuracy or adequate and correct data processing and analysis). From a counterfactual point of view (first introduced to biostatistics by Neyman 1923), determining the average causal effect of the novel product (a therapeutic drug, for example) would require exposing each study participant simultaneously only once to both exclusively the drug with the active substance *and* an indistinguishable version without that substance (placebo), which is impossible (reflecting what is sometimes referred to as the "fundamental problem of causal inference"). In any factual experiment, participants must instead be randomized to active treatment *or* to placebo/control. The potential outcomes model (Rubin 1974) provides a conceptual and formal framework of causal inference, grounded in counterfactual logic and accounting for the inter-individual variability of treatment responses. It provides coherent definitions to describe causal effects as they occur in empirical research. These include individual as well as average causal treatment effects and specifications of key concepts like randomization, selection bias, confounding, or compliance, and allow one to state conditions and to specify assumptions, under which factual statistics provide valid causal treatment effect estimates.

A key assumption for drawing valid conclusions from experiments (cf. West et al. 2008) is ignorability (unconfoundedness), implying that potential outcomes are independent of the assigned treatment. Even though sometimes neglected, ignorability depends on a sufficient sample size for randomization to play out. Other important assumptions are stable unit treatment value (SUTV—based on the absence of treatment variation across units and on non-interference of treatment effects across units), exclusion restriction (any effect of randomization is transmitted through the experimental exposure/treatment, which often implies the requirement of blinding of personnel and participants with regard to the allocated treatment to avoid performance bias), full compliance (post-randomization adherence to treatment regimen) and completeness (i.e., no missing data, including no post-randomization sample attrition). Fisher's agricultural research fits, unsurprisingly enough, remarkably well with these "ideal experiment" assumptions, which his methodology in fact requires to yield valid conclusions. While indeed plots of land rarely exhibit noncompliance, this is not necessarily so with all types of experimental units, particularly not with humans, irrespective of whether they are subjects, patients, or consumers.

5 Treatment Effects

Evaluating the effects of a treatment (e.g., a drug) in a blinded manner (mainly to avoid differential ascertainment) based on an ideal RCT relies basically on comparing it statistically, with regard to an endpoint, directly (i.e., without statistical adjustment) to some control treatment (e.g., a placebo). Under the assumptions of all baseline characteristics being equally distributed across the comparison groups through randomization to the novel $(R = 1)$ or control treatment $(R = 0)$, no noncompliance, and no missing data, the experimental results are automatically (i.e., without the need for any mechanistic understanding, theory, or additional assumptions) turned into evidence of a causal treatment effect, i.e., an efficacy claim—the core strength of the randomized-experimental method in terms of internal validity. The mechanism of randomization renders the impact of the actual treatment (i.e., of $A = 1$ as compared to no treatment or to an alternative treatment, $A = 0$) on the potential outcomes $Y(A = a)$ "ignorable" and participants "exchangeable" across groups (Rosenbaum and Rubin 1983), i.e., $Y(a) \perp A$. Ideal RCT is, however, a rather simplistic concept, as in real clinical trials compliance of study participants and completeness of data is rarely one hundred percent. This raises questions on how to deal with non-compliant participants (even treatment crossover might occur, meaning that patients randomized to the experimental treatment may have received (and actually taken) the control medication, $R = 0$, $A = 1$, or *vice versa*, $R = 1$, $A = 0$) and incomplete data.

The intuitive response to broken randomization due to noncompliance $(A_i \neq R_i$ for some individuals i) and missing data would be to simply restrict the analysis to compliant patients with complete records. This "per-protocol" analysis strategy can provide "proof" of a therapeutic effect by answering the "can it work" (somewhere) question (cf., Cartwright 2011), i.e., for a specific outcome (Y), study and context, by demonstrating that *here* the outcomes were more pronounced in patients treated with the novel treatment than in those treated with the control treatment, i.e. $E(Y|A = 1, R = 1) > E(Y|A = 0, R = 0)$, which corresponds to estimating efficacy as it might occur under ideal circumstances (Fig. 1).

Unfortunately, per-protocol effect estimates can be biased, as the contrasted groups are not any longer solely based on randomized treatment allocation, but also on post-randomization compliance. As factors that determine compliance can also influence the treatment effect (or can, in turn, be influenced by compliance and treatment effect), the magnitude of the association between type of treatment and effect can be confounded by such factors. The apparent benefit of the treatment can therefore be biased (typically overestimated), as the target population would be composed of a different, possibly less responsive and/or tolerant case mix than the per-protocol study population. While a per-protocol analysis does not require analyzing the details of noncompliance, it does bear the risk of introducing (self-selection) bias as the ignorability assumption cannot be maintained, and rigidly dismissing incomplete or noncompliant records always implies a loss of information and power. Also, when otherwise protocol-adherent records have missing data

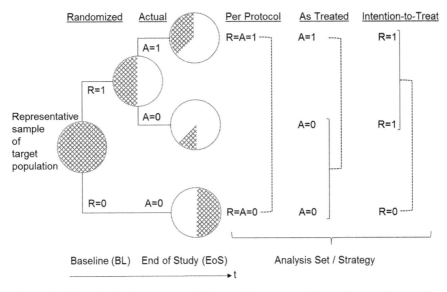

Fig. 1 Generic randomized two-arm parallel group therapy superiority study example, assuming one-sided non-compliance (patients in the control group are assumed not having access to the novel treatment). Half of the sample is randomized to the novel treatment ($R = 1$), the other half to the control treatment ($R = 0$). There is a chance that the observed treatment effect is biased by non-compliance, as 25% of the patients randomized to the novel treatment actually take the control treatment ($R = 1$, $A = 0$). There are three options to assess the effect of the novel treatment: (i) Taking into account both randomization and compliance—the per-protocol analysis; (ii) ignoring randomization—the as-treated analysis; (iii) ignoring compliance—the intention-to-treat (ITT) strategy. In an ITT analysis, patients are analyzed according to their randomized treatment, irrespective of whether they take it or not

only in variables of minor importance or if missingness can be assumed being completely at random across participants, then excluding such records from the analysis is not a very convincing strategy.

Thus, it might be considered preferable to analyze participants according to the treatment that they have actually received, i.e., according to the "as-treated" analysis strategy, aiming at demonstrating a treatment effect on outcome Y in a specific study and context by showing that $E(Y|A = 1) > E(Y|A = 0)$. As-treated is the only viable analysis of non-randomized (observational) cohort studies, and RCT-based safety data are usually also analyzed according to treatment received. Also, as-treated is the standard approach for analyzing preventive vaccine trials (Hudgens et al. 2004). When randomization cannot be relied on (or is absent in the first place) it is usually attempted to establish conditional exchangeability, i.e., $Y(a) \perp A|C$ by conditioning the effect estimation on measured potential confounders (C). Conditioning can be achieved by some form (or combination of) adjustment, stratification, standardization, or matching. In order to correctly specify actual treatment (exposure) groups, an as-treated analysis necessitates the need to analyze the details of noncompliance with regard to whether treatment has simply not been taken, has been taken, but not according to the protocol, has been replaced (or supplemented) by alternative treatment(s), the correct dosing and timing of the treatment has been followed, and whether possibly physicians were noncompliant as well. The details of this pre-analysis depend to a large degree on the particular research question and circumstances, including whether or not compliance was measured in the control group and whether or not the active drug was accessible to the control group or some (active) control treatment was accessible to the treatment group. The likelihood of such complications is increased in large, long, and complex studies, in non-prescription settings, when the treatment under investigation is already on the market, under open-label treatment, and when the study is ambulatory rather than conducted in confinement.

Another classic response to protocol violations is to abstain from comparing groups according to the treatment actually received, but according to the intention-to-treat (ITT) principle. ITT analyses compare all participants according to the group to which they were randomized. Even though the approach is generally straightforward, in reality methodological problems are often encountered, as for example the need to deal with missing outcome data when participants are lost to follow up. As previously with the RCT methodology in general, the ITT approach faced considerable opposition, in particular by clinicians. This might have possibly been related to the need to statistically treat noncompliant patients as if they had taken the investigational drug, which from a clinical point of view could indeed appear being a "bizarre assumption" (Sheiner 1991, p. 4). Again like with RCTs, ITT is to date often referred to as a "gold standard", and sometimes—less flattering—as having become gospel (Salsburg 1994). In 1990, the International Conference on Harmonisation of Technical Requirements for Registration of Pharmaceuticals for Human Use (ICH), in which regulatory authorities of Europe, Japan and the United States and experts from the pharmaceutical industry participate, set out to harmonize regulation on the evaluation of medicinal products for market approval. Their 1996 E6 Good Clinical Practice guidance on clinical trials to demonstrate efficacy and safety of medicinal products acknowledges the role of statistics in trial design and analysis, which is detailed in the E9 guidance aimed at harmonizing the principles of clinical trial statistical methodology. It supports (ICH 1998, p. 28) the "intention-to-treat ideal" and states that "Preservation of the initial randomization in analysis is important in preventing bias and in providing a secure foundation for statistical tests. In many clinical trials, the use of the full analysis set provides a conservative strategy. Under many circumstances, it may also provide estimates of treatment effects that are more likely to mirror those observed in subsequent practice." The authors of the Consolidated Standards of Reporting Trials (CONSORT; Schulz et al. 2010) recommend ITT analysis of parallel group RCTs for unbiased treatment effect estimates. Similarly, the Cochrane Collaboration (Higgins and Green 2011, Sect. 16.2.1) points out that "ITT analyses are generally preferred as they are unbiased, and also because they address a more pragmatic and clinically relevant question." Modifications of the ITT approach, e.g. by excluding, after randomization, patients that were misdiagnosed or never had received any treatment, have been criticized for possibly introducing bias (Montedori et al. 2011).

From a causal effect estimation point of view, ITT is a form of instrumental variable analysis. In fact, the instrument (randomized treatment allocation) satisfies the key prerequisites for the validity of an instrumental variable (Greenland 2000), i.e., it is clearly linked to the actual treatment, but is unrelated to observed or unobserved prognostic factors as well as to the outcome (other than through the actual treatment; "exclusion restriction", i.e., $Y(R,A) = Y(A)$). In this case, any confounding of the association between actual treatment and outcome is rendered irrelevant with respect to the association between the instrument (randomization R) and the potential outcomes, i.e., $Y(a) \perp R$. The reason is, based on causal-analytical considerations (Greenland and Pearl 2011), that the backdoor-path from the outcome to the instrument is blocked by the actual treatment, on which the effects of randomization and potential confounders collide; unless (incorrectly so), the ITT effect estimation would be conditioned on the actual treatment, which would open the backdoor path and (re)introduce confounding.

As pointed out above, the ITT principle to analyze the data of all participants as randomized has gained the status of the *de facto* standard (or even "gold standard"; Armijo-Olivo et al. 2009) for the primary analysis of randomized superiority clinical therapy trials and is broadly supported by regulatory and other authoritative bodies (Ten Have et al. 2008). There are downsides, however. The counterintuitive aspect of ITT is to some degree supported by an inherent asymmetry, which is that a treatment might be efficacious without being effective (due to a large nonadherence level). From this it can be deduced that an analysis which is exclusively based on ITT cannot provide sufficient insight into treatment effects. This is related to the fact that an ITT estimate, while avoiding confounding by self-selection through ignoring compliance, is by no means independent of compliance. In superiority settings, ITT estimates of treatment effects are being increasingly biased towards the null, i.e., diluted (compared to compliance-based estimates) as noncompliance increases. The simplicity of conducting an ITT analysis is largely restricted to parallel-group superiority designs, while deviations (e.g. crossover-designs) pose substantial conceptual and methodological problems. Moreover, for safety analyses ITT appears to be generally inappropriate (Robins and Greenland 1994). When post-randomization drop-outs occur, the ITT approach obliges some form of adjustment to avoid selection bias due to differential loss to follow-up. One of the simplest and most frequently applied forms of adjustment is by simply replacing missing outcome data points by the last known value (LOCF) of the participant. Although this is often considered to be a very conservative approach, it can introduce bias in either direction and always leads to overestimating the precision of the ITT effect estimates (Altman 2009). Under open-label conditions, the assumption that ITT provides pure estimates of effects of treatment offer/allocation does not hold anymore, as expectation effects can then introduce bias (e.g., Rosenthal, Hawthorne, and/or placebo effects). Due to the dilution of treatment effects by extending the assessment to noncompliant participants, ITT effect estimates are usually smaller than those of per-protocol and as-treated analyses, which increases the likelihood of underestimating or even failing to confirm a real effect (increased false negative/type II error rate). As a consequence, the conservativeness of ITT, compared to per-protocol and as-treated, does not extend to non-inferiority or equivalence studies, where it tends to favor equality of treatments and therefore to increase the type I (false positive) error. This becomes evident in a hypothetical study where perfect equivalence would be guaranteed under complete non-compliance of all study participants, at least as long as no additional success criterion (e.g., a minimal effect magnitude) is implemented. Even in superiority trials, to warrant external validity (generalizability, transportability) of ITT estimates, the assumption of similar levels and patterns of noncompliance under study and real-world conditions is required to hold.

Probably more importantly, however, the ITT approach addresses a different research question than non-ITT approaches. While per-protocol provides answers with respect to the effect of receiving a treatment as assigned to and in line with the protocol, and as-treated on the effect of receiving a treatment (irrespective of randomization and protocol-adherence), both are providing efficacy measures aiming at explaining effects. In contrast, ITT aims at quantifying the effect of *being assigned* to a treatment, regardless of whether it is received. ITT therefore does not address treatment efficacy and clinical meaning, but rather pragmatically quantifies the effectiveness of treatment *allocation*. This has in fact been considered an asset with regard to similarity to the real-world clinical practice and its value for informing policy decisions. However, the properties of RCT-based ITT estimates need to be handled with great care and assessed in context, in particular when comparing them to results from observational studies. An example is the controversy on the impact of hormone replacement therapy on the risk of coronary heart disease, where an observational cohort study (the Nurses Health Study) looking at more than 30,000 postmenopausal women suggested a substantial risk reduction, which was not confirmed by two subsequent RCTs (cf. Tannen et al. 2008). As Hernán et al. (2008) demonstrated, the results from the observational study estimated a different effect in a different population, and when reanalyzed by calculating an ITT-analogue effect in the sub-cohort of new hormone users and accounting for time since menopause and length of follow-up, the apparent discrepancies vanished.

While the conservativeness of ITT is often considered a major advantage, as it would protect against overestimating therapy effects, this very property might increase the risk of seriously disadvantageous public health strategies. Feinman (2009) has illustrated this point based on data from the Artery Bypass Surgery trial (Newell 1992). ITT analysis suggested a modest mortality advantage of surgery over medical treatment (5.3% vs. 7.8% mortality, respectively), while per-protocol and (more pronounced) as-treated showed a more than twofold higher mortality under medical treatment. An indifferent clinical practice regarding the therapy decision, in-line with the ITT results, might miss out on the potentially highly relevant option of embarking on an orchestrated action plan that would aim at allocating as many patients as possible to surgery. Not doing so effectively implies assuming that noncompliance rates and patterns cannot be influenced and will necessarily remain at what had been seen in the trial.

6   Consumer Products

In the medical world, treatment allocations are to a large degree made by clinicians, and patients are largely restricted to following this external allocation; they are in need of therapy and are being made an offer that they cannot easily decline. Thus, randomization appears to be an appropriate model of the external real-world. This is reflected in Fig. 2a, where the typical situation for an RCT on a therapeutic drug is summarized prior to the drug being marketed. Study participants selected from the target population in accordance with pre-specified inclusion and exclusion criteria are randomized to the novel drug (R = 1) or to some comparator (R = 0). If there is

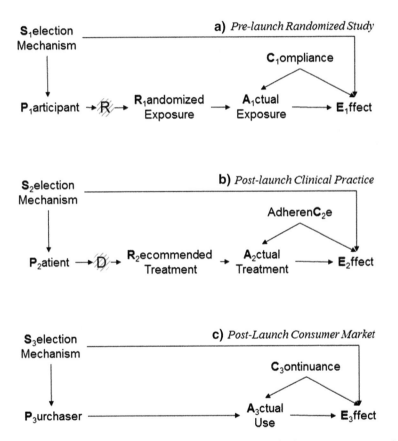

Fig. 2 Basic causal diagrams of (**a**) pre-launch effects of therapeutic drugs or consumer products in randomized parallel-group studies, of (**b**) clinical practice effects of prescription drugs, and of (**c**) in-market effects of consumer products. In the drug-therapy context, a close structural match between pre-launch clinical therapy research and post-launch clinical practice of components S, P, R, A, C, and E, to be justified on a case-by-case basis, provides support for the generalizability of the in-study findings (external validity). In consumer product contexts, the correspondence between pre-launch research and post-launch market is far more questionable, in particular with regard to the absence of external product allocation (component R) in consumer product contexts

(i) no access to the novel product in those randomly allocated to the control group, i.e. a zero probability of actually taking the novel product, $Pr(A = 1|R = 0) = 0$, (ii) allocation to either group is equally probable through $Pr(R = 1) = 0.5$, and (iii) in-study exposure occurs in a double-blind and non-discriminable manner, then the effect in the study sample is essentially a function of actual treatment (exposure) and, as pointed out above, compliance.

By comparing this with Fig. 2b, denoting the situation after the therapeutic drug is on the market and can be prescribed by doctors, it becomes clear that the causal relationships are quite similar. The in-study randomization (R) corresponds to the post-market allocation of the drug by the doctor (D). All things being, while not fully equal but largely comparable, it can be expected that the study results have a good potential of predicting the real-world effectiveness of the drug once it is being marketed. Of course, in order to generalize study effects to real world effectiveness, the requirement of C1=C2 is critical: If real-world adherence to prescription differs from in-study compliance, then the study simply does not reflect the real world in that respect, and the in-study findings cannot accurately predict the post-market situation.

Transposing the above from pharmacotherapy to consumer product clinical trial settings is difficult. The first problems become evident when it comes to sampling study participants. In any research area, for generalizability, a study sample is required that represents some specific real-world population of interest. Consequently, a prerequisite of any study is that by some adequate selection mechanism S on a certain target population, a representative sample of participants P is included in the study, i.e., a sample having the same joint probability distribution over all relevant variables as the target population. Identifying and selecting participants into high-quality RCTs is in either case based on prudently defined procedures and inclusion/exclusion criteria. Drug trials typically build on the additional criterion of a confirmed medical diagnosis as well as related restrictions regarding co-morbidities and concomitant medications. Also, in particular when patients expect to benefit from the novel treatment, participation rates, i.e. $Pr(P = 1| S = 1)$, are likely higher than when consumer products are tested for which potential study participants feel no immediate need. Target populations of drug trials are therefore likely to be more narrowly defined than those of consumer product trials. This implies that the representativeness of therapy study populations tends to be better warranted than under consumer product premises. When the rate and severity of adverse events under novel drug treatment is low and a lack of effects is not easily discernable by patients in the control group, compliance, i.e. $Pr(A = R)$, might in general also be higher in drug as compared to consumer product trials.

Some consumer products aim at alleviating symptoms and conditions (like a cream aimed at moisturizing dry skin or a standardized diet, fitness program, or massaging device to address obesity). However, most health-related issues that are linked to consumer products are related to whether or not the use of (or exposure to) a certain consumer product is associated with improved wellbeing (rather than disease proper), or with increased or decreased risks of *future* adverse health-effects in currently healthy consumers. The range of consumer products and product categories that may be subjected to health-related research questions is quite broad and fuzzy, bordering on matters of lifestyle patterns, "alternative therapies", and over-the-counter drugs. Examples are specific diets, certain fast-food items, snacks, ready-made nutrition products, sugar-enhanced soft drinks, functional food supplements, fitness programs, cosmetic products, sunglasses, alcoholic beverages, bicycle helmets, toothpaste, or tobacco products such as cigarettes. Depending on the type of consumer product tested in an RCT as outlined in Fig. 2a with regard to its health-impact, the feasibility of blinding or concealing the actual exposure is very likely generally lower (and often non-existent) than in a typical pharmaco-therapy context. Also, the access to the (active) control product, which may already be on the market and then is typically freely accessible, depends very much on the study design, duration, and procedures. If the study is conducted in an ambulatory manner, all study participants typically would have access to the control product (other than in research on prescription drugs). For tobacco products, for example, this implies that all (presumably adult) noncompliant study participants randomized to the novel product (e.g., a candidate modified risk tobacco product, MRTP) would be able to obtain and consume the control product (e.g., conventional cigarettes), whereas the reverse would not be possible, as long as the novel product would not be on the market.

A key aspect of transposing research concepts from pharmacotherapy to consumer products is that prescription drugs are just that: prescribed, i.e., externally allocated. Even when consumer product RCTs follow the principles of a pharmacotherapy trial as laid out in Fig. 2a, pretty much the opposite of external allocation takes place under consumer market conditions, with largely unmediated and unrestricted product access through self-selection, i.e., consumer-internal product exposure allocation (Fig. 2c). Compared to the clinical practice world of prescription drugs, in the post-market consumer product world there are typically no diseases, no doctors, no treatments, and no patients, and products are not prescribed but freely chosen. The lack of anything only barely resembling prescription renders ITT and per-protocol based effect estimates meaningless, as there is nothing in the consumer product world that would correspond with the underlying concepts; all there is in the post-launch consumer product world is actual use (cf. Weitkunat et al. 2016, for a more detailed assessment of ITT estimates in the context of consumer product trials). In order to render an RCT-based as-treated effect estimate a valid predictor of the effect of actual use in the consumer market, it would be required that S, P, C, A, and E are identical under study and market conditions. As a comparison of Fig. 2(a) and (c) clarifies, this essentially necessitates that $R1 = S3$, i.e., that the self-selection to $A = 1$ and $A = 0$ under consumer market conditions is an unbiased version of what would be achieved by randomization.

7 Allocation vs. Preference

How can the problem of in-RCT randomization possibly not reflecting in-market self-selection in consumer product research be consolidated? It appears that accounting for consumer preferences is at the core of the issue. Even in the context of therapy research, concerns have been raised against randomization when external treatment allocation conflicts with patient preferences. In particular in contexts of impractical or incomplete blinding, external but also internal validity may be compromised through preference-related recruitment and compliance (King et al. 2005), and consequently preference-incorporating study designs have been proposed (e.g. Brewin and Bradley 1989; Zelen 1990; Wennberg et al. 1993). Irrespective of its relevance in therapy research, considering preference in the design of consumer studies might provide a possibility to reconcile randomization with relevance to and correspondence with the real world. By randomizing not the allocation to a certain product *per se*, but rather (as in the preference arm of the Wennberg et al. design) the option to choose a novel product to replace a previously used comparator product, the consumer market situation would be mirrored by the study design. Data obtained from this randomized choice option (RCO) design would lend themselves to an ITT-analogue analysis, which could be denoted as option-to-use or (for the sake of terminological similarity) intention-to-use (ITU) analysis. What ITU would estimate is actually the effect of offering a consumer product in a consumer market—something that cannot be achieved by an ITT analysis which is based on participants being externally allocated to a certain product through direct randomization. As with ITT in the therapy-research context, ITU would have the advantage of being randomization-protected against confounding by baseline variables, which of course requires analysis strictly according to randomization, irrespective of actual product choice. A critical prerequisite of ITU to provide valid effectiveness estimates is evidently the correspondence of in-study and real-world self-selection patterns and levels, which is in fact a rather strong assumption, although it can in principle be validated after the product has been launched by comparing in-study users with in-market consumers of the novel and of the comparator product. In addition to effectiveness (through ITU analysis), efficacy can be estimated from RCO data by analyzing actual use (AU)–outcome associations in the choice-option arm, necessarily by accounting for potential confounding (which corresponds to a classical observational cohort study).

From a practical point of view, the RCO design has the advantage that only those participants who are randomized to the product choice option need to be informed of the novel product, whereas the control group would reflect a market to which the novel product would never have been introduced. In addition, the RCO design provides use prevalence rate estimates based on real volitional behavior rather than solely relying on proxies of behaviors, like attitudes or intention-to-use declarations. As it may be adequate in many contexts to randomize a distinctly smaller number of consumers to the no-choice-option condition, the efficiency of an RCO design is likely comparable to a traditional RCT with direct (individual-level) randomization to a certain product. It appears worthwhile to point out that reversing the order of RCO events by first selecting participants based on their preference for the novel product (or, a weaker variant, their willingness to being randomized to it), while possibly leading to higher in-study adoption and compliance rates, will not achieve the same study-to-real-world correspondence and will lead to a very different (i.e., preference-selected) sample of participants (even though the ITT-analogue effect of product use allocation in those preferring the product can then be estimated, under the usual randomization-based protection from baseline confounding). A sensible extension of the RCO design appears to be adding a second randomization step to the scheme, allocating participants of the choice option arm who had previously expressed their preference for the novel product to actual product access versus to no access. Estimating the ITU effect of offering the product as well as estimating the AU effect would still be possible (by a slightly more complicated combination of the comparison groups), but now also a randomization-protected product effect could be estimated in those choosing the product offer and having versus not having actual access to the product.

8 Real World

Although it is often claimed that ITT would provide an effect estimate reflecting the real-world effectiveness of an intervention, this must, even under circumstances where the underlying logic applies, not be confused with population health impact estimation; ITT is restricted to quantifying effectiveness at the individual level. To quantify population-level effects, population impact measures are required, which can be based on estimates of the risk (cumulative incidence or prevalence) or rate (incidence rate) difference between the actually exposed and unexposed study groups. To estimate the population attributable risk (PAR), this risk difference (or attributable risk) is multiplied by the proportion of the total population that is actually exposed (i.e., is actually taking the drug that is investigated, or is actually using the consumer product under consideration). By multiplication with the population size, the PAR can be converted to a headcount estimate. To obtain valid PAR estimates, these calculations must be conducted in accordance with the exposure and risk strata that actually occur in the target population. If, for example, the impact of an exposure/therapy/consumer product on the outcome depends on sex, age, dose, or other factors, then stratum-specific risks as well as stratum-specific exposure prevalence estimates must be obtained in order to estimate the integrative population attributable risk (cf. Weitkunat et al. 2015).

When the generalization of therapy study results to the target population as a whole is assumed to be valid, then—in theory—a study-based ITT effect might be considered being a valid estimate of the attributable risk as it will occur in the target population, when the proportion of patients randomized to the drug in the study corresponds to the proportion of patients that the treatment will later be prescribed to and when in-study compliance corresponds to clinical practice adherence patterns and levels. Based on the considerations given to the generalizability of findings from therapy RCTs to target populations, this is, even under very favorable circumstances, a dauntingly long shot. For consumer products, it appears to be an impossible one. Here, but probably also for drug contexts, a population health impact assessment based on actual use effect estimates appears to be much more logical. What is required are stratum-specific AU estimates, based on studies where exposure-response data have been obtained for all strata (or contexts) of relevance, in particular with regard to various levels of dose, as they occur in the real world, as well as prevalence data regarding the size of all strata of relevance in the total population.

Even though this is somewhat beyond scope, contemplating the logic of how to analyze consumer product RCTs ultimately raises the question as to how useful this design is in the first place. It appears that for biomarkers of exposure or other objective short-term effects, the advantages of a randomized experimental approach apply essentially in full, even though the usually unquestioned assumption of baseline covariate balance being quasi-automatically achieved by randomization is somewhat problematic with regard to a single RCT (cf. Worrall 2007). Whenever the exposure period exceeds a few days or weeks, and whenever the outcomes are more complex (including subjective and behavioral endpoints, let alone long-term health outcomes), the question arises about what is actually being achieved through randomization. Seligman (1995, p. 974) has voiced the concern that random treatment allocation may be "less than useless" in mental disorder therapy research. In such circumstances, the likelihood of protocol deviations, allocated exposure contamination, and participants dropping out in a non-ignorable manner increases markedly, and both efficacy and effectiveness become ambiguous concepts, implying that valid analyses of outcomes cannot be conducted without accounting for post-randomization bias. Factually, the described complications render studies that have been conceived as experiments essentially observational in nature, necessitating the application of bias-correcting analysis methods, rather than a simple (sometimes denoted "naïve") endpoint comparison across study groups. Such approaches aim at establishing conditional independence through unconfounding and include, by considering dynamic exposure as well as baseline and time-varying covariates, adjustment, inverse probability of treatment weighting, stratification for actual use patterns (irrespective of randomization), matching, propensity-score weighting (or adjustment), instrumental variable analysis, marginal structural modeling, or g-estimation (Schafer and Kang 2008, for an overview). According to Hernán and Hernández-Diaz (2012) and Hernán et al. (2013), outpatient therapy RCTs on effects of sustained interventions over long periods in real-world clinical care settings ("pragmatic trials") conducted in large samples tend to suffer from non-differential noncompliance and sample attrition, and effectively become observational studies that require analyses beyond ITT; the authors suggest to analyze them as observational studies. It might, depending on the degree of deviation from the ideal RCT, indeed be more adequate to designate them as closed prospective cohort studies with baseline randomization.

To summarize: Clinical trials can contribute to consumer product assessment and research related to the health and wellbeing of consumers. The methodology was originally developed for and is most widely deployed in therapy research. It cannot be simply copied for consumer product research. Rather, careful consideration is required as to whether it can indeed provide sensible answers to the specific research questions at hand. Many of the critical aspects of using clinical research methods in consumer product research relate to the specific conditions of consumer's access to freely available products. Other than patients with serious diseases, consumers usually do not have an inevitable need to use or consume a certain product and their sovereignty to choose is largely unrestricted. Such differences have far-reaching methodological implications, including the meaning of statistical data analysis strategies. To account for consumer preferences, behaviors, and contexts, study designs may more likely than not need to be adopted or even newly developed in rather unconventional ways. In general, planning and conducting research must be guided by considering whether a specific set of methods actually addresses the scientific questions at hand. Only then then collected data can have meaning, i.e., can provide evidence.

References

Altman, D. (2009). Missing outcomes in randomized trials: Addressing the dilemma. *Open Medicine, 3*, 2.

Armijo-Olivo, S., Warren, S., & Magee, D. (2009). Intention to treat analysis, compliance, dropouts and how to deal with missing data in clinical research: A review. *The Physical Therapy Review, 14*, 36–49.

Brewin, C. R., & Bradley, C. (1989). Patient preferences and randomized clinical trials. *British Medical Journal, 299*, 313–315.

Campbell, D. T., & Stanley, J. C. (1963). *Experimental and quasi-experimental designs for research.* Chicago: Rand-McNally.

Cartwright, N. (2010). What are randomized controlled trials good for? *Philosophical Studies, 147*, 59–70.

Cartwright, N. (2011). A philosopher's view of the long road from RCTs to effectiveness. *Lancet, 377*, 1400–1401.

Cochrane, A. L. (1972). *Effectiveness and efficiency: Random reflections on health services.* London: Nuffield Provincial Hospitals Trust.

DeVries, J. G., & Berlet, G. C. (2010). Understanding levels of evidence for scientific communication. *Foot & Ankle Specialist, 3*, 305–309.

Doll, R., & Hill, A. B. (1950). Smoking and carcinoma of the lung: Preliminary report. *British Medical Journal, 2*, 739–748.

Doll, R., & Hill, A. B. (1964). Mortality in relation to smoking: Ten years' observations of British doctors. *British Medical Journal, 1*, 1399–1410.

Feinman, R. D. (2009). Intention-to-treat. What is the question? *Nutrition and Metabolism, 6*, 1.

Fisher, R. A. (1925). *Statistical methods for research workers.* Edinburgh: Oliver and Boyd.

Gadenne, V. (2013). External validity and the new inductivism in experimental economics. *Rationality Markets and Morals, 4*, 1–19.

Grahame-Smith, D. (1995). Evidence based medicine: Socratic dissent. *British Medical Journal, 310*, 1126–1127.

Greenland, S. (2000). Instrumental variables for epidemiologists. *International Journal of Epidemiology, 29*, 722–729.

Greenland, S., & Pearl, J. (2011). Causal diagrams. In M. Lovric (Ed.), *International encyclopedia of statistical science* (pp. 208–216). Berlin: Springer.

Gupta, S. K. (2011). Intention-to-treat concept: A review. *Perspectives in Clinical Research, 2*, 109–112.

Hernán, M. A., & Hernández-Diaz, S. (2012). Beyond the intention to treat in comparative effectiveness research. *Clinical Trials, 9*, 48–55.

Hernán, M.A., Alonso, A., Logan, R., Grodstein, F., Michels, K. B., Stampfer, M. J., Willett, W. C., Manson, J. E., & Robins, J. M. (2008). Observational studies analyzed like randomized experiments: An application to postmenopausal hormone therapy and coronary heart disease. *Epidemiology, 19*, 766–779.

Hernán, M. A., Hernández-Diaz, S., & Robins, J. M. (2013). Randomized trials analyzed as observational studies. *Annals of Internal Medicine, 159*, 560–562.

Higgins, J. P. T., & Green, S. (Eds.). (2011). *Cochrane handbook for systematic reviews of interventions (V5.1.0)*. The Cochrane Collaboration. Accessed August 15, 2016. http://handbook.cochrane.org/

Hill, A. B. (1955). *Principles of medical statistics* (6th ed.). London: Lancet.

Hill, A. B. (1990). Suspended judgment: Memories of the British Streptomycin Trial in tuberculosis. The first randomized clinical trial. *Controlled Clinical Trials, 11*, 77–79.

Ho, P. M., Peterson, P. N., & Masoudi, F. A. (2008). Evaluating the evidence. Is there a rigid hierarchy? *Circulation, 118*, 1675–1684.

Hoffmann, J., Schirra, T., Lo, H., Neeb, L., Reuter, U., & Martus, P. (2015). The influence of weather on migraine—are migraine attacks predictable? *Annals of Clinical and Translational Neurology, 2*, 22–28.

Hudgens, G., Gilbert, P. B., & Self, S. G. (2004). Endpoints in vaccine trials. *Statistical Methods in Medical Research, 13*, 1–26.

ICH. (1998). *Guidance for industry: E9 Statistical principles for clinical trials*. Rockwell: US Department of Health and Human Services, Food and Drug Administration. Accessed August 15, 2016, from http://www.fda.gov/downloads/Drugs/GuidanceComplianceRegulatory Information/Guidances/ucm073137.pdf

King, M., Nazareth, I., Lampe, F., Bower, P., Chandler, M., Morou, M., Sibbald, B., & Lai, R. (2005). Impact of participant and physician intervention preferences on randomized trials. *JAMA, 293*, 1089–1099.

Lewis, J. A., & Machin, D. (1993). Intention to treat—who should use ITT? *British Journal of Cancer, 68*, 647–650.

Montedori, A., Bonacini, M. I., Casazza, G., Luchetta, M. L., Duca, F. C., & Abraha, I. (2011). Modified versus standard intention-to-treat reporting. *Trials, 12*, 58.

Morabia, A. (2013). Hume, Mill, Hill, and the sui generis epidemiologic approach to causal inference. *American Journal of Epidemiology, 178*, 1526–1532.

MRC Medical Research Council Streptomycin in Tuberculosis Trials Committee. (1948). Streptomycin treatment of pulmonary tuberculosis. *British Medical Journal, 2*, 769–783.

Newell, D. (1992). Intention-to-treat analysis: Implications for quantitative and qualitative research. *International Journal of Epidemiology, 21*, 837–884.

Neyman, J. (1923). On the application of probability theory to agricultural experiments. Essay on principles (Section 9). *Statistical Science, 5*, 465–472.

Neyman, J., & Pearson, E. S. (1933). On the problem of the most efficient tests of statistical hypotheses. *Philosophical Transactions of the Royal Society of London Series A, 231*, 289–337.

Popper, K. (1935). *Logik der Forschung*. Wien: Springer.

Robins, J. M., & Greenland, S. (1994). Adjusting for differential rates of PCP prophylaxis in high- versus low-dose AZT treatment arms in and AIDS randomized trial. *Journal of the American Statistical Association, 89*, 737–749.

Rosenbaum, P., & Rubin, D. B. (1983). The central role of the propensity score in observational studies for causal effects. *Biometrika, 70*, 41–55.

Rubin, D. B. (1974). Estimating causal effects of treatments in randomized and nonrandomized treatments. *Journal of Education & Psychology, 66*, 688–701.

Rothman, K. J. (2014). Six persistent research misconceptions. *Journal of General Internal Medicine, 29*, 1060–1064.

Sackett, D. L. (1989). Rules of evidence and clinical recommendations on the use of antithrombotic agents. *Chest, 95*(Suppl 2), 2–4.

Sackett, D. L., & Wennberg, J. E. (1997). Choosing the best research design for each question. *BMJ, 315*, 1636.

Salsburg, D. (1994). Intent to treat: The reduction ad absurdum that became gospel. *Pharmacoepidemiology and Drug Safety, 3*, 329–335.

Schafer, J. L., & Kang, J. (2008). Average causal effects from nonrandomized studies: A practical guide and simulated example. *Psychological Methods, 13*, 279–313.

Schulz, K. F., Altman, D. G., & Moher, D. (2010). CONSORT 2010 statement: updated guidelines for reporting parallel group randomised trials. *Journal of Clinical Epidemiology, 63*, 834–840.

Seligman, M. E. (1995). The effectiveness of psychotherapy. The Consumer Reports study. *American Psychologist, 50*, 965–974.

Sheiner, L. B. (1991). The intellectual health of clinical drug evaluation. *Clinical Pharmacology & Therapeutics, 50*, 4–9.

Steckler, A., & McLeroy, K. R. (2008). The importance of external validity. *American Journal of Public Health, 98*, 9–10.

Tannen, R. L., Weiner, M. G., Xie, D., & Barnhart, K. (2008). Perspectives on hormone replacement therapy: The Women's Health Initiative and new observational studies sampling the overall population. *Fertility and Sterility, 90*, 258–264.

Ten Have, T. R., Normand, S. L. T., Marcus, S. M., Brown, C. H., Lavori, P., & Duan, N. (2008). Intent-to-treat vs. non-intent-to-treat analyses under treatment non-adherence in mental health randomized trials. *Psychiatric Annals, 38*, 772–783.

Tolman, E. C. (1932). *Purposive behavior in animals and men.* New York: Appleton.

Victor, T. W., Hu, X., Campbell, J. C., Buse, D. C., & Lipton, R. B. (2010). Migraine prevalence by age and sex in the United States: A life-span study. *Cephalalgia, 30*, 1065–1072.

Weitkunat, R., Lee, P. N., Baker, G., Sponsiello-Wang, Z., González-Zuloeta Ladd, A. M., & Lüdicke, F. (2015). A novel approach to assess the population health impact of introducing a Modified Risk Tobacco Product. *Regulatory Toxicology and Pharmacology, 72*, 87–93.

Weitkunat, R., Baker, G., & Lüdicke, F. (2016). Intention-to-treat analysis but for treatment intention: How should consumer product randomized controlled trials be analyzed? *International Journal Statistics Medical Research, 5*, 90–98.

Wennberg, J. E., Barry, M. J., Fowler, F. J., & Mulley, A. (1993). Outcomes research, PORTs, and health care reform. *Annals of the New York Academy of Sciences, 703*, 52–62.

West, S. G., Duan, N., Pequegnat, W., Gaist, P., Des Jarlais, D. C., Holtgrave, D., Szapocznik, J., Fishbein, M., Rapkin, B., Clatts, M., & Mullen, P. D. (2008). Alternatives to the randomized controlled trial. *American Journal of Public Health, 98*, 1359–1366.

Worrall, J. (2007). Why there's no cause to randomize. *British Journal for the Philosophy of Science, 58*, 451–488.

Zelen, M. (1990). Randomized consent designs for clinical trials: An update. *Statistics in Medicine, 9*, 645–656.

Epidemiological Product Assessment

Olivier Ethgen and Olivier Bruyère

1 Introduction

Policy makers and regulators have increasingly expressed an interest in obtaining more safety data and guidance on the use of consumer products. A number of concerns have been raised about the potential health risks associated with the consumption of consumer products or exposure to some of their components. The products that have received scrutiny cover quite a large range, including all sorts of commercial products, home products, personal care products, children's products, and food products.

This increased interest has led to a greater emphasis on the use of observational methods to understand the safety profile of products after they are marketed. With the development of new technologies, increasingly available biomonitoring data have provided evidence of widespread human exposure to large numbers of chemical, microbiological, and physical agents. Epidemiological methods and studies can contribute to assessments of the health risks posed by consumer products.

The objectives of this contribution are to introduce key notions of epidemiological research and to show how these notions can be applied to consumer products.

O. Ethgen (✉)
Department of Public Health, Epidemiology and Health Economics, University of Liège, CHU Sart-Tilman B23, Avenue de l'Hôpital n°3, 4000 Liège, Belgium

SERFAN Innovation, Rue F. Terwagne n°30A, 5020 Namur, Belgium
e-mail: o.ethgen@serfan.eu; o.ethgen@ulg.ac.be

O. Bruyère
Department of Public Health, Epidemiology and Health Economics, University of Liège, CHU Sart-Tilman B23, Avenue de l'Hôpital n°3, 4000 Liège, Belgium

Bone and Cartilage Metabolism Unit, University of Liège, Polycliniques Brull, Quai G. Kurth n°45, 4020 Liège, Belgium

© Springer International Publishing AG 2017
G. Emilien et al. (eds.), *Consumer Perception of Product Risks and Benefits*,
DOI 10.1007/978-3-319-50530-5_5

2 Epidemiological Concepts

2.1 Definition and Purpose of Epidemiology

Epidemiology is the study of the distribution of diseases and their determinants in human populations (Silman 1995; Friedman 2004). The key principle is to compare health-related events such as deaths, accidents, diseases, or injuries, between groups of individuals that are exposed or not exposed to specific factors. Epidemiology is not necessarily solely concerned with adverse health outcomes; it also identifies positive health effects and assesses methods for improving and maintaining health. Thus, the results of epidemiological studies can be used to promote healthy behavior (e.g., physical activity or a healthy diet) or discourage unhealthy behaviors (e.g., smoking, alcohol consumption, or a sedentary lifestyle).

Epidemiology plays a particularly important role in safety evaluations for medicines. A classic example of how pioneering research has applied epidemiologic methods to safety evaluations is the discovery of the relationship between thalidomide and limb defects in babies born in the Federal Republic of Germany in the 1950s. In 1961, Lenz (1961) and McBride (1961) suggested a possible correlation between congenital defects and the use of thalidomide during pregnancy. The drug was removed from the market in Germany, and several other countries, between 1961 and 1962. However, by that time, around 10,000 children had been born worldwide that were affected by thalidomide. The thalidomide tragedy dramatically changed the way we currently assess the primary and side effects of drugs. Prior to thalidomide, there were no statutory requirements for implementing epidemiologic studies.

2.2 The Notion of Risk in Epidemiology

Risk refers to the probability of an adverse outcome over a specific period of time. Risk is a quantifiable, but dimensionless concept. We may talk about the risk of death or the risk of a heart attack, in general, but risk can vary with the time-period under consideration. Therefore, it is essential to specify the period used to assess risk.

A prerequisite for the quantification of risk is to quantify exposure to a so-called risk-factor. This is not necessarily an easy task. Exposure may depend on the characteristics of the factor of interest. The characteristics might include chemical, radioactive, nutritional, environmental, occupational, or behavioral properties. When the factor is a substance, exposure also depends on whether natural barriers or specific equipment can be used to prevent exposure or mitigate the degree of exposure. Exposure also depends on how the substance is adsorbed, metabolized, and excreted by the body.

Table 1 Different ways to categorize exposure

Categorization types	Response types (Example: alcohol consumption)
Dichotomous (yes/no)	At least once
	Never
Rank	Never
	Very rarely (1 or 2 glasses per month)
	Occasionally (1 or 2 glasses per week)
	Frequently (every day)
Continuous	
Stratification	$\leq$ 5 glasses per week
	5–14 glasses per week
	15–24 glasses per week
	$\geq$ 25 glasses per week
Statistical[a]	1st quartile
	2nd quartile
	3rd quartile
	4th quartile
Continuous	The quantity of alcohol consumed per week

Adapted from Silman (1995)
[a]Quartile or any other percentile of a continuous variable, like the milliliters of alcohol consumed per week

Exposure can be defined by its intensity, its frequency (and duration), and its route. There are multiple ways to categorize exposure (Table 1). The simplest approach is dichotomous, where exposure is defined according two modalities (yes/no or at least once/never). However, epidemiologists are usually more interested in comparing multiple degrees of exposure. Thus, they typically prefer to use multi-modal categorizations, when possible and practical.

After an association is found, it is necessary to determine the extent of causality between an exposure (cause) and the occurrence of an event (effect). This determination requires a great deal of effort from the epidemiologist. The Bradford Hill criteria are used to assess evidence of a causal relationship between an exposure and an event (Table 2). In particular, it is important to consider the temporal relationship: the cause (i.e., the exposure) must precede the occurrence of the disease or the event of interest. Although the timing might appear to be self-evident at first glance, difficulties arise when exposures and outcomes are measured at the same time. Finally, the exposed population (i.e., the "population at risk") must be clearly defined.

When an association is thought or proven to be causal, epidemiologists use the term "risk factor". Risk factors represent any product characteristic, individual characteristic or behavior that can increase the likelihood of an event. Risk factors are categorized as modifiable (e.g., behavior) or non-modifiable (e.g., gender, age, ethnicity, genetics, or environment). Age is a risk factor for many diseases, but some of the strongest risk factors are behavioral. Examples include an unhealthy diet, smoking, alcohol abuse, or lack of physical activity.

Table 2 The Bradford Hill criteria for causation

Criteria	Description
Strength (effect size)	How strong is the association between the cause and the effect? A strong association is good evidence of causality, but small effects might also represent strong associations.
Consistency (reproducibility)	An association reported in nearly all studies can provide a basis for causation. Consistent findings across different studies support the possibility of an effect.
Specificity	Causation is very likely when there is no other credible explanation.
Temporality	Cause (exposure) must precede the effect (disease). When a delay is expected between the cause and effect, then the effect must occur after that delay.
Biological gradient	Higher (lower) exposure should lead to higher (lower) incidence of the effect. This is also known as the dose-response phenomenon.
Plausibility	The effect must be biologically plausible and explainable. Nonetheless, the understanding of the mechanism between cause and effect might be limited by current knowledge.
Coherence	Coherence between laboratory experiments (in which all variables are controlled) and epidemiological findings increases the likelihood of a causal effect. Nonetheless, a lack of laboratory experimental evidence cannot nullify epidemiological associations.
Experiment	Very strong evidence of cause and effect comes from the results of experiments, where many significant variables are held stable to prevent interference with the results.
Analogy	When a factor is thought to cause an effect, then other similar factors should also be considered in a list of possible causes.

Bradford Hill (1965)

It is important to note that, typically, there is not a one-to-one relationship between a risk factor and a particular disease. A given risk factor may cause multiple diseases and a disease may have multiple causes. Finally, exposure to some factors may promote good health by preventing adverse outcomes. In those cases, the terminology "protective factor" is preferred.

2.3   Measures of Risk

Several measures are used by epidemiologists to quantify risk (Table 3). The measures most commonly used are the incidence and the relative risk (i.e., the ratio of incidences in exposed and non-exposed individuals). The incidence must be distinguished from the prevalence, another commonly reported measure in epidemiology. The incidence is the rate of occurrence, and the prevalence is the proportion of individuals with a specific health condition at a given point in time.

Many medical endpoints are reported as binary outcomes; i.e., outcomes that reflect the occurrence or non-occurrence of a particular event or disease. A convenient way to represent and compare binary outcomes across two groups is to use a

Table 3 Measures of risk in epidemiology

Measures of risk	Formulae	Definition
Incidence (or absolute risk)	$I = \frac{N_{NC}}{N_T}$	The proportion of individuals that experience the disease (N_{NC}), among a group of individuals initially free of the disease of interest (N_T), over a given period of time. For instance, incidence refers to new cases of disease that occur in individuals that were initially free of the disease. The incidence is the best way for individuals, epidemiologists, and clinicians to understand how risk factors impact health.
Relative risk (or risk ratio)	$RR = \frac{I_E}{I_{NE}}$	The ratio of the incidence in exposed individuals (I_E) to the incidence in non-exposed individuals (I_{NE}). The RR estimates the fold-increase in the likelihood of contracting the disease, among exposed individuals compared to non-exposed individuals (i.e., $I_E = RR \cdot I_{NE}$).
Attributable risk (or risk difference)	$AR = I_E - I_{NE}$	The difference between the incidences of disease in exposed individuals (I_E) and non-exposed individuals (I_{NE}). The AR estimates to what extent the incidence of the disease is attributable to exposure (i.e., $I_E = I_{NE} + AR$).
Population-attributable risk	$PAR = AR \times P$	The product of the AR multiplied by the prevalence P of exposure to the risk factor. The PAR measures the excess incidence of a disease associated with the degree of exposure to a risk factor in the population.
Population-attributable fraction	$PAF = \frac{PAR}{I_T}$	The ratio of the PAR to the incidence of the disease in the total population (I_T). The PAF determines what fraction of the disease in a population is attributable to exposure to a risk factor.

Adapted from Silman (1995) and Fletcher et al. (2014)
N_{NC} Number of new cases of the disease over a given period of time, N_T Total number of individuals initially free of the disease in the group followed over that given period of time, I_E Incidence of the disease in exposed individuals, I_{NE} Incidence of the disease in non-exposed individuals, I_T Incidence of the disease in the total population (i.e., those who are exposed plus those who are not exposed), P Prevalence of exposure to the risk factor in the population

2×2 contingency table (Fig. 1). Typically, a group of individuals exposed to a risk (or protective) factor, such as smoking (or a healthy diet), is compared to a group of individuals that are not exposed to this risk (or protective) factor. The relative risk can then be readily computed to measure the association between exposure and the risk of occurrence of the event or disease of interest (Fig. 1).

The odds ratio (OR) is another measure of the association between a risk factor and the occurrence of disease. The OR is also readily computed from a contingency table. The odds that an event will occur is usually numerically close to the probability that an event will occur when the event rate is low. It is the ratio of the odds in the exposed group to the odds in the non-exposed group (Fig. 1). The OR approximates the RR when the event rate is low (typically below 10%). In general, an OR provides a more extreme estimate of the effect (i.e., more different

	Health impact				Risks	Odds
		Disease	No disease	Total		
Exposure	Exposed (E)	a	b	a+b	a/(a+b)	a/b
	Non-exposed (NE)	c	d	c+d	c/(c+d)	c/d
	Total	a+c	b+d	N_T	$(a+c)/N_T$	

Relative risk (RR) $$RR = \frac{I_E}{I_{NE}} = \frac{\frac{a}{a+b}}{\frac{c}{c+d}} \iff I_E = RR.I_{NE}$$	<1	Risk in exposed group is lower than in the unexposed group; i.e., exposure decreases the risk of disease	
	=1	Risks in both groups are the same; i.e., there is no effect of exposure on the risk of disease	
	>1	Risk in exposed group is higher than in the unexposed group; i.e., exposure increases the risk of disease	
Odds ratio (OR) $$OR = \frac{O_E}{O_{NE}} = \frac{\frac{a}{b}}{\frac{c}{d}} = \frac{ad}{bc} \iff O_E = OR.O_{NE}$$	<1	Odds in the exposed group are lower than in the unexposed group; i.e., exposure decreases the risk of disease	
	=1	Odds in both groups are the same; i.e., there is no effect of exposure on the risk of disease	
	>1	Odds in the exposed group are higher than in the unexposed group; i.e., exposure increases the risk of disease	

Fig. 1 Medical outcomes in a contingency table can be used to compute relative risk (RR) and odds ratio (OR). (*Top*) Contingency table shows how formulas are derived; (*bottom*) formulas and potential values are shown with standard interpretations. Note: $N_T = a + b + c + d; I_E = \frac{a}{a+b}; I_{NE} = \frac{c}{c+d}; I_T = \frac{a+c}{a+b+c+d} \neq I_E + I_{NE}$

from 1) as the event rate increases. Generally, ORs are used for cross-sectional and retrospective studies, while RRs can be calculated for prospective studies.

3 Epidemiological Studies and Risk Assessment

A number of different study designs can be used to assess causal relationships between exposure to risk factors and the occurrence of an event or disease. In all instances, it is essential to have clear definitions of the event or disease of interest and the exposure. In the absence of clear definitions, it can be difficult to design and interpret an epidemiological study.

3.1 Cross-Sectional, Retrospective, and Prospective Designs

Epidemiological studies can be cross-sectional, retrospective, or prospective (Fig. 2). A cross-sectional study measures exposure and disease in a specific population at a particular point in time. A survey is a typical example of a cross-sectional study. With survey information, concurrent exposed and non-exposed

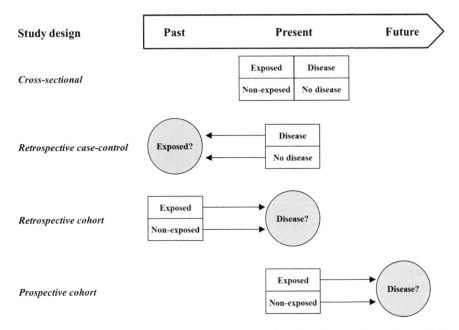

Fig. 2 Cross-sectional, retrospective, and prospective study designs (Adapted from Silman 1995)

groups can be compared for their disease status or vice versa (Silman 1995). The main purpose of surveys is to determine prevalence, both of exposure and of outcomes. While being the simplest design, cross-sectional studies cannot properly discern whether an exposure is the potential cause of a disease. Ideally, exposure status should be documented before disease onset. In retrospective studies, exposure is recorded after the outcome.

In a retrospective study, the event or disease of interest has already occurred before the start of the study, but epidemiologists look backward in time to determine the exposure status. Case-control studies and retrospective cohort studies are typical examples of retrospective studies (Fig. 2). In a prospective study, the event or disease of interest has not yet occurred. Individuals free of the event or disease are followed forward in time. Prospective cohort studies, such as clinical trials, are typical examples (Fig. 2).

In cohort studies, individuals are followed to see how the subsequent occurrence of an event or the development of new disease cases differs between exposure and non-exposure groups. Attributable and relative risks can be estimated. This type of study provides the best evidence to support the causation of disease. Although conceptually simple, cohort studies represent a major undertaking. They may require long follow-up periods as many exposures are long-term in nature. The difficulty is further increased when there is a long induction period between the first exposure to a hazard and the eventual manifestation of a disease, as with most carcinogens, for instance.

Case-control studies provide another way to investigate the causes of diseases. They recruit individuals with the disease of interest and a comparable control group of individuals without the disease. The study then compares the extent of past exposure to the suspected risk factor between groups. An important consideration in case-control studies is the identification of an appropriate and comparable control group. The cases and controls should belong to the same general population. Exposures should be measurable to the same degree of accuracy in controls and cases.

Absolute risk and relative risk cannot be determined directly from case-control studies, because the incidence of disease is not known in either the exposed or the unexposed population. However, as mentioned above, ORs can be calculated to determine the association between exposure and the risk of disease. Note that a case-control approach is preferred when studying rare diseases, because a relatively large number of individuals would be necessary to draw conclusions from a cohort study.

Finally, it should be noted that retrospective studies are typically much less expensive and time consuming than prospective studies. The costs of retrospective studies can occasionally be further reduced by using historical cohorts, identified on the basis of records of previous exposure. This type of investigation is then called a historical cohort study, because all exposure and disease status data have been collected before the study was planned. This sort of design is relatively common for studies on cancers related to occupational exposures.

3.2   Observational Versus Interventional (Experimental) Studies

Observational studies allow nature to take its course. The researchers observe, measure, and analyze, but they do not intervene. Observational studies are generally descriptive or analytical. A descriptive study documents the occurrence of a disease in a population. It is often the first step in an epidemiological investigation. For instance, descriptive epidemiology determines the distribution over time of health outcomes, in individuals grouped by age, gender, socioeconomic status, levels of exposure, etc. An analytical study goes a step further. It examines the potential relationships between health outcomes and other variables. The aim is to investigate which factors might be responsible for increasing or decreasing the risk of occurrence of a specific event or disease. In other words, descriptive studies are concerned with the prevailing distribution of variables. They do not test hypotheses or make inferences concerning possible causality. In contrast, analytical studies test for a hypothesized causal relationship and focus on the identification and quantification of specific risk factors.

In experimental (or interventional) studies, the researchers intend to assess the effect of a specific intervention on health outcomes. The researchers define the nature of the intervention, the selection/exclusion criteria for enrollment into the study, the length of follow-up, and a plan for proper management of the study population during the follow-up period. Experimental studies are necessarily prospective cohort studies. They are more controlled and managed than cohort studies. They are usually referred to as clinical trials, when the exposure is to a treatment that is designed to protect individuals against the occurrence of the event of interest, such as premature death, myocardial infarction, or cancer relapse.

A randomized controlled trial is an investigational epidemiological experiment, where the enrolled individuals are randomly allocated to the intervention group or the control group (e.g., placebo or active-control). Randomization promotes a balance between groups with regard to both known and unknown confounding and prognostic factors. Therefore, randomization guarantees that the only difference in outcomes between the groups lies in the treatment given; other characteristics are assumed to be evenly distributed with the randomization process. Thus, a causal relationship between outcome and treatment can be established. When randomization is accompanied by double-blinding (neither the investigator nor the subject know to which group the subject belongs), the study is less subject to "noise" or bias.

Randomized clinical trials are the gold standard among study designs for assessing intervention effects. When well designed and conducted, they provide the most compelling evidence of cause and effect. However, they are subject to extra constraints. Ethical considerations are of paramount importance. It is not acceptable to expose subjects deliberately to potentially serious hazards, and no one should be denied appropriate intervention as a result of participation in an experiment. The intervention tested must be acceptable in the light of current knowledge. Finally, properly informed consent from participants must be sought and obtained.

Of note, in the context of consumer products, randomized trials are mostly conducted with healthy individuals. In these cases, the goal is to assess risk or prevention effects. Notwithstanding, randomization to the use of a consumer product is often very difficult, impractical, or even totally unrealistic.

3.3   Meta-Analysis

The term 'meta-analysis' refers to an analysis where a collection of pooling and weighting methods are applied to the results of two or more independent individual studies to provide an overall combined estimate. The result is essentially the quantitative component of a systematic review of the relevant literature. The rationale behind a meta-analysis is to provide an estimate with more power than the estimates provided by the separate studies. Simply said, a meta-analysis increases the statistical power, due to an increased sample size.

A critical question is which studies should be included or excluded from the meta-analysis. In fact, the quality of a meta-analysis depends on the quality of the individual studies and the integrity of the process used to combine them. Another important point to consider is the potential heterogeneity across the selected studies. Studies are typically different in design, population, degree of exposure, etc., and when data are combined assuming a unique global effect, the results could be misleading. One approach to this problem is to use statistical random effect models that take into account the heterogeneity across studies.

The use of meta-analyses in epidemiology has increased in recent years, due to ethical reasons, cost issues, and the need to estimate the overall effect of a particular intervention or factor. These reasons are particularly true for clinical trials, where the sample sizes of individual trials are often too small to permit drawing a robust conclusion from any single trial. In addition, results from multiple studies may sometimes be conflicting. Thus, a meta-analysis might be able to increase statistical power, improve the precision of the effect estimate, and provide an overall summary measure.

3.4 Sources of Concerns

There are few sources of concerns to be aware of when designing and interpreting epidemiological studies.

3.4.1 Confounding

When studying the association between an exposure and the risk of a disease, confounding can occur when another exposure is present in the studied population, and it is associated with both the disease and the exposure being studied. Confounding can have very profound effects. It can even change the apparent direction of an association. A variable that appears to be protective may in fact be harmful after controlling for confounding factors. Confounding might also create the appearance of a causal relationship that does not actually exist. For instance, antioxidant supplementation is relatively popular among the lay population. Laboratory experiments and studies on individuals that take antioxidants on a regular basis have suggested that antioxidants can prevent cardiovascular disease and even certain cancers. However, careful randomized studies, which are able to avoid confounding factors, have routinely found little effect of antioxidants. In fact, results showed that, compared to individuals that do not take antioxidants, individuals that regularly take antioxidants are more conscious of their health in general, are more likely to exercise more frequently, tend to watch their weight, eat more vegetables, and avoid smoking. It might well be that all of these activities, not solely the intake of antioxidants, lead to better health outcomes in non-randomized studies on antioxidants.

Several methods are available to control for confounding factors (Table 4). These methods can be applied either during the study design and conduct

Table 4 Methods of controlling for confounding factors in epidemiological studies

Methods	Description
Randomization	In prospective investigational studies, randomization is the ideal method for ensuring that potential confounding variables are equally distributed among the groups being compared. With randomization, individuals have an equal chance of falling into any of the groups.
Restriction	Individuals that are recruited in a study can be limited to only those with a predetermined, narrow range of characteristics. This procedure ensures that certain characteristics are similar in the groups being compared.
Matching	Individuals in an exposed group are matched by selecting one or more individuals with the same characteristics for the comparison group. Subjects are typically matched for age and sex, because these variables are often strongly related to risk or prognosis in many diseases. Matching on the severity of disease or the socioeconomic status can also provide meaningful results.
Stratification	Groups of individuals can be divided into sub-categories (i.e., strata) according to similar risks or disease prognoses, other than the major exposure of interest.
Standardization	Groups can be compared by weighting (or adjusting for) the potential confounder. In the analysis, a standard set of weights is applied to different groups to ensure that they are compared "fairly" (i.e., free of the effects of different proportions in the various groups). Subject groups are typically standardized according to age.
Statistical modeling	Multivariable statistical analysis can adjust for the effects of many variables simultaneously on the outcome of interest. Logistic regression or Cox proportional hazard analyses are typical examples of multivariable statistical models that can be used to adjust (control) for the effects of multiple variables simultaneously to determine the independent effect of one.

Adapted from Fletcher et al. (2014)

(randomization, matching, restriction) or during the data analysis (standardization, stratification, statistical modeling).

3.4.2 Bias

Bias (or systematic error) occurs when results differ in a systematic manner from the true values. Bias has been defined as "an error in the conception and design of a study or in the collection, analysis, interpretation, publication, or review of data, leading to results or conclusions that are systematically (as opposed to randomly) different from the truth" (Porta 2008). The possible sources of bias in epidemiology are many and varied. Over 30 specific types of bias have been identified. The principal biases are confounding (see above), selection bias, and measurement (or classification) bias.

Selection bias occurs when there is a systematic difference in characteristics between groups, other than those under study. That is, two groups that differ in a specific characteristic of interest (i.e., the degree of exposure) might also differ in other characteristics. When these other characteristics are related to the outcome, the comparison is biased (Fletcher et al. 2014). Thus, the independent effect of the characteristic of interest cannot be properly assessed, because the difference might actually be due to the differences in other characteristics. For example, not all subjects selected for a study will necessarily fully complete or return the questionnaire. This is a potential source of selection bias, because the study might only evaluate individuals that fully participated in the study. Another source of selection bias is when participants volunteer for a study, because either they feel unwell or they are particularly worried about their exposure to a risk factor. The possibility of selection bias should always be considered when defining a study sample.

A measurement bias occurs when individual measurements of a disease or exposure are inaccurate; i.e., when the instruments do not correctly measure what they are intended to measure. There are many sources of measurement bias, and the importance of the effect is variable. For instance, biochemical or physiological measurements are never completely accurate, and different laboratories often produce different results on the same specimen. When specimens from exposed and control groups are analyzed randomly by different laboratories, the chance of a systematic measurement bias is lower than when all specimens from the exposed group are analyzed in one laboratory and all those from the control group are analyzed in another laboratory.

Another type of measurement bias, the recall bias, is a particular concern in retrospective case-control studies. Indeed, the ability to recall information may be different between case and control groups. For example, diseased individuals might be more likely to recall past exposure than healthy individuals, particularly when they have a disease that is clearly suspected to be associated with exposure. Recall bias can either exaggerate or minimize the degree of association between exposure and disease, depending on whether affected subjects are, respectively, more or less likely than controls to admit or recall past exposure.

Finally, it should be kept in mind that meta-analyses are sensitive to publication bias. Publication bias is a form of selection bias, because some results have a higher probability of being published than others (Ioannidis 2008). For example, studies that show a statistically significant effect have a higher likelihood of getting published than studies that show no significant effect. Publication bias can be addressed with a funnel plot (i.e., the plot of each study effect against its respective level of precision). The funnel plot should be symmetric, and it should converge to the true effect size in the absence of publication bias.

Nearly all epidemiological studies are subject to bias of one sort or another. This does not mean that they are scientifically unacceptable, or that they should be disregarded. However, it is important to be aware of biases and to assess their potential impact when drawing conclusions from a study.

3.4.3 Statistical Power

One problem that often arises in epidemiological investigations is how to determine an adequate sample size to address a specific research question. The sample size must be large enough to provide appropriate statistical power (i.e., the ability to demonstrate a significant association, if one exists). Sample size calculations are based on a number of study design factors, such as the prevalence of the outcome, the acceptable statistical error, and a meaningful difference required for detection.

3.4.4 Representativeness

Observations about exposure and disease are based on groups of individuals sampled from the population of interest. Thus, epidemiologists must ensure that the selected individuals are representative of the population. The sample characteristics must correspond, as much as possible, to the characteristics of the original population. Ideally, each member of the population should have an equal chance of being selected in the study sample.

3.4.5 Generalizability

The findings of a study should be applicable, and thus generalizable, to individuals elsewhere. It is important to define precisely how the studied subjects were selected from what population of interest. Detailing the baseline characteristics of the studied subjects (such as age, gender, or duration and severity of symptoms, for instance) is a prerequisite in a study report. With this information, the extent of similarity between the studied population and the original population can be gauged.

4 Case Studies

This section presents a selected series of case studies that illustrate how findings from epidemiological reports can be used to assess the risk associated with the consumption of consumer products.

4.1 *Health Products*

Oral contraceptives are known to reduce the incidence rate of endometrial cancer (Collaborative Group on Epidemiological Studies on Endometrial Cancer 2015).

However, it is uncertain how long this effect lasts after use ceases or whether it is modified by other factors. The *Collaborative Group on Epidemiological Studies on Endometrial Cancer* investigated the association between the use of oral contraceptives and the subsequent risk of endometrial cancer. The Group used data from 36 epidemiological studies on endometrial cancer. In all, 27,276 women with endometrial cancer and 115,743 controls were analyzed. In both groups, the proportion of women that used oral contraceptives was comparable (35% of cases versus 39% of controls). The protective effect of oral contraceptives was confirmed. Women that had consumed oral contraceptives had a relative risk (RR) of 0.69 (95% confidence interval [CI]: 0.67–0.72) for endometrial cancer compared to women that had never consumed oral contraceptives. Moreover, this study showed a positive association between the duration of oral contraceptive consumption and protection from endometrial cancer. The longer women had used oral contraceptives, the greater the reduction in risk of endometrial cancer. Every 5 years of use was associated with a risk ratio of 0.76 (95% CI: 0.73–0.78). The study also showed that, at 75 years of age, women that had never used oral contraceptives had a cumulative incidence of endometrial cancer of 2.3 per 100 women. This cumulative incidence decreased to 1.7, 1.3, and 1.0 per 100 women among women that had consumed oral contraceptives for 5, 10, and 15 years, respectively. The authors concluded, by extrapolation, that oral contraceptive consumption could have prevented more than 400,000 endometrial cancers, in 21 countries around the world, between 1965 and 2014, and half of these cancers had occurred over the last 10 years.

4.2   Food Products

Butter is known to have a cholesterol-raising effect, and it has often been included as a negative control in dietary studies. Nonetheless, the effect of moderate butter intake was unclear, until the study by Engel and Tholstrup (2015). The authors compared the effects of moderate butter intake, moderate olive oil intake, and a habitual diet on blood lipids, high-sensitivity C-reactive protein (hsCRP), glucose, and insulin. The study was a controlled, double-blinded, randomized, 2×5-week crossover dietary intervention study with a 14-day run-in period, during which subjects consumed their habitual diets. The study included 47 healthy men and women that substituted part of their habitual diets with 4.5% of energy from butter or refined olive oil. Butter intake increased the levels of total cholesterol and LDL cholesterol more than the olive oil intake, compared to the run-in period. Butter also increased HDL cholesterol compared to the run-in period. No effects were observed on triacylglycerol, hsCRP, insulin, or glucose concentrations. The intake of saturated fatty acids was significantly higher in the butter period than in the olive oil and run-in periods. The authors concluded that individuals with hypercholesterolemia should maintain minimum consumption of butter, but individuals with normocholesterolemia may consider moderate butter intake in the diet.

Fractures during childhood are common. The risk of fracture can be influenced by both genetic and environmental factors. The identification of detrimental dietary patterns early in life may contribute to reducing the high incidence of fractures among healthy children. To test this hypothesis, Danish and Australian researchers conducted a systematic review and meta-analysis of observational studies that examined the association between dietary intake or serum nutritional concentrations and childhood fractures (Händel et al. 2015). The authors identified 18 observational studies that were primarily case-control in design. Randomized controlled trials were absent, potentially due to the unethical nature of randomly assigning children to dietary exposures that could increase later fracture rates. The authors found that the absence of breastfeeding, the non-consumption of milk, the consumption of fat cheeses and highly-caloric soft drinks may be risk factors for sustaining fractures between 2 and 13 years of age. The authors speculated that the effect of calcium intake on the risk of fracture would follow a U-shape curve, with increased risk at low and high calcium intakes.

4.3   Internet Usage

The internet has become part of our daily life. It is widely available, often unregulated, and it provides ready access to a broad range of information and communication with strangers around the world. The high intensity of internet usage has given rise to concerns about how it may negatively impact vulnerable individuals, notably those with suicidal tendencies (Mok et al. 2015). In this context, Mok et al. (2015) reviewed the literature to assess the use of the internet for suicide-related issues. Those authors reported that many individuals used the internet to search for suicide-related information and to discuss suicide-related problems with others. However, the causal link between suicide-related internet use and suicidal thoughts and behaviors remains unclear. There is a lack of studies that focus on internet users with suicidal tendencies. Only case studies are available that have examined the influence of suicide-related internet use on suicidal behaviors. No studies have specifically assessed the influence of pro-suicide or suicide prevention websites. Although online professional services might be useful for reinforcing suicide prevention, more work is required to demonstrate their efficacy. Currently, further research is needed, particularly research involving direct contact with internet users, to improve our understanding of the impact of both informal and professionally moderated suicide-related internet use.

4.4   Psychoactive Drugs

Over the past 20 years, epidemiological studies have provided ample information on how regular cannabis use in young adulthood has adverse effects on mental health and psychosocial outcomes. The Christchurch Health and Development Study (CHDS) made a particularly valuable contribution to this field (Wayne 2015). That study followed the life course, from birth, of 1000 New Zealanders, and found that 80% of those individuals had used cannabis by their mid-20s. Nearly a third had consumed cannabis regularly and for long periods. That number was sufficient to enable an assessment of potential associations between regular cannabis use and adverse psychosocial and mental health outcomes. Daily cannabis consumers consistently attained lower levels of education and employment in young adulthood, compared to non-consumers. Compared to non-consumers, daily consumers were also more likely to consume other illicit drugs, to report symptoms of psychosis or depression, and to commit suicide. Many of these risks increased with the intensity of cannabis use. Moreover, these risks persisted after statistically adjusting for plausible confounding factors. The study also showed that the adverse health effects of cannabis were mostly concentrated among daily users, which comprised nearly 20% of all individuals that had ever consumed cannabis. This risk pattern was most common among individuals that began cannabis consumption in their mid-teens and continued to consume it daily throughout young adulthood.

In the US, the Centers for Disease Control and Prevention (CDC) have published noteworthy data on polysubstance abuse trends involving alcohol, opioid pain relievers, and benzodiazepines (Ogbu et al. 2015). The CDC report was based on the 2010 data retrieved from the Drug Abuse Warning Network (DAWN). DAWN had randomly sampled 237 hospitals to collect data on alcohol use, illegal drug use, prescription and over-the-counter medication use, emergency department (ED) visits, and deaths. In 2010, they reported that 438,718 ED visits in the US had been associated with opioid abuse, and of these, 18.5% had also involved alcohol consumption. Alcohol involvement was even higher for ED visits related to benzodiazepine abuse; of the 408,021 ED visits associated with benzodiazepine, 27.2% also involved alcohol consumption. Opioid-related ED visits involving alcohol were the highest (20.6%) among individuals aged 30–44 years. Benzodiazepine-related ED visits involving alcohol were highest (31.1%) among individuals aged 45–54 years. Of the 3833 opioid-related deaths and 1512 benzodiazepine-related deaths, 22.1% and 26.1% involved alcohol, respectively. Opioid-related deaths involving alcohol were highest among those aged 40–49 years (25.2%) and 50–59 years (25.3%). Benzodiazepine-related deaths were highest among individuals aged 60 years and older (27.7%). However, the DAWN data had a number of limitations. The most important limitations were the lack of accurate drug identification, the lack of accurate quantification of alcohol consumption, and the failure to distinguish between medical and non-medical uses.

4.5 Food Supplements

An increasing number of individuals use dietary supplements to promote health. For instance, calcium-collagen chelate (CC) is a dietary supplement that can contribute to preventing osteoporosis among postmenopausal women with osteopenia (Elam et al. 2015). Elam et al. (2015) randomly assigned 39 women to receive either 5 g of CC containing 500 mg of elemental calcium + 200 IU of vitamin D or 500 mg of calcium + 200 IU vitamin D. Both groups received the dietary supplement daily over a 12-month period. The loss of whole body bone mineral density in women that received CC was substantially lower than that of the control group at 12 months. Moreover, the CC group had significantly better results in bone biomarker assessments compared to the control group. The authors concluded that the CC supplement improved bone health in terms of bone density and bone turnover, in postmenopausal women with osteopenia.

4.6 Injuries

Head injuries are relatively common among alpine skiers and snowboarders. It was hypothesized that helmets might prevent these injuries. However, helmets might also increase head injuries by reducing the field of vision, impairing hearing, and giving skiers a false sense of security. To obtain more definitive evidence of the actual effects of helmet use, investigators in Norway conducted a case-control study (Sulheim et al. 2006). Both cases and controls were selected from visitors to eight major Norwegian alpine ski resorts during the 2002 winter season. The cases comprised 578 individuals that had sustained head injuries, according to ski patrol reports. The controls comprised a sample of individuals that were waiting in line at the bottom of the main ski lift at each of the eight resorts. For both cases and controls, investigators recorded other factors that might confound the relationship between helmet use and head injury, including age, gender, nationality, type of equipment, previous ski school attendance, rented or owned equipment, and skiing ability. After taking confounders into account, helmet use was associated with a 60% reduction in the risk of head injury.

5 Perspectives

5.1 Summary of Key Messages

Currently, people are exposed daily to a multitude of potentially hazardous agents from consumer products. In the evolving policy and regulatory landscape, concerns are being raised about the health risks associated with these exposures. An essential component in evaluating health risks is to estimate the magnitude, frequency, and duration of exposure. This task is challenging, because many exposures are mixed and long-term in nature. The amount of product used (or misused) by individuals (i.e., how much, how frequently, and under what conditions) is often either unknown or varies substantially among individuals. An individual's exposure to a risk factor may vary with the setting (e.g., the workplace vs. home) and the timing (e.g., variations from season to season or from day to day).

This contribution has reviewed the main epidemiological concepts and methods employed to establish a potential causal relationship between exposure and the occurrence of disease, injury, or adverse outcomes. Selecting the appropriate study design is critical for epidemiological investigations. It should be kept in mind that each study design has different strengths and limitations. Prospective randomized trials remain the gold standard for therapeutic research. However, in the field of consumer products, they may not be practical or feasible.

Prospective, non-randomized cohort studies can provide valuable information about the causation of diseases from specific exposures. However, a large number of individuals must be followed up over long periods of time to accrue sufficient cases for statistically meaningful results. This is particularly true when investigating the causation of chronic diseases, such as cancer, coronary heart diseases, or diabetes. The difficulty is intensified, when there is a long induction period between the first exposure and the clinical manifestation of disease.

Case-control studies can also be valuable, when designed effectively. In this approach, one of the most difficult tasks is to identify an appropriate control group. The degree of exposure should be determined in the same manner for both groups. Case-control studies can estimate the relative risk of disease, but they cannot determine the absolute incidence of disease.

5.2 Recommendations for Future Epidemiological Product Assessments

It is critical for epidemiological research to assess exposure to the risks spawned by consumer products in a reliable manner. However, this is probably the greatest challenge that epidemiologists must face. Professionals from relevant disciplines (e.g., chemists, engineers, toxicologists, and even behavioral scientists and sociologists) should be involved in the design of monitoring programs for epidemiological studies to ensure they provide suitable exposure assessments. We also encourage greater collaborations between epidemiologists and regulators. Indeed, it is worthwhile to present the results of epidemiological studies in a form that can be readily utilized by regulators, and in turn by policymakers, to support the establishment of consumption policies and safeguards.

5.3 Implications for Consumer Risk Perceptions, Behaviors, and Decisions

Many people actually use, consciously or unconsciously, epidemiologic information in daily life to reduce their health risk. For instance, when we decide to quit smoking, to use the stairs instead of the elevator, or to order vegetables instead of fries, we are influenced by epidemiologists' assessment of risks to our health. Findings from epidemiological studies are directly relevant to the choices we make every day to promote our health and well-being. In other words, the knowledge of epidemiologically identified risk factors can steer our lifestyle, with health-related decisions and behaviors. Concerns about health risk reduction are currently publicized through a multiple of channels, including television, newspapers, magazines, and a myriad of web sites. The emergence of the internet has provided consumers unlimited access to product information, usage recommendations, and cautionary statements. There is little doubt that all this information increasingly drives our consumer decision-making processes.

6 Conclusion

Regulators are increasingly faced with the necessity of correctly informing and protecting consumers about the potential hazards of consumer products. Accurate characterizations of exposure to risk factors are essential for guiding policies and safety recommendations. However, it is challenging to assess the effects of exposure to a multitude of risk factors embedded in consumer products. Human behavior, social factors, and complex product characteristics play important roles in exposure. Improving the reliability of individual exposure assessments will enhance the evidence that can be generated through epidemiological studies. In turn, this evidence can provide a basis for consumers and policymakers to make better-informed consumption choices and policies.

References

Bradford Hill, A. (1965). The environment and disease: Association or causation? *Proceedings of the Royal Society of Medicine, 58*, 295–300.

Collaborative Group on Epidemiological Studies on Endometrial Cancer. (2015). Endometrial cancer and oral contraceptives: An individual participant meta-analysis of 27,276 women with endometrial cancer from 36 epidemiological studies. *The Lancet Oncology, 16*, 1061–1070.

Elam, M., Johnson, S., Hooshmand, S., et al. (2015). A Calcium-Collagen Chelate dietary supplement attenuates bone loss in postmenopausal women with osteopenia: A randomized controlled trial. *Journal of Medicinal Food, 18*, 324–331.

Engel, S., & Tholstrup, T. (2015). Butter increased total and LDL cholesterol compared with olive oil but resulted in higher HDL cholesterol compared with a habitual diet. *The American Journal of Clinical Nutrition, 102*, 309–315.

Fletcher, R. H., Fletcher, S. W., & Fletcher, G. S. (2014). *Clinical epidemiology* (5th ed.). Baltimore: Wolters Kluwer Lippincott Williams & Wilkins.

Friedman, G. D. (2004). *Primer of epidemiology* (5th ed.). New York: Appleton and Lange.

Händel, M. N., Heitmann, B. L., & Abrahamsen, B. (2015). Nutrient and food intakes in early life and risk of childhood fractures: A systematic review and meta-analysis. *The American Journal of Clinical Nutrition, 102*, 1182–1195.

Ioannidis, J. P. (2008). Interpretation of tests of heterogeneity and bias in meta-analysis. *Journal of Evaluation in Clinical Practice, 14*, 951–957.

Lenz, W. (1961) Fragen aus der Praxis: kindliche Missbildungen nach Medikament Einnahme während der Graviditat? *Dtsch MedWochenschr, 86*, 2555–2556.

McBride, W. G. (1961). Thalidomide and congenital abnormalities. *Lancet, 278* (7216), 1358.

Mok, K., Jorm, A., & Pirkis, J. (2015). Suicide-related Internet use: A review. *The Australian and New Zealand Journal of Psychiatry, 49*, 697–705.

Ogbu, U., Lotfipour, S., & Chakravarthy, B. (2015). Polysubstance abuse: Alcohol, opioids and benzodiazepines require coordinated engagement by society, patients, and physicians. *The Western Journal of Emergency Medicine, 16*, 76–79.

Porta, M. (2008). *Dictionary of epidemiology* (5th ed.). New York: Oxford University Press.

Silman, A. J. (1995). *Epidemiological studies: A practical guide*. Cambridge: Cambridge University Press.

Sulheim, S., Holme, I., Ekeland, A., et al. (2006). Helmet use and risk of injuries in alpine skiers and snowboarders. *JAMA, 295*, 919–924.

Wayne, H. (2015). Challenges in minimizing the adverse effects of cannabis use after legalization. *Social Psychiatry and Psychiatric Epidemiology, 50*, 1013–1015.

Individual and Population Risks

Viviane Kovess-Masfety

1 What Is Risk?

Risk is defined as the proportion of new cases and the number of individuals at risk of becoming a case, during a certain period of time. For example, in the case of a disease that occurs only among women like uterine cancer, men are not included in the denominator. Also, women who have had a hysterectomy are removed from the denominator. While the above definition of risk can be used for a variety of situations, most health issues require a measure of association. It is then necessary to measure disease occurrence among those exposed and those not exposed. Relative risk is a risk ratio obtained by dividing the risks of those exposed and those not exposed. When individuals are sampled with and without the disease of interest and retrospectively assessed for their exposure status, as in a case control study, the odds ratio is calculated as an estimate of the relative risk. In any case, reliable measures of both exposure and disease status are necessary, which can be difficult to achieve. Estimating risk is a complex task and has often led to controversy. While researchers are bound by high scientific standards and are faced with peer-reviews prior to publication, the media largely ignore scientific limitations of any given study and are often not aware of methodological pitfalls. Also, the epidemiological definition of risk is far from the public's understanding of risk. The general population is mostly interested in the implications of exposure for individuals and their immediate surroundings. It is therefore important that health authorities carefully address the communication of risk estimates to the general population.

V. Kovess-Masfety (✉)
Department of Epidemiology and Biostatistics for Decision Making in Public Health, Ecole des Hautes Etudes en Sante Publique (EHESP), Universite Paris V (Rene Descartes), 20 avenue George Sand, 93210 La Plaine St Denis, France
e-mail: vKovess@gmail.com

© Springer International Publishing AG 2017   105
G. Emilien et al. (eds.), *Consumer Perception of Product Risks and Benefits*,
DOI 10.1007/978-3-319-50530-5_6

2   Risk Assessment and Regulation

2.1   The Case of Formaldehyde

In the U.S. during the 1970s, urea-formaldehyde foam insulation (UFFI) was used in many homes, often in the form of pressed-wood products containing formaldehyde resins. Although the short-term health effects of formaldehyde exposure were well known, less was known about its potential long-term health effects. In 1980, laboratory studies showed that exposure to formaldehyde could cause nasal cancer in rats. This raised the question of whether formaldehyde exposure could also cause cancer in humans and suspicion of formaldehyde started to present a risk for professionals exposed to the substance. The long-term effects of formaldehyde exposure have been evaluated in epidemiologic studies attempting to uncover the patterns and causes of disease in groups of people. In cohort studies, groups of people varying in their level of exposure to formaldehyde were followed over time to determine whether or not they developed a disease. Also, case-control studies compare people who were already diagnosed with a disease (cases) with people who do not have the disease (controls), in an attempt to identify differences in exposure to formaldehyde that might explain why the cases developed the disease while the controls did not.

Studies have first focused on certain professions that are often exposed to the substance, such as anatomists and embalmers. A study, carried out among funeral industry workers who had died between 1960 and 1986, compared those who had died from hematopoietic and lymphatic cancers and brain tumors with those who died from other causes. This analysis showed that those who had performed the most embalming and those with the highest estimated formaldehyde exposure had the greatest risk of myeloid leukemia (Hauptmann et al. 2009). Another study, conducted by the US National Institute of Cancer (NCI), examined 25,619 workers in industries with the potential for occupational formaldehyde exposure and estimated each worker's exposure to the chemical (Hauptmann et al. 2003). The results showed an increased risk of death due to leukemia, particularly myeloid leukemia, among workers exposed to formaldehyde. This risk was associated with increasing peak and average levels of exposure, as well as with the duration of exposure, but was not associated with cumulative exposure. An additional 10 years of data on the same workers were used in a follow-up study (Beane Freeman et al. 2009). The analyses supported a probable link between formaldehyde exposure and cancers of the hematopoietic and lymphatic systems, particularly myeloid leukemia. As in the initial study, the risk was highest earlier in the follow-up period. Risk declined steadily over time, such that the cumulative excess risk of myeloid leukemia was no longer statistically elevated at the end of the follow-up period. The researchers noted that similar patterns of risk over time had been seen for other agents known to cause leukemia. Finally, several case-control studies, as well as analysis of the large NCI industrial cohort (Beane Freeman et al. 2009), have found an association between formaldehyde exposure and nasopharyngeal cancer, although other studies have not. However, data from the extended follow-up of the NCI cohort found that the excess of nasopharyngeal cancer observed in the earlier report persisted (Hauptmann et al. 2004).

As a consequence, in 1987 in order to protect workers, the U.S. Occupational Safety and Health Administration (OSHA) established a federal standard that reduced the amount of formaldehyde to which workers can be exposed over an 8-h workday from 3 ppm to 1 ppm. In May 1992, the standard was amended, and the formaldehyde exposure limit was further reduced to 0.75 ppm. In order to protect exposure in homes the U.S. Environmental Protection Agency (EPA) recommends the use of "exterior-grade" pressed-wood products to limit formaldehyde exposure in homes. These products emit less formaldehyde because they contain phenol resins, not urea resins. Pressed-wood products include plywood, paneling, particleboard, and fiberboard and are not the same as pressure-treated wood products, which contain chemical preservatives and are intended for outdoor use. However since this substance is also present in many products in homes, buyers are required to ask about the formaldehyde content of these products before purchasing pressed-wood products, including building materials, cabinetry, and furniture. Furthermore, the population was informed that formaldehyde levels in homes can also be reduced by ensuring adequate ventilation, moderate temperatures, and reduced humidity levels through the use of air conditioners and dehumidifiers.

Formaldehyde has been classified as a probable carcinogen by the U.S. Occupational Safety and Health Administration (CIRC) since 2004, although it is classified as a potential carcinogen in Europe. Where concentrations repeatedly reach peaks at 5000 $\mu g/m^3$ the risk of such cancers is multiplied by 2; where exposure over 8 h is over 1230 $\mu g/m^3$ there is a risk to develop such cancers; between 250 and 1230 $\mu g/m^3$ the risk could not be excluded, and below 250 $\mu g/m^3$ the risk is negligible. Germany has set up a threshold at 124 $\mu g/m^3$ in order to prevent irritant effects which precede carcinogenic effects.

Such norms have been set for industry, however health authorities have yet to define values to guide decisions, which would prevent the population from any negative health effects. The French environmental authority AFSSET has proposed 50 $\mu g/m^3$ for a 2-h exposure and 10 $\mu g/m^3$ for long-term exposure. These thresholds protect against eye and nose irritations and possibly respiratory effects, which have not been established but may not be sufficient for those who are particularly sensitive. The World Health Organization (WHO) proposed to set the level at 100 $\mu g/m^3$ for 30 min. Values have been proposed for professionals as well for different periods of exposure: 250 $\mu g/m^3$ for 8 h; 500 $\mu g/m^3$ for 15 min.

As outlined above, regulations concerning toxic substances vary across countries and contribute to tough discussions when unified market treaties are negotiated. In the E.U., in order to improve the protection of human health and the environment through the improved identification of the intrinsic properties of chemical substances, a new directive called "REACH" (EC 1907/2006) has been established in 2006 by the European Parliament and the Council. It defines four processes: the Registration, Evaluation, Authorization and Restriction of Chemicals. REACH aims to enhance innovation and competitiveness of the European chemical industry by the "No data, no market" concept. By doing so, REACH regulation places responsibility on the industry to manage the risks from chemicals and to provide safety information on substances. Manufacturers and traders are required to gather information on the properties of the chemical substances and to register the information in a centralized database with the European Chemicals Agency (ECHA). The Agency is the central point in the REACH system: it manages the databases necessary to operate the system, co-ordinates the in-depth evaluation of suspicious chemicals and is building a public database in which consumers and professionals can find hazard information. REACH also calls for the progressive substitution of the most dangerous chemicals (referred to as "substances of very high concern") when suitable alternatives have been identified. One of the main reasons for developing and adopting the REACH regulation was that a large number of substances have been manufactured and placed on the market in Europe for many years, sometimes in very large amounts, and yet there is insufficient information on the hazards that they pose to human health and the environment. The process aims to fill these information gaps in order to ensure that the industry is able to assess hazards and risks of the substances, and to identify and implement the risk management measures to protect humans and the environment (http://ec. europa.eu/environment/chemicals/reach/).

The case of formaldehyde illustrates how a complex process evolved over the years, from experimental work on animals to guidelines that will affect the entire population. Indeed, animal experiments raised suspicion that formaldehyde may be carcinogenic; then observational studies were used to compare workers exposed to the different levels of the substance, followed by prospective cohort studies of funeral industry workers to eventually set up norms for industry. Regulations were then extended to the general public though norms, which however vary across countries due to different views of health authorities regarding the acceptability of risks.

2.2   The Case of Nuclear Risks

Dangers for health have been described for different levels of nuclear radiation at short and long term, resulting in people's fear of radiation. Studies on events involving radiation and risk perception show that exposure, whether real or perceived, is conflated with nuclear weapons and the bombings of World War II (Bromet et al. 2011). According to the EPA, ionizing radiation has sufficient energy to cause damaging chemical changes in cells. Some cells may die or become abnormal, either temporarily or permanently. By damaging the genetic material (DNA) of cells, radiation can cause cancer. Fortunately, our bodies are extremely efficient at repairing cell damage. The extent of the damage to the cells depends on the type, dose and duration of the exposure, as well as on the organs exposed.

A very large dose of radiation over a short period of time can cause sickness or even death within hours or days. Such acute exposures are extremely rare and may occur during nuclear accidents in people directly involved with the nuclear site. In most cases, a large acute exposure to radiation causes both immediate radiation sickness and delayed effects such as cancer or death. Chronic continuous or intermittent exposure to radiation over a prolonged period of time can affect a larger number of individuals than those directly involved with a nuclear site. With chronic exposure, there is a delay between the start of the exposure and the observed health effects, such as cancer, benign tumors, cataracts, and potentially harmful genetic changes. Nuclear events are very frightening because radiation may not be adequately measured and people may ignore their exposure levels and the effects may only appear years later, making people feel very insecure about the future. Current science suggests that there is some cancer risk from any exposure to radiation. However, it is very hard to tell whether a particular cancer was caused by very low doses of radiation or by something else (https://www.epa.gov/radiation/radiation-health-effects).

While experts disagree over the exact definition and effects of "low dose", U.S. radiation protection standards are based on the premise that any radiation dose carries some risk, and that risk increases directly with dose. As stated at the beginning of this contribution, risk is the probability of injury, disease or death from exposure to a hazard. Radiation risk may refer to all excess cancers caused by radiation exposure (incidence) or to excess fatal cancers (mortality). A 1% excess risk of cancer incidence can equivalently be expressed as a 1 in a hundred (1/100) surplus risk or an excess risk of 0.01. For radiation, the method of estimating risk is called the "linear no-threshold model". It is based on the assumption that the risk of cancer increases linearly as radiation dose increases. This means, for example, that doubling the dose doubles the excess risk and that even a small dose could result in a small risk. That being said, it is currently impossible to know what the actual risks are at very small doses. In addition, the risk of cancer from radiation also depends on age, sex, and factors such as tobacco use. Pregnant women and children are especially sensitive to radiation exposure. The cells in children and fetuses divide rapidly, providing more opportunity for radiation to disrupt the process and to cause cell damage. EPA accounts for these differences in sensitivity due to age and sex when revising radiation protection standards.

Evaluating the effects of radiation on health is a rather complex process in case of a nuclear accident. It requires understanding the type of radiation exposure (alpha, beta, gamma, x-ray), the manner in which a person is exposed (external vs. internal), the dose and the duration. This type of information is difficult to communicate to a population when nuclear accidents occur, since individual risks may be quite different following a particular accident, depending among others on meteorological factors, physical factors (housing type and place where they resided at the time of the accident) and on personal health factors. Nuclear accidents lead to emergency decisions concerning evacuation by delimitating perimeters where people are not allowed to stay, perimeters where people could spend some time but not live, and so on. People are not infrequently traumatized, confused and misinformed regarding the complexities of specific risks. After analyzing different nuclear accidents, Bromet (2011) stressed how communication to the public has been inadequate and was responsible for considerable damages, mainly regarding the mental health of the affected populations. This assessment is based on analyzing in detail some toxic disasters, among them the three more recent nuclear disasters: Three Mile Island (TMI) (1979), Chernobyl (1986) and more recently Fukushima (2011).

Looking back at the Three Mile Island accident (March 28, 1979, 4:00 a.m.), Bromet described the communication as follows: the Governor of Pennsylvania advised that pregnant women and preschool children evacuate the 5-mile area near TMI (later extended to 20 miles), and 144,000 people (just under half of population) left the area.

Starting on March 28, TMI, the Governor's office, NRC, and scientists of various stripes made contradictory statements reported in the media. On March 30, the NY Times title "The Credibility Meltdown". "Credibility was not enhanced by public statements... Was it a little leak, a bigger leak—or a general emergency? The reactor's operators said one thing, state officials another, Federal officials yet another, not to mention the contributions of equipment manufacturers and politicians. Who is to be believed? The profusion of explanations and of contradictory statements has meant troubling confusion."

As a consequence, fears contradicted facts. For example, the anti-nuclear community predicted that over 300 cancers would occur, a PhD physicist from the University of Pittsburg showed data indicating there was an increase in stillbirths downwind of TMI. Rumors spread about three-legged cows, kittens born without eyes, and other such phenomena.

The President's Commission Report in December 1979 stated that the maximum individual dose estimate was equal or below 1 millisievert, leading to 1–2 excess cancers possible among the plant workers and that the biggest impact was on mental health mainly due to misinformation.

Based on the Presidential Commission report Bromet's research team focused on the long-term psychological aftermath among three groups:

- Mothers of young children living in the 10 miles radius of TMI
- TMI workers
- Psychiatric outpatients in the public mental health system

Their main findings regarding the Three Mile Island disaster were that 25% of mothers versus 14% of controls had clinical depression or generalized anxiety in the year following the incident (Bromet 1982). Symptoms of distress remained high over 10 years. Ten years later, mothers still continued to worry about the health impact of the incident: 42% believed their health was affected, another 68% were concerned about their children's health. Risk perceptions were significantly correlated with distress and poor self-rated health. Other studies have confirmed the long-term psychological impacts (Dew and Bromet 1993).

By comparing the three nuclear disasters, Bromet described common patterns: deeply rooted fear of radiation and lack of understanding, on one hand radiation safety experts using jargon to communicate the "facts" and on the other anti-nuclear proponents airing graphic, alarmist "facts". The case of nuclear disasters demonstrates the importance of communication and information: results have to be presented in person clearly and consistently to local stakeholders in open forums.

Scientists have to contribute to better communicating science, which in the end might lower the level of distrust towards them, and ultimately can help people knowing how to differentiate good from bad information and what questions they should be asking. The media play a key role and bear the responsibility of translating scientific information into accessible messages to the public while avoiding sensationalism.

3 Individual Versus Collective Risk

3.1 Sick Individuals and Sick Populations

A seminal paper by Rose (2001) focused attention on the importance of reasoning at the level of the population instead of the individual to investigate causality.

He pointed out that clinicians typically rely on case control or cohort studies to investigate causality. In this "individual centered approach" a relative risk is estimated dividing the risk of exposed by the risk of non exposed; the higher the ratio the higher the risk for a particular disease when exposed.

The author argues that this reasoning is neither adequate for etiological research nor for a public health approach. Indeed, to be able to identify a risk factor, this risk factor needs to be highly prevalent in one group of people and such methods are based on the assumption of heterogeneity of the distribution of the risk factor in the population. Rose gave the example of tobacco smoking and lung cancer: if everybody smoked 20 cigarettes a day the exposure would be constant and the distribution of cases would be determined by individual factors. One could then conclude that lung cancer has a genetic origin, which may not be totally wrong, except that this genetic susceptibility may not be expressed without exposure to tobacco. As a consequence, the more widespread the cause of a disease is, the less it will explain the distribution of cases. Consequently, the probability of finding a cause decreases when the cause is universally present which is why Rose claimed that control group or cohort studies are not pertinent in causal research.

To illustrate the concept, Rose compared the distribution of systolic blood pressure in two populations; London civil servants and Kenyan nomads. The two curves have a normal distribution with a peak and a bell shape. However, the London curve had its peak at 140 mm/Hg while the Kenyan curve at around 120 mmHg. In each population, some people have above average blood pressure. Hence, risk factors for high blood pressure exists within both populations, where genetic variation and to a lesser extent environmental and behavioral differences explain the variation. However, the most public health pertinent question which is why Kenyan nomads have lower blood pressure than London civil servants would be missed. What accounts for that most important difference is not individual susceptibilities within both populations but the shift of the population distribution towards higher values in the London population.

Rose provided another example: Serum cholesterol in Finland is high and coronary heart disease is frequent, while in Japan cholesterol levels are much lower and coronary heart disease is relatively rare. Again in each country there are individual differences produced by genetic susceptibility and other causes, but these do not explain the large differences between the two countries. Differences between the two populations may regard diet, which is very different between the two countries. However, since within countries people have a relatively similar diet, this factor may not be found, other than when comparing populations where diet is different. Only by comparing populations where diets are very different, becomes possible to show strong associations between population mean values for saturated fat intake versus serum cholesterol levels and coronary health disease rates, for sodium intake and blood pressure or for energy intake and overweight.

Thus, what causes a case is not necessary the same factor that determines the incidence of the disease. The consequences on risk factor research are very important since any factor that is uniformly distributed in a population will escape identification, and research will focus on individual susceptibilities only and miss the point. In some cases exposure varies within the population and can then be identified, such as for tobacco and lung cancer. Because not everybody smokes in a population, researchers could identify smoking as the risk factor. However, this situation is not too frequent. Genetic factors are widely distributed within populations and do not differ so much between populations, while for environmental factors the reverse is the case. Indeed immigrants who could be genetically very different acquire the disease rates of the country they immigrated to, because after some time they are exposed to the same environmental factors than the non-immigrant population.

Rose points out that the causes of many non-infectious diseases remain unknown. Some personal characteristics of individuals who are at greater risk are known, but what influences incidence rates is not known. In addition, non-infectious disease rates fluctuate over time: duodenal ulcer in Britain was quite frequent during the first half of the twentieth century then rose steadily to then decrease to near disappearance nowadays, without any documented determinants for these changes. Since many diseases fluctuate between populations and over time, studying incidence changes may be more a promising research focus.

These considerations have a tremendous impact on prevention strategies. "High risk" strategies attempt to identify a subpopulation at risk using screening techniques and then proceed to offer risk reduction interventions such as for example treating hypertension. Rose describes the advantages of this strategy: to be appropriate for the individual, to motivate the subject as well as the physician, to be a cost-effective use of resources, and to have a favorable risk/benefit ratio. On the other hand, there are disadvantages such as the difficulties and costs of screening and the fact that the effect is only palliative and temporary, as the cause is not eradicated, implying that the strategy needs to be maintained with no end in sight. Even if we know certain risk factors, the ability to predict individual future disease cases is very weak. People "at risk" can remain well and people not "at risk" may develop the disease, since relative risk does not determine outcome. Rose reports being impressed with the ability of the Framingham study to distinguish high and low risk groups at baseline (Kannel et al. 1971). However, at follow-up there were no significant differences in cholesterol levels among those who developed coronary disease and those who did not. Indeed, there may be very few individuals at high risk while the great majority is at low risk, potentially leading to a greater number of cases in the latter group. Lastly, the "high risk" strategy may be inappropriate when dealing with behavioral factors like eating, smoking, exercise and other life style characteristics which are constrained by social norms. It is very difficult to provide effective health education based on individual needs because people find it hard to step out of line with their peers.

"Population" strategies attempt to identify and manage the determinants of incidence and can be preferable. These strategies attempt to control the determinants of incidence to lower the mean risk levels in order to shift the whole distribution of exposure in a favorable direction. The advantages include the following: removing the underlying cause; with a relatively small shift in distribution of risk a large number of cases are avoided and it is more effective to manage behavioral factors with population strategies (for example banning smoking in public places). Such enthusiasm is moderated by the disadvantages of the approach: the individual benefit is small, since most people would have been well anyway, but are required to change their habits. The author calls this phenomenon the "prevention paradox": a preventive measure which brings much benefit at the population level might offer very little to the individual. If individual benefits have to be visible and immediate, the populations approach can fail. Immunization does not show any individual positive measurable effect that people can directly feel or be proud of, while quitting smoking can be viewed as an accomplishment. Consequently the population approach leads to poor motivation of individuals, including physicians, who may play an important role in the process. Some doctors were enthusiastic about anti-smoking education, but achieving 5–10% cessation rates is too low to be rewarding; in addition, they likely lack the skills to provide for effective behavioral counseling. The medical community is more familiar with an individual patient-oriented approach and not very sensitive to population issues.

Rose concludes that both approaches will continue to co-exist and emphasizes that the priority should be to identify and manage the causes of incidence. Another conclusion that can be drawn is that individual and population risks are two rather different concepts.

3.2   Vaccinations and Epidemics

Balancing the risks and benefits of vaccination is an emblematic example to illustrate the aspects of individual versus collective risks. In this case the epidemiologic approach shows that the key variable for understanding the relationship between individual risk and societal risk is the size of the population. A risk may be very small at the individual level, but be a strong collective risk if millions of people are exposed.

For example, models have been proposed on risks and benefits of small pox vaccination (Meltzer 2003), suggesting that most individuals in the general population would not accept pre-exposure smallpox vaccination and support the U.S. recommendation to stop routine childhood immunization against smallpox. The study warns that a factor such as new information (e.g., reported cases of vaccine-related adverse events) could alter the perception and valuation of risks and that public health officials must always be prepared to assess how new information and communication alter the risks involved.

For other more common and less severe infectious diseases, the vaccine is both an individual and collective protection: by reducing the number of infected people, the risk of contagion for each individual is reduced. The heart of the debate is then: to protect the group, is it acceptable that some pay the price and experience significant side effects? The doctor's role is to vaccinate an individual after weighting the potential benefits and risks. The public health officer argues at the population level, focusing on the collective level, the benefits outweighing the risks. But the issue is complex; there is no universal standard in place, which explains why each country according to its culture, its resources, its beliefs and its values has a vaccination policy of its own.

A recent survey titled the "Vaccine confidence Project" (www. vaccineconfidence.org) revealed the levels of confidence in the safety of vaccinations in 67 countries. France is the most distrustful country of the survey: 41% of French people think that vaccines are not safe as compared to 13.5% in the U.S.A., 15.8% in China, 8.7% in the U.K., 4.2 in Portugal, 5.4% in Australia. However, in some countries such as Russia (27.5%), Greece (25.4%), Japan (25.1%) or Iran (22.6%), the distrust is quite high and in some others like Bangladesh (0.2%) it is quasi absent.

In countries like Bangladesh people might have been able to see how widespread vaccinations have improved children health. In France, the high level of distrust has been attributed to a mixture of pharmaceutical industry scandals such as excessive profits from vaccines and conflicts of interest within health authorities, a mandatory vaccination system, plus the quasi military organization of H1N1 vaccination, which excluded general practitioners who are the closest to the population, the hepatitis B vaccination fiasco, and many mistakes in the communication to the public added to a distrust towards the general practitioners themselves (Verger et al. 2015). In addition, the media have been accused of stressing the negative effects without quoting the positive effects.

However, France is not the only country where defiance is important, especially in Europe; measles is resurging as endemic in the U.K. due to the lack of vaccination. In Europe, where the distrust is high, people forget that most severe diseases such as poliomyelitis or smallpox have been eradicated thanks to vaccination, and that these could reappear if vaccination is no longer generally accepted.

3.3 Societal Aspects

Vaccination is not solely a medical issue. It questions the way we organize our society.

In 1423, the Venetians introduced quarantines to prevent the risk of plague they rightly suspected arriving with ships from the Far East. The use of quarantines was a breakthrough for two reasons. First, quarantines are based on collective protection, rather than on an individual perspective of illness. Second, religious faith was no longer the only approach to protection, but an organized community effort was put in place to ensure safety, with it the idea of a "public health force", since it required to set up a police to ensure the effectiveness of the decisions.

There are questions about the legal obligation to vaccinate, as it is the case in France, where distrust is high. Other societal questions are relevant such as the religious taboos around vaccination. In the above confidence survey, Asians were most likely to consider that religion does not allow vaccination (Vietnam, Thailand and Mongolia, 26–46%) while this was not the case in Saudi Arabia (2%) and Brazil (3%). However 15% of the people around the world estimated that their religion did not allow them to be vaccinated. Women were more prone than men to find vaccination important, as were those over 65 years versus young people.

With the fear of biological terrorism and the possible resurgence of the most severe diseases the vaccination level of a population could become a serious issue, and some governments or health authorities are currently taking steps to try to reverse the tendency and to increase the level of confidence in vaccination.

Infectious diseases could also introduce tensions when, on behalf of the group's protection, personal freedom is restricted. This was the case during the Ebola threat to the United States in New York, where Ebola infected a physician who worked in Liberia before returning to the US in October 2014.

This led several governors to decide that health professionals returning from epidemic countries should be routinely quarantined upon their return for 3 weeks. An article in the New England Journal of Medicine (Drazen et al. 2014) refuted the idea, classifying it in the "false good idea" category. Regarding emotions management, often mobilized by politicians, the authors emphasize a management based on biological and epidemiological evidence.

Indeed scientists have demonstrated that to catch the virus, mucous or skin with an open wound have to be in contact with a high concentration of virus. Such concentration is only present in symptomatic patients (fever, vomiting, diarrhea, deteriorated general health state) in their stools, their sweat, their tears, and their blood. When symptoms progress and viral load increases towards the end of their life, more patients become hyper-contagious. This was the case for the only nurses who had been contaminated by a patient in Dallas, because she took care of him at the end of his life; in contrast, for the persons who shared housing with the patient when he was not feverish, risks were small and they were not contaminated.

Unfortunately, there are no absolute truths: in most cases the carriers of the virus are not infectious when they have no fever, but can we certify that this is true for

100% of cases? No; so we must acknowledge some uncertainty and therefore authorities may be right to be cautious. In reality, judgment must result from a systemic reasoning, analyzing all the risks and benefits of a decision.

On one hand, the fight against epidemics should be guided by science and not purely by political considerations. On the other hand, the history of epidemics teaches that it is by acting on their epicenter that best limits their spread. If voluntary caregivers are discouraged from travelling to epidemic areas, this may create the conditions for a pandemic. This illustrates how much risks are not risks "per se" but are embedded into societal values and intertwined into rather complex interactions (Zylberman and Flahault 2009). It is another example of how different risks can be at the level of the individuals versus that of populations.

4 Risk Uncertainty

In some cases there are no comprehensive data to evaluate a risk: either data are completely lacking, contradictory, not interpretable, or believed to be produced by parties with conflicts of interest. Two attitudes can be contrasted: One considers that it is necessary to reduce uncertainty before any action. The other advocates acting with caution before all the evidence is gathered. A recent article (Peretti-Watel et al. 2013) illustrates this question, using French data on the perception of health risks linked to electromagnetic waves, including electricity, mobile phone waves, Wi-Fi and microwave ovens. These non-ionizing waves share common characteristics: they are everywhere in our environment, they are invisible, undetectable without a measuring device, but are related to visible emitters such as high voltage or relay antennas.

The effects of waves differ depending on the type of field (electric or magnetic) and frequency. Most studies focused on waves with a frequency over 400 MHz, which corresponds to mobile phones. A lot of studies did not apply robust methodological procedures to measure dosage or its biological effects. The studies that did failed to provide evidence of any genotoxic or carcinogenic effect, effects on the immune system, on the nervous system or on the reproductive system (https://interphone.iarc.fr/UICC).

In addition, an important international study has been conducted in 13 countries, Australia, Canada, Denmark, Finland, France, Germany, Israel, Italy, Japan, New Zealand, Norway, Sweden, and the UK, using a common core protocol. "Interphone" was the largest case–control study to date investigating risks related to mobile phone use and to other potential risk factors for the tumors of interest and included 2765 glioma, 2425 meningioma, 1121 acoustic neuroma, 109 malignant parotid gland tumor cases and 7658 controls. In addition to a detailed history of mobile phone usage, information was collected on a number of known and potential risk factors for the tumors of interest. The study concluded that overall, there was no increase in risk of glioma or meningioma observed with use of mobile phones. There was no increase in risk of acoustic neuroma with regular use of a mobile phone or for users who began regular use 10 years or more before the reference date. Elevated odds ratios observed at the highest level of cumulative call time could be due to chance, reporting bias or a causal effect. As acoustic neuroma is usually a slowly growing tumor, the interval between the introduction of mobile phones and the occurrence of the tumor might have been too short to observe an effect, if there is one (INTERPHONE 2010; Swerdlow et al. 2011).

The French government agency AFSSET published a report to state that no risks have been demonstrated. Despite this publication, the controversy continued and groups of people continue to oppose antennas and base stations, claiming that waves are a risk for health.

Peretti-Watel et al. (2013) investigated lay risk perceptions related to exposure to electromagnetic fields (from an electric power-line, a TV, a cellular phone or micro-wave oven) in France. Answers to an opened-ended questions suggested that many people worry about such exposures: they believe that it may interfere with natural electricity circulating in the human body, disturb the nervous system and cause cancer. Statistical analyses showed that risk perception related to these four devices were strongly correlated with one another and shared common predictors. The results suggest that these risk perceptions are built within the same perceptive frame. The authors advise not to consider them as "false beliefs" as they are based on consistent conceptions of the body, health and disease, they are fueled by the contemporary leveling of knowledge, and they reflect the difficulties experienced by many people living in a changing world. It also seems that the understanding of the way electromagnetic waves can affect health is not a matter of knowledge and education, since in this survey the most educated were the ones who feared the power lines the most. Indeed the "educational" approach is unlikely to convince, because two factors play a role in structuring opinions and behavior firstly, emotions and representations and secondly, confidence that health is not sacrificed over economic interests.

Again we see how much trust in government and health authorities is essential in all these individual versus collective tensions. Society needs projects for its economic development: people need electricity, internet, mobile phones, antennas and relays. Independent research is required to establish risks, but independence is difficult to establish and many "independent" committees have been accused of having shared interest with one of the stakeholders. The education system is a key element as well: when a survey shows that the most educated are those who are the most fearful, it is quite surprising to see how much ignorance concerning health matters and scientific reasoning might be abundant in very highly educated people, including those who could have responsibilities related to health matters. A basic health education could render citizens more able to make judgments about their risks and the decisions to be made for staying healthy.

5   Amount of Risk

The International agency for research on cancer IARC (www.iarc.fr), the WHO agency responsible for assessing the evidence for the carcinogenicity of environmental or dietary exposures, has classified red meat as "probably carcinogenic to humans" (group 2A of the scale of evidence) and processed meat after salting, fermentation or maturation as "somewhat carcinogenic to humans" (group 1). Although the agricultural sector has declared that they do not believe in the data, supporting a causal relationship between the consumption of any red meat and any cancer, the WHO's decision resulted from a long process of expertise and multidisciplinary scientific data on some 800 published studies. Indeed, the IARC scale is not a risk scale, but a scale classifying the level of evidence available for the existence of a danger. "Probably carcinogenic" means that there are strong arguments in favor of a role of consumption of red meat in the occurrence of cancer in humans, but that we cannot conclude with certainty on the causal link. IARC assesses the dangers, but not the risk, although in this case, the agency provides guidance on the relationship between the level of consumption and cancer risk.

Danger, or hazard, is the ability of a substance to cause an adverse effect. It is a potentiality. This says nothing about the degree of realization of this potential. Red meat is probably dangerous, however it does not mean that all those who eat it will develop cancer (we are talking about digestive and prostate cancers). The frequency at which a danger is realized is the risk. For processed meat, the estimate is an increase in the excess relative risk of cancer of about 0.2 per 50 g serving. That is, by consuming 100 g, the baseline absolute risk multiplies by 1.4, etc. To consume 250 g per day doubles the risk of cancer, which still can be described as moderate. Indeed, another fundamental element is that cancer is a multifactorial disease. Cancer develops in the interplay of genetic, biological, behavioral and environmental factors. It is difficult to distinguish with the current knowledge the contribution of each of these factors.

In terms of safety, one must not only consider the danger of exposure, but also think in terms of the level of risk. Clearly, a danger scale is not a risk scale. It is often asked why there isn't a universal risk scale? The answer is that such a scale is impossible to define because the level of risk actually depends on several parameters such as the amount ingested (dose), on co-exposures, personal characteristics, age, gender, etc. Another important factor, but not quantified for all cancers, is the family history of cancer. In sum, cancer risk is a function of each of the above factors, exposure to carcinogens and genetic heritage.

In addition, the amount of meat eaten per day matters; IARC experts concluded that each daily serving of 50 g of processed meat increases the risk of gastrointestinal cancer, including colon and rectal cancer, by about 20 %. Thus, 150 g of cold cuts consumed daily result in an increased risk of 60%. This means that instead of an annual colorectal cancer risk of 1 in 10,000, a person consuming that quantity increases his or her risk to reach 1.6 per 10,000. In epidemiology, such an increase of a low baseline risk can be described as small. Moreover, two facts must be kept in mind: the average lifetime risk of developing any cancer is about 33%, while eating meat has nutritional benefits. No rational decision to risk prevention can be taken without carefully considering the magnitude of the risk.

6   The Precautionary Principle

Uncertainty about risks generally leads to a preventive approach to avoid known and possible risks. Indeed, many new technologies and products may convey risks that have not yet been assessed because we are lacking knowledge on their short and long-term effects, or the instruments or tests to measure their effects are non-existent. Alternatively, some of these risks have been measured, but the results are not coherent, so they may have an effect but the effect may not be solidly grounded. What to do? The tolerance to risk is very low, but "zero risk" does not exist, since any action or product induces a risk. However, when there is some information about a risk, even in the absence of proof, a new attitude has become prevalent: "The precautionary principle".

In the EU, the precautionary principle has been detailed since 2000 in the Treaty on the Functioning of the European Union (EU). The precautionary principle enables rapid response in the face of a possible danger to human, animal or plant health, or to protect the environment. In particular, where scientific data do not permit a complete evaluation of the risk, recourse to this principle may, for example, be used to stop distribution or to order withdrawal from the market of products likely to be hazardous. Since the definition of the principle may have a positive impact at international levels it has been recognized by various international agreements, notably in the Sanitary and Phytosanitary Agreement (SPS) concluded in the framework of the World Trade Organization (WTO).

The precautionary principle may only be invoked upon consideration of three preliminary aspects: identification of potentially adverse effects, evaluation of the scientific data available and the extent of scientific uncertainty. In most cases, European consumers and the associations which represent them, must demonstrate the danger associated with a procedure or a product placed on the market, except for medication, pesticides and food additives. However, in the case of an action being taken under the precautionary principle, the producer, manufacturer or importer may be required to prove the absence of danger. This possibility is examined on a case-by-case basis. It cannot be extended generally to all products placed on the market (http://eur-lex.europa.eu).

There are views suggesting that precautionary principle may do more harm than good. The principle induces concerns regarding the dangers of certain human exposures to agents in the environment, which requires that these exposures are considered dangerous until proven otherwise. The principle can induce in the public a feeling of insecurity fueled by the slightest warning. For others, the principle is fundamentally reassuring. It provides assurance that uncertainty must benefit primarily the protection of the health of the population and create trust.

To evaluate the effects, a large international study was conducted in students of social sciences and humanities (Wiedemann et al. 2013), about 400 in each country in Australia, Brazil, Germany, India, Japan, the Netherlands, South Africa, the United Kingdom, and the United States. The study focused on possible risks of radio frequency mobile phones and base stations. Its main objective was to measure the impact on risk perception following information about the possible risks of electromagnetic waves. The research questions were:

Does informing about precautionary measures affect risk perception differently across various countries? Does it make a difference whether the precautionary measures refer to cell phones or to base stations? Does precautionary information framed in terms of safety have a different effect on risk perception compared to information framed in terms of risk?

The question wording to evaluate the risk perception was:" All in all, how threatened do you feel by electromagnetic radiation emissions from <base stations/cell phones>? (1 = I don't feel threatened at all; 7 = I feel very threatened)".

The mean risk perception level for both base stations and cell phones varied across countries, with the Netherlands having the lowest ratings and India the highest. Except for India and Japan, perceived risk for base stations was higher than for cell phones. Compared with cell phones as target of precautionary measures, where the effect was quite weak, it seems that informing about precaution has a stronger effect when targeting base stations, albeit in the direction of increasing the perceived risk. The data suggest that informing people about precautionary measures aiming at base stations does not decrease concern. Rather, results point in the opposite direction.

The only variable that in all countries, except for Japan, consistently showed significant correlations with perceived risk was perceived personal benefit. The higher the perceived personal benefit of cell phones, the lower the perceived risk. Interestingly, the amount of daily use of cell phones was not associated with perceived risk. Gender also showed no statistically significant correlation with perceived risk, except for Japan, where women tended to have higher perceived risks than men. Attitudes towards science and technology were also not consistently related to perceived risks of cell phones, but when they were, a more favorable attitude towards science and technology was associated with lower perceived risk.

With regard to the association of perceived risks of base stations, the direction of the associations was the same as for cell phone risk perceptions. Framing the information on precautionary measure as "protecting public health" versus "avoiding health risks" did not result in different risk perceptions. The authors concluded that "Public health authorities should not expect that precautionary measures are sufficient in and of themselves to increase confidence in risk management and thus reduce the perception of risk. If the intention is to reassure the public, information about precautionary measures is likely to lead to failure". This study is obviously not sufficient to evaluate the effects or applying the precautionary principle to perceived risks, but it underlines that a measure which is supposed to be positive and aimed at reassuring people can have opposite effects. However, even though the precautionary principle is apparently not reassuring, it has become highly present in people's life. Ironically, for a lot of risks that are well documented, governments have failed to agree and take the necessary decisions because of a lot of conflicting interests, including on issues regarding global warming or armed conflicts, while for potential risks that may have very small effects, a lot of debate has occurred and decisions to suspend projects have been made.

7 Mental Disorders

Stress is an inherent part of the life; reactions to stress have been first described by H. Selye (Rosch 2016) who stated that the organism is in equilibrium and that any change will stimulate the system to adapt; he proposed to refer to these changes as "stressors" and the mechanisms to adapt as "stress". Since stressors are inevitable, humans are programmed to face them to survive, but if the stressors are too important or too frequent, the adaptation can fail and can create detrimental effects on health. However, people have different levels of resistance and their ability to face high stressor levels is called resilience, as opposed to vulnerability.

Selye studied mainly the physical reactions associated with stress. Brown and Harris opened (Brown 1978) the field of psychosocial stressors and depression, studying large cohorts of vulnerable women in non-affluent areas in suburban London. They described how vulnerability factors starting from childhood, such as the loss of one's mother before the age of 11 years, interact with protective factors such as having a job or a satisfactory relationship with a partner, when a negative event occurs, precipitating or not the person into clinical depression. Moreover, the authors described how specific events such as humiliation or entrapment could be more precipitating to depression than others. They also documented how a "fresh start", that is a positive event, could help a person recover.

All of this work is at the interface of personal versus population risks. Indeed, it demonstrates that a population risk such as poverty, which leads to poor housing for example, is a risk factor for depression in general, but that for the individual this factor becomes a risk only if the person has certain characteristics that renders her vulnerable. For the general population, poverty increases the prevalence of depression, but only because certain vulnerable individuals could not cope with the event because of their own vulnerability, and become depressed.

Another illustration of this interaction comes from work on Post-Traumatic Stress Disorder (PTSD). North et al. (2012) have studied 15 disasters over 25 years and followed over 3500 survivors, directly exposed to a disaster. They classified disasters into Natural disasters: floods, tornado, earthquake and hurricane; Technological accidents: dioxin contamination, plane crash and firestorm; Intentional acts/terrorism: 4 mass murders; OKC bombing; bombing of US Embassy in Nairobi, Kenya; 9/11 attacks on NYC; bioterrorism (anthrax) on Capitol Hill.

The authors found that after disasters many persons experience symptoms, but few meet diagnostic criteria and that most symptoms disappear with time. Moreover, following the Oklahoma City bombing, those who met full diagnostic criteria had pre-trauma disorders including PTSD, major depressive episode, panic disorder and generalized anxiety disorder. Curiously, no new incident cases were found for alcohol and drug use disorders, although an increase of alcohol consumption has been documented. Similar results have been reported by Galea regarding depressive symptoms (Contractor et al. 2015) in soldiers confronted with traumatic events in Afghanistan: half of the soldiers did not have any symptoms, some had symptoms which faded over time, and those who either had an increase of symptoms or a chronic level of symptoms have had experienced childhood adversity and a high number of lifetime traumatic events prior to the exposure.

These studies converge to demonstrate the interaction of individual risk factors such as genetics, childhood and adult traumas. Once confronted with a stressor, the combination of these factors determine whether that stressor develops into a disease in a certain individual, while at the population level these traumas per se increase the prevalence of disorders.

This has consequences in terms of prevention; it may be more efficient to screen for those at high risk and to offer an intervention to those who had one rather than offering interventions to all individuals confronted to a traumatic event. Indeed, this may become an approach recommended in case of a disaster or tragic event. Instead of trying to propose help to everybody, it can be preferable, based on rapidly screening those at risk, concentrate efforts on those at individual risk. On the other hand, these high-risk strategies do not exclude population-based interventions aimed at reinforcing trust, as they may affect population-level well-being and thus reduce the incidence of mental disorders.

8 Conclusions

Evaluating risks is a fairly difficult task. Societies are becoming highly sensitive to risks and the development of technologies increases both risks and the ability to detect them. Sophisticated statistical methods, together with the capacity to follow large samples of the population, allow the calculation of attributable risks, but they are not easily transformed into individual risks. Indeed, evaluating individual risks is currently a quasi-impossible task as a number of factors are involved, including personal history and background, health practices and access to care, which interact with collective, mostly environmental risks.

Notwithstanding these difficulties, the psychological aspects of risks are constantly underestimated, as are mental health problems in general. Whatever the circumstances, the most psychologically fragile will always be those most at risk, and a risk management policy should take care of this specific dimension. In cases of disasters or highly traumatic events, general psychosocial interventions will benefit most people, but only some of them should be offered specialized care, possibly after effective screening. Finally, gap between scientific knowledge and policy has to be bridged since a lot of decisions are made under political pressures, often ill-informed about major scientific facts. Communication skills and consideration of ethical principles have to be improved at each level to avoid generating unnecessary panic. Ideally, all parties should join forces involving representatives of those impacted to elaborate actions and messages that reflect the best available knowledge, in a language that is accessible to each citizen.

References

Beane Freeman, L. E., Blair, A., Lubin, J. H., Stewart, P. A., Hayes, R. B., Hoover, R. N., et al. (2009). Mortality from lymphohematopoietic malignancies among workers in formaldehyde industries: The National Cancer Institute Cohort. *Journal of the National Cancer Institute, 101* (10), 751–761. doi:10.1093/jnci/djp096.

Bromet, E. (2011). Lessons learned from radiation disasters. *World Psychiatry, 10*(2), 83–84.

Bromet, E. J., et al. (1982). Mental health of residents near the Three Mile Island reactor: A comparative study of selected groups. *Journal of Preventive Psychiatry, 1*(3), 225–276.

Bromet, E. J., Havenaar, J. M., & Guey, L. T. (2011). A 25 year retrospective review of the psychological consequences of the chernobyl accident. *Clinical Oncology, 23*(4), 297–305. doi:10.1016/j.clon.2011.01.501.

Brown, G. H. T. (1978). *Social origins of depression*. London: Tavistock.

Contractor, A. A., Elhai, J. D., Fine, T. H., Tamburrino, M. B., Cohen, G., Shirley, E., et al. (2015). Latent profile analyses of posttraumatic stress disorder, depression and generalized anxiety disorder symptoms in trauma-exposed soldiers. *Journal of Psychiatric Research, 68*, 19–26. doi:10.1016/j.jpsychires.2015.05.014.

Dew, M. A., & Bromet, E. J. (1993). Predictors of temporal patterns of psychiatric distress during 10 years following the nuclear accident at Three Mile Island. *Social Psychiatry and Psychiatric Epidemiology, 28*(2), 49–55. doi:10.1007/bf00802091.

Drazen, J. M., Kanapathipillai, R., Campion, E. W., Rubin, E. J., Hammer, S. M., Morrissey, S., et al. (2014). Ebola and Quarantine. *New England Journal of Medicine, 371*(21), 2029–2030. doi:10.1056/NEJMe1413139.

Hauptmann, M., Lubin, J. H., Stewart, P. A., Hayes, R. B., & Blair, A. (2003). Mortality from lymphohematopoietic malignancies among workers in formaldehyde industries. *Journal of the National Cancer Institute, 95*(21), 1615–1623.

Hauptmann, M., Lubin, J. H., Stewart, P. A., Hayes, R. B., & Blair, A. (2004). Mortality from solid cancers among workers in formaldehyde industries. *American Journal of Epidemiology, 159* (12), 1117–1130. doi:10.1093/aje/kwh174.

Hauptmann, M., Stewart, P. A., Lubin, J. H., Beane Freeman, L. E., Hornung, R. W., Herrick, R. F., et al. (2009). Mortality from lymphohematopoietic malignancies and brain cancer among embalmers exposed to formaldehyde. *Journal of the National Cancer Institute, 101*(24), 1696–1708. doi:10.1093/jnci/djp416.

INTERPHONE. (2010). Brain tumour risk in relation to mobile telephone use: results of the INTERPHONE international case-control study. *International Journal of Epidemiology, 39*(3), 675–694. doi:10.1093/ije/dyq079.

Kannel, W. B., Garcia, M. J., McNamara, P. M., & Pearson, G. (1971). Serum lipid precursors of coronary heart disease. *Human Pathology, 2*(1), 129–151.

Meltzer, M. I. (2003). Risks and benefits of preexposure and postexposure smallpox vaccination. *Emerging Infectious Diseases, 9*(11), 1363–1370. doi:10.3201/eid0911.030369.

North, C. S., Oliver, J., & Pandya, A. (2012). Examining a comprehensive model of disaster-related posttraumatic stress disorder in systematically studied survivors of 10 disasters. *American Journal of Public Health, 102*(10), e40–e48. doi:10.2105/AJPH.2012.300689.

Peretti-Watel, P., Vergélys, C., & Hammer, B. (2013). Ces ondes qui nous menacent. Perceptions profanes des risques associés à quatre dispositifs émettant des ondes électromagnétiques. *Natures Sciences Sociétés, 21*(3), 282–292. doi:10.1051/nss/2013110.

Rosch, P. J. (2016). http://www.stress.org/about/hans-selye-birth-of-stress. Accessed 09/13/2016.

Rose, G. (2001). Sick individuals and sick populations. *International Journal of Epidemiology, 30* (3), 427–432. doi:10.1093/ije/30.3.427.

Swerdlow, A.J., Feychting, M., Green, A.C., Leeka Kheifets, L.K., & Savitz, D.A. (2011). Mobile phones, brain tumors, and the interphone study: where are we now? *Environmental Health Perspectives, 119*(11), 1534–1538.

Verger, P., Fressard, L., Collange, F., Gautier, A., Jestin, C., Launay, O., et al. (2015). Vaccine hesitancy among general practitioners and its determinants during controversies: A national cross-sectional survey in France. *eBioMedicine, 2*(8), 891–897. doi:10.1016/j.ebiom.2015.06. 018.

Wiedemann, P. M., Schuetz, H., Boerner, F., Clauberg, M., Croft, R., Shukla, R., et al. (2013). When precaution creates misunderstandings: The unintended effects of precautionary information on perceived risks, the EMF case. *Risk Analysis, 33*(10), 1788–1801. doi:10.1111/risa. 12034.

Zylberman, P., & Flahault, A. (2009). *Des épidémies et des hommes.* France: Coédition Editions de La Martinière/Cité des Sciences et de l'Industrie.

Risk Communication

Hye Kyung Kim

1 Introduction

Product labeling, patient information leaflets inserted in product packaging, product warning labels—all of these represent ways in which consumers commonly encounter product-related risk information in their daily lives. Today, it is not only considered good business practice to inform consumers of potential risks associated with consumer products, but numerous laws and regulations—varying by product type and jurisdiction—also mandate risk communication to protect consumers from potential harm. Properly done, the communication of product-related risks also implicates actors from across the spectrum of product fabrication and use, including scientists, regulators, legislative representatives, and end users. Considering the highly interdisciplinary nature of the field, practitioners who communicate product risk should be able to understand the complex dynamics of risk communication from a number of vantage points, at both the individual and societal levels.

This contribution starts with a definition of risk communication that should help identify key features of effective risk communication. Those definitional aspects are followed by a section on the risk communication process, which provides practical examples for addressing product-related risks. The remainder of the contribution explores approaches for understanding how people perceive and interpret risk, and how producers might effectively communicate risk to consumers. Several theories have been proposed to explain why people evaluate and respond differently to risks and hazards. Thus, the contribution divides the major theoretical

H.K. Kim (✉)
Division of Communication Research, Wee Kim Wee School of Communication and
Information, Nanyang Technological University, Singapore, Singapore
e-mail: hkkim@ntu.edu.sg

© Springer International Publishing AG 2017
G. Emilien et al. (eds.), *Consumer Perception of Product Risks and Benefits*,
DOI 10.1007/978-3-319-50530-5_7

approaches into three groups: psychological approaches, sociological approaches, and interdisciplinary approaches.

Psychological approaches to understanding risk communication focus on factors that influence perceptions of risk at the individual level. In this contribution, both cognitive (unrealistic optimism) and affective (risk as feelings and affect heuristic, functional emotion theory) factors are introduced and their implications for risk communication are discussed. Scholars tend to emphasize the importance of risk information-seeking and processing as tools for making better risk decisions; the contribution thus explains important considerations for promoting those information behaviors. Beyond individual-level risk, this contribution also explores sociological contributions to risk factors at the group level (cultural theory), and it evaluates interdisciplinary (social amplification of risk) approaches to understanding perceptions of risk. Each sub-section concludes with practical insights for communicating risk.

2 Defining Risk Communication

Risk communication refers to an exchange of information about the "risks caused by environmental, industrial, or agricultural processes, policies, or products among individuals, groups and institutions" (Glik 2007, p. 34). Although risk communication comes in many different forms, in this contribution, the term refers to the communication of health, safety, or environmental risks associated with consumer products. Previously, risk communication had been considered a one-way form of communication, with consumers being told what the experts or companies consider important. With growing demand for consumer involvement in risk management, however, risk communication is now considered a two-way, interactive process involving informational exchanges between different groups of key players, including consumers, experts, companies, organizations, and institutions.

The primary objective of risk communication is to improve the match between the actual magnitude of a risk issue and the magnitude of risk that consumers perceive and to which they respond. Thus, to act as a bridge between the experts/companies and consumers, communication practitioners should develop a strong understanding of the risk issue as well as consumers' concerns, feelings, and reactions toward the risk issue. Recognizing the reasons behind a perceptual gap between the consumers and the expert/company constitutes one of the most critical enterprises in the practice of risk communications. Furthermore, communicating risk often involves information or messages that may be threatening to consumers, and which may trigger defensive reactions, unnecessary fear, misunderstanding, or suspicion. Risk communicators must therefore be able to diffuse these potential consequences by showing empathy and exercising negotiation skills, while also protecting their credibility and trustworthiness with the public.

Fig. 1 Risk
communication process

3 Processes of Risk Communication

As outlined above, risk communication is an interactive process involving informational exchanges between different stakeholders to address potential hazards or
risks associated with consumer products. Several steps are involved in the development and execution of an effective risk communication program. As Fig. 1
illustrates, the process starts with identifying and assessing potential risks, and
finishes with program evaluation.

3.1 Step 1: Identify and Assess Risk

Risk identification refers to the process of determining potential threats to the
environment or human safety and health (in this contribution, as posed by consumer
products). This critical first step in the risk management process allows companies
to prevent product returns and recalls, and it reduces the threat of litigation that may
arise if consumers are placed in danger. The objective is the early and continuous
identification of product risks that may cause harm to consumers and their environments. To meet that objective, risk assessments are performed at different
stages, from the product design to manufacturing. In many parts of the word,

product risk assessments of this sort are not mandatory, but in other jurisdictions, companies may be required by law to conduct product risk assessments (e.g., for toys in the US and EU). For example, governments frequently adopt into legislation elements from the international standard *ISO 10377: Consumer product safety—Guidelines for suppliers*, which offers practical guidance about product risk assessment such as hazard identification, the development of injury scenarios, and evaluations of the probability and potential severity of injuries.

3.2 Step 2: Determine Communication Needs and Objectives

Not all product risks can be eliminated, even after their identification through risk assessment. The subsequent step, then, in cases where some level of product risk persists, is to inform consumers of those potential product risks. A successful risk communication should have a defined purpose and set of objectives, because the tactics used to communicate risk may differ according to distinct goals. Potentially five different objectives may be established for risk communication (Kasperson et al. 1992): (1) to diagnose and maintain public trust; (2) to increase awareness of risks; (3) to improve public understanding of risk; (4) to develop mediating skills; and (5) to mobilize the public. Risk communication can further be divided into several categories depending on its purpose: care communication, consensus communication, crisis communication, and product communication (Lundgren and McMakin 2013; Ng and Hamby 1997).

3.2.1 Care Communication

The purpose of care communication is to inform consumers about potential risks and to educate end users on the effective means to reduce such risks, based on scientific evidence. As an example of the importance of relying on scientific information, coffee drinking was associated with an increased cancer risk as early as the 1980s. However, twenty-five years after classifying coffee as a possible carcinogen leading to bladder cancer, the World Health Organization removed coffee from the list of cancer causes in light of cumulative evidence suggesting no link between cancer and coffee drinking. Conversely, shampoo and other body care products routinely inform consumers about the dangers associated with swallowing; this is intended to reduce proven risks of intestinal illness or discomfort as a result of ingestion.

3.2.2 Consensus Communication

Consensus communication aims to inform and encourage relevant stakeholders to work together in order to make a decision about how the risk should be managed

(Lundgren and McMakin 2013). Typically, consensus communication involves activities such as panel discussions, public consultations, and audience interactions. Engaging in this sort of public involvement enables an organization or company to improve its decision-making processes, but just as importantly, it enhances the firm's local credibility. Communities are also more likely to accept decisions made with their input, which may reduce the likelihood of legal delays and political pressure (Sandman 1985). An example would be a citizens' advisory panel, a group of experts, and representatives from a governmental agency working together to decide on the location for a new nuclear energy facility.

3.2.3 Crisis Communication

Crisis communication aims to manage perceptions around unpredictable events that might threaten the product-related expectations of key stakeholders; such events include disease outbreaks and natural/human-caused disasters. Communication objectives during a crisis may seek to inform, convince, or motivate certain stakeholders to take some form of essential action, though the key objective in these circumstances is often damage control—an effort to prevent drastic negative changes in the relationship between stakeholders (Sturges 1994). The Tylenol crisis in 1982, which involved a series of poisoning deaths resulting from drug tampering in Chicago, constitutes an exemplary case of successful crisis communication (Lazare 2002). Johnson & Johnson immediately warned the public of poisoning risks and proactively issued a nationwide recall of Tylenol products. This incident led to reforms in over-the-counter substance packaging and in federal anti-tampering laws (Mitchell 1989).

3.2.4 Product Communication

Product communication intends to inform consumers about product risks particularly when introducing a new product. This type of risk communication is often mandated by regulations and has become more important as failure to properly inform consumers of product risks puts companies at exposure to large-scale lawsuits. Chemical companies, for instance, communicate potential hazards of their products through product labels, product health/safety bulletins, and material safety data sheets (MSDS). An example would be creating public awareness around the environmental and health risks associated with using pesticides. According to WHO specifications (WHO 1985), pesticides should be packaged and labeled in English or in the local language, and labels should indicate the contents, the proper safety instructions (warnings) to follow, and possible measures to take in the event of contamination or swallowing.

Pharmaceutical manufacturers also use product labeling (the Summary of Product Characteristics, SmPC), patient information leaflets (package inserts), and product warning labels to inform consumers about product risks. One of the major challenges to product communication is delivering the risk information in an easy-to-understand format while also ensuring that the instructions are comprehensive and accurate. In developing a patient information leaflet, for instance, it would be important to avoid using technical jargon that only medical experts can interpret.

3.3   Step 3: Selecting Potential Audiences

Owing to the fact that a wide range of individuals and groups have a stake in the risk-related aspects of any product, it is important to properly identify these stakeholders and to understand their distinct views and concerns. In developing a communication program, risk communicators may prioritize target audiences depending on their roles and the magnitude and probability of the risks they face. For instance, in communicating risks related to children's products (e.g., toys), parents are the primary target audience as they make purchase decisions and serve as caregivers for the children who cannot make proper risk-related decisions themselves.

Communicative approaches—in terms of the content, tactics, and strategies—differ based on the intended audience largely as a function of their knowledge of the issue, their attitudes toward the company, and their reading level and numeracy skills. Understanding the intended audiences' perception of risk is thus an essential step in creating successful risk communication. Risk perception refers to "people's beliefs, attitudes, judgments and feelings, as well as the wider social or cultural values and dispositions that people adopt, towards hazard and their benefits" (Pidgeon et al. 1992, p. 89). As indicated in this definition, because each audience tends to have some commonality or shared identity, risk perception should be understood against the societal and cultural background, beyond the individual-level process.

For instance, the cultural theory of risk (Douglas and Wildavsky 1983) suggests that social aspects and cultural adherence shape how we perceive and respond to risk. Accordingly, variation in social participation can be accounted for by the interaction between the two dimensions: (1) the strength of allegiance to a group (the group axis) and (2) the extent of regulation within or outside of the group (the grid axis). Using the group-grid scheme, four kinds of social environments exist: individualism ("low grid, low group", protecting individual freedom) versus fatalistic ("high grid, low group", indifferent about risk), and hierarchical ("high grid, high group", relying on experts) versus egalitarian ("low grid, high group", striving for equality). Risk communicators should take these distinct social and cultural environments into account when developing strategies for effective risk communication.

3.4 Step 4: Develop Risk Messages

3.4.1 Comprehension and Accuracy

Risk information or messages should be appropriately suited to audiences' reading levels, prior risk experience, and perceptions/feelings about risk, in order to enhance comprehension. Instead of using technical terms that are unfamiliar to an audience, risk communicators should develop more easily understood terms with clear definitions. Using comparisons is a common strategy to enhance comprehensibility, as people often find it difficult to understand probability-based risk estimates (Slovic 1987). For instance, the risk associated with a particular new product can be compared to similar products' risks, to natural background levels, or to regulatory standards. To ensure comprehensibility, it is always desirable to pretest the developed risk messages through focus groups or in-depth interviews with members of the target audience prior to implementation.

Risk communication inevitably involves some degree of uncertainty. When delivering research findings in particular, uncertainties should be clearly acknowledged by addressing the study's limitations and caveats, expert disagreements, and inconsistencies. Because uncertainty can be perceived as incompetence, risk communicators should deliver factual information supported by cumulative research evidence and reviewed by an expert panel.

3.4.2 Fear Appeal

Fear inducing messages are often used, particularly in health campaigns, to promote protective behaviors or to deter unhealthy behaviors. The process of inducing fear works by raising the prospect of personal risk vulnerability, and by underscoring the severity of harm associated with unhealthy behaviors. According to the Extended Parallel Process Model (EPPM; Witte 1994), there are potentially two different coping strategies that audiences may adopt when they face fear-inducing messages: danger control and fear control. Danger control allows audiences to take precautionary actions to reduce personal risk, whereas fear control leads to maladaptive behaviors (e.g., avoiding risk information) as a self-defense mechanism. When fear is aroused, audiences can activate danger control, instead of fear control, only when they perceive themselves as capable of managing the risk. To promote protective behaviors using fear appeal, risk communicators should provide information on effective ways to reduce the risk (*response efficacy*) and on the audience's competence to perform those actions (*self-efficacy*).

3.4.3 Message Framing

Persuasive outcomes differ depending on how messages are framed. Although not all risk communication involves persuasion, message framing can be useful for changing perceptions of and solutions to risk. For instance, news framing research suggests that news coverage featuring an individual who suffers from a problem (episodic frame) makes readers more likely to attribute responsibility to the individual than to society, compared to coverage that focuses on the issue's overall impact in society (thematic frame) (Iyengar 1991). When the objective is to promote society-wide solutions to a risk issue (e.g., to establish a new policy), it might thus be useful to employ a thematic frame as opposed to an episodic frame; doing so would likely serve to emphasize society-level responsibilities in addressing the risk issue.

Many persuasion scholars have investigated the relative persuasive efficacy of gain- and loss-framed messages. A gain-frame focuses on the benefits and positive outcomes of taking the recommended action, whereas a loss-frame focuses on the costs and negative outcomes of not taking the recommended action. According to Prospect Theory (Kahneman and Tversky 1979), people tend to seek risks when the message is loss-framed and to avoid risks when the message is gain-framed. For instance, a loss-frame tends to perform better in promoting detection behaviors (e.g., cancer screenings), which involve the potential to receive negative risk information (Rothman and Salovey 1997). In promoting prevention behaviors aimed at achieving desirable outcomes (e.g., regular exercise), on the other hand, a gain-frame tends to be more persuasive than a loss-frame (Rothman and Salovey 1997).

Prior research suggests that the relative efficacy of gain- and loss-frames differs by individual predispositions, such as one's cultural worldview. In particular, evidence suggests that loss-frames are more effective than gain-frames at increasing policy support to address risk for those with a hierarchical worldview; however, the reverse appears to be true for those with an egalitarian worldview (Nan and Madden 2014). Combined with the cultural theory of risk (Douglas and Wildavsky 1983) explained earlier, gain-loss framing could be useful in risk communication when matched with the intended audience's cultural worldview.

3.4.4 Visual Presentations

Proper use of visuals can significantly improve an audience's understanding and recall of risk information. The use of bar graphs and pie charts in product labels, for instance, has been shown to improve consumer comprehension of nutrition information, compared to text-only product labels (Geiger et al. 1991). Visuals also help clarify abstract or complex concepts in risk information by allowing audiences to construct mental models (Graber 1990).

Product warning labels, such as those used for prescription drugs and household chemicals, often utilize visuals and graphics to convey product risks. For instance, graphic warning labels on cigarette packages have been found to improve consumer knowledge about the risks from smoking (Hammond et al. 2006); thus, such warning labels are now mandated in many countries. The United Nations Economic Commission for Europe and its partners developed a worldwide voluntary guideline for labeling chemical hazards, which requires specific symbols on labels to indicate particular hazards (e.g., a white jagged star inside a human silhouette to indicate a health hazard). These symbols can be applied to pharmaceutical packages to prevent children or pregnant women from taking certain medications. Because symbols may have different meanings in different cultures and industries, it is important to pre-test those symbols with target audiences prior to actual implementation.

3.5   Step 5: Select a Media Vehicle and Execute

Risk communicators utilize multiple media platforms, from traditional media (e.g., newspaper, radio, television) to social network platforms, to disseminate risk information through advertisements and press releases. Beyond diverse media outlets, risk communicators also frequently adopt more interactive approaches that involve public participation such as community meetings, panel discussions, and public consultation. Other tactics include brochures, information packets, fact sheets, newsletters, videotapes or slide shows, product inserts, and warning labels.

The selection of an appropriate media vehicle and tactic largely depends on the objective of risk communication and the characteristics of the intended audience. For example, mass media-based advertisements are typically effective at disseminating risk information. News coverage, conversely, is useful for increasing the salience of a particular risk issue in the public's mind. Because preferences over the outlet type and exposure levels vary by the audience, audience analysis can assist with the selection of appropriate forms of media through which to communicate risk.

3.6   Step 6: Evaluate the Communication Program

The evaluation of an overall risk communication program is an important final step that allows risk communicators to learn from their experience and mistakes. Evaluation can begin at the early stages of a program in order to identify issues and to make adjustments regarding the remaining program components. Like many other communication practices, however, it is a challenging task for risk communicators to document actual changes in knowledge, perceptions, and behaviors that result from program exposure. Thus, it is desirable to establish a baseline or comparison group in order to draw the most accurate conclusions possible about the effects of a risk communication program. Feedback from the audience, gathered through post-program surveys, focus groups, or interviews, can help to identify issues such as definitional problems, conflicting expectations, and communication barriers, and thus to ensure the continual improvement of the risk communication program.

4 Unrealistic Optimism and Debiasing Risk Communication

People tend to believe they are not vulnerable or less likely than similar others to experience illness, injury and other negative health issues (Weinstein 1980). Unrealistic optimism about personal risk is a well-documented phenomenon in the literature across a wide range of topics and different populations. By negating one's own vulnerability, individuals are able to maintain positive self-view (e.g., healthy) and reduce anxiety that may be caused by thinking of uncontrollable future occurrences (Taylor and Brown 1988). However, underestimating one's own risk could be problematic because it may reduce attention to risk information and the performance of risk-reducing behaviors (e.g., Radcliffe and Klein 2002).

4.1 Conceptualization and Consequences

Understanding the consequences of optimism about personal risk (or perceived invulnerability) requires a careful examination of how the construct is conceptualized. People can be optimistic about their risk either *absolutely,* by considering their own risk to be lower than the actual level of risk they face, or *comparatively,* by believing their own risk to be lower than what they believe to be the average risk. Scholars have less frequently investigated absolute optimism by dint of the evidentiary difficulties that arise in obtaining the actual level of risk to which risk judgments can be compared in gauging the existence of absolute errors. Comparative risk is considered psychologically important given that people's understanding of risk in terms of odds and probabilities is limited and subject to cognitive errors (Slovic 1987). Also, social comparisons constitute an important part of how people understand their own personal risk.

Scholars have emphasized the importance of distinguishing optimism from bias or illusion (Dillard et al. 2009). While people typically consider themselves to be less vulnerable to risk in a comparative or an absolute sense, this estimation may be either correct (realistic) or incorrect (unrealistic optimism or unrealistic pessimism), depending on the individual's actual level of risk (Dillard et al. 2009). For example, if an individual estimates his or her own risk of pesticide poisoning to be

Table 1 Categorization scheme for identifying unrealistic optimism

Comparative risk perception	Actual comparative risk		
	Below average	Average	Above average
Own < Other's risk	Realists	Unrealistic optimists	Unrealistic optimists
Own = Other's risk	Unrealistic pessimists	Realists	Unrealistic optimists
Own > Other's risk	Unrealistic pessimists	Unrealistic pessimists	Realists

low because the person does not use pesticides (i.e., low actual risk), then it would be inappropriate to consider this person as unrealistic.

Comparative optimism and unrealistic optimism have often been conflated in studies, yet they differ critically. The former refers to a relative risk judgment irrespective of the accuracy of that belief, while the latter refers to a *mistaken* belief that one's risk is lower than that of other people or of one's actual risk (Radcliffe and Klein 2002). The appropriate identification of such biases thus requires an objective criterion for measurement and comparison (e.g., actual comparative or absolute risk). To determine whether "being biased" is consequential, one must be capable of identifying distorted risk perceptions at the individual level. Table 1 shows the categorization scheme for identifying unrealistic optimism.

Emerging evidence exists to suggest that unrealistic optimism, but not comparative optimism, has negative health consequences. Researchers have suggested that people's comparative risk judgments are often ordinally accurate and do not have negative implications; that suggests little need for making comparative judgments the target of interventions (e.g., Radcliffe and Klein 2002). Although high-risk individuals like smokers or siblings of cancer patients do tend to underestimate their own personal risk, they at least tend to estimate their risk to be higher than that of low-risk individuals such as non-smokers or people without a family history of cancer (e.g., Strecher et al. 1995).

Distinctly different patterns have been reported with respect to unrealistic optimism. Unrealistic optimists, as defined in terms of identifying bias, tend to perceive themselves to be at lower risk despite their actual high risk standing (Radcliffe and Klein 2002). More importantly, evidence indicates that unrealistic optimists often employ ego-protective strategies that help them to sustain their unrealistic beliefs, such as avoiding risk information and downplaying the riskiness of their behavior (Radcliffe and Klein 2002; Klein 1996). In a longitudinal study using a sample of college students, unrealistic optimism about alcohol-related negative events was associated with a greater number of respondents who actually experienced those events at subsequent time periods (Dillard et al. 2009).

4.2 Psychological Mechanisms and Interventions

Weinstein (1984) recommended several strategies to better endorse risk-reducing behaviors by changing risk perceptions such as emphasizing the association between behavior and susceptibility, providing specific behavioral objectives, and offering others' preventive actions. Although some interventions were successful, many theory-driven intervention strategies have failed to change the bias in personal risk assessments (e.g., Weinstein and Klein 1995; Klein 1996). A better understanding of the psychological mechanisms related to how unrealistic optimists become biased serves an important starting point for tackling such biased perceptions.

Unrealistic optimism is thought to originate from multiple psychological factors that are quite difficult to tease apart. The most prominent explanations include (1) self-serving motivations to protect and maintain a positive self-image, and (2) cognitive errors in processing risk information due to egocentrism (which leads to a failure to think carefully about others' risk status), a lack of information about other's self-protective behaviors, and selective focus on one's risk-reducing factors (e.g., Weinstein 1980).

Egocentric thinking in the context of risk judgment refers to an inability to access information about other's risk levels while focusing exclusively on one's own risk factors. Based on the assumption that unrealistic optimism results from unmotivated errors in understanding the risk that people face—particularly others—, providing individuals with risk information that they had been unaware of or had overlooked is frequently cited as a remedy for such misunderstanding (e.g., Weinstein and Klein 1995). This informational approach has not always been successful in changing risk perceptions, however, suggesting that unrealistic optimism is not caused solely by unmotivated cognitive errors.

People tend to adopt various cognitive strategies to justify their own past unhealthy behaviors and to maintain a positive self-view (Klein 1996). This self-serving motivation often creates a situation in which unrealistic optimists resistant to correction via information interventions (Klein 1996; Weinstein and Klein 1995). Instead, addressing overlooked personal risk factors could actually prompt defensive information processing and interpretation, particularly in contexts in which an individual is motivated to self-defend (Weinstein and Klein 1995). For instance, when comparative optimism was directly challenged in research studies, people tended to hold on to their superiority either by distorting their memory about their own past unhealthy behaviors or by lowering the relevance or importance of these behaviors to their health (Klein 1996).

4.3   Practical Insights

Considerable evidence suggests that both cognitive and motivational factors contribute to the emergence of unrealistic optimism about personal risk. Informing individuals about the risk status of others or about behaviors for reducing risk is likely to reduce comparative risk judgments by lowering risk estimates about others, but those strategies are unlikely to influence personal risk estimates. As previously discussed, however, comparative optimism is typically of less concern given that it is associated with rather positive outcomes. Thus, no strong grounds exist to argue in favor of providing other's low-risk information as a strategy for changing an individual's unrealistic optimism about personal risk. Instead, it seems crucial to identify those who have unrealistic risk judgments and to inform these individuals about their personal risk standing. The key to this process would be the reduction of possible defensive reactions, considering that unrealistic optimists are likely to be defensive.

Two intervention strategies have the potential to bring unrealistic optimists' perceived risk in line with their actual risk level: (1) eliminating the need for self-defense (via self-affirmation) before exposure to personalized risk information, and (2) providing vicarious experiences through narratives that depict a person who shares a similar risk profile with the audience. In the context of alcohol-related problems among college students (Kim and Niederdeppe 2016), for example, providing risk information to unrealistic optimists while also protecting their self-concept via either self-affirmation or narratives, tends to reduce defensive reactions and to align their perceived risk more closely with their actual risk. These intervention strategies are based on an educational approach (rather than using deception techniques), which can be applied to risk communication campaigns.

5 The Role of Affect in Risk Communication

Emotions are generally viewed as internal, mental states representing evaluative, valenced reactions to events, agents, or objects that vary in intensity (Ortony et al. 1988). Emotions are thought to be specific, focused, and foregrounded in consciousness; this puts emotions in contrast to mood, which is often viewed as a diffuse background affect of uncertain cause (Dillard and Peck 2000). Risk communication scholars have emphasized the role of emotions in interpreting and responding to potential hazards and risks. In this section, major concepts and theories relevant to the role of emotions are outlined and their implications for risk communication are discussed.

5.1 Risk-as-Feelings and the Affect Heuristic

Because emotions and affective reactions are triggered automatically, often before conscious evaluation of a risk, they offer important information about how individuals perceive risk situations. Scholars who investigate the role of affect in decision-making processes have noted a distinction between anticipated affect and anticipatory affect, especially in response to risks and uncertainties (e.g., Loewenstein et al. 2001). While anticipatory affect is "immediate visceral reactions (e.g., fear, anxiety, dread) to risks and uncertainties" (Loewenstein et al. 2001, p. 267), anticipated affect does not include immediacy but expected to be experienced in the future. The risk-as-feelings perspective (Loewenstein et al. 2001) posits that factors such as anticipated outcomes (including anticipated affect) and subjective probability related to a risk influence an individual's feelings about the risk. This emotional reaction to risky situations, in turn, leads to a behavioral response to the risk either with or without mediation from cognitive evaluations about the risk. When emotional reactions are not in agreement with cognitive assessments of risk, the emotions often drive behavioral responses to those risks.

The affect heuristic explains how an individual's affect can change the way he or she makes risk decisions. People tend to make those risk decisions relying on their current emotion or "affect pool" as a cue about the judgment of a risk (Finucane et al. 2000); this subconscious process occurs quickly and efficiently as it allows the individual to shorten the decision-making process. The affect heuristic is often, then, used to make judgments about the risks and benefits of a particular situation or object based on the positive or negative feelings that people relate to that situation/object. Specifically, the negative relationship between perceived risk and benefit is closely related to the strength of positive or negative affect associated with the situation/object. For instance, if an individual's feelings toward a particular consumer product are negative, he or she will be more likely to judge the risk as high and the benefits low. In contrast, if an individual's feelings toward the product are positive, he or she is likely to evaluate the risks as low and the benefits high, even when doing so is logically unwarranted for that product. This suggests that a strong affective response toward a consumer product can change an individual's judgment about the product's risks and benefits, which could be an illogical judgment.

5.2 Functional Emotion Theory and Crisis Emotions

Functional emotion theory explains how different emotions influence the mobilizing and allocating of mental and physical resources for person-environment interactions. Generally, emotions operate as basic information processing systems designed to deal with a certain, limited set of person-environment relationships (Lazarus 1991); they signal the mobilization of psychological and physiological resources in response to that context (Dillard and Peck 2000). This action tendency is related to physiological changes, which in turn influence future perceptions, cognitions, and behaviors in accordance with the goal set by the action tendency (Lazarus 1991).

Emotions play an important role in how individuals respond to risk information in the sense that emotions serve as a frame, influencing the way in which information is gathered, stored, recalled, and used to make risk judgments. When emotion is evoked, its associated action tendency guides information processing and influences selective attention and recall (Nabi 2003). For instance, the public would be more open to mobilization efforts and stronger penalties for criminal offenses if an anger frame is repeatedly used with crime stories focusing blame on perpetrators.

This suggests that message-relevant emotions can lead to selective processing of emotion-relevant information, and, in turn, to decision-making.

Fear is typically considered an avoidance emotion, while anger is treated as an approach motivation that triggers action on the part of the consumer (Frijda et al. 1989). Because different emotions trigger different action tendencies, it is important to identify discrete emotions associated with a risk event, particularly a crisis that may trigger stronger emotional reactions. Emotions can be broadly divided into two categories, negative and positive.

5.2.1 Negative Emotions

Four primary negative emotions are associated with a crisis (Jin and Cameron 2007): anger, sadness, fright, and anxiety. In response to the September 11 terrorist attacks, anger, sadness and fear were the three most dominant negative emotions (Fredrickson et al. 2003). Based on the functional emotion theory, negative emotions promote selective processing of available information about a crisis and guide decision-making, which then influences attitudes toward the issue and the organization in crisis. For example, anger aroused by a toxic waste dumping story is associated with greater support for punishing goals compared to goals relating to systemic change or helping victims.

5.2.2 Positive Emotions

The role of positive emotions in a crisis has been largely neglected in the literature, in large part because they are considered to be less intense and less enduring than negative emotions. However, scholars emphasize that people in stressful situations experience both negative and positive emotions (Fredrickson et al. 2003); while positive emotions may seem inappropriate in the context of crisis, positive emotions indeed co-occur alongside negative emotions. For instance, gratitude, interest, and love were the three most frequent positive emotions noted in studies following the September 11 tragedy (Fredrickson et al. 2003).

Positive emotions not only provide more pleasant subjective experiences than negative emotions, but they also help reduce the focus on negative emotions. More specifically, they tend to work as a "breather" by undoing physiological arousal and enhancing broadminded coping (Fredrickson et al. 2003). As opposed to negative emotions that narrow people's attention to specific action tendencies (e.g., attack), people's attention, thinking, and behavioral repertoires are widened by positive emotions (Fredrickson et al. 2003). Applying these effects to the crisis context, positive emotions can aid an organization by allowing stakeholders to be more flexible in interpreting a crisis situation and to be more open-minded in the processing of relevant information. Positive emotions might also mitigate the impact of negative emotions on organizational reputation and may encourage stakeholders to engage in active communication.

5.3 Practical Insights

Emotions play a key role, often times more than cognitive evaluations of risk, in interpreting and responding to risks. Furthermore, because people tend to evaluate risk by relying on their current emotion as a heuristic cue, their risk decisions do not always correspond to the actual level of risk that they face. To promote more accurate evaluations of risk, practitioners would thus need to address illogical conclusions that could be drawn from heuristic thinking and to encourage consumers to consider probability-based assessments of product risk. In light of functional emotion theory, it would be also beneficial to understand the specific types of emotions that could be triggered by a particular risk issue or crisis, along with the associated action tendencies. For instance, the core action tendencies of fear and anxiety are changing plans in order to enhance protection or learning (Dillard and Peck 2000). Thus, if fear and anxiety are the dominant emotions to emerge in a crisis situation, risk communicators would need to provide information that reduces uncertainties or that offers other means to address protection and learning goals.

6 Risk Information Seeking and Processing

Information seeking and processing are critical components of risk decision-making, yet individuals vary greatly in their capability and motivation to engage in these processes. It is thus important to understand when individuals are likely to seek out risk information and how they are likely to process it. The risk information seeking and processing model (RISP; Griffin et al. 1999) explores predictors of these risk information behaviors guided by the heuristic-systematic model (HSM; Chen and Chaiken 1999) and the theory of planned behavior (TPB; Ajzen 1991). In this section, key components and predictions of the RISP model are introduced and its implications for risk communication are discussed. Fig. 2 offers a visual representation of the model.

6.1 The RISP Model

6.1.1 Information Seeking and Processing

In keeping with the dual processing models in psychology (e.g., HSM, Chen and Chaiken 1999), two types of information processing exist: systematic and heuristic. These two processes differ in the amount of mental energy an individual exerts to process the information at hand. Systematic processing requires both cognitive ability and motivation to process information in a relatively analytic and

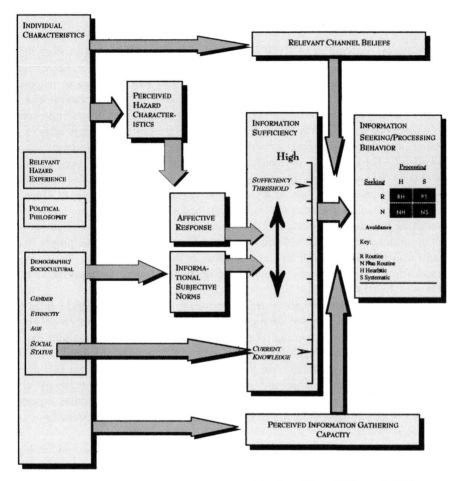

Fig. 2 Risk information seeking and processing model (adopted from Griffin et al. 1999)

comprehensive manner. On the other hand, heuristic processing makes fewer cognitive demands on the individual, as it relies primarily on cognitive shortcuts or "heuristics". While utilizing a mental shortcut has pragmatic benefits, it may also lead to flawed or biased risk decisions. Not surprisingly, compared to heuristic processing, systematic processing has been found to promote more long-lasting attitudinal and behavioural changes (e.g., Chaiken et al. 1989).

Information seeking refers to a volitional process of attempting to obtain desired information by selecting relevant information channels. Like processing, RISP suggests that information seeking can involve more or less mental effort: one could heuristically seek risk information through routine media exposure such as watching a TV news program after dinner, or, on the other hand, one might purposefully search for particular risk information via nonroutine media channels. The latter would be an example of engaging in systematic information seeking.

6.1.2 Model Components and Predictions

The primary proposition of RISP is that individuals seek out and process risk information depending on their subjective assessments of the gap between what they know about a risk and the extent to which they feel sufficient to respond adequately to that risk (*information insufficiency*). Based on "accuracy motivation" (Eagly and Chaiken 1993), systematic information seeking and processing occur only when one is sufficiently motivated to engage in the tasks required to achieve a desired degree of judgmental confidence regarding a risk decision (*sufficiency threshold*). Thus, a low sufficiency threshold activates heuristic seeking and processing, whereas a high sufficiency threshold promotes systematic seeking and processing. In a meta-analytic study (Yang et al. 2014), current levels of knowledge, rather than a sufficiency threshold, explained a larger share of the variance in predicting information seeking and processing. That suggests that individuals may not accurately estimate the amount of information they need to make proper risk decisions when dealing with less familiar risks, so the RISP model may have more practical utility in addressing risks that are relatively familiar to the respondents (Yang et al. 2014).

Informational subjective norms (ISN), derived from TPB (Ajzen 1991), refer to perceived normative pressure to engage in information seeking and processing. Based on "impression motivation" (Eagly and Chaiken 1993), individuals are more likely to seek and process risk information when they are under greater normative influence from close confidantes or loved ones. Evidence indicates that ISN does influence information seeking and processing, both directly and indirectly via changing information insufficiency (Kahlor 2010). Meta analytic studies suggest that ISN is the strongest predictor of risk information seeking and processing (e.g., Yang et al. 2014).

Two other major components in the RISP model moderate the relationship between information insufficiency and information behaviors: perceived information gathering capacity and relevant channel beliefs. *Relevant channel beliefs (RCB)* refers to perceptions about the nature and quality of available information (e.g., useful, unbiased, trustworthy). Individuals are more likely to utilize a particular information channel when they perceive that channel to deliver information that is most relevant to them. Information seeking typically involves multiple channels, which may vary by the context and information needs. Due to the corresponding challenges in conceptualizing and operationalizing RCB in clear and consistent ways, recent RISP studies (e.g., Kahlor 2007, 2010) have adopted the concept of behavioral beliefs, derived from TPB (Ajzen 1991), to assess people's beliefs about information seeking behaviors.

The RISP model accounts for the capacity, in addition to the motivations, that individuals possess to seek and process risk information. *Perceived information gathering capacity (PIGC)* refers to the perceived ability to acquire needed risk information from information channels. Similar to the concept of self-efficacy (Ajzen 1991), which has been suggested as an important predictor of behaviors, individuals with higher capacity will find it easier to identify the most relevant and valuable information needed for their risk decision-making. Although the original RISP model suggests that PIGC is a key factor in promoting systematic information seeking and processing (and reducing heuristic processing), studies have found inconsistent evidence in support of that claim (e.g., Kahlor 2007), suggesting that PIGC may play a marginal role in the model (Yang et al. 2014).

The RISP model also proposes several antecedents to information insufficiency including cognitive evaluations of and affective responses to a particular risk. Cognitive evaluations of risk are termed *perceived hazard characteristics,* and are commonly conceptualized based on two dimensions: perceived likelihood and severity. Although the RISP model also includes affective responses to risk, particularly in the form of worry, the model focuses more heavily on cognitive factors. Other individual-level difference factors in the RISP model (e.g., demographic factors, past experience) serve as distal predictors of information behaviors, but their predictive power has been relatively small compared to other RISP factors (Yang et al. 2014).

6.2   Practical Insights

The RISP model offers useful insights for the design of risk messages and campaigns. For instance, practitioners who communicate risks should address the key potential motivators of risk information seeking and processing, such as accuracy motivation (relevant to information insufficiency) and impression motivation (relevant to ISN) (Eagly and Chaiken 1993). In light of the meta-analytic findings suggesting that ISN is the strongest predictor of information behaviors (Yang et al. 2014), it would be most useful to emphasize what is expected of the audiences by important referent groups, for instance, by increasing the salience of social environment where they can observe the behaviors and expectations of important others. Perceptions about the quality of an information channel can also play an important role in seeking and processing risk information from that channel. Thus, in selecting media vehicles, risk communicators should take into account the credibility and relevance of the media source in order to improve the likelihood that the intended audience will indeed be exposed to the message. Although the RISP model addresses both systematic and heuristic processing, the heuristic processing variables in the model show only limited explanatory power (Yang et al. 2014). More work is needed to better understand the factors associated with heuristic processing and the manner in which heuristic processing shapes risk assessments.

7 Social Amplification of Risk

Many risk scholars have been interested in understanding the gap between how experts and lay audiences assess risk. In particular, relatively minor risk events as evaluated by experts often elicit public panic and concern, thereby generating significant social consequences. Why might experts and lay audiences interpret risk events so differently? The social amplification of risk framework (SARF; Kasperson et al. 1988), a conceptual framework for understanding the processes of amplification and attenuation of public risk perceptions, offers plausible explanations to answer this question. Since its introduction in 1988, this framework has received widespread attention from both scholars and practitioners, serving as a useful conceptual tool for examining the social experience of risk. Figure 3 visually presents the framework.

7.1 Social Amplification of Risk Framework

The SARF describes the social mechanisms underlying the communication of risk messages, while integrating the cultural-, societal-, and individual-level structures that shape the public experience of risk. Its primary proposition is that risk events interact with psychological, societal and cultural processes to amplify or attenuate public risk perceptions and related behaviors. These, in turn, produce secondary consequences at the societal level, such as changes in political climate and risk monitoring/regulation, which may also amplify or attenuate the perceptions of risk. Secondary impacts then prompt social groups and individuals to engage in another stage of amplification spreading or "rippling" to other social parties. Thus, the

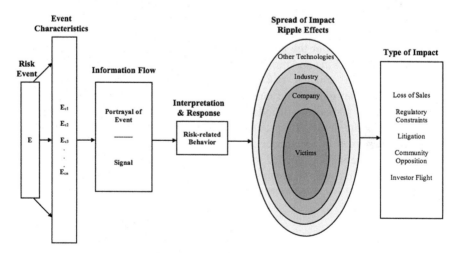

Fig. 3 Social amplification of risk (adopted from Kasperson et al. 1988)

social amplification of risk refers to a dynamic phenomenon of "the social structures and processes of risk experience, the resulting repercussions on individual and group perceptions, and the effects of these responses on community, society, and economy" (Kasperson et al. 1988, p. 179).

7.1.1 Socially Constructed Risk

Proponents of SARF suggest by way of criticism that the concept of risk, often conceptualized as the multiplication of the probability of risk events by the severity of the event consequences, has been too narrow and technical to serve as a useful guideline for making policy decisions. Instead, they emphasize a socially constructed definition of risk, which is shaped by individuals and social groups learning to create interpretations of hazards (Renn et al. 1992). These interpretations depend largely on how risk information is communicated via various social and individual amplification "stations", including scientists, risk-management institutions, the news media, opinion leaders within social groups and personal networks. Amplification or attenuation occurs during the transmission of information through these "stations" at both the information reception and recoding stages.

7.1.2 Two Stages of Social Amplification of Risk

The SARF includes two major stages: the transmission of risk information and the response mechanisms of society. Most people do not experience risks directly; instead they learn about the risk from others and the media. Attributes such as the volume of information, the amount of dramatization and dispute, and the symbolic connotations of information are all involved in the transmission stage of the social amplification of risk. For example, repeated media coverage and dramatization direct public attention toward a particular risk issue, which may trigger public fear about the risk. Disagreement among experts and disputes covered in the news media may also increase public uncertainty about unknown hazards, which can serve to amplify the public perception of risk. The risk event amplification process is typically assigned a signal value, which may not always correspond to the signal value of the risk itself (Slovic 1987). One essential role of the media comes in repackaging the signal value of a risk event and transmitting it to the general public, but the incentives of media outlets may not militate in favor of a true or appropriate signal value (Kasperson et al. 1988).

The second stage of the social amplification of risk addresses four components that formulate public reactions to risk events: heuristics and values, social group relations, signal value, and stigmatization (Kasperson et al. 1988). These mechanisms explain how risk information is understood and how values are assigned within social and cultural contexts. For instance, individuals evaluate risks using their mental shortcuts or values in order to respond to those risks in an efficient manner. Social group relationships also shape public responses to risks as those risk events enter the political agenda. When a risk event becomes an important political issue, creating conflict among social groups, it gathers more public attention. The signal value characterizes the risk event; high-signal events mean that more serious risk is introduced than was previously known. Negative imagery associated with the risk can create stigmatization of social groups or individuals who were influenced by the risk.

7.2 Practical Insights

The SARF is a useful conceptual tool for understanding the complex social processes involved in the amplification and attenuation of public perceptions of risk. This framework is particularly useful for identifying communication pathways through which risk information is transmitted. Given their central role as amplification stations in the transmission of risk information, the news media has received much attention from communication scholars and researchers. Risk communicators should regularly monitor and evaluate the volume of coverage in the media, the amount of dispute, and the news angles and frames to prevent misrepresentation of risks by the news media. Because disagreements and disputes among experts tend to amplify perceptions of risk, it is important to reach a consensus before communicating risk to the public. Furthermore, owing to the crucial role that opinion leaders play within social groups, risk communicators need to identify these opinion leaders and properly address their concerns. The SARF highlights the news media as an important amplification station, but the role of other types of media has not been clearly established. Insofar as many people learn about risks through personal networks or social media, future work should examine other types of channels, beyond the news media, that might amplify or attenuate perceptions of risk.

8 Conclusion

Risk communication is a dynamic and interactive process involving informational exchanges between different stakeholders. To act as a bridge between relevant stakeholders, communication practitioners must have a strong understanding of both the risk issues and the concerns and reactions of consumers related to those risks. Recognizing the perceptual gap between consumers and the expert or company responsible for the product constitutes a crucial first step for an effective risk communication. Guided by psychological and sociological approaches, this contribution introduced theoretical frameworks that could serve as useful lenses for designing risk communication programs. In outlining those frameworks, the contribution offers a better understanding of the complex dynamics involved in risk communication, both at the individual and societal levels.

References

Ajzen, I. (1991). The theory of panned behavior. *Organizational Behavior and Human Decision Process, 50*, 179–211.

Chaiken, S., Liberman, A., & Eagly, A. H. (1989). Heuristic and systematic information processing within and beyond the persuasion context. In J. S. Uleman & J. A. Bargh (Eds.), *Unintended thought* (pp. 212–252). New York: Guilford.

Chen, S., & Chaiken, S. (1999). The heuristic-systematic model in its broader context. In S. Chaiken & Y. Trope (Eds.), *Dual-process theories in social psychology* (pp. 73–96). New York: Guilford.

Dillard, J. P., & Peck, E. (2000). Affect and persuasion: Emotional responses to public service announcements. *Communication Research, 27*, 461–495.

Dillard, A. J., Midboe, A. M., & Klein, W. M. (2009). The dark side of optimism: Unrealistic optimism about problems with alcohol predicts subsequent negative event experiences. *Personality and Social Psychology Bulletin, 35*, 1540–1550.

Douglas, M., & Wildavsky, A. (1983). *Risk and culture: An essay on the selection of technological and environmental dangers*. London: University of California Press.

Eagly, A. H., & Chaiken, S. (1993). *The psychology of attitudes*. Fort Worth, TX: Harcourt Brace.

Finucane, M. L., Alhakami, A., Slovic, P., & Johnson, S. M. (2000). The affect heuristic in judgment of risks and benefits. *Journal of Behavioral Decision Making, 13*, 1–17.

Fredrickson, B. L., Tugade, M. M., Waugh, C. E., & Larkin, G. R. (2003). What good are positive emotions in crises? A prospective study of resilience and emotions following the terrorist attacks on the United States on September 11th, 2001. *Journal of Personality and Social Psychology, 84*, 365–376.

Frijda, N. H., Kuipers, P., & Schure, E. (1989). Relations among emotion, appraisal, and emotional action readiness. *Journal of Personality and Social Psychology, 57*, 212–228.

Geiger, C. J., Wise, B. W., Parent, C. R. M., & Hanson, R. G. (1991). Review of nutrition labeling formats. *Journal of the American Dietetic Association, 91*, 808–815.

Glik, D. C. (2007). Risk communication for public health emergencies. *The Annual Review of Public Health, 28*, 33–54. doi:10.1146/annurev.publhealth.28.021406.144123.

Graber, D. (1990). Seeing is remembering: How visuals contribute to learning from television news. *Journal of Communication, 40*, 134–155.

Griffin, R. J., Dunwoody, S., & Neuwirth, K. (1999). Proposed model of the relationship of risk information seeking and processing to the development of preventive behaviors. *Environmental Research, 80*, S230–S245.

Hammond, D., Fong, G. T., McNeill, A., Borland, R., & Cummings, K. M. (2006). Effectiveness of cigarette warning labels in informing smokers about the risks of smoking: Findings from the International Tobacco Control (ITC) Four Country Survey. *Tobacco Control, 15*, iii19–iii25.

Iyengar, S. (1991). *Is anyone responsible? How television frames political issues*. Chicago: University of Chicago Press.

Jin, Y., & Cameron, G. T. (2007). The effects of threat type and duration on public relations practitioner's cognitive, affective, and conative responses in crisis situations. *Journal of Public Relations Research, 19*, 255–281.

Kahlor, L. (2007). An augmented risk information seeking model: The case of global warming. *Media Psychology, 10*, 414–435.

Kahlor, L. (2010). PRISM: A planned risk information seeking model. *Health Communication, 25*, 345–356.

Kahneman, D., & Tversky, A. (1979). Prospect theory: Analysis of decision under risk. *Econometrica, 47*, 263–291.

Kasperson, R. E., Renn, O., Slovic, P., Brown, H. S., Emel, J., Goble, R., Kasperson, J. X., & Ratick, S. (1988). Social amplification of risk: A conceptual framework. *Risk analysis, 8*, 177–187.

Kasperson, R. E., Golding, D., & Tuler, S. (1992). Social distrust as a factor in siting hazardous facilities and communicating risks. *Journal of Social Issues, 48*, 161–187.

Kim, H. K., & Niederdeppe, J. (2016). Effects of self-affirmation, narratives, and informational messages in reducing unrealistic optimism about alcohol-related problems among college students. *Human Communication Research, 42*, 246–268.

Klein, W. M. (1996). Maintaining self-serving social comparisons: Attenuating the perceived significance of risk-increasing behaviors. *Journal of Social and Clinical Psychology, 15*, 120–142.

Lazare, L. (2002). Crisis triggered brilliant PR response. *Chicago Sun-Times*. Sun-Times News Group. Accessed July 13, 2016, from https://www.highbeam.com/doc/1P2-1457273.html

Lazarus, R. S. (1991). *Emotion and adaptation*. New York: Oxford University Press.

Loewenstein, G. F., Weber, E. U., Hsee, C. K., & Welch, N. (2001). Risk as feelings. *Psychological Bulletin, 127*, 267–286.

Lundgren, R. E., & McMakin, A. H. (2013). *Risk communication: A handbook for communicating environmental, safety, and health risks* (5th ed.). Hoboken, NJ: Wiley.

Mitchell, M. (1989). The impact of external parties on brand name capital: The 1982 Tylenol poisonings and subsequent cases. *Economic Inquiry, 27*, 601–618.

Nabi, R. L. (2003). Exploring the framing effects of emotion. *Communication Research, 30*, 224–247.

Nan, X., & Madden, K. (2014). The role of cultural worldviews and message framing in shaping public opinions toward the human papillomavirus vaccination mandate. *Human Communication Research, 40*, 30–53.

Ng, K. L., & Hamby, D. M. (1997). Fundamentals for establishing a risk communication program. *Health Physics, 73*, 473–482.

Ortony, A., Clore, G. L., & Collins, A. (1988). *The cognitive structure of emotions*. New York: Cambridge University Press.

Pidgeon, N. F., Hood, C., Jones, D., Turner, B., & Gibson, R. (1992). Chapter 5: Risk perception. In *Risk analysis, perception and management: Report of a Royal Society Study Group* (pp. 89–134). London: The Royal Society.

Radcliffe, N. M., & Klein, W. M. P. (2002). Dispositional, unrealistic, and comparative optimism: Differential relations with knowledge and processing of risk information and beliefs about personal risk. *Personality and Social Psychology Bulletin, 28*, 836–846.

Renn, O., Burns, W., Kasperson, R. E., Kasperson, J. X., & Slovic, P. (1992). The social amplification of risk: Theoretical foundations and empirical application. *Social Issues, 48*, 4, Special Issue: Public Responses to Environmental Hazards, 137–160.

Rothman, A. J., & Salovey, P. (1997). Shaping perceptions to motivate healthy behavior: The role of message framing. *Psychological Bulletin, 121*(1), 3–19.

Sandman, P. M. (1985). Getting to maybe: Some communications aspects of siting hazardous waste facilities. *Seton Hall Legislative Journal, 9*, 242–265.

Slovic, P. (1987). Perception of risk. *Science, 236*, 280–285.

Strecher, V. J., Kreuter, M. W., & Kobrin, S. C. (1995). Do cigarette smokers have unrealistic perceptions of their heart attack, cancer, and stroke risks? *Journal of Behavioral Medicine, 18*, 45–54.

Sturges, D. L. (1994). Communicating through crisis: A strategy for organizational survival. *Management Communication Quarterly, 7*, 297–316.

Taylor, S. E., & Brown, J. D. (1988). Illusion and well-being: A social psychological perspective on mental health. *Psychological Bulletin, 103*, 193–210.

Weinstein, N. D. (1980). Unrealistic optimism about future life events. *Journal of Personality and Social Psychology, 39*, 806–820.

Weinstein, N. D. (1984). Why it won't happen to me: Perceptions of risk factors and susceptibility. *Health Psychology, 3*, 431–457.

Weinstein, N. D., & Klein, W. M. (1995). Resistance of personal risk perceptions to debiasing interventions. *Health Psychology, 14*, 132–140.

Witte, K. (1994). Fear control and danger control: A test of the extended parallel process model. *Communication Monographs, 61*, 113–134.

World Health Organization. (1985). *Specifications for pesticides used in public health: Insecticides, molluscicides, repellents, methods* (6th ed.). World Health Organization: Geneva.

Yang, Z. J., Aloe, A. M., & Feeley, T. H. (2014). Risk information seeking and processing model: A meta-analysis. *Journal of Communication, 64*, 20–41.

Part II
Perception of Product Risks and Benefits

Comprehension of Products and Messages

Christopher L. Cummings

1 Factors Affecting Consumer Perception

Consumers constantly face decisions regarding product choices, product uses, and how to respond to product messages. Such decisions weigh heavily for the consumer as well as for industry and policymakers. Decisions that consumers face are often difficult and are constantly changing given the advent of new products and technologies, the diversity of product alternatives, and increased information from a variety of competing message sources. Foundationally, the field of marketing is centered on improving product comprehension through strategic efforts to communicate information about a product to stimulate positive reactions and demonstrate how a product might satisfy consumers' desires, or persuade potential consumers to engage in behaviors like purchasing a new product, or referring others to consider a specific product over its competitors.

Besides marketers, product comprehension is also important to quality and safety regulators who seek to improve consumer understanding of potential risks and benefits associated with product use. Agencies in the United States like the Consumer Product Safety Commission (CPSC), the Department of Agriculture (USDA), and the Food and Drug Administration (FDA) guide policy creation and govern necessary product information needs and labelling criteria to improve comprehension of products and their messages. Often these groups require product sponsors to conduct comprehension studies to ensure that consumers understand risk information and warnings about a product and to identify areas where such important consumer information can be presented more simply and clearly to improve comprehension among literate and low-literate individuals. These

C.L. Cummings (✉)
Wee Kim Wee School of Communication and Information, Nanyang Technological University, Singapore, Singapore
e-mail: ccummings@ntu.edu.sg

© Springer International Publishing AG 2017
G. Emilien et al. (eds.), *Consumer Perception of Product Risks and Benefits*, DOI 10.1007/978-3-319-50530-5_8

agencies provide detailed guidelines to product developers to assist in the development of product risk information, labelling, and mandatory and voluntary instructions for product use.

Still other groups and individuals are motivated to influence product comprehension among potential consumers and may attempt to persuade consumers to view a product negatively or avoid or boycott the use or development of specific products. Anti-product messaging about vaccines and other medical products, genetically modified foods, and products using emerging science applications like nanotechnology and synthetic biology have garnered significant public attention in recent decades and have heavily influenced product comprehension and often miscomprehension, where some consumers come to hold beliefs and attitudes about products that are incongruent to scientific consensus regarding product safety (Scheufele and Lewenstein 2005; Van Eenennaam and Young 2014). Ultimately, consumer products and messages live within a chaotic array of competition for attention and comprehension of a product is likely influenced by motivations of information providers—be them product proponents, opponents or otherwise.

Increased mass media coverage of product quality and safety issues have given rise to increased desires of consumers to have more information about products they consume—this has also corresponded with a similar rise in beliefs that consumers should hold the right to be better informed about choices and safety regarding products (Jacoby and Hoyer 1987). However, it is also established that more information does not equate to better comprehension, especially regarding the potentially hazardous consequences of some product's use (Sjöberg 1999). The increased uncertainty that arises from the influx of information around products leaves consumers with a challenging task to first comprehend products and their messages before they ultimately make decisions about product intentions, purchases, and use.

Although preceded by exposure and attention, comprehension of a product is commonly considered the crux of the product-consumer relationship and is succeeded by consumer motivations, intentions, and purchasing decisions. Comprehension is the baseline from which consumers derive attitudes, make judgments about risks and benefits, and produce intentions to engage or avoid a product or service. The first half of this contribution unpacks the terminology associated with consumer comprehension of products and messages into two distinct approaches where (1) comprehension is equated with knowledge outcomes, and (2) where comprehension is equated with sense-making processes. This foundational section provides historic examples of each approach and details how comprehension has been conceptualized and measured across disciplines. The second half of this contribution details how the process of comprehension is complex and bounded by a variety of factors including (1) communication processes and approaches, (2) information asymmetry and the role of branding and labelling as a comprehension heuristic, (3) individual consumer differences and vulnerable consumer groups, and (4) types of products. Understanding the cognitive and social processes from which consumers comprehend and then make judgments about products and their messages is vital to improving consumer relations both from an industry standpoint, as well as for regulators and communicators who drive initiatives to inform consumers regarding potential benefits and risks of products.

2 Unpacking Product Comprehension

Much of the scholarly work concerning 'consumer product comprehension' is suitably published in the fields of business, advertising, and marketing. However many of the concepts and methods used to understand and measure comprehension are drawn from other fields including psychology, communication, economics, risk analysis, public policy, and governance; leaving consensus of the meaning of 'product comprehension' obfuscated by overlapping terminology across this multidisciplinary landscape. The term 'product comprehension' has maintained a pernicious history over the past century and has been used to signify different meanings to different groups. It is important to formally 'unpack' these ontological differences concerning product comprehension, noting how the term has been used in different ways, so that we can better understand the opportunities and constraints of the distinct conceptions of consumer comprehension.

Foundationally, the term 'comprehension' stems from the Latin *comprehensiō*, comprised of the prefix *com-* meaning 'together' and the verb *prehendō* meaning 'to grasp, or embrace'. The basic linguistic meaning of the term is that comprehension is the ability to understand a phenomenon based through intelligent reasoning and thought. Comprehension is also noted as the process of matching referents or concepts related with a specified target with cognitive representations based on previous knowledge that can be stored as memory (Quillian 1968). From these premises, it is of value to note that at its core, comprehension has been used as verb and noun; process and outcome. This is reflected in its scholarly applications to consumer product comprehension. Comprehension is the process and totality of understanding an individual holds with regards to any particular phenomenon, be it physical or abstract. Concerning products and their messages, comprehension can be thought of as a knowledge outcome stemming from messaging about a product, or as a process of sense-making with regard to a given product. Both of these distinct approaches to product comprehension and messages have been employed across disciplines and are further detailed below.

2.1 Comprehension as Knowledge

The majority of studies, and most early studies of products and message comprehension focused on comprehension from a positivist paradigm approach. This approach asserts that consumers would come to form correct or incorrect memories about products by applying reason and logic while interpreting messages. This positivist perspective equates comprehension to 'correct' knowledge production and recall of that assumed knowledge as a function of memory. This form of comprehension as 'correct knowledge' has been acknowledged as "objective comprehension" (Mick 1992). This *comprehension as knowledge* approach is both simple and intuitive, which has its benefits and limitations.

The *comprehension as knowledge* approach is appealing for various reasons. First, this approach allows for easy conceptualization where comprehension becomes a unidimensional construct that interrogates if consumers could accurately identify and later recall certain elements of a product or message. Second, the measurement of this conceptualization is quite simple as well, amounting to post-product message exposure evaluation in the form of true-false quizzes about the message contents, or interviews that assess if respondents could identify salient features of the product message.

The history of use of the *comprehension as knowledge* approach is far reaching and was the primary form of social scientific research in the field of consumer product comprehension stemming from roots in assessing listening and reading comprehension beginning in the 1930s. Concerning mass media, others have adopted this approach by measuring recall of message claims post-stimulus using television advertisements. Rather than study comprehension of product messages, Jacoby et al. (1980) chose to focus upon "miscomprehension" which they note to be "the evocation of a meaning not contained in or logically derivable from the message" pertaining to television advertisements (p. 32). Specifically they tested for

> the accuracy of memory traces (in the form of meaning structures represented by beliefs and impressions) which our receivers described after exposure to a particular phenomenon. We were note concerned with the receiver's ongoing perception of the communication itself, i.e., or subjects were not asked to describe their mental contents as they viewed a given communication. Rather, what was examined instead was the accuracy of their comprehension of that communication shortly after then had finished attending to it, i.e., we assessed the beliefs they held regarding what the communication said or implied (p. 32).

Miscomprehension was assessed via a six-item true-false quiz "developed to assess the core meanings contained in each communication" (Jacoby and Hoyer 1987, p. 7). The authors note that measuring miscomprehension was likely to be more relevant and pressing for regulatory agencies and consumer activists who hold motivations to improve miscomprehension regarding products and messages, rather than industry who hold other persuasive motivations. A sample quiz reported by Jacoby et al. (1980) is recreated in Table 1 below.

As can be noted from Table 1, such measurement is limited in scope and focuses solely on 'correct' comprehension—there is no major distinction between counting the number of 'correct' responses of a true-false quiz given by a consumer than alternatively counting the number of 'incorrect' responses. The choice to highlight 'misconception' over 'correct' conception is a measurement of the same variable and remains little more than rhetorical flourish.

While the positivist *comprehension as knowledge* approach has had a long history of use, it has also been criticized for its conceptualization of comprehension and measurement. Conceptually, this approach disregards consumer-based

Table 1 Example sample quiz

	True-False questions	True	False
1.	The technician in this scene is analyzing a new sound effects record.	[ ]	[ ]
2.	Charlie's Angles figure the call came from long distance.	[ ]	[ ]
3.	The technician in the scene is telling Charlie's Angels which airline is best to fly.	[ ]	[ ]
4.	According to the airport noises, the commuter flight terminal is near the International Terminal.	[ ]	[ ]
5.	The technician decided that the sounds came from outside the airport, near the Terminals.	[ ]	[ ]
6.	The technician says the sounds are from the San Francisco Airport.	[ ]	[ ]

meaning of a product or message, and instead focuses solely on the saliency of message characteristics as determined by the researcher. In this sense, this approach only conceptualizes the consumer's ability to adequately distil prespecified facts or meanings from a message *as intended by the message creator or researcher*. This discounts all potentially-relevant and salient knowledge and meaning that may be created and reported by the consumer, but is not accounted for by the researcher's conceptualization and measurement of their decided-upon 'correct' responses. This approach also is likely to be confounded by memory effects including memory retention and retrieval in their comprehension assessment (Mick 1992).

2.2 Comprehension as Sense-Making

Others have adopted an approach toward product comprehension that originates from a constructivist or hermeneutic paradigm where comprehension equates to consumer experience in sense-making and inference processing when exposed to a product or message. The key determinant in the constructivist approach is that it relies on the consumer's view of the product in question without predetermining what 'correct' comprehension means, and instead focuses on consumer experience in assessing how consumers come to understand a product or message. This constructivist *comprehension as sense-making* approach has been less frequently applied to the field of consumer perceptions and behavior than the positivist approach but has garnered greater attraction and use in recent years.

The consumer *comprehension as sense-making* approach originates from the work of Herbert Krugman (1965) who noted that people experienced mass media in distinct ways. Specifically he notes there are:

> two entirely different ways of experiencing and influenced by mass media. One way is characterized by lack of personal involvement... The second is characterized by a high degree of personal involvement. By this we do not mean attention, interest, or excitement but the number of conscious "bridging experiences," connections, or personal references per minute that the viewer makes between his own life and the stimulus (p. 355).

Krugman's seminal conceptualization that some people had "bridging experiences, connections, or personal references" noted that people rely on memory and come to make sense of stimuli through cognitive elaboration and instantiation of new meanings of how stimuli fit with their current state of being or experience.

Greenwald (1968) adopted Krugman's sense-making approach and including it into his theorization of product comprehension that focused on consumer-generated meanings rather than rote memory recall of 'correct' knowledge about a product. In a subsequent study Greenwald and Leavitt (1984) examined the role of audience involvement in advertising. Here they conceptualize comprehension as a level of involvement that includes "syntactic analysis" which "analyzes speech or text by constructing a propositional representation of it" and precedes further elaboration, inference-making, or integration of message contents with existing conceptual knowledge (p. 854). Their conceptualization of message comprehension follows from Krugman's (1965) examination of low versus high involvement within their larger elaborative framework outlining peripheral and central routes to persuasion. Greenwall and Leavitt note that "the comprehension level requires symbolic word codes for construction of propositional representations" and precedes conceptual analysis (p. 587).

Celsi and Olson (1988) examined the role of involvement in attention and comprehension processes. In their study they adopt Greenwald and Leavitt's (1984) framework that separates comprehension from elaboration, and they conducted an experiment to test effects of intrinsic and situational sources of personal relevance on attention and comprehension processes. Their findings are much less influential for this contribution than their operationalization of comprehension where the note, "after viewing the pair of ads in each product category, subjects were told to write the thoughts they had while processing each ad. We considered the total number of thoughts in each subject's cognitive response protocol as a measure of comprehension effort exerted during ad processing" (p. 217). This quantitative measure equates comprehension to perceptual elaborations, or the number of thoughts an individual has about a product. This is a significant departure from the positivist approach that assessing if respondents accessed memory functions to recall any assumed 'correct' knowledge about the product and instead defines comprehension as cognitive elaboration, or inference-making that occurs as consumers consider a product or message.

This comprehension as inference conceptualization has been further explicated by Graeff and Olson (1994) and Graeff (1995) who argue that the positivist approach of product comprehension "is independent of context and situational factors" (p. 29) and that product comprehension involves assimilating product-related information from external sources and "supplementing given information with inferences so that the product information fits with our existing knowledge, makes sense, and has a coherent meaning" (p.30).

This constructive *comprehension as sense-making* process resituates the locus of "meaning" from residing in the product message itself or of researcher derived 'correct' meaning, to residing in the consumer's cognitive evaluation of the product message. This approach helps to explain how individuals can form different

Fig. 1 Depiction of means-end chain theory

meanings about the same product message as consumers vary in their experiences and perceptual filters to the degree that each consumer likely forms a personal interpretation of a product that is "correct" to them but potentially quite distinct from other consumers (Graeff 1995, p. 30).

The *comprehension as sense-making* process has been incorporated into larger approaches including the Means-End Chain (MEC) approach to note how individuals assess product attributes, their functional and psychological consequences, and make value-based judgments upon this chain prior to ultimate intention to engage or avoid a product or service (Olson and Reynolds 2001). Figure 1 below depicts the MEC:

Measurement of the *comprehension as sense-making* approach is much more challenging than for the positivist approach. Rather than simple post-stimulus measures as witnessed in the previous section, assessing how consumers come to make sense of a product or message is more involved and most often has been undertaken using qualitative methods including in-depth surveys, focus groups, and ethnographies, although some quantitative experiments have been conducted as well (Graeff 1997).

Most scholars using this constructivist *comprehension as sense-making* approach have relied on qualitative laddering interview techniques to prompt consumers to respond to a series of semi-structured questions designed to elicit opportunities for researchers to better assess how consumers come to comprehend a product or message. The typical laddering interview is comprised of two processes, (1) the researcher must first seek to identify primary criteria that consumers may employ when considering a potential product among a set of alternatives, and (2) the researcher should seek to learn why these consumer-derived criteria are salient and meaningful to the consumer. To do so, most laddering interviews ask a series of "why" questions that probe the consumer to seek out higher-order, abstract reasons for why certain salient features of a product or message were considered important for consumer judgments. Laddering techniques urge consumers to consider how product attributes (A) are linked to more abstract consequences (C) of product use, which in turn are associated with core values (V) the consumer holds. For instance when considering the anti-lock braking system of a new car, a consumer may note the consequence of this product attribute to be an increase in safety compared to alternative cars without anti-lock braking systems, and thus may comprehend that this car is superior because they hold beliefs and values that safety

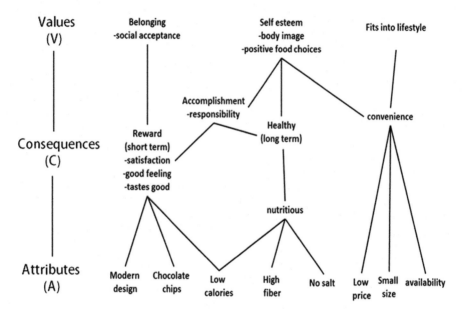

Fig. 2 Hierarchical laddering depiction of granola bars

is of primary importance with their choice of car as they want to protect their own lives and those who may also ride in the car.

Assessing consumer responses from laddering techniques often appear as scaffolded hierarchical value maps that follow the A-C-V format and move from baseline product attributes (A) to consequences (C), that represent abstract values (V). Figure 2 below depicts a hypothetical hierarchical values map for granola bars where the base is comprised of identified product attributes (A) that correspond to higher-order consequences (C), which ultimately represent values identified by the potential consumer (V).

Many versions of MEC and A-C-V laddering techniques have been adopted that employ qualitative forms of inquiry. While they have been lauded in their ability to assess a greater breadth and depth of consumer sense-making of products, they also hold particular limitations. One of the most pressing limitations is that such exercises produce forced exposure to product messaging and then continually seek further elaboration from the consumer being evaluated. As Hoeffler (2003) notes, it is "always a concern when people have been guided to think about products in ways they would not during the product adoption decision. Careful evaluation of a product concept can change consumers' preferences and perceptions" (p. 419). Qualitative techniques like these may be more prone to produce social desirability biases among consumers who may report a greater tendency to respond to researchers in ways they believe will be desired by the research rather than reflect their true feelings and perceptions (Paulhus 1991).

In sum, comprehension of products and messages has been approached from two distinct perspectives; *comprehension as knowledge* and *comprehension as sense-*

making. The former posits that comprehension is an outcome of cognitive processing and recall of specified salient product attributes, while the latter contests that comprehension is an evolving process of inference-making that is not bounded to recall of 'correct' product features. As the field of product comprehension moves forward it is important to note these distinct ontological differences as each perspective provides its own opportunities and constraints to evaluating how members of the public come to comprehend products and their messages. Key determinants of communication and cognition, as well as major challenges should be well defined and understood by researchers and practitioners regardless whether studying comprehension as knowledge, or comprehension as sense-making. The latter half of this contribution introduces the reader to some of the challenges and opportunities of comprehending products and messages.

3 Communicating About Products: Processes and Approaches

In order for a consumer to comprehend a product or message, there must first be some initial sense of the product's existence. Comprehension is predicated by message exposure and attention. Without a primary form of sensorial experience, there is no basis for a consumer to further comprehend of a product or message. The tradition of advertising has relied heavily on a linear model of communication for depicting how consumers come to experience a product through targeted advertising messages. In this model, a message sender (often a marketer) encodes messages made up of symbols that carry intended meanings, and transmits those messages through various media to message receivers (consumers) who decode the symbolic message and thusly comprehend the product to some degree or another. The linear model of communication highlights the dual functions of message creator encoding, and receiver-based decoding, which can be muddled by message characteristics and noise.

Each message has various characteristics that both provide opportunities for comprehension, and constrain understanding and sense-making. Messages are bound by the physical limits within which a message receiver tangibly experiences a message. Physical characteristics can include message intensity, volume, color, numbers, and any other physically delimiting factor that influences the *in situ* environment of message exposure and attention. Other characteristics, like the simplicity or complexity of message contents, the credibility and trustworthiness of the perceived message source, and congruity of the message with pre-existing perceptions all can influence ultimate message comprehension.

Another constraint to comprehension is noise; the distortion of intended messages between senders and receivers. Noise can come in four main forms along the linear pathway from message instantiation of the message sender through the decoding process of the message receiver. First, noise can be semantic in nature,

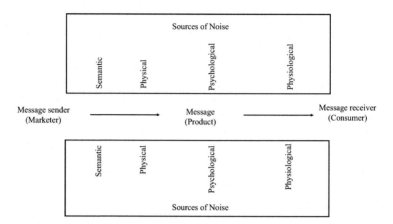

Fig. 3 The linear model of consumer communication

where the symbolic use of language chosen by the sender may not suitable for decoding by the receiver. Second, noise can come in the form of physical, external influence on message reception. This is commonly seen when targeted product messages are physically limited by the scope, market space, and competing messages within which they attempt to reach consumers. A third form of noise, psychological noise, refers to the consumers' values predispositions, prejudices, moods and transient affective states, and biases that influence the message decoding process. The fourth form of noise is physiological noise, which refers to the human biological influences on message processing, for instance message attention and decoding processes are likely to be influenced by illness, fatigue and the like. The linear model which has dominated much of the last 75 years of advertising theory is depicted below, however, within the communication discipline such linear models are notably dated and have been mostly abandoned for more modern transactional and dynamic models that are becoming more widely accepted across disciplines (Fig. 3).

The linear model typifies a person as either only sender or receiver. This holds true for many product messaging initiatives in the forms of advertisements, product warnings, and the like, but this model does not account for all forms of product messaging. Consumers experience products often through targeted- and non-targeted messages. In the linear model, meaning is transmitted from marketer to consumer, without the consumer providing any messaging themselves (except in the form of purchasing). However, many consumers today have direct communication with product creators and engage in ongoing dialogues about products. Also many consumers have turned to peer-to-peer communication to make-sense of products and to better comprehend them together (Jarvis 1998). Such messages are often seen as product reviews, testimonials, and ratings that are not created by marketers or quality and safety regulators, but are from other potential consumers who have shared experiences (Huang et al. 2014). Given these larger

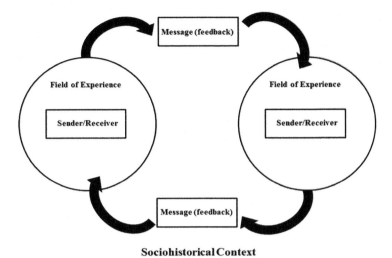

Fig. 4 Barnlund's transactional model of communication

communicative arenas, an expanded view of communication itself helps to improve upon the shortcomings of the linear model of communication that has dominated the field of product advertising and influenced how product comprehension has been defined and measured.

Barnlund's (2008) transactional model of communication shifts focus toward creating shared meaning through simultaneous sending and receiving of symbolic messages. Communicators gain greater comprehension through messaging and feedback as each party continually encodes and decodes messages. Unlike the linear model, this model notes that both parties are responsible for the effectiveness of communication and can influence the comprehension process for themselves and others. Further, this model incorporates past experience and the larger sociohistorical context as an important factor in creating greater shared understanding. One message builds upon previous messages and there is interdependency between communicators who negotiate a shared field of experience regarding the product or message (Fig. 4).

Barnlund's model is likely to be more reflective of the role of digital and social media in the consumer comprehension process. This model provides a greater sense of the role of sociohistorical context as a primary factor in decision-making, which has been often described as significantly influential in product decision making, and a primary concern for product comprehension is the larger context of alternative choices consumers have in the market.

It is also of value to note that consumers also are not always acting on individual bases. Consumers may take the form of groups, organizations, and even institutions that make purchasing decisions collectively, or at the call of decision-makers, for instance company accounts, sales personnel, or agency leaders. Consumers of all types can engage in communicating about products and have the power to influence other consumers.

To date, consumers have unprecedented access to product information in various forms and from various sources ranging from marketers, to quality and safety regulators, to peers. This evolution in communication media about products poses new opportunities for consumers to consciously seek out greater amounts of information as they make sense of products and messages. However this abundance of information can also become overwhelming and may produce biases that stem from heuristic processes in sense-making. Heuristics are mental shortcuts that function to ease cognitive load and simplify comprehension and decision-making processes. In a recent experiment, Aljukhadar et al. (2010) noted that as information load increased among consumers, they were more likely to employ heuristics and default to basic recommendations from others when confronted with larger amounts of information about a consumer product. While there are many forms of heuristics, the next section will examine the role of branding and labelling as heuristic cues that may spur comprehension and decision-making within the asymmetric information context consumers face when trying to comprehend products.

4   Information Asymmetry—Brands and Labelling

The principle of information asymmetry assumes that at least one party within any communication environment holds less pertinent and relevant information than others, which may leave that party susceptible to making judgments without the resources to consider all relevant information. This is especially true of consumers who often hold little information when exposed to products and messages and then must attempt to comprehend and make decisions about products. In today's markets, there may be a great deal of product information, both promotionally as well as pertaining to quality and safety, but the majority of consumers are on the receiving end of very little of such information and they ultimately make product choices based upon this dearth of information.

Within this information asymmetric context, many consumers default to product cues in the forms of brands in order to better comprehend a product. Product brands are symbolic messages aimed to distinguish one product from another while conveying salient concepts from which consumers can derive greater comprehension of the what the product is, what it means to the consumer, and its value. In this sense, branding serves a heuristic function that influences consumers' process of comprehension under low information contexts. Van Dam and van Trijp (2007) note that consumers

> associate brand names to facts, thoughts, feelings, perceptions, images, and experiences. Associations also combine the brand to various usage situations. Brands may also signal social dimensions of the product, as brand awareness implies that the brand has a reputation within the consumer's social network or within society as a whole. Through its various associations, brand name awareness may render the particular brand salient in the face of a

consumer decision problem. This means that brands come to mind at the very moment of product choice and that they are more likely to feature in the consumer's consideration set, out of which a final product choice is being made (p. 156).

In terms of comprehension, brands serve as potentially salient product attributes that may spur sense-making processes regarding consumer's perceptions of the value and quality of the product. Brand awareness is likely to also guide information processing through vicarious learning, where brands with increased awareness may serve as a heuristic cue and be comprehended as more socially valuable or intrinsically better. Brands are also likely to serve a vital function in comprehension situations where consumers have high information asymmetry (hold low knowledge) and are confronted with high variability of product choices. Under such decisions, brands with higher awareness or familiarity are likely to be comprehended more favorably than other similar products, as has been demonstrated in taste studies where consumers are asked to rate brands on taste alone, yet those with greater brand awareness trump other products in purchasing intentions (Hoyer and Brown 1990). Indeed, as consumers make-sense of what a product is and its value, a successful brand becomes a touchstone with which consumers perceive unique and sustainable added values over other similar products and are more likely to feel that the product aligns to their needs.

While certainly similar to brands in many aspects, product labels, and product packaging serve a different role for products. Labels name products and define specific product attributes, while packaging providing tangible cues from which the consumer experiences products and messages. Labels are often affixed to product packages themselves. Product packaging serves as an important signboard that influences the physical experience a potential consumer has with the product and message. However, labels may not be limited to direct product packaging placement, but can also exist as spoken or visual information about a product. Unlike brands, labels typically describe objective product attributes including country or region of origin or manufacture of the product, use, shelf-life, or other criteria that may be either voluntarily labelled or be mandated by quality and safety governing agencies (van Dam and van Trijp 2007).

Quality labels are often governed by certification organizations or governmental agencies, and some quality labels incur extra costs to the producer, which in turn may be passed on to consumers at higher market pricing. Quality labels also simplify comprehension processes by pre-evaluating the value of a product and serving as a quick information source from which consumers can come to understand a product's worth and fit. However, like all information, comprehending brands and labels can be challenging for many consumers and labels are often miscomprehended, or go unnoticed or unused by consumers as they process information.

5 Special Subgroups

It should come as no surprise that consumers vary in their ability to comprehend products and their messages, and some consumer groups are more vulnerable to the persuasive qualities of product messages than others. Consumer may become vulnerable because of "uncontrollable conditions related to physical, cognitive, motivational or social characteristics" (Bonifield and Cole 2007, p. 430). Two age groups are identified as holding lower comprehension capabilities than the typical consumer, older adults and children.

5.1 Older Adults

Older adults are a growing population around the world and are a market segment that will be increasingly targeted with product messages. This group is more likely to be vulnerable to certain product messages when their previous knowledge and experience does not fully compensate for declines in cognitive abilities associated with increased aging (Bonifield and Cole 2007). Older adults face significant deficits concerning memory recall of product messages, regarded above in the *comprehension as knowledge* domain. Older adults recall less than their younger counterparts when it comes to rational persuasive messages and knowledge-based appeals for products. This decline of cognitive ability is especially pronounced as people transition from become young-old adults (65–74) middle-old (75–84) and old-old adults (over 85 years of age) where linear declines in fluency, memory, and perceptual speed are commonly observed. Repetition of product messages improves recall of product claims among older adults, but also can dissuade younger segments (Singh and Cole 1993). Interestingly for older adults, repetition of a product claim as false improved recall that the claim was false in the short term, but later made this vulnerable group more likely to remember the product claim as true following a three day delay (Skurnik et al. 2005). This switch from comprehending the claim as false in the short term, but miscomprehending the claim in a longer-term was not observed among younger demographics. Older adults have lower working memory function and often have difficulty in comprehending complex or similar information. Older consumers proved less capable of making good nutritional choices as compared to their younger counterparts, even when encouraged to focus on particularly relevant information. It has also been identified that older adults are more likely to use heuristic information processes to comprehend product messages and thus may be less likely to base decisions out of deliberative processes (Hess et al. 2001).

5.2   Children

Like many older adults, children hold lower cognitive abilities to comprehend products and messages, yet they are also directly targeted by many product messages. The average child is exposed to over 20,000 product advertisements annually in the United States. As children grow, so too does their ability to encode and decode messages and to accurately form memories and recall product message features. Very young children have difficulty comprehending the difference between television programming and advertising. By age 5, roughly half of children are able to correctly comprehend the difference between advertisements and programs. This jumps to above 60% around age 10, and is near 100% among adults.

Also, most children under the age of 8 are unable to comprehend the persuasive intention of product messaging, and this too increases as children develop, where by age 9 roughly 90% of children understood that television product advertisements held persuasive intentions. Internet-based product message comprehension is less understood among children, although younger generations are more readily using such media to greater extents than their older counterparts. Morrison (2004) noted that children aged 9–11 had little understanding of the persuasive nature of product websites and the children primarily viewed the websites as informative rather than commercial in nature.

5.3   Safeguarding Special Groups

In order to safeguard vulnerable populations, some groups and individuals have called for greater ethical considerations and legislation regarding product message exposure. Nwachukwu et al. (1997) discuss the need for establishing an ethical premise of consumer sovereignty when it comes to assessing how vulnerable consumer groups comprehend products and their messages. While the basis for consumer sovereignty notes that knowledgeable, critical consumers with adequate resources are mostly autonomous and freely base decisions out of individual need, there are other groups who may not be able to easily comprehend product messaging and are more susceptible to making decisions based out of unethical persuasive claims from others (Drumwright 2007).

In order to assess consumer sovereignty, Smith (1993) promotes a three dimensional test. First, the cognitive capabilities of the consumer should be assessed. For example, Walsh and Mitchell (2005) found that certain consumer clusters who were older and of lower educational attainment were less able to comprehend product differences among similar products, thus leaving this group more vulnerable to "mistaken and misinformed purchases" (p. 140). Second, the availability and quality of product information should be evaluated to ensure that consumers are not forced into overly asymmetric information deficits where comprehension and decision-making is based from little information. Third, Smith advocates for determining if consumers have opportunity to make informed choices about alternate products, and that tests should involve "switching costs" from one product to another (p. 30).

Besides advocating for increasing sovereignty among these groups, some groups and agencies have made strides to limit advertising initiatives that target children and older adults. In the 1970s, the United States Federal Trade Commission (FTC) favored banning of all television advertisements to children under the age of 8 as they do not yet hold the mental faculties to adequately comprehend the differences between programming and product advertisements, however the proposal was defeated on the backs of strong arguments that such legislation would infringe upon the rights of advertisers to free speech under the First Amendment. Later the US Congress would pass the Children's Television Act in 1990 that limited the amount of commercial airtime to 12 minutes per hour on weekdays and 10.5 minutes per hour on weekends. More recently in 2006, the FCC has also introduced rulings that websites being referenced during children's programming must adhere to specific criteria and must contain non-commercial related content that is clearly divided from commercial portions of product websites.

Older adults have been the targets of unethical telemarketing activities—an activity that has been estimated to cost roughly $40 billion in fraudulent sales annually. One survey found that 56% of telemarketing fraud victims were 50 years of age or older, and that upward of 10% of all telemarketing firms in the United States may be fraudulent (Aziz et al. 2000). In 1997, the National Fraud Information Center reported three to four reports per hour of older adult fraud victims whose average total losses were around $5000 (Elder Fraud Task Force 1997). Although there are no directly limiting legislations pertaining to advertisements targeting older adults, initiatives have been taken to diminish the miscomprehension of fraudulent advertisers among this group in the US. In 2003, the FTC established the National Do Not Call Registry which prohibited commercial telemarketers from calling potential consumers who had opted-out of the call system. Other agencies have helped to provide greater consumer knowledge and programming for older adults to make informed decisions about products and messages. The Financial Fraud Enforcement Task Force (FFETF) provides many resources aimed at improving the comprehension and recall of potentially fraudulent advertisers among older adults.

6 Product Types

Comprehension of products and their messages vary also by the type of product under evaluation by consumers. Many consumer protection laws have been created to ensure that consumers' rights and safety are maintained, and that consumers maintain a right to be informed about products, which in turn is thought to stimulate greater comprehension of products, their messages, and consequences.

In the US most products fall under the jurisdiction of the CPSC with some exceptions. Agricultural and food products are governed by the USDA, medical devices and medicines by the FDA, automobiles by the National Highway Traffic Safety Administration, and rightly alcohol, tobacco, firearms, and explosives are overseen by the Bureau of Alcohol, Tobacco, Firearms, and Explosives (ATF). This section details two distinct product classes that have been investigated regarding their comprehension: food products and nutrition labels, as well as medical devices, products, and drugs.

6.1 Food Products and Nutrition Labels

Food is the staple product and a great deal of research has been conducted to evaluate the role of nutrition labelling on consumer comprehension of food products. Nutrition labels have been mandated for use following the Nutrition Labeling and Education Act of 1990 that gives the FDA authority to regulate labelling of most food products and ensure that nutritional content claims (e.g. "low fat") ascribe to FDA regulations.

While nutrition labels have been added to many food products to help improve consumer comprehension of the nutritional value of foods, studies have demonstrated that consumers pay little attention to the labels, often lack the ability to correctly interpret them, and are more likely to use heuristics based on branding and product appearance than on cognitive evaluations of the nutritional aspects of food products (Graham and Mohr 2014). Some initiatives, like the use of summary information (e.g. average or range information) along with numerical nutrition data regulated for use within the nutrition label improves correct comprehension of nutrition label information, but this improvement is diminished when multiple competing brands are portrayed (Viswanathan 1994). Sinclair et al. (2013) evaluated if consumers could correctly estimate the calorie content of a food product based upon nutrition label information and found that participants of lower education, lower income, and above 64 years of age were significantly less likely to correctly comprehend the number of calories in portrayed food products. The researchers also noted that consumers of higher education, higher income, and white ethnicity were significantly more likely to correctly comprehend the percent daily value of nutritional aspects of the food products as given by the nutrition label.

Besides the FDA, the USDA's Agricultural Marketing Service (AMS) oversees programs for standardization, grading, and marketing news of agricultural products across five domains including cotton and tobacco, dairy, fruits and vegetables, livestock and seed, and poultry. The AMS National Organic Program (NOP) also oversees labelling standards for organic agricultural products and is the accrediting agency that inspects and certifies the production and handling procedures necessary for USDA certification standards.

6.2   Medical Devices, Products, and Drugs

Older adults consume significantly more prescription and non-prescription medicines than other subgroups, yet this group is known to have greater difficulties comprehending product messages including medical instructions for use that if not comprehended correctly could have severe consequences and even result in death (Park et al. 1992). Comprehension of medical product use can be increased by pairing written instructions with verbal consultations and that face-to-face communication from a health care provider that directs attention to particular aspects of medical product use (e.g. how often to take a prescription pill) improves consumer comprehension and recall of salient product features and uses (De Tullio et al. 1986).

Wolf et al. (2010) evaluated the use of "enhanced print" on prescription drug warning labels and found that the addition of uses of icons was useful in conveying meaning to lower literate adults while simple and explicit language use increased correct consumer comprehension of the desired understand of the product warning. For example, rather than saying the standard line used on many warning labels, "For external use only," the simpler diction "use only on your skin" increased correct comprehension that the product was not intended for internal consumption.

The FDA oversees medical product messaging and provides guidance for industry to provide detailed descriptive, operating, and troubleshooting information for consumers and lay caregivers, as well as additional information through product messages across a variety of labelling formats including patient brochures, leaflets, user manuals, and videotapes that are intended to be supplied to and used by consumers with or without additional professional guidance. The FDA notes that such materials should include risk/benefit information as well as instructions for proper product use.

7   Summary

Consumer comprehension begins with exposure and attention to products and their messages. As detailed in this contribution, comprehension has been used to conceptualize correct and incorrect knowledge outcomes and recall of product features like label information and warnings, or particular salient features of a product message. Comprehension has also been used to conceptualize the sense-making process enacted by consumers when they are exposed to a product or message. This perspective highlights the asymmetric context consumers face along with adaptive inference-processes through which consumers solidify what a product means to them individually, which may be different from how marketers and regulators would envision them comprehending a particular product, its attributes, or consequences. Both perspectives are valuable for quality and safety regulators who seek to improve evaluation of the influences that messages have on providing crucial information to consumers that influences how they come to comprehend a product. Evolving communication technologies provide greater opportunities for consumers to access product information, although this appears to only be of use of more literate segments of today's population. This parallels evolutions in communication models that help to explain the larger sociohistorical context in which product messaging exists and is accessed. Safeguards to protect more vulnerable consumer groups should continue to evolve as well in to improve comprehension among the increasing population of older adults while limiting potentially unethical product messaging to children. Understanding that product types like food and medical products also face significant challenges highlights a greater need to continue to develop the field of consumer comprehension studies in order to maximize the efficacy of consumers to comprehend warnings and nutrition information that can have significant impact on human health.

References

Aljukhadar, M. Senecal, S., & Daoust, C. (2010, September 30). *Information overload and usage of recommendations*. Paper presented at the ACM RecSys Workshop on User-Centric Evaluation of Recommender Systems and Their Interfaces (UCERSTI), Barcelona, Spain.

Aziz, S.J., Bolick, D.C., Kleinman, M.T., & Shadel, D.P. (2000). The National telemarketing victim call center: Combating telemarketing fraud in the United States. *Journal of Elder Abuse and Neglect, 12*(2), 93–98

Barnlund, D. C. (2008). A transactional model of communication. In C. D. Mortensen (Ed.), *Communication theory* (2nd ed., pp. 47–57). New Brunswick: Transaction.

Bonifield, C., & Cole, C. (2007). Advertising to vulnerable segments. In G. Tellis & T. Ambler (Eds.), *The Sage handbook of advertising* (pp. 430–444). Thousand Oaks, CA: Sage.

Celsi, R. L., & Olson, J. (1988). The role of involvement in attention and comprehension processes. *Journal of Consumer Research, 15*, 210–224.

De Tullio, P., et al. (1986). Patient medication instruction and provider interactions: Effects on knowledge and attitudes. *Health Education Quarterly, 13*(1), 51–60.

Drumwright, M. (2007). Advertising ethics: A multi-level theory approach. In G. Tellis & T. Ambler (Eds.), *The Sage handbook of advertising* (pp. 399–415). Thousand Oaks, CA: Sage.

Elder Fraud Task Force. (1997). *Report of the New Jersey Division of Consumer Affairs*. Dept. of Law and Public Safety, Office of the Attorney-General, New Jersey, USA.

Graeff, T. R. (1995). Product comprehension and promotional strategies. *Journal of Consumer Marketing, 12*(2), 28–39.

Graeff, T. R. (1997). Comprehending product attributes and benefits: The role of product knowledge and means-end chain inferences. *Psychology and Marketing, 14*, 163–183.

Graeff, T. R., & Olson, J. C. (1994). Consumer inference as part of product comprehension. In C. Allen & D. Roedder (Eds.), *Advances in consumer research* (pp. 201–207). Provo, UT: Association for Consumer Research.

Graham, D. J., & Mohr, G. S. (2014). When zero is greater than one: Consumer misinterpretations of nutrition labels. *Health Psychology, 33*(12), 1579–1587.

Greenwald, A. G. (1968). Cognitive learning, cognitive response to persuasion, and attitude change. In A. G. Greenwald et al. (Eds.), *Psychological foundations of attitudes* (pp. 147–169). New York: Academic Press.

Greewald, A. G., & Leavitt, C. (1984). Audience involvement in advertising: Four levels. *Journal of Consumer Research, 11*, 581–592.

Hess, T. M., et al. (2001). Motivation and representational processes in adulthood: The effects of social accountability and information relevance. *Psychology and Aging, 16*, 629–642.

Hoeffler, S. (2003). Measuring preferences for really new products. *Journal of Marketing Research, 40*(4), 406–420.

Hoyer, W., & Brown, S. (1990). Effects of brand awareness on choice for a common, repeat purchase product. *Journal of Consumer Research, 17*(2), 141–148.

Huang, L. Q., et al. (2014). Comprehension and assessment of product reviews: A review-product congruity proposition. *Journal of Management Information Systems, 30*(3), 311–343.

Jacoby, J., & Hoyer, W. (1987). *The comprehension and miscomprehension of print communications*. New York: The Advertising Education Foundation.

Jacoby, J., et al. (1980). *The miscomprehension of televised communication*. New York: American Association of Advertising Agencies.

Jarvis, C. (1998). An exploratory investigation of consumers' evaluations of external information sources in prepurchase search. *Advances in Consumer Research, 25*, 446–452.

Krugman, H. (1965). The impact of television advertising: Learning without involvement. *The Public Opinion Quarterly, 29*(3), 349–356.

Mick, D. G. (1992). Levels of subjective comprehension in advertising processing and their relations to ad perceptions, attitudes, and memory. *Journal of Consumer Research, 18*(4), 411–424.

Morrison, K. L. (2004). Children reading commercial messages on the Internet: Web Sites that merge education, information, entertainment, and advertising. *Dissertation Abstracts International, Section A: Humanities and Social Sciences, 64*(11A), 3957.

Nwachukwu, S. L. S., et al. (1997). Ethics and social responsibility in marketing: An examination of the ethical evaluation of advertising strategies. *Journal of Business Research, 39*, 107–118.

Olson, J. C., & Reynolds, T. J. (2001). The means-end approach to understanding consumer decision making. In J. C. Olson & T. J. Reynolds (Eds.), *Understanding consumer decision making: The means-end approach to marketing and advertising strategy* (pp. 3–20). Mahwah, NJ: Erlbaum.

Park, D., Morrell, R., Frieske, D., & Kincaid, D. (1992). Medication adherence behaviors in older adults: Effects of external cognitive supports. *Psychology and Aging, 7*, 252–256.

Paulhus, D. L. (1991). Measurement and control of response biases. In J. P. Robinson et al. (Eds.), *Measures of personality and social psychological attitudes*. San Diego: Academic Press.

Quillian, M. R. (1968). Semantic memory. In M. Minsky (Ed.), *Semantic information processing*. Cambridge, MA: MIT.

Scheufele, D., & Lewenstein, B. (2005). The public and nanotechnology: How citizens make sense of emerging technologies. *Journal of Nanoparticle Research, 7*, 659–667.

Sinclair, S., Hammond, D., & Goodman, S. (2013). Sociodemographic differences in the comprehension of nutrition labels on food products. *Journal of Nutrition Education and Behavior, 45*(6), 767–772.

Singh, S., & Cole, C. (1993). The effects of length, content, and repetition on television commercial effectiveness. *Journal of Marketing Research, 30*(1), 91–105.

Sjöberg, L. (1999). Risk perception by the public and by experts: A dilemma in risk management. *Research Human Ecology, 6*(2), 1–9.

Skurnik, I., et al. (2005). How warnings about false claims become recommendations. *Journal of Consumer Research, 31*, 713–724.

Smith, N. C. (1993). Ethics and the marketing manager. In N. C. Smith, J. A. Quelch, & D. Richard (Eds.), *Ethics in marketing*. Homewood, IL: Irwin.

van Dam, Y., & Trijp, H. (2007). Branding and labelling of food products. In L. Frewer & H. van Trijp (Eds.), *Understanding consumers of food products*. New York: CRC Press.

Van Eenennaam, A. L., & Young, A. E. (2014). Invited review: Prevalence and impacts of genetically engineered feedstuffs on livestock populations. *Journal of Animal Science, 92*, 4255–4278.

Viswanathan, M. (1994). The influence of summary information on the usage of nutrition information. *Journal of Public Policy & Marketing, 13*, 48–60.

Walsh, G., & Mitchell, V. (2005). Consumer vulnerability to perceived product similarity problems: Scale development and identification. *Journal of Macromarketing, 25*(2), 140–152.

Wolf, M., Davis, T., Bass, P., Curtis, L., Lindquist, L., Webb, J., Bocchini, M., Bailey, S., & Parker, R. (2010). Improving prescription drug warnings to promote patient comprehension. *Archives of Internal Medicine, 170*(1), 50–56.

Perception of Product Risks

Arnout R.H. Fischer

1 Introduction

By the end of the 1960s it had become clear that the public often perceives risks and benefits considerably different from experts. This implies that an expert view on risk does not suffice for understanding risk perceptions of the public. Consumers are often seen as non-rational decision makers by experts. If it is, however, taken into account that a logical weighing of arguments requires substantial topical knowledge, mental resources, attention, and motivation it can be understood why consumers do not always follow the argumentation of experts. In addition, experts tend to appraise risks within a fairly narrowly defined quantified definition of risk, that does not allow for many ethical or social deliberations, that may be central to consumers perceptions of risks (Gupta et al. 2015).

Following the realization that consumer risk perception consistently deviates from that of experts, a considerable amount of research into consumer or lay perceptions of risk developed. The research of risk perception was developed across several domains from the 1970s onwards. Different traditions of risk perception research look at how the public responds to risks in society they have little control over. Throughout these research agendas there tended to be a twofold aim, first of all to understand the regularities in where consumer risk perception deviates from expert assessments, and secondly to figure out how consumer and expert assessments could better be aligned (Hansen et al. 2003). The research of risk perception has also investigated what properties in products increase perceived risks. For responsible business practice it is important that consumer make informed choices about which products and service they choose to purchase. Good understanding of

A.R.H. Fischer (✉)
Wageningen University, Marketing and Consumer Behaviour Group, Hollandseweg 1, 6706, KN, Wageningen, The Netherlands
e-mail: arnout.fischer@wur.nl

consumer risk perception can support producers in selecting the information that is relevant to consumers to inform themselves, and present this information in such a way that consumers are best helped in evaluating risks in a way that is relevant to their decision.

2   Risk Perception Models

2.1   Unrealistic Optimism

Generally, people underestimate the risks they run in a large number of health threatening behaviors (Weinstein 1989). In particular it appears that consumers consistently underestimate the risks they take in their personal behavior, while they more or less accurately perceive the risk that a member of the general population takes when exhibiting the same type of behavior (Frewer et al. 1994). There is some evidence that this optimistic bias about perceived health risks to the person depends on the multitude of risky behaviors that did not lead to negative consequences in the past. The subsequent positive feedback loop leads to stable, overly optimistic risk perceptions that are not easily influenced. When people suffer from the negative consequences, by for example falling ill due to improperly prepared food, optimistic bias tends to decrease. This effect is however short-lived and risk perception quickly reverts to original, overly optimistic levels when the subsequent behavior does not lead to additional negative consequences (Parry et al. 2004).

There are several properties that set this type of risk perception apart from other risks. First of all, the risks are immediately related to behavior of the involved individual. This implies there might be the feeling of personal control about the situation. Secondly, these behaviors tend to be repeated behaviors. In many of these behaviors, safeguarding oneself against risk is possible, but it takes effort, again and again every time the behavior is conducted. This makes it very tempting to take short cuts, and find ways to limit effort by skipping risk reducing practices. Once such short cuts work, and no negative consequences are suffered from skipping risk reducing practices, individuals are likely to take the short cut again and again and add another short cut, and another, until they settle at a level where they feel to run justifiable risks (Wilde 1994) which may be much higher than recommended by experts. The combination of having no ill effects of the risky behavior, in combination with the effort involved to avoid risks, every time over again, steers to an equilibrium.

2.2 Psychometric Approach

The psychometric model first applied in the late 1970s shows that in general consumers perceive higher risks if a product or situation is seen as leading to dreadful consequences (Slovic 1987). This dread dimensions is high for situation that contain risks that are fatal, have global impact, whose effects are not fairly distributed, have influence on future generations, are uncontrollable and involuntary. A second dimension that increases perceptions of risks are those risks that are uncertain; i.e. not observable, uncontrollable, new and unknown to science (Slovic 1987). The classification of a long list of applications in this scheme gives an intuitively plausible overview of why some risks (e.g. of nuclear reactors and airplane crashes) are perceived higher than others. The psychometric approach has been applied with some success to specific groups of products, such as foods (Fife-Schaw and Rowe 2000), where similar factors could be found, indicating that risks of fat and sugar tended to be underestimated and those of hormone and pesticide residues overestimated. At an even more detailed level, risk perceptions of nanotechnology applications could be placed in a similar dimensional map (Siegrist et al. 2008).

Through the dimension lack of control and uncertainty, the psychometric approach can explain the generally heightened risk perception related to the introduction of new technologies into society, such as nuclear power plants, the introduction of consumer products such as genetic modification, mobile phones, hydrogen as energy carrier. These topics have in common that individual consumers have little influence about the risk they take, as the placement of nuclear power plants, allowing unlabeled genetically modified foods in the food chain, the placement of base stations of mobiles phones and the introduction of hydrogen in normal traffic are taken at a policy level. Potential negative consequences, do, however, also influence consumers who have not chosen for this option themselves; and in several cases the benefits accrue to stakeholders not immediately close to the risks. Generally, it seems that these risks are perceived higher by the public than by experts, which can be explained in part because the consumer does not perceive control over these risks (cf. Slovic 1987).

While the psychometric paradigm provides an intuitively plausible classification of products in relation to perceived risks and underlying rationale why the risk for a product is perceived as higher or lower, it only explains part of the variation in risk perception observed across the population (Sjöberg 2002).

2.3 Risk Aversion

Another line of research takes the point of view that in all choices there is a level of uncertainty, which invokes the risk of making the wrong choice (Kahneman and Tversky 1979). Initially much of this research investigated to what extent monetary losses are considered in relation to the same gains, and found that in general losses and risks are perceived as larger than the same monetary gains (Kahneman and Tversky 1979). The ideas have later been extended to situations where the risks are not as easily monetarized, with much the same results. This suggests that people in general may be risk, or loss averse when choosing between alternatives. It therefore also seems that in many cases people base their judgment more on limiting the amount of regret and disappointment they expect, (Loomes and Sugden 1987) rather than aligning their choice with the highest possible gain. From an evolutionary point of view this makes sense as in our past many risks could be instantly fatal, so avoiding those at all costs makes sense. The consequence in the current situation is that many people tend to be overly risk averse however (Tversky and Kahneman 1991). In addition this research program also showed discounting of extreme values. That is that linearly increasing monetary gains/losses lead to a gradual reduction in the perceived increase in gains losses, in other words. The difference between 10 and 11 Euros is seen as larger than between 1000 and 1001 Euros.

2.4 Risk Seeking

Besides a general tendency to be risk averse, some people tend to seek risks (Weber and Milliman 1997). Two types of risk seeking can be distinguished, a first type where people have an uncontrollable, emotional urge to engage in highly stimulating behavior (Zaleskiewicz 2001). Stimulating risk seeking tends to neglect negative consequences and focusses on positive arousal associated with the risky behavior. The decision to engage in such risky behavior is largely impulsive and unconscious. This is the type of risk seeking where individuals go out for thrill seeking experiences, a type of behavior that is exhibited more by adolescents than by either children or adults (Defoe et al. 2015). A second type of risk seeking relates to long term, rational decisions and focusses on avoiding possible losses while gaining most profit. The decision to seek such risk for long term benefit is more instrumental and is more based on rational deliberation compared to the impulsive decision to engage in stimulating risky behaviors (Zaleskiewicz 2001).

2.5 Individual Differences

Another approach to understand differences in risk perception focusses on differences in risk perception between individuals. Individual differences are suggested by some to be more relevant than differences in risk perception related to product or service attributes (Marris et al. 1998). Specific personality traits are known to affect risk perception. People who score high on neophobia, a propensity to dislike new products, tend to perceive the risks of new products and technologies as considerably higher than others. People with a personality trait aimed at risk aversion exhibit lower willingness to take risks (Weber and Milliman 1997). Risk aversion appears fairly strongly related to demographic variables, where females are often shown to be generally more risk averse than men. This translates to risk perception where men tend to perceive lower risks than females, and (at least in countries where the upper class is dominantly white) white people tend to perceive lower risks than non-whites (Marshall et al. 2006). Although the same demographic variables relate to higher risk aversion and higher risk perception, some care with equating risk aversion to risk perception is warranted. Especially in financial risk taking, there is evidence that it is not the risk perception that distinguishes risk averse individuals from individuals more open to risk seeking, but instead the risk attitude; that is the evaluation to what extent and how negatively the perceived risk contributes to the overall evaluation of the decision to be taken (Pennings and Smidts 2000).

2.6 Cultural Cognition

Besides demographic differences in risk aversion and risk perception, it has been proposed that the formation of risk perception depends to a substantial extent on socio-cultural differences between population groups. This goes beyond proposing that specific population groups perceive higher (or lower) risks in the same situation, but argues that there is a difference between cultural population groups in how the same risk information is processed. The cognition of individuals is in part cultural (Kahan et al. 2009). The cultural cognition approach has been used to explain differences in risk perception across sub-populations in the United States regarding nanotechnology, gun control and the climate debate (Kahan et al. 2011).

By adopting the cultural cognition approach, trust in the source of communication becomes related to risk perception in a structured way. Following cultural cognition, population groups whose values and preconceptions align with those of the communicator (i.e. who trust the communicator) are more likely to adopt the proposed information and conclusions and use these as a basis for risk perception. Population groups whose values conflict with those of the communicator may reject the provided arguments, and may even consider the arguments as colored by the values of the communicator. This could lead to reinterpretation of arguments of the communicator as indication of their opposite; and thus a message intended to mitigate perceptions of risk may be re-construed and result in increased risk perception (Kahan et al. 2009). Cultural cognition also provides a framework to understand the finding that risk perception often predicts that we trust those confirming our perceptions and values, rather than that we update our perceptions based on information from those we trust (Poortinga and Pidgeon 2005). Cultural cognition explains observed confirmation biases, where we do not seek for, ignore or even actively deny counter-attitudinal information (Jonas et al. 2001). By accounting for cultural cognition risk information can be framed and developed to serve specific groups. The main conclusion from cultural cognition is that to communicate risks to a specific population group content, framing and communicator should align with the cultural values of that group.

The cultural cognition theory has been posited as a comprehensive theory that explains much of the variance risk perception. This positioning of cultural cognition as such a broad and a comprehensive theory has raised criticism. While the effects predicted by cultural cognition appear to be generally robust, the effects are relatively small (as shown in a meta-analysis by Xue et al. 2014). The limited predictive power of cultural cognition compares to criticism on earlier cultural approaches to risk perception (Sjöberg 2002) and suggests that the contribution of cultural cognition to understanding risk perception is more modest than sometimes suggested. A theoretical criticism is that cultural cognition relies on overgeneralization of a multitude of effects shown in very specific conditions. The abundance of covered effects and the abstract level of presentation makes it hard to empirically assess the cultural cognition hypothesis. Therefore it is argued the theoretical assumptions underlying cultural cognition should be critically assessed and if necessary re-evaluated to further develop cultural cognition into a fully-fledged cognitive theory (van der Linden 2016).

3 The Rationality of Lay Risk Perception

The models above present an overview when and how lay people perceive risks in a systematically different way than experts. It does, however, not address the issue to what extent lay risk perceptions are rational, right or wrong.

Many experts argue that since lay perceptions deviate from their "objective" models, these lay perception must be wrong and irrational (see e.g. Hansen et al. 2003). There are however arguments against this view. First, it is important to realize that expert risk assessment models are based on a number of assumptions about what should be included in a risk assessment and how strongly each of these elements should weigh. These decisions are, at least to some extent, subjective (Hansen et al. 2003), which unavoidably makes the outcomes of any risk assessment based on such starting points subjective as well. From public consultations it becomes clear that the public desires that, besides measures of for example public health burden, moral and ethical values such as integrity of nature are also important in determining risks. Most expert models do not incorporate such values, in part because it is nigh impossible to measure this impact quantitatively and objectively, in part because there is little agreement on what is ethically or morally desired. In addition, individuals may (either consciously or unconsciously) assign different weight to dimensions of risks than expert models. For example, the fear of social exclusion may cause high risk perceptions associated to exhibiting a specific, conspicuous behavior that deviates from the norm in the own peer group. As both the aspects of a product or service included in assessing the risk, and the weights assigned to these aspects bear at least some level of subjectivity, the claim that the difference between expert risk assessment and lay risk perception is due to fallacies in lay risk perception should be carefully reconsidered (Hansen et al. 2003).

It is often claimed that lay individuals are susceptible to biases and miscalculations when forming risk perception. In this context it is important to realize that human mental capacity is limited, and that humans therefore rely on bounded rationality, rather than brute calculating power. Bounded rationality relies on heuristics that have been formed within a realistic decision context for human beings. These heuristics can lead to fallacious decisions, for example when stepping outside of realistic decision contexts from the human perspective (Gigerenzer and Todd 1999). This happens when people are presented with information on a risk topic that appears to be relevant, but is not. In such cases, people will still integrate the information into their perception. In addition, when people are confronted with numbers as proportions or percentages, they tend to deviate substantially from technical risk assessment, while the same information presented in natural numbers leads to substantially better risk estimates (Gigerenzer and Todd 1999). Bounded rationality suggests that as long as information is tailored to capitalize on, or fits within the scope of existing heuristics and decision rules, individual risk perceptions are often rational. While the resulting risk perceptions of the heuristic process are often rational, the actual judgment process is based on heuristics—which is a process that does not follow the general idea of a rational judgment process based on formal logic and mathematical weighing of evidence.

Individuals are often risk averse and forego larger gains, or they are unrealistically optimistic when they should not be. It is important to distinguish between risk aversion and unrealistic optimism that aggregate to irrational behavior at a societal (macro) level and those that are irrational at the individual (micro) level. The well-known prisoner dilemma illustrates this. Mutual collaboration (not admitting anything) leads to the best collective outcome (total number of years imprisonment for all accused together is lowest; i.e. at societal level the lowest negative consequence is taken). Hence, it would be rational for the collective of accused parties to collaborate. Both one and mutual sided defection (accusing the other) leads to a larger collective negative consequence (more years imprisonment), but a lower individual penalty. For the individual it is always rational to defect, and this is what is often observed. Similarly, risk aversion may well be a rational, short term survival trait for the individual but not for society as whole. Unrealistic optimism may create problems for individuals, but it also provides confidence required for making decisions and take action. Such short term individual rewards may results in a relatively large proportion of risk averse tendencies in the gene pool (Tversky and Kahneman 1991; Kahneman and Tversky 1979). Irrationally high risk perception may also be detrimental for individuals. This is the case with phobias and anxiety disorders, which lay outside the scope of normal consumer behavior.

To recap, the rationality of lay risk perception should be considered while taking account of (1) the subjectivity of expert inclusion and weighing of risks factors (2) The fact that lay risk perception often exhibits outcome rationality, but not process rationality; but that this only works within a more or less normal situations (3) That societal and individual risks cannot always be equated.

4 Risk Perception in Context

4.1 Risk Information Seeking

People require sufficient and relevant risk information to form an adequate risk perception. Since looking for, interpreting and evaluating information requires substantial effort, it is unlikely people will expend that effort unless they feel the need to do so. The risk information seeking and processing model (RISP e.g. Griffin et al. 2004) provides a framework that predicts when people will look for and use risk information. At the heart of the RISP lies a perception of information sufficiency. Information sufficiency is defined as the gap between the current knowledge level and a knowledge level felt as sufficient. If there is a substantial gap between current knowledge and the sufficient knowledge level information search is instigated to fill this knowledge gap (Griffin et al. 2004).

The sufficiency threshold is determined by the social norms imposed on by peers and the affective response people have towards a risky situation. Situations that incorporate risk increasing properties, for example those relating to the psychometric dread dimensions, are likely to create an effective response and through that the requirement for information. Socio-cultural and other individual characteristics predict the current knowledge level but also influence trust in information sources, and perceived capacity to gather information. Depending on this interplay of perceived information gap, belief in information channels and perceived information gathering capacity, routine or non-routine information search will be instigated and the information will be processed in a heuristic or systematic way (cf. Trumbo 1999) to arrive at a more informed risk perception. The risk information seeking and processing framework is fairly robust in predicting that risk information will be sought and processed in a systematic way in situations where a large knowledge gap is experienced (Yang et al. 2014).

4.2 Benefit Perception and Attitudes

Risk perception is sometimes considered as the evaluation of negative or risky elements of a situation. If only risks are considered when planning behavior, each situation that holds some risks would then be evaluated as negative; and the only relevant behavior would be to avoid the situation. In practice, people often engage in situations that contain at least some risks. Risk perceptions therefore have to be offset by perception of positive elements of the situation, or benefit perceptions (see e.g. Bredahl 2001). More specifically it appears that for the acceptance of potentially risky products the benefits to the end user need to be clear and tangible for that end user, rather than long term abstract benefits that accrue to society as a whole ore others (Johnson 2003). This need to offset risks with benefits relevant to the end-user followed the realization that the benefits of genetic modification going to producers and possibly society as a whole, did not feature in consumer deliberation to accept the technology at all. As a consequence of this lack of perceived benefits, all risks were perceived as too large by large groups in the public. The need for clear and tangible benefits for the end-user may also help to understand NIMBY (not in my backyard) effects where individuals are unwilling to accept interventions that benefit society as a whole but impose some risk to them. To understand the effect of risk perception in context, we should also understand benefit perception (Johnson 2003). However, where much research since the 1970s has focused on understanding risk perception, but such effort for understanding benefit perception is largely lacking.

When risks and benefit perceptions are studied together it is shown that risk and benefit perceptions for realistic products are often negatively correlated. This negative correlation between risk and benefit perception is unexpected. If risk and benefit perception were fair representations of actual risk and benefit, as it would imply that most of the products on the market that impose considerable risks to consumers have low consumer benefits. It is unlikely that such low benefit-high risk products will make for a profitable market proposition and remain on the market for a long time. Since this negative correlation between risk and benefit perceptions was found across several products, it was concluded that there must be something in the mind of the consumers that connects the perceptions of both risk and benefits, thus creating a spurious negative correlation (Finucane et al. 2000).

4.3   Emotions

Much of the early work on risk perceptions was based in more or less rational, cognitive deliberations of the risks, and biases (Kahneman and Tversky 1979) or psychological dimensions (Slovic 1987) that influence how an actual risks is filtered to form a risk perception. The importance of issues like fear and dread do however already suggest that risk perception is at least partially caused by feelings or emotions. Perhaps the most obvious examples of this is the emotions of fear that is felt in situations where there is a high risk for the self or disgust which is evoked when confronted with (obviously) spoiled food. Negative feelings in forming risk perception can be combined with cognitive deliberations in forming risk perceptions (Loewenstein et al. 2001). Feelings, or affect can also be seen as a main driver of risk perception. Negative affect is considered a driver for higher risk perception and lower benefit perceptions and positive affect to lower risk perception and higher benefit perception (Finucane et al. 2000). This way the underlying affect causes the negative correlation between risk and benefit perception. The affect heuristic to understand risk perception, highlighted the issue whether risk perception is a predominantly cognitive and conscious process, or whether it is more of an automatic unconscious process (Slovic et al. 2002). While risk perception the affect heuristic considers risk-perception as predominantly affective phenomenon, the observation that the negative correlations between risk and benefit perceptions are generally low (see e.g. Finucane et al. 2000), suggests there is a substantial part of risk perception (and for that matter benefit perception) that cannot be attributed to the affect heuristic.

4.4 Social Amplification of Risk

The social amplification of risk framework brings together risk perception theories based on properties of products or situations (such as the psychometric model or prospect theory) with communication theory and risk perception theories based on personal values and cultural differences (Kasperson et al. 1988). By bringing together these approaches, the social amplification of risks framework aims to understand why the same situations sometimes lead to high perceived risks, and at other times do not. The social amplification of risk framework starts with a risky situation that is perceived in according to its properties. This will lead to an initial response or behavior by those involved with the risky situation. The outcomes of these initial actions then may or may not spread in society, for example because of other people being confronted with the outcome of the behavior, or the media starting to report on the case. If the impact remains with those originally involved with the risk event, and little media coverage is generated, it is unlikely that risk perceptions in society will increase. However, if substantial media coverage is created and people outside those originally involved are affected, the perception of risk may be amplified. This amplification of risk may create a ripple effect where involved companies may suffer beyond the affected situation (for example through loss of brand equity of the parent company). If the risks are further amplified, other actors in the same sector may be affected and a whole industry may be perceived as risky. Further amplification may even affect situations only loosely related to original situation. An example is that of nuclear power following the Chernobyl disaster in 1986. The Chernobyl accident is to date the most disastrous nuclear power plant accident in history and substantially surpasses the 2015 Fukushima disaster. While the Chernobyl disaster was caused by human error, the media attention catalyzed the already heated debate on nuclear power and resulted in shelving of many plans for new nuclear power plants. The effects rippled beyond the nuclear power industry and negatively affected the perceptions of food irradiation, a technology based on ionizing radiation aimed at eliminating microbial food hazards.

The social amplification of risk framework is frequently used to interpret how media attention amplifies perceptions of risk in society. It should be noted though, that the framework was developed in the 1980s when the media consisted of the (classical) printed media, radio and television. The media arena has changed substantially since with the emergence of the internet. It has changed even more with the introduction of internet 2.0 which allows everyone to post personal viewpoints on blogs and fora. Social media like Twitter and Facebook have created different dynamics in how events are communicated, and what information is generated and shared among the public. It is suggested that the social amplification of risk framework may not fully capture the new dynamics and may require an update to align it with this new media landscape (Kasperson 2015).

5   Risk Perceptions and Consumer Products

So far this contribution has dealt with risk perception theories in general. To understand how people look at products and services, we should look more specifically what in products makes for risk perception.

To do so, we distinguish different paths of deliberation that lead towards product evaluations (Fischer et al. 2013); which we apply to risk perceptions. The first path is about properties of specific product attributes, and whether such properties induce such a high perceived risk that other attributes of the product no longer matter. In other words, the risk perceptions of parts form a non-compensatory risk for the whole. Secondly there is a path where risk perceptions of product attributes are integrated with perceptions of other attributes to form a comprehensive perception of the product. This distinctions may help us to recognize the different approaches in published research.

The first path of risk perception heavily depends on the risk perception of a single attribute. If risks of such an attribute are perceived as high this may lead to categorical rejection of products. Obvious examples are those of allergic people, who will reject an unknown product if there is even a chance of holding the allergen. Risk perception research on the acceptance of novel technologies has also frequently taken this path, where it is assumed that high risk perception of a technology used to create a product would be decisive in consumer decisions towards the product, regardless of other product properties. In this vein, it has been shown that many consumers deem the risk of irradiation of food as creating an unsurmountable risk and hence as a reason to reject any product produced in this way out of hand. Another example from food, is the case of genetic modification. Genetic modification of, in particular, food products received a lot of attention in academia in the 1990s and the 2000s. Much of this research focused on outright rejection of genetically modified plant or animals by the public based. Risks of genetic modification are often perceived as high (Siegrist 2000; Frewer et al. 2013) and these perceptions may block consumer willingness to even consider production of thus created plants or animals even if there are clear societal benefits (Frewer et al. 2013). The use of growth hormone in dairy production also sparked some outrage and subsequent categorical rejection of products based on this technology. It is the general rejection of several technologies as being unnatural and hence risky to health that makes consumer groups reject many foods and opt for the organic option. Other examples where the perceived risk of the technology as a whole may form a barrier against consumer acceptance of specific products is the introduction of hydrogen based fuel cells, where associations with, for example, the Hindenburg disaster and the H-bomb impact consumer response towards the introduction of personal cars based on hydrogen fuel cells.

Many technologies that are considered as unacceptably risky are considered as such because of their potential for major societal impact; and not so much because the immediate risk to the end-user. For example, for nuclear power the risk is not so much about the electricity that is provided in the home (the product) but the chance of a nuclear power plant melt-down. For mobile phones, most of the risk perception is not so much about the radiation caused by the receivers, but by the ground stations and masts. Similar concerns about the risk for nature were also found as reasons to categorically reject genetically modified foods.

In other cases technologies where not categorically rejected. But nevertheless the technology may be perceived as somewhat negative, as is for example the case with nanotechnology. This brings us to the second way in which risk perception of products may play a role—through product attribute perceptions. This approach assumes that the overall perception of risks of a product is not based on a single attribute or technology but on the product as a whole. This can either imply that risks and benefits may be offset against each other and some overall judgment of the product is formed or that a first impression of a product as a whole is dominant. As long as no single attribute creates unacceptable risk perception (i.e. triggers categorical rejection), the top down overall impression of the product influences the perception of the attributes (Grunert 2002). In extremis this can mean that risky attributes of a product are completely overlooked in favor of the overall perception of the product as whole. This is most likely to happen with frequently used products like food leading to obesity, unsafe preparation practice (Parry et al. 2004) or car driving behavior (Wilde 1994). When this is less extremely so, the attribute risk perception can than still be integrated into the overall evaluation of the product, but will have only limited influence. This approach is similar to that of a rational decision maker who weighs risks against benefits and converges onto an overall assessment, where risks can be compensated by sufficiently large benefits. This has been applied to research into the acceptability of genetically modified organisms as well with some success, especially when there were clear benefits to the end-user (De Steur et al. 2012). The obvious benefits to the user may also play an important role in the reason why mobile phone sets are readily adopted in spite of initial discussion about the risks caused by the electro-magnetic radiation (EMR) required for these products to operate. In fact, the risk of EMR for mobile phones is perceived as generally low compared to other sources in the environment and this specific risk of mobile telephony is even hardly noticed by people who have not been accustomed to land lines prior to the introduction of mobile phones (Van Kleef et al. 2010).

6   Risk Perception and Behavior

To understand the role of risk perception in behavior, we can consider human behavior as the outcome of a process where the world is perceived, the status of the world is evaluated, and behavior is exhibited to achieve goals. This allows us to consider risk perception in relation to behavior. It also makes explicit that the relation between risk perception and behavior is not clear cut. Some approaches place risk perception at the first stage and position consider it as a perception filter that translates real world observations into mental representations. It could be argued that prospect theory that proposes a perception function for losses and gains takes this approach (Kahneman and Tversky 1979). Other studies consider risk perception as part of the evaluation of the situation; where the perceived real world observations are already integrated into some kind of risk evaluation. In these cases risk perceptions are sometimes considered a part of a larger evaluation or attitude. Risk perception research from social or consumer psychology perspective tends to take this approach (e.g. Siegrist 2000). While in practice the distinction between perception and evaluation are not always explicitly made; both approaches consider risk perception as a precursor of the formation of behavioral intention, and as such as an indirect predictor of actual behavior.

Self-regulatory approaches, and approaches that rely on automatic, habitual behavior suggest a more direct relation between risk perception and behavior. In situations of where frequent behavior with high perceived personal control occurs, risk perception gradually diminishes and the barrier against risky behavior is lowered as long as no negative consequences are encountered. In many cases this tends to converge on behavior that is relatively risky (e.g. unrealistic optimism Weinstein 1989; target risk, Wilde 1994). On the other hand phobia's and extreme risk aversion may completely inhibit behavior whatever the benefits are; and fear induced by a risky situation may trigger automatic response without conscious perception of the risk. The extent to which risk perception has a direct or indirect, conscious or unconscious impact on behavior depends on whether the behavior is more deliberate or more automated.

7   Conclusions

The risk perception literature presents several insights that explain risk perception in different situations. Frequently repeated, lifestyle related risky behaviors tend to result in unrealistic optimism, and hence risky behavior. Properties of products and situations that have dreadful consequences, or are unknown increase perceptions of risks. Some people tend to actively seek out risks, but there are also personality traits that make people avoid risk at all costs. On average, people are somewhat risk averse resulting in more attention to avoiding risks than gaining benefits. Cultural context determines what information about risk is interpreted in what way.

Together these insights can explain lay risk perception to a considerable extent. In addition, if we should keep in mind that selecting and weighing elements of a situation depends on personal priorities, that risk perception is geared at individual, rather than societally, relevant decisions, and that human decision making depends on bounded rational heuristics that require the information which fits the natural context of the individual.

In the larger context of human decision making, it helps to figure out when individuals will engage in risk information seeking, and when they process this information. It makes sense to study risk and benefit perception together and to include affective and emotional perceptions of risk. The influence of the media on the amplification of risks and ensuing ripple effects beyond the original situation are important in understanding public response to incidents. When people are asked to choose a product or service, it is important to study perceived risks about the risky attribute as such an attribute may sometimes lead to categorical rejection of the product. It is also important to study risky attributes embedded in a product context, as the consumer may adopt a product with a risky attribute when other attributes bring sufficient benefits to offset the risk.

Understanding risk perception in isolation is not the end goal. It is important to understand risk perception of consumers, and we need to do research to increase its understanding. Ultimately, as long as risk perception remains a mental process in the mind of consumers, risk perception research has to contribute to understanding consumer behavior. This brings us back to William James who in 1890 already stated that *"My thinking is first and last and always for the sake of my doing."*. Risk perception as evaluation in a more or less deliberate decision, or as trigger for automatic behavior are ways in which risk perception influences behavior. The situation and the individual consumer will determine what behavior is adopted. To fully understand risk perception we should therefore always consider the real life behaviors that consumers may, or may not decide upon as a consequence of the risks they perceive.

References

Bredahl, L. (2001). Determinants of consumer attitudes and purchase intentions with regard to genetically modified foods—results of a cross-national survey. *Journal of Consumer Policy, 24* (1), 23–61.

De Steur, H., Gellynck, X., Feng, S., Rutsaert, P., & Verbeke, W. (2012). Determinants of willingness-to-pay for GM rice with health benefits in a high-risk region: Evidence from experimental auctions for folate biofortified rice in China. *Food Quality And Preference, 25* (2), 87–94.

Defoe, I. N., Dubas, J. S., Figner, B., & Van Aken, M. A. G. (2015). A meta-analysis on age differences in risky decision making: Adolescents versus children and adults. *Psychological Bulletin, 141*(1), 48–84. doi:10.1037/a0038088.

Fife-Schaw, C., & Rowe, G. (2000). Extending the application of the psychometric approach for assessing public perceptions of food risks: Some methodological considerations. *Journal of Risk Research, 3*(2), 167–179.

Finucane, M. L., Alhakami, A. S., Slovic, P., & Johnson, S. M. (2000). The affect heuristic in judgments of risks and benefits. *Journal of Behavioral Decision Making, 13*(1), 1–17.

Fischer, A. R. H., van Trijp, H. C. M., Hofenk, D., Ronteltap, A., Esjberg, L., & Tudoran, A. A. (2013) Collation of scientific evidence on consumer acceptance of new food technologies: Three roads to consumer choice. Wageningen, NI, RECAPT EU FP7.

Frewer, L. J., Shepherd, R., & Sparks, P. (1994). The interrelationship between perceived knowledge, control and risk associated with a range of food-related hazards targeted at the individual, other people and society. *Journal of Food Safety, 14*(1), 19–40.

Frewer, L. J., Kleter, G. A., Brennan, M., Coles, D., Fischer, A. R. H., Houdebine, L. M., Mora, C., Millar, K., & Salter, B. (2013). Genetically modified animals from life-science, socio-economic and ethical perspectives: Examining issues in an EU policy context. *New Biotechnology, 30*(5), 447–460.

Gigerenzer, G., & Todd, P. M. (1999). *Simple Heuristics that make us smart.* Oxford: Oxford University Press.

Griffin, R. J., Neuwirth, K., Dunwoody, S., & Giese, J. (2004). Information sufficiency and risk communication. *Media Psychology, 6*(1), 23–61.

Grunert, K. G. (2002). Current issues in the understanding of consumer food choice. *Trends in Food Science and Technology, 13*(8), 275–285.

Gupta, N., Fischer, A. R. H., & Frewer, L. J. (2015). Ethics, risk and benefits associated with different applications of nanotechnology: A comparison of expert and consumer perceptions of drivers of societal acceptance. *NanoEthics, 9*(2), 93–108. doi:10.1007/s11569-015-0222-5.

Hansen, J., Holm, L., Frewer, L. J., Robinson, P., & Sandoe, P. (2003). Beyond the knowledge deficit: Recent research into lay and expert attitudes to food risks. *Appetite, 41*(2), 111–121.

Johnson, B. B. (2003). Further notes on public response to uncertainty in risks and science. *Risk Analysis, 23*(4), 781–789.

Jonas, E., Schulz-Hardt, S., Frey, D., & Thelen, N. (2001). Confirmation bias in sequential information search after preliminary decisions: An expansion of dissonance theoretical research on selective exposure to information. *Journal of Personality and Social Psychology, 80*(4), 557–571.

Kahan, D. M., Braman, D., Slovic, P., Gastil, J., & Cohen, G. (2009). Cultural cognition of the risks and benefits of nanotechnology. *Nature Nanotechnology, 4*(2), 87–90.

Kahan, D. M., Jenkins-Smith, H., & Braman, D. (2011). Cultural cognition of scientific consensus. *Journal of Risk Research, 14*(2), 147–174. doi:10.1080/13669877.2010.511246.

Kahneman, D., & Tversky, A. (1979). Prospect theory: An analysis of decision under risk. *Econometrica, 47*(2), 263–292.

Kasperson, R. E. (2015) Social amplification of risk: Progress and new issues. In Society for risk analysis annual meeting, Alrington, VA.

Kasperson, R. E., Renn, O., Slovic, P., Brown, H. S., Emel, J., Goble, R., Kasperson, J. X., & Ratick, S. (1988) The social amplification of risk: A conceptual framework. *Risk Analysis, 8*(2), 177–187. doi:10.1111/j.1539-6924.1988.tb01168.x.

Loewenstein, G. F., Weber, E. U., Hsee, C. K., & Welch, N. (2001). Risk as feelings. *Psychological Bulletin, 127*(2), 267–286.

Loomes, G., & Sugden, R. (1987). Testing for regret and disappointment in choice under uncertainty. *Economic Journal Supplement, 97*, 118–129.

Marris, C., Langford, I. H., & O'Riordan, T. (1998). A quantitative test of the cultural theory of risk perceptions: Comparison with the psychometric paradigm. *Risk Analysis, 18*(5), 635–647.

Marshall, B. K., Picou, J. S., Formichella, C., & Nicholls, K. (2006). Environmental risk perceptions and the white male effect: Pollution concerns among deep-South coastal residents. *Journal of Applied Social Science, 23*(2), 31–49.

Parry, S. M., Miles, S., Tridente, A., & Palmer, S. R. (2004). Differences in perception of risk between people who have and have not experienced *Salmonella* food poisoning. *Risk Analysis, 24*(1), 289–299.

Pennings, J. M. E., & Smidts, A. (2000). Assessing the construct validity of risk attitude. *Management Science, 46*(10), 1337–1348.

Poortinga, W., & Pidgeon, N. F. (2005). Trust in risk regulation: Cause or consequence of the acceptability of GM food? *Risk Analysis, 25*(1), 199–209.

Siegrist, M. (2000). The influence of trust and perceptions of risks and benefits on the acceptance of gene technology. *Risk Analysis, 20*(2), 195–204. doi:10.1111/0272-4332.202020.

Siegrist, M., Stampfli, N., Kastenholz, H., & Keller, C. (2008). Perceived risks and perceived benefits of different nanotechnology foods and nanotechnology food packaging. *Appetite, 51* (2), 283–290.

Sjöberg, L. (2002). Are received risk perception models alive and well? *Risk Analysis, 22*(4), 665–669.

Slovic, P. (1987). Perception of risk. *Science, 236*(4799), 280–285.

Slovic, P., Finucane, M. L., Peters, E., & MacGregor, D. G. (2002). Rational actors or rational fools: Implications of the affect heuristic for behavioral economics. *Journal of Socio Economics, 31*(4), 329–342.

Trumbo, C. W. (1999). Heuristic-systematic information processing and risk judgment. *Risk Analysis, 19*(3), 391–400.

Tversky, A., & Kahneman, D. (1991). Loss aversion in riskless choice: A reference-dependent model. *The Quarterly Journal of Economics, 106*(4), 1039–1061.

van der Linden, S. (2016). A conceptual critique of the cultural cognition thesis. *Science Communication, 38*(1), 128–138. doi:10.1177/1075547015614970.

Van Kleef, E., Fischer, A. R. H., Khan, M., & Frewer, L. J. (2010). Risk and benefit perceptions of mobile phone and base station technology in Bangladesh. *Risk Analysis, 30*(6), 1002–1015.

Weber, E. U., & Milliman, R. A. (1997). Perceived risk attitudes: Relating risk perception to risky choice. *Management Science, 43*(2), 123–144.

Weinstein, N. D. (1989). Optimistic biases about personal risks. *Science, 246*(4935), 1232–1233.

Wilde, G. J. S. (1994). *Target risk.* Toronto: PDE Publications.

Xue, W., Hine, D. W., Loi, N. M., Thorsteinsson, E. B., & Phillips, W. J. (2014). Cultural worldviews and environmental risk perceptions: A meta-analysis. *Journal of Environmental Psychology, 40*, 249–258. doi:10.1016/j.jenvp.2014.07.002.

Yang, Z. J., Aloe, A. M., & Feeley, T. H. (2014). Risk information seeking and processing model: A meta-analysis. *Journal of Communication, 64*(1), 20–41. doi:10.1111/jcom.12071.

Zaleskiewicz, T. (2001). Beyond risk seeking and risk aversion: Personality and the dual nature of economic risk taking. *European Journal of Personality, 15*(1 special issue), S105–S122.

Measuring Risk Perception

Stefan Cano and Thomas Salzberger

1 Key Concepts

1.1 Objective Versus Perceived Risk

The risk associated with the use of products is important to government, legislative and regulatory bodies, such as the US Food and Drug Administration. "Objective risk" can be assessed, for example, by epidemiological studies examining products that have been on the market for some time. Such studies may reveal hitherto unanticipated risks and trigger new guidelines or amended legislation. For products subject to regulatory approval prior to their introduction to the market, risk assessment is equally crucial. However, opportunities to appraise objective risk are limited to small experiments or clinical studies. While providing some insight, these studies do not allow for a reliable assessment of the long-term risks to the individual and population at large. Whereas the individual use of pharmaceutical products, such as prescription drugs, can be controlled to a large extent, the situation is different for products, such as gambling or tobacco and other nicotine-containing devices. Once approved by regulatory bodies, there is little control of who uses the product (or service) and to what extent. In this situation, an assessment of perceived risk as a subjective evaluation can be helpful to better understand expected usage patterns, in terms of who will adopt the product and how intensely it will be consumed.

S. Cano (✉)
Modus Outcomes, Suite 210b, Spirella Building, Letchworth Garden City SG6 4ET, UK
e-mail: stefan.cano@modusoutcomes.com

T. Salzberger
Institute for Statistics and Mathematics, Institute for Marketing Management, Vienna University of Economics and Business, Welhandelspl. 1, 1020 Wien, Austria
e-mail: Thomas.Salzberger@wu.ac.at

© Springer International Publishing AG 2017   191
G. Emilien et al. (eds.), *Consumer Perception of Product Risks and Benefits*,
DOI 10.1007/978-3-319-50530-5_10

"Objective" and "perceived" risk differ in many respects. Perceived risk is not confined to products used by the individual or already on the market. However, it seems plausible that risk perception might be better elaborated when products are familiar to the individual. In contrast to objective risk, perceived risk is a subjective reality to the individual. Risk perception is a psychological, predominantly cognitive concept, which cannot be observed directly. In the social sciences, such concepts are represented by one or a set of latent variables. We need observations from which we infer the latent variable. Manifest observations can be created by means of questionnaires (or self-report instruments). Respondents are offered a number of response categories, assumed to be ordered by intensity, associated with a statement or question (also referred to as an 'item'). The observed choice is scored and analyzed by a measurement model. The discipline of psychometrics provides models that relate manifest scores and measures of latent variables in a way as to infer measures of a latent concept.

1.2   Perceived Risk as a Latent Variable

Compared to other latent variables, risk perceptions are somewhat more complicated. A personality trait defines one property that resides within the individual. An attitude comprises an internal disposition with respect to an outside object. Risk perception also refers to an external object, which could also be a behavior, but at the same time requires a subject, whose risk is perceived. In other words, there are three entities involved: the object that implies the risk, the individual who is affected by the risk, and the individual who perceives the risk. The subject affected by the risk and the subject perceiving the risk can, but need not, be the same person. For example, the risk of driving a car as perceived by the driver can refer to the risk to the driver (the personal risk to the individual) or to an abstract driver (the general risk to others).

Perceptions of risk related to the consumption of tobacco products can vary based on whether one is comparing oneself to a specific reference group (e.g., similar in age, race or smoking status), the time frame being considered (e.g., lifetime, 10 years, etc.), and conditional on whether one stops or continues to smoke. Weinstein (1998) found individuals typically believe they are less at risk personally of experiencing an undesirable life event than are other people. This finding makes clear the importance of recognizing the distinction between people's beliefs about the health risks of smokers in general, and their beliefs about their own personal health risks of smoking. Most smokers agree smoking poses a serious health risk, yet many continue to smoke. To better understand these issues, the appropriateness of risk perception measures is particularly important to ensure valid and generalizable results.

2   Measurement

2.1   Current Approaches

In general, studies investigating tobacco product risk perception classify perceived risk as a multidimensional variable. For example, Rindfleisch and Crockett (Rindfleisch and Crockett 1999) describe perceived risk as being made up of: (1) addiction risk (e.g., the risk of a smoker wanting to quit but fearing that he or she will be unable to, and the danger of developing a lifelong smoking habit); (2) health risk (e.g., lung cancer, heart disease); (3) social risks (e.g., the adverse impact of a smoker's interpersonal interactions or how he or she is perceived by others); (4) financial risk (e.g., wasting money or needing to borrow money for tobacco); and (5) time risk (e.g., wasting time, losing time). However, the majority of existing studies have primarily focused on health risk perceptions (Romer and Jamieson 2001a, b; Shiffman et al. 2001; Lyna et al., 2002; Halpern-Felsher et al. 2004; Oncken et al. 2005; Weinstein et al. 2005; Tilleczek and Hine 2006; Song et al. 2009; Morrell et al. 2010; Wagener et al. 2010; Dillard et al. 2012). Many published studies have focused on personal risk perceptions (Lyna et al. 2002; Halpern-Felsher et al. 2004; Song et al. 2009; Morrell et al. 2010; Wagener et al. 2010; Dillard et al. 2012), general risk perceptions (Shiffman et al. 2001; Weinstein et al. 2005) or a combination of both (Romer and Jamieson 2001a, b). In addition, risk perceptions have been assessed in relation to different products or cessation (e.g., Romer and Jamieson 2001a, b; Weinstein et al. 2005; Song et al. 2009; Lyna et al. 2002; Oncken et al. 2005; Tilleczek and Hine 2006; Wagener et al. 2010; Dillard et al. 2012). The most common assessments of risk perceptions have been in the form of single items (Romer and Jamieson 2001a, b; Lyna et al. 2002; Halpern-Felsher et al. 2004; Oncken et al. 2005; Weinstein et al. 2005; Tilleczek and Hine 2006; Song et al. 2009; Wagener et al. 2010), which have included a variety of response options types (e.g., Likert-type (Budd and Preston 2001); numeric rating scale (Rees et al. 2001)). Most existing multi-item self-report instruments contain items about risk perception as part of a wider battery of issues (Budd and Preston 2001; Heishman et al., 2003; Jeffries et al. 2004; Lewis-Esquerre et al. 2005; Park et al. 2009; Rees et al. 2009). Four commonly used instruments typify the wider research field.

2.1.1   Attitudes and Beliefs About the Consequences of Smoking Scale

Budd and Preston (2001) developed a 27-item instrument including four subscales: attitudes and beliefs about smoking related to emotional benefits, health hazards, self-confidence, and body image. In this instrument, risk perceptions fall under the term "health hazards", covering short and long term risks (i.e., smoking accelerates the effects of aging; smoking causes lung cancer; smokers are sick more often; smoking is addictive; smoking makes your breath smell bad; smoking causes shortness of breath; smoking is a cause of heart disease; smoking causes people to die at a young age; smoking and other drugs are frequently used together).

2.1.2 Smoking Behavior Questionnaire

Gilliard and Bruchon-Schweitzer (2001) developed a 42-item instrument including four subscales (7-items each): dependence, social integration, regulation of negative affect, and hedonism. In this instrument, addiction risk is the primary focus.

2.1.3 Smoking Consequences Questionnaire

The Smoking Consequences Questionnaire (SCQ) was initially developed to measure outcome expectancies related to cigarette smoking in college students (Brandon and Baker 1991). An adult version of the SCQ (SCQ-A) was developed for assessing expectancies in more typical, older, nicotine-dependent smokers (Copeland et al. 1995), and psychometrically evaluated by Jeffries et al. (2004). Lewis-Esquerre et al. (2005) modified the SCQ-A for adolescent nonsmokers and current smokers. They proposed a seven sub-scale factor structure including: negative affect reduction, taste/sensorimotor manipulation, social facilitation, weight control, negative physical feelings, boredom reduction and negative social impression.

2.1.4 Risk Perception Questionnaire

Park et al. (2009) used a cross-sectional study in the US to develop a 10-item risk perception questionnaire to measure perceived lifetime risk of lung cancer and other smoking-related diseases (SRDs). An individual's risk perception profile was constructed on respondents' views of personal and comparative risk. The authors suggest that since each informs and influences the other, individuals' personal risk reports (own risk) as well as their comparative risk reports (risk in relation to others) should be included.

2.2 Future Directions

The US Institute of Medicine makes three key recommendations for measuring risk perception in relation to modified risk tobacco products (MRTP; Institute of Medicine 2012). First, measures of perception of tobacco-related outcomes should include the perception of short- and long-term risks and addiction, including issues such as overall risk of harm or addiction, as well as perceptions of specific harm, such as risk of lung cancer or heart disease. Second, self-report instruments should use the most appropriate scale type (e.g., log linear, lexical, comparative). Third, the measurement of risk perception should allow for comparison of an MRTP with existing tobacco products and comparison among different smoking statuses (i.e., people who have never used a tobacco product; people who have used any tobacco product in the past, but not currently; people who currently use a tobacco product and do not intend to quit; and people who currently use a tobacco product and do intend to quit).

All the self-report instruments described in the previous section have some level of psychometric evidence supporting their use in group-level studies. However, none checked all the boxes for comprehensive instrument development (Mokkink et al. 2010). Also, there exists no self-report instrument developed specifically to compare risk perceptions across different tobacco product types, importantly newer products such as e-cigarettes or MRTPs. Also, in general, the validity of current instruments is questionable, given the broad lack of rigorous qualitative research supporting content and the non-existence of clear conceptual frameworks. In addition, none were developed using modern psychometric methods, which open them up to further potential criticism (see below). Thus, new self-report instruments are required. This necessitates a consideration of best practice self-report instrument development methodology and psychometrics.

3   Instrument Development

3.1   Methodology

To be fit for purpose, self-report instruments must be conceptually meaningful and scientifically sound. A questionnaire that is conceptually meaningful addresses those issues considered important by key stakeholders (e.g., the most relevant and important issues that reflect risk perceptions of tobacco products for consumers, researchers and regulators). Scientific soundness refers to the demonstration of reliable, valid, and responsive measurement of the concept of interest. Conceptual meaningfulness does not guarantee scientific soundness, and vice versa. Of particular relevance is the field of quality of life research, in which a series of texts and articles have been published on the subject of methodology (Mokkink et al. 2010). In particular, given the regulatory issues, guidelines for the development of new patient reported outcome (PRO) instruments have been published by the US Food and Drug Administration's (FDA), which lay out the scientific requirements for use in clinical trials (US Food and Drug Administration 2009). To optimally measure risk perceptions, new instruments should ideally undergo careful and extensive development and psychometric evaluation. There are usually three stages to this process.

Stage 1 defines the conceptual framework and generates a pool of items to ensure all important areas are considered for inclusion in the final instrument. To develop these, qualitative research is required. The item pool is then pre-tested (or piloted) in a small sample of subjects to clarify ambiguities in the wording of items, confirm appropriateness, and determine acceptability and completion time. In Stage 2, field-testing is performed on a larger sample of subjects with the goal to select the best items for inclusion in the final instrument. Items are eliminated or revised according to psychometric criteria. In Stage 3, psychometric validation of the instrument is performed. Here, the instrument, in its final form, is administered to a large group of subjects.

At a broad level, self-report instruments should be psychometrically assessed against the following criteria: data quality, scaling assumptions, targeting, reliability, validity, and responsiveness (Hobart and Cano 2009). Indicators of data quality, such as item non-response and percent computable scores, reflects respondents' understanding and acceptance of a self-report instrument and helps to identify items that may be irrelevant, confusing, or disturbing to subjects. Tests of scaling assumptions determine whether it is legitimate to generate scores for a self-report instrument using the algorithms proposed by the developers. Targeting is the extent to which the spectrum of the concept of interest measured by a self-report instrument matches the distribution of concept in the study sample and is determined simply by examining score distributions. The reliability of a self-report instrument is the degree to which it is free from random error. Validity is the extent to which a self-report instrument measures what it intends to measure. The distinction between reliability and validity is important, because an instrument may be reliable (i.e. always yield the same score), but may not be valid, as it may be consistently measuring the same thing but not what it is supposed to measure. Finally, responsiveness is the extent to which the instrument can detect change. How each of these criteria are evaluated depends on the psychometric approach taken.

3.2 Psychometric Theories

3.2.1 Classical Test Theory

The dominant psychometric paradigm for the development of self-report instruments is classical (or traditional) test theory (CTT), the foundations of which were laid down by Charles Spearman. Classical Test Theory posits that an observed score (O) is the sum of a True score (T) and an error score (E), assuming the relationship between these is additive (e.g. as opposed to multiplicative). Data from self-report instruments is analyzed to ascertain the appropriateness that items can be summed, without weighting or standardization, to produce a score. Between the turn and the middle of the twentieth century, CTT related methodology developed further (e.g., Kuder-Richardson's coefficients for internal inconsistency, Cronbach's alpha, correlations between replicated measurements). The key traditional psychometric properties commonly associated with CTT became: data quality, scaling assumptions, targeting, reliability, validity, and responsiveness (these are described more fully elsewhere (US Food and Drug Administration 2009; Hobart and Cano 2009)).

As a psychometric approach, CTT is useful for broad analyses of item-level data in self-report instruments. However, despite its dominance, there are some long time acknowledged limitations of CTT (Cano and Hobart 2011): (1) observed data are always ordinal rather than interval; (2) scores for persons and samples are scale-dependent; and as such (3) psychometric properties, such as reliability and validity, are sample-dependent; (4) data support group-level inferences but, importantly, not individual subject measurement.

3.2.2 Rasch Measurement Theory

Georg Rasch, a Danish mathematician, argued that social measurement should parallel the rules of physical measurement, and be concerned with invariant comparison. He developed the simple logistic model (now known as the Rasch model), and demonstrated that his approach met the stringent criteria for measurement used in the physical sciences (Rasch 1960). The term Rasch Measurement Theory (RMT) encompasses instrument development methods that use the Rasch model to evaluate the legitimacy of summing items to generate measurements, and their reliability and validity. Through this approach items of an instrument are examined to assess the extent to which observed data (subjects' responses to items) "fit" with predictions of those responses from a mathematical (Rasch) model. Thus, the difference between what should happen (expected) and what does happen (observed) indicates the extent to which measurement is achieved.

There are seven key measurement properties that should be considered: thresholds for item response options; item fit statistics; item locations; differential item functioning (DIF); correlations between standardized residuals; person separation index (PSI), individual person change statistics. We describe these in more detail elsewhere (Hobart and Cano 2009). Importantly RMT address each of the four limitations of CTT described above. First, the approach offers the ability to construct linear measurements from ordinal-level data, thereby addressing a major concern of using self-report instruments as outcome measures. Second, RMT methods provide item estimates that are independent of the sample distribution and person estimates that are independent of the scale distribution, thus allowing for greater flexibility in situations where different samples or test forms are used. Third, the methods allow for the use of subsets of items of each scale rather than requiring all items of the scale, without compromising the comparability of measures made using different sets of items. This is the foundation for item banking and computerized adaptive testing. Fourth, RMT enables estimates suitable for individual person analyses rather than only for group comparison studies.

3.2.3 Item Response Theory

Item Response Theory (IRT) is another psychometric approach that involves the statistical estimation of item and person parameters on a latent continuum (Lord and Novick 1968). There are three main IRT models. The one parameter (1P) model is essentially identical in structure to the Rasch model. Mathematical models relating the probability of a response to an item, to the person's location, the item's difficulty and the item's discrimination are known as two parameter (2P) models. The addition of a third parameter (a person guessing parameter) to the basic 2P model results in the 3P model. The general approach in IRT focuses on mathematical models that explain the observed data. The reasoning behind model selection is empirical evidence of model suitability to account better for the data. In relation to the four shortcomings of CTT, IRT only haphazardly and indirectly overcomes these, depending on whether the data at hand are found to fit a one-parameter (Rasch) model.

4 Conclusions and Recommendations

Risk perception is a significant indicator for better understanding the uptake and use of tobacco products. As a means to quantifying and understand risk perception, self-report instruments are part of the future of tobacco-related research and marketing practices. Traditional psychometric methods, based on classical test theory, form the current dominant paradigm for developing such instruments. But there are now newer methods (e.g., Rasch Measurement Theory, Item Response Theory) increasingly being used, which will help extend the utility of risk perception instruments. It is, therefore, essential that professionals working in this area are aware of the scientific issues surrounding the appropriate development and use of self-report instruments. In this way, these key stake holders can be directly involved in how these methods are used to shape the future of risk perception measurement.

References

Brandon, T., & Baker, T. (1991). The smoking consequences questionnaire: The subjective expected utility of smoking in college students. *Psychological Assessment, 3*, 484–491.

Budd, G., & Preston, D. (2001). College student's attitudes and beliefs about the consequences of smoking: Development and normative scores of a new scale. *Journal of the American Academy of Nurse Practitioners, 13*(9), 421–427.

Cano, S., & Hobart, J. (2011). The problem with health measurement. *Patient Preference and Adherence, 5*, 279–290.

Copeland, A., Brandon, T., & Quinn, E. (1995). The smoking consequences questionnaire—Adult: Measurement of smoking outcome expectancies of experienced smokers. *Psychological Assessment, 7*, 484–494.

Dillard, A., Ferrer, R., Ubel, P., & Fagerlin, A. (2012). Risk perception measures' associations with behavior intentions, affect, and cognition following colon cancer screening messages. *Health Psychology, 31*(1), 106–113.

Food and Drug Administration (FDA). (2009). Patient reported outcome measures: use in medical product development to support labelling claims. http://www.fda.gov/downloads/Drugs/Guidances/UCM193282.pdf.

Gilliard, J., & Bruchon-Schweitzer, M. (2001). Development and validation of a multidimensional smoking behaviour questionnaire. *Psychological Reports, 89*(3), 499–509.

Halpern-Felsher, B., Biehl, M., Kropp, R., & Rubinstein, M. (2004). Perceived risks and benefits of smoking: Differences among adolescents with different smoking experiences and intentions. *Preventive Medicine, 39*, 559–567.

Heishman, S., Singleton, E., & Moolchan, E. (2003). Tobacco craving questionnaire: Reliability and validity of a new multifactorial instrument. *Nicotine and Tobacco Research, 5*(5), 645–654.

Hobart, J., & Cano, S. (2009). Improving the evaluation of therapeutic intervention in MS: the role of new psychometric methods. *Monograph for the UK Health Technology Assessment Programme, 13*(12), 1–200.

Institute of Medicine. (2012). *Scientific standards for studies on modified risk tobacco products.* Washington, DC: The National Academies Press.

Jeffries, S., Catley, D., Okuyemi, K., Nazir, N., McCarter, K., Grobe, J., & Ahluwalia, J. (2004). Use of a brief Smoking Consequences Questionnaire for Adults (SCQ-A) in African American smokers. *Psychology of Addictive Behaviors, 18*(1), 74–77.

Lewis-Esquerre, J., Rodrigue, J., & Kahler, C. (2005). Development and validation of an adolescent smoking consequences questionnaire. *Nicotine and Tobacco Research, 7*(1), 81–90.

Lord, F. M., & Novick, M. R. (1968). *Statistical theories of mental test scores.* Reading, MA: Addison-Wesley.

Lyna, P., McBride, C., Samsa, G., & Pollak, K. (2002). Exploring the association between perceived risks of smoking and benefits to quitting—Who does not see the link? *Addictive Behaviors, 27*, 293–307.

Mokkink, L., Terwee, C., Patrick, D., Alonso, J., Stratford, P., Knol, D., Bouter, L., & de Vet, H. (2010). The COSMIN checklist for assessing the methodological quality of studies on measurement properties of health status measurement instruments: an international Delphi study. *Quality of Life Research 19*, 539–549.

Morrell, H., Song, A., & Halpern-Felsher, B. (2010). Predicting adolescent perceptions of the risks and benefits of cigarette smoking: A longitudinal investigation. *Health Psychology, 29*(6), 610–617.

Oncken, C., McKee, S., Krishnan-Sarin, S., O'Malley, S., & Mazure, C. (2005). Knowledge and perceived risk of smoking-related conditions: A survey of cigarette smokers. *Preventive Medicine, 40*, 779–784.

Park, E., Ostroff, J., Rakowski, W., Gareen, I., Diefenbach, M., Feibelmann, S., & Rigotti, N. (2009). Risk perceptions among participants undergoing lung cancer screening: Baseline results from the National Lung Screening Trial. *Annals of Behavioral Medicine, 37*, 268–279.

Rasch, G. (1960). *Probabilistic models for some intelligence and attainment tests.* Copenhagen: Danish Institute for Education Research (Expanded edition (1980) with foreword and afterword by B.D. Wright, Chicago: The University of Chicago Press, 1980. Reprinted Chicago: MESA Press, 1993. Available from www.rasch.org/books.htm).

Rees, G., Fry, A., & Cull, A. (2001). A family history of breast cancer: women's experiences from a theoretical perspective. *Social Science and Medicine, 52*, 1433–1440.

Rees, V., Kreslake, J., & Cummings, K. (2009). Assessing consumer responses to potential reduced-exposure tobacco products: A review of tobacco industry and independent research methods. *Cancer Epidemiology Biomarkers & Prevention, 18*(12), 3225–3240.

Rindfleisch, A., & Crockett, D. (1999). Cigarette smoking and perceived risk: A multidimensional investigation. *Journal of Public Policy & Marketing, 18*, 159–171.

Romer, D., & Jamieson, P. (2001a). Do adolescents appreciate the risks of smoking? Evidence from a national survey. *Journal of Adolescent Health, 29*, 12–21.

Romer, D., & Jamieson, P. (2001b). The role of perceived risk in starting and stopping smoking. In P. Slovic (Ed.), *Smoking: Risk, perception, & policy* (pp. 64–80). Thousand Oaks, CA: Sage.

Shiffman, S., Pillitteri, J., Burton, S., Rohay, J., & Gitchell, J. (2001). Smokers' beliefs about "Light" and "Ultra Light" cigarettes. *Tobacco Control, 10*(1), 17–23.

Song, A., Glantz, S., & Halpern-Felsher, B. (2009). Perceptions of second-hand smoke risks predict future adolescent smoking initiation. *Journal of Adolescent Health, 45*, 618–625.

Tilleczek, K., & Hine, D. (2006). The meaning of smoking as health and social risk in adolescence. *Journal of Adolescence, 29*, 273–287.

Wagener, T., Gregor, K., Busch, A., McQuaid, E., & Borrelli, B. (2010). Risk perception in smokers with children with asthma. *Journal of Consulting and Clinical Psychology, 78*(6), 980–985.

Weinstein, N. (1998). Accuracy of smokers' risk perceptions. *Annals of Behavioral Medicine, 20* (2), 135–140.

Weinstein, N., Marcus, S., & Moser, R. (2005). Smokers' unrealistic optimism about their risk. *Tobacco Control, 14*, 55–59.

The Perception Risk Instrument (PRI)

Thomas Salzberger and Stefan Cano

1 Introduction

Consumer behavior typically involves consequences that the consumer cannot anticipate with certainty. Some of them are likely to be unpleasant (Stone and Grønhaug 1993). The notion of perceived risk has been proposed as a hypothetical construct that captures the consumer's assessment of adverse consequences of buying behavior and product use. Risk perceptions by consumers, or laymen, often deviate considerably from expert perceptions (for a detailed treatise of risk perception see Fischer 2017). While experts often rely on a narrow definition of risk invoking the concept of probability, the general public entertains a broader perspective of risk comprising aspects that cannot be captured by a simple probability. Therefore, what consumers perceive as risk typically is uncertainty that does not allow for attaching probabilities to future events (Stone and Grønhaug 1993). Even though expert risk perception does not necessarily reflect "true", or "objective", risk (Fischer 2017), the lack of agreement of expert assessment and consumer risk perception implies that expert judgment cannot replace subjective consumer risk perception. Furthermore, it has to be noted that no objective risk assessment is possible for products that have not been marketed yet (Cano and Salzberger 2017).

Risk perceptions are influenced by a number of mechanisms. As a rule, people tend to underestimate their individual risk resulting in an unrealistic optimism, specifically in relation to health consequences (Weinstein 1989; Weinstein et al.

T. Salzberger (✉)
Institute for Statistics and Mathematics, Institute for Marketing Management, Vienna University of Economics and Business, Welthandelspl. 1, 1020 Wien, Austria
e-mail: Thomas.Salzberger@wu.ac.at

S. Cano
Modus Outcomes, Suite 210b, Spirella Building, SG6 4ET Letchworth Garden City, UK
e-mail: stefan.cano@modusoutcomes.com

© Springer International Publishing AG 2017
G. Emilien et al. (eds.), *Consumer Perception of Product Risks and Benefits*,
DOI 10.1007/978-3-319-50530-5_11

2005). The observation that the perceived risk of exhibited hazardous behavior is likely to be downplayed is also line with cognitive dissonance theory (Festinger 1957). What is more, the formation of risk perception may take the form of an ex-post rationalization when the decision to engage in a particular behavior precedes the formation of risk perception (Slovic 1987). In contrast to optimism regarding one's own risk, the risk incurred by others exhibiting the same behavior is perceived more accurately suggesting that risk perceptions have to be differentiated in terms of individual (personal) risk and general risk affecting members of the general population.

Rather than relying on objective data, people rely on heuristics that may lead to biases (Kahneman et al. 1982). Valid risk perceptions are further hampered by difficulties in understanding what probabilities mean, by restricted access to information, and by improper consideration of personal experiences (see Slovic 1987). Risk perceptions are also impacted by affective heuristics (Slovic et al. 2004). The role of personal experiences, individual affect and cognitive processing implies that risk perceptions differ between individuals. The inter-individual variability may be more relevant than variability due to risk-related product attributes (Fischer 2017).

The notion of perceived risk as a hypothetical construct accommodates the characteristics of risk perception. Risk perceptions are inherently subjective and thus need to be assessed at the level of the individual. The complex and multifaceted nature of risk perceptions, which transcend one specific behavioral consequence comprising a multitude of outcomes, implies a challenge to the empirical assessment of perceived risk. The psychometric paradigm lends itself as a framework for developing a measurement instrument for perceived risk represented by potentially multiple latent variables (Cano and Salzberger 2017).

2 Risk Perception in Tobacco Research

The use of tobacco is an example of a behavior associated with a range of highly unpleasant consequences. Tobacco use may harm nearly every organ in the human body. What is more, the adverse consequences of tobacco are not confined to the user but also affect non-users through second-hand smoking. The use of tobacco, most notably by smoking cigarettes, therefore represents one of the biggest health concerns worldwide. In many countries, public initiatives have been devised that are to encourage users of tobacco to stop smoking, which is the best way to reduce the adverse health consequences of smoking (U.S. Department of Health and Human Services 1990). Smoking cessation is difficult to achieve, though; and relapse remains a frequent threat. Therefore, the class of modified risk tobacco products (MRTPs; Institute of Medicine 2012) has been proposed as a complementary harm reduction strategy of alleviating the detrimental effects of tobacco use to the society (Royal College of Physicians 2007). MRTPs imply reduced exposure to tobacco toxicants and/or reduced risk of developing tobacco-related diseases. The Food Drug Administration (FDA) drafted guidelines for application of modified risk tobacco products (MRTPs) (Food and Drug Administration (FDA) 2012). The FDA draft guidance highlights the importance of perceived risks and their measurement among tobacco users and non-users as risk perception is seen as an important determinant of product use. Specifically, the assessment of perceived risks of MRTPs in comparison to perceived risks of cigarette smoking, using cessation aids, and quitting all tobacco use is crucial. Thus, a valid, trustworthy measure of perceived risk is essential to assist and inform public smoking initiatives and authorities concerned with the regulation of MRTPs. Such an instrument needs to capture the dimensions of perceived risk that are more important to consumers. Salzberger et al. (2016) have carried out a literature search on available measurement instruments of perceived risk. The authors reached the conclusion that no instrument is fit for purpose specifically with regard to comparative measurement of perceived risk associated to a range of products. Therefore, a new instrument, the Perceived Risk Instrument (PRI), has been developed. The scale development project was sponsored by Philip Morris Product S.A.

3 The Perceived Risk Instrument (PRI) Scale Development

3.1 Objectives

The project aimed at developing a self-report instrument, easy to administer, to measure the perceived risks associated with the use of tobacco-related products. The instrument should be generic allowing for the comparative assessment of perceived risks associated with a broad range of tobacco-related products including nicotine replacement therapy, and potential MRTPs. The proposed instrument should capture the domains of perceived risk that are most relevant and meaningful to users and non-users. Further objectives were the applicability of the instrument to different subpopulations including current users of the products, former users as well as never users, and the applicability to the perceived risk to the individual user of the product and to users in general.

The development of the instrument was to reflect the state-of-the-art in psychometrics and take the criteria of good self-report instruments into account (see Cano and Salzberger 2017). This implied: (1) the development of a conceptual framework of the construct of perceived risk based on existing research and qualitative investigation; (2) the generation of items representing suggested dimensions of perceived risk and the qualitative assessment of their appropriateness; and (3) the investigation of the psychometric properties of the proposed instrument based on the Rasch model for measurement (Rasch 1960; Andrich 1988). Finally, while the validity of the proposed instrument was assessed in the USA, the conceptualization should allow for future applications of the instrument in other countries as well.

3.2 Conceptualization of the Construct

The conceptual framework defined the domains of perceived risk and explained their content. The conceptualization followed the best practice guidelines for developing patient reported outcome (PRO) instruments (Scientific Advisory Committee of the Medical Outcomes Trust 2002; Food and Drug Administration (FDA) 2009), including the current widely quoted US Food and Drug Administration's (FDA) scientific requirements for PROs in clinical trials (Revicki 2007). The development of the conceptual framework was based on input from a literature review, focus groups and expert opinion (for a detailed description see Salzberger et al. 2016). The literature review comprised two stages. First, it was to reveal existing self-report instruments (see Cano and Salzberger 2017). Based on the existing instruments' applicability to various smoking status groups (i.e., smokers, former smokers, never smokers), tobacco-related products, their content coverage and psychometric properties, it was concluded that none of the existing instruments were suitable to assess risk perceptions in a directly comparable way across different smoking status groups and tobacco-related products. Second, the key themes of risk perception were extracted from published studies. During this stage, health risk (to the person using the tobacco-related product as well as health hazards to third persons), social risk, financial risk and time risk were identified as potential dimensions.

Focus groups with consumers were the second source of qualitative data that informed the conceptualization of the construct. In order to provide the best possible basis for future extension of the instrument's applicability to other countries, discussions were initially conducted in the UK (nine groups with a total of 72 participants), Italy (four groups with a total of 32 participants), and Japan (four groups, 32 participants). Subsequently, additional focus groups were run in the USA (twelve groups, 93 participants) in order to establish the appropriateness of the conceptual framework in the USA, too. The analysis of the focus group results revealed 88 concepts that were grouped into three thematic clusters: health and addiction risks, societal and social risks, and material and financial risks. Thus, the literature review and the focus groups converged on the same themes that were important to consumers.

Subsequently, input from experts in the field of risk research was sought serving two purposes. First, it was another source of input to the formation of the conceptual framework. Second, it was to facilitate the consolidation of all input gathered. The expert panel agreed on the proposal of the domains of physical risk (health issues), addiction risk, social risk, emotional risk, and practical risk (risks associated with time and financial resources).

The broad agreement of the preliminary conceptual framework based on the literature review and the focus groups and the outcome of the open elicitation phase with experts provided strong support in terms of triangulation. As a result, the consolidation of all sources of input was non-critical (see Salzberger et al. 2016, for details). Thus, the conceptual framework based on qualitative input from the literature, focus groups in four countries, and expert opinion comprised the following domains of perceived risk:

Perceived Health Risk. The perceived negative risk (or impact) of product use to the user's physical health, going from minor immediate concrete manifestations of health risk (e.g. having poor gum health) to more serious long terms ones (e.g. having lung cancer);

Perceived Addiction Risk. The perceived negative risk (or impact) that product use may have on the user's sense of being addicted to using the product;

Perceived Health Risk to Others. The perceived negative risk (or impact) to the physical health of non-smokers when being around during product use;

Perceived Social Risk. The perceived negative risk (or impact) that product use will affect interpersonal interactions adversely or how the user is perceived by others;

Perceived Practical Risk. The perceived negative risk (or impact) that product use may have on the user's time and finances.

3.3 Item Generation

Based on focus group discussions, existing literature, and input from experts, items were generated for each of the five domains proposed by the conceptual framework. In this context, the term item denoted a symptom, a disease, a condition, or, generally speaking, an adverse consequence of using a tobacco-related product. In addition, a sentence stem shared by all items in a domain was generated. For each previously defined smoking status group, slight adaptations were made in order to tailor formulations to the smoking behavior and thus enhance cognitive orientation. Moreover, reflecting the differentiation between risk to the individual (referred to as personal risk) and risk to a user of a product in general (referred to as general risk) discussed in the literature, two versions of the instrument were developed. Since the necessary adaptation was minimal and limited to the sentence stem, potential comparability of the measures to be derived was preserved. As a response scale, a five-point fully verbalized rating scale was used. The verbal labels explicitly refer to the level of risk ranging from "no risk" to "very high risk". This offered the opportunity to express a medium level of risk by endorsing the middle category labelled "moderate risk". In order to avoid enforcing a response if respondents did not relate to the content of the item and therefore lacked a genuine perception, the option "don't know" was added.

Cognitive debriefing interviews (CDIs) were carried out in order to review the respondents' comprehension and interpretation of the items and the sentence stems, as well as the appropriateness of the response scale. For the English version of the instrument, CDIs were conducted in the UK (40 CDIs) and in the US (48 CDIs). The CDIs entailed minimal changes to the items. After the CDIs, the final draft versions of the perceived risk instrument (PRI), one for personal risk (PRI-P) and one for general risk (PRI-G), comprised a total of 67 items each. The items related to five domains: Perceived Health Risk (30 items, plus 1 item confined to nicotine replacement therapy), Perceived Health Risk to Others (3 items), Perceived Addiction Risk (11 items), Perceived Social risk (13 items), and Perceived Practical Risk (9 items).

3.4   Psychometric Scale Formation

3.4.1   Objectives, Study Design and Methods

The psychometric analysis aimed at the empirical confirmation of the conceptual framework and the assessment of the proposed items. Specifically, the applicability of the draft PRI to various tobacco and nicotine-related products across product users and non-users was to be investigated. To this end, a pilot study and two surveys were conducted in the USA administered online as web-surveys (see Cano et al. 2016, for details). In all studies, four subpopulations based on their self-reported smoking status (current smokers with no intention to quit, current smokers with intention to quit, former smokers, and never smokers) accounted for approximately 25% of the total sample in order to assess item properties for each group. Within each subpopulation, quota sampling based on gender, age group and education was implemented. In addition, for former smokers, proportions for recent quitters and long-term quitters were defined. The purpose of the small-scale pilot study (n = 233 completers) was to gain insight in terms of the feasibility of developing the proposed five scales in parallel. While Survey 1 (total n = 2020 completers) aimed at scale formation and assessment, Survey 2 (total n = 1640 completers) served as a cross-validation. In the psychometric analyses, the polytomous Rasch model for measurement (Rasch 1960; Andrich 1988) was used. The basic principles and requirements are described in Cano and Salzberger (2017).

In the pilot study and in Survey 1, respondents completed the proposed PRI applied to conventional cigarettes (CC), a tobacco heating system (THS) 2.2 (a candidate MRTP developed by Philip Morris Product S.A.), nicotine patch and cessation (defined as having successfully stopped smoking and not using any tobacco and nicotine-containing product). In Survey 2, the draft PRI was also applied to e-cigarettes, while nicotine patch was replaced by nicotine replacement therapy (NRT) as a general category. In the following, the tobacco and nicotine-related products as well as cessation are referred to as "objects". Half of the study participants responded to the PRI applied to the risk for the individual user (personal risk, PRI-P) and half of the participants to the PRI applied to the risk for the user in general (general risk, PRI-G).

Apart from the draft PRI, additional measures were administered for convergent validity assessment (the Short-Term and Long-Term Smoking Risks Questionnaire by Slovic (2000); visual analogue scales (VAS) as overall measures of selected domains of perceived risk).

3.4.2 Findings: Pilot Study

For items related to perceived social and perceived practical, the pilot study revealed considerable floor effects (lack of perceived risk) when applied to products other than conventional cigarettes. For this reason, it was decided to restrict further quantitative field tests to the three health-related domains (i.e., perceived health risk to self, perceived addiction risk, perceived health risk to others), which also were the most frequently addressed themes in the literature and most often reported in focus groups.

3.4.3 Findings: Surveys 1 and 2

An important prerequisite of the assessment of the validity of the PRI is the acceptability of the instrument to the participants. In both surveys, the acceptability of the PRI in terms of complete responses was very high. In survey 1, 98% of all participants who completed the whole survey provided responses to all PRI items. In survey 2, the proportion was 99%. At the item level, missing responses were extremely scarce with a proportion of 0.1% at most.

Given the objective of the development of an instrument that is broadly applicable to different subpopulations and products (or objects), the psychometric analysis of Survey 1 data suggested the omission of some items due to a lack of fit to the measurement model or other problems such as different functioning of the item for different subpopulations or objects. As a result, an 18-item Perceived Health Risk scale and a 7-item Perceived Addiction Risk scale were derived. One item assessing Perceived Addiction Risk was confined to cessation, for which addiction risk referred to the remaining addiction to cigarettes. Both scales showed excellent psychometric performance. Items related to Perceived Health Risk to Others did not form a separate scale and also could not be co-calibrated with items addressing Health Risk to the user of the product. These items were therefore interpreted as single items providing additional information to the two scales of the Perceived Risk Instrument (PRI).

The analysis of the 18-item Perceived Health Risk scale and 7-item Perceived Addiction Risk scale data in Survey 2 confirmed the psychometric properties of the scales. Importantly, no DIF was observed based on gender, age group, education, object, and type of risk (personal versus general risk). Thus, the scale provided perfectly comparable measures of perceived risk. The adequacy of the five-category response format was addressed by the investigation of the item threshold order. All item thresholds, marking the transition from one response option to the adjacent option, were properly ordered demonstrating that the scored responses did indeed represent an increasing amount of the perceived risk. Finally, the PRI scales adequately captured the risk perceptions of study participants providing satisfactory precision of measurement (Cano et al. 2016).

3.4.4 Further Evidence of Validity

Besides assessing the fit of the data to the Rasch model for measurement, further evidence of validity was provided based on convergent, discriminant and known-group validity (see Cano et al. 2016, for details). In terms of convergent validity, correlations of the 18-item Perceived Health Risk measure for conventional cigarettes with each of the five items of the Short- and Long-Term Smoking Risks Questionnaire (Slovic 2000), which were not supposed to form a summative scale, were in the expected direction for both personal and general risk. The size of the correlations was mostly weak to moderate, though, illustrating the limitations of single items as stand-alone measures. Correlations of the VAS and PRI measures for both perceived health risk and perceived addiction risk were higher (in the range of 0.52 to 0.68 for CC, THS 2.2, E-Cigarettes and NRT). Discriminant validity was examined by computing correlations between the two domains of Perceived Health Risk and Perceived Addiction Risk separately for each object and type of risk (personal versus general risk). The Pearson correlation coefficients were between 0.67 and 0.78 (depending on the object, Survey 2 data) indicating distinct yet related measures of perceived risk. Finally, as assessment of known-group validity, mean differences between subpopulations or types of risk were investigated that were to be expected based on previous studies in the literature. For example, current smokers perceived their personal health risk of smoking cigarettes as lower than the health risk for smokers in general. For more details, see Cano et al. (2016).

3.5 Estimation of Perceived Risk Measures

The estimation of measures of perceived risk is facilitated by a conversion table that converts the simple unweighted raw score across all items in a scale into a linear, i.e. interval-scaled measure (Fischer 1995). Missing responses or responses in the don't know category, which are to be set to missing, can be replaced by the respondent-specific mean response to other items in the scale provided at least 50% of the items have been responded to in valid response options. This score has then to be rounded to the nearest integer. For ease of interpretation, the metric of the linear measure is transformed into a 0-to-100 scale. The bottom end at 0 represents the lowest possible measure of perceived risk as assessed by the PRI. It indicates that all responses are in the "no risk" category. The mid-point at 50 implies a moderate risk, while 100 means that the respondent perceives a very high risk on all items.

Table 1 PRI items (examples) and response scale

PRI Health Risk
Having poor gum health
Having lung cancer
PRI Addiction Risk
Being unable to quit cigarettes
Having to smoke cigarettes to feel better
PRI response scale and scoring
No risk (0); Low risk (1); Moderate risk (2); High risk (3); Very high risk (4);
Don't know (set to missing)

4 The PRI: Purpose and Application

4.1 Purpose of the PRI

The PRI consists of two scales assessing Perceived Health Risk (18 items) and Perceived Addiction Risk (7 items) of using a tobacco or nicotine-related product (see Table 1 for examples). While the items remain the same regardless of the tobacco or nicotine-related product the instrument is applied to, the sentence stem for each scale provides the reference to the product to be assessed as well as the type of risk (personal risk—PRI-P, general risk—PRI-G). Furthermore, if applicable, the sentence stem accommodates the smoking status (see Table 2 for sentence stem examples).

The PRI establishes a continuum of perceived risk allowing for a direct comparability of measures in terms of (1) different tobacco and nicotine-related products, (2) different subpopulations based on smoking status, and (3) perceived risk to the individual user versus perceived risk to the user in general. In addition, comparisons across gender, age groups and education can be made. While these comparisons are made at a particular point in time, the PRI can also be used in order to track risk perception for a product over time. This is of particular interest in the context of newly developed products, such as MRTPs, where consumers have limited information and understanding of the product. The PRI helps assess the impact of new information, such as communication messages, labels or labelling, on the risk perception by consumers. In the following, we present illustrative examples of applications of the PRI-P and the PRI-G to various tobacco and nicotine-related products across different subpopulations. Furthermore, we demonstrate the usage of the PRI as a predictor of product trial and its utility to assess the impact of communication messages.

Table 2 PRI Sentence stems (examples)

PRI-P Health Risk applied to conventional cigarettes
Smokers with no intention to quit or with intention to quit:
What do you think is the risk, if any, to you personally of getting the following (sometime during your lifetime) because you smoke cigarettes …
Former smokers:
If you were to resume smoking, what do you think would be the risk, if any, to you personally of getting the following (sometime during your lifetime) because you smoke cigarettes …
Never smokers:
If you were to start smoking, what do you think would be the risk, if any, to you personally of getting the following (sometime during your lifetime) because you smoke cigarettes …
PRI-P Health Risk applied to cessation
Smokers with no intention to quit or with intention to quit:
If you were to successfully quit smoking, what do you think would be the risk, if any, to you personally of getting the following (sometime during your lifetime) because you smoked cigarettes in the past …
Former smokers:
If you remain a former smoker, what do you think is the risk, if any, to you personally of getting the following (sometime during your lifetime) because you smoked cigarettes in the past …
PRI-G Health Risk applied to conventional cigarettes
All subpopulations:
In general, what do you think is the risk, if any, to smokers of getting the following (sometime during their lifetime) because of smoking cigarettes …

4.2 Application of the PRI to Different Tobacco and Nicotine-Related Products

Figure 1 shows the means of Perceived Health Risk (personal risk) across all smoking status groups for all five objects the PRI-P has been applied to in Survey 2. Conventional cigarettes are perceived as the riskiest tobacco product. THS 2.2 ranks second and is perceived to be slightly riskier than e-cigarettes. Study participants perceive NRT as the product with the lowest health risk. The cessation scenario is associated with the second-lowest perceived health risk. NRT being less risky than cessation may seem counterintuitive. However, NRT is meant to be applied for a limited time only. It is, in the end, a cessation scenario, too. More importantly, cessation refers to the risk due to smoking in the past while the perceived risk of NRT emphasizes the future use of NRT.

4.3 Application of the PRI to Different Subpopulations

The applicability of the PRI to different subpopulations based on smoking status is illustrated by a comparison of the perceived health risk of using conventional cigarettes and THS 2.2 (see Fig. 2) based on Survey 2 data. Within all four smoking

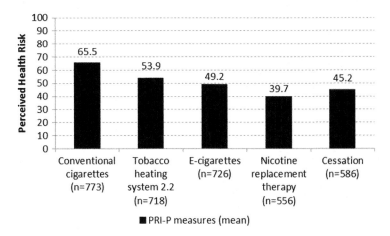

Fig. 1 PRI-P measures of Perceived Health Risk across objects

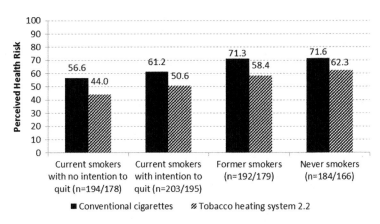

Fig. 2 PRI-P measures of Perceived Health Risk across subpopulations

status groups, conventional cigarettes are perceived as riskier than THS 2.2, even though for never smokers the difference is the smallest. The means reveal big differences between the smoking status groups. While the risk perceptions of former smokers and never smokers are rather similar, current smokers, particular those with no intention to quit, are considerably lower. Former and never smokers perceived THS 2.2 as riskier than current smokers with no intention to quit perceive conventional cigarettes.

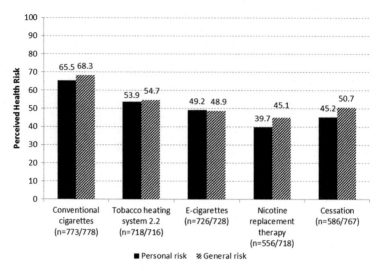

Fig. 3 PRI-P and PRI-G measures of Perceived Health Risk

4.4 Application of the PRI to Different Types of Risk

The measures of the PRI-P assessing the perceived risk to the individual user and the PRI-G measuring the perceived risk to product users in general refer to the same latent continuum of perceived risk. The measures are expressed in the same metric and are thus directly comparable. Figure 3 exemplifies the comparison across types of risk for perceived health risk. For conventional cigarettes, nicotine replacement therapy and cessation, the perceived health risk is higher for the user in general than for the individual participant. By contrast, no such differences prevail for THS 2.2 and e-cigarettes.

4.5 Application of the PRI as a Predictor of Product Use

Perceived risk is one potential antecedent to usage behavior (Ajzen 1991; Bandura 1998). In the context of the scale development project, the predictive power of the PRI was investigated with regard to initiation of THS 2.2. Since the product is new and not yet available on the market, actual usage could not be investigated. Since the intention to use the product continuously arguably depends on how the consumer experiences the product during a trial phase, the intention to try THS 2.2 was considered as the predicted behavior. Intention to try was assessed using a single item with six response categories labelled definitely not, very unlikely, somewhat unlikely, somewhat likely, very likely, and definitely. For the purpose of investigating predictive power, intention to try was dichotomized by retaining the definitely not category and collapsing the other categories. Thus, intention to try meant the slightest chance to try THS 2.2. Among the participants assessing personal perceived risk, across all smoking status groups, 40% of participants (Survey 2) said they would definitely not try the product. In the general risk sample, 44% had definitely no intention.

A logistic regression of the intention to try on the conversion table-based linear measures of the PRI of Perceived Health Risk and Perceived Addiction Risk revealed a significant relationship of the PRI measures and intention to try for both personal and general risk in the expected direction. Thus, a higher score on the PRI implies a lower intention to try. The impact of Perceived Health Risk (odds ratio 0.90 in case of personal risk, and 0.86 in case of general risk) and Perceived Addiction Risk (odds ratio 0.89 in case of personal risk, and 0.88 in case of general risk) was in a similar range. In total, the strength of the relationship was limited. The reasons were twofold. First, the vast majority of never smokers (80% in the personal risk sample, 88% in the general risk sample) ruled out any intention to try. Similarly, 64% (personal risk) and 70% (general risk) of former smokers did definitely not want to try THS 2.2. Second, lacking any personal product experience and more detailed information on the product, many participants might not have been able to state a valid intention to try. This could change when consumers receive more information and the product is available on the market. The assessment of how new information influences the risk perception of the product constitutes another application of the PRI.

4.6 Application of the PRI to Assess the Impact of Communication

Risk perception depends on how much and what kind of information consumers possess. In case of new products, such as MRTPs, it is, from a regulatory point of view, crucial how communication messages impact on risk perception. The PRI allows for the assessment of their effect. In a study on the effect of messages about THS 2.2 on risk perception, Beacher et al. (2016) used the PRI-P to assess the Perceived Health Risk of THS 2.2 and comparators. Figure 4 shows the means of Perceived Health Risk in various smoking status groups as a result of different messages. While message 1 was a reduced exposure claim (reduction in harmful chemicals while pointing out that a risk reduction has not been demonstrated), message 5 was a reduced risk claim (switching from cigarettes to THS 2.2 reduces the risks of tobacco-related diseases while pointing out that reduced risk does not mean no risk).

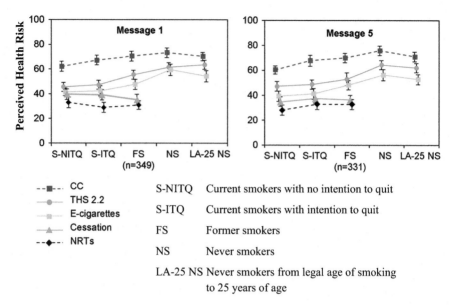

Fig. 4 PRI-P measures of Perceived Health Risk as a function of different messages

5 Limitations of the PRI

When applying the PRI, researchers should be aware for limitations that constrain the use of the instrument. The limitations are related to the order in which products are assessed, to the meaningfulness of the administration of the PRI given the smoking status of the respondent, and to the characteristics of tobacco and nicotine-related products.

5.1 Carry-over Effects

In experimental research, carry-over effects may occur when the exposure to an experimental condition affects another condition the subject is exposed to subsequently. While the presence of carry-over effects is rarely investigated in survey research, the application of the PRI to multiple objects raises the question whether risk perceptions are altered depending on the order in which objects are assessed. In Survey 2, the order of objects was randomized allowing for analyses shedding light on this potential problem. To this end, mean comparisons (Wellek and Blettner 2012) were carried out for all objects when presented first versus second or later in the sequence. For CC, THS 2.2 and e-cigarettes no differences were detected. However, for cessation, both personal and general Perceived Health Risk were higher when cessation was presented as the first object compared to it being presented after at least one other object. For NRT, a similar effect was found for general risk, with the level of risk being higher when NRT was assessed first.

The indication of carry-over effects for cessation and NRT suggests care should be taken when administering the PRI to a sequence of objects including cessation or NRT. In particular, comparisons of perceived risk across studies that applied the PRI to products in a different order might be adversely affected. Based on findings from Survey 2, carry-over effects may best be accommodated by a fixed order of objects to which the PRI is applied to. The best-known product, typically CC, should be presented first, as it helps the participant setting a meaningful reference point. Subsequently, further applications of the PRI to other tobacco products should be administered in decreasing order in terms of product familiarity. Reflecting the transition from product use to non-use, objects related to quitting smoking should be presented at the end. In particular, cessation (not involving any use of NRT) should be presented as the very last object.

5.2 Applicability to Cessation

The assessment of perceived risk of the use of a product should be meaningful to the respondent. It turned out that never smokers have extreme difficulties to imagine a personal smoking history for which they state their risk perceptions. Similarly, never smokers found it hard to relate to the personal use of NRT, which almost all participants ruled out categorically. For these reasons, the PRI-P was not administered to cessation and NRT for never smokers when assessing personal risk. However, never smokers had no issues with stating their risk perceptions with regard to a smoker in general who stopped smoking or started using NRT. Therefore, it is recommended not to apply the PRI-P to cessation or NRT in case of never smokers, while the PRI-G may be applied under these conditions.

The assessment of the perceived risk of cessation is affected by another intricacy related to its time reference. While all other objects refer to the risk due to prospective product use, cessation pertains to the risk of smoking behavior in the past. For this reason, the perceived health risk of using NRT (referring to a relatively short usage period in the future) was lower than the perceived health risk of cessation (referring to a possibly very long period of using cigarettes). Therefore, NRT and cessation should be used as alternative endpoints of lower risk on the continuum of perceived risk depending on the purpose of the study.

5.3 Applicability to Further Products

The scale development project considered a broad range of products the PRI was applied to. The psychometric properties were assessed for conventional cigarettes, electronic cigarettes that vaporize a liquid, an MRTP that heats but does not burn tobacco, and a concrete NRT product (nicotine patch) as well as NRT as a product category. In addition, the past but successfully discontinued use of cigarettes was considered (cessation). It is to be expected that the PRI would also be applicable to further tobacco or nicotine-related products. However, if such products are based on a different technology that was not covered by the studies undertaken, it is recommended to confirm the psychometric properties of the PRI.

5.4   Applicability to Novel Products

The formation of risk perceptions requires that respondents possess at least some understanding of the product. If respondents feel unable to state their perceived risk, they should not be forced to respond. For this reason, a "don't know" category was offered. While study participants made little use of this category in case of familiar products, such as conventional cigarettes, it was more often resorted to when assessing the unfamiliar THS 2.2. While responses in the "don't know" category represent valuable qualitative information, they do not contribute to the estimation of a participant's measure of perceived risk. If less than half of the items are responded to in the "don't know" category, the responses can be replaced by the respondent's mean response to the remaining items. Otherwise, no estimation of perceived risk is possible for such respondents. Therefore, when assessing novel products, a reduced sample size is to be expected as far as the estimation of measures of perceived risk is concerned.

6   Conclusions

Adequate measurement of perceived risk at the level of the individual consumer informs regulatory decision making specifically with regard to the risk reduction strategy that complements efforts to facilitate smoking cessation. The appraisal of the effects of introducing MRTPs benefits from comparative perceived risk assessment across different tobacco and other nicotine-containing products and across different smoking status groups. Since existing instruments did not adequately meet the requirements of direct comparability, a new instrument to measure perceived risk was developed following a multistep process.

At first, a conceptual framework of perceived risk was developed. Subsequently, quantitative studies were conducted in the USA aiming at forming scales for the most relevant domains of perceived risk. The scale development project resulted in the Perceived Risk Instrument (PRI) consisting of two scales: the Perceived Health Risk scale and the Perceived Addiction Risk scale. Both scales can be applied to personal risk (PRI-P) and general risk (PRI-G). The strengths of the PRI lie in its ease of administration and the high acceptability by the respondents, its versatility in terms of tobacco and nicotine-related products it can be applied to, and the straightforward comparability of the estimated measures.

The application of the PRI should observe a few constraints. The administration of the PRI to cessation or NRT in case of never smokers is not advised when referring to their own individual risk rather than general risk. Care should be exercised when applying the PRI to multiple products at a time as carry-over effects may be present. It is recommended to start the assessment with the most familiar product, typically conventional cigarettes, and assess NRT and cessation at the end. The applicability of the PRI has been demonstrated for a broad range of products suggesting its suitability for products other than those considered in the scale development project. However, when applying the PRI to products with a new technology, the psychometric properties should be re-evaluated. Finally, the formation of perceived risk may be impeded in case of novel products where consumer knowledge and understanding are meagre. A higher proportion of responses in the "don't know" category is then to be expected.

The PRI fills a critical gap and lends itself to be used in clinical and population-based studies. Future empirical studies utilizing the PRI promise to expand the knowledge-base and provide more insight into the understanding of risk perception data. In particular, the PRI will be useful for the investigation of how risk perception impacts behavior or behavioral intention including switching behavior or product initiation among non-users or former users. The PRI may also inform studies on the effects of risk communication on the understanding of risk and product perception and thereby allow for recommendations as to how to contribute to realistic risk perceptions.

The development of the PRI demonstrates that complex constructs such as perceived risk, which involve the consumer as the subject and the product as the object, can be measured allowing for comparative assessment of perceived risk. The approach lends itself as a template for scale development in risk research in general. Whenever perceived risks of consumer behavior are to be measured using a self-report instrument, the development of the PRI can serve as a roadmap. The scheme outlines the developmental process starting with the generation of a conceptual framework informed by a multiple sources, followed by item generation and qualitative pre-testing of the of items, and ultimately concluded by the psychometric analysis of quantitative data from the administration of the new instrument. In a broader context, measurement in health research is expected to benefit from new scale development in line with the development of the Perceived Risk Instrument. The PRI and a calibrated scoring table will be available through MAPI Research Trust (http://www.mapi-trust.org/).

References

Ajzen, I. (1991). The theory of planned behavior. *Organizational Behavior and Human Decision Processes, 50*(2), 179–211.

Andrich, D. (1988). A general form of Rasch's extended logistic model for partial credit scoring. *Applied Measurement in Education, 1*(4), 363–378.

Bandura, A. (1998). Health promotion from the perspective of social cognitive theory. *Psychology and Health, 13*(4), 623–649.

Beacher, F., Magnani, P., Ramazzotti, A., Weitkunat, R., Kallischnigg, G., Coleman, S., & Alfieri, T. (2016, March 2–5). *Study to Quantitatively Assess Tobacco Heating System 2.2 potential messages.* Poster presented at the Society for Research on Nicotine and Tobacco (SRNT) 2016 Annual Meeting, Chicago, USA.

Cano, S., & T. Salzberger (2017). Measuring risk perceptions. In G. Emilien, R. Weitkunat, & F. Lüdicke (Eds.), *Consumer perception of product risks and benefits.* Chapter II.3 (pp. XX–XX).

Cano, S., Chrea, C., Salzberger, T., Alfieri, T., Emilien, G., Mainy, N., Ramazzotti, A., Lüdicke, F., & Weitkunat, R. (2016). *Development and validation of a new instrument to measure perceived risks associated with the use of tobacco and nicotine-containing products.* Unpublished manuscript at the time of writing.

Festinger, L. (1957). *A theory of cognitive dissonance.* Stanford: Stanford University Press.

Fischer, G. H. (1995). Derivations of the Rasch model. In G. H. Fischer & I. W. Molenaar (Eds.), *Rasch models* (pp. 15–38). New York: Springer.

Fischer, A. R. H. (2017). Perception of product risks. In G. Emilien, R. Weitkunat, & F. Lüdicke (Eds.), *Consumer perception of product risks and benefits.* Chapter II.2 (pp. XX–XX).

Food and Drug Administration (FDA). (2009). *Patient reported outcome measures: Use in medical product development to support labeling claims.* Accessed May 19, 2016, from http://www.fda.gov/downloads/Drugs/Guidances/UCM193282.pdf

Food and Drug Administration (FDA). (2012). Guidance for industry—modified risk tobacco product applications (draft guidance) [online]. Accessed May 19, 2016, from http://www.fda.gov/downloads/TobaccoProducts/GuidanceComplianceRegulatoryInformation/UCM297751.pdf

Institute of Medicine. (2012). *Scientific standards for studies on modified risk tobacco products.* Washington, DC: The National Academies Press.

Kahneman, D., Slovic, P., & Tversky, A. (Eds.). (1982). *Judgement under uncertainty: Heuristics and biases.* New York: Cambridge University Press.

Rasch, G. (1960). *Probabilistic models for some intelligence and attainment tests.* Copenhagen: Danish Institute for Education Research (Expanded edition (1980) with foreword and afterword by B. D. Wright, Chicago: The University of Chicago Press, 1980. Reprinted Chicago: MESA Press, 1993).

Revicki, D. (2007). FDA Draft guidance and health-outcomes research. *Lancet, 369*, 540–542.

Royal College of Physicians. (2007). *Harm reduction in nicotine addiction: Helping people who can't quit.* A report by the Tobacco Advisory Group of the Royal College of Physicians. London: RCP.

Salzberger, T., Chrea, C., Cano, S., Martin, M., Emilien, G., Mainy, N., Ramazzotti, A., Weitkunat, R., & Lüdicke, F. (2016). *Development of a conceptual framework of perceived risks associated with the use of tobacco and nicotine-containing products.* Unpublished manuscript at the time of writing.

Scientific Advisory Committee of the Medical Outcomes Trust. (2002). Assessing health status and quality of life instruments: Attributes and review criteria. *Quality of Life Research, 11*, 193–205.

Slovic, P. (1987). The perception of risk. *Science, 236*(4799), 280–285.

Slovic, P. (2000). What does it mean to know a cumulative risk? Adolescents' perceptions of short-term and long-term consequences of smoking. *Journal of Behavioral Decision Making, 13*(2), 259–266.

Slovic, P., Finucane, M. L., Peters, E., & MacGregor, D. G. (2004). Risk as analysis and risk as feelings: Some thoughts about affect, reason, risk, and rationality. *Risk Analysis, 24*(2), 311–322.

Stone, R. N., & Grønhaug, K. (1993). Perceived risk: Further considerations for the marketing discipline. *European Journal of Marketing, 27*(3), 39–50.

U.S. Department of Health and Human Services. (1990). The Health Benefits of Smoking Cessation. US Department of Health and Human Services Public Health Service Centers for Disease Control Center for Chronic Disease Prevention and Health Promotion Office on Smoking and Health 1990. DHHS Publication No. (CDC) 9O-8416.

Weinstein, N. D. (1989). Optimistic biases about personal risks. *Science, 246*(4935), 1232–1233.

Weinstein, N. D., Marcus, S., & Moser, R. (2005). Smokers' unrealistic optimism about their risk. *Tobacco Control, 14*, 55–59.

Wellek, S., & Blettner, M. (2012). On the proper use of the crossover design in clinical trials: Part 18 of a series on evaluation of scientific publications. *Dtsch Arztebl Int, 109*(15), 276–281.

Role of Emotions in Risk Perception

W. Gerrod Parrott

1 Introduction

It is possible to conceive of risk in terms that are completely unemotional: risk is the undesirability of an event, weighted by its probability; increasing either the probability or the undesirability of the event will increase the risk (see, e.g., von Neumann and Morgenstern 1944). Such a formulation uses abstract concepts and mathematical calculation to elide the emotional qualities inherent in the psychology of risk perception. An abstract term, "undesirability," neutralizes the emotional associations that are inherent in more specific and vivid terms such as danger, disease, pain, suffering, harm, injury, death, or loss. The obvious connection between these terms and emotion provides an intuitive reason why it is necessary to consider the emotional aspects of risk to understand how consumers perceive product risks.

More rigorous proof that emotion is related to risk perception may be found in a classic laboratory experiment. Johnson and Tversky (1983) asked participants to read one of several newspaper reports about the death of a young adult; the reports described the cause of death—either leukemia, fire, or homicide—in a detailed manner that induced anxiety and worry in readers, who subsequently were asked to estimate the frequency of various causes of death that were either similar to or dissimilar from to the one described in the newspaper. The participants estimated the risk of death to be much higher than did participants in a control condition who read only mundane newspapers reports that did not induce negative emotions. Most importantly, the participants perceived increased risk from all causes of death, regardless of whether they were similar to the cause of death that they read about.

W.G. Parrott (✉)
Department of Psychology, Georgetown University, 3700 P Street, NW, Box 571001, Washington, DC 20057, USA
e-mail: parrottg@georgetown.edu

© Springer International Publishing AG 2017
G. Emilien et al. (eds.), *Consumer Perception of Product Risks and Benefits*,
DOI 10.1007/978-3-319-50530-5_12

For example, participants who read about a death from leukemia were just as likely to perceive elevated risk from electrocution or lightning as from other types of cancer. Subsequent studies demonstrated that elevated perceptions of risk extended to non-lethal life problems such as bankruptcy or divorce; that newspaper accounts of non-lethal sad events such as job stress and romantic breakup could raise perceptions of lethal risk as much as did a story about a homicide; and that a newspaper article about a person's good fortune (admission to medical school) decreased perceptions of the risk of all manner of bad events. From these experiments, Johnson and Tversky (1983) concluded that the mechanism influencing participants' perceptions of risk was not the specific information in the newspaper, nor was it cognitive inference about particular risks, but rather it was the emotions that were aroused by the newspaper report that led to an increased or decreased sense of vulnerability to all kinds of problems.

During the decades since Johnson and Tversky's (1983) article, researchers have greatly refined our understanding of the ways that emotions are related to risk perception and other judgments. These decades witnessed a transformation in theory and research on emotions, including research on how emotions are related to perception, memory, attention, and other cognitive processes. The purpose of the present contribution is to explore how emotions affect the perception of risk. It will first summarize the advances in the theory of emotion that have occurred since Johnson and Tversky's (1983) research. It then will describe the principal theoretical frameworks for understanding emotions' effects on judgments of risk, survey the empirical support for these theories, and apply these findings to the specific issue of how emotions influence consumers' perceptions of product risks and benefits.

2   Risk Perception and the Nature of Emotion

The concept of emotion has long been accorded an ambivalent status in the Western cultural tradition, from the ancient Romans to the present day. On the one hand, emotion has been opposed to reason and characterized as irrational, primitive, and biased; on the other hand, emotion has been opposed to mechanical detachment and characterized as caring, intuitive, sensitive, and motivated (Lutz 1988). Researchers' approach to emotion's role in risk perception has been similarly ambivalent. Risk experts sometimes disparage the way that emotion affects the general public's perceptions of risk; the public's aversion to nuclear energy, or its willingness to abandon freedoms and allocate resources to combat rare acts of terrorism may be viewed by experts as irrational and disproportionate, whereas the public's acceptance of indoor air pollution or automobile crashes seems dangerously blasé. The general public, in turn, often distrusts the judgments of experts (Slovic 1999).

The perspective of modern research on emotions can help resolve this ambivalence. Two fundamental conclusions from contemporary emotion research are that emotion and reason cannot be sharply distinguished, and that emotions generally function in ways that are adaptive and beneficial (Frijda 1986; Lazarus 1991). Rather than contrast dispassionate experts with an emotional public, it is more accurate to characterize experts and public as applying different ideologies and values to their assessments of risk, with emotions being involved for both experts and general public alike (Slovic 1999).

2.1 Components and Levels of Analysis of Emotion

These two conclusions derive from the renewed study of emotion that began in psychology in the mid-1970s and continues today, having spread to most academic disciplines in the social and biological sciences, as well as in the humanities. An essential breakthrough was the development of a conceptual framework that allows coordination of biological, cognitive, and social research while accommodating the somewhat imprecise definition of emotion. Essentially, the solution entailed conceiving of emotions as involving a set of components that can each be analyzed fruitfully regardless of whether the overall category is itself precisely defined. This approach treats emotion as a fuzzy concept that, prototypically, incorporates a set of components, none of which is essential or sufficient to constitute emotion, but which are frequently present in any given emotional state. There is considerable agreement among theorists about the components of emotion, although there are slight differences between theorists (Parrott 2007; Scherer 1984).

Emotions may be considered to be valenced reactions to events. A valenced reaction is one that may be described as positive or negative in some sense, whether it be a judgment of being in accord or opposed to one's wishes, a feeling of pleasure or displeasure, or a motivation to approach or withdraw. Emotions are more than simple valence, however. Emotions may be characterized as entailing five components: feelings, cognition, action tendencies, expression, and self-regulation.

The first and most traditional component is *feeling*, the conscious experience of being emotional in some way. Whether the feeling is of a specific emotion, such as fear, anger, or satisfaction, or whether it is a vaguer sense of well-being or unhappiness, this feeling is part of what people typically mean when they say they are experiencing a mood or emotion. In this contribution the word *emotion* will be used generically to encompass all such affective states. Feeling sometimes appears to be the central feature of emotion, but at other times is only one aspect part of emotion, and at other times is not essential at all—consider an emotion that a person is unaware of (such as unacknowledged shame or repressed anger), or emotions in animals, which are studied by researchers despite the impossibility of assessing the animal's subjective experience. As shall be discussed later in this contribution, feeling is central to one major approach to understanding the effect of emotion on risk perception, the "affect heuristic" (Finucane et al. 2000).

The second component, *cognition*, are part of emotions in two ways, one being the interpretation that gives rise to an emotion and sustains it (known in psychology as 'appraisal'), the other being the alteration in subsequent thinking that occurs once an emotion is underway (which may be termed "emotional cognition"). Appraisals differ from other perceptions and beliefs because they relate situations and events to a person's cares, concerns, and values, and they are central to another major approach to understanding the role of emotion in risk perception, the "appraisal-tendency framework" of Lerner and Keltner (2000).

The third component, *action tendencies*, refers to the variety of ways that emotions alter motivation (Frijda 1986). Emotions do not result in fixed behavioral responses, but rather potentiate behavioral and cognitive tendencies. These tendencies may include preparation or readiness for action, either physically in the world or mentally with respect to attention, perception, memory, or reasoning. Action tendencies are the primary way that emotions can be useful and adaptive because they prepare an organism for behavior and cognition that are likely to be functional given the appraisal of circumstances that gave rise to the emotion. The anxiety that arises from an appraisal of heightened threat includes cognitive attentional vigilance and behavioral preparedness for escape, both of which are likely to promote survival and flourishing under the circumstances.

The incorporation of cognitive processes within appraisal and action tendencies demonstrates why researchers no longer make a sharp distinction between emotion and reason. Although it is possible to distinguish emotional cognition from unemotional cognition, it does not make sense to characterize emotion as being non-cognitive because the appraisal of events is intrinsic to emotion itself, as is the redirection of attention, memory, and perception that emotion initiates (Parrott and Schulkin 1993).

The fourth component of emotion is *expression*, the observable changes that communicate an organism's emotional state to others. Expression introduces a means by which emotion can spread from one person to another, as well as a means of inducing complementary or reactive emotions in others. Emotional communication can occur via facial expressions, tone of voice, posture, movement, and gesture.

Finally, most emotions involve a component of *self-regulation* by which the emotion's nature, intensity, duration, and expression are modified to suit the circumstances in which it occurs. Although some theorists maintain that regulation should not be considered to be part of the thing being regulated, many psychologists argue that emotions are shaped from beginning to end in ways that cannot be separated from other aspects of emotion, and therefore that regulation and emotion are one (Kappas 2011). Emotions related to risk perception are continuously monitored and adjusted in light of the changing characteristics and demands of the circumstances.

A key feature of the componential approach is that each component can be analyzed at multiple levels of analysis (Parrott 2007). There is no fixed number of levels, but this idea can be illustrated by distinguishing three levels: the individual, the social, and the biological. Emotions are often examined on the individual level of analysis, which considers an isolated person's consciousness, thoughts, feelings, and actions when in an emotional state such as anger, fear, or happiness. Emotions can also be examined at the social level of analysis, which would situate the anger, fear, or happiness within the dynamics of a particular social interaction involving members of a group, set of groups, and culture. Although the participants in the social interaction would all be having emotions describable at the individual level, their interaction gives rise to social phenomena that are more than the sum of the individual reactions. An example of risk perception that requires explanation at the social level of analysis would be public panics that start with an isolated case or an unsubstantiated rumor but rapid social dissemination spreads fear and results in elevated perceptions of risk (Loewenstein and Mather 1990). These social and cultural phenomena require their own terminology and principles of organization, and often their own research methodologies as well. Finally, there is the biological level of analysis, which addresses the same set of five components in terms of hormonal, neural, and bodily activity. For example, if damage to a specific region of the brain alters risk perception, then biological changes can be mapped onto individual perception and behavior. As with the social level of analysis, the terminology, concepts, and research methods appropriate to biological processes differ markedly from those appropriate to the individual level. The optimal level of analysis for describing the effects of emotions on risk perception will vary depending on the type of influence and the way in which it is measured.

2.2 Emotions' Potential to be Functional

The idea that emotions are functional and adaptive stems from both theoretical and empirical roots. Many lines of evidence point to emotions having an evolutionary basis. Emotions rely on neurological and hormonal systems that have a genetic basis and that have analogs in non-human species; some expressions of emotion can be recognized cross-culturally in humans and develop with minimal experience in infants. Evolutionary theory postulates that an elaborate and calorically costly system would not continue to exist unless it provided some adaptive benefits that outweighed these costs (Tooby and Cosmides 1990). Emotions' modification of action tendencies, thought processes, expressions, and conscious awareness can facilitate adaptive functioning in the situations in which they occur (Frijda 1986). Functionalist theories of emotion posit that emotions exist in order to be useful; unpleasant emotions typically arise in situations where obstacles need to be confronted, where dangers require vigilance or escape, where relationships are threatened and must be monitored or repaired, where loss or failure requires the abandonment of prior attachments, where social transgression requires submissiveness and making amends; positive emotions typically arise when there is opportunity to take advantage of opportunities when things are going well (Parrott 2014). The purpose of emotions is not to make people feel pleasant but rather to motivate and guide actions that optimize responses to the problems and opportunities at hand. This idea represents quite a break from the psychology of the mid-twentieth-century in which emotions were considered to be disruptions that disorganize behavior. The claim is not that emotions cannot be dysfunctional and lead to erroneous and maladaptive perceptions of risk. Rather, functionalist theories claim that the purpose of each type of emotion is to be adaptive, and that accurate appraisal and appropriate regulation maximize the probability that an emotion will be aroused in circumstances in which it can be beneficial (Parrott 2002).

One well-known empirical demonstration of emotions effectiveness in guiding risk perception comes from research on patients who have damage to the ventro-medial prefrontal cortex (VMPFC) of the brain (Damasio 1994). Damage to this brain region does not impair attention, working memory, cognitive estimation, language, or social knowledge, but does cause difficulty in feeling and expressing emotion. Remarkably, patients with damage to the VMPFC also tend to be less avoidant of risk and to experience difficulty in making decisions. In laboratory studies, decision making that involves uncertainty, risk, and reward has been studied by presenting these patients with a gambling task that required participants to select from one of four decks of cards to obtain a card that would reveal either a financial reward or a penalty (Bechara et al. 1997). Unknown to the participant, two of the decks contained high rewards but on occasion even higher penalties, so on average those decks yielded a net loss, whereas the other two decks contained low rewards but even lower penalties, so on average those decks allowed the participant to make money. The gambling task was repeated for 100 trials so that participants could get experience with the outcomes. The cards were too variable to allow a participant to figure out the exact rule for each deck, but repeated trials led healthy controls to develop a preference for cards from the safe, profitable decks. In contrast, patients with damage to the VMPFC did not develop this preference. The patients prefered the risky, losing decks throughout the task (Bechara et al. 1997). Although these findings are consistent with a variety of explanatory mech-anisms (Dunn et al. 2006), they suggest that emotional reactions to choices under conditions of uncertainty and risk can affect risk perception in ways that benefit decision making.

2.3   *Integral, Incidental, and Anticipated Emotions*

When discussing the ways that emotions affect risk perception it must be noted that the emotion can be related to the risk in several distinct ways. In the case of the gambling task described in the preceding paragraph (Bechara et al. 1997), the emotion (fear) was elicited by the risky choice itself (whether to choose a card from a deck that has delivered large financial losses). Emotions that arise from the decision at hand have been termed "integral emotions" (Lerner and Keltner 2000).

Emotions can affect risk perception in others ways, however. An emotion that is aroused by one source can influence how risk is perceived in other, unrelated domains. For example, in the classic studies of risk perception that were described in the present contribution's Introduction (Johnson and Tversky 1983), an emotion (anxiety) that was elicited by a newspaper article about a person's death (from, say, leukemia) led to elevated perception of risk for a wide variety of unrelated bad outcomes, ranging from other diseases to accidents to divorce or bankruptcy. When an emotional state caused by one situation influences risk perception about an unrelated situation, the emotion can be termed "incidental emotion" (Lerner and Keltner 2000).

This contribution is concerned with the ways that ongoing emotional states affect risk perception, so all possibilities are encompassed by the twin categories of integral and incidental emotions. It is worth mentioning, however, that emotion can influence risk perception in less direct ways as well (Loewenstein and Lerner 2003). For example, a third way that emotion can be related to risk perception is by being anticipated and thereby shaping the perceived riskiness of a decision or course of action. For example, if a consumer anticipates that buying an expensive new hat might lead to regret over the wasted money or to sadness about not getting two less expensive hats or to embarrassment when confronted by an angry spouse, then the possibility of unpleasant emotion becomes part of the risk that the consumer perceives. This relationship of emotion to risk differs from the previous two in that it does not involve an ongoing emotional state; the emotion is not present at the time of decision making but rather is considered as a future possibility. Some research has addressed anticipated emotions and risk. For example, Zeelenberg et al. (1996) found that consumer decision making could be influenced by the possibility of later feelings of regret about the decision, and that risk aversion is distinct from regret aversion. The focus of this contribution is on the effects of ongoing emotional states, however, so there is no need for further review of the literature on anticipated emotions.

The effects of integral and incidental emotions on risk perception have been explained from two theoretical perspectives. One considers the effects of the appraisal and action tendency components of emotions; it is known as the "appraisal-tendency framework" (Lerner and Keltner 2000). The other focuses on the feeling component of emotions, specifically on how feelings provide information that is incorporated into risk perception. There are several variants on this approach that are known variously as the "affect heuristic" (Finucane et al. 2000), as "affect as information" (Clore 1992), or as the "risk-as-feelings hypothesis" (Loewenstein et al. 2001). Considered as a group, they may be referred to as "affect as information" theories. Each of these theoretical perspectives applies the theory of emotion to risk perception. The remainder of this contribution will describe each perspective in turn, and review some of the research that demonstrates how it has been applied to understanding consumers' perception of risk.

3   The Appraisal-Tendency Framework

The appraisal-tendency framework was initially proposed by Lerner and Keltner (2000), and has continued to be tested and refined in subsequent years (Han et al. 2007; Lerner et al. 2015). The aim of this theory is to account for how emotional appraisals and action tendencies modify judgment and decision making, including risk perception. The primary innovation of this theory was to account for differential effects of various emotions that share the same valence (positive or negative). Whereas prior theories tended to assert that all negative emotions (e.g., fear, anger, disgust, sadness) would have the same effects on risk perception, the appraisal-tendency framework applied the theory of discrete emotions outlined above to explain why emotions sharing the same valence could have different effects.

The name "appraisal-tendency framework" refers to the theory's linking aspects of an emotion's appraisal to their effect on risk perception. Part of the appraisal for fear, for example, is an assessment of low certainty and low control in a situation, whereas the appraisal for anger includes an assessment of high certainty and high situational control. Given that prior research had demonstrated that risk perception is heightened when hazards seem uncertain and uncontrollable (Slovic 1987), the appraisal-tendency framework predicts that fear will tend to increase perceived risk whereas anger will tend to decrease it.

The first test conducted by Lerner and Keltner (2000) verified these predictions by using the same risk questionnaire that had been used in 1983 by Johnson and Tversky, but assessing participants' fear and anger. The researchers found that fear and anger levels predicted strikingly different effects: whereas fear correlated with higher assessments of risk, anger correlated with lower assessments of risk. A subsequent study added a measure of happiness and found that it, like anger, lowered risk perception, a finding that was consistent with the appraisal for happiness involving perceptions of certainty and control (Lerner and Keltner 2001).

In a more rigorous test that experimentally manipulated emotional states, Lerner and Keltner (2001) randomly assigned participants to perform a task that would make them either fearful or angry. Subsequent assessments confirmed that anger activated higher appraisals of certainty than did fear, and that appraisals of control mediated the effect of emotion on risk perception.

The appraisal-tendency framework has since proven remarkably applicable to a variety of laboratory and real-life situations. In a national field experiment conducted a few months after the September 11, 2001 terrorist attacks in the United States, in the midst of the anthrax crisis, real-life fear was found to increase perceived risk of terrorism whereas anger decreased the perceived risk (Lerner et al. 2003).

Emotions also change people's memory of past perceptions of risk. A year after the September 11, 2001 terrorist attacks in the United States, Americans who were induced to feel fear recalled having experienced high levels of risk during that prior time, whereas those who were induced to feel anger remembered experiencing low levels of risk (Fischhoff et al. 2005). That is, emotions produced a hindsight bias in memories for previous judgments of risk.

The association between happiness and greater risk taking has been studied using a subtle manipulation. Rapid thought speed is known to be a symptom of mania, and some research indicates that fast thinking induces a positive mood. In research on risk, thought speed was manipulated by varying the rate at which volunteers read neutral text. It was found that participants who read the text quickly took more risks with actual money and reported more intention to engage in risky behaviors such a using illegal drugs and engaging in unprotected sex in their own lives (Chandler and Pronin 2012).

The appraisal-tendency framework addresses more than appraisal. It also takes into account the action tendencies of emotions. Anxious individuals have been found to show more risk-averse behavior than do non-anxious individuals (Maner and Gerund 2007). In a laboratory study in which participants had to choose between a riskier choice with a high reward and a less risky choice with a low reward, anxious participants were more risk averse than were controls; in contrast, sad participants chose greater risk than did controls (Raghunathan and Pham 1999). Although happiness is associated with decreased risk perception, when risks are recognized happiness is similar to anxiety and unlike anger in being associated with heightened risk aversion (Blanchette and Richards 2010).

4 Feelings as Information

The idea that affective feelings can shape judgment by acting as a source of information focuses on different aspects of emotion than does the appraisal-tendency framework. Feelings are informative because they serve as a heuristic guide to cognitive assessments that may be too complex, quick, or not fully conscious to access directly. The nature of appraisal is that it assesses the significance of a situation in terms of a person's cares and concerns. Any resulting affective feeling may therefore serve as a heuristic for the overall outcome of that assessment. The idea was first put forth in a classic set of studies by Schwarz and Clore (1983) who telephoned people at random on sunny days or cloudy days and asked them to rate their overall life satisfaction. On average, life satisfaction was reported significantly higher on sunny days (which elevate mood) than on cloudy days (which depress mood). In another condition the pollster first nonchalantly asked people about the weather outside, and then asked about their life satisfaction; in this condition there was no significant difference between the life satisfaction reported on sunny and cloudy days. The affect-as-information theory explains these results in terms of attribution theory. Mood did not alter cognitive processes involved in judgments of life satisfaction so much as it provided a quick source of information that could be relevant to answering what is a rather vague question. If not reminded about the weather, respondents answered the pollster's question by noting that they felt in a good or bad mood and interpreting that feeling as information about the quality of their life overall. In the condition in which they were first asked about the weather, the respondents were reminded that weather was a possible cause of their moods and therefore that their mood was not a valid heuristic for the overall quality of their lives. Thus, moods and emotions will be used as a source of information for a judgment if they are believed to be valid indicators, but otherwise they will not (Clore 1992).

The idea that affective feelings can serve as information is at the core of two leading approaches to risk perception. The "affect heuristic" suggests that emotional feelings are used both for judging risks and for judging benefits (Finucane et al. 2000). The theory therefore predicts that if providing information only about benefits improves mood, then the mood will have the effect of also decreasing the perception of risk; likewise, if providing information about risks depresses mood, then the mood will have the effect of also decreasing the perception of benefits. Finucane et al. (2000) tested this hypothesis by providing information about nuclear power; four separate conditions stated either that nuclear power's benefits are high, its benefits are low, its risk is low, or its risk is high. In each case, perception of risk changed inversely with perception of benefit, suggesting that the emotion, created by the information about either risks or benefits, mediated the effect. Furthermore, forcing participants to make their decisions under time pressure strengthened the inverse relationship between perceived risks and benefits.

The risk-as-feelings hypothesis addresses similar relations between emotion and risk perception (Loewenstein et al. 2001). For example, in research in which participants were asked to assess the likelihood that they would avoid a risky situation (such as getting out of a taxi driven by a drunk driver), participants rated themselves as more worried and more likely to exit the taxi than an unspecific average person. Risk-as-feelings theory predicted this result based on the idea that people are less likely to project their emotions onto an abstract other person (Loewenstein et al. 2001).

Research has examined positive mood and gambling behavior and shown that participants in a positive mood are more risk averse and loss averse than controls (Isen and Patrick 1983). This effect cannot be explained in terms of the availability heuristic because happy moods should make positive outcomes more available and thus encourage greater risk taking. So the mechanism is most likely a mood-as-information account of perceived utility, such that the happy mood works by making the reward seem less valuable—if everything is fine then there is no need to take risk in order to get more reward (Blanchette and Richards 2010).

In sum, the feelings as information approach explains perception of risk in terms of the heuristic that one's feelings convey relevant information about the riskiness of a situation or object. If the feeling is thought to be invalid, or is not thought to pertain to a judgment or to another person, then the feeling will not be used as information and will not influence the perception of risk.

5   Conclusions

Emotion theory accounts for two general ways in which emotional states influence consumer's perceptions of risk. One is by shaping the way in which events are perceived and the motivational tendencies for dealing with risk. The other is by providing a source of information about the present circumstances that is used as a heuristic for evaluating risk. Both have found support from research on a range of emotions using a variety of methodologies. These theories suggest an important role of emotion in consumers' perceptions of product risks and benefits.

References

Bechara, A., Damasio, H., Tranel, D., & Damasio, A. R. (1997). Deciding advantageously before knowing the advantageous strategy. *Science, 275*, 1293–1295.

Blanchette, I., & Richards, A. (2010). The influence of affect on higher level cognition: A review of research on interpretation, judgement, decision making and reasoning. *Cognition and Emotion, 24*, 561–595.

Chandler, J. J., & Pronin, E. (2012). Fast thought speed induces risk taking. *Psychological Science, 23*, 370–374.

Clore, G. L. (1992). Cognitive phenomenology: Feelings and the construction of judgment. In L. L. Martin & A. Tesser (Eds.), *The construction of social judgments* (pp. 133–163). Hillsdale, NJ: Erlbaum.

Damasio, A. R. (1994). *Descartes' error: Emotion, reason, and the human brain*. New York: Grosset/Putnam.

Dunn, B. D., Dalgleish, T., & Lawrence, A. D. (2006). The somatic marker hypothesis: A critical evaluation. *Neuroscience and Biobehavioral Reviews, 30*, 239–271.

Finucane, M. L., Alhakami, A., Slovic, P., & Johnson, S. M. (2000). The affect heuristic in judgments of risks and benefits. *Journal of Behavioral Decision Making, 13*, 1–17.

Fischhoff, B., Gonzalez, R. M., Lerner, J. S., & Small, D. A. (2005). Evolving judgments of terror risks: Foresight, hindsight, and emotion. *Journal of Experimental Psychology: Applied, 11*, 124–139.

Frijda, N. H. (1986). *The emotions*. Cambridge: Cambridge University Press.

Han, S., Lerner, J. S., & Keltner, D. (2007). Feelings and consumer decision making: The appraisal-tendency framework. *Journal of Consumer Psychology, 17*, 158–168.

Isen, A. M., & Patrick, R. (1983). The effect of positive feelings on risk taking: When the chips are down. *Organizational Behavior and Human Performance, 31*, 194–202.

Johnson, E. J., & Tversky, A. (1983). Affect, generalization, and the perception of risk. *Journal of Personality and Social Psychology, 45*, 20–31.

Kappas, A. (2011). Emotion and regulation are one! *Emotion Review, 3*, 17–25.

Lazarus, R. S. (1991). *Emotion and adaptation*. New York: Oxford University Press.

Lerner, J. S., & Keltner, D. (2000). Beyond valence: Toward a model of emotion-specific influences on judgment and choice. *Cognition and Emotion, 14*, 473–493.

Lerner, J. S., & Keltner, D. (2001). Fear, anger, and risk. *Journal of Personality and Social Psychology, 81*, 146–159.

Lerner, J. S., Gonzalez, R. M., Small, D. A., & Fischhoff, B. (2003). Effects of fear and anger on perceived risks of terrorism: A national field experiment. *Psychological Science, 14*, 144–150.

Lerner, J. S., Li, Y., Valdesolo, P., & Kassam, K. S. (2015). Emotion and decision making. *Annual Review of Psychology, 66*, 799–823.

Loewenstein, G., & Lerner, J. S. (2003). The role of affect in decision making. In R. J. Davidson, K. R. Scherer, & H. H. Goldsmith (Eds.), *Handbook of affective sciences* (pp. 619–642). New York: Oxford University Press.

Loewenstein, G., & Mather, J. (1990). Dynamic processes in risk perception. *Journal of Risk and Uncertainty, 3*, 155–170.

Loewenstein, G., Weber, E. U., Hsee, C. K., & Welch, N. (2001). Risk as feelings. *Psychological Bulletin, 127*, 267–286.

Lutz, C. (1988). *Unnatural emotions: Everyday sentiments on a Micronesian atoll and their challenge to western theory*. Chicago: University of Chicago Press.

Maner, J. K., & Gerend, M. A. (2007). Motivationally selective risk judgments: Do fear and curiosity boost the boons or the banes? *Organizational Behavior and Human Decision Processes, 103*, 256–267.

Parrott, W. G. (2002). The functional utility of negative emotions. In L. F. Barrett & P. Salovey (Eds.), *The wisdom in feeling: Psychological processes in emotional intelligence* (pp. 341–359). New York: Guilford Press.

Parrott, W. G. (2007). Components and the definition of emotion. *Social Science Information, 46*, 419–423.

Parrott, W. G. (2014). Feeling, function, and the place of negative emotions in a happy life. In W. G. Parrott (Ed.), *The positive side of negative emotions* (pp. 273–296). New York: Guilford Press.

Parrott, W. G., & Schulkin, J. (1993). Psychophysiology and the cognitive nature of the emotions. *Cognition and Emotion, 7*, 43–59.

Raghunathan, R., & Pham, M. T. (1999). All negative moods are not equal: Motivational invluences of anxiethy and sadness on decision making. *Organizational Behavior and Human Decision Processes, 79*, 56–77.

Scherer, K. R. (1984). On the nature and function of emotion: A component process approach. In K. R. Scherer & P. Ekman (Eds.), *Approaches to emotion* (pp. 293–317). Hillsdale, NJ: Erlbaum.

Schwarz, N., & Clore, G. L. (1983). Mood, misattribution, and judgments of well-being: Informative and directive functions of affective states. *Journal of Personality and Social Psychology, 45*, 513–523.

Slovic, P. (1987). Perception of risk. *Science, 236*, 280–285.

Slovic, P. (1999). Trust, emotion, sex, politics, and science: Surveying the risk-assessment battlefield. *Risk Analysis, 19*(4), 689–701.

Tooby, J., & Cosmides, L. (1990). The past explains the present: Emotional adaptations and the structure of ancestral environments. *Ethology and Sociobiology, 11*, 375–424.

Von Neumann, J., & Morgenstern, O. (1944). *Theory of games and economic behavior*. New York: Wiley.

Zeelenberg, M., Beattie, J., Van der Pligt, J., & De Vries, N. K. (1996). Consequences of regret aversion: Effects of expected feedback on risky decision making. *Organizational Behavior and Human Decision Processes, 65*, 148–158.

Rational Choice and Bounded Rationality

Ronald E. Goldsmith

1 A Prolegomena to Consumer Decision Making

Life is filled with problems to solve. Not all problems are consumption problems, but many are. The focus of this contribution is on consumer problem solving by making decisions. One way consumers solve problems is by *creative thinking*, that is, by devising a novel solution to the problem. One example would be using an empty can and some wire to fix a broken muffler. Such novel and ingenious problem solving is highly valuable and highly praised. Another way consumers solve problems is by *critical thinking* and *decision-making*. These problem solutions require consumers to analyze the problem situation, develop a set of possible solutions, and select the solution that best solves the problem. An example would be buying new muffler to replace the old one, but having to choose a muffler shop to do the work. Both approaches to problem solving are ubiquitous and common. The present contribution focuses on the latter type of problem solving, judgment and decision-making, leaving the creative thinking for others to discuss (e.g., Csikszentmihalyi 1997).

Much of life involves making decisions, both consumption and otherwise. We must all decide all the time. Many decisions are easy, requiring little time, thought, or information; and the outcomes are of no great import. Examples would be whether to watch TV or take a walk. Some of these decisions are major life choices, such as which college to pick, whom to marry, or what model car to buy. These

"*Logic: The art of thinking and reasoning in strict accordance with the limitations and incapacities of the human misunderstanding.*" Ambrose Bierce
"*The heart has its reasons, of which reason knows nothing.*" Blaise Pascal

R.E. Goldsmith (✉)
Department of Marketing, Florida State University, College of Business, 505 Rovetta Building A, Tallahassee, FL 32306-1110, USA
e-mail: rgoldsmith@cob.fsu.edu

© Springer International Publishing AG 2017
G. Emilien et al. (eds.), *Consumer Perception of Product Risks and Benefits*,
DOI 10.1007/978-3-319-50530-5_13

Table 1 A decision-making continuum

Relatively minor decisions	Relatively major decisions
Only a minor impact on life course	Major impact
Little information needed	More information needed
Reliance on memory for information	External sources of information
Requires little thought	Requires more thought
Minor evaluation of consequences	Major evaluation of consequences
Situation or criteria salient at time of	Situation or criteria at time of
The decision is very important	The decision is less important
Risk of poor decision minor	Risk of poor decision major

"Consumption Examples: Candy bar, Lunch, New shirt, Kitchen appliance, Vacation, Car, House"

decisions can be hard to make, require a great deal of time and energy to make, require a body of information, and have major consequences for the life course. Some decisions, of course, fall in between these extremes. Thus, we can think of decision-making as a continuum of tasks ranging from minor to major, distinguished by the relative impact of a variety of aspects that characterize the decision. Table 1 presents this decision continuum.

The background for consumer decision-making lies in the *motives* or *needs* that drive behavior. These motives provide the energy that compels consumers to solve their problems by making a variety of decisions on a daily basis. Although scholars have offered several schemes to describe the types of human motivations (e.g., Maslow 1970; Lawrence and Nohria 2002), for the purposes of understanding consumer decision-making, we can propose a list of consumer motives or needs derived from these and other sources that is parsimonious, intuitive, useful, and justifiable:

- Physiological (e.g., food, drink, safety, security).
- Social (e. g., friendship, love, belonging, sex)
- Cognitive (e.g., curiosity, need for cognition, understanding)
- Hedonic (e.g., pleasurable sounds, sights, tastes, smells, and touch)
- Experiential (e.g., fun, excitement, pleasure, stimulation)
- Psychological (e.g., self-esteem, subjective well-being, self-concept)
- Spiritual (e.g., connection with some transcendent other)

Each human is born with these needs, but individuals differ in the intensity with which these needs drive behavior. These individual differences stem from unique genetic inheritances plus the individual's learning experiences (such as socialization) during the circumstances of life, such as the family, social class, or culture in which one is born; and specific learning histories accumulated through life experience. Moreover, we can further distinguish between this small number of global, inherent needs characterizing all consumers and the vastly more numerous and varied *wants* derived from the needs. For example, every consumer more or less needs food (a physiological need); the specific food an individual wants depends on

Table 2 The five-stage decision-making process

1. Problem Recognition—the consumer notes a difference between the ideal situation and the real situation (e.g., the gas gauge says the tank is nearly empty)
2. Search for Information (the driver remembers the location of a preferred gas station, spots a sign identifying a gas station, or asks a passenger to tell him or her where the best place to get gas is)
3. Alternative Evaluation (the set of potential gas stations is evaluated along some criteria, such as price, brand name, nearness, long lines, etc.)
4. Choice (from the set of alternatives, a fueling station is chosen)
5. Outcomes (after filling up the driver may be reinforced that the favorite station again served well, may be satisfied with the choice, or may become dissatisfied with it)

the aforementioned sources of individual differences. A hungry German might want a bratwurst, while a hungry Mexican might want a taco (perhaps sometimes vice versa).

When consumers make their consumption decisions, seeking to solve their problems (satisfy their needs and wants), they enter the marketplace to exchange their resources for the products and services that satisfy their needs and wants. The four major resources or assets consumers' possess are their money, time, physical energy, and cognitive energy. The dilemma is that these resources are not unlimited; even billionaires cannot buy more time. Most consumers have distinct limits on their resources so that their decision-making is more than simply choosing options to satisfy their needs and wants. *Consumer decision making* describes how consumers allocate their limited resources in exchange for a shopping basket of goods and services intended to satisfy their needs and wants. They have to expend their money, time, and energies in a series of decisions that they think will be the most effective use of their resources. Moreover, consumers face risks when they make decisions arising from both uncertainty about the outcome of the decision and the severity of the consequences of a wrong decision. How people make these consumption decisions is a subset or variety of the ways people make decisions across all aspects of their lives (e.g., work, family, spiritual). The basic decision process can be modeled as a sequence of five-steps that describe the tasks a decision maker performs. Table 2 presents a model of the generic decision making process.

Obviously, decision makers, especially consumers, neither explicitly nor consciously go through all five steps for every decision they make, but the model does provide valuable insight into the psychological processes taking place when people make decisions. For the minor consumer decisions, consumers rapidly notice they have a problem, search their memories for relevant information, and quickly pick an option. Mid-level problems might require more time and cognitive energy, but as decision makers, consumers tend to follow a "cognitive miser" strategy by which they expend as little time and energy needed to make their decisions. Finally, most likely, only the most important decisions call for the full model. This contribution focuses on the fourth stage of the model; that is, having resourced sufficient information to create a selection of possible solutions, how do consumers actually make their choices?

Keep in mind that the model is a global generalization, so that individuals differ in how closely they follow the model, yielding individual differences in decision-making strategies. Moreover, no one expects consumers to use the same strategies for every decision. People differ overall in their preferences for making decisions and they switch between strategies depending on the type of product they are buying and depending on external situational influences, such as the purpose of the purchase, the time of year, and presence of other people. So the question remains, how do consumers actually make decisions? Economists pioneered the study of decision-making and proposed a model to describe the optimal way to make decisions, termed *rational decision-making*. This model is the foundation or touchstone used to describe and explain how consumers and others make decisions (Yang and Carmon 2010).

2   The Concept of Rationality and Its Denial

The rational model of decision-making is a highly formalized (prescriptive) description of an ideal decision making process. It's most detailed formulation by von Neumann and Morgenstern (1944) is termed *Expected Utility theory*. It makes a number of assumptions about the decision maker and proceeds to draw conclusions about the outcomes of the decision process based on these assumptions. This standard benchmark of consumer decision making is often called *homo economicus* or economic man (Yang and Carmon 2010). Its roots can even be traced back to Jeremy Bentham's notions of utilitarianism. The rational model essentially assumes that (1) consumers have complete and accurate information available prior to making their decisions; (2) they face no risks, that is, there are no bad outcomes from making the decision; (3) they are capable of using this information (processing it) effectively; (4) their goal is to make optimal decisions, that is, outcomes that optimize the utility of the decision; and (5) the optimal solution is not influenced by situational or context factors. The highly formal and unrealistic nature of these assumptions suggests that consumers rarely are capable of making their decisions in this way. Consequently, more psychologically realistic models of rational decision-making were subsequently formulated into *subjective expected utility* theories by Edwards (1954) and Savage (1954).

2.1   Subjective Expected Utility

The rational decision-making model assumes that consumers seek to optimize the *utility* they receive by exchanging their resources (money, time, energy) for the benefits that goods and services provide. Utility here refers to the outcomes of the exchange in terms of the satisfaction of consumer needs and wants. When formulated as *subjective expected utility* or SEU, the model consists of a probability assessment of the decision outcome based on each person's subjective criteria (guided by the individual's needs and wants). The model assumes that consumers will assess all the options from which they are choosing using all the available information and use this information rationally to choose the option that has the highest expected utility. SEU also assumes that consumers factor risks into their assessments when making the decision. Thus, the SEU model argues that consumers always strive to make the best decision they can make where "best" is defined to be the decision that optimizes the utility or value of the choice outcomes. Consumer, however, rarely seem to make decisions according to the SEU model. Two different categories of factors explain why.

2.2 The Ideal Denied

One set of reasons why consumers fall short of rational models of decision-making lies in the assumptions they make. Contrary to the assumptions of the rational model, consumers might not be aware of the all the options available from which to choose. They are certainly not likely to have all the information, and much of the information they do have is likely incomplete, inaccurate, or difficult to evaluate. This is why decision-making is usually referred to as "decision making under uncertainty." How this information is processed to yield the optimal choice follows strict optimization rules that do not describe how the human brain works when making decisions. Consumers are not good at assessing their risks and so cannot adequately incorporate risk into their decisions (Gigerenzer and Selten 2001). Finally, the rational models assume that decisions are made in the absence of any situational contexts that might influence the outcome; and they leave out the influence that emotions or affect might play. In short, rational models are ideal descriptions of how decisions would be made in order to arrive at the optional solution to a choice problem, but "rational models are psychologically unrealistic" (Kahneman 2003, p. 1449). One reason rational models are unrealistic lies in the assumptions they make. In addition, rational models are poor descriptions of how consumers actually make decisions for reasons other than the unrealistic assumptions they make about decision makers.

3 Why Don't Consumers Make Rational Decisions?

A second set of reasons why consumers fail to follow the Rational Model of decision-making stems from the difficulty consumers have in thinking critically. Rational decision-making refers to decision-making that strives to follow the standards of what might be termed *critical thinking*. Long, complex definitions of critical thinking exist (Hastie and Dawes 2010), and the term has slightly different meanings for different people. Combining and synthesizing many of these different definitions yields a description of critical thinking that has five elements or stages.

- define the decision problem correctly
- determine the relevant information needed to make the decision
- evaluate the quality of the available information
- use the information correctly to solve the problem by making the decision
- evaluate the process and improve it if necessary

Although rational decision-making is not identical to critical thinking, it shares many of its features. For our purposes, a simple summary definition ties critical thinking to rational problem solving. We can describe critical thinking informally as "the application of good reasoning strategies to reasoning problems" (Bishop 2012). Good reasoning, or rational decision-making, follows the rules of logic and mathematics (probability) when evaluating and using information to make decisions. So what accounts for the difficulty consumers have in thinking critically and therefore prevents them from following rational models even if the assumptions the models make were not so unrealistic? We can identify three candidates that prevent consumers from thinking rationally derived from their evolutionary heritage, the absence of good models to follow, and the failure of education to impart these skills.

3.1   The Role of Evolution

In the judgment of those who study this problem (e.g., Gilovich 1991; Kahneman 2003), the human mind has not evolved to think rationally when evaluating information and making decisions. The human brain consists of two separate systems for reasoning, judgment, and decision-making (Evans 2008). The evolutionarily older of the two, System 1, is unconscious, rapid, automatic, and high capacity while the evolutionarily younger System 2 is conscious, slow, and deliberative. Many consumer decisions are made by first system, which does not use the Rational Model. Rational decision-making is located in System 2. Consumers may strive to use the second system for some decisions, but as we shall see, even then they fail to be fully rational owing to a variety of flaws in the decision-making apparatus over all. Most authors on this topic reach similar conclusions in this regard:

- Evolution has given us powerful intellectual tools for processing vast amounts of information with accuracy and dispatch, and our questionable beliefs derive primarily from the misapplication or overutilization of generally valid and effective strategies for knowing. Just as we are subject to perceptual illusions in spite of, and largely because of, our extraordinary perceptual capacities, so too are many of our cognitive shortcomings 'closely related to, or even an unavoidable cost of, [our] greatest strengths' (Gilovich 1991, p. 2).

- We all have natural tendencies to search for and evaluate evidence in a faulty manner (Kida 2006, p. 15).

Thus, the basic reason people are poor in critical thinking ability is not that they are ruled by their emotions rather than by reason; both faculties are needed for good decision-making, but out-of-control emotions are not the basic source of suboptimal decisions. Neither are people fundamentally irrational or incapable of reasoning, although some people are better than others are at reasoning. The basic reason is that human rationality is bounded or limited (Gilovich 1991). This means that even when trying to make a rational decision, many people fall prey to the inherent limitations of their rational minds (Kahneman 2003). In the words of Piattelli-Palmarini (1994, p. 142): *"The systematic failure of many of our 'judgments under uncertainty' is not argument against the canons of rationality, but rather a demonstration that we frequently, without being aware of it, adopt strategies and mental intuitions that vary quite a bit from the formulas prescribed by those rational rules. . . . We have come to see that our minds spontaneously follow a sort of quick and easy shortcut, and that this shortcut does not lead us to the same place to which the highway of rationality would bring us."*

In summary, making rational consumer decisions assumes that consumers have the ability to think rationally (follow the rules of logic and probability) so that they can use the information available to make optimal choices. In reality, our evolutionary history has not equipped consumers with the mental apparatus needed to make rationally optimal decisions. Instead, consumers often make suboptimal decisions because they use their System 1 thinking or when they try to use System 2, their minds simply aren't up to the task of optimizing the outcome. However, this is not the whole story of why consumers fail to make rational decisions. When consumers try to make rational decisions, they are often given defective information to work with and poor examples of rational decision making to follow.

3.2 The Influence of Others

Second reason consumers have difficulty in making rational a decision is that many actors or agents in society promote irrational and poor thinking. Politicians, marketers, pollsters, journalists, and the media in general should be held accountable for a constant barrage of violations of critical thinking (Blastland and Dilnot 2010; Seife 2010). Sometimes they do this out of ignorance, simply repeating the mistakes that many people naturally make; sometimes out of carelessness, not taking the trouble to apply critical thinking skills to a problem; but often deliberately, in an effort to persuade or mislead in pursuit of some goal that benefits them. The media is especially guilty in this regard, preferring to report the outrageous, the astonishing, the facile, and the conventional aspects of the story rather than critically analyze it and judge its soundness (Seife 2010). Given the constant barrage of misinformation, misleading information, self-serving efforts to persuade consumers to make poor decisions, and outright lies, it is no wonder that consumers often make suboptimal decisions. Many people (conmen, politicians, or any agent with a vested interest) out there benefit from these poor decisions and actively seek to promote them.

3.3 The Failure of Education

A third contributor to the failure of consumers to adhere to the rational model is that, given the fact that we are not born with the mental apparatus to make rational decisions, education to make up for this deficit is also lacking. It is well documented that college students, who might be expected to excel in rational decision-making, actually perform poorly on standardized assessments (e.g., Stein and Haynes 2011). This is most likely because colleges devote little effort to explicitly teaching these skills and focus on discipline content instead. Consumers who are not innately rational, who are constantly exposed to examples and encouragements that lead them away from rational thinking, and who are never explicitly trained in it cannot be expected to follow the models proposed by economists when they make consumer decisions. Nevertheless, how do consumers make their decisions if not rationally? Researchers have identified a variety of ways consumers make decisions that do not follow rational models (e.g., Evans 2008; Hastie and Dawes 2010; Kahneman 2003).

4 Alternative Decision Strategies

The realization that consumers fall short when it comes to conforming to the rational decision-making model of *homo economicus*, has led to a variety of theories to explain how consumers actually make decisions. We start with theories that relax some of the more restrictive assumptions of rational theory models and progress toward theories that emphasize non-rational and unconscious psychological processes. What follows are short summaries of several of the most prominent theories. Table 3 presents a continuum of these theories.

4.1 Satisficing and Bounded Rationality

The work of Edwards (1954) and Savage (1954) attempted to preserve the basic model of rational decision making by relaxing some of its more restrictive assumptions while preserving the formal, mathematical modeling approach pioneered by von Newman and Morgenstern. A more radical approach to describing decision making was subsequently proposed by Herbert A. Simon (Sent 2005). In contrast to

Table 3 A continuum of decision making theories

Eight prominent decision-making theories

Rational decision making[a]	Subjective expected utility[b]	Satisficing bounded rationality[c]	Compensatory reasoning[d]	Emotional decision making[e]	Compulsive impulsive consumption[f]	Unconscious decision making[g]	Behavioral ecology foraging[h]
Formal Reasoning High			← - - - - - →		Formal Reasoning Low		
Situational influences Low			← - - - - - →		Situational influences High		
Decision Making Time High			← - - - - - →		Decision Making Time Low		

[a]von Newmann and Morgenstern (1944)
[b]Edwards (1954) and Savage (1954)
[c]Simon (1995), Kahneman (2003), and Gigerenzer and Selten (2001)
[d]Chernev and Hamilton (2009)
[e]Chaudhuri (2006)
[f]Faber (2010)
[g]Koch (2012)
[h]Foxall (2007) and Hantula (2012)

the economists, Simon approached decision making from the administrative or organizational perspective. He argued that the rational models lacked empirical support and sought to replace them with models that more closely resembled actual decision making given the human limitations already noted above. The most widely known concepts firmly associated with Simon are "bounded rationality" and "satisficing" (Sent 1997). Bounded rationality describes humans making decisions within the constraints of incomplete and imperfect information, limited time, and restricted computational ability. Rationality is thus "bounded" by their limitations even though people try to decide rationally. Satisficing is the term Simon coined to describe decisions that fall short of optimizing and instead are "good enough" for the purposes of the decision maker.

In addition, according to Simon (1995), "recognition" and "heuristic search" "explain not only everyday problem solving but also such phenomena as intuition, insight, and the cognitive aspects of creativity." Recognition refers to the ability of decision makers to quickly recognize a piece of information for its relevance to the problem and match it to a pattern stored in memory. Heuristic search is using rules of thumb to quickly search through large stores of information in memory to find the most relevant and useful bits to guide the decision process. Both these processes are keys to understanding expert decision making because they are the result of experience and expertise. Simon popularized the concept of heuristic decision-making that was subsequently adopted by others, especially in the field of consumer behavior, but with an important twist. Simon and his predecessors tried to modify the rational economic model; his most important successors "started from the rationality assumption that has characterized mainstream economics and next analyzed departures from this yardstick, rather than developing and alternative one" (Sent 2005, p. 230).

4.2 Decision-Making Using Heuristics

Rational choice models and even bounded rationality assume that the decision maker is implementing rational and logical rules during the decision process. Some theorists propose that instead of a systematic and logical process, many decisions are made using *heuristics*, or rule of thumb. These simple shortcuts to making decisions are not likely to yield the optimal outcome proposed by the rational models, but they have the advantages of being easy to implement (thereby conserving scarce cognitive resources) and to explain as a justification for the decision. The two major versions of this theory of decision-making are those proposed by Kahneman and Tversky (Kahneman 2003) and by Gigerenzer (Gigerenzer and Selten 2001).

Over a period of several decades, Daniel Kahneman worked with his colleague Amos Tversky to develop an extensive description of the heuristics commonly used by ordinary decision makers. Kahneman (2003) summarizes this body of work. Instead of modifying the rational model as Simon tried to do and retain as much rationality as possible, Kahneman and Tversky argued that humans make decisions that are qualitatively different from the rational model. Building on the distinction between System 1 thinking and System 2 thinking outlined earlier, Kahneman and Tversky developed a comprehensive theory of human decision making called "prospect theory" to describe decision making under uncertainty using heuristics. They and a host of subsequent researchers have documented a variety of heuristics decision-makers use. Prominent heuristics include *availability*, the tendency to use the ease with which instances of a particular event or situation come to mind as an indication of the likelihood of the event occurring; and the *validity effect*, whereby repeated statements are judged to be more valid, thus forming better evidence to justify a decision. Also important are framing effects, which describes the influence of minor, superficial features of a decision problem that lead people to make different judgments about otherwise equivalent options. These examples only touch upon the vast body of findings regarding the influence heuristics and biases have on decision-making. Most notably, this stream of research posits that intuitive, System 1, ways of making decisions distort the results away from the most beneficial outcomes and lead to sub-optimal results.

In contrast, Gerd Gigerenzer shares with Kahneman and Tversky the opinion that decision theorists have not really adhered to Simon's ideas, but differs from him by proposing that that simple heuristics often lead to better decisions than theoretically optimal procedures (Gigerenzer and Selten 2001). In his view, rules of thumb can be effective guides for making decisions given the uncertainty and lack of information characteristic of so many of them. His body of work contains many illustrations and guidelines for making better decisions that often rely on presenting the available information in ways that facilitate good, if not the optimally best, outcomes (Fox 2015). Notably, examples of helpful decision-making shortcuts are 1/N and the *recognition* heuristic. The former applies to investing money (a highly important type of decision for many people) by allocating available funds equally among the N funds in a retirement plan (it appears to work nearly as well as an optimization technique). The latter states that less information is often better than more information. In some judgment situations, better outcomes can be achieved by relying on the most recognized information, on the assumption that it must be the most valuable.

Moreover, Gigerenzer opposes Kahneman's interpretation of most people's poor decision making when they are presented with probabilistic problems. He argues that the human mind is not naturally equipped to think in terms of probabilities, especially conditional probabilities. However, when the same problems are presented using frequencies or absolute numbers (integers) they draw better conclusions. Framing decision problems in the more "natural" terms of frequencies makes them fit more closely to human information processing capabilities (Gigerenzer 2002). Overall, Gigerenzer's approach is to emphasize using fast and frugal, simple rules of thumb to arrive at the best, maybe the most 'satisficing,' outcome. Thus, the Kahneman and Gigerenzer models in their own ways start by critiquing rational models and argue for more psychologically based descriptions of how humans make decisions.

4.3   Non-Compensatory and Compensatory Reasoning

Consumer psychology textbooks frequently describe consumer decision making using two types of models: non-compensatory and compensatory. The former is comprised of various rules for choosing from a set of brands the consumer has collected from all those available to him or her after an initial search for information. Non-compensatory models describe methods by which consumers evaluate these alternatives, eliminating one after another until the best option is chosen for purchase. Thus, these non-compensatory decision rules reside in the same family of heuristics as those discussed earlier. The four most frequently mentioned rules for evaluating alternative brands are the conjunctive, disjunctive, lexicographic, and elimination by aspects. Each rule uses a set of purchasing criteria, fixed cut-off points on them, and follows a decision rule that either retains or discards brands until the most favored brand remains for purchase. These rules are non-compensatory because low brand evaluations on any criterion cannot be off-set by high evaluations on other criteria.

In contrast, the second family of decision rules is termed "compensatory" because deficiencies in one criterion of a brand can be compensated for by strengths or advantages on other criteria (see Chernev and Hamilton 2009). In contrast to the non-compensatory rules consumers sometimes use, compensatory strategies emphasize balance and trade-offs between options as consumers feel their way to a choice. For example, consumers might use "covariance-based inferences" that assume that an option's performance on an attribute that they are unable to evaluate is linked to an attribute they can evaluate. Assuming product quality is positively linked to (high) price, to brand name, or to length of warranty are examples (Chernev and Hamilton 2009, p. 135). Sheth et al. (1991) provide a detailed theory of consumer choice that is compensatory throughout. They argue that consumers strive to achieve valued states classified into five areas: functional, social, emotional, epistemic, and conditional (varying by situation). Note the similarity to the basic motives described early in this contribution. Sheth et al. (1991) demonstrate that if they operationalize their theory by measuring consumers' evaluations of the five value types and using discriminant analysis, they can explain and predict consumer choices with remarkable accuracy. The high and low value ratings offset one another so that final choices are the result of compensatory tradeoffs.

4.4   Emotion and Decision Making

Western culture has traditionally viewed emotion and reason as opposite and mutually exclusive forces. From the Greeks to Freud, these two opponents have been pitted against each other in competition to drive behavior. Many consumer decisions, however, result from the combination of emotions and rational or semi-rational factors at work. Chaudhuri (2006) cogently argues that instead of antagonistic foes, emotion and reason are "two separate yet often complementary means of gaining knowledge about the world" (p. 2). Not to be confused with Kahneman's Systems 1 and 2, the duality of emotion and reason refers to two different brain mechanisms that operate independently, but whose cooperation is needed for effective decision making. Pure reason alone does not work; it needs the emotional component to function. Likewise, without the guiding hand of reason, purely emotional decisions would often be sub-optimal. "Thus, these systems of behavior control interact and inform each other, leading to goal-direct behavior" (p. 5). Chaudhuri (2006) presents several empirical studies demonstrating the contribution of emotions to a variety of consumer decisions, such as forming attitudes toward which brands to buy and how much risk to take in a consumer decision. His work, however, does not address two types of emotional decisions, compulsive and impulsive buying, the latter of which is a very common illustration of the absence of rational decision-making.

The role of the unconscious in consumer decision making is currently and active field of research where new technologies are being applied. Combining traditional laboratory behavioral experimental procedures with functional neuroimaging and formal economic modeling, decision neuroscience is emerging as an innovative approach to understanding how consumers make decisions by uncovering the neuronal substrate mechanisms that underlie the phenomenal processes only glimpsed by previous researchers. For instance, Shiv et al. (2005) studied three groups of subjects: normals, patients with damage to their ventromedial region of the prefrontal cortex, and those with substance dependency. The latter are known to be poor at making decisions owing to their impaired ability to evaluate future consequences rationally. They found that in an investment decision-making task, the substance dependence group, who suffered from abnormalities in the neural circuitry critical for processing emotion owing to an impaired emotional system, actually made better rational investment decisions than the normals. This was because they ignored the risks of losing which hindered the normals, who responded emotionally by becoming conservative. Such studies highlight the role of emotion in decision-making and point to the future of this study.

4.5   Compulsive and Impulsive Consumption

Closely related to the description of consumer decision-making described by the role of emotions are two unique types of consumer consumption: compulsive consumption and impulsive consumption. These behaviors are not identical types of decision-making, but share certain similarities and are often confused. Both compulsive and impulsive buying, however, can be thought of as types of consumer decision making that are far removed from the deliberate and careful patterns described by previous theories, all of which invoke some degree of cognitive processing. While true compulsive purchasing is relatively rare, most of us have made an impulsive purchase at some time in our consumer lives.

Researchers actually distinguish different understandings of compulsive buying. One way researchers describe this type of consumption is revealed by the term "compulsive buying disorder" or CBD. Black (2007, p. 14) describes CBD as "excessive shopping cognitions and buying behavior that leads to distress or impairment." In this sense, compulsive buying is a clinical disorder needing professional psychiatric treatment. Black (2007, p. 14) goes on to state: "Subjects with CBD report a preoccupation with shopping, prepurchase tension or anxiety, and a sense of relief following the purchase. CBD is associated with significant psychiatric comorbidity, particularly mood and anxiety disorders, substance use disorders, eating disorders, and other disorders of impulse control." Black (2007) estimates that CBD has a 5.8% prevalence in the general U.S. population. Thus, this pattern of consumption can be considered not as a voluntary variety of decision-making, but instead is a pathology much like hoarding behavior.

A less clinical understanding of compulsive buying describes it as an individual difference, more a continuum of behavior akin to a personality variable. In this sense, Desarbo and Edwards (1996) and Palan et al. (2011) understand compulsive buying as "an episodic urge to buy" (Palan et al. 2011, p. 83). They treat compulsive buying as a continuously distributed variable representing degrees to which consumers differ from each other in this pattern of behavior. This approach is consistent with Rook's (1987) presentation of a continuum of buying behavior ranging from a low of "completely rational choice" based on perfect planning to the extreme of "compulsive buying" as the clinical disorder. Compulsive buying in this sense is consistently associated with the consumer characteristics of materialism, status seeking, and a variety of other personality characteristics (see Desarbo and Edwards 1996).

Moreover, Edwards (1954), Desarbo and Edwards (1996), and Palan et al. (2011) distinguish impulsive buying from compulsive buying. Impulsive purchases can also be thought of as "unplanned purchases" Faber (2010). Impulsive buying seems to be more situational than compulsive buying, which seems to be more of a general tendency. External stimuli such as offering a premium, a coupon, or a deal often stimulate impulsive buying. In addition, being in a good mood or having depleted willpower can trigger an impulsive purchase (Faber 2010). Willpower and the ability to resist marketing's blandishments appear to play a major role in impulsive buying.

4.6 Unconscious Decision Making

All the preceding descriptions of decision-making, and especially consumer decision-making, assume that the decision makers are making their decisions *consciously*, that is, with full self-awareness of what they are doing. This assumption is surely accurate in the case of organizations or group decisions and with most consumer decisions on the right side of Table 1. An alternative view of decision making that has much in common with Kahneman and Tversky's System 1 (in that they are mostly quick and rely on little information), argues that many decisions are actually made unconsciously. The key difference in these two interpretations is that Kahneman and Tversky's System 1, while relying on heuristics, is still conscious decision-making in the sense that people are aware that they are making a decision. Note that the evidence supporting the heuristic interpretation of how people make decisions employs tasks in which the experimental subjects are consciously engaged (see Evans 2008; Kahneman 2003). The interpretation of unconscious decision-making described in this section argues that much of mental life, including the judgments and decisions people make, is unavailable to consciousness (Koch 2012). That is, part of the brain is performing a huge variety of activities of which the conscious part of the brain is not aware and has no access to; but our interpretation of our behavior is that it is under conscious control. This view of decision-making argues that part of the brain to which we have no access is reacting to environmental stimuli and making decisions after which we become consciously aware as the illusion of self-control. This view of decision-making is compatible with many of the mechanisms described by the "alternative decision strategies" in this contribution. The extreme form of this argument is that consciousness itself is an illusion, just as the external world is a virtual reality created by neural mechanisms (Koch 2012).

4.7   Behavioral Ecology and Foraging Theory

Our final alternative to rational decision-making's description of how consumers make decisions can be found in the newly emerging discipline of behavioral ecology and especially the area of *foraging theory*. This approach sets aside considerations of the psychological (i.e., rational or emotional) processes taking place in the consumer brain and focuses on how the decision maker is interacting and responding to the environment when making decisions. According to the International Society for Behavioral Ecology (http://www.behavecol.com/pages/society/welcome.html:), "*Behavioral ecology is the study of the fitness consequences of behavior. Research in this field poses the basic question: what does an animal gain, in fitness terms, by doing this rather than that? It combines the study of animal behavior with evolutionary biology and population ecology, and more recently, physiology and molecular biology. Adaptation is the central unifying concept.*" The study of behavior includes four principle areas:

(1) the use of ecological and evolutionary processes to explain the occurrence and adaptive significance of behavior patterns and life history strategies;
(2) the use of behavioral processes to predict ecological patterns, and
(3) comparative analyses relating behavior to the environment in which it occurs or investigating the pattern of evolution.
(4) the mechanisms underpinning costs and benefits of variable behavioral or life history strategies.

   This perspective on consumer behavior interprets how consumers behave as how any organism would behave in its natural environment. According to Hantula (2012), foraging theory offers a description and explanation for consumer decision-making that is economic in nature, but an alternative to the rational process model. Instead of emphasizing the internal workings of a rational mind, foraging theory (as part of behavioral ecology) looks to the environment as the explanation for how and why decisions are made. Foraging is "a general purpose set of rules and strategies for adapting to environmental risk and uncertainty, yielding both prey items and information" (Hantula 2012, p. 549). In the consumer context, foraging describes how consumers acquire information and products (goods and services) in exchange for their resources of time, money, and energies. Hantula points out that behavioral ecology offers an explanation for consumer decision-making that challenges both the rational decision-making model and the heuristics and biases (or quasi-rational) model proposed by Kahneman. While the former argues that when people fail to follow the formal rational model they are behaving irrationally, the latter proposes that people try to be rational but fail owing to their limited cognitive abilities and use heuristics instead of formal reasoning. Behavioral ecology avoids this issue altogether by focusing on the adaptation of the consumer organism to its environment and proposes that when consumers make decisions they are foragers.

   Briefly, foraging theory describes decision-making not as an irrational, but as a strategic behavior. It consists of three major phases: searching, handling, and consumption. Foraging rests on two major assumptions. The "currency assumption" assumes that foragers (consumer decision makers) spend money, energy, and time as currency that they had to earn. The second assumption is the "constraint assumption": "All foragers have limitations that constrain their ability to forage, and a successful forager is one the works within its constraints" (Hantula 2012, p. 554). Moreover, foraging takes place in an environment of risk and uncertainty. Thus, foragers expend their limited resources in attempts to gain benefits that meet their needs following rules that try to "match" their expenditures to their rewards that optimize their rates of return on asset of options. To do so they use time delay discounting as the mechanism behind the matching. Thus, consumer decision making consists of naturally selected decision strategies inherited from an evolutionally past because they have served to meet the needs of the species in general.

   Researchers have developed several mathematical models of foraging behavior that describe animal behavior and consumer behavior quite well (see Pirolli 2007; Smith and Hantula 2003). They view choices as evolved preferences. This view of consumer decision-making is highly congruent with Foxall's (2007) behavioral economics approach because it emphasizes the environment and evolved interactions with the environment rather than mental processes and psychological theories to explain choice. Moreover, both behavioral ecology and behavioral economics descriptions of consumer decision-making imply that people are largely unaware of why they are behaving in the ways they do, supporting the argument that much of the actual decision-making is taking place unconsciously with little conscious insight into the actual mechanisms involved.

5   Rational Choice, Bounded Rationality, and Marketing

Many marketing activities require highly rational behavior from consumers, and consumers do sometimes make decisions in ways that seem to follow the prescriptions of the rational model. For instance, many consumer decisions require that gathering information prior to making choices, especially where the product cannot be evaluated prior to its consumption. The emerging field of "information economics" addresses situations in which "different parties to a transaction often have different amounts of information regarding the transaction, and this information asymmetry has implications for the terms of the transaction and the relationship between the parties" (Kirmani and Rao 2000, p. 66). Focusing specifically on the need for consumers to assess product quality, Kirmani and Rao (2000) describe the theoretical justification for various managerial strategies that attempt to resolve the problem of information asymmetry by "signaling" or using such marketing mix elements as prices, brand names, store names, amount of advertising, and so forth to communicate the quality of brands. These signals are used by consumers to form perceptions of quality that guide their brand choices. "Signaling posits a 'rational' consumer who expects a firm to honor the implicit commitment conveyed through a signal because not honoring the commitment is economically unwise" (Kirmani and Rao 2000, p. 66). Signaling high quality and then disappointing the consumer obviates future purchases by that consumer and risks retaliation in the form of negative word-of-mouth. Thus, firms adopt profitable signaling strategies, "making it rational for consumers to infer that the firm that transmits a signal is the high-quality provider" (Kirmani and Rao 2000, p. 68).

On the other hand, some managerial strategies might require irrational consumers, that is, those who are not following the rational model but rely on one or more of the other types of decision-making. For instance, loyalty programs that reward consumers for repeat purchases are common. Whether they are the best option for consumers depends on how they are used. Consumers might remain loyal to a firm chiefly to gain the loyalty reward and thereby miss purchasing a more rational option from a competitor. Dubner and Levitt (2007) review several instances of violations of the rational model that potentially work to the advantage of the firm owing to irrational consumer behavior. U.S. consumers buy and give billions of dollars in gift cards each year that are not redeemed or when used are accompanied by additional spending by the card user. Many consumers purchase gym memberships they don't use. Moreover, gift themselves can be viewed by an economist as a suboptimal use of resources.

It is important for marketing management to understand the role of reason, emotion, and the influence of the environment on consumer decision making. As the preceding review shows, consumer decision making is complex and cannot be comprehensively described by any current theory. At least there is no universal agreement among scholars as to which theory is the best; each theory has its own advocates. However, instances can be found in which they appear to behave in ways described by each of the other theories. The traditional emphasis on compensatory and non-compensatory reasoning as taught to undergraduates in courses in consumer behavior seems to do a good job of explaining and predicting many instances of consumer choice (Sheth et al. 1991). Sometimes emotion seems to be the primary input to the decision (Chaudhuri 2006). Many behaviors correspond closely to the patterns described by Foxall's (2007) behavior modification theory or by foraging theory (Pirolli 2007). This wide variety of competing explanations allows scholars and practitioners considerable latitude to choose which theory they want to emphasize.

6 The Future of Consumer Decision Making

How do consumers make decisions? The position of this contribution is that they do so in a variety of ways, some of which tend to a rational, logical, thoughtful direction and others tending toward the thoughtless, emotional, often unconscious direction. No one theory seems to describe all types of consumer decisions. Not only is this due to inter-person variability, where people can be arrayed in a distribution from one extreme to the other, but also because of intra-variability, where the same person might make a highly rational decision in one instance but clearly make an illogical decision in another, making use of various heuristics all the time. Moreover, the influence of both product category and situational influences must be accounted for in trying to understand how given consumers are making their decisions.

What does the future hold for consumer decision making? We can venture a few guesses based on recent social and technological trends. First, we can argue that providing decision-making education and experience will improve consumer decision making toward the rational side of the continuum. Certainly, financial and nutritional educations strive to achieve this goal. As individuals are exposed to marketing and the marketplace earlier and earlier, they should gain experience that helps them make better (more rational) decisions. Consumers can certainly improve their decision-making ability over time and pass on their wisdom to the young.

Decision makers of all types appear to use the rational decision making model rarely if at all. However, the model did stimulate one method of making decisions under uncertainty that is both rational and feasible and thus is widely used in organizational settings. Collaboration among mathematicians, statisticians, and engineers yielded a type of decision making called "decision analysis," which is a family of problem solving approaches that systematically formulate problems, develop possible solutions, analyze each solution using Bayesian probabilities and optimization techniques to yield the solutions with the highest expected utility (Fox 2015). Note the similarity between decision analysis and the summary of critical thinking presented earlier. According to Fox (2015), this approach to decision making is highly appropriate to the big decisions organizations make with long investment horizons. This example suggests another possibility for the future of consumer decision making.

Accelerating technological progress in developing smarter computer algorithms, faster processing capacity, and greater availability of data through the Internet will yield computerized decision makers to take over the job of making many consumer decisions. Apple's Seri and her cohorts will assume a greater role in making consumer decisions. Similar to the way that artificial intelligence programs are used to assist doctors in making diagnoses and prescribing treatments, consumers might give up many of their decisions to technology, with the goal of achieving the rational ideal of the optimal decision. From the marketing perspective, managers can tailor their strategies to any style of type of decision-making. Marketing can present formal arguments to persuade at the rational end of the continuum and play more on the emotions at the other end of the continuum. It can employ more situational influencers at the right side of the continuum and more cognitive influencers at the other end. As more is learned about decision-making, strategies will be tailored more specifically to the circumstances of target consumers.

References

Bishop, M. (2012). *Thinking about critical thinking.* Presentation, May 22, 2012, Florida State University.

Black, D. W. (2007). A review of compulsive buying disorder. *World Psychiatry, 6*(1), 14–18.

Blastland, M., & Dilnot, A. W. (2010). *The numbers game: The commonsense guide to understanding numbers in the news, in politics, and in life* (1st paperback trade ed.). New York: Gotham Books.

Chaudhuri, A. (2006). *Emotion and reason in consumer behavior.* Burlington, MA: Elsevier Butterworth-Heinemann.

Chernev, A., & Hamilton, R. (2009). Compensatory reasoning in choice. In M. Wänke (Ed.), *Social psychology of consumer behavior* (pp. 131–147). New York: Psychology Press.

Csikszentmihalyi, M. (1997). *Creativity: Flow and the psychology of discovery and invention* (1st HarperPerennial ed.). New York: HarperPerennial.

DeSarbo, W. S., & Edwards, E. A. (1996). Typologies of compulsive buying behavior: A constrained clusterwise regression approach. *Journal of Consumer Psychology, 5*(3), 230–262.

Dubner, S. J., & Levitt, S. D. (2007, January). The gift-card economy. *The New York Times Magazine, 7*(2007), 16–17.

Edwards, W. (1954). The theory of decision making. *Psychological Bulletin, 51*(4), 380–417. doi:10.1037/h0053870.

Evans, J. (2008). Dual-processing accounts of reasoning, judgment, and social cognition. *Annual Review of Psychology, 59*, 255–278. Palo Alto, CA: Annual Reviews.

Faber, R. J. (2010). Impulsive and compulsive buying. In R. P. Bagozzi & A. A. Ruvio (Eds.), *Wiley international encyclopedia of marketing* (pp. 183–184). Chichester: Wiley.

Fox, J. (2015). From "economic man" to behavioral economics. *Harvard Business Review, 93*(5), 78–85.

Foxall, G. R. (2007). *Explaining consumer choice.* Basingstoke: Palgrave Macmillan.

Gigerenzer, G. (2002). *Calculated risks: How to know when numbers deceive you*. New York: Simon & Schuster.

Gigerenzer, G., & Selten, R. (2001). *Bounded rationality the adaptive toolbox*. Cambridge, MA: MIT.

Gilovich, T. (1991). *How we know what isn't so*. New York: The Free Press.

Hastie, R., & Dawes, R. M. (2010). *Rational choice in an uncertain world* (2nd ed.). Los Angeles, CA: SAGE.

Hantula, D. A. (2012). Consumers are foragers, not rational actors: Towards a behavioral ecology of consumer choice. In V. Wells & G. Foxall (Eds.), *Handbook of developments in consumer behaviour* (pp. 549–577). Cheltenham: Edward Elgar.

Kahneman, D. (2003). Maps of bounded rationality: Psychology for behavioral economics. *American Economic Review, 93*(5), 1449–1475.

Kida, T. (2006). *Don't believe everything you think: The 6 basic mistakes we make in thinking*. Amherst, NY: Prometheus Books.

Kirmani, A., & Rao, A. R. (2000). No pain, no gain: A critical review of the literature on signaling unobservable product quality. *Journal of Marketing, 64*(2), 66–79.

Koch, C. (2012). *Consciousness: Confessions of a romantic reductionist*. Cambridge, MA: MIT.

Lawrence, P. R., & Nohria, N. (2002). *Driven: How human nature shapes our choices*. San Francisco, CA: Jossey-Bass.

Maslow, A. H. (1970). *Motivation and personality* (2nd ed.). New York: Harper & Row.

Palan, K. M., Morrow, P. C., Trapp Ii, A., & Blackburn, V. (2011). Compulsive buying behavior in college students: The mediating role of credit card misuse. *Journal of Marketing Theory & Practice, 19*(1), 81–96. doi:10.2753/MTP1069-6679190105.

Piattelli-Palmarini, M. (1994). *Inevitable illusions*. New York: Wiley.

Pirolli, P. (2007). *Information foraging theory: Adaptive interaction with information*. Cary, NC: Oxford University Press.

Rook, D. W. (1987). The buying impulse. *Journal of Consumer Research, 14*(2), 189–199.

Savage, L. (1954). *The foundations of statistics*. New York: Wiley.

Seife, C. (2010). *Proofiness: The dark arts of mathematical deception*. New York: Viking.

Sent, E.-M. (1997). Sargent versus Simon: Bounded rationality unbound. *Cambridge Journal of Economics, 21*(3), 323–338.

Sent, E.-M. (2005). Simplifying Herbert Simon. *History of Political Economy, 37*(2), 227–232. doi:10.1215/00182702-37-2-227.

Sheth, J. N., Newman, B. I., & Gross, B. L. (1991). *Consumption values and market choices: Theory and applications*. Cincinnati, OH: South-Western.

Shiv, B., Loewenstein, G., & Bechara, A. (2005). The dark side of emotion in decision-making: When individuals with decreased emotional reactions make more advantageous decisions. *Cognitive Brain Research, 23*(1), 85–92. doi:10.1016/j.cogbrainres. 2005.01.006.

Simon, H. A. (1995). The information-processing theory of mind. *American Psychologist, 50*(7), 507–508.

Smith, C. L., & Hantula, D. A. (2003). Pricing effects on foraging in a simulated Internet shopping mall. *Journal of Economic Psychology, 24*(5), 653–674. doi:10.1016/S0167-4870(03)00007-2.

Stein, B., & Haynes, A. (2011). Engaging faculty in the assessment and improvement of students' critical thinking using the CAT. *Change: The Magazine of Higher Learning, 43*(2), 44–49.

von Neumann, J., & Morgenstern, O. (1944). *Theory of games and economic behavior* (2nd 1947 ed.). Princeton, NJ: Princeton University Press.

Yang, H., & Carmon, Z. (2010). Consumer decision making. In R. P. Bagozzi & A. A. Ruvio (Eds.), *Wiley International encyclopedia of marketing* (pp. 79–88). Chichester: Wiley.

Temporal Discounting of Future Risks

Chengyan Yue and Jingjing Wang

1 Concept of Temporal Discounting

Temporal discounting describes people's tendency to lower the subjective value of future outcomes. A consumer might choose a smaller and more immediate reward over a larger but delayed reward because the present value of the delayed reward is discounted (Myerson and Green 1995; Chapman and Elstein 1995). Standard discounted utility theory assumes that consumers make rational tradeoffs between immediate rewards and delayed rewards and captures consumers' intertemporal choices using discount rates (Grossman 1972). Some researchers have argued that temporal discounting might reflect the increased risks involved in waiting for a future outcome (Myerson and Green 1995; Chapman and Elstein 1995; Hardisty and Weber 2009). For example, Dasgupta and Maskin (2005) suggested that when uncertainty is involved in the realization time of the payoffs, the corresponding intertemporal preferences may entail hyperbolic discounting.

Overall, temporal discounting is useful in explaining how an individual consumer or a society acts when there are future financial, health, or environmental risks/benefits. For example, hyperbolic discounting models are often used to explain an individual's unhealthy behaviors such as addiction to alcohol and tobacco (Scharff and Viscusi 2011; Roewer et al. 2015) as well as health outcomes such as obesity (Richards and Hamilton 2012; Scharff 2009). Studies also have investigated how temporal discounting affects environmental outcomes such as air

C. Yue (✉)
Department of Horticultural Science, University of Minnesota, 305 Alderman Hall,
1970 Folwell Ave, St Paul, MN 55108, USA
e-mail: yuechy@umn.edu

J. Wang
Department of Applied Economics, University of Minnesota, St Paul, MN, USA

© Springer International Publishing AG 2017   253
G. Emilien et al. (eds.), *Consumer Perception of Product Risks and Benefits*,
DOI 10.1007/978-3-319-50530-5_14

quality deterioration and water quality improvement (Hardisty and Weber 2009). Therefore, understanding consumer temporal discounting behavior for future risks/ benefits is very important in designing, evaluating, and implementing financial, environmental, and health policies and strategies.

1.1 Exponential and Hyperbolic Discounting

In general, two major types of models have been used to characterize the temporal discounting of future outcomes. According to the standard discounted utility theory, the utility of future outcomes is discounted to the present using a constant discounting factor in which the individual's choices between two future outcomes are independent from the time when future outcomes occur. In this case, consumers' intertemporal choices are assumed to be time-consistent, which can be explained by exponential discounting models in the following functional form:

$$V(A, t) = A\, e^{-kt},$$

where V is the present value of the delayed reward, A is the delayed amount of reward, t is the delayed time, and k is the discount rate.

However, extensive studies have revealed that consumers' intertemporal behaviors violate rational choice theory and that exponential discounting models cannot explain the mechanisms underlying the intertemporal decision-making (Loewenstein and Prelec 1992; Hardisty and Weber 2009). First of all, temporal discounting rate is not fixed but appears to vary over time. In particular, discount rates for longer delays are lower than those for shorter delays. The tendency to choose more immediate alternatives, also called impulsivity or temporal myopia, is more aligned with the hyperbolic patterns of discounting (Frederick et al. 2002).

Moreover, evidence of "preference reversals" has been found in both laboratory and field experiments, which is not consistent with exponential discounting model. For instance, when people are asked to choose between two future rewards, $105 in a year and a day or $100 in 1 year, they often choose the larger amount. But 1 year later, when they are asked to choose between getting $100 now and getting $105 tomorrow, they become impatient and choose to get $100 immediately. Such preference reversals, as presented in Fig. 1, have been extensively discussed in pervious literature. One theory consistent with preference reversals is "diminishing impatience," where subjects discount the future with a declining discount rate. Experiments conducted by both behavioral economists and psychologists using various rewards such as money, durable goods, and sweets also suggest that impatience at the present time is higher than impatience with respect to trade-offs occurring in the future (e.g., Frederick et al. 2002).

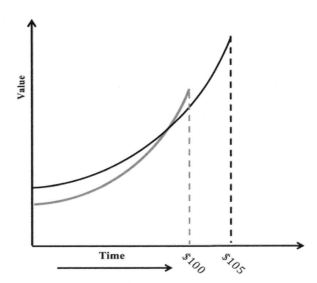

Fig. 1 Discounting curves for two rewards of different sizes available at different times (preference reversals) (Adapted from Figure 1 in Ainslie, 1975)

Time-inconsistent discounting models such as hyperbolic discounting and quasi-hyperbolic discounting functional forms are often used to capture people's tendency to give higher weight to payoffs that are closer to the present time when weighing trade-offs between two future moments. The hyperbolic discounting model, for example, has the following functional form:

$$V(A,t) = \frac{A}{1 + kt}$$

where V is the present value of the delayed reward, A is the delayed amount of reward, t is the delayed time, and k is the discount rate (Ainslie, 1975).

As shown in Fig. 2, the discount factor in hyperbolic discounting falls very rapidly at short-delayed periods but falls slowly at longer-delayed periods, which is different from exponential discounting, where discount factor falls by a constant rate per unit of delay. Numerous studies have shown that temporal discounting behavior can be better described by a hyperbolic rather than an exponential discounting model (e.g., Green and Myerson 2004; Richards and Hamilton 2012).

Quasi-hyperbolic discounting is also introduced and explored in intertemporal choice studies where the value of rewards declines rapidly over the short run but at a slower rate over the long run, or the short-term impulses supersede long-term goals (Loewenstein and Prelec 1992). In other words, subjects exhibit a strong present bias for earlier payoffs. Present-biased preferences have also been interpreted in terms of self-control problems (Ainslie 1975) or a lack of self-awareness (Frederick et al. 2002). The quasi-hyperbolic model developed by Laibson (1997) is also known as the $\beta - \delta$ model, where the discount function is a discrete time function with values $\phi(t) = \{1, \beta\delta, \beta\delta^2, \beta\delta^3, \ldots, \beta\delta^t, \ldots\}$ for time from present $t = \{0, 1, 2,$

Fig. 2 Comparison of the
discount functions of
hyperbolic and exponential
discounting (Adapted from
Figure 1 in Laibson, 1997)

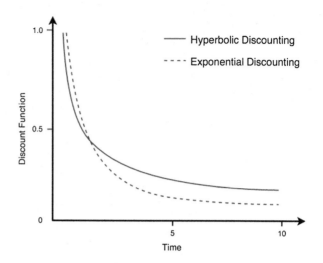

$3, \ldots, t, \ldots\}$, $\beta \in (0, 1)$ is the short-run discount factor capturing the present bias, and $\delta \in (0, 1)$ is the long-run discount factor.

Other hyperbola-like models, such as the generalized hyperbolic discounting model, were also proposed and widely discussed in both theoretical and empirical studies to explain distinct consumer behaviors in intertemporal choice decisions. Specifically, Loewenstein and Prelec (1992) suggested the generalized hyperbolic discount function to be $\phi(t) = (1 + \alpha t)^{-\frac{\beta}{\alpha}}$, $(\alpha > 0 \text{ and } \beta > 0)$, where α is the parameter capturing the degree of decreasing impatience, which determines how much the function departs from the exponential discounting.

1.2 Contributions from Cognitive Neuroscience

Although hyperbolic discounting provides a useful quantitative measure of intertemporal discounting, it only focuses on stimulus input and behavioral output and is limited in explaining different temporal discounting phenomena. Specifically, the hyperbolic discounting model does not account for various discounting behaviors across situations, and it fails to illustrate the cognitive processes of decision-making. Recent studies suggest that neuroscience-based theory can demonstrate the cognitive process of intertemporal choices at the brain level.

Neurobiology frameworks suggest that decision-making takes place in several basic stages (Bos and McClure 2013). In the past decade, brain-imaging techniques such as functional magnetic resonance imaging (fMRI) have frequently been used in decision-making tasks to determine the relative brain activation areas and explore the specific areas of the brain used. Brain-imaging studies have consistently shown that temporal discounting involves activities in different regions of the brain, such as subcortical and cortical regions. These regions are commonly divided into two networks: a valuation network and a control network (Bos and McClure 2013). The valuation network is involved in estimating the incentive value of the different options, and the control network is involved in action selection, maintaining future goals, and inhibiting prepotent responses.

The valuation network consists of some important nodes, such as the ventromedial prefrontal cortex (vmPFC), ventral regions of striatum (VS), amygdala, and the posterior cingulate cortex (PCC). Several human neuroimaging studies have shown that various brain areas are associated with the brain's dopamine system. Particularly, greater activities in the VS, vmPFC, and PCC are related to more impulsive choices. These areas also show a clear present bias tendency when receiving signals of future rewards. Although there is still debate on the role of vmPFC, many studies in cognitive neuroscience agree that the vmPFC works at the intersection of the valuation and control networks. Information from each of these two systems is integrated in the vmPFC to determine behaviors. Findings also suggest that the VS and possibly other areas are central components of a valuation network that biases behavior toward immediate rewards (Bos and McClure 2013).

The control network includes the dorsal anterior cingulate cortex (dACC), dorsal and ventral lateral prefrontal cortex (dlPFC/vlPFC), and the posterior parietal cortex (PPC). Among the control network, dACC supports the selection and maintenance of behavior directed toward long-term goals. Activities in the LPFC and PPC are associated with an increase in the likelihood of choosing larger, delayed outcomes over smaller, sooner outcomes (Bos and McClure 2013).

Overall, the control network has been found to be involved in guiding behaviors to plan for the future and to seek rewards with significant delays. In the context of intertemporal choice, the dominant effect of increased control is to bias behavior in favor of larger, later outcomes.

Moreover, distinct pathways are associated with temporal discounting. For instance, Bos et al. (2014) suggest that reward-based and goal-oriented decisions rely on the striatum and its interactions with other cortical and subcortical networks. Using connectivity analyses in both structural and functional MRIs, their results indicate that connectivity between the striatum and the lateral prefrontal cortex is associated with increased patience, whereas connectivity between subcortical areas and the striatum is associated with increased impulsivity.

When facing intertemporal choices, imagining or simulating the benefit from a future reward plays an important role since it is impossible to experience future rewards at the time of making choices. Hakimi and Hare (2015) suggested that the quality of reward imagination might affect the degree of temporal discounting of future outcomes. Using fMRI to monitor the brain activities of subjects, they found that the vmPFC responds actively when subjects are imagining receiving primary rewards, which is correlated with reduced monetary temporal discounting.

Bos and McClure (2013) conclude that the brain-based model shows how cognitive models can be linked to hyperbolic discounting curves in a very natural way. The neuroscience-based model integrates the cognitive models and quantitative measures of temporal discounting. Furthermore, it can help clarify why a particular brain region may dominate choice behavior in one situation but not in others.

2 Empirical Findings

2.1 Domain Differences in Temporal Discounting

Many previous studies in temporal discounting considered all goods and services (for example, health, air quality, etc.) to be potentially tradable with money, assuming that future outcomes in different domains are therefore discounted at the same rate. Some research, however, has shown that temporal discounting may vary across different domains and that it is inappropriate to use one general estimation of discount rate for all situations (Chapman and Elstein 1995). For example, Hendrickx and Nicolaij (2004) concluded that temporal discounting is less pronounced for environmental risks than for other types of risks. Hardisty and Weber (2009) found that health gains are discounted more than monetary and environmental gains. Lawless et al. (2013) suggested that discount rates for health are higher than those for money in both social and private contexts.

We compared temporal discounting across three different domains (financial, environmental, and health) using an online experiment with 697 U.S. consumers to study their intertemporal preferences in terms of rewards with short-term (6 months) and long-term (24 months) delays. In the choice experiment, participants were presented with a series of hypothetical choices between receiving a smaller reward sooner or a larger reward later (the rewards are money for the financial domain, square feet of park improvement for the environmental domain, and days of relief from chronic back pain for the health domain).

We found that, on average, participants had the highest discount rates in the health domain, followed by environmental domain and financial domain, for both the short-term and long-term delays. The discount rates for the financial and environmental domains are quite similar, but the short-term discount rate in the environmental domain is slightly higher than that in the financial domain. The pairwise t-test results show that the discount rates in the health domain are significantly higher than those in the other two domains, which is consistent with previous findings that the discount rates for health gains are higher than those for monetary and environmental gains (Lawless et al. 2013; Hardisty and Weber 2009). Overall, the short-term environmental discount rate is more correlated with the short-term discount rate in the health domain than that in the financial domain. The correlations between the long-term environmental discount rate and the long-term discount rates in the other two domains are not significantly different from one another. For both short-term and long-term discount rates, very low correlations (0.3 for short-term outcomes and 0.36 for long-term outcomes) are found between financial and health domains, indicating that discount rates in these two domains may not be good substitutes for each other.

Consistent across domains, we found that the short-term temporal discounting rate is higher than the long-term temporal discounting rate, which implies that temporal discounting is significantly influenced by the realization time of future rewards and that temporal myopia is less pronounced for longer delays.

2.2 Individual Differences in Temporal Discounting

In addition to the variation across domains, temporal discounting also varies considerably across individuals. Demographic characteristics have significant impact on temporal discounting behavior. For instance, Weller et al. (2008) found that obese women show greater temporal discounting than women in the control group, but obese and healthy-weight men do not differ significantly in temporal discounting.

Several studies also find individual heterogeneity in temporal discounting using the quasi-hyperbolic $(\beta - \delta)$ model. Andreoni and Sprenger (2012) found average values of δ in the range of 0.74–0.8, and only 16.7% of their respondents were characterized as present biased. More evidence of individual differences in temporal discounting has been found in the neuroscience studies. For example, individual differences in the quality of reward imagination are significantly correlated with the temporal discounting rate of future monetary rewards; enhanced activity in vmPFC during reward imagination can predict choice behavior differences between and within individuals (Hakimi and Hare 2015).

Even within individuals, temporal discounting behaviors could be distinct in different situations. Tsukayama and Duckworth (2010) found that adults discount delayed rewards they find particularly tempting more steeply than less tempting rewards.

Our experimental results also show that consumer socio-demographic characteristics affect temporal discounting behaviors in different domains in different ways.

Our results indicate that discount rates in the financial domain tend to decrease as participants get older. Female participants tend to discount future financial outcomes more compared to male participants. Additionally, participants with higher education levels have lower discount rates, and participants with higher household income are more likely to have lower discount rates. As suggested by Becker and Mulligan (1997), poverty increases an individual's need for immediate income more than future income. Therefore, participants with higher household income discount less for future financial rewards due to their patience. The presence of children under the age of 12 also has a significant impact on participants' discount rates in the financial domain. Other variables—such as marital status, household size, and home location—do not significantly impact their financial discount rates.

As for the environmental temporal discounting, our experimental results suggest that age is not a significant factor. Similar to the results in the financial domain, having a graduate school education greatly decreases participants' discount rate, while the influence of college education is not statistically significant. The presence of children also has a negative and significant effect on the environmental discount rate, suggesting that families with children discount less and care about future environmental outcomes.

Notably, our results suggest that age has a positive effect on health discount rate, which is different from the results in the other two domains. Older participants have higher discount rates compared to younger participants in the health domain (i.e., older participants would like to receive a sooner, albeit small, health reward compared to younger respondents), which was also found by van der Pol and Cairns (2001). Our results indicate that college education does not significantly affect the health discount rate, but graduate school education decreases health discount rate by a similar amount to that in the environmental domain. The income effect is less prominent in the health domain. Moreover, the presence of children does not significantly affect an individual's discount rate in the health domain, indicating that having a child may not change an individual's preference for future health rewards.

2.3 Temporal Discounting on Addiction and Unhealthy Behaviors/Outcomes

Numerous studies have demonstrated the relationship between temporal discounting and addictive behaviors such as smoking, drinking, and drug use. In general, many studies found that decision-makers value future health outcomes (such as high probability of getting cancer or obesity) much less than present outcomes (consumption of tobacco, alcohol, or unhealthy food). Subjects with addictive behaviors discount the future steeply or have higher temporal discount rates compared to those without addictive behaviors (Scharff and Viscusi 2011; Harrison et al. 2010; Bos and McClure 2013). In neuroscience-based studies, there are clear associations between impulsivity and dopamine function in patients with dopamine-related disorders such as addiction and attention-deficit/hyperactivity disorder (ADHD) (Bos and McClure 2013).

Many studies find significant relationships between temporal discounting and smoking. Scharff and Viscusi (2011) found that the individual discount rate is higher for smokers than nonsmokers, or smokers are more present biased than non-smokers. However, omitted variables such as severity of addiction, self-efficacy, and social support among others may confound the analysis. Both individual characteristics and current smoking status influence temporal discounting behaviors. Harrison et al. (2010) found that male smokers have significantly higher temporal discount rates than male non-smokers, but the rates are not significantly different between female smokers and female non-smokers. Roewer et al. (2015) suggested that heavy smokers respond more slowly when making intertemporal choices after nicotine deprivation.

Furthermore, studies suggest that drinking behaviors are correlated with temporal discounting rates; people who frequently consume alcohol tend to discount future outcomes more and are more impulsive to enjoy sooner rewards (Vuchinich and Simpson 1998). For instance, Vuchinich and Simpson (1998) found that the hyperbolic discounting function described temporal discounting behavior of alcohol consumption more accurately than exponential functions. They also suggest that light drinkers are less impulsive and more future-oriented compared to heavier drinkers.

Some unhealthy outcomes, such as obesity, have been well examined by temporal discounting models (Richards and Hamilton 2012; Scharff 2009). In particular, consumers suffering from self-control problems often ignore the unforeseeable health outcomes of overeating, drinking, and other unhealthy behaviors. They often fail to consider the long-term health goals when making tradeoffs between immediate and future consequences. Obesity, for example, is often related to steeper temporal discounting (or impulsivity for immediate rewards over delayed rewards). Many previous studies have found significant correlations between obesity and temporal discounting of monetary rewards (e.g., Richards and Hamilton 2012; Scharff 2009). For instance, using quasi-hyperbolic models to capture time-inconsistent preferences, Courtemanche et al. (2014) found that both long-run discount factor and present bias significantly impact an individual's body mass index; thus both rational intertemporal tradeoffs and time inconsistency are associated with obesity.

It is also worth noting that many studies compared addiction and unhealthy behaviors with the discount rate in monetary rewards (as a proxy for temporal discounting). As previously discussed, intertemporal preferences may vary across different domains, and these studies potentially fail to differentiate temporal discounting behavior in the health and financial domains, which might lead to biased results.

3 Scope

Empirical findings suggest that, in many situations, more distant future rewards are discounted less than rewards in the near future. In other words, consumers exhibit more temporal myopia (or impatience) when facing short-term delays compared to long-term delays. Decreased temporal discounting rates given longer delays suggest that temporal discounting is inconsistent over time and more likely to have a hyperbola shape; therefore, employing appropriate temporal discounting models is critical in explaining consumers' time-inconsistent behaviors. Hyperbolic and quasi-hyperbolic discounting models are found to be more appropriate than exponential discounting models in explaining individuals' intertemporal choice behavior. The neuroscience-based models account for contextual factors that are known to affect individuals' intertemporal preferences and demonstrate the cognitive process of intertemporal choices at the brain level. The neuroscience-based model preserves much of the functional form of the hyperbolic discounting models but overcomes their limitations, such as the ignorance of contextual effects and the inability to capture the cognitive process of decision-making.

The inconsistent temporal discounting models, such as hyperbolic and quasi-hyperbolic discounting models, can be used to explain a wide range of anomalies in individuals' life-cycle consumption, such as consumption discontinuities at retirement and under-saving (Laibson 1997). To help individuals overcome temporal myopia and self-control problems, commitment mechanisms can be introduced. For instance, Laibson (1997) illustrated how impatience could be overcome by mandatory investment of a portion of income into illiquid assets. Other studies (for example, Basu 2011) introduced saving programs as commitment devices, where the majority of participants successfully increased their saving toward retirement.

The findings of temporal discounting and brain activities from neuroscience are critical for understanding addictions and ADHD. In particular, the valuation system is thought to develop during early adolescence, while the control system is developed later and more gradually (Bos et al. 2014). The imbalance in the development of these two systems may result in steeper temporal discounting and greater impulsivity, as is the case with ADHD. Therefore, it is necessary to understand how different neural systems contribute to intertemporal preferences and impulsive behavior.

Previous studies suggest that temporal discounting rates are different across different domains, indicating that temporal discounting should be domain-specific. Much of the previous research on temporal discounting simply used the discount rate for monetary outcomes as a proxy to measure the temporal discounting for environmental outcomes or health outcomes (e.g., Richards and Hamilton 2012). However, our conclusions suggest that using one universal discount rate for different domains may not be appropriate and thus might lead to biased results. Even within a specific domain, temporal discounting may also be different. Previous studies estimated discount rates ranging from negative to several thousand percent per year for environmental outcomes, and it is still unclear what discount rate should be used in many cases. Similarly, temporal discounting rates for health outcomes vary significantly depending on the delay of illness or health improvement as well as the severity of the health outcomes (Chapman and Elstein 1995; Pol and Cairns 2001). Therefore, it is helpful for policy makers to distinguish the temporal discounting rates for different future outcomes and understand which temporal discounting rates individuals use when facing future rewards.

Understanding consumers' time-inconsistent discounting behaviors has important implications for environmental organizations and policy makers. The positive discount rates for future environmental rewards indicate that individuals put less weight on future environmental outcomes. Compared to temporal discounting in other domains, environmental risks or benefits often take effect in an even more distant future, sometimes in decades or hundreds of years. As a consequence, future environmental outcomes are highly discounted, resulting in little present value and losing almost all significance. The presence of temporal myopia may lead individuals to overlook the effect of environmental risks for future generations; therefore, it is crucial for individuals to understand the benefit of environmental sustainability in the long run. Public policies and education could help consumers understand that supporting the environment may only take little daily efforts. In particular, public media and environmental organizations could educate consumers about the long-run environmental benefits of everyday behaviors such as recycling and using energy-saving and water-saving technologies/devices.

Furthermore, these findings can provide useful implications for health policy makers as well as individual consumers. Consumers discount future health outcomes more compared to future outcomes in other domains. Many studies have investigated consumers' temporal discounting behaviors in drug or alcohol use and concluded that addicted individuals may be more myopic (Ainslie 1975). When making tradeoffs between current rewards (for example, gratification from consuming unhealthful products) and future health outcomes, myopic individuals tend to put less weight on future outcomes. The high discount rates in the health domain also suggest that health improvement in the future is discounted and valued so little that many individuals may not engage in preventive behaviors. The analysis of smoking behavior using temporal discounting models could generate implications about the effectiveness of public policies. For instance, if the temporal discounting behaviors for addictive smokers are mostly time-inconsistent, policies such as increasing cigarette taxes and anti-smoking campaigns may not work well (Lawless et al. 2013). Public policies should also promote generally healthy behavior and introduce commitment mechanisms to help addicted individuals overcome their self-control problems.

Additionally, individuals with temporal myopia should be educated about the future health risks of current behaviors such as overeating and eating an unhealthful diet. Public health policies could also focus on improving people's awareness of future health risks. For example, helping consumers understand the relationship between temporal myopia and obesity could improve their recognition of self-control problems when consuming food. As Richard and Hamilton (2012) suggested, to deal with obesity, public policy could target behaviors associated with impatience and immediate gratification instead of focusing only on nutritional education or fitness messages. More specifically, in the weight-control effort, consumers are suggested to purchase limited quantities of unhealthy foods or buy smaller quantities of food during each shopping trip. Moreover, commitment devices can be used for those consumers who lack the self-control to overcome their inconsistent time preferences. For example, peer groups such as Weight Watcher programs are often useful to reinforce an individual's self-control (Scharff 2009).

In summary, temporal discounting—the tendency for individuals to prefer immediate but small rewards to future but sizable rewards—is far from a simple matter. On-going research in this area is being conducted by researchers around the globe. Both behavioral economics and neuroscience studies have found solid evidence that temporal discounting affects individuals' intertemporal preferences. Accumulated evidence indicates that temporal discounting is not consistent over time. Appropriate temporal discounting models need to be investigated and adopted when examining consumers' discounting behaviors. Moreover, individual heterogeneity and domain differences should be considered when studying temporal discounting behaviors.

References

Ainslie, G. (1975). Specious reward: A behavioral theory of impulsiveness and impulse control. *Psychological Bulletin, 82*(4), 463–496.

Andreoni, J., & Sprenger, C. (2012). Estimating time preferences from convex budgets. *American Economic Review, 102*(7), 3333–3356.

Basu, K. (2011). Hyperbolic discounting and the sustainability of rotational savings arrangements. *American Economic Journal: Microeconomics, 3*(4), 143–171.

Becker, G., & Mulligan, C. (1997). The endogenous determination of time preference. *The Quarterly Journal of Economics, 112*(3), 729–758.

Chapman, G. B., & Elstein, A. S. (1995). Valuing the future: Temporal discounting of health and money. *Medical Decision Making, 15*(4), 373–386.

Courtemanche, C., Heutel, G., & Mcalvanah, P. (2014). Impatience, incentives and obesity. *Economic Journal, 125*, 1–31.

Dasgupta, P., & Maskin, E. (2005). Uncertainty and hyperbolic discounting. *American Economic Review, 95*(4), 1290–1299.

Frederick, S., Loewenstein, G., & O'Donoghue, T. (2002). Time discounting and time preference: A critical review. *Journal of Economic Literature, 40*(2), 351–401.

Green, L., & Myerson, J. (2004). A discounting framework for choice with delayed and probabilistic rewards. *Psychological Bulletin, 130*(5), 769–792.

Grossman, M. (1972). On the concept of health capital and the demand for health. *Journal of Political Economy, 80*(2), 223.

Hakimi, S., & Hare, T. A. (2015). Enhanced neural responses to imagined primary rewards predict reduced monetary temporal discounting. *Journal of Neuroscience, 35*(38), 13103–13109.

Hardisty, D. J., & Weber, E. U. (2009). Discounting future green: Money versus the environment. *Journal of Experimental Psychology: General, 138*(3), 329–340.

Harrison, G. W., Lau, M. I., & Rutström, E. E. (2010). Individual discount rates and smoking: Evidence from a field experiment in Denmark. *Journal of Health Economics, 29*(5), 708–717.

Hendrickx, L., & Nicolaij, S. (2004). Temporal discounting and environmental risks: The role of ethical and loss-related concerns. *Journal of Environmental Psychology, 24*(4), 409–422.

Laibson, D. (1997). Golden eggs and hyperbolic discounting. *The Quarterly Journal of Economics, 112*(2), 443–478.

Lawless, L., Drichoutis, A. C., & Nayga Jr., R. M. (2013). Time preferences and health behaviour: A review. *Agricultural and Food Economics, 1*(17), 1–19.

Loewenstein, G., & Prelec, D. (1992). Anomalies in intertemporal choice: Evidence and an interpretation. *The Quarterly Journal of Economics, 107*(2), 573–597.

Myerson, J., & Green, L. (1995). Discounting of delayed rewards: Models of individual choice. *Journal of the Experimental Analysis of Behavior, 64*(3), 263–276.

Richards, T., & Hamilton, S. (2012). Obesity and hyperbolic discounting: An experimental analysis. *Journal of Agricultural and Resource Economics, 37*(2), 181–198.

Roewer, I., Wiehler, A., & Peters, J. (2015). Nicotine deprivation, temporal discounting and choice consistency in heavy smokers. *Journal of the Experimental Analysis of Behavior, 103*(1), 62–76.

Scharff, R. L. (2009). Obesity and hyperbolic discounting: Evidence and implications. *Journal of Consumer Policy, 32*(1), 3–21.

Scharff, R. L., & Viscusi, W. K. (2011). Heterogeneous rates of time preference and the decision to smoke. *Economic Inquiry, 49*(4), 959–972.

Tsukayama, E., & Duckworth, A. L. (2010). Domain-specific temporal discounting and temptation. *Judgment and Decision Making, 5*(2), 72–82.

Van den Bos, W., & McClure, S. M. (2013). Towards a general model of temporal discounting. *Journal of the Experimental Analysis of Behavior, 1*(99), 1–16.

Van den Bos, W., Rodriguez, C. A., Schweitzer, J. B., & McClure, S. M. (2014). Connectivity strength of dissociable striatal tracts predict individual differences in temporal discounting. *Journal of Neuroscience, 34*(31), 10298–10310.

Van der Pol, M., & Cairns, J. (2001). Estimating time preferences for health using discrete choice experiments. *Social Science & Medicine, 52*(9), 1459–1470.

Vuchinich, R. E., & Simpson, C. A. (1998). Hyperbolic temporal discounting in social drinkers and problem drinkers. *Experimental and Clinical Psychopharmacology, 6*(3), 292–305.

Weller, R. E., Cook, E. W., Avsar, K. B., & Cox, J. E. (2008). Obese women show greater delay discounting than healthy-weight women. *Appetite, 51*(3), 563–569.

Cognitive Styles and Personality in Risk Perception

Eric Ping Hung Li

1 Introduction

Does risk perception shaped by culture, consumers' cognitive styles and personality? Do consumer's consumption patterns influenced by different personality and cognitive styles? In the past few decades, consumer researchers have examined how cognitive styles and personality influence decision making processes (e.g., Myers and McCaulley 1985; White et al. 2003) or examined how culture affects consumers' risk perception (Hsee and Weber 1999; Keh and Sun 2008). However, not many studies provides a holistic approach to explore the role of cognitive styles and personality in the context of risk perception.

This chapter examines the link between consumer personality and cognitive styles in the context of risk perception. An extensive literature review on the Big Five personality model as well as different conception of cognitive styles illustrate the interconnection of these two prominent psychological dimensions and their influences on consumers' risk perception. The last part of this chapter highlights some cross-cultural studies on personality, cognitive styles and risk perception. In summary, this chapter extends our understanding of the socio-psychological development of risk perception and sheds light to future research directions on this topic.

E.P.H. Li (✉)
University of British Columbia – Okanagan, Kelowna, BC, Canada
e-mail: eric.li@ubc.ca

© Springer International Publishing AG 2017   267
G. Emilien et al. (eds.), *Consumer Perception of Product Risks and Benefits*,
DOI 10.1007/978-3-319-50530-5_15

2 Role of Cognitive Styles in Consumer Research

Built on the foundation of Allport (1937), James (1890), Galton (1884), and Jung (1923), cognitive styles historically has referred to stable attitudes, preferences, or habitual strategies that represent consistent individual differences in how individual perceive, remember, think, solve problems, learn, take decisions and related to others, particularly with respect to acquiring and processing information. In the field of consumer research, White et al. (2003) define the term "cognitive style" as "the relatively stable mental structures or processes that people prefer when they perceive and evaluation information" (p. 64). Cognitive style therefore is considered to be an important attribute that influence consumers' decision making process as it reflects an individual's underlying values and assumptions.

Prior literature identified six cognitive personality traits that related to individual differences in processing information, perceiving risk, and decision-making. These six traits include: (i) tolerance for ambiguity—the tendency to perceive ambiguous or inconsistent situations as desirable, (ii) rigidity—the intolerance for ambiguity, (iii) cognitive style—individual's tendency to react to uncertain or inconsistent information, (iv) need for cognitive clarity—need for cognitive certainty, (v) self-esteem—confidence in ability to evaluate alternatives and make purchase decisions (Cox 1967b), and (vi) trait anxiety—the stress level at which individuals can effectively function in decision-making tasks.

2.1 Tolerance for Ambiguity

In the field of consumer research, the concept of tolerance for ambiguity has been linked to information processing and to new product acceptance. Blake et al. (1973) found that intolerant individuals tended to perceive a typical products as newer, and that perceived product newness was positively related to purchase intention among tolerant individuals, but negatively related among intolerant ones. Consumers' familiarity of products or products categories also affect their acceptance and tolerance level. In other words, tolerance for ambiguity is very much driven by consumers' knowledge and exposure to certain products or features.

2.2 Rigidity and Trait Anxiety

Rigidity is a personality trait that refers to the degree of inflexibility in a person. It is characterized by the qualities such as inhibition, conservatism, social introversion, anxiety, and guilty. Previous research has shown a link between rigidity and behavior. For example, Blake et al. (1973) reported that the more intolerant person perceived the atypical products as newer than did the tolerant one. Their study also showed that perceived product newness tended to be positively related to willingness to buy among tolerant individuals, but negatively related among intolerant ones (p. 239). Similarly, Schaninger and Sciglimapglia (1981) found that individuals with lesser tolerance for ambiguity or greater rigidity are less relied on information. In other words, consumers with a more rigid personality are expected to have higher risk perception and are tended to employ risk reductions strategy in their decision making process.

Other studies found that perceived risk can induce anxiety. In his study on personality and innovation proneness, Jacoby (1971) argued that highly dogmatic mental systems represent a cognitive-psychodynamic network of defenses against anxiety. Dogmatism, according to Jacoby, is functional: the more persistently anxious or threatened the individual, the more he or she manifests a closed mind. Previous studies on consumer decision processes indicates that brand-switching usually entails some perceived risk which increases when switching to a new brand or product is contemplated (Cox 1967b). In this sense, high dogmatics are less likely than low dogmatics to try new products.

2.3 Cognitive Styles and Need for Cognitive Clarity

Kelman and Cohler (1959) defined the concept of need for cognitive clarity as "the degree to which a person is made uncomfortable by ambiguity and incongruity which motivates him/her to restore a state of cognitive clarity in which the different elements fit together and make sense." They suggest two different cognitive styles of dealing with ambiguity and incongruity—"Clarifiers" (seeking new information for clarification) versus "simplifiers" (avoiding or rejecting incongruous information). Previous studies reported that simplifiers tended to resist changing their product preferences following additional information (e.g., Cox 1967a). In alternative, individuals high in need for cognitive clarity (clarifiers) were more likely to incorporate new information and to change their prior product evaluations. Clarifiers are expected to access more information to evaluate unfamiliar product or services before finalize their decisions (Schaninger and Sciglimpaglia 1981). Need for cognitive clarity can also be considered as a measure of the consumer's desire for certainty. Yilmaz (2014) reported that there is a positive relation between perceived risk and need for cognitive clarity. In this sense, an individual with a high need for cognitive clarity is likely perceived higher risk and is expected to have a stronger desire to reduce uncertainty in their decisions.

2.4 Self Esteem

Coppersmith (1967) refers self-esteem to "the evaluation which the individual makes and customarily maintains with regard to himself: it expresses an attitude of approval or disapproval, and indicates the extent to which the individual believes himself to be capable, significant, successful, and worthy" (p. 4). Self-esteem is positively related to the sense of freedom, personal authority, and role-taking ability. Previous research on perceived risk and self-esteem found that high self-esteem related to low levels of risk engagement (Donnellan et al. 2005). However, people may sometimes engage in risky behaviors to increase or maintain self-esteem, or to reduce the threat of having low self-esteem.

3 A Comprehensive Personality Model: The "Big Five" Model

Previous studies reported that personality is an important driver to consumer choices. The term *personality* is generally defined as "an individual's characteristic patterns of thought, emotion, and behavior, together with the psychological mechanisms—hidden or not—behind those patterns" (Funder 1997, pp. 1–2). Built on previous studies on personality and individual differences, Digman and Takemoto-Chock (1981) developed the "Big Five" model of personality to illustrate the five major personality traits: (1) extraversion or surgency; (2) agreeableness or likeability; (3) conscientiousness, control, or constraint; (4) emotional stability or neuroticism; and (5) openness or intellect. This Big Five taxonomy provides useful integrative framework for examining individual differences. Table 1 summarizes key characteristics of each factor of the Big Five model.

The first factor, *extraversion/intraversion* or *surgency*, indicates consumers' inner world of thoughts and ideas as well as their responses to outer world of events and actions. This factor frequently refers to personality traits such as being sociable, gregarious, assertive, talkative, active, initiative, surgency, ambition, impetuous, expressive. Vollrath and Torgersen (2002) reported that individuals scoring high on extraversion were particularly inclined to engage in multiple, risky behaviors. In other words, it could be expected that extroverts should possibly view deviant personal or social behaviors in a more lenient way than introverts do. Worrying about risky behaviors may not only take time away from extroverts' action-oriented lifestyle, but it could also possibly limit its range (Chauvin et al. 2007, p. 173).

The second factor, *agreeableness* or *likeability*, associates with traits such as being courteous, flexible, trusting, good-natured, cooperative, forgiving, soft-hearted, tolerant, proper conduct as well as non-violence and care for others and the environment. Vollrath et al. (1999) reported that more agreeable individuals are less likely to engage in risky behaviors than others. Also, it is expected that more agreeable individuals should possibly consider pollution, violence, and illnesses as more undesirable and risky than the less agreeable individuals due to their greater ability to empathize with people who are often involuntarily affected by these threats.

The third factor, *conscientiousness* or *conscience*, reflects the cautiousness, orderliness, dutifulness, and precaution nature of an individual. The concept usually refers to being careful, thorough, responsible, organized, planful, determined,

Table 1 The five factors of personality

Factors	Characteristics
Extroversion or surgency	Extraverted versus introverted
	Talkative versus silent
	Active versus inactive
	Energetic versus unenergetic
	Sociable versus reclusive
	Bold versus timid
	Assertive versus unassertive
	Adventurous versus cautious (or unadventurous)
	Open versus secretive
Agreeableness or likeability	Agreeable versus disagreeable
	Warm versus cold
	Good-natured versus irritable
	Cooperative versus uncooperative (or negativistic)
	Kind versus unkind
	Generous versus stingy
	Mild/gentle versus headstrong
	Trustful versus distrustful
	Unselfish versus selfish
	Not jealous versus jealous
Conscientiousness	Conscientious versus negligent
	Responsible versus irresponsible (or undependable)
	Organized versus disorganized
	Scrupulous versus unscrupulous
	Practical versus impractical
	Persevering versus quitting
	Hardworking versus lazy
	Thorough (or fussy/tidy) versus careless
	Thrifty versus extravagant
Emotional stability or neuroticism	Calm versus anxious (or angry)
	Not envious versus envious
	Stable versus unstable
	Contented versus discontented
	Unemotional versus emotional
	Composed versus excitable
	Not hypochondriacal versus hypochondriacal
	Relaxed/poised/at ease versus nervous/tense
Openness or intellect	Intelligent versus unintelligent
	Analytical versus unanalytical
	Reflective versus unreflective
	Curious versus uninquisitive
	Artistic versus nonartistic
	Creative versus uncreative
	Imaginative versus unimaginative (or simple/direct)
	Polished/refined versus crude/boorish
	Sophisticated versus unsophisticated

controlled, and effective manner as well as traits such as hardworking, achievement-oriented, and preserving. Hampson et al. (2000) reported that more conscientious individuals are less likely to engage in risky health behavior such as unprotected sex, smoking, and drinking than less conscientious individuals. In this sense, individuals who score higher on conscientiousness would be more likely to perceive the hazard factor of risky behaviors.

The fourth factor, *emotional stability* or *neuroticism*, associates with a set of avoidance, withdrawal, and flight behaviors. Traits associated with this factor include being anxious, depressed, angry, embarrassed, emotional, worried, and insecure. The essence of this factor related to the idea of fearlessness in many circumstances. A negative relationship is expected between emotional stability and risky behaviors and decisions. Chauvin et al. (2007) stated that well-trained and better-educated individuals (i.e., individuals who are politically more conservative, having higher household incomes, higher perceived control over risks, and higher trust in government/authority) see less risk in the world. These individuals are likely considered themselves more tranquil, more moderate, and tougher (more calm even in tense situations) than others (p. 174).

The fifth factor, *openness* or *intellect*, is largely related to the way that the individual perceives the world as well as concepts of curiosity and intellectuality. Traits commonly associated with this factor include being imaginative, cultured, curious, original, broad-minded, intelligent, and artistically sensitive. The focus of this factor is related to an individual's open-mindedness. It could be expected that more open individuals should consider behaviors such as free sex and consumption of substances as less problematic and less risky than others.

4   Personality-Cognitive Styles Relationship

Myers and McCaulley (1985) identified four dimensions of cognitive style among individuals: extrovert versus introvert, judging versus perceiving, sensing versus intuiting, and thinking versus feeling. These dimensions then play a major influence on studies on consumer information processing and decision making. For instance, the *extrovert-introvert* dimension refers to "individual's preferences for interacting with others when making a decision". In this sense, others' opinion is a key influencer of extroverts' interpretation and decision-making process than its impact on introverts (Jung 1923; White et al. 2003).

The *judging-perceiving* dimension of cognitive style refers to "individual preferences with regard to proactiveness when making a decision" (White et al. 2003, p. 66). Individuals with judging cognitive styles tend to be more proactive, adaptive, organized and purposeful in decision-making. On the contrary, individuals with perceiving cognitive style tend to postpone a decision because of the fear of missing critical information.

McIntyre and Meloche (1995) refer *sensing and intuition* to "how people find out the world". According to Mokwa and Evans (1984), sensors emphasize detailed, sensory input such as data and hard facts about a divisible, concrete reality while intuitors rely on imagination and conceptualization to construct holistic realities beyond the abilities of direct sensation, and often accept possibilities and ideals as reality. Sensors are practical, good with detail and numbers, and like tangible objects, while intuitors find patterns and trends and are quite at home with intangibles.

The fourth dimension, *thinking* and *feeling*, refers to decision making or information processing functions. For instance, thinkers emphasize the role of conventional, deductive logic in decision making. Mokwa and Evans (1984) describe thinkers as seeking formal and general explanations relatively independent of human qualities and values. On the other hand, feelers accentuate values and conflict in decision making. Feeling, in this sense, is portrayed as a process of individualization and questioning, as well as the search for justification and human realization. Characteristics of feeling are most evident in conventional expressions of aesthetics, ethics, politics, and religion. Feelers therefore are expected to be more subjective, personal, empathizing as well as are more able to accept and deal with ambiguity, while thinkers are tended to be more objectives, impersonal, and analytical. Table 2 illustrates some salient characteristics of the four cognitive styles.

The above cognitive styles also play important roles to consumers' perception of risk. Previous studies reported that extroverts are more likely to evaluate social risk before making their consumption decision while consumers with judging cognitive styles tend to have high tolerance to risk. White et al. (2003) connect the sensing-intuiting and thinking-feeling dimensions of cognitive style to "a person's tolerance for ambiguity and risk propensity" (p. 66). They argue that individuals with more intuiting and thinking cognitive styles are more adaptive, imaginative, and eager to

Table 2 Characteristics of the cognitive styles

ST (sensory-thinker)	NT (intuitive-thinker)
Seeks certainty, precision	Relies on ideas and calculation
Concrete orientation	Builds interesting alternatives
Seek to find the "right" answer	Inventive and imaginative
Detached from work	Seeks to solve the puzzle
Concerned with methods and techniques	Focus on alternatives and outcomes
An impersonal perspective	A theoretical perspective
A technical specialist	A generalists
Relies on observation and measurement	Oriented toward the future
Oriented toward the present	
SF (sensory-feeler)	**NF (intuitive-feeler)**
Relies upon and seeks intense personal experience	Relies on feeling and emotions
Active and experiential	Constructs ideal social systems
Seeks to get the job done	Empathetic and idealistic
Concerned with actions	Systematic orientation
A behavioral perspective	Seeks to address the real problem
A pragmatist	Concern with people's problems
Live in present, here and now	Focus on social impacts
	Takes a personal-social perspective
	An idealist
	Oriented to future

Adapted from McIntyre and Meloche (1995) and Mokwa and Evans (1984)

explore new experiences, and ambitious. These individuals tend to have more tolerance to risk. In contrast, individuals with more sensing and feeling cognitive styles tend to prefer a more stable environment and prefer complete control, certainty, and specificity.

5 Personality Factors and Risk Perception

The main objective of this contribution is to connect factors like personality and cognitive styles to consumers' risk perception. In this section I discuss the definition of risk and how this concept associate to individual differences. The term "perceived risk", according to Cox and Rich (1964), refers to "the nature and amount of risk perceived by a consumer in contemplating a particular purchase decision" (p. 33). They argue that perceived risk is closely related to buying goals in which a consumer is motivated to make a purchase in order to attain some set of buying goals. In a similar vein, Keh and Sun (2008) define the concept as "the subjective expectation of a loss" (p. 122). These definitions, however, are primarily focused on consumers' uncertainty judgment and assumed negative outcomes will occur if consumers make a wrong decision.

Prior studies shown that risk preference is inferred through choices (Hsee and Weber 1999). Different forms of risks that consumers experienced were reported during the decision making or consumption process. For example, in his study on consumers' risk perception and willingness to try new products, Popielarz (1967) found that willingness to try a new product is associated with a preference for errors of inclusion rather than errors of exclusion while unwillingness to try a new product involves a preference for errors of exclusion. His study also reported that early adopters usually possess high levels of social, educational, and geographic mobility; have high needs for achievement, change, exploration, and dominance; and are somewhat dissatisfied with their self-images but realistic in their aspirations (p. 368). Similarly, Cox and Rich (1964) found that consumers developed their own characteristics or cognitive style to reduce uncertainty.

Other researchers assessed how commercial products and services affect consumers' risk perception in domains such as health and well-being, food, and tobacco products. In their study on risk assessment regarding a local depository of nuclear waste and three personality factors, Sjöberg and af Wahlberg (2002) found that the more neurotic a person declared himself/herself, the more he/she perceived the depository as risk in general. In his other study on risk assessment and unsuitable dietary habits, Sjöberg (2003) found that the more conscientious a person declared himself/herself, the less this person perceived unsuitable dietary habits as risky for himself/herself. Various antecedents such as motivational antecedents, affective antecedents, cognitive antecedents, and contextual antecedents that associated to consumers' emotion, self-control, past experience and judgment were identified. However, it is important to provide a holistic framework to understand the interconnection of these individual psychological attributes and cultural factors.

6 Cultural Influences on Cognitive Styles and Personality

Previous sections primarily focused reviewing literature on the influence of personality and cognitive styles on consumers' risk perception. This section will focus on discussing how culture affect these psychological constructs. Previous studies suggested that culture has played an important role in shaping consumer behavior. Our behavior was shaped by a network of rules such as myths, norms, and other cultural ideologies and artefacts. Sternberg (1997), for instance, suggested that culture may influence the development of an individual's cognitive style in addition to factors such as gender, age and education. In cross-cultural psychological studies, researchers often refers to three major frameworks: the Hofstede's (1980, 2001) cultural dimension framework, the Schwartz's (1994) value dimension framework and Markus and Kitayama's (1991) independent/interdependent self-construal framework.

In his study on national cultures, Hofstede (1980, 2001) employed five cultural dimensions: power distance, individual-collectivism, uncertainty avoidance, masculinity-femininity, and short-time versus long-time orientation to differentiate cultures across the world. For Hofstede, *power distance* refers to the extent to which individuals accept that power in institutions and organizations is distributed unequally. The *individual-collectivism* dichotomy, on the contrary, demonstrates the degree to which a person is integrated into groups. While *individualism* refers to the preference for a loosely knit social framework, *collectivism* reflects the preference for a tightly knit social framework in which individuals expect support and loyalty within the group. The third dimension, *uncertainty avoidance,* refers to the extent to which people feel uncomfortable with uncertainty and ambiguity. The *Masculinity-femininity* dichotomy describes the distribution of emotional roles. For instance, *masculinity* refers to the preference for achievement, heroism, assertiveness, and material success while *femininity* refers to the preference for relationships, modesty, caring for the weak, and quality of life. The fifth dimension, *long-term orientation,* is an expression of the sense of persistence, thrift, modesty and respect for tradition.

Unlike Hofstede's cultural dimension framework, Schwartz (1992) proposed a cultural framework which centers on cultural values at the individual level. His framework is organized into four value domains along two bipolar dimensions: *self-transcendence* versus *self-enhancement* and *conservation* versus *openness* to change. The former dimension captures the degree to which cultural values motivate people to promote the welfare of others (*self-transcendence*) while the latter focuses on elaborating which cultural values enhance individuals' personal interests even at the expense of others (*self-enhancement*). For Schwartz, *self-transcendence* comprises the values of universalism (i.e., understanding, appreciation, tolerance, and protection of the welfare of all people and nature) and benevolence (i.e., preservation and enhancement of the welfare of people in close relationships). *Self-enhancement*, on the contrary, are the values of power (e.g., social status and prestige, control or dominance over people and resources) and achievement (e.g., personal success through competence).

Compare to Hofstede and Schwartz's cultural dimension frameworks, Markus and Kitayama (1991) proposed a simple distinction among self by introducing concepts of *independent* and *interdependent self-construal* to illustrate how individuals define the self in relation to others. The *independent self-construal* defines the individual in terms of unique attributes and characteristics that distinguish him or her from others, whereas the *interdependent self-construal* defines the individual in terms of social roles and relationships with others. Shavitt et al. (2008) suggested that national cultures such as the United States, Canada, Germany, Denmark that celebrate the values of independence are categorized as individualistic societies in which an independent self-construal is common. On the contrary, collectivistic societies such as China, Korea, Japan, and Mexico tend to nurture the values of fulfilling one's obligations and responsibilities over one's own personal wishes or desires. In other words, interdependent self-construal is common in these collectivistic societies (see also Hofstede 1980, 2001; Markus and Kitayama 1991).

Prior studies on cross-cultural differences in information processing reported that cognitive styles varies across culture. For instance, Doktor (1983) describes "Japanese cognition" as non-abstract, based on concrete perception, reliance on sense data, emphasizing the particular (not the universal) with sensitivity towards relationships and the environmental context. "American cognition", in alternative, was described as being based on logic and sequential connections, and abstractions to represent universals. In a similar vein, Nisbett et al. (2001) examined the hypothesized dichotomy between the rational, analytical, "left-brained" West and the intuitive, holistic, "right-brained" East.

Risk assessment is a social phenomenon based upon culturally determined ideas. Social and cultural factors determine what risks are salient. According to cultural theory, risk perception is ideologically driven whether it be the lay public, the media, the government or the scientific elite. Risk perceptions are an expression of four different socially determined "thought worlds" or ideologies: (i) the "atomized" perspective, which is expressed through a fatalistic attitude; (ii) the hierarchical view, characterized by trust in authority; (iii) the individualistic or rational view; and (iv) the egalitarian or critical view.

In cross-cultural or cross-national comparison, researchers tended to choose countries that stand at opposite ends of the continuum (North American versus Asian cultures, European versus Asian cultures) in respect to political system and traditional cultural values (e.g., Hsee and Weber 1999). Previous studies have systematically reported cross-national differences in many fundamental psychological effects such as the independent/interdependent construal of the self (Markus and Kitayama 1991) and cultural dimensions such as individualism and collectivism. For instance, independent relationships and pursuing personal goals are preferred in individualistic cultures (e.g., American and Western European cultures) while interdependent relationships and pursuing collective goals and benefits are preferred in collectivistic cultures) (Hofstede 1980, 2001).

In their cross-cultural study between Americans and Chinese in the context of making investment, medical, and academic decisions, Hsee and Weber (1999) found that Chinese consumers are more risk seeking than consumers in the United States in the context of financial investment. Their study also suggest that consumers in collectivist society such as China are more likely to receive financial help if they are in need because of their huge social network ("cushion hypothesis") therefore they are less risk averse than consumers in an individualistic society such as the United States (p. 165). In other words, consumers' risk perception is sometime influence by the consumption task in different cultural context.

In their cross-cultural studies on risk evaluation among Singaporean and Chinese consumers, Keh and Sun (2008) reported that two cultural dimensions (self-transcendence/self-enhancement versus conversation/openness to change) and individual contextual factors (involvement and face consciousness) exert differential effect on consumer perceived risk in the two studied countries (p. 120). In a similar vein, Tinsley and Pillutla (1998) suggest that the self-enhancement versus self-transcendence cultural dimension is consistent with the individualism-collectivism construct. Their findings show that consumers with high self-transcendence are more concerned that their choices might not be approved by other members in their social network and might perceive high social and psychological risks. On the contrary, the cultural value of conservation might compatible with conformity to the status quo and well-established cultural customs as openness to change emphasizes freedom and risk taking. Consumers with a high level of conservation might feel more threatened by ambiguous conditions and whereas consumers with lower level of conservation tend to tolerate uncertainty and engage in risk-taking activities. In summary, the extended consumer risk perception framework emphasizes that cultural influence and individual difference are interconnected.

Kleinhesselink and Rosa (1991) employed the seven risk dimensions (controllable-uncontrollable, calm-dread, not catastrophic-catastrophic, and voluntary-involuntary, known-unknown to the individual, old-new, and know-unknown to science) to compare and contrast risk perception among Japanese and American. Their findings show that Japanese rated more of the examined risks (e.g., prescription drugs, motor vehicle accidents, coal mining accidents) as uncontrollable, dreaded, and catastrophic compared to the American. They also found Japanese were considerably less benign in their perceptions of the purity and safety of food, drug products, and transportation than the American students. The authors explained that the American's higher self-efficacy in these domains mitigated the anxiety (p. 26). In summary, these seven risk dimensions provide additional insights to understand how consumers of different cultural background interpret risks in their everyday lives.

7   New Developments and Future Directions

7.1   The Extended Model on Consumer Risk Perception

The extended consumer risk perception model (Fig. 1) addressed the interconnection among different cultural and individual constructs. Seeing culture as the macro factor that influence the construction of individual personality and cognitive styles, this contribution takes an integrative approach to map out key determinants of consumers' risk perception. Based on the extended review of prior literature, this contribution conceives personality and cognitive styles are key influencers of consumers' risk perception and willingness to try or purchase new products/services. The framework also suggests that culture shaped individuals' personality and cognitive styles.

Through the articulation of different cultural dimension, the framework highlights some important intersections and relationships:

(1) Hofstede's (1980, 2001) cultural dimensions addresses the differences in terms of worldviews and social structure of different societies or cultural societies therefore provides a foundation of understanding the development of individual personality and cognitive styles. Schwartz (1992), and Markus and Kitayama (1991) cultural dimension models provide additional theoretical foundation to understanding the differences between social roles and relationships.

(2) Based on the most-established personality framework (Big Five Model) and prior literature on cognitive personality relationship, the proposed framework addresses the intra-cultural diversity and suggests that these individual differences are closely connected to the affiliated cultural system.

(3) The proposed framework also illustrate how cognitive styles affect consumers' perceived risk and risk-taking behaviors as well as consumers' willingness to

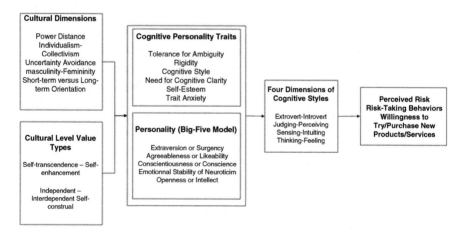

Fig. 1   An extended consumer risk perception framework

try or purchase new products and services. These behavioral outcomes can be interpreted as the consequences of a complex interaction between culture and individual psychology. These behavioral outcomes can be seen as individuals' responses to the current cultural and social situation.

7.2 Limitations and Future Research Directions

Since the integrated framework was developed based on prior literature, future empirical research is encouraged. Prior literature shows significant differences in term of cultures among Asian countries. For example, China, Japan, and Korea are highly collectivist and homogeneous society while South-east Asian countries such as Singapore, Malaysia, and Indonesia are multicultural. Experimental studies, survey, and longitudinal studies are suggested to examine the framework. Qualitative inquiries and mixed method approaches are recommended to unpack the complexity of the framework. For instance, cultures might implicitly shape consumers' perception of risk and their cognitive styles and personality. Social interaction and other situational factors might also influence consumers' risk preferences and choices. In this sense, future research should explore the connection between macro and micro-levels of consumption.

Future research can also examines how different personality and cognitive styles affect different forms of risks (e.g., personal risks versus non-personal) in different cultural context. A deeper level of analysis may potentially enrich the theoretical and practical understandings of the topic. For instance, how cognitive bias, over-confidence, illusion of control, and other social or situational factors after consumers' risk perception and decision-making will provide additional insights to understand the construction and responses to risks.

In addition to the cultural dimensions, gender and age differences in consumers' risk perception and the changes of consumers' personality and cognitive styles over time will be interesting areas to further explore based on the current topic. Cross-sectional studies can detect the differences in risk perception based on gender and age while longitudinal studies can track changes on personality, cognitive styles, and risk perception over time. The interrelationship between the above constructs and consumers' learning styles, and knowledge accumulation or transfer activities can enrich the depth and breadth of the study.

Last but not least, future studies can revisit the descriptive adjectives of the personality-traits and cognitive styles in different languages and cultural context. Since all the current personality models and scales are built in the English language system. It is important for researchers to examine the translatability of these constructs among different languages and cultural systems. In this sense, this chapters provides a methodological advancement in the cross-cultural studies.

8 Conclusion

This chapter suggests that marketing and consumer researchers have to recognize the complexity of risk perception at the individual and cultural levels. To better manage cross-cultural differences in risk perception, researchers have to understand the inter-connections of individual and cultural concepts. For instance, social risk are expected to be an important risk factor in collectivist cultures such as East Asian and Latin American societies. Consumers in these cultures are tended to be more aware of others' opinion and evaluation therefore they are less likely to purchase products that will expose them to high social risk. This could be explained by their interdependent self-construal. On the contrary, consumers in more individualistic cultures such as North America and Western Europe are more concerns psychological risk. Therefore, consumers in these cultures tend to avoid products or services that against their personal interests or will harm their ego. Marketers have to pay attention to communicate product or service benefits to consumers with high self-enhancement character.

There are two other focal areas that marketers and researchers should pay attention to in managing cultural differences. First, marketers should pay attention to the structure of the social network and the society as a whole. For instance, Hsee and Weber's (1999) study shows that Chinese consumers have higher risk-taking behavior in financial investment context because of the "cushion" effect. Consumers in collectivist cultures, in this case, are willing to take certain risk because of the closely knitted social network and expected support from other in-group members (e.g., family, relatives, and friends). The sense of reciprocity and altruism also influence consumers' perceived risk. It is recommended that marketers should further investigate norms and social structure of different cultures and explore how consumers define and manage risks at an individual and collective level.

Second, marketers should recognize the intracultural differences. Many societies are no longer in a mono-culture setting. Immigrations and generation differences transform countries and cities into multicultural societies. Global cities like New York, Boston, Los Angeles, Toronto, Vancouver, Dubai, London, and Brussels are shaped by their multicultural population. Marketers, therefore, have to pay attention to the dialectic relationship between home and host cultures, dominant and minority cultural ideologies, as well as mainstream and sub-culture in these new cultural setting. Instead of segmentation the population with well-established construct such as individualist versus collectivist nations, marketers have to pay attention to the social interactions among consumers of different cultural backgrounds and their transformation in the new consumer cultural landscape.

In conclusion, the contribution of this chapter is threefold. First, this chapter presents an integrated framework to show the impact of culture on consumers' cognitive styles and personality and its effect on risk perception. Prior literature reported that consumers respond differently in any risk-involved decision making process and consumption condition. Their responses were very much driven by their cognitive style and personality. Second, this chapter views culture as key determinant to shape consumers' cognitive styles and personality. Other factors such as purchasing condition and social interaction shall be added to this framework. Finally, this chapter presents the complexity of cultural influence on consumer risk perception. In addition to applying binary comparisons such as individualist versus collectivist societies, this chapter highlights the connection of cultural dimensions and individual differences (in terms of cognitive styles and personality) that shape consumers' risk perception.

References

Allport, G. W. (1937). *Personality: A psychological interpretation.* New York: Holt.

Blake, B. F., Perloff, R., Zenhausern, R., & Heslin, R. (1973). The effect of intolerance of ambiguity upon product perceptions. *Journal of Applied Psychology, 58*(2), 239–243.

Chauvin, B., Hermand, D., & Mullet, E. (2007). Risk perception and personality facets. *Risk Analysis, 27*(1), 171–185.

Coppersmith, S. (1967). *The antecedents of self-esteem.* San Francisco, CA: W.H. Freeman.

Cox, D. F. (1967a). The influence of cognitive needs and styles on information handling in making product evaluations. In D. F. Cox (Ed.), *Risk taking and information handling in consumer behavior* (pp. 370–393). Boston, MA: Graduate School of Business Administration, Harvard University.

Cox, D. F. (1967b). Synthesis-perceived risk and information handling. In D. F. Cox (Ed.), *Risk taking and information handling in consumer behavior* (pp. 603–639). Boston, MA: Graduate School of Business Administration, Harvard University.

Cox, D. F., & Rich, S. (1964). Perceived risk and consumer decision-making. *Journal of Marketing Research, 1*(4), 32–39.

Digman, J. M., & Takemoto-Chock, N. K. (1981). Factors in the natural language of personality: Re-analysis, comparison, and interpretation of six major studies. *Multivariate Behavioral Research, 16*, 149–170.

Doktor, R. (1983). Some tentative comments on Japanese and American decision making. *Decision Sciences, 14*, 607–612.

Donnellan, B. M., Trzesniewski, K. H., Robins, R. W., Moffitt, T. E., & Caspi, A. (2005). Low self-esteem is related to aggression, antisocial behavior, and delinquency. *Psychological Science, 16*, 328–335.

Funder, D. C. (1997). *The personality puzzle.* New York, NY: Norton.

Galton, F. (1884). Measurement of character. *Fortnightly Review, 36*, 179–185.

Hampson, S. E., Andrews, J. A., Barckley, M., Lichtenstein, E., & Lee, M. E. (2000). Conscientiousness, perceived risk, and risk-reduction behaviors: A preliminary study. *Health Psychology, 19*, 496–500.

Hofstede, G. (1980). *Culture's consequences: International differences in work-related values.* Beverly Hills, CA: Sage.

Hofstede, G. (2001). *Culture's consequences: Comparing values, behaviours, institutions, and organizations across nations* (2nd ed.). Thousand Oaks, CA: Sage.

Hsee, C. K., & Weber, E. U. (1999). Cross-national differences in risk reference and lay predictions. *Journal of Behavioral Decision Making, 12*, 165–179.

Jacoby, J. (1971). Personality and innovation proneness. *Journal of Marketing Research, 8*(2), 244–247.

James, W. (1890). *The principles of psychology.* London: Macmillan.

Jung, K. (1923). *Psychological types.* New York: Harcourt Brace.

Keh, H. T., & Sun, J. (2008). The complexities of perceived risk in cross-cultural services marketing. *Journal of International Marketing, 16*(1), 120–146.

Kelman, H.C., & Cohler J. (1959). *Reaction to persuasive communications as a function of cognitive needs and style.* In Paper presented to the meeting of the Eastern Psychological Association, Atlantic City, April 3.

Kleinhesselink, R. R., & Rosa, E. A. (1991). Cognitive representation of risk perceptions: A comparison of Japan and the United States. *Journal of Cross-Cultural Psychology, 22*(1), 11–28.

Markus, H. R., & Kitayama, S. (1991). Culture and the self: Implications for cognition, emotion, and motivation. *Psychological Review, 98*, 224–253.

McIntyre, R. P., & Meloche, M. S. (1995). Cognitive style and customer orientation. *Journal of Business and Psychology, 10*(1), 75–86.

Mokwa, M. P., & Evans, K. R. (1984). Knowledge and marketing: exploring the foundations of inquiry. In S. W. Brown & R. P. Fisk (Eds.), *Marketing theory: Distinguished contributions* (pp. 170–179). New York, NY: Wiley.

Myers, I. B., & McCaulley, M. H. (1985). *Manual: A guide to the development and use of the Myers-Briggs type indicator.* Palo Alto, CA: Consulting Psychologists Press.

Nisbett, R. E., Peng, K., Choi, I., & Norenzayan, A. (2001). Culture and systems of thought: Holistic versus analytic cognition. *Psychological Review, 108*, 291–310.

Popielarz, D. T. (1967). An exploration of perceived risk and willingness to try new products. *Journal of Marketing Research, 4*(4), 368–372.

Schaninger, C. M., & Sciglimpaglia, D. (1981). The influence of cognitive personality traits and demographics on consumer information acquisition. *Journal of Consumer Research, 8*, 208–216.

Schwartz, S. H. (1992). Universals in the content and structure of values: Theoretical advances and empirical tests in 20 countries. In M. Zanna (Ed.), *Advances in experimental social psychology* (Vol. 25, pp. 1–65). New York, NY: Academic Press.

Schwartz, S. H. (1994). Beyond individualism/collectivism: New cultural dimensions of values. In U. Kim, H. C. Triandis, C. Kagitcibasi, S. C. Choi, & G. Yoon (Eds.), *Individualism and collectivism: Theory, methods, and applications* (pp. 85–119). Thousand Oaks: Sage.

Shavitt, S., Lee, A. Y., & Johnson, T. P. (2008). Cross-cultural consumer psychology. In C. P. Haugtvedt, P. M. Herr, & F. R. Kardes (Eds.), *Handbook of consumer psychology* (pp. 1103–1131). New York, NY: Lawrence Erlbaum Associates.

Sjöberg, L. (2003). Distal factors in risk perception. *Journal of Risk Research, 6*, 187–211.

Sjöberg, L., & af Wahlberg, A. (2002). Risk perception and new ages beliefs. *Risk Analysis, 22*, 751–764.

Sternberg, R. J. (1997). *Thinking styles.* Cambridge: Cambridge University Press.

Tinsley, C. J., & Pillutla, M. M. (1998). Negotiating in the United States and Hong Kong. *Journal of International Business Studies, 29*(4), 711–727.

Vollrath, M., & Torgersen, S. (2002). Who takes health risks? A probe into eight personality types. *Personality and Individual Differences, 32*, 1185–1197.

Vollrath, M., Knoch, D., & Cassano, L. (1999). Personality, risky health behaviour, and perceived susceptibility to health risks. *European Journal of Personality, 13*, 39–50.

White, J. C., Varadarajan, P. R., & Dacin, P. A. (2003). Market situation interpretation and responses: The role of cognitive style, organizational culture, and information use. *Journal of Marketing, 67*(3), 63–79.

Yilmaz, H. (2014). Perceived risk, risk reduction methods and personality. *International Review of Business and Economic Studies, 1*(1), 1–18.

Consumer Values and Product Perception

Katrin Horn

1 Meaning of Value

The meaning of a product to a consumer and what it stands for, rather than rational assessment of functionality, has long been recognized as a crucial element for its interpretation, evaluation and any purchase and usage decision. The concept of value offers several angles to grasp this meaning from a consumer perspective.

Research on value has been approached from different perspectives. On one hand, cultural constructions of value have been examined as a socio-cultural blueprint of consumer behavior. On the other hand, a stream of research has focused on the measurement of *customer value*, i.e. the benefit of a product or service to a customer, and factors influencing this perception. Within this dichotomic view on value, the first research area represents a more general perspective on human behavior and a broader application to consumption situations, encompassing also non-purchase situations. A cultural value system, developed by consumers as part of an enculturation process (i.e. learning about desirable and undesirable behaviors and preferable outcomes through growing up in a particular culture), influences general dispositions of consumers through a broad-based belief system.

The second research perspective on the concept of value concentrates on evaluations of concrete consumption experiences, as well as assessing the benefit consumers connect with the interaction with products and services. In contrast to cultural concepts of value, this perception relates to product-specific attitudes. Research on their relationship has shown that values as an abstract social cognition are an influencing factor in the development of more product-specific attitudes and behavioral intentions. Based on this, the first perspective on value can be seen as an

K. Horn (✉)
The Semiotic Alliance, London, UK
e-mail: katrin.horn@fh-kufstein.ac.at

© Springer International Publishing AG 2017
G. Emilien et al. (eds.), *Consumer Perception of Product Risks and Benefits*,
DOI 10.1007/978-3-319-50530-5_16

Fig. 1 Socio-cultural
values and customer value.
Source: Author's own

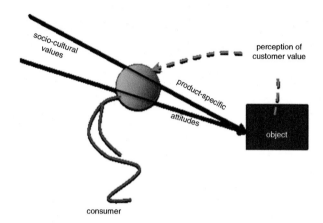

input factor, *influencing* the interaction between consumer and object, while the
second perspective qualifies as an output factor, *resulting from* the consumer-
object-interaction (Fig. 1). Both the perspective of general, culturally derived
values and the perception of customer value in the sense of an assessment of benefit
gained from a consumption experience will explored separately as well as with
regard to their relationship.

2 Consumer Values: Culture and Consumer Behavior

Values are defined as a relatively stable, "permanent belief of a person" (Daghfous
et al. 1999, p. 317). Schwartz and Bilsky (1987, p. 551) state that "values (a) are
concepts or beliefs, (b) about desirable end states or behaviors, (c) that transcend
specific situations, (d) guide selection or evaluation of behavior and events, and
(e) are ordered by relative importance". From this definition it follows that culturally derived values are more general than the evaluation of a specific product or
consumption experience, and that they cannot be analyzed in isolation. But
although their direct input has been contested, values have been shown to impact
behavioral intentions (Kahle et al. 1986). As values further form an important part
of consumer identity, they are highly relevant for understanding consumer
decisions.

How do consumers develop their views on desirable and undesirable end states?
Consumers are exposed to the dominant belief system of their surrounding culture
though the process of enculturation, and the relative importance of preferable states
of being is conveyed by socialization agents including parents, teachers and friends
(Solomon 2009). Durkheim theorized three aspects of the bond between society and
culture: logical, functional, and historical. He understood culture as a dimension of
stability for society, establishing common ground via rituals and beliefs and
through this maintaining social order (structural functionalism): in fact Durkheim
calls culture the "collective conscience". Taking their impact on behavioral

Fig. 2 Schein's three levels of culture. Source: Based on Schein (1996)

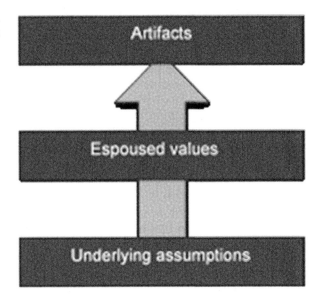

intentions through attitudes into account, values can therefore be seen as an intervening variable between culture and individual behavior, which contributes to shaping consumer behavior, decisions and evaluations.

The following model illustrates the relationship between products and their assessment, values, and their roots in culture. Schein's seminal model assumes that culture consists of three levels (Fig. 2). The most accessible level at the top is represented by cultural *artifacts*, which constitute the visible manifestation of *values*. These values are shaped by basic underlying *assumptions* or belief systems stemming from the cultural environment (Schein 1996). While originally referring to organizational cultures, Schein's model adds an important perspective to the discussion of culture and values: the materialization of otherwise hidden and often uncodified rules and values in visible manifestations such as products, brands or institutions.

Due to this assumed function of visualizing more abstract beliefs and values, goods and the individual use of their carefully constructed symbolism can serve to negotiate and manage complex social relationships such as association to groups, role transitions, affection, or love.

2.1 Culture as the Source of Values

Despite criticisms of insufficient operationalization, culture has been used in a large number of studies: almost 10% of articles published in 13 major business journals between 1996 and 2001 have used culture as an independent variable (see Lenartowicz and Roth 2004, p. 47 for a list of the reviewed journals). A longitudinal review of cross-cultural research by Sojka and Tansuhaj (1995) revealed three main modes of operationalization: (i) via language, (ii) via artifacts and (iii) via values and belief systems. This indicates the mutual importance of culture and values.

Values and their influence on consumer behavior are rooted in a cultural context. To understand values of consumers, an analysis of the cultural context in which these values have developed is essential. Sheth and Sethi (1973) regard "cultural lifestyle" as one of the most important constructs in their model on consumer innovation and describe it as "those 'cultural universals' which are salient to consumption behavior." (ibid., p. 11). De Mooij and Hofstede (2011, p. 181) state that "most aspects of consumer behavior are culture-bound". Moreover, if the perception of products is understood as manifestation of cultural artifacts (see Schein model above), then an exploration of the underlying values shaping the perception and evaluation of consumer symbols amounts to a cultural analysis. Culture is therefore fundamental to the understanding of values and consequently to the transfer of meaning through consumer goods.

Culture is often explained as a system of shared values and resulting norms for behavior. Geertz (1973) proposes an interpretation of culture as providing specific control mechanisms—ranging from very prescriptive programs to more flexible advice. These mechanisms direct, but do not determine, human behavior. He also points out the dependence of mankind to culture in order to make sense of and react appropriately to external stimuli of the environment (Geertz 1973). Without culture as a guiding "rulebook", actions of others as well as products and services rooted within a culture remain at least not fully intelligible.

An overview over differences between definitions of culture not only shows the historical development of the conceptualization of culture, but also the dissension that surrounds these definitions. This is illustrated in Kroeber and Kluckhohn's (1952) list of 166 approaches to define culture. One stream of research focuses on the function of culture to create shared meaning through language, symbols and events:

> "Culture consists of patterns, explicit and implicit, of and for behavior acquired and transmitted by symbols, constituting the distinctive achievement of human groups, including their embodiments in artefacts [. . .]." (Kroeber and Kluckhohn 1952, p. 181)

Triandis (2007, pp. 64–65) summarizes the large array of definitions for culture: "First, culture emerges in adaptive interactions between humans and environments. Second, culture consists of shared elements. Third, culture is transmitted across time periods and generations." It is therefore necessary to identify in what way culture can influence human behavior. In search for a conceptualization of the relationship between culture and actual behavior, values have been identified as an intervening variable: If culture is defined as shared webs of meaning, then values as an intervening variable to shape the interpretation of symbols and arrive at a communal construction of connotations provide the highest potential especially for cross-cultural comparisons.

As evident in Schein's model, visible artifacts of culture and their assessment are determined by underlying values. Research on value in the field of culture has therefore concerned itself with the search for values as a possibility to define and differentiate between cultures. From this perspective, culture can be seen as a system of symbols, norms and practices, which shapes the values of consumers—and vice versa.

2.2 Value Systems

The *relative* importance of values varies per individual and forms an important part of their self-identity (Schwartz and Bilsky 1987). Consequently, values are a defining variable both on a macro-level (differentiating between cultures, see Sect. 2.1) and on a micro-level (segmentation, detecting individual differences). While most researchers differentiate between values on the individual and country/national culture level, there has also been evidence for a single scale covering both levels (Fischer and Poortinga 2012).

Research in the area of value fields is concerned with the compilation of a set list of universally valid values, as well as the relationship between them. Several classification systems have been developed, and a number of these stress the fact that values, as defining and guiding construct, are culturally shared, thereby relying on a cross-culturally valid and finite list of values. The most prominent value frameworks will be briefly discussed and contrasted below.

Rokeach Value Survey The relative importance of individual values can only be understood through their position in relation to other values (Schwartz and Bilsky 1987; Rokeach 1973). Consequently, the Rokeach Value Survey (RVS) requires respondents to rank values.

Rokeach distinguishes between terminal and instrumental values, differentiating between a person's beliefs about a desirable end-state (terminal) or a desirable mode of conduct (instrumental). In his system of values, instrumental values lead to a smaller number of terminal values. Within terminal values, Rokeach theorizes that there are personal and social values, or in other terms intrapersonal and interpersonal values, and that individuals differ in the relative importance of one over the other type of value (Rokeach 1973). Within instrumental values, Rokeach distinguishes between moral values and competence values. Here, moral values refer to values concerned with interpersonal relationships and "doing the right thing". Competence values on the other hand are related by Rokeach to "doing the best you can": "Their violation leads to feelings of shame about personal inadequacy rather than to feelings of guilt about wrongdoing" (Rokeach 1973, p. 8). The result of Rokeach's research is a list of 18 instrumental and 18 terminal values. The RVS served as a basis for both Kahle's List of Values (LOV) and the Schwartz Value Survey (SVS) and represents a seminal contribution to later research on classification systems for values (Table 1).

List of Values and Lifestyles (VALS) and List of Values (LOV) VALS, a classification system of different lifestyle groups based on values derived from Maslow's hierarchy of needs, was developed by SRI International and continues to

Table 1 Rokeach's instrumental and terminal values

Instrumental values	Terminal values
Ambitious	A comfortable life
Broad-minded	An exciting life
Capable	A sense of accomplishment
Cheerful	A world of beauty
Clean	A world at peace
Courageous	Equality
Forgiving	Family security
Helpful	Freedom
Honest	Happiness
Imaginative	Inner harmony
Independent	Mature love
Intellectual	National security
Logical	Pleasure
Loving	Salvation
Obedient	Self-respect
Polite	Social recognition
Responsible	True friendship
Self-controlled	Wisdom

Source: Rokeach (1973, pp. 360–361)
n.b. Values are listed here in alphabetic order

Table 2 List of Values (LOV)

Values
Sense of belonging
Excitement
Warm relationships with other
Self-Fulfillment
Being well respected
Fun and enjoyment of life
Security
Self-Respect
A sense of accomplishment

Source: Kahle and Kennedy (1989, p. 8)

be popular in an applied professional context. Kahle et al. (1986) attribute part of the attractiveness of the model to the vivid and colorful description of the prototypes of the lifestyle groups, but criticize it for its proprietary scoring system and the non-disclosure of the full instrument, which makes a scientific replication and review impossible (ibid.).

Kahle et al. (1986) condensed the RVS by disregarding the 18 instrumental values (understood to be personality traits or desirable behavior rather than values as desirable end states), reducing the 18 terminal values and aligning them with Maslow's hierarchy of needs (see Table 2). The resulting list of values is therefore strictly related to the individual and has a greater predictive power for actual consumer behavior trends. This may also be related to the inclusion of demographic variables in LOV (Novak and MacEvoy 1990).

Both VALS and LOV focus on market segmentation, enabling researchers to cluster consumers into groups based on their value preferences. While this explains their strong appeal to practitioners, both classification systems suffer from a limited acceptance in more fundamental, academic research.

Schwartz Value Survey (SVS) The research conducted by Schwartz and colleagues, resulting in the Schwartz Value Scale, was based on the Rokeach Value Survey. It is at the forefront of the representation of values in a coherent system and their mutual interdependency. While the Schwartz Value Scale features individual-level values, an extensive body of comparative studies has confirmed their cross-cultural validity (Knafo et al. 2011). This allows their usage on the level of culture.

Schwartz and Bilsky (1987) have developed a circular structure based on Rokeach's list of values. Refining and further developing the concept of Rokeach and the terminal and instrumental distinction between values, Schwartz's model puts values into a motivational context. In this construct values are sorted into motivational domains and arranged depending on their mutual (non-) compatibility. The motivational domains were first developed from existing research on values and motivation and then confirmed in several large-scale cross-cultural studies.

Motivational domains are here understood as principles, which guide human behavior and aim to satisfy three universal requirements: personal needs, social interactional motives and social institutional motives (Schwartz and Bilsky 1987). Motivational domains comprise several different values, taken from Rokeach, as "markers" for this motivation (see Fig. 3). The result is a circular structure along the two axes Openness to Change versus Conservation, and Self-Enhancement versus Self-transcendence (ibid.), confirmed in several cross-cultural studies with more than 100,000 participants. These two dimensions organize 44 values into the

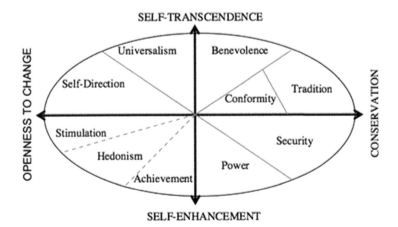

Fig. 3 Schwartz Value Scale (SVS). Source: Based on Schwartz and Bilsky (1987)

10 motivational domains of Universalism, Benevolence (Self-Transcendence pole), Achievement, Power (Self-Enhancement pole), Tradition, Conformity, Security (Conservation pole), Stimulation, Self-Direction (Openness to Change pole) and Hedonism. Hedonism occupies a special position, as it informs both Openness to Change and Self-Enhancement, and is therefore situated between these fields.

Maio et al. (2009) confirm the general validity of the circular arrangement, where values are positioned according to their compatibility or mutual opposition. While the cross-cultural validity of the Rokeach Value Survey has been doubted, the Schwartz Value Survey has in particular been important for its contribution to the research on cross-culturally valid determinants of individual behavior (Horn 2005). The values have been tested in 47 different cultures, which confirmed their transcultural validity; and cultures can be differentiated through the relative importance of the values.

While the measurement of values with the Schwartz Value Survey has been criticized as relatively complicated and time-consuming, possibly the most important contribution of Schwartz has been the introduction of a structural view at values, identifying their proximity or mutual exclusivity through the arrangement in a circular space. The circular structure allows an analysis of how values either support or oppose each other (Schwartz and Bilsky 1987), offering further insight into motivational conflicts. The aspect of opposing values also enhances research on sacrifice and opportunity costs: a stronger focus on one value field automatically implies that opposing values are not pursued. Consumers therefore do not only endorse certain values, but by this reject other values too.

Summarizing the above frameworks, the primary aim of the research on values has been the establishment of a cross-culturally valid, universal set of basic human values. The identification of universal values allows not only for an assessment of the relation between behavior (i.e. consumption choices) and values, but also for measurement and comparison of values across cultures. If values are shaped by the surrounding culture and have a direct impact on consumer choice and perception, a closer understanding of the importance of certain values of a particular target group establishes an important link between culture and consumer choice. Research into values therefore holds particular interest for international marketing.

2.3   Values as Link Between Culture, Consumer Behavior and Perception

Empirical evidence suggests systematic differences dependent on an individual's value structure (cf. Gatignon et al. 1989; Hofstede 1980; Schwartz 1992).

While the lack of research on the exact impact of cultural factors on consumer behavior has been pointed out, the general importance of culture for consumer behavior is undisputed (Arnould and Thompson 2005). Culture has an important role to play both in the shaping of consumer objects as visible artifacts of culture, as

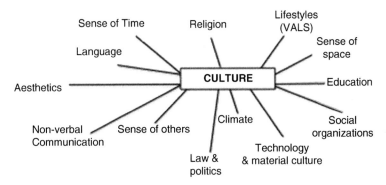

Fig. 4 Facets of culture. Source: Horn (2005), p. 27

well as consumers' perception and evaluation of them. Cultural categories "are the conceptual grid of a culturally constituted world" (McCracken 1986, p. 71).

But what are these categories? A wide variety of disciplines, among them social anthropology, linguistics or developmental psychology, have pursued the question of cross-cultural universals versus cultural relativity. The inability to arrive at a generally accepted definition of culture leads to a conceptual ambiguity, which makes a further breakdown into categories and specific 'building bricks' of culture difficult.

In relation to consumer behavior, Horn (2005) discusses the aspects in Fig. 4 as a starting point to understand the multi-faceted impact of culture, and subsequently of culturally shaped values, on consumer behavior and perception, including aspects of time perception, space perception, aesthetics as well as non-verbal communication.

Figure 4 therefore illustrates the broad influence of culture on aspects permeating everyday lives of consumers. Culture as a web of meaning simultaneously impacts the development of social institutions, practices and goods, and the way consumers evaluate and perceive these through their own, culturally shaped value system. Culture can therefore be seen as an all-encompassing background to the perception of a particular object and the assessment of the meaning and the benefit of it.

If consumption choices are the visible expression of culturally informed values, these can be used for market segmentation and thus for a description of consumer preferences and behavioral intentions of particular market segments (Kamakura and Novak 1992). Henry (1976) proved a predicatory relationship between culturally determined values and ownership in the automobile category. Using four cross-cultural value dimensions discussed by Kluckhohn and Strodtbeck (1961, in Henry 1976, p. 122): (i) Man's relation to nature, (ii) Time dimension, (iii) Personal activity and (iv) Man's relation to others, the direct relationship between these value dimensions and the attitudes towards specific product categories illustrates the relevance of cultural values for concrete consumer behavior decisions.

3 Customer Value: Attitudes and the Value of Things

The concept of consumer values needs to be distinguished from *customer* value as the concept of product-specific customer attitudes. While the values of consumers as discussed above represent a kind of broad socio-cultural compass, which consists of a general disposition towards general goals (e.g. a world at peace, a comfortable life), another aspect of value is the perception and assessment of the benefit a customer connects with a specific object: a product, a service, a brand, or a consumption experience. In accordance with existing literature in this field, this kind of product-specific benefit perception and assessment—e.g. with regard to quality or price—will be discussed as 'customer value'.

One definition of customer value, which has found widespread acceptance, has been proposed by Zeithaml (1988 p. 14): "the customer's overall assessment of the utility of a product based on perceptions of what is received and what is given". Zeithaml points out, that the most relevant aspects of consumer value in her research, namely price, quality and their relation to each other, are concepts, which are difficult to define and separate from each other, as they depend on a subjective assessment. The objective price of a product is encoded by the customer into a subjective price, including an evaluation of the monetary price and its transformation into categories ("cheap", "expensive") as well as a broader conception of the sacrifice necessary to obtain the product (nonmonetary component, ibid.)

In sum, the value customers derive from products in terms of a function of price and quality is dependent on individual and subjective conceptions of the parameters of price and quality themselves, as well as the assessment of their relation to each other. In conjunction with culture as an underlying influence on more general belief systems, the perception of what constitutes quality and its relative importance have to also be considered under the influence of culture.

3.1 Customer Value Characteristics

From their review of the literature on customer value Leroi-Werelds et al. (2014) derive a number of key characteristics of the concept: customer value is personal as well as situation-dependent. The value that consumers attach to objects is therefore also a reflection of personal values. In other words, consumers may use products to confirm and communicate their interpretation of themselves—which is in itself dependent on their culturally shaped values (see part 1)—to themselves and to others.

Leroi-Werelds et al. (2014) also point out, that customer value is created in an interactive process. As such, customer value is a key concept to measure the outcome of a consumer experience. Holbrook (1996) defines customer value as:

1. interactive: interaction between product and person,
2. relativistic: customer value is

(a) comparative among objects,
(b) personal (different between persons),
(c) situational (context-specific),

3. preference-based: dependent on the general value system of an individual, measurable by different value scales. Via this link to values, customer value is indirectly influenced by culture.
4. experience-dependent: customer value is not created by the purchase, but the consumption of a product.

Holbrook (1996) discusses eight different types of value, which can be gained from the consumption experience by consumers. While the list is not assumed to be exhaustive, it provides a useful overview over the different values customers can draw from an experience. Table 3 shows an overview of these values and their sources as well as a short explanation.

The focus on perceived customer value represents a change from a utilitarian, purchase-dominated perspective to a more hedonic view, in which a purchase constitutes a possible, but not necessary outcome of the consumption situation. Holbrook contrasts the traditional C-A-B (Cognition-Affect-Response) framework with his C-E-V (Consciousness-Emotion-Value) construct of consumer perception. A product or brand can be understood as the stimulus, which impacts the consumer's cognitive (consciousness) and affective (emotional) experience, and through this his appreciation of the customer value derived from the consumption experience.

For some consumers, either certain types of products or one particular product can hold significant value that is not transferable to other consumers. This individual value is derived from heightened interest in a certain product category (e.g. collectors) or from the enhancement of products with memories and/or special experiences. Special possessions derive their value not from any more or less objective assessment of material value, but from the meaning that they carry. As representatives of memories, old teddy bears and concert tickets have the power to transport underlying values and belief systems and make them visible.

Table 3 Customer value according to Holbrook

Value	Explanation	Source
Efficiency	Match of expected with actual performance	Extrinsic values, based on rational assessment
Excellence	High quality of product or service	
Status	Status markers	
Esteem	Enhancing esteem in the eyes of others	
Play	Hedonic consumption, three F's (fantasies, feelings, fun)	Intrinsic values, based on emotion assessment
Esthetics	Appreciation of beauty	
Ethics	Appreciation of ethical aspects as marker of superiority	
Spirituality	Magical experiences, transcendent value	

Source: Holbrook (1996)

3.2   Consumption Experience: The Interactive Process of Customer Value Creation

In times when it becomes more and more difficult to distinguish products and services on the basis of benefits alone, the *experience* connected to a product is seen as an increasingly important factor of differentiation. Simultaneously, as consumers are bombarded with more and more marketing messages, it can be argued that effectiveness of advertising decreases. Therefore, marketers turn to concepts of co-creation, and the design of a shopping *experience* that customers will value and remember is proposed as one solution to beat the marketing noise and create customer value (Gilmore and Pine 2002).

Lewis and Chambers (2000, p. 46) see an experience as "the total outcome to the customer from the combination of environment, goods, and services purchased". Berry et al. (2002, p. 85) similarly state, that an experience involves "orchestrating all the 'clues' that people detect in the buying process". Both of these definitions take a processual perspective, understanding an experience as a *process* of interaction on several, connected levels, encompassing the product with all its facets and through this creating the value of a service, a product, or any other form of interaction between consumer and commercial offering.

The focus on experiences as a contributor to or even dominant factor in creating customer value has been most notably discussed in the context of hedonic consumption. Gilmore and Pine (2002) discuss a transition of economic value from commodities over products and services to experiences, which are seen as replacing functional with sensory and emotional values. By thus extending the spectrum of potential interaction with the consumer, possible points of differentiation to competitors are also increased. This is particularly important in a situation, where the fulfillment of a utilitarian need has become the norm and is not sufficient for differentiation anymore.

The consumption experience can be split up into four stages, equivalent to the ubiquitous five-stage consumer decision making process: (i) the pre-consumption experience, (ii) the purchase experience, (iii) the core consumption experience and finally (iv) the remembered consumption or nostalgia experience. The last stage links to special and sacred possessions as customer value that is derived from consumption experiences that carry a distinct connotation for an individual.

3.3   Perception of Risk

As shown above, the engagement with a particular product offers consumers important hedonic and utilitarian benefits. The potential gain in form of this

Table 4 Risk sensitivity

Consumer groups at risk	Type of risk	Product category
Consumers with relatively low wealth	**Monetary risk**	Relatively expensive purchases
Consumers focusing on utilitarian customer value	**Functional risk**	Products requiring exclusive commitment
Consumers who are aware own physical limitations	**Physical risk**	Products with potential to inflict physical harm: food, beverages, medical, electrical
Consumers with lower self-esteem and higher insecurity	**Social risk**	Symbolic and publicly visible products: clothes, jewelry, cars
Consumers lacking status and affiliation to relevant groups	**Psychological risk**	Status symbols and personal luxuries

Source: Based on Solomon (2009)

customer value however runs counter to the perception of risk attached to the product. Perception of risk is dependent on two aspects: (a) a product-based perspective, where particular attributes make a purchase more risk-prone, and (b) a consumer-related angle, in that the pursuit of specific values makes consumers more or less vulnerable to certain types of risk at conflict with the achievement of this desirable end-state.

In general, five types of risks can be distinguished: monetary, functional, physical, social, and psychological risk (Solomon 2009). In each case, particular product categories are associated with each type of risk, and simultaneously particular consumer groups feel more vulnerable with regard to this risk category. Table 4 shows the relationship between types of risk in relation to product category and consumer groups.

Just as the assessment of customer value, the perception of risk is therefore not an objective aspect. Rather, it is a subjective appraisal by consumers, which is dependent on their individual outlook on life. Due to its potential impact on purchase intentions and search behavior, understanding risk perception from the consumer perspective is crucial. While traditionally, risk evaluation has been viewed as an almost mathematical formula of perceived customer value and loss expectancy, it has been suggested, that risk perception is (a) highly subjective and (b) more powerful at explaining consumer behavior than potential customer value: as consumers tend to be loss-averse, there has been evidence that they rate potential losses higher than potential gains (Chiu et al. 2014).

With regard to risk-reducing strategies, firms need to understand the risk capital consumers possess (capacities to offset any perceived risk). Risk perception is linked to personal circumstances (e.g. wealth, see Table 4). At the same time, the evaluation of how much risk a purchase carries has also been examined with regard to more general predispositions. Hofstede's dimension of Uncertainty Avoidance offers an obvious way to connect risk aversion with cultural value dimensions (Chiu et al. 2014).

While the assessment of risk is typically framed as the 'cost' of a purchase, which has to be regarded vis-à-vis the potential gain through customer value, it has also been pointed out, that in some categories and for some consumers, risk itself can also *add* to the perceived value of a product. It is important to note, that a purely negative conceptualization of risk fails to grasp risk-seeking behavior of consumers, e.g. in areas of sports and experiential leisure. The "Berlyne curve" indicates a preference of actions associated with increased risk. In following studies, this behavior has been related to novelty seeking (Mitchell 1999). Conceptually close is also innovation diffusion theory, which examines the willingness of different groups to accept innovations—and thereby with products carrying an increased risk due to uncertainty of their performance and lack of previous experience. While there are few cross-culturally valid traits to identify innovators as the first 2.5% to accept an innovation, the function of culturally induced values as motivational construct guiding individual perception and serving as a general guideline for behavior indicates that risk-seeking behavior, the perception of risk and the acceptance of innovation can also be explained along a value construct such as Schwartz' Value Survey (Steenkamp et al. 1999), especially with the dimension Openness to change versus Conservation.

4 Conclusion

Consumers face complex decisions. While some of these decisions seem to promise pleasurable, hedonistic outcomes as well as utilitarian benefits, consumers have to determine prior to the purchase, if the desired end state will be achieved. This is why several layers of risk are attached to any decision for—or against—a product, service, or experience. With regard to the product itself, risks perceived by consumers relate to the expected result (satisfaction of expectation), to the cost involved, and to any actual, physical risk.

The consumer assessment of these risks has to be analyzed on two levels. Firstly, any risk evaluation is dependent on mostly imperfect information (consumers will typically access a selection of all available information) as well as on the subjective interpretation of this information: very few consumers can actually decode technical information to a degree that would allow them to achieve a near-objective assessment of functional or physical risk connected to a technological or medical product. Rather than an objective assessment, their evaluation of the risk is therefore a subjective perception.

Secondly, the relevance of this information to individual consumers is dependent on their general predisposition to rate certain end states and behaviors as more desirable than others. This is influenced by their value system, which they develop as a consequence of their personality, their immediate environment, and the cultural frame of reference in which they are encultured. While some consumers are in general more risk-averse and value tradition and security, others are more open to change and may be willing to accept a higher risk as it supports their predilection for stimulation.

On a more personal level, consumers also have to weigh psychological and social risks, affecting their self-image and their status in society, against their personal value system. Persons with strategies to alleviate certain risk types may be able to engage in more risk-prone behavior—but on the other hand, they might then not perceive the risk they take as being particularly high. Both assessment of risk attached to a product, as well as the decision whether to engage with a certain level of risk are therefore dependent on individual circumstances and perception.

The question of risk perception therefore leads back to a more fundamental research debate of the congruence between objective and subjective understandings of risk. Consumers construct their world through their individual value system, which serves as a guideline and a benchmark for their decisions and their behavior. The relative importance of some values over others, as well as their supporting or opposing position to each other, impacts their assessment of product attributes and their overall evaluation of customer value—what they get from interaction with a product, service or experience—and perceived risk. The complex interaction of these personal evaluations means that the resultant assessment is highly dependent on personal factors, which are themselves shaped by culture.

The role of culture for understanding the world of consumers cannot be overestimated. Through the process of enculturation, we develop a general value system, which is hierarchical and forms a coherent structure, in which certain values can only be pursued at the expense of others. Culture shapes our perception of what is important and what is not. Culture also influences what is interpreted as good quality, a fair price, or too much risk. While the relationship between culture and values is clear, a more in-depth investigation of the impact of culture on risk perception and customer value concepts, as well as validated frameworks to measure cultural determinants of risk perception will offer a deeper understanding of consumer perception of risk for specific product categories.

References

Arnould, E., & Thompson, C. (2005). Consumer culture theory (CCT): Twenty years of research. *Journal of Consumer Research, 31*(4), 868–882.

Berry, L., Carbone, L., & Haeckel, S. (2002). Managing the total customer experience. *MIT Sloan Management Review, 43*(3), 85–89.

Chiu, C., Wang, E., Fang, Y., & Huang, H. (2014). Understanding customers' repeat purchase intentions in B2C e-commerce: The roles of utilitarian value, hedonic value and perceived risk. *Information Systems Journal, 24*(1), 85–114.

Daghfous, N., Petrof, J., & Pons, F. (1999). Values and adoption of innovations: A cross-cultural study. *Journal of Consumer Marketing, 16*(4), 314–331.

de Mooij, M., & Hofstede, G. (2011). Cross-cultural consumer behavior: A review of research findings. *Journal of International Consumer Marketing, 23*(3/4), 181–192.

Fischer, R., & Poortinga, Y. (2012). Are cultural values the same as the values of individual? An examination of similarities in personal, social and cultural value structures. *International Journal of Cross Cultural Management, 12*(2), 157–170.

Gatignon, H., Eliashberg, J., & Robertson, T. (1989). Modelling multinational diffusion patterns. *Marketing Science, 8*(3), 231–247.

Geertz, C. (1973). *The interpretation of cultures.* New York: Basic Books.

Gilmore, J., & Pine, B. (2002). Customer experience places: The new offering frontier. *Strategy & Leadership, 30*(4), 4–11.

Henry, W. (1976). Cultural values do correlate with consumer behavior. *Journal of Marketing Research, 13*(2), 121–127.

Hofstede, G. (1980). Culture and organizations. *International Studies of Management & Organization, 10*(4), 15–41.

Holbrook, M. (1996). Special session summary. Customer value—a framework for analysis and research. In K. Corfman & J. Lynch (Eds.), *NA—Advances in Consumer Research* (Vol. 23, Issue, 2, pp. 138–142).

Horn, S. (2005). *Interkulturelle Kompetenz im Zugang zu japanischen Konsumenten: Eine empirische Untersuchung zur Einordn ung japanischer Akkulturationsstrategien im Zeichen globaler Consumscapes* [Intercultural competence in accessing Japanese consumers: An empirical study on Japanese acculturation strategies in the context of global consumscapes]. Wiesbaden: Deutscher Universitäts-Verlag.

Kahle, L., & Kennedy, P. (1989). Using the list of values (LOV) to understand consumers. *The Journal of Consumer Marketing, 6*(3), 5–12.

Kahle, L., Beatty, S., & Homer, P. (1986). Alternative measurement approaches to consumer values: The list of values (LOV) and values and life style (VALS). *Journal of Consumer Research, 13*(3), 405–409.

Kamakura, W., & Novak, T. (1992). Value-system segmentation: Exploring the meaning of LOV. *Journal of Consumer Research, 19*(1), 119–132.

Knafo, A., Roccas, S., & Sagiv, L. (2011). The value of values in cross-cultural research: A special issue in honor of Shalom Schwartz. *Journal of Cross-Cultural Research, 42*(2), 178–185.

Kroeber, A., & Kluckhohn, C. (1952). Culture: A critical review of concepts and definitions. Papers. Peabody Museum of Archaeology & Ethnology, Harvard University. [Online]. [Accessed 03.06.2016]. Available from https://archive.org/details/papersofpeabodymvol47no1peab.

Lenartowicz, T., & Roth, K. (2004). The selection of key informants in IB Cross-cultural studies. *Management International Review, 44*(1), 23–51.

Leroi-Werelds, S., Streukens, S., Brady, M. K., & Swinnen, G. (2014). Assessing the value of commonly used methods for measuring customer value: A multi-setting empirical study. *Journal of the Academy of Marketing Science, 42*(4), 430–451.

Lewis, R., & Chambers, R. (2000). *Marketing leadership in hospitality: Foundations and practices.* New York: Wiley.

Maio, G., Pakizeh, A., Cheung, W., & Rees, K. (2009). Changing, priming, and acting on values: Effects via motivational relations in a circular model. *Journal of Personality and Social Psychology, 97*(4), 699–715.

McCracken, G. (1986). Culture and consumption: A theoretical account of the structure and movement of the cultural meaning of goods. *Journal of Consumer Research, 13*(1), 71–84.

Mitchell, V. (1999). Consumer Perceived Risk: Conceptualisations and models. *European Journal of Marketing, 33*(1/2), 163–195.

Novak, T., & MacEvoy, B. (1990). On comparing alternative segmentation schemes: The list of values and values and life styles. *Journal of Consumer Research, 17*(1), 105–109.

Rokeach, M. (1973). *The nature of human values.* New York: The Free Press.

Schein, E. (1996). Culture: The missing concept in organisation studies. *Administrative Science Quarterly, 41*(2), 229–240.

Schwartz, S. (1992). Universals in the content and structure of values: Theory and empirical tests in 20 countries. In M. Zanna (Ed.), *Advances in experimental psychology, 25*(1), 1–65. New York: Academic Press.

Schwartz, S., & Bilsky, W. (1987). Toward a universal psychological structure of human values. *Journal of Personality and Social Psychology, 53*(3), 550–562.

Sheth, J., & Sethi, S. (1973). Theory of cross-cultural buyer-behavior. Faculty Working Paper. 115. College of Commerce and Business Administration, University of Illinois. [Online]. [Accessed 12.01.2016]. Available from https://www.ideals.illinois.edu/bitstream/handle/2142/27767/theoryofcrosscul115shet.pdf?sequence=1.

Sojka, J., & Tansuhaj, P. (1995). Cross-cultural consumer research: A twenty-year review. *Advances in Consumer Research, 22*, 461–461.

Solomon, M. (2009). *Consumer behavior: Buying, having, and being.* Upper Saddle River, NJ: Pearson Education International.

Steenkamp, J., Hofstede, F., & Wedel, M. (1999). A Cross-national investigation into the individual and national cultural antecendents of consumer innovativeness. *Journal of Marketing, 63*(2), 55–69.

Triandis, H. (2007). Culture and psychology: A history of the study of their relationship. In S. Kitayama & D. Cohen (Eds.), *Handbook of cultural psychology* (pp. 59–76). New York: Guilford.

Zeithaml, V. A. (1988). Consumer perceptions of price, quality, and value: A means-end model and synthesis of evidence. *The Journal of Marketing, 52*, 2–22.

Part III
Consumer Behavior

Perception, Attitudes, Intentions, Decisions and Actual Behavior

Arnout R.H. Fischer

1 Introduction

The variation in disciplinary background of research in consumer behavior has resulted in a range of different, sometimes difficult to align theories and insights. For the research into consumer choice, consumer behavior research has drawn mainly on the fundamental disciplines of social psychology and economic psychology. In addition it uses insights from other applied disciplines such as behavioral economics, health interventions and usability research in human computer interaction research. This broad range of backgrounds has resulted in a seemingly fractured field that brings numerous different models to predict consumer behavior. In my view, the most important difference lies whether models predict intention to adopt a product based on evaluation of that product on its own or whether the model predicts the choice for a product in competition with another product. Models in economic psychology tend to focus on this latter strategy, and derive part worth of product attributes from choices made by consumer who have been asked to select between carefully selected pairs of product, that differ on only a few attributes. In such models the process underlying the evaluation of the product is implied as the cause for the preference; but the actual process of forming this evaluation and how it relates to choice is not the topic of study. Most models that have their background in social psychology, on the other hand, investigate how a consumer evaluates a single product and to what extent the consumer claims the intention to purchase that product. The central question is to study how product evaluation occurs and leads to intention to choose a product. While such approaches give insight into how an opinion and an intention is formed, it does not necessarily predict which product

A.R.H. Fischer (✉)
Wageningen University, Marketing and Consumer Group, Hollandseweg 1, 6706 KN, Wageningen, The Netherlands
e-mail: arnout.fischer@wur.nl

© Springer International Publishing AG 2017
G. Emilien et al. (eds.), *Consumer Perception of Product Risks and Benefits*,
DOI 10.1007/978-3-319-50530-5_17

will be chosen if a consumer is confronted with two (or more) similar products, which is often the case in a realistic retail environment. Hence both approaches have their benefit, the choice paradigm may be better suited to investigate which products will be selected among similar alternative, while the evaluation process approach gives a better idea how this preference is formed. As the latter approach focusses more on the processes underlying preference formation, the current contribution will focus on this approach and discuss current issues with the relation between perception of a product, formation or activation of an attitude towards this product, and how this results in intention or actual behavior.

Consumer behavior is often considered as the outcome of a more or less linear and rational process. A product is presented to a consumer who perceives the product. Following these perceptions the product is evaluated and an attitude about the adoption, procurement or use of the product is formed. This attitude informs intentions to act in relation to the product, leading to a decision when and how to act, which shows itself as consumer behavior (Ajzen 1991).

Linear models starting with product perception and ending with product usage hold a strong appeal to consumer research for several reasons. (1) They are simple because limited to the timespan between the moment of presenting a product to a consumer to the moment the consumer acts. (2) They assume that consumers base their behavior on the product as presented. (3) They allow for intervention by product developers and marketers as change in product presentation should lead to predictable changes in behavior. As a consequence, many practitioners use these models to straightforwardly predict consumer choice based on a product, without including context or consumer personality or experience. In the last decades there has been increasing insight that predictions based on such models only predict actual behavior to some extent. This suggests that there may be more subtleties involved in using such models, or even that some of the assumptions of these models do not fit with all situations to which they are applied The current contribution will therefore review these models and discuss some of the subtleties that underlie these seemingly simple models, as well as some more fundamental criticisms that are voiced in relation to these models. To do so, a number of influential, linear consumer behavior models will be briefly introduced, the theory of planned behavior, the technology acceptance model, the norm activation model. These models have in common that they have attitude or a similar summary evaluation at a pivoting role in bringing together perceptions and leading to behavior. Underlying assumptions of these models will be discussed. Subsequently current discussions in the field of evaluations that have focused on attitudes will be discussed in relation to the consequences for consumer behavior research. I will then go into reasons why evaluations as elicited by much consumer research may be less predictive of behavior than often hoped for and what alternative approaches are currently explored to predict actual behavior. The contribution will conclude with a reflection on where we stand and where we may want to go in the near future.

2 Consumer Behavior Models

Among the most influential models in consumer behavior is the Theory of Planned Behavior (TPB Ajzen 1991). The Theory of Planned Behavior predicts that the (stated) intention to adopt behavior will result in the behavior, at least in situations where sufficient behavioral control allows for this behavior. Behavioral intention in turn is predicted by a combination of attitudes towards the behavior, subjective norms and perceived behavioral control. Attitude, norms and perceived control are in turn determined by considering salient product attributes relevant to choice. Attitude, norms, and control are then the sum of individual's beliefs about whether the object contains the attribute and the evaluation whether that attribute is positive or negative. The Theory of Planned Behavior in itself is an expansion of an earlier influential consumer behavior model: the Theory of Reasoned Action. The main addition of TPB over TRA is that it includes perceived behavioral control, i.e. the belief that one can actually achieve the behavior if wanted.

The Theory of Planned Behavior is among the most frequently used theories in product choice. When a search was conducted on 27 January 2016 using the search term "theory of planned behavior" OR "theory of planned behavior" OR "TPB" in Topic for Web of science (apps.webofknowledge.com) and in Article Title—Abstract—Keywords for Scopus (scopus.com); the theory of planned behavior was found to be the topic of about 12,000 papers in Web of Science and about 7000 in Scopus addressing the topic; with about 12,000 citations in Web of Science and about 15,500 in Scopus to Icek Ajzen's 1991 paper and there exist several meta-analyses (see e.g. Armitage and Conner 2000). The theory can be adapted to some extent to fit specific research questions. For example, subjective norm is sometimes considered the combination of social (peer response) and personal moral norms (Hübner and Kaiser 2006). Antecedents predicting attitude in more detail based on, for example risk and benefit weighing and personality characteristics (Bredahl 2001) or the addition of anticipated regret (Sandberg and Conner 2008) can be included within the framework of TPB. Cultural differences and differences in occupation can be introduced as moderators to explain different influence of norms, perceived control and attitude on intention (Frewer et al. 2008). Such adaptations give the Theory of Planned Behavior the opportunity to be adapted to specific research questions that may not be fully addressed by the basic version of the model.

Prior to the 1970s the leading position on consumer behavior, was that individual consumer choose the products with the highest perceived utility. TPB differs from this approach by including the social, normative context beyond the evaluation of the product, and that it includes the perception of whether the intended behavior is indeed under control of the individual as a determinant of behavior. As such the TPB goes beyond a purely functional utilitarian model. Nevertheless the evaluation of the product, the attitude within the TPB could easily be considered a rational weighing based on the partial utilities of all attributes of a product. This is, however, not what the TPB claims. First of all, evaluating all attributes in detail would make for an infeasibly complex task and it is unlikely consumers will engage in such deliberation, especially for the purchase of simple goods where a satisficing solution may be within grasp. The original attitude model embedded within the TPB accounts for this, as it is explicitly stated that only a limited set, of relevant attributes are considered. We should immediately realize that this bounded evaluation reduces the explanatory values of our methods, as in a real life situation, different consumers will consider different attributes as relevant when forming an opinion. This subtlety is often overlooked in experimental research where only one or a few attributes are changed, and these are assumed to be salient to all consumers. A second deviation from the utility idea, lies in the fact that attitude within the Theory of Planned Behavior, does not only consists of a reasoned, deliberated weighing of the product and its attributes, but also includes affective feelings and experiences based on past behavior (Ajzen 1991). These additions make the TPB on the one hand more applicable and more predictive, on the other hand this would require that the questions asked are tailored to individual consumers, making a product specific TPB approach at individual level less relevant (Kaiser et al. 2007).

Another frequently used model, the Technology Acceptance Model (TAM; Davis 1989) shares many assumptions about how consumers form an intention to adopt product use with the Theory of Planned Behavior. Similar to the Theory of Planned Behavior the use of a product is predicted from intentions based on properties of the product. In the case of the TAM the intention is mainly based on perceived usefulness and ease of technology usage. The central role of ease of use and usefulness in the technology acceptance model can be understood by taking account of the moment in time, and the class of products for which TAM was developed: consumer interaction with complex electronics and computer technology in the 1980s. Until the 1980s, such technology had mainly been limited to interested hobbyists; but by the mid 1980s programmable videorecorders (VCR's) and the early generations personal computers had become widespread among consumers. TAM was one of the first models to address consumer behavior in the context of complex electronics, and has played an important role in the development of more user-friendly devices in specific and the development of the field of human computer interaction in particular. While, TAM has mostly been used in the context of interactive systems, some of its insights have been used outside of the domain of interactive electronics (Ronteltap et al. 2007). Since its original conception, the Technology Acceptance Model has been repeatedly extended and its most recent versions includes a multitude of predictors based on a number of models of consumer behavior making the successors of TAM among of the most comprehensive models (see e.g. Venkatesh et al. 2012). This approach of adding evermore predictors has lead in turn to the criticism that, while adding additional predictors to existing models unavoidably increases explained variance in samples, it does not help us to developed unanswered issues in the heart of the model, the evaluation of the product and the formation of intention (Bagozzi 2007).

TPB and similar models start with the properties of a product or behavior to determine attitude, subjective norms and perceived behavioral control; and more or less implicitly introduces goals, motivations and values of consumers through beliefs and evaluations. These models are applicable to the average consumer, but not very well suited to understand context and person-to-person difference in intention of a product (Kaiser et al. 2007). A different approach was taken to develop the norm activation model for explaining altruistic behavior (Schwartz 1994). Since there is no obvious utility or value in altruistic behavior, some motivation to engage in such behavior has to come from the consumer, rather than from the involved product. The norm activation starts with the activation of a normative desirable state, which then leads to a set of motivations against which the product or behavior is evaluated and behavior follows. This makes it important to know which norms are activated, especially in the context of altruistic or pro-environmental behavior. In most situations, personal values of the individual (Schwartz 1994) are assumed to drive such motivations—where a person with more altruistic and pro-environmental values is likely to make different choice in comparable situations than egoistic individuals (Schwartz 1994). The norm activation model has since been mostly applied to situations where consumer behavior cannot be understood by a direct benefit to the individual such a pro-environmental behavior. In spite of its relevance in starting with personal values of the consumer, and looking at consumer behavior from personal motivations and goals, the norm activation model shows a generally weak relation between personal values and observed behavior, and tends to explain behavior only in cases where values do play a major role (such as in sustainable behavior).

While these three models introduced above differ whether the starting point is the product, or the values of the individual, in all the models behavior is predicted by intention, which is in turn largely based on a summary evaluation of the product. There is broad consensus that attitudes do describe summary evaluations of products or services (Eagly and Chaiken 1993), there is however still ongoing debate what an attitude exactly is (Gawronski and Bodenhausen 2011). Therefore in the next section, I will focus on different angles in attitude research.

3   Attitudes: What Summary of What Evaluation?

Attitudes have been studied in social psychology in order to understand opinion and behavior of individuals since the 1930s. Attitudes have likewise held an important position in consumer psychology since the inception of the field. For such a central and often studied concept, there is however, remarkably much, ongoing debate on what exactly an attitude is (Gawronski and Bodenhausen 2011). There is general agreement that an attitude should, at a high level of abstraction been seen as a valenced—either positive or negative—evaluation of an attitude object (Eagly and Chaiken 1993).

In consumer research, attitude models traditionally adopted the approach that product attributes are weighed independently and summed to from some overall evaluation. This view was further refined in the Fishbein attitude model (See: Ajzen 1991) that distinguished beliefs whether the attitude object would or should lead to some outcome, and the evaluation of (the desirability or value) of that outcome. To account for limited cognitive resources, from the inception of the Fishbein attitude model, it has been assumed that not *all* attributes of a product are part of the evaluation. In fact, only attributes that are salient for the individual consumer at the moment of planning their behavior are assumed to play a role. The combinations of belief and evaluation of the salient product attributes to meet those beliefs are result in positive or negative values that are summed to form an overall attitude. Attitude as such is thus a summary judgment across salient product attributes and is either positive, or negative. It is however, less clear what makes up the beliefs and evaluation. There are several researchers who define attitudes as a more or less elaborately, information based construct that is mainly based on cognitive beliefs and evaluations (e.g. Fazio 2007). Others argue that attitudes are predominantly emotional and affective constructs (Clore and Schnall 2005), based on intuitive and affective response to the product and its properties. The majority of researchers tend to agree that both affect and cognition evaluation matter for attitudes (e.g. Eagly and Chaiken 1993; Ajzen 1991). Some support the view that besides cognitive and affective evaluation, past behavior and subsequent experience with the product forms a third, important element of attitudes (Eagly and Chaiken 1993).

Models that study attitude change, such as the Elaboration Likelihood Model (Petty and Cacioppo 1986), suggest that high motivation and availability of resources is required for factual information to be integrated into the attitude in an elaborate, lasting way that results in predictable behavior. In the absence of sufficient motivation and cognitive resources, the elaboration likelihood predicts people may still change their attitude, but will do this based on heuristic information used in a peripheral way. Such peripheral attitude change only has a short term effect, and is not expected to lead to temporally stable attitude change, and attitudes thus influenced are hence unlikely to allow prediction of future behavior.

Even if we follow the idea that attitudes consist of both cognitive and affective components, there is some debate on whether an attitude should be considered to be a single construct with an affective and a cognitive component (e.g. Ajzen 1991), or that we should consider the affective and cognitive attitudes as different evaluations, i.e. dual attitudes that in competition or agreement determine intention and behavior (e.g. Lee et al. 2005). There are some who claim that affect is generally faster and therefore frequently the dominant attitude (e.g. Crano and Prislin 2006), although there is evidence that some stimuli and situations are more easily, and faster judged cognitively, and others situations more easily in an affective way; in other words that the specific situation determines whether the cognitive or affective process is faster and dominant. This aligns with the idea that the cognitive and affective components of attitudes are filled in by somewhat different processes, but that the end result still is one attitude.

Another issue under debate is whether and if so how attitudes are stored in memory. One position is that attitudes towards and object or product can be stored as such valenced, positive or negative summary evaluations linked to a specific attitude object. When the consumer is confronted with the object the associated summary evaluation, but not the underlying arguments and knowledge are retrieved, which implies that consumers may give a positive or negative judgment without being able to reconstruct how they came to this decisions. Others, take a different position and claim that stored attitudes do not exists, or at least are not relevant as no situation is ever exactly the same and that opinion is always, but not necessarily consciously, constructed on the spot in response to external event based on associations with the object and the situation (e.g. Conrey et al. 2005). Faster and less conscious attitude retrieval would then not signify stored evaluations, but instead highly practiced neural networks, that allow very fast and consistent recombination of associations to come up with consistent, unconscious, and quickly reconstructed attitudes (Schwarz 2007). The MODE model (Fazio 2007) takes a middle ground and assumes that with repeated exposure, attitudes become stored evaluations in their entirety, while new objects are evaluated on the spot using the available information, associations, and partially relevant attitudes. The MODE model thus assumes that existing evaluation can be flexibly used to form new attitudes. In addition within MODE it is assumed that attribute-evaluations are stored in memory, as without such attribute-evaluation associations, attitude construction would be very demanding (Fazio 2007). Attribute-evaluations can be seen as, attitudes towards the attribute, and if those can be stored there seems no reason to assume why attitudes to more complex objects cannot also be stored.

Whether attitudes are retrieved in their entirety or reconstructed on the spot, in both cases there is a difference between well established, crystallized attitudes and new attitudes that have not yet been learned (Schuman and Presser 1996). This distinction is important in the context of consumer behavior research as well established, strong attitudes are generally good predictors of behavior, while decisions based on weak attitudes are easily influenced by context (Holland et al. 2002). Strong attitudes tend to be stable over time and cannot easily be changed by providing additional, counter-attitudinal information on a product at least not easily or quickly (Tormala and Petty 2002). Thus, for practical purposes it is relevant to take account of both the valence (positive or negative) and the strength of attitudes.

Attitude strength has been argued to consist of several dimensions such as extremity of the attitude, certainty about the attitude, level of non-commitment, affective-cognitive consistency, and lack of ambivalence in general both within cognition or affect, or between affect and cognition (Krosnick et al. 1993). Attitudinal ambivalence has a special place in relation to attitude strength, as it assumes the existence of opposing positive and negative evaluations towards a product at the same time. Thus rather than a weak attitude that exists because someone has no opinion, no knowledge or no associations with the situation or product, ambivalence relates to an unpredictable, and possibly unstable attitude because someone has fairly strong opposing views on different attributes of the situation. Adopting the simple sum score of attitude (e.g. Ajzen 1991) such ambivalent attitudes would average out to a more or less neutral attitude. Ambivalent attitudes are, however much more complex (Jonas et al. 2000), as it is based on relatively strong opposing attribute-evaluation links. When someone holds an ambivalent attitude and is asked to make a decision, a distinctly uncomfortable situation is experienced, and people will strive to solve this experienced cognitive dissonance either definitively by creating a consistent, non-ambivalent attitude and story that or more incidentally, by picking just one option for the decision in hand (Nordgren et al. 2006). As a consequence, attitudinal ambivalence may lead to unexpected, seemingly erratic switching of extreme attitudes between situations; where a "true" neutral attitude would remain more or less neutral whatever happens, and a neutral attitude based on lack of information would be formed using the provided information in a more or less structured way.

So far, this discussion has mainly addressed attitudes regardless of whether these are unconscious or under conscious control. One criticism on much attitude research has, however, been that social desirable answering is not reflecting the true attitude of an individual; and that first gut responses are often predictive of behavior, but not recognizable in expressed attitudes (Haidt 2007). First gut responses are often related to the final affective attitude component. This seems less straightforward however, as for example first cognitive responses to well-known objects that evoke little strong responses tend to be close to final cognitive attitudes, while for these object first affective responses are much less so (Van Giesen et al. 2015). The first response is nevertheless considered a good indication of the earliest evoked response that is not under conscious control; and hence not likely to evoke social desirable responses. Social desirable response appears to be predominantly the case for interpersonal stereotyping such a racial, gender or age stereotyping, and it is for such applications that initial effort into tapping into unconscious attitudes were mostly directed. The idea behind accessing unconscious attitudes is to make use of the mental structure in which attitudes are stored. If an attitude is more closely related to a positive evaluation, than accessing other positive stimuli should results in faster and less error prone responses than negative stimuli. This assumption has led to a number of methods for measuring unconscious attitudes. Most notably affective priming, where an attitude object, the prime, is presented first followed by a positive or negative target. The response time on the target should than provide an indication where the faster response time indicated to what valence of evaluation the attitude object is linked to (Fazio 2001). Another often used method, the implicit association test (IAT: Greenwald et al. 1998) takes a slightly different approach where participants are asked to classify attitude objects and evaluative words to the same response. If the evaluative words align with the attitude object this should be faster and less error prone. There are also other methods that have a similar approach (Goodall 2011).

While these implicit methods have a certain appeal in their claim that they measure the true, unconscious attitudes, it is now generally accepted that the conscious control that maybe responsible for socially desirable answering, may also ensure that people do not act on their implicit attitudes alone (Gawronski and Bodenhausen 2011). It should be realized that including implicit attitudes does introduce complexities, in part methodological. In spite of the effort invested in these implicit measures over the last 15 years there are still considerable methodological issues in developing a reliable, and easily applicable tool based on these methods (Lebel and Paunonen 2011). Therefore a study of implicit attitudes may be particularly warranted to understand how disagreement between expressed, socially desirable and implicit attitudes are resolved (Gawronski and Bodenhausen 2011), as in case where there is no disagreement between implicit and expressed attitudes we can simply rely on expressed attitudes. Meta-analyses of the use of implicit in consumer research suggests that the difference between explicit, consciously controlled attitude, and implicit attitudes is often very small, especially compared to interpersonal stereotyping (Greenwald et al. 2009; Hofmann et al. 2005).

In summary, while attitudes are among the most frequently applied constructs to predict consumer behavior, there is substantial variation in the way attitudes are conceptualized. Attitude strength and attitudinal ambivalence determine how predictable an attitude is, and how well it predicts behavior. Distinctions are made between affective and cognitive attitudes or attitude components. Distinctions are made between implicit, unconscious attitudes and explicit, self-reported attitudes.

4   Attitude Behavior Links

Consumer behavior models of the class presented in this contribution aim to predict intention, and actual behavior to act based on product evaluation. In practice, however, the link between intention and actual behavior is often weak, especially when it concerns behavior that provides no immediate benefits to the consumer, such as sustainable consumption decisions (Vermeir and Verbeke 2006). This attitude behavior gap decreases the practical applicability of the proposed models. Understanding why this gap exists and under what situations it is most prominent is therefore important in order to gain most from the strengths and limitations of these models.

If predictive power of these models is limited, there is much to be said for the argument that the attitude as measured is not as relevant to behavior as assumed. There is a number of reasons; both in the way attitudes are measured, as in our behavior that may account for this.

One element that may play a role is that of lack correspondence between the attitude and behavior object. In much research, attitudes are measured at the level of a broad product category; while in reality consumer do not buy a broad category of products but a specific product. This seems to be particularly the case for behavior based on abstract attitudes such as attitude towards sustainability (Kaiser et al. 1999), or socially responsible behavior, where attitudes are often measured at the level of being in favor of sustainable/responsible behavior in general. Such broader attitudes are easily measured, tend to be more stable than those towards a specific product, and can be applied for several products without having to re-asses very specific products. Nevertheless, the predictive power of such broad attitudes is unavoidably low as it only addresses one property of a product. For example when looking at the purchase of an organic apple, a positive attitude towards sustainability may predict some of the consumer behavior towards this apple, but without knowing whether he likes apples at all, this will only provide a limited prediction of intention and purchase behavior. The attitude (general sustainable behavior) and the behavior level (buying apples that happen to be sustainable) do only correspond to a limited amount, which reduces explanatory power.

Lack of correspondence is a frequently occurring issue. From the literature it is not always clear what causes this, and we suspect that this in part due to imprecise operationalization of the object of research (Reinders et al. 2013). If this shift is the unintentional consequence of adopting existing measures leading to differences in objects studied in perception, attitude, intention, and behavior, explained variance will drop because of the unavoidable introduction of different associations (i.e. noise) at different steps in the model. There are however situations where general attitudes are more useful, as these may lie closer to personal values and may be more stable and lasting predictors, useable for a larger range of objects compared to attitudes towards a single specific object. In those cases a lower predictive values may be acceptable, but this consequence should be accepted before engaging in the study. Even in cases where generic broad attitudes are preferred it may be possible to maximally reduce lack of correspondence by measuring the broad attitude at the same level of specificity as the actual behavior (Kaiser et al. 1999). A hybrid form of including general attitudes and personal values could be to add those as predictors for specific product attitudes. The more general, abstract attitudes then become a more distal predictors of those product attitudes and behaviors.

Another, related, reason why attitudes as measured in most consumer research have limited predictive power for behavior is that when people fill out surveys they are typically thinking at a different level from the purchase moment. When people fill out surveys they tend to consider a hypothetical future situation and speculate how that should unfold. In such situations consumers are thinking about a desirable future situation and will report their assessment based on what they feel as desirable. In a real life situation, short term concrete context demands foremost that the behavior is feasible in the context, so decision taking in this situation will be more based on feasibility of behavior than on desirability alone. This suggests that the way in which we are customarily investigating attitudes is accessing evaluations at a different level than those we use in actual purchase behavior. Self-reported attitudes tend to address more abstract, hypothetical, temporally, socially and geographically distal desirability's which leads to these attitudes to be construed at a high level. As actual behavior tend to be concrete, actual, now, for the consumer themselves and here, the decision immediately leading to behavior is made at a lower construal level. This difference in construal levels may explain why attitudes lack predictive power for actual choice (Trope and Liberman 2010).

But even if we could assume that an attitude is sufficiently specific, corresponds to the behavior and is construed at a similar level of abstraction, and a relevant intention has been formed and memorized, the predictive power of attitudes may still be limited. For such previously planned intention to result in behavior, the intention needs to be activated at the moment that the behavior should be done. This often requires deviation from normal routines which requires substantial cognitive control (Ouellette and Wood 1998). Many of us have experienced that a plan was made to go for a specific purchase on the way home from work, realizing after turning the key in the front door that once we went into our routine trip home, we passed the shop without executing the planned behavior. There are indeed many reasons, why intentions stored in prospective memory do not activate the relevant behavior at the right time. Routines taking over, being interrupted in the sequence planned to lead to the intended behavior and having to focus attention on other tasks rather than the intended behavior are factors that were shown to interfere with intended behavior (Dismukes 2012).

Intentional behavior, based on attitudes as described in the theory of planned behavior assumes planning (sic). Planning tends to be an elaborate process. In real life situations, people may revert to less intense decision making approaches and may rely on environmental cues that nudge their behavior with any planning, heuristics and automatisms, rather than applying the much more intensive system that facilitates conscious deliberation (Kahneman 2003). In fact, transferring much of our basis tasks to automatisms has long been considered a very efficient way of freeing up mental resources for more important tasks. In fact much of our daily behavior, and especially frequently repeated behavior like food purchases, and notably addictions maybe the outcome of habits and other automatized behavior. Such automatic, habitual behaviors may lead to situations where an evaluation of the product or behavior (Aarts and Dijksterhuis 2000), nor conscious behavioral goals are guiding behavior. While some claim the attitude concept could be expanded to include habitual and automatic behavior (Bamberg et al. 2003), others argue this results in a different class of consumer behavior, in which attitudes towards the product and intentions to buy that product play a minor role. This class of consumer behavior could better be understood as based on a different mode decision making relying on heuristics and associations rather than elaboration (Kahneman 2003). This may explain both habitual and automatic behavior as well as other decisions outside conscious control, like impulse buying. In practice marketers use many techniques relating to these unconscious, unplanned behavior to entice consumers to exhibit behavior (see e.g. Cialdini 2006). Nevertheless while theories for planned behavior are fairly mature and complete, theoretical views on this type of unconscious, heuristic and automatic decision making remain remarkably underdeveloped to date (Glöckner and Witteman 2010).

5 Reflection

Models of consumer behavior that start with the perception of the products and its attributes, the evaluation of this product along its attributes to form or activate an existing attitude, which then leads to formation of a behavioral intention and ultimately behavior have dominated consumer behavior research for several decades. These models are intuitively easy to understand as they are linear, and follow a logical chain of arguments going from product to behavior. These models do however only explain some part of actual consumer behavior. This in to some extent unavoidable, as human beings are complex entities and their behavior at any moment in time is influenced by many more personality factors and contextual and personal situation than can be meaningfully captured in a simplified model of consumer behavior.

An approach that may lead to improvement might be to think of consumer decision making as a way to reach goals and fulfil motivations. While many consumer models implicitly take account of goals and motivation, this subordinate role does not give them their full place. In the practice of consumer research the focus of many studies of attitudes is even conducted largely independent from personal and context based influence. To improve predictive relevance of attitudes on behavior, inclusion of goals and motivations both during decision making as well as during the actual behavior into our models is needed. It has, for example, been shown that a lot of the behavior consumers exhibit is motivated by a desire to conspicuously show yourself to others. Consumer behavior in those case is thus often motivated by an identity confirmation goal (Oyserman 2009); either a personal identity (I behave like this, hence I am being consistent with what I am) or a social identity (I behave like this, hence I am a clear member of this social group). The identity of the consumer may lead to more extreme, coherent and behavior predictive attitudes towards attitude congruent behavior.

There are considerable differences in the way attitudes and intentions are measured (Reinders et al. 2013). Such differences in measures makes it difficult to compare consumer behavior studies and judge the value of them in comparison to each other. In addition, the use of a broad range of scales, often validated in different ways makes it hard to judge the quality of used instruments. As in all sciences in consumer science as well, the quality of any data depends on the quality of the measurement instruments and their calibration. Therefore, I want to re-emphasize the importance of developing and using high quality measures that are adequate, reliable and valid operationalizations of the constructs we aim to measure (Churchill 1979). This will make the development of surveys and questionnaires more labor intensive and requires a high level of expertise. If we take our science as a serious discipline we should be prepared to make this investment as this will also lead to more robust, better, and more comparable outcomes—which will benefit the field of consumer behavior research as a whole.

Research into heuristic and unconscious predictors of consumer behavior has taken flight since the mid 1990s. There has been much attention to developing new techniques to measure consumer thoughts, such as the implicit association test, biometric data, eye-gaze analysis and neuroimaging (fMRI) being. Many of these techniques are reaching a level of maturity where relevant response can be measured. Nevertheless theoretical understanding of what part of consumer decision making these new measures actually address is lagging behind (Glöckner and Witteman 2010). For consumer behavior, the added value for consumer behavior research, purely based on measuring such unconscious measures seems limited to date (Greenwald et al. 2009). Nevertheless these measures may give important novel insights if they lead to better understanding of underlying decision making processes, which requires that the theory is developed. In consumer research it will be one of the challenges for the coming years to connect unconscious and conscious decision making.

In spite of all their shortcomings, consumer behavior models that present a linear progression from perception, to attitude, to intention, to behavior can still provide a meaningful tool for consumer behavior experts to describe and predict consumer behavior, if applied within their boundaries, while accepting the limitations. One caveat with the use of these models is that behind a seemingly simple model, many subtle assumptions are hidden. Some of these have been discussed in the current contribution (e.g. determination of salient attributes, specifying relevant level of correspondence/abstraction, whether the studied behavior falls within the remit of the chosen model). To make the best use of these models, consumer behavior experts should be aware of these assumptions and consciously chose to what extent it matters whether and to what extent they matter or not.

References

Aarts, H., & Dijksterhuis, A. (2000). The automatic activation of goal-directed behaviour: The case of travel habit. *Journal of Environmental Psychology, 20*(1), 75–82.

Ajzen, I. (1991). The theory of planned behavior. *Organizational Behavior and Human Decision Processes, 50*(2), 179–211.

Armitage, C. J., & Conner, M. (2000). Efficacy of the theory of planned behaviour: A meta-analytic review. *British Journal of Social Psychology, 40*, 471–499.

Bagozzi, R. P. (2007). The legacy of the technology acceptance model and a proposal for a paradigm shift. *Journal of the Association of Information Systems, 8*(4), 244–254.

Bamberg, S., Ajzen, I., & Schmidt, P. (2003). Choice of travel mode in the theory of planned behavior: The roles of past behavior, habit, and reasoned action. *Basic and Applied Social Psychology, 25*, 175–187.

Bredahl, L. (2001). Determinants of consumer attitudes and purchase intentions with regard to genetically modified foods—results of a cross-national survey. *Journal of Consumer Policy, 24* (1), 23–61.

Churchill, G. A. J. (1979). A paradigm for developing better measures of marketing constructs. *Journal of Marketing, 16*, 64–73.

Cialdini, R. B. (2006). *Influence: The psychology of persuasion* (Revised ed.). New York: Harper Business.

Clore, G. L., & Schnall, S. (2005). The influences of affect on attitude. In D. Albarracín, B. T. Johnson, & M. P. Zanna (Eds.), *Handbook of attitudes* (pp. 437–490). Mahwah, NJ: Erlbaum.

Conrey, F. R., Sherman, J. W., Gawronski, B., Hugenberg, K., & Groom, C. J. (2005). Separating multiple processes in implicit social cognition: the quad model of implicit task performance. *Journal of personality and social psychology, 89*(4), 469.

Crano, W. D., & Prislin, R. (2006). Attitudes and persuasion. *Annual Review of Psychology, 57*, 345–374.

Davis, F. D. (1989). Perceived usefulness, perceived ease of use, and user acceptance of information technology. *MIS Quarterly, 13*(3), 319–340.

Dismukes, R. K. (2012). Prospective memory in workplace and everyday situations. *Current Directions in Psychological Science, 21*(4), 215–220. doi:10.1177/0963721412447621.

Eagly, A. H., & Chaiken, S. (1993). *The psychology of attitudes*. Fort Worth, TX: Harcourt Brace Jovanovich.

Fazio, R. H. (2001). On the automatic activation of associated evaluations: An overview. *Cognition and Emotion, 15*(2), 115–141.

Fazio, R. H. (2007). Attitudes as object-evaluation associations of varying strength. *Social Cognition, 25*(5), 603–637.

Frewer, L. J, Fischer, A. R. H, van den Brink, P. J., Byrne, P., Brock, T., Brown, C., Crocker, J., Goerlitz, G., Hart, A., Scholderer, J., & Solomon, K. (2008) Potential for the adaptation of probabilistic risk assessments by end-users and decision–makers. *Human and Ecological Risk Assessment, 14*, 166–178.

Gawronski, B., & Bodenhausen, G. V. (2011). The associative-propositional evaluation model. Theory, evidence, and open questions. *Advances in Experimental Social Psychology, 44*, 59–127.

Glöckner, A., & Witteman, C. (2010). Beyond dual-process models: A categorisation of processes underlying intuitive judgement and decision making. *Thinking and Reasoning, 16*(1), 1–25.

Goodall, C. E. (2011). An overview of implicit measures of attitudes: Methods, mechanisms, strengths, and limitations. *Communication Methods and Measures, 5*(3), 203–222.

Greenwald, A. G., McGhee, D. E., & Schwartz, J. L. (1998). Measuring individual differences in implicit cognition: The implicit association test. *Journal of personality and social psychology, 74*(6), 1464.

Greenwald, A. G., Poehlman, T. A., Uhlmann, E. L., & Banaji, M. R. (2009). Understanding and Using the Implicit Association Test: III. Meta-Analysis of Predictive Validity. *Journal of Personality and Social Psychology, 97*(1), 17–41.

Haidt, J. (2007). The new synthesis in moral psychology. *Science, 316*(5827), 998–1002.

Hofmann, W., Gawronski, B., Gschwendner, T., Le, H., & Schmitt, M. (2005). A meta-analysis on the correlation between the Implicit Association Test and explicit self-report measures. *Personality and Social Psychology Bulletin, 31*(10), 1369–1385.

Holland, R. W., Verplanken, B., & Van Knippenberg, A. (2002). On the nature of attitude-behavior relations: The strong guide, the weak follow. *European Journal of Social Psychology, 32*(6), 869–876.

Hübner, G., & Kaiser, F. G. (2006). The moderating role of the attitude-subjective norms conflict on the link between moral norms and intention. *European Psychologist, 11*(2), 99–109.

Jonas, K., Broemer, P., & Diehl, M. (2000). Attitudinal ambivalence. *European Review of Social Psychology, 11*, 35–74.

Kahneman, D. (2003). A perspective on judgment and choice: Mapping bounded rationality. *American Psychologist, 58*(9), 697–720.

Kaiser, F. G., Woelfing, S., & Fuhrer, U. (1999). Environmental attitude and ecological behaviour. *Journal of Environmental Psychology, 19*(1), 1–19.

Kaiser, F. G., Schultz, P. W., & Scheuthle, H. (2007). The theory of planned behavior without compatibility? Beyond method bias and past trivial associations. *Journal of Applied Social Psychology, 37*(7), 1522–1544.

Krosnick, J. A., Boninger, D. S., Chuang, Y. C., Berent, M. K., & Carnot, C. G. (1993). Attitude strength: One construct or many related constructs? *Journal of Personality and Social Psychology, 95*(9), 1132–1151.

Lebel, E. P., & Paunonen, S. V. (2011). Sexy but often unreliable: The impact of unreliability on the replicability of experimental findings with implicit measures. *Personality and Social Psychology Bulletin, 37*(4), 570–583.

Lee, C. J., Scheufele, D. A., & Lewenstein, B. V. (2005). Public attitudes toward emerging technologies: Examining the interactive effects of cognitions and affect on public attitudes toward nanotechnology. *Science Communication, 27*(2), 240–267.

Nordgren, L. F., van Harreveld, F., & van der Pligt, J. (2006). Ambivalence, discomfort, and motivated information processing. *Journal of Experimental Social Psychology, 42*(2), 252–258.

Ouellette, J. A., & Wood, W. (1998). Habit and intention in everyday life: The multiple processes by which past behavior predicts future behavior. *Psychological Bulletin, 124*(1), 54–74.

Oyserman, D. (2009). Identity-based motivation: Implications for action-readiness, procedural-readiness, and consumer behavior. *Journal of Consumer Psychology, 19*(3), 250–260.

Petty, R. E., & Cacioppo, J. T. (1986). *Communication and persuasion: Central and peripheral routes to attitude change*. New York: Springer.

Reinders, M. J., van der Lans, I. A., Fischer, A. R. H., & van Trijp, H. C. M. (2013) A review to collate information on external communication as a basis of innovation success. Connect4Action Deliverable. Wageningen.

Ronteltap, A., van Trijp, J. C. M., Renes, R. J., & Frewer, L. J. (2007). Consumer acceptance of technology-based food innovations: Lessons for the future of nutrigenomics. *Appetite, 49*(1), 1–17.

Sandberg, T., & Conner, M. (2008). Anticipated regret as an additional predictor in the theory of planned behaviour: A meta-analysis. *British Journal of Social Psychology, 47*(4), 589–606. doi:10.1348/014466607x258704.

Schuman, H., & Presser, S. (1996). Attitude strength and the concept of crystallization. In H. Schuman & S. Presser (Eds.), *Questions and answers in attitude surveys; experiments on question form, wording, and context* (pp. 251–273). Thousand Oaks, CA: Sage.

Schwartz, S. H. (1994). Are there universal aspects in the structure and contents of human values? *Journal of Social Issues, 50*(4), 19–45.

Schwarz, N. (2007). Attitude construction: Evaluation in context. *Social Cognition, 25*(5), 638–656.

Tormala, Z. L., & Petty, R. E. (2002). What doesn't kill me makes me stronger: The effects of resisting persuasion on attitude certainty. *Journal of Personality and Social Psychology, 83*(6), 1298–1313.

Trope, Y., & Liberman, N. (2010). Construal-level theory of psychological distance. *Psychological Review, 117*(2), 440–463. doi:10.1037/a0018963.

Van Giesen, R. I., Fischer, A. R. H., Van Dijk, H., & Van Trijp, H. C. M. (2015). Affect and cognition in attitude formation toward familiar and unfamiliar attitude objects. *PLoS ONE, 10* (10). doi:10.1371/journal.pone.0141790.

Venkatesh, V., Thong, J. Y. L., & Xu, X. (2012). Consumer acceptance and use of information technology: Extending the unified theory of acceptance and use of technology. *MIS Quarterly Management Information Systems, 36*(1), 157–178.

Vermeir, I., & Verbeke, W. (2006). Sustainable food consumption: Exploring the consumer "attitude—Behavioral intention" gap. *Journal of Agricultural and Environmental Ethics, 19* (2), 169–194.

Consumer Products and Consumer Behavior

Antony Davies

1 Theoretical Approaches to the Study of Consumer Behavior

Most research into consumer behavior follows one of five approaches depending on the tools and assumptions employed: economic approach, psychodynamic approach, behaviorist approach, cognitive approach, and humanistic approach.

The economic approach takes as its starting point that consumers are economic agents who seek to maximize their happiness subject to constraints. The economic approach assumes that humans are rational and that they correctly employ information available to them. The psychodynamic approach assumes that consumer behavior arises from biologically driven instinct. In modeling man as a rational animal, the economic approach tends to ignore the "animal" part in favor of the "rational" part, while the psychodynamic approach tends to ignore the "rational" part in favor of the "animal". The behaviorist approach is akin to the psychodynamic approach in that it tends to regard human choice as being driven by impulses rather than cognition. Unlike the psychodynamic approach, the behaviorist approach holds that human behavior is not driven by biology but by learned responses to external stimuli. Where the psychodynamic approach regards human behavior as the playing out of imperatives arising from who we are, the behaviorist approach regards human behavior as the playing out of imperatives arising from what we have experienced. The cognitive approach assumes that human behavior arises largely from cognition wherein the person processes information gleaned from his environment and society. In this branch of thought, emphasis is placed on the processes of perceiving stimuli, encoding those stimuli as memory, thinking about the memories, and developing motivations for action from thought and

A. Davies (✉)
Duquesne University, 130 Green Lane, Greenburg, PA 15601, USA
e-mail: antony@antolin-davies.com

© Springer International Publishing AG 2017
G. Emilien et al. (eds.), *Consumer Perception of Product Risks and Benefits*,
DOI 10.1007/978-3-319-50530-5_18

emotion. The humanistic approach is more holistic in that it assumes that the human is, together, rational, emotional, spiritual, and animal. Consequently, not only is human behavior is influenced by all these factors together, but through self-awareness, the person can choose his behavior rather having it thrust upon him by biology, stimulus, or logic.

2 Consumer Choice in the Presence of Incomplete Information

Popular conceptions of industries tend toward the extreme and theoretical cases of industry structure: perfect competition and monopoly. On one hand, people tend to accept the theoretical case of monopoly without question. Much concern about "reining in markets" revolves around concern that this theoretical case is, if not real, is a real possibility. On the other hand, people tend to dismiss the theoretical case of perfect competition. When told that competition is good because it encourages low prices and large selection, people commonly respond, "well, that might be true in theory".

Interestingly, in both of these extreme cases, the consumer plays only the nominal role of purchaser. Neither case requires any contribution on the part of the consumer beyond purchasing the product. In perfect competition, there are so many firms and the products, service, and support are so similar that consumers simply look for the lowest price. The result is that all firms end up charging the same price for the same product. The consumer's choice reduces to a simple binary: buy or don't buy. In the case of monopoly, the consumer's role is largely unchanged. The monopoly firm has no competitors, so (as with perfect competition) the consumer faces a single price for a single product. Again, the consumer's choice is largely binary: buy or don't buy. Monopoly firms will attempt to extract additional revenue by offering "upgrade" variations that cost the firm little. Economists call this, "price discrimination." The purpose of price discrimination is to encourage each consumer to pay the maximum that consumer is willing to pay. But the consumer's choice as to which level of upgrade to purchase usually comes after the consumer has already determined that he will buy the product at all.

Consumer choice becomes interesting in the intermediate cases. Fortunately (at least for consumer behavior researchers), the intermediate cases comprise the overwhelming majority of cases. In contrast to the extremes of monopoly and perfect competition, most industries are better characterized as monopolistically competitive. For the purpose of this discussion, oligopoly industries can be included in the discussion of monopolistic competition when consumers regard the oligopolists' products as heterogeneous.

Monopolistically competitive firms produce a variation (or multiple variations) of a product that is distinguished, if not in an objective sense then at least in the minds of the consumers, from other variations. Each variation is called a "brand."

The term is not to be confused with, "brand name" which refers to the manufacturer. Two brands may come from different manufacturers (e.g., Nike sports shoes versus Reebok sports shoes), or the same manufacturer (Toyota Sienna versus Toyota Highlander), or may be variations on the same product from the same manufacturer (e.g., Sherwin-Williams flat white latex paint versus Sherwin-Williams gloss white latex paint). Brands vary according to *salient attributes*—attributes that the consumer deems important enough to influence the consumer's choice. Where consumer behavior is concerned, it doesn't matter whether brands differ objectively. All that is necessary is that consumers believe that they differ. Taste tests of bottled water versus tap water bear this out. When told they are tasting bottled versus tap, subjects report that the bottled water tastes better. But in blind taste tests, subjects report no difference in taste (Teillet et al. 2010). As consumers don't purchase water under blind conditions, it is their beliefs that matter, not the objective reality. These beliefs will drive more complex behaviors than we observe in either monopoly or perfectly competitive markets.

When faced with the many brands of a monopolistically competitive industry, the consumer encounters an information problem that does not manifest in the extreme cases of monopoly and perfect competition. In a monopolistically competitive industry, the many differing brands present a triple problem for the consumer. First, there are many brands, each of which the consumer perceives to be meaningfully different from the others. Second, given the large number of brands, it is too costly for the consumer to obtain the information necessary to make the best purchase decision because (a) brands may exist of which the consumer is unaware and, (b) even for brands which the consumer knows to exist, the consumer may be unsure of the qualities of the brands' salient attributes. For example, a typical consumer is aware of many, but not all, brand names of beers. Also, the same consumer may have never tried some of the brands he could name and so may have no first-hand knowledge of the qualities of those brands' salient attributes. Third, the consumer is aware of his incomplete knowledge and so knows that he is making an imperfect choice (Kivetz and Simonson 2000).

As in voter-behavior models, the consumer faces a rational ignorance problem wherein the best decision the consumer can make is one made without full information because, beyond a certain point, the marginal benefit of having additional relevant information is less than the marginal cost of obtaining the information (Caplan 2001; Bettman 1971). Many products come with costs other than price. For example, cigarettes come with health costs, small cars come with safety costs, computers come with obsolescence costs. The term "benefit" used throughout this contribution is benefit net of these expected costs. For example, the benefit a smoker anticipates from a cigarette is, for the purposes of this analysis, the satisfaction the smoker receives from smoking a cigarette less the (present discounted value of) damage the smoker expects to his health, the psychic cost to his worrying about his health, etc.

So long as the marginal benefit of having additional information exceeds the marginal cost of acquiring the information, the consumer will expend more effort on collecting and processing information. The marginal benefit of having additional information takes two forms: a reduction in *external uncertainty* and a reduction in *internal uncertainty*. External uncertainty arises from the consumer's incomplete information about what brands exist and the brands' salient attributes (price in understood to be a salient attribute). Internal uncertainty arises from the consumer's incomplete information about the utility, or satisfaction, he will obtain from a given set of attributes (Davies and Cline 2005).

For example, the benefit to having more information about competing brands of chewing gum is relatively small. While there are likely brands of chewing gum of which the consumer is unaware, the attributes of chewing gum (regardless of the brand) are small in number and tend not to vary overly much across brands. Thus, the consumer faces little external uncertainty. Similarly, assuming the consumer has had chewing gum before, there will be little internal uncertainty as to the utility the consumer will receive from a given set of chewing gum attributes. Hence, the consumer experiences relatively little internal uncertainty. Facing little uncertainty, the consumer does not stand to gain much from acquiring additional information about chewing gum brands and attributes. Compounding this is the fact that the cost of making an erroneous purchase decision is low—at worst, the consumer selects a brand that he ends up hating and is out the price of a pack of gum. So, we would expect the consumer to expend about as much energy as it takes to scan the shelf in front of him and grab the first pack that he recognizes. That is, the consumer will expend very little effort acquiring more information about competing brands.

Conversely, the benefit to having more information about competing brands of cars is relatively large. Given advertising and the fact that people see many cars every day, it is unlikely that there exist brands of which the consumer is unaware. However, the consumer is very likely to be unaware of all the brands' salient attributes (external uncertainty), and is unlikely to be sure about his reactions to those attributes (internal uncertainty). For example, a consumer might be aware that some brands have all wheel drive and even know exactly how all-wheel drive works. But, if the consumer has never owned a car with all-wheel drive, the consumer may incorrectly judge his reaction to the attribute. That is, the consumer may not know how much he likes (or dislikes) all-wheel drive until he actually experiences driving an all-wheel drive car over time and under varied road conditions. In addition to internal uncertainty, the consumer faces external uncertainty. Number of seats, engine power, mileage, safety features, sound system, warranty, expected maintenance costs, color, detailing, available upgrade packages, price, and financing options are just a few of the salient attributes about which the consumer will likely have limited knowledge. Where a car is concerned, not only does the consumer likely experience significant uncertainty, but the cost of making an erroneous purchase decision is high. Consequently, the consumer will tend to expend significant effort acquiring more information about competing brands (Petty and Cacioppo 1990).

3   Consumer Choice and Observed Context Effects

Faced with a choice from among many heterogeneous variations on a product, not only can it be irrational for the consumer to collect all the information necessary to make the best purchase decision, but the consumer will be aware that it is irrational yet forced to make a decision nonetheless. Experimental evidence suggests, however, that the consumer does not make the choice blindly but rather relies on low-cost heuristics to guide him to a better choice. The consumer constructs these heuristics from his perception of how the brands are positioned relative to each other according to their salient attributes. In the consumer behavior literature, these heuristics are known as *context effects*. Context effects are the effects on the likelihood of consumer choice due to the juxtaposition of brands according to the similarities of their salient attributes.

The importance of context effects in the consumer choice process is well-documented (Payne 1982; Huber and Puto 1983; Simonson and Tversky 1992; Heath and Chatterjee 1995; Slovic 1995; Bhargava et al. 2000). Several context effects identified through experimentation are:

- *Attraction Effect*: The likelihood of consumer choice for a target brand increases when a new, but strictly inferior, brand is positioned close to the target brand.
- *Substitution Effect*: The likelihood of consumer choice for a target brand decreases when a new, but asymmetrically inferior, brand is positioned close to the target brand.
- *Compromise Effect*: The likelihood of consumer choice for two target brands decreases when a new brand is positioned between the two target brands.
- *Lone-Alternative Effect*: The likelihood of consumer choice for a set of similar target brands decreases when a new brand is positioned far from the existing brands.
- *Polarization Effect*: The likelihood of consumer choice for two disparate target brands increases when a new brand is positioned between the target brands.

Experimental research largely focused on the existence of context effects. The original stream of experimental literature left largely unaddressed the question of *why* the context effects exist. The answer, of course, lies in consumer psychology. Attempts to explain individual context effects include Parducci's range-frequency theory, categorization effects, social judgment theory, rank based preferences, and tradeoff contrast (Parducci 1965; Kardes et al. 1989; Simonson and Tversky 1992; Pan and Lehmann 1993; Prelec et al. 1997; Davies and Cline 2005; Sinn et al. 2007). However, these explanations were post-hoc and applied to individual context effects only. Davies and Cline (2005) proposed a set of heuristics that derived from psychological principles and explained all observed context effects in a single general framework. Subsequent discussion in this contribution draws from their framework.

4 Consumer Choice and Uncertainty

The consumer choice process is complicated by two categories of uncertainty: external and internal. These uncertainties create a discrepancy between the satisfaction a consumer expects to receive from consuming a brand and the satisfaction the consumer actually receives. These uncertainties make it difficult for the consumer to make the optimal purchase decision.

External uncertainties arise from the consumer's incomplete knowledge about brands' objective salient attributes:

- *Partial information.* The consumer is unaware of all the brands that exist.
- *Measurement error.* The consumer incorrectly evaluates brands' salient attributes.
- *Obsolete information.* The consumer fails to update his evaluation of brands' salient attributes as those attributes change over time.

Internal uncertainties arise from the consumer's incomplete knowledge about the consumer's subjective reactions to brands' salient attributes:

- *Absolute utility error.* The consumer is uncertain as to the amount of satisfaction he will receive from a brand's given salient attribute.
- *Relative utility error.* The consumer is uncertain as to the rate of tradeoff of satisfaction derived from one salient attribute versus another.

For example, a consumer who is choosing a brand of beer may not be aware of all the brands that exist and are available to him (partial information). For those beers of which the consumer is aware, the consumer may think that a particular brand is high in calories when it isn't, or has a hoppy taste when it doesn't (measurement error). For those beers of which the consumer is aware and for which the consumer has correctly evaluated the salient attributes, the consumer may be unaware that a particular brand altered its formula and now contains more calories than before (obsolete information). Each of these sources of uncertainty contribute to the likelihood of the consumer making a sub-optimal choice when selecting a brand of beer.

Even if the consumer has full information about all the brands and their salient attributes—that is, the consumer experiences no external uncertainty—the consumer is still subject to internal uncertainty. For example, the consumer may believe that he likes hoppy beers. But perhaps from changing tastes, what he is eating with the beer, the environment in which he is drinking it, or even how many hoppy beers he has recently consumed, the consumer realizes upon tasting the beer that he is not getting the satisfaction he expected from the hoppiness. This is absolute utility error. Unlike with measurement error, the consumer has not misjudged the beer's hoppiness—the consumer would report that the beer is precisely as hoppy as he expected. Rather he has misjudged his reaction to the hoppiness—the consumer would report that, upon trying the beer, he realizes that he isn't "in the mood" for a hoppy beer.

With relative utility error, the consumer doesn't misjudge his reaction to the beer's salient attributes but rather his willingness to trade off those attributes. For example, the consumer may have full information about the taste and the calories of two beers (i.e., the consumer has no external uncertainty). The consumer may also correctly anticipate his reaction to each of the beers' tastes and to each of the beers' calorie contents (i.e., the consumer has no absolute utility error). The consumer knows the extent to which he prefers the taste of brand A to that of brand B and also knows that brand A has 10 percent more calories than brand B. But, the consumer misjudges the extent to which he is willing to trade off better taste for fewer calories and so erroneously chooses to consume brand B.

5 Representing the Consumer's Mental Map of the Product Market

The reason a consumer cares about brand attributes at all is because the consumer believes he will obtain different levels of satisfaction from different levels of each salient attribute. Were that not the case, the attribute would not be salient and, therefore, not of interest to the consumer. Note that what matters is the consumer's belief, not the reality, as it is the belief that affects his behavior. For example, a consumer who believes that genetically modified organisms (GMOs) are not harmful, or who is unaware of controversies surrounding GMOs, will ignore whether competing brands contain GMOs—even if GMOs are, indeed, harmful. Similarly, a consumer who believes that "frost brewing" beer improves its taste will compare competing brands based on whether they are frost brewed—even if frost brewing has no effect on taste but is simply a marketing gimmick. This is not to say that consumers will remain in a state of ignorance. Over time, consumers will tend to revise their beliefs based on experience and new information (Akcura et al. 2004). However, at the moment in time when the consumer makes a purchase decision, the consumer is bound by his current beliefs. Beer provides a good example of this sequence of belief-trial-revision. Some beer producers described their beers as "fire brewed." Much marketing effort went into convincing consumers that fire brewing generated a better taste. For a while, many consumers responded by associating fire brewing with better taste. With experience, consumers determined that fire brewing had no real effect on taste. Marketers then described beers as "ice brewed." The same sequence of consumer response followed by realization that ice brewing had no appreciable effect on taste ensued. Similarly used terms include "premium," and "lite"—neither one of which has an agreed definition, but are simply used to alter consumers' beliefs about the beers.

Because the satisfaction gained from levels of the salient attributes is what matters to consumers, consumers will mentally position brands relative to each other according to the satisfaction the levels of the salient attributes represent. For example, suppose a consumer is about to purchase a gallon of milk. The consumer

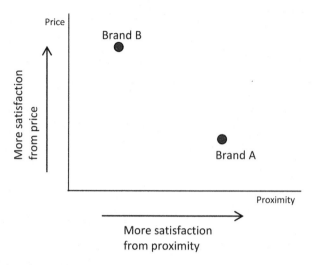

Fig. 1 Depiction of the utility obtained from a brand's attributes

is concerned with price but is also concerned with helping local businesses and so wants to buy local goods where possible. If there is no other attribute that is important enough to the consumer to alter the consumer's purchase decision, then the consumer recognizes two salient attributes: price and proximity. The consumer gets greater satisfaction from a lower price and greater satisfaction the closer is the manufacturer's location to the consumer's home.

Figure 1 depicts the consumer's mental map of these brands. Distance along the axis denotes the consumer's expected satisfaction from the level of the attribute, not the level of the attribute itself. For example, in this map, the further up the vertical axis a brand is located, the greater is the satisfaction the consumer receives from the brand's price. That is, the further up the axis the brand is, the lower is its price. The further to the right a brand is located, the greater is the satisfaction the consumer receives from the brand's manufacturer's proximity to the consumer. That is, the further to the right the brand is, the closer is its manufacturer.

Representing the consumer's mental map in this way gives us the means to express easily directional changes in satisfaction the consumer gets from changes in levels of the salient attributes (up is better than down, right is better than left) without having to quantify the changes. Also left unaddressed is how the consumer resolves tradeoffs. For example, the figure shows that the consumer receives more satisfaction from Brand A's proximity than from Brand B's proximity, but more satisfaction from Brand B's price than from Brand A's price. The figure shows that the consumer will have to weigh the tradeoff of Brand A's better proximity for Brand B's better price, but does not indicate which the consumer will prefer.

6   Brand Clustering

Humans' natural proclivity for pattern recognition causes consumers (consciously or subconsciously) to group the brands of which they are aware according to similarities in the levels of the brands' salient attributes. This is called, *brand clustering* (Bettman 1971). Reinforcing consumers' tendencies to mentally cluster brands, producers will produce brands with salient attribute levels that match consumers' preferences. To the extent that consumers' preferences are heterogeneous but clustered, brands' attributes will also be clustered. For example, suppose a large number of consumers prefers coats that are very stylish, but aren't concerned with durability. Another large number of consumers prefers coats that are very durable, but aren't concerned with style. However, few consumers prefer coats that are moderately stylish and moderately durable. In an attempt to maximize their market shares, coat manufacturers will produce brands that cluster around one or the other of these two attributes, but will tend not to produce brands that are midway between the two. As a counterargument, one can imagine waiting until next season to get this season's stylish coats at a lower price. However, that argument either (a) introduces a third salient attribute, "current season," and again we'll see clustering but this time in three dimensions, or (b) muddles the definition of "stylish" as style itself is a function of time. Consequently, clustering of consumer preferences leads to brand clustering (Fig. 2).

Figure 3 shows a consumer's mental mapping of the four brands of which the consumer is aware. The axes measure utility derived from the indicated attributes. Consequently, the further up a brand is located, the more utility the consumer derives from the brand's style (i.e., the brand is more stylish). The further to the right a brand is located, the more utility the consumer derives from the brand's price (i.e., the brand is <u>less</u> expensive).

Brands A and B are similar in that their styles provide the consumer much satisfaction while their prices provide the consumer little satisfaction. Brands C and D are similar in that their styles provide the consumer little satisfaction while their

Fig. 2 Four brands arranged into two clusters

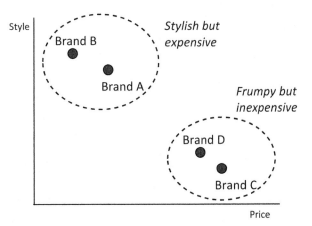

Fig. 3 The cluster frontier is formed by combining the best attributes of the brands perceived to exist within the cluster

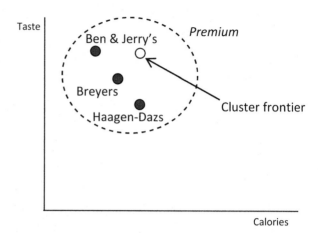

prices provide the consumer much satisfaction. Mentally, the consumer will regard Brands A and B as the "stylish but expensive" brands, and Brands C and D as the "frumpy but inexpensive" brands.

Of course, it is possible that consumer preferences do not cluster for some products and some attributes but are rather uniformly distributed along some salient attributes. For example, consumers don't perceive much meaningful difference between Internet bandwidth of 6 and 10 Mbps, so providers sell bandwidth in discrete chunks (6, 30 Mbps, etc.). Meanwhile, consumers do perceive meaningful difference between 5 gallons of gas and 6 gallons of gas, so retailers sell gasoline in whatever quantity each individual consumer wants. The result is that, while quantity is a salient attribute for both bandwidth and gasoline, Internet service brands cluster according to quantity of bandwidth but gasoline retailers do not cluster according to quantity of gasoline.

7 Non-compensatory Consideration and Compensatory Choice

A high-involvement purchase decision is one in which is there is a high opportunity cost to selecting a sub-optimal brand, and it is costly to obtain information necessary for selecting the optimal brand or it is cognitively costly to weigh the tradeoffs of various brands' different attribute levels.

When a consumer faces a high-involvement purchase decision in the presence of many competing brands, the consumer's choice process divides into two phases: non-compensatory and compensatory decision making (Biehal and Chakravarti 1986; Kardes et al. 1993). The term, "compensatory" refers to the consumer's willingness to tradeoff a lesser level of one salient attribute for a greater level of another. A salient attribute is non-compensatory when the consumer regards some minimal level of an attribute as necessary. When an attribute is non-compensatory, there is no increase in the level of another attribute that can compensate for a decrease in the level of the non-compensatory attribute.

For example, a consumer who is part of a family of four is looking to purchase a house and requires three bedrooms. Suppose the consumer finds five bedrooms more desirable than four. The consumer would be willing to tradeoff five bedrooms for four in exchange for a more desirable location, or a bigger yard, or a lesser price. But, the consumer is unwilling to tradeoff four bedrooms for three no matter how desirable the other attributes. In the consumer's mind, the salient attribute, "number of bedrooms," is non-compensatory at four, but compensatory above four.

Because weighing attribute tradeoffs is cognitively costly, consumers will use non-compensatory attribute levels to reduce the number of brands they must compare. This leads naturally to a two-stage choice process. In the first stage (called *consideration*), the consumer eliminates from consideration all groups (or *clusters*) of brands that do not satisfy the minimum non-compensatory attribute requirements. For example, the consumer will eliminate from consideration all houses with less than four bedrooms. The consideration phase is less cognitively costly because the consumer is eliminating whole clusters of brands based on a simple rule. In the consideration phase, the consumer does not weigh attribute level tradeoffs, and need not examine all of a brand's attributes—if a brand fails to meet the minimum acceptable attribute level for any one attribute, that brand is removed from consideration regardless of the levels of its other attributes.

The second phase of the consumer choice process is choice-given-consideration, or simply, "choice." The choice phase is cognitively costly because the consumer must consider each salient attribute for each brand and weigh tradeoffs among those attributes. This problem can easily become intractable. For example, for just five competing brands of ice cream with just three salient attributes (taste, calories, and price), the consumer would need to make 30 unique comparisons—each of which requires weighing the satisfaction the consumer expects to get from two attributes—in order to determine which brand was best. For example, there are more than 220 brands of beer in the US. If there were only three salient attributes for beer (for example, price, taste, aroma), a consumer would have to make more than 72,000 comparisons to determine which beer was best. A consumer who could make one comparison per second would require 20 hours to decide which beer to buy. That we don't take hours to make most purchase decisions indicates that consumers are eliminating large numbers of brands from consideration prior to weighing attribute tradeoffs.

8   Product Market Characteristics

Consumers juxtapose what information they (believe they) have about the brands they are aware exist to create a perceived product market. Experimental evidence suggests that consumers use these product market characteristics to form heuristics that guide their decision-making. Characteristics of the perceived product market include:

- *Cluster size*: The number of brands the consumer perceives to exist in each cluster.
- *Cluster variance*: The degree of difference among the brands within a cluster of the values of the brands' salient attributes.
- *Cluster frontier*: The (possibly) hypothetical ideal brand that is an agglomeration of the best observed salient attribute values among the brands in a cluster.
- *Brand variance*: The degree of uncertainty about a brand's true salient attribute values.
- *Granularity*: The ratio of the degree of brand dissimilarities between clusters to brand similarities within clusters.

The first two characteristics (cluster size, cluster variance) influence the consideration phase of the consumer choice process. The more brands a person perceives to exist within a cluster, the more consumers the person perceives are choosing brands within the cluster. In this way, the number of brands serves as a proxy for what others are purchasing. For example, if a person perceives that greater numbers of consumers are choosing Androids over iPhones then, other things constant, the person would be more apt also to choose an Android. This is a variation on the social behavior principle that, if a crowd of people gathers, others will join so as to partake in whatever is attracting the rest of the crowd.

9   Consideration

A person may have a predilection for brands in a cluster that has nothing to do with the number of brands in the cluster. For example, a person may be more likely to consider a suburban apartment to an urban one because the person grew up in a suburban environment—even though the person perceives that a larger number of available apartments exist in the urban environment. However, *changes* in the number of brands the person perceives to exist in a cluster will alter the likelihood of the consumer considering brands within the cluster (Hedgcock and Rao 2009). For example, regardless of where the person grew up, the more ads the person sees for urban apartments (relative to suburban apartments) the greater will be the likelihood of the person considering urban apartments. This gives us the first behavioral heuristic, the cluster size heuristic:

9.1   Cluster Size Heuristic

As the number of brands within a cluster of which a consumer is aware rises, the probability of the consumer considering the cluster increases.

Table 1 A consumer's mental mapping of brands known to the consumer according to attributes the consumer regards as salient

Brand	Price	Resolution		
Logitech C920	$62	1080 p		High-price/high-resolution cluster
Microsoft LifeCam	$52	1080 p		
Logitech C615	$47	1080 p		
Logitech C525	$32	720 p		Low-price/low-resolution cluster
Logitech C310	$32	720 p		
Microsoft HD-3000	$24	720 p		
Logitech C270	$20	720 p		

This cluster size heuristic requires that the brands within a cluster be obviously similar in some meaningful way. For example, various brands of Android phone (Google Nexus, HTC One, Samsung Galaxy S6) are very similar to each other. But various brands of economy cars (Honda Civic, Mazda3, Chevrolet Volt) are less so. Consequently, the cluster size heuristic will tend to be a more useful heuristic when considering Android phones than when considering economy cars. Thought of another way, the more dissimilar brands are within a cluster, the more likely it will seem to the person that the person has incorrectly grouped together into a single cluster brands that properly belong in separate clusters.

For example, suppose a consumer who is looking to purchase a webcam is aware of seven brands and perceives only two salient attributes: price and resolution. Table 1 shows the consumer's mental mapping of the seven brands.

Based on this information, the consumer mentally groups the webcams into two clusters: high-price/high-resolution (Logitech C920, Microsoft LifeCam, Logitech C615), and low-price/low-resolution (Logitech C525, Logitech C310, Microsoft HD-3000, Logitech C270). That there are more brands in the low-price/low-resolution cluster tells us nothing about the consumer's likelihood of considering one cluster over the other. Factors external to the salient attributes of price and resolution will determine the consumer's "baseline" likelihood of consideration for the two clusters. For example, the consumer may be on a tight budget or have limited use for a webcam (which would cause the consumer to favor the low-price/low-resolution cluster), or the consumer may be a professional photographer or an early adopter (which would cause the consumer to favor the high-price/high-resolution cluster). Perhaps through advertising or word-of-mouth, the consumer then becomes aware of an eighth brand, the HP HD 4310. Table 2 shows the consumer's updated mental map.

This new brand is similar to the brands the consumer has already mentally grouped in the high-price/high-resolution cluster. The consumer's awareness of the additional brand triggers the cluster size heuristic and so the likelihood of the consumer considering the high-price/high-resolution cluster increases.

Table 2 The consumer's updated mental map after the consumer becomes aware of an eight brand

Brand	Price	Resolution
HP HD 4310	$62	1080 p
Logitech C920	$62	1080 p
Microsoft LifeCam	$52	1080 p
Logitech C615	$47	1080 p
Logitech C525	$32	720 p
Logitech C310	$32	720 p
Microsoft HD–3000	$24	720 p
Logitech C270	$20	720 p

Table 3 The consumer's updated mental map after the consumer becomes aware of a different eighth brand

Brand	Price	Resolution
Logitech C930e	$95	1080 p
Logitech C920	$62	1080 p
Microsoft LifeCam	$52	1080 p
Logitech C615	$47	1080 p
Logitech C525	$32	720 p
Logitech C310	$32	720 p
Microsoft HD-3000	$24	720 p
Logitech C270	$20	720 p

Alternatively, suppose that the eighth brand of which the consumer becomes aware is not the HP HD 4310, but instead the Logitech C930e. Table 3 shows the consumer's updated mental map when the additional brand is the Logitech C930e rather than the HP HD 4310.

Clearly, the Logitech C930e belongs in the high-price/high-resolution cluster. But notice that, unlike the HP HD 4310, it stands out as markedly more expensive than the other brands in the high-price/high-resolution cluster. More so than with the HP HD 4310, adding the Logitech 930e to the perceived product market may cause the consumer to question whether he has mentally grouped the brands correctly. For example, perhaps there are really three clusters: low-price/low-resolution, medium-price/high-resolution, and high-price/high-resolution. Or, adding the Logitech 930e to the perceived product market may cause the consumer to wonder that he has overlooked the existence of a third salient attribute that is causing the price of the C930e to be so high.

In short, introducing the C930e to the perceived product market increases the cluster size for the high-price/high-resolution cluster, but also causes the consumer to question his mental grouping of the brands. To the extent that the consumer is uncertain about his mental groupings, he will rely less on heuristics based on those groupings. And this gives us the cluster variance heuristic:

9.2 Cluster Variance Heuristic

As dissimilarities among brands in a cluster increase, the probability of the consumer considering the cluster decreases.

10 Choice Given Consideration

In the first phase of the consumer choice process, the consumer uses low-cost non-compensatory criteria to select one cluster of brands for consideration. In the second phase of the choice process, the consumer employs cognitively expensive compensatory criteria to choose a single brand from within the considered cluster. The consumer begins by forming (either consciously or subconsciously) a perception of the perfect brand—a brand that embodies the best levels of the salient attributes of all the brands observed in the considered cluster. For example, suppose a consumer perceives two salient attributes for vanilla ice cream: taste and calories. The consumer mentally divides brands of vanilla ice cream into two clusters: premium (better taste but higher calories) and discount (worse taste but lower calories). In the first stage of the choice process, the person eliminates the discount brands from consideration, leaving the premium cluster. Within the premium cluster, the consumer is aware of the salient attributes of three brands of ice cream (where the taste attribute reflects what the person believes the taste to be— whether from personal experience, word-of-mouth, or some other source). Table 4 shows the consumer's mental map of the brands of which he is aware according to the attributes the consumer regards as salient.

Because the consumer is aware that there are additional brands of which he is unaware, as the consumer considers tradeoffs between taste and calories within the premium cluster, the consumer forms a perception (given his available information) of the ideal brand. In the example in Fig. 3, the ideal brand is an ice cream that has the taste of Ben & Jerry's but the calories of Haagen-Dazs. The location of the ideal brand within the cluster is called the *cluster frontier*.

In this example, the consumer is only aware of three brands. While the consumer can form an image of the ideal brand, he does not know whether the ideal brand actually exists. Table 5 shows the customer's mental mapping of the known brands and the ideal brand. Regardless of whether it actually exists, the ideal brand serves as a standard against which the consumer evaluates the brands of which he is aware.

Table 4 A consumer's mental mapping of brands known to the consumer according to attributes the consumer regards as salient

Brand	Taste (1 = low, 5 = high)	Calories
Ben & Jerry's	5	250
Breyers	4	200
Haagen-Dazs	3	150

Table 5 Comparison of the brands of which the consumer is aware to the consumer's perception of the ideal brand

Brand	Taste (1 = low, 5 = high)	Calories
Ideal Brand	*5*	*150*
Ben & Jerry's	5	250
Breyers	4	200
Haagen-Dazs	3	150

Fig. 4 The consumer perceives that a technological constraint imposes limits on the possible locations of the ideal brand

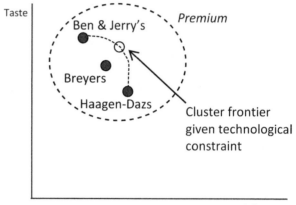

Cluster frontier given technological constraint

Table 6 The consumer's awareness of technological constraints imposes limits on the ideal brand's location

Brand	Taste (1 = low, 5 = high)	Calories
Cluster Frontier	*4.5*	*160*
Ben & Jerry's	5	250
Breyers	4	200
Haagen-Dazs	4	150

Depending on the salient attributes and the consumer's knowledge, the consumer may believe that there are limits, called *technological constraints* that restrict where the ideal brand can be located. Such limits are depicted in Fig. 4. For example, the consumer may believe that good taste and high calories are necessarily related. So, the consumer may believe that it is not possible for a brand to exist that has a taste of 5 and calories of 150. Depending on the consumer's beliefs about the technological constraints, the consumer will mentally shift the location of the cluster frontier to account for the constraints. For example, the consumer may believe that, while a 5–150 combination of taste and calories isn't possible, a "second-best" of 4.5–160 is. Therefore, the consumer's awareness of technological constraints alters the consumer's mental mapping of the brands from that shown in Table 5 to that shown in Table 6.

The consumer's goal is to choose the brand that maximizes his satisfaction. The brands are arranged in the cluster according to the satisfaction that their attributes impart. Therefore, the closer a given brand is to the cluster frontier, the more satisfaction the consumer can expect to receive from the brand. This gives us the cluster frontier heuristic:

10.1 Cluster Frontier Heuristic

The closer a brand is positioned to the cluster frontier, the greater is the probability of choice-given-consideration for that brand. The cluster frontier heuristic requires that the consumer be able to evaluate exactly each known brand's salient attributes. There are many reasons why this might not be possible. It may only be possible to evaluate the salient attribute subjectively (e.g., taste). A consumer's subjective evaluation can vary because of factors external to the brand. For example, if the consumer has recently eaten something sweet, he may rate the taste of low-fat ice creams lower than if he had not. Thus, the consumer's repeated subjective evaluation of a brand's attribute may change making the consumer unsure of the brand's attribute level. Even if the salient attribute can be evaluated objectively (e.g., calories), the consumer may not have a first-hand evaluation of the attribute and so must rely on others' reported evaluations. If those evaluations differ, the consumer will be unsure of the brand's attribute level. Even if others' evaluations agree, the consumer must believe the others' evaluations. If the consumer has reason to suspect that the evaluations, despite the fact that they agree, are not honest or accurately measured, then the consumer will be unsure of the brand's attribute level.

This lack of surety as to a brand's attribute's level is called *brand variance*. In the same way that cluster variance causes the consumer to be less sure of his mental grouping of brands into clusters, brand variance makes the consumer less sure of his positioning of brands within a cluster and, by extension, the position of the cluster frontier. The less sure the consumer is of the brands' positions relative to the cluster frontier, the less able the consumer is to rely on the cluster frontier heuristic. This gives us the brand variance heuristic:

10.2 Brand Variance Heuristic

The greater is a brand's variance, the lesser is the effect of the cluster frontier heuristic.

11   Usefulness of Heuristics

The heuristics are only useful to a consumer to the extent that the consumer is able to mentally group brands into clusters according to their salient attributes. It is the first step—consideration—that simplifies the consumer choice process by whittling down a large number of competing brands to a set small enough that the consumer is willing to apply the cognitively costly evaluation of attribute level tradeoffs. If the consumer is less able (perhaps because of limited knowledge or perhaps because competing brands have not carved out unique market niches) to mentally cluster the brands, then the consumer will be less able to rely on the clustering heuristics. This gives us the final heuristic:

11.1   Granularity Heuristic

The lesser is the ratio of the brand differences within clusters to brand differences across clusters, the lesser are the effects of the cluster size and cluster variance heuristics.

A comparison of a consumer's mental mapping exhibiting high and low granularity is shown in Fig. 5. Compared to high granularity, low granularity implies possible flaws in how the consumer has mentally mapped the brands. It is less clear to the consumer whether Brands A and D belong in the same cluster or different clusters. Also, the larger distances within the clusters hint at possibly more numerous brands the consumer has not observed.

12   Gaining Information: The Iterative Choice Process

Modeling repeated consumer behavior in the presence of incomplete information requires examining the stages of consumer choice and what factors influence each stage. Howard and Sheth (1969) described a process in which a consumer, influenced by external stimuli and moderated by preferences and habit, move from the need to fulfill a desire to the purchase of a product to satisfy that desire. Consumption of the purchased product provides information and experience that influence future purchase decisions. Davies and Cline (2005) present the following iterative choice process that draws on the Howard and Sheth model.

Brands have true attributes that may or may not match the consumer's perception of those attributes. The consumer will gain true satisfaction from consuming a brand that may or may not match the satisfaction the consumer anticipates gaining from that brand. The consumer's perceptions of brands' attributes differ from the true brand attributes due to external uncertainty. The consumer's anticipated satisfaction differs from the satisfaction the consumer will actually attain due to internal uncertainty. Due to these uncertainties, the consumer develops an imperfect mental

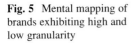

Fig. 5 Mental mapping of brands exhibiting high and low granularity

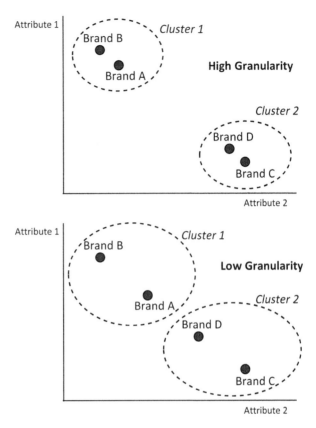

map of the competing brands. The product-market characteristics formalize the mental picture. The consumer uses cognitively inexpensive heuristics that can be described using these product-market characteristics to whittle the competing brands down to a manageable cluster of brands. This is the consideration phase and the manageable set the consumer selects is the considered cluster. The consumer then employs more cognitively expensive heuristics to choose a single brand from among the considered cluster. After the consumer makes a choice and consumes the brand, the consumer gains information. With this information, the consumer can reduce his external and internal uncertainties. This iterative choice process is depicted in Fig. 6.

13   Examples and Applications

Ben Cohen, of Ben & Jerry's ice cream, happily says, "Never trust a skinny ice cream man." Calories, of course, are one of ice cream's few negative attributes. Fundamental marketing principles dictate that a company should not draw attention

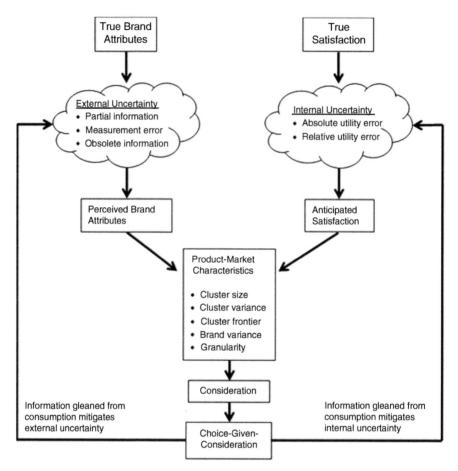

Fig. 6 The iterative consumer choice process

to its products' negative attributes. Yet, there is a case in which such an admission could actually help Ben & Jerry's market share. Suppose the salient attributes for ice cream are taste and calories, and that Ben & Jerry's is flanked within the premium ice cream cluster by two competitors, Brands A and B, as shown in Fig. 7.

Before announcing, "Never trust a skinny ice cream man," the consumer imagines the ideal premium ice cream as having Brand A's taste but Brand B's calories. The announcement reminds the consumer, not simply that Ben & Jerry's ice cream has a lot of calories, but more importantly, that great taste comes at a price of high calories. In short, the announcement reminds consumers that there is a technological constraint that prohibits the existence of a brand of ice cream that has Brand A's taste but Brand B's calories. Consumers now perceive a technological constraint that restricts the location of the cluster frontier as shown in Fig. 8.

Provided Ben & Jerry's is located between two extreme brands, the announcement pushes (in the consumers' minds) the cluster frontier closer to Ben & Jerry's.

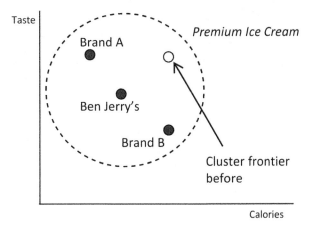

Fig. 7 A consumer's perception of the premium ice-cream cluster in the absence of technological constraints

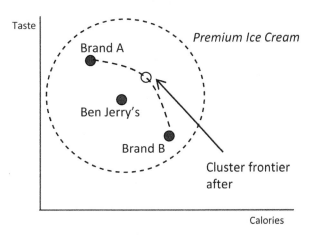

Fig. 8 A consumer's revised perception of the premium ice-cream cluster in the presence of a technological constraint

By the cluster frontier heuristic, this increases the probability of choice-given-consideration for Ben & Jerry's. What we should observe is an increase in Ben & Jerry's market share at the expense of Brands A and B, but not at the expense of brands outside the premium ice cream cluster because the technological constraint has no effect on the consideration phase of the choice process—the probability of consideration for the premium ice cream cluster is unchanged.

In the mid 1990s, the Miller Brewing Company launched a new brand of beer, Red Dog. On attributes of taste and price, the new brand was positioned to be similar but inferior to Miller's flagship brand, Miller Genuine Draft (MGD). At the time, analysts contended that the entrant would simply siphon market share away from MGD to no net benefit for Miller. Suppose that, with the two salient attributes of price and taste, consumers mentally divide beer brands into two clusters: "domestic" (i.e., lower price and lesser taste) and "imported" (i.e., higher price and better taste). Figure 9 depicts a consumer's perceived product market for beer.

Fig. 9 A consumer perceives four brands of beers existing in two clusters

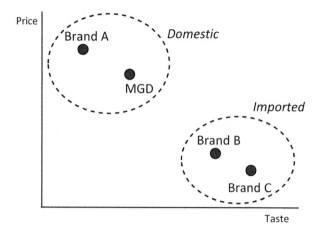

Fig. 10 The consumer's perception of the product market for beer updated for the discovery of a new brand

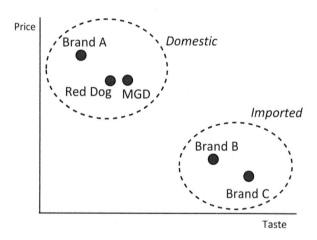

Beer consumers often form consideration sets on the basis of "import" versus "domestic," and consumers tend not to move often between the clusters. Introducing Red Dog and heavily advertising its entry, increased the number of brands consumers perceived to exist in the domestic cluster. The introduction of Red Dog causes our example consumer to update his mental map of the product market from that shown in Fig. 9 to that shown in Fig. 10. By the cluster size heuristic, the introduction of the new brand increased the probability of consumers considering the domestic cluster. Because Red Dog was positioned to be strictly inferior (though similar) to MGD, Red Dog's introduction had no effect on the domestic cluster's frontier. Thus, Red Dog had no effect on the probability of choice-given-consideration among domestic beers. The result, according to these positioning and salient attribute assumptions is that Red Dog's introduction would increase market shares for all brands in the domestic cluster at the expense of those in the imported cluster.

The consumer choice process and heuristics find application anywhere a consumer is faced with choosing one option from among many in a high-involvement setting. In selecting a mate, consumers follow the same heuristics—immediately eliminating from consideration whole groups of potential mates based on various salient attributes like looks, health, earning potential, personality. Politicians deliberately position themselves relative to their competitors in an attempt to gain votes. Voters, in turn, employ heuristics by considering only those candidates who satisfy some non-compensatory criteria (membership to a certain party, economic platform, social platform, looks, speaking voice), and then consider tradeoffs for only a small number of politicians who satisfy the non-compensatory criteria.

14   Brand Image and Consumer Behavior

Brand image can influence and, in the extreme, short-circuit the consumer choice process by causing the consumer to use the brand name as a replacement for some (or all) of the salient attributes. For example, if Toyota can successfully develop in the consumer's mind a brand image of reliability, then the consumer can come to regard the salient attribute of "reliability" as being binary—a brand is reliable if and only if it carries the Toyota name. At the consideration phase, this means that the consumer could mentally cluster brands not by reliability but by the presence or absence of the Toyota name. Toyota advertising, by bringing the brand name to the consumer's mind, can have the same effect as an increase in the number of brands within the reliability (now Toyota) cluster. In sum, when the company's name is associated with a salient attribute in the consumer's mind, advertising can increase the probability of consideration for the company's brand by making the company's brand's cluster appear to be larger.

At the choice-given-consideration stage, repeated advertising could cause the consumer to mentally reposition competing brands further away from the cluster frontier. For example, if the consumer associates the salient attribute of reliability exclusively with the Toyota name, then additional advertising by Toyota can reinforce in the consumer's mind that non-Toyota brands are not reliable and so are, consequently, located further from the cluster frontier along the reliability dimension. In sum, when a company's name is associated with a salient attribute in the consumer's mind, advertising can increase the probability of choice-given-consideration for the company's brand by causing the company's brand to appear to be relatively closer to the cluster frontier.

15   Conclusion

Decades of experimental marketing research have revealed patterns in how consumer choice is affected by brand positioning, collectively known as context effects. Recent economic psychology research has proposed an underlying behavioral framework for explaining context effects as functions of behavioral heuristics. Future research into the framework itself could include determining the degree to which consumer involvement (perhaps due to emotion, to purchase price relative to disposable income, or to frequency of purchase) can strengthen or mitigate the heuristics. Future research into applications of this framework include modeling and predicting voter choices among political candidates given changes in candidates' positions on salient issues, and investor choices of stocks wherein, along with objective attributes such as financial ratios and risk measures, investors' perceptions of other investors' expectations becomes a salient attribute. This latter application could yield insight into the formation and bursting of market bubbles.

References

Akcura, M., Fusun, F., & Petrova, E. (2004). Consumer learning and brand valuation: An application on over-the-counter drugs. *Marketing Science, 23*(1), 156–169.

Bettman, J. (1971). The structure of consumer choice processes. *Journal of Marketing Research, 8* (4), 465–471.

Bhargava, M., Kim, J., & Srivastava, R. (2000). Explaining context effects on choice using a model of comparative judgment. *Journal of Consumer Psychology, 9*(3), 167–177.

Biehal, G., & Chakravarti, D. (1986). Consumers use of memory and external information in choice: Macro and micro perspectives. *Journal of Consumer Research, 13*(March), 382–405.

Caplan, B. (2001). Rational ignorance versus rational irrationality. *Kyklos, 54*(1), 3–26.

Davies, A., & Cline, T. W. (2005). A consumer behavior approach to modeling monopolistic competition. *Journal of Economic Psychology, 26*(6), 797–826.

Heath, T., & Chatterjee, S. (1995). Asymmetric decoy effects on lower-quality versus higher-quality brands: Meta-analytic and experimental evidence. *Journal of Consumer Research, 22* (December), 268–284.

Hedgcock, W., & Rao, A. R. (2009). Trade-off aversion as an explanation for the attraction effect: A functional magnetic resonance imaging study. *Journal of Marketing Research, 46*(1), 1–13.

Howard, J., & Sheth, J. N. (1969). *The theory of buyer behavior.* New York: Wiley.

Huber, J., & Puto, C. (1983). Market boundaries and product choice: Illustrating attraction and substitution effects. *Journal of Consumer Research, 10*(June), 31–44.

Kardes, F. R., Herr, P., & Marlino, D. (1989). Some new light on substitution and attraction effects. *Advances in Consumer Research, 16*, 203–208.

Kardes, F. R., Kalyanaram, G., Chandrashekaran, M., & Dornoff, R. J. (1993). Brand retrieval, consideration set composition, consumer choice, and the pioneering advantage. *Journal of Consumer Research, 20*(June), 62–75.

Kivetz, R., & Simonson, I. (2000). The effects of incomplete information on consumer choice. *Journal of Marketing Research, 37*(4), 427–448.

Pan, Y., & Lehmann, D. R. (1993). The influence of new brand entry on subjective brand judgments. *Journal of Consumer Research, 20*(June), 76–86.

Parducci, A. (1965). Category judgment: A range-frequency model. *Psychological Monographs, 72*(6), 407–418.

Payne, J. W. (1982). Contingent decision behavior. *Psychological Bulletin, 92*, 382–402.

Petty, R. E., & Cacioppo, J. T. (1990). Involvement and persuasion: Tradition versus integration. *Psychological Bulletin, 107*, 367–374.

Prelec, D., Wernerfelt, B., & Zettelmeyer, F. (1997). The role of inference in context effects: Inferring what you want from what is available. *Journal of Consumer Research, 24*(June), 118–125.

Simonson, I., & Tversky, A. (1992). Choice in context: Tradeoff contrast and extremeness aversion. *Journal of Marketing Research, 29*(August), 281–295.

Sinn, F., Milberg, S. J., Epstein, L. D., & Goodstein, R. C. (2007). Compromising the compromise effect: Brands matter. *Marketing Letters, 18*(4), 223–236.

Slovic, P. (1995). The construction of preference. *The American Psychologist, 50*(May), 364–371.

Teillet, E., Urbano, C., Cordelle, S., & Schlich, P. (2010). Consumer perception and preference of bottled and tap water. *Journal of Sensory Studies, 25*(3), 463–480.

Consumer Resistance: From Anti-Consumption to Revenge

Marcelo Vinhal Nepomuceno, Mina Rohani, and Yany Grégoire

1 Introduction

There are many examples of consumers resisting consumption, marketing practices and questionable corporations. For example, adepts of voluntary simplicity prefer to offer something they themselves made for Christmas rather than to buy gifts at the store. After the Volkswagen crisis about the diesel engine, some owners swore they would never buy another car from this company. In addition, many of them complained aggressively about the "dishonest" German manufacturer on social media. Although the manifestations of consumer resistance are omnipresent, this area of research has received limited attention in the academic literature. The current contribution aims to fulfill this gap by providing state-of-the-art reviews on two streams of research—consumer anti-consumption and revenge—that are closely associated with consumer resistance.

In this contribution, consumer resistance refers to the voluntary opposition to marketing activities or corporations that leads consumers to engage in a variety of anti-consumption actions (Lee et al. 2009) and revenge behaviors against corporations (Grégoire and Fisher 2008; Grégoire et al. 2010). Generally speaking, research on consumer resistance focuses on the unbalanced power that exists between consumers and firms (Price and Penaloza 1993), and the current contribution investigates two types of actions—anti-consumption and revenge—that consumers may use to regain some of their perceived lost power (Price and Penaloza 1993). Although both anti-consumption and revenge behaviors are driven by a similar feeling of opposition toward corporations and marketing, these two types of behaviors also possess different characteristics, as illustrated in Fig. 1. Given

M.V. Nepomuceno • M. Rohani • Y. Grégoire (✉)
Department of Marketing, HEC Montréal, 3000, chemin de la Côte-Sainte-Catherine, Montréal, Québec H3T 2A7, Canada
e-mail: yany.gregoire@hec.ca

© Springer International Publishing AG 2017
G. Emilien et al. (eds.), *Consumer Perception of Product Risks and Benefits*,
DOI 10.1007/978-3-319-50530-5_19

345

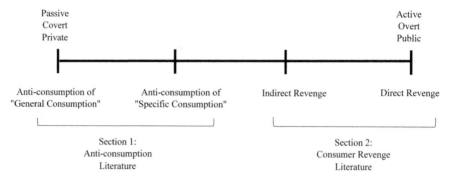

Fig. 1 Consumer resistance behaviors and the arrangement of this contribution

their differences, the two literatures dealing with these behaviors are reviewed separately in the first two sections of this contribution. In our concluding remarks, the similarities between these two types of behaviors and their links with the notion of resistance are discussed further.

Anti-consumption literally means "against consumption," and this literature examines consumers who are strongly opposed to the acquisition, use and dispossession of goods and brands (Lee et al. 2009). The first section of the contribution focuses on the refusal to consume brands and products as a lifestyle. Specifically, this section discusses different typologies of anti-consumption lifestyles as well as the antecedents and consequences of these lifestyles. Compared to the revenge responses, anti-consumption behaviors can be viewed as more private and passive in nature (see Fig. 1). These actions constitute a form of "quiet" (but persistent) refusal to go along with consuming products or services. Most of these behaviors are not primarily designed to hurt corporations, although firms (like Volkswagen) could suffer from these behaviors (e.g., boycott) as a byproduct. Most of anti-consumptions are also covert because managers may not be aware of the existence of these consumers.

The second section of this contribution proposes a comprehensive model of consumer revenge—which is defined as consumers' efforts to punish and cause inconvenience to corporations for the damages they have caused (Grégoire et al. 2009). Revenge behaviors—made in person or through social media—are strong manifestations of consumer resistance; when consumers endeavor to get revenge, they invest time, energy and even money to get back at firms. This second section of the contribution discusses the cognitive and emotional antecedents leading to a desire for revenge as well as the most common revenge manifestations (indirect and direct). Revenge behaviors—especially the direct form which includes vindictive complaining and marketplace aggression—are arguably the strongest and most active form of consumer resistance. Given the overt nature of direct revenge, these actions are difficult to ignore by firms and managers.

2 Anti-Consumption Lifestyles

2.1 Typologies of Anti-Consumption Lifestyles

Marketing is inherently biased to investigate what makes consumers buy, as this facilitates the creation of persuasive communication strategies, as well as the development of products and services tailored to consumers' needs and wants. Research in marketing focuses mostly on investigating the reasons for consuming (Chatzidakis and Lee 2013). However, the reasons for consuming are not necessarily the logical opposite of the reasons against consuming (Chatzidakis and Lee 2013). A study might conclude that consumers bought a given brand because it represents environmental values, but one should not conclude that consumers who did not buy the same brand are not environmentally concerned. Therefore, it is important for marketing to study not only the "reasons for" a given behavior, but also the "reasons against" this same behavior. In addition, behaviors are better explained when individuals are asked both whether they intend to do something and whether they are against doing something (Chatzidakis and Lee 2013). For example, while the intention to reduce consumption is driven by environmental concerns, the intention to maintain current consumption may be motivated by a desire to maintain current lifestyles. This reinforces the importance of studying not only why consumers buy, but also why they refuse to buy products or services.

In light of these points, the first part of this contribution reviews research on anti-consumption and focuses on its two motivations (Iyer and Muncy 2009): societal and personal. Consumers who refuse to consume for societal reasons believe that society at large would be improved if consumers reduced their consumption. For them, consumption is not simply the act of buying. They believe that consumption has much broader implications, impacting society and the well-being of a community. Consumers who resist consuming for personal reasons are motivated to satisfy private concerns. For instance, they may reduce consumption in response to personal ethical beliefs or to avoid the pain they experience when spending.

Anti-consumption also has two principal objects: general consumption and specific consumption (Iyer and Muncy 2009). Consumers who resist general consumption will avoid all consumption, reducing the acquisition of all types of products and services. Conversely, consumers who resist specific consumption are against acquiring specific brands or product categories because of what such brands and products symbolize. By combining the two objects and the two motivations of anti-consumption, Iyer and Muncy (2009) proposed four types of anti-consumers. We briefly summarize them below.

First, *global impact consumers* resist general consumption for societal reasons. They want to reduce all consumption to benefit the society or the environment. They believe that social inequalities are too strong and that current eco-systems cannot cope with present levels of over-consumption.

Second, *market activists* resist acquiring specific products and brands for societal reasons. They believe that consumers should boycott certain brands or products because they represent a menace to general well-being. These consumers blame certain brands or products for low wages and illegal or immoral practices as well as for environmental degradation. They believe that consumers should use their wallets to force companies to make positive social changes.

Third, *anti-loyal consumers* resist acquiring specific products or brands for personal concerns. They avoid purchasing particular brands and products because of perceived inferiority or because they had negative experiences with the product or brand. Their resistance to consumption is not motivated by societal concerns; rather, it is based on their own personal experiences. These consumers may also resist buying certain products and brands because of their associated negative image.

Fourth, *simplifiers* resist general consumption for personal reasons. They reduce all their consumption to satisfy self-centered goals. They believe that consumption distracts them from more important life goals, and that consumption is not an important source of happiness. Therefore, they resist consumption to live simpler and have more meaningful lives. They are also motivated by personal ethical concerns, and they reject consumption as focusing too much on self-serving activities.

Of note, in line with recent research (Nepomuceno and Laroche 2015a), we argue that consumers may resist all consumption for personal reasons other than those related to voluntary simplicity. For example, consumers could reduce consumption because they feel pleasure when saving or pain when spending. These consumers are known respectively as being frugal and tightwad (Nepomuceno and Laroche 2015a). Taking the existence of these consumers into account opens the scope of research on anti-consumption; it expands the limited view that resisting all consumption is due only to personal motivations related to simplicity.

Now that we have briefly presented the different types of anti-consumers, we turn our attention to the drivers leading these individuals to adopt such lifestyles. In particular, we summarize antecedents that have been found to correlate with a person's inclination to resist consumption. The next section provides insights into which traits explain people's willingness to resist consumption.

2.2 Antecedents of Anti-Consumption Lifestyles

Specifically, we review the following traits: materialism, self-control, long-term orientation and environmental concern. Note that we do not present an exhaustive list of the antecedents of anti-consumption; we focus on the most important ones according to prior research.

Materialism describes how much a given person attributes importance to possessions. A materialistic person believes that possessions are an important source of happiness, that possessions signal success, and that acquiring possessions is a central goal in their lives (Richins 2004). Extensive research has shown that materialism is an important predictor of a person's intention to consume or resist consumption. Materialism correlates negatively with anti-consumption lifestyles, such as tightwadism, voluntary simplicity and frugality (Lastovicka et al. 1999; Nepomuceno and Laroche 2015a). While low materialism is associated with resistance to consumption, high materialism is associated with increased consumption. Though research has investigated instances in which materialists might resist consumption (Nepomuceno and Laroche 2015b), research strongly suggests that endorsing materialistic values makes it difficult for consumers to resist consumption.

Research has also paid particular attention to the role of self-control as an antecedent of anti-consumption. Self-control is the ability to override, alter, or inhibit behaviors that would normally occur because of undesired physiological processes, learning, habits or situations (Tangney et al. 2004). Studies looking at the effect of self-control on consumption have found that impulsive consumption correlates negatively with self-control. In addition, a self-control scale designed to measure consumer spending self-control correlates positively with frugality and tightwadism. Overall, research indicates that self-control is an important antecedent of anti-consumption lifestyles (Tangney et al. 2004; Nepomuceno and Laroche 2015b) because the dominant culture in the west is that consumer expenditures are desirable (Borgmann 2000), so one needs to exert self-control to avoid falling into consumerist temptations.

Authors have also examined how long-term orientation is associated with anti-consumption. Long-term orientation refers to how much a person is focused on obtaining future gains and benefits (Bearden et al. 2006). A long-term oriented person values planning, hard work, and perseverance. Given that in the west materialism is desirable and endorsed (Borgmann 2000), a long-term oriented individual will be more likely to resist temptations in the present to obtain greater gains in the future. For example, long-term oriented individuals might save today to buy something in the future.

A final important antecedent of anti-consumption is environmental concerns. This construct measures how much individuals are concerned about the environment and how much they believe that human development threatens the availability of resources necessary for survival (Fransson and Gärling 1999). Interestingly, individuals concerned with environmental risks endorse altruistic values and the well-being of other humans (Slimak and Dietz 2006). Given that environmentally concerned individuals endorse altruistic values, and considering that they believe that current consumption levels pose a threat to the environment and society, it is likely that environmental concerns are an important motivation for some consumers to endorse anti-consumption lifestyles. For example, global impact consumers may be motivated to improve society by reducing their own environmental impact through what they consume. Likewise, market activists may believe they can improve the well-being of society by refusing to buy brands that threaten the environment and society at large. In sum, environmental concerns are likely an important antecedent of endorsing an anti-consumption lifestyle.

2.3   Consequences of Anti-Consumption Lifestyles

What if large consumer segments were to resist consumption? How would that affect a given economy? The current zeitgeist is that consumption is "good" and that economies grow stronger if consumers increase their consumption levels (Borgmann 2000). Given this rationale, it is logical to conclude that economies would shrink if consumers were to resist consumption.

Here, we wish to point out another outcome that could occur with resisting consumption. At a macro-level, anti-consumption could be beneficial for some economies. Let's consider oil as an example. This commodity serves many purposes: oil is used to generate power and its derivatives are widely used in many industries. A country that is not self-sufficient in the production of oil is especially dependent on international suppliers. Given that oil derivatives are used in many products (such as plastics, synthetic materials, and chemical products), a given country could gain an economic advantage if its population were to voluntarily reduce its overall consumption. In this case, the country would become less dependent on foreign suppliers. Even a country that is self-sufficient on oil could benefit from a reduction in consumption; it would allow this country to have more oil derivatives to export—which in turn would generate greater national revenues. Therefore, by motivating consumers to resist consumption, policy makers could create strategic commercial advantages. In short, our argument is that strong macro-economic advantages may arise if consumers reduce their consumption.

To illustrate additional benefits of resisting consumption, consider the recent work by Nepomuceno and Laroche (2015a). These authors found that voluntary simplicity negatively correlates with personal debt. This finding suggests that resisting consumption leads to greater account balances and lower inclination to obtain debt. Conversely, individuals who do not voluntarily resist consumption are more likely to encounter and suffer from financial difficulties. Also important, consumer debt has been positively correlated with negative emotions, mental disorder, depression, and suicidal completion (Richardson et al. 2013). Thus, by motivating consumers to voluntarily resist consumption, governments and other institutions could also assist them to live happier and more meaningful lives.

Research has indicated that resistance to consumption leads to increased well-being. Thrift consumers and consumers who spend money wisely (Dunn et al. 2011) are more likely to experience well-being. This finding directly contradicts the Western belief that possessions are a source of happiness (Richins 2004). Interestingly, research suggests that one is happier because, after resisting consuming, one experiences a greater sense of authenticity and greater ease in self-expression (Black and Cherrier 2010). In addition, consumption has a displacement effect. That is, it forces individuals to work longer hours, distracting them from leisure activities and time devoted to family, community, or religion (Borgmann 2000). Given that consumers are likely to enjoy happier lives if they resist consumption, research on consumer resistance and anti-consumption can produce knowledge that might be used to improve consumers' lives (Nepomuceno and Laroche 2015b).

An additional benefit of resisting consumption is the potential impact on sustainability. Authors have suggested that resistance to consumption should reduce the constraints on the environment. They argue that when consumers systematically reduce consumption, the strains on the environment are reduced as the demand for resources is also reduced (Sheth et al. 2011). Therefore, policy makers motivated to tackle growing environmental challenges should consider the promotion of anti-consumption values and educate consumers about the benefits of resisting consumption for society and themselves. In short, research on anti-consumption has the potential to produce knowledge that might assist in achieving sustainability outcomes (Sheth et al. 2011).

2.4   Consumer Resistance and Marketing Practices

In the early twentieth century, marketing was highly focused on the products developed. The goal was to mass market a product and make it appealing to consumers. Fortunately, marketing has come a long way since then. As competition grew in the marketplace, the shift changed from the products being sold to the consumers. Quickly, marketers noticed that consumers had "needs and wants" to be satisfied, and products that best satisfied these "needs and wants" were more popular among consumers (Narver and Slater 1990). Segmentation was a natural evolutionary step, as practitioners attempted to group consumers in homogeneous groups, providing tailored solutions. When companies started to focus on consumer segments, the competition within these segments grew, forcing companies to focus on smaller and smaller segments as well as niche marketing (Sheth et al. 2000).

The fact that niche marketing has grown in importance demonstrates that practitioners are increasingly aware that consumers have diverse goals, ambitions, and motivations. In particular, consumers are increasingly concerned about the environment (Brown and Wahlers 1998), sustainability (Hinton and Goodman 2010), and social responsibility (Mohr et al. 2001), to the point that they take these issues into consideration when selecting a product. These changes in consumer profile and marketplace competition have pushed companies to perceive consumer resistance in a different way. Companies are now realizing that consumers who want to resist consumption are still consumers and will need to purchase solutions for their needs and wants. Therefore, companies should not ignore consumers who voluntarily resist consumption. In fact, companies should attempt to provide solutions that will satisfy these consumers. Companies that fail to do so risk losing space to competitors. Reinforcing this point, research has found that 18% of the general population scores as high on frugality as subscribers of a book promoting a thrift lifestyle (Lastovicka et al. 1999). These convincing results indicate that consumers resisting consumption are a sizeable group.

Of note, this substantially large group is particularly important for the banking industry. Consumers who adopt an anti-consumption lifestyle are expected to spend less money, as they resist acquiring new possessions. This has been shown in recent research demonstrating that frugal consumers have larger account balances, possibly because of their different lifestyle (Nepomuceno and Laroche 2015a). Because anti-consumption leads to less consumption, the money saved after resisting consumption must be kept somewhere. Naturally, individuals would deposit their savings in financial institutions and either invest or simply leave the money in their bank accounts. Therefore, practitioners working in financial institutions should pay particular attention to anti-consumption lifestyles.

2.5 Anti-Consumption and Consumer Revenge

The next section covers consumer revenge (see Fig. 1), defined as the effort made by consumers to punish companies for the damages they have caused. Some typologies of anti-consumption seem to have overlapping behaviors with consumer revenge. In particular, market activists refuse to consume because they believe that by doing so they will improve society at large, whereas anti-loyal consumers might refuse to consume because they had negative experiences with a company. Similarly, consumer revenge might occur because consumers had negative experiences with the company and because they believe that by punishing the company they will improve society. So, anti-consumption and consumer revenge might be motivated by personal and societal concerns. However, while anti-consumption lifestyles involve the refusal to purchase from a given company or buy a particular brand, consumer revenge leads individuals to act more actively against the company and to spend time and energy in order to get even with it.

3 Consumer Revenge: Another form of Resistance

After discussing different anti-consumption lifestyles, we now turn to consumers who take the extra steps in their opposition by retaliating against firms. Here, we focus on consumers getting "their" revenge and the psychological process leading to these extreme responses. For instance, the revelations of Volkswagen's diesel engine car emissions ignited a great deal of anger among auto wholesalers, private dealers, and, of course, owners. Car dealers now have to handle a flood of angry calls, emails and tweets from the owners (cbsnews.com). It has been estimated that the whole crisis could cost Volkswagen 87 billion dollars (money.cnn.com).

People are increasingly getting revenge through online applications. Most people have already seen examples of this recent form of revenge (which started about 10 years ago). For example, there are plenty of examples on Facebook and Twitter of consumers who were overcharged by mobile phone operators, or who missed a connection for a delayed flight. How did these consumers feel? Why did they engage in revenge behaviors—that is, actions motivated by a desire to harm the firm for what it did in the first place (Grégoire and Fisher 2008)? In this section, we examine what leads consumers to get revenge against firms when a company fails to serve them properly or violates important societal norms (such as care for the environment).

We propose a general framework to better understand the cognitive and emotional drivers of consumer revenge behaviors (see Fig. 2 for the model and Table 1 for recent work on this issue). The proposed framework draws on the well-established cognitive appraisal theory of Lazarus (1991) in order to better explain how consumers' assessment of failures affect their cognitive, emotional, motivational, and behavioral responses (see Fig. 2). Accordingly, this section tries to answer the following questions: What are the cognitive, emotional and motivational antecedents to consumer revenge? What are the different ways that consumers can enact revenge? How should firms respond when consumers get revenge? Once we understand why consumers engage in vengeful behaviors, we can better understand what firms should do to manage their occurrences.

Previous research illustrates that consumer revenge can be caused by a service failure (i.e., a service situation that brings dissatisfaction) or a societal failure (i.e., a company's misbehavior that negatively affects the whole society, like an oil spillage). In both cases, the process is almost the same, and it involves similar cognitions and emotions. A service failure is experienced when a product or service is not performing as it should (e.g., luggage damage by an airline). Indeed, experiencing both a service failure and a poor recovery is the context that leads to 96% of online complaints (Grégoire et al. 2009). Societal marketing refers to firms' efforts to reach company goals by considering society's long-term interests and benefits. Accordingly, consumers may hold a grudge against firms that neglect to consider the best interest of society—that is, a societal failure.

The revenge process strongly relies on Lazarus' appraisal theory, in which consumers' judgments about a negative event precede their emotions (Lazarus 1991). Specifically, consumers initially form a moral judgment about a service or

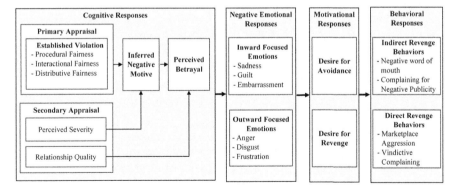

Fig. 2 Conceptual framework for the revenge process

Table 1 Review of consumer revenge work in marketing

Author(s)/Journal	Theoretical approach	Findings/contributions
McColl-Kennedy and Sparks (2003) *Journal of Service Research*	Justice theory	(1) Adapting a fairness theory for studying consumers' emotions during a service recovery. (2) Studying the role consumers' counterfactual thinking and accountability according to the procedural, interactional, and distributive justice, on their emotional response.
Grégoire and Fisher (2008) *Journal of the Academy of Marketing Science*	Justice theory Social exchange theory	(1) Perceived betrayal is the key motivational force that leads consumers to restore fairness by all means possible. (2) Relationship quality moderates the link between a consumer perception of a service fairness and betrayal.
Grégoire et al. (2009) *Journal of Marketing*	Forgiveness theory	(1) Explores the effects of time and relationship quality on the evolution of consumer grudge in online public complaining contexts. (2) Time affects consumer negative motivational responses differently. (3) In contrast to low relationship quality consumers, consumers with strong relationship quality with the firm are more amenable to any level of recovery attempt.
McColl-Kennedy et al. (2009) *Journal of Retailing*	Affective Events Theory (AET) Cognitive Appraisal Theory	(1) Develops scales for consumers' emotions, expressions, and behaviors. (2) Different forms of consumer rage emotions lead to different types of expressions and behaviors.
Grégoire et al. (2010) *Journal of the Academy of Marketing Science*	Appraisal Theory Justice Theory Attribution Theory	(1) Incorporates inferred negative motives as the key drivers of consumers' desire for revenge, (2) Categorizes consumers' vengeful behaviors as direct vs. indirect. (3) Explains the antecedents of consumers' direct and indirect revenge behaviors.

societal failure. This judgment then creates negative emotional responses, such as anger, that lead to the development of antisocial motivations (such as a desire for revenge) and behavioral responses (e.g., negative word of mouth or marketplace aggression). This model is explained in the following subsections.

3.1 The Cognitive Antecedents Leading to Revenge

Lazarus (1991) identified two levels of cognitive appraisal: (a) the primary appraisal is about the unfairness of the situation, and (b) the secondary appraisal concerns the assessment of the failure severity and the prior level of relationship quality (before the failure). While the primary appraisal focuses on the general assessment of the negative event, the secondary appraisal is more specific and it helps in selecting the appropriate coping mechanism (Zourrig et al. 2009). Building on justice theory, the primary appraisal is shaped according to three dimensions: procedural fairness (i.e., firms' policies and procedures to address the failure), interactional fairness (i.e., employees' interactions in the recovery process), and distributive fairness (i.e., the compensation or the outcome that consumers receive) (Tax et al. 1998).

The secondary appraisal includes severity, which is defined as the magnitude of the loss or the inconvenience of a failure (Grégoire and Fisher 2008). This category also refers to the prior assessment (before the failure) of relationship quality, which is defined as consumers' trust (i.e., confidence that the firm can be relied on), commitment (i.e., a willingness to preserve a relationship with the firm), and social benefits (i.e., a perception of a "one-to-one" connection through personalization and customization of services).

Moving downward in the model (see Fig. 2), Grégoire et al. (2010) found that the more consumers perceive procedural and interactional unfairness, the greater they infer that a firm has negative motives. Here, inferred negative motive is defined as the extent to which a consumer believes a firm intended the wrongdoing to maximize its own benefits and take advantage of the situation (Grégoire et al. 2010). This judgment has been found to be one of the most powerful cognitions leading to anger and a desire for revenge. When a failure occurs, consumers act as jurors and they infer whether or not the firm had negative motives for causing the failure. If so, they will then judge that the firm deserves to be punished for its actions.

If consumers perceive they have been unfairly treated—on the basis of the three dimensions—they may also perceive a sense of betrayal (Grégoire and Fisher 2008). Betrayal is defined as the extent to which a consumer perceives that a firm has intentionally violated the norms regulating their relationships (Grégoire et al. 2009). Unlike dissatisfaction, consumers' perceived betrayal is strongly associated with anger and a desire for revenge; this variable is also a powerful antecedent causing revenge. In addition, the results of a longitudinal research study with online complainers (Grégoire et al. 2009) indicate this assessment is influenced by the prior level of relationship quality (perceived by a consumer). Relationship quality is positively related to consumers' perceived betrayal, and this effect is persistent over time. In other words, when consumers perceive a high level of prior relationship quality, they experience a greater sense of betrayal—this phenomenon is called the "love becomes hate" effect.

3.2   The Emotional Antecedents to Consumer Revenge

According to the appraisal theory, emotions are created by the cognitive appraisal of a situation. These emotions ultimately lead them to choosing a coping behavior in order to reduce emotional dissonance (Haj-Salem and Chebat 2013; Lazarus 1991). This mechanism is aligned with the cognitive change theory that argues that individuals try to integrate the stressful experience within their current reference system, also called their "inner" model. Accordingly, individuals have two options. Either they can face the stressful event and try to solve the problem, or they can try to manage their negative emotions and establish a new inner model that matches the stressful event better. As can be seen in Fig. 2, consumers' perceptions of negative motives and/or betrayal lead them to experience diverse negative emotions (Lazarus 1991).

Lazarus (1991) introduced two distinct categories of negative emotions: namely, inward vs. outward. This distinction is based on the attribution of agency, which refers to the attribution of the stressor to self vs. others (Haj-Salem and Chebat 2013). Inward negative emotions occur when individuals believe they are responsible for the negative event. They blame themselves and feel that they could have done better. Consumers who perceive that they are more responsible for a negative outcome (e.g., selecting the wrong service provider) are more likely to feel inward negative emotions such as sadness, guilt, and embarrassment (Haj-Salem and Chebat 2013).

In turn, outward negative emotions occur when an individual puts the blame on the other party for the occurrence of a negative event (Lazarus 1991). In a consumer context, the more consumers blame a firm for a failure, the greater they should feel outward negative emotions, such as anger, disgust, or frustration (Haj-Salem and Chebat 2013). According to the model proposed in this section, the more consumers perceive betrayal and infer a firm's negative motives, the more they feel outward negative emotions (such as anger) rather than inward negative emotions. In contrast, if consumers perceive that they are responsible for the situation and the negative outcome, they feel more inward negative emotions.

Grégoire et al. (2010) demonstrate that consumers' inferences of a firm's negative motives (such as greed) are very influential cognitions that drive anger, which is defined as an intense negative emotion that leads consumers to strongly respond to the source of anger (McColl-Kennedy et al. 2009). In addition, consumers' perception of the severity of a failure has both direct and indirect effects on anger. In sum, anger (and perhaps rage) is definitely the strongest emotional driver leading consumers to consider revenge as an appropriate coping mechanism.

3.3   Key Motivational Responses: A Desire for Revenge vs. A Desire for Avoidance

Consumers' cognitions and negative emotions about an unfair experience drive them to have some negative motivational responses, such as a desire for revenge, a desire for avoidance, or both (Grégoire et al. 2009). A consumer's desire for revenge is a felt need to punish and cause harm to a firm because of the damages it has caused in the first place (Grégoire et al. 2009). Desire for avoidance, which is mostly caused by dissatisfaction, is defined as a consumer's motivation to keep as much distance as possible between him/her and the firm. A desire for revenge is the major force leading consumers to engage in extremely negative behaviors, such as negative word-of-mouth or vindictive complaining.

Generally speaking, consumers can cope with a stressful situation (e.g., service or societal failure) in two ways: problem-focused versus emotion-focused coping (Lazarus 1991). The first coping strategy refers to managing the environment or the situation in order to reduce its impact or try to resolve the problem. In the second coping strategy, individuals try to manage and regulate their emotions in order to adjust their inner model. By avoiding the firm (i.e., developing a desire for avoidance), consumers may try to ignore the service failure and escape from the uncomfortable emotional states caused by anger (Grégoire et al. 2009). Alternatively, consumers may decide to confront the firm and seek to cause it harm in order to get even (i.e., developing a desire for revenge) (Grégoire et al. 2009, 2010). In other words, consumers may hold a desire for revenge, a desire for avoidance, or both to show their lack of forgiveness when they experience a severe failure.

For instance, an angry consumer can hold a grudge against a firm by stopping purchasing from the company and switching to a competitor (i.e., an avoidance approach). In the meanwhile, this consumer can also blog negatively about the transgressing firm (i.e., a revenge approach). Although consumers' desire for revenge and desire for avoidance are correlated, they are also conceptually distinct and can simultaneously coexist (McCullough et al. 1998).

Because of their different natures, these two desires follow different evolutionary patterns over time (Grégoire et al. 2009). As illustrated in Fig. 3, when a firm does not take action after receiving an online complaint, consumers' desire for revenge is high but tends to fade away over time, although it never disappears. The diminishing desire for revenge is replaced by consumers taking their business elsewhere and a growing desire for avoidance over time.

The different effects of time on consumers' desires for revenge and avoidance are also moderated by the level of relationship quality that consumers perceive to have with a firm (Grégoire et al. 2009). High relationship quality consumers are firms' best and most loyal consumers, with strong emotional connections with firms. In turn, low relationship quality consumers are casual consumers who only make periodic purchases and do not have strong emotional attachments with firms. In an online complaining context, consumers with high relationship quality hold their desire for revenge over a longer period of time, compared to low relationship

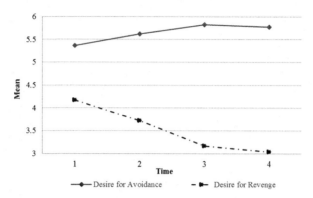

Fig. 3 Evolution of revenge and avoidance over time. Source: Adapted from Grégoire et al. (2009). Note: This study was conducted in a series of four questionnaires over a 2-month period (every 2 weeks). The initial sample of participants was 431. Then, 300 participants completed the survey at time 2, and 215 at time 3. Overall, 172 participants completed all four waves. For both desires, the scale varies between 1 (lowest) and 7 (highest)

quality consumers (see Fig. 4, Panel A). Meanwhile, the desire for avoidance of high relationship quality consumers amplifies more rapidly over time, compared to those with low relationship quality (see Fig. 4, Panel B). This set of patterns has been described as a longitudinal "love becomes hate" effect.

Fortunately, Grégoire et al. (2009) demonstrate that high relationship quality consumers are also more amenable to any form of post-complaint recovery—although these consumers hold a longer grudge when no recovery is offered. High relationship quality consumers tend to care more about firms' efforts to resolve a problem than the monetary value. In contrast, low relationship quality consumers are mainly concerned about the size of a compensation. While low relationship quality consumers require high value compensations, high relationship quality consumers are more interested in the social value of a recovery.

3.4 Consumer Revenge Behavioral Responses and Firms' Interventions

The cognitive-emotion process leads consumers to have negative motivational responses (i.e., desires for revenge or avoidance) toward the wrongdoing firm. In that case, consumers may engage in different types of vengeful behaviors to get even with the transgressing firms and "make them pay" with concrete actions (Grégoire and Fisher 2008; Grégoire et al. 2010). The behaviors could vary from passively exiting the relationship to engaging in aggressive behaviors, such as slamming the door and insulting employees (McColl-Kennedy et al. 2009; Grégoire et al. 2010). With the fast rise of social media, consumers' vengeful behaviors are becoming more salient, and the resulting inconvenience could be even more severe

Fig 4 Interaction effects between relationship quality and time on revenge and avoidance. Source: Adapted from Grégoire et al. (2009); Note: see Fig. 3

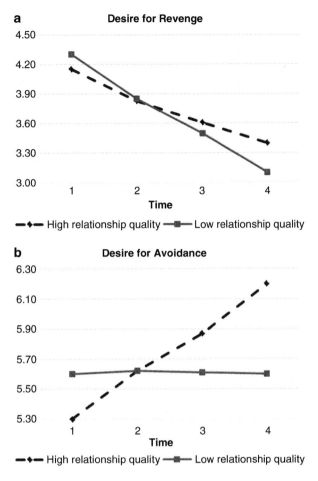

for firms. The side effects can be so important that in some cases even major recovery efforts are insufficient to stop the online crisis. For example, in the case of Dave Carrol—a musician whose guitar was broken during baggage handling on a United Airlines flight in 2009—the airline suffered from serious public relations humiliation and brand damages. And the damages still continue: The YouTube video "United Breaks Guitars" is still viral in 2016, and it has been viewed more than fifteen million times!

As mentioned earlier, consumers may engage in different vengeful behaviors to get even with firms. A key question then becomes: How should managers deal with each type of revenge behavior? Understanding different types of revenge behaviors is important because it provides guidance to managers about the best ways to intervene and offer tailored solutions for each form of behavior. Previous research identifies two distinct categories of revenge behaviors: direct vs. indirect (Grégoire et al. 2010). These two categories require different interventions from firms, since each one has different effects on firms.

First, *direct revenge behaviors* include consumers' actions that occur within a firm's borders and that directly target its employees and operations. A firm is necessarily aware of these actions. Vindictive complaining (e.g., insulting front-line staff) and marketplace aggressions (e.g., physical actions, such as hitting an object or damaging firms' properties) are two types of frequent direct revenge behaviors (Grégoire et al. 2010). Vindictive complaining refers to consumers' complaining behaviors that occur to cause inconveniences to and abuse of frontline employees (Grégoire and Fisher 2008). All sorts of direct retaliatory behaviors (e.g., physical aggression and vandalism) can be viewed as direct revenge.

It is not hard for firms to recognize consumers' direct revenge behaviors, as many examples easily come to mind. Because these behaviors may put pressure on the frontline employees, they could lead to an increase in the rate of absenteeism and turnover (Grégoire et al. 2010). For manifestations of direct revenge, managers are able to take immediate actions to rectify the situation and prevent the recurrence of these behaviors. In other words, this set of behaviors is more identifiable and manageable and, in that regard, less dangerous for firms. In addition, these behaviors do not have the potential to spread in viral and uncontrollable ways.

While most direct revenge behaviors occur in a face-to-face context, the *indirect types* include actions that happen "behind a firm's back" (Grégoire et al. 2010). For instance, negative word-of-mouth and online complaining for negative publicity are two popular forms of indirect revenge behaviors. Negative word-of-mouth refers to consumers' efforts to denigrate a firm to their family and friends to convince them to stop patronizing the transgressing firm (Grégoire et al. 2010). In turn, online public complaining for negative publicity occurs when consumers use online applications to inform the public about firms' misbehaviors (Grégoire et al. 2010).

In contrast to the direct type, frontline employees are not the target for the indirect revenge behaviors (Grégoire et al. 2010). As the qualifier suggests, indirect revenge behaviors are harder to recognize and control because they occur beyond a firm's borders. These behaviors can drastically damage a firm's reputation by indirectly influencing a larger number of potential consumers. It should be noted that the advent of the Internet and social media has made this form of behavior more dangerous than ever before in the history of consumption.

Now that we understand the different categories of revenge behaviors, the question becomes: What are the specific drivers leading to direct vs. indirect revenge behaviors? Consumers' desire for revenge naturally leads them to engage in both direct and indirect revenge behaviors (Grégoire et al. 2010). However, these two types of behaviors also have different and distinct antecedents. First, a multi-stage study (Study 2 in Grégoire et al. 2010) reveals that perceived severity has a significant effect only on the *indirect* revenge behaviors. When the inconveniences of a failure are major, it creates a strong internal pressure that leads consumers to share their stories by all means possible.

In addition, consumers' perceived power has main and moderating effects only on the *direct* revenge behaviors (Grégoire et al. 2010). Consumers' perceived power is defined as the extent to which a consumer perceives being able to influence a firm in an advantageous manner. In other words, if consumers perceive themselves to be "powerless," they are less likely to engage in direct revenge behaviors. This effect is explained because these consumers may fear counter-retaliation from firms. Given the overt nature of direct revenge behaviors, powerless consumers may be afraid that firms could quickly recognize them and engage in counter-retaliation actions—these actions could make the situation even worse for consumers. In turn, if consumers perceive they are powerful enough to engage in direct revenge actions, they may assume that firms will be reluctant to counter-react in an unpredictable manner (Grégoire et al. 2010). Such consumers perceive that firms need their patronage more than the consumers need the firms' products or services, so they feel comfortable in retaliating in an aggressive manner.

3.5 An Overview of the Revenge Model

This review—presented in the second section—contributes to a better understanding of consumers' vengeful responses in the context of service and societal failures. Drawing on cognitive appraisal theory (Lazarus 1991), we propose a general conceptual framework that synthesizes previous research in a marketing context (see Fig. 2). Accordingly, the conceptual framework explains consumers' cognitive, emotional, motivational, and behavioral responses once they experience a failure. Overall, the conceptual model argues that consumers cognitively process an unfair experience, which consequently may lead them to perceive firms' negative motives and/or betrayal. The cognitive responses of these consumers drive them to experience various inward (e.g., sadness, guilt) or outward (e.g., anger) negative emotions in relation to the failure. The negative feelings, especially anger, motivate consumers to hold a grudge (i.e., desire for revenge, desire for avoidance) against firms. Finally, aggrieved consumers may engage in various revenge behaviors (i.e., direct vs. indirect) to get even with the transgressing firm.

4 Two Facets of Consumer Resistance: Concluding Remarks

In this contribution, we review two facets of consumer resistance—a phenomenon we broadly define as consumers' sense of opposition toward consumption, marketing, and corporations. As we explained in the anti-consumption section, this opposition can be general (toward all forms of consumption) or specific (toward a specific brand or product), and it can strongly influence a person's lifestyle. The first stream of literature that we reviewed is more abstract and sociological in nature, and the emergence of the four anti-consumption lifestyles is strongly explained by general values that consumers possess toward materialism, long-term orientation, and environmental concerns. Broadly speaking, the anti-consumption movement has been described as more passive and covert than the revenge responses (see Fig. 1) because this movement refers to a quiet (but persistent) refusal to go along with consuming goods or services.

In turn, the second section of this contribution refers to consumer revenge (i.e., the actions to hurt a firm), which constitutes another distinct way that consumers can use to express their opposition toward firms. In contrast with the anti-consumption section, we study revenge under a psychological (rather than a sociological) lens. In this second section, we try to understand the internal process—in terms of cognitions, emotions, and motivations—that lead consumers to engage in direct and indirect revenge. Although revenge behaviors can be especially aggressive and confrontational, these extreme responses are also short-lived. Revenge relies on extreme cognitions (betrayal and motives) and emotions (anger) that are unhealthy to sustain over time. So, revenge behaviors and anti-consumption lifestyles also differ on the basis of their duration; lifestyles are based on routine behaviors that are much more permanent than revenge actions.

Despite the differences between the anti-consumption and revenge literatures, we wish to conclude this contribution by highlighting their commonalities. First, both behaviors can be motivated by personal or societal reasons. Indeed, consumers can engage in anti-consumption or revenge because a firm fails them personally (through a product or a service failure); or even worse, it fails to respect important societal values (such as respecting basic human rights). Second, both types of behaviors are motivated by a strong sense of opposition toward firms (and marketing), and both behaviors are grounded in a strong desire to regain power over firms. Through these behaviors, consumers reclaim their power, and they communicate that marketing or consumption will not dictate the way they should live.

References

Bearden, W. O., Money, R. B., & Nevins, J. L. (2006). A measure of long-term orientation: Development and validation. *Journal of the Academy of Marketing Science, 34*, 456–467.

Black, I. R., & Cherrier, H. (2010). Anti-consumption as part of living a sustainable lifestyle: Daily practices, contextual motivations and subjective values. *Journal of Consumer Behaviour, 9*, 437–453.

Borgmann, A. (2000). The moral complexion of consumption. *Journal of Consumer Research, 26*, 418–422.

Brown, J. D., & Wahlers, R. G. (1998). The environmentally concerned consumer: An exploratory study. *Journal of Marketing Theory and Practice*, 39–47.

Chatzidakis, A., & Lee, M. S. (2013). Anti-consumption as the study of reasons against. *Journal of Macromarketing, 33*, 190–203.

Dunn, E. W., Gilbert, D. T., & Wilson, T. D. (2011). If money doesn't make you happy, then you probably aren't spending it right. *Journal of Consumer Psychology, 21*, 115–125.

Fransson, N., & Gärling, T. (1999). Environmental concern: Conceptual definitions, measurement methods, and research findings. *Journal of Environmental Psychology, 19*, 369–382.

Grégoire, Y., & Fisher, R. J. (2008). Customer betrayal and retaliation: When your best customers become your worst enemies. *Journal of the Academy of Marketing Science, 36*, 247–261.

Grégoire, Y., Tripp, T. M., & Legoux, R. (2009). When customer love turns into lasting hate: The effects of relationship strength and time on customer revenge and avoidance. *Journal of Marketing, 73*, 18–32.

Grégoire, Y., Laufer, D., & Tripp, T. M. (2010). A comprehensive model of customer direct and indirect revenge: Understanding the effects of perceived greed and customer power. *Journal of the Academy of Marketing Science, 38*, 738–758.

Haj-Salem, N., & Chebat, J. C. (2013). The double-edged sword: The positive and negative effects of switching costs on customer exit and revenge. *Journal of Business Research, 67*, 1106–1113.

Hinton, E. D., & Goodman, M. K. (2010). Sustainable consumption: Developments, considerations and new directions. In M. R. Redclift & G. Woodgate (Eds.), *The International handbook of environmental sociology* (p. 245). London: Edward Elgar.

Iyer, R., & Muncy, J. A. (2009). Purpose and object of anti-consumption. *Journal of Business Research, 62*, 160–168.

Lastovicka, J. L., Bettencourt, L. A., Hughner, R. S., & Kuntze, R. J. (1999). Lifestyle of the tight and frugal: Theory and measurement. *Journal of Consumer Research, 26*, 85–98.

Lazarus, R. S. (1991). Progress on a cognitive-motivational-relational theory of emotion. *American Psychologist, 46*, 819.

Lee, M. S., Motion, J., & Conroy, D. (2009). Anti-consumption and brand avoidance. *Journal of Business Research, 62*, 169–180.

McColl-Kennedy, J. R., & Sparks, B. A. (2003). Application of fairness theory to service failures and service recovery. *Journal of Service Research, 5*, 251–266.

McColl-Kennedy, J. R., Patterson, P. G., Smith, A. K., & Brady, M. K. (2009). Customer rage episodes: Emotions, expressions and behaviors. *Journal of Retailing, 85*, 222–237.

McCullough, M. E., Rachal, K. C., Sandage, S. J., et al. (1998). Interpersonal forgiving in close relationships: II. Theoretical elaboration and measurement. *Journal of Personality and Social Psychology, 75*, 1586.

Mohr, L. A., Webb, D. J., & Harris, K. E. (2001). Do consumers expect companies to be socially responsible? The impact of corporate social responsibility on buying behavior. *The Journal of Consumer Affairs, 35*, 45–72.

Narver, J. C., & Slater, S. F. (1990). The effect of a market orientation on business profitability. *The Journal of Marketing, 54*, 20–35.

Nepomuceno, M. V., & Laroche, M. (2015a). The impact of materialism and anti-consumption lifestyles on personal debt and account balances. *Journal of Business Research, 68*, 654–664.

Nepomuceno, M. V., & Laroche, M. (2015b). When materialists intend to resist consumption: The moderating role of self-control and long-term orientation. *Journal of Business Ethics, 68*, 1–17.

Price, L. L., & Penaloza, L. (1993). Consumer resistance: A conceptual overview. *Advances in Consumer Research, 20*, 123–128.

Richardson, T., Elliott, P., & Roberts, R. (2013). The relationship between personal unsecured debt and mental and physical health: A systematic review and meta-analysis. *Clinical Psychology Review, 33*, 1148–1162.

Richins, M. L. (2004). The material values scale: Measurement properties and development of a short form. *Journal of Consumer Research, 31*, 209–219.

Sheth, J. N., Sisodia, R. S., & Sharma, A. (2000). The antecedents and consequences of customer-centric marketing. *Journal of the Academy of Marketing Science, 28*, 55–66.

Sheth, J. N., Sethia, N. K., & Srinivas, S. (2011). Mindful consumption: A customer-centric approach to sustainability. *Journal of the Academy of Marketing Science, 39*, 21–39.

Slimak, M. W., & Dietz, T. (2006). Personal values, beliefs, and ecological risk perception. *Risk Analysis, 26*, 1689–1705.

Tangney, J. P., Baumeister, R. F., & Boone, A. L. (2004). High self-control predicts good adjustment, less pathology, better grades, and interpersonal success. *Journal of Personality, 72*, 271–324.

Tax, S. S., Brown, S. W., & Chandrashekaran, M. (1998). Customer evaluations of service complaint experiences: Implications for relationship marketing. *Journal of Marketing, 62*(2), 60–76.

Van Cleave, K., & Angry, V. W. (2015, September 24). Dealers and owners want answers—now. Accessed October 16, 2015. Online at http://www.cbsnews.com/news/angry-vw-dealers-and-owners-want-answers-now/

Zourrig, H., Chebat, J. C., & Toffoli, R. (2009). Consumer revenge behavior: A cross-cultural perspective. *Journal of Business Research, 62*, 995–1001.

Motivation

Gregory Bonn

1 Introduction

Why do people do what they do? Why do individuals often behave in ways that are contrary to their long-term health or well-being? How does motivation influence product perception, and eventually use? And, vice-versa, how does product perception impact motivation? Over the years the topic of human motivation has been approached from numerous different perspectives. Some approaches have focused their attention on biological and psychological *needs*. Others have focused on *learning*, or how the individual is trained to behave in certain ways by contingencies within their environment. Further approaches place more weight on the *cognitive* processes involved in how each individual understands and evaluates the costs and benefits of behaviors. Still other approaches focus more on the dynamic interplay between emotion and intellect, or how conscious and unconscious factors play varying roles in motivation. The first several sections of this contribution provide a brief overview of different types of motivational theories. Following this we will look at the influence of self-understanding and self-regulatory factors as well as personality differences in motivation, some practical implications, and finally how we might reconcile these many different approaches.

G. Bonn (✉)
Department of General Studies, King Fahd University of Petroleum and Minerals, Dhahran, Saudi Arabia

Japan Society for the Promotion of Science, Nagoya University, School of Education and Human Development, Nagoya, Japan
e-mail: gbbonn@hotmail.com

© Springer International Publishing AG 2017
G. Emilien et al. (eds.), *Consumer Perception of Product Risks and Benefits*,
DOI 10.1007/978-3-319-50530-5_20

2   Needs Theories

From the earliest days of psychology, innate needs, or instincts, have been presumed by most theorists to play an important role in human motivation. Early theorists such as William James (1890) and William McDougall (1912) proposed that instincts of various sorts are primary factors in human motivation. McDougall, for example, suggested such instincts as curiosity, nurturing, laughter, lust, and seeking comfort were essential to human behavior. James, as well as Sigmund Freud (1923), focused more on Darwinian instincts—those that are specifically related to survival and reproduction such as cleanliness, fear, anger, and sex/love. Though there were differences among these early theories as to the exact details of how instincts influence motivation, the essence of all was that biological, or innate, drives are the foundation of human motivation; a foundation that is built upon through experience. Throughout the twentieth century, a number of influential theories were proposed along these lines.

2.1   Maslow's Hierarchy of Needs

Probably the most well-known of the more modern needs-based theories of human motivation is Maslow's "hierarchy of needs" (1943). Maslow suggested that, in general, humans seek to satisfy basic physiological needs such as those for food and shelter first. Once those simple physiological needs are met then people turn their attention to other more long-term concerns such as security and safety: Concerns such as being free from the threat of violence and alleviating financial as well as health concerns become of primary concern. Following this, Maslow proposed that humans become free to concentrate on so-called higher order needs such as love/belonging and esteem. Once more fundamental physiological and security concerns are taken care of, people are strongly driven to connect with others. They seek quality relationships such as those between friends, family members, and romantic partners. Upon developing such relationships, the individual, in Maslow's thinking, should eventually form a healthy sense of self-esteem. Humans, he argued, want to be valued and respected by others and, when they experience such respect, they learn to respect themselves.

Once the previously mentioned needs are mastered, Maslow argued, a person becomes more driven to pursue self-actualization, or self-transcendence. Essentially this is a motivation to create, or to express the inner self. Maslow suggested the ultimate goal for humans is to transcend narrow self-interest, but in order to be able to do so, the individual must first master their selfish, individual needs. It is important to note here that, although, the hierarchy of needs is often portrayed as a straight progression from one level to the next, Maslow's thinking was more nuanced. He suggested that, in reality, the levels of personal development and motivation do not progress in a simple linear fashion. Most levels, such as belongingness and self-esteem for example, are interdependent. Also, there are many times when people forsake more fundamental needs such as security or health for theoretically higher order needs such as love or belongingness.

2.2   ERG Theory: Existence, Relatedness, Growth

Alderfer (1969) reworked Maslow's theory into a simpler non-hierarchical model, which he called ERG Theory. Taking into account the previously mentioned inter-relatedness among Maslow's different levels, Alderfer proposed just three essential need categories: Existence, relatedness, and growth. Existence needs include all physiological and safety needs. Relatedness describes needs for relationships and belonging as well as for respect (i.e. being respected by others). Growth needs include internal aspects of esteem (i.e. self-respect or self-esteem), as well as self-actualization and self-expression related motivations. Alderfer argued that these need categories are not necessarily progressive. Instead all three types of needs operate simultaneously, although the relative importance of particular needs might vary between individuals and depending on the context. The ERG model suggests that if specific needs are not met, or not perceived as attainable, individuals will compensate by focusing more intensely on other needs. For example, if a person's need for personal growth is frustrated, they might focus intensely on social needs or gaining approval from others. Alternatively, if a person is very socially isolated, they might focus their attention on artistic pursuits (self-expression or growth-related needs) or on earning a lot of money (existence or security-related needs). In this way ERG theory can be used to explain some individual and group differences in motivational style, where individuals learn to compensate for per-ceived shortcomings in their personal or social situations by focusing more intently on other types categories of needs or desires.

2.3   McClelland's Learned Needs

David McClelland, similarly built upon Maslow's work by suggesting a set of three essential motivating needs: *achievement, affiliation,* and *power.* McClelland's theory, however, emphasizes how individuals differ in their focus on each of these primary needs, and how social and cultural background shapes individuals' need profile. McClelland suggested that the emphasis on certain motivators is learned: Everyone is motivated to some degree by needs for achievement, affilia-tion and power, but we learn over time which are preferred by our cultural surroundings and which we individually are more inclined towards. Thus, each persons' dominant motivations are shaped by their individual experiences as well as by their socio-cultural environment.

2.4   Self-Determination Theory

More recently, Deci and Ryan (2000) have proposed Self-Determination Theory (SDT) which argues that humans have an innate psychological need for autonomy, competence, and relatedness. Essentially, according to SDT, humans want to feel that their actions are freely chosen; that they can function effectively in the areas that are important to them; and they crave high-quality, continuing relationships with other people. To the degree that these needs are satisfied over time, humans tend to function effectively and experience well-being. However, when these needs are thwarted, people tend to exhibit less than optimal functioning and lower levels of life satisfaction. SDT considers many of the less-desirable aspects of human behavior; addiction, aggression, and prejudice for example, to be compensatory reactions to the denial of basic needs, either throughout the course of development or contextually.

2.5   Intrinsic vs Extrinsic Motivation

Ryan and Deci (2000) have also written extensively on the distinction between intrinsic, or internally driven, and extrinsic, or externally driven, motivations. In many cases, external factors such as rewards (say, money or promotions), punishments, or the opinions of others are sources of motivation. Because they are more easily manipulated, such external motivators have been the focus of most learning and motivational theory. Often, however, humans, as well as other animals, are driven by internal factors such as curiosity, enjoyment, interest, and, perhaps, deeply-held values. Intrinsic motivations are not necessarily associated with external rewards. Nevertheless, they can be the source of much long-term effort and creativity.

Research also indicates (see Ryan and Deci for a review) that, depending on various personal and environmental contingencies, motivations can change over time from extrinsic to intrinsic and vice-versa. For example, in some cases, when rewards are provided for an activity that was previously motivated intrinsically, people actually exhibit lower levels of motivation. Other studies have shown that mild threats or risks associated with a behavior can make that behavior more internally motivating (Wilson and Lassiter 1982). Thus, a certain level of risk can actually be motivating. Possibly because the associated excitement is internally rewarding, or possibly because prohibitions can stimulate curiosity which is also, as will be discussed later, an internal motivating factor.

2.6   Basic Emotions and Motivation

From the very early days of psychology, scholars such as William James and Carl Lange have argued for the primacy of physiological states which we interpret as emotions in how humans interpret and react to their surroundings. In recent decades, research on affective neuroscience, or the biology of emotion, has supported the contention that humans, similar to other animals, have fundamental core motivations that are based in neurobiological circuitry. In accord with previously discussed theories, a primary drive to form relationships with other people, or attachments, exists from infancy (Bowlby 1988). Humans are born with specialized neurological circuits that have evolved specifically for social purposes, such as recognizing faces, understanding speech, detecting others' emotions, and mimicking or learning from others' behavior. Essentially, humans are hard-wired from birth to seek out contact with and learn from other humans (Schore 1994). Throughout the lifespan this drive to interact smoothly with others, whom we are evolutionarily dependent upon for survival, actually shapes neural connections within the brain such that humans unconsciously absorb and adhere to social norms of behavior and thought (Quinn 2003).

Expanding further into understanding emotions as fundamental motivators Panksepp (2005) has identified seven human emotions each of which is associated with unique, underlying neural circuitry. These are: Seeking, which is essentially curiosity; a motivational urge towards exploring and understanding one's environment. Fear, a self-protective drive to avoid perceived threats. Nurturing, a drive to connect with and care for others. Panic, anxiety that occurs when interpersonal connections are threatened. Lust, or sexual desire. Rage, or aggression, which is a drive to actively defend against perceived threats (distinct from fear, which motivates one to hide or to flee). Finally, Play which encourages the development of various social and physical skills through active engagement with others. All of these primary emotions are, by nature, innately motivational, though of course, they may at times conflict with each other. Fear or anger, for example, in most situations, will override emotional drives towards seeking/exploring or play. Also, reminiscent of Maslow, physiological needs such as hunger or sleep will generally dull the intensity of emotional drives. Curiosity/seeking and play, for example, are notably reduced when subjects are experiencing hunger or deprived of sleep (Fig. 1).

3   Learning Processes

3.1   Conditioning

The most basic concept involved in learning is generalized in the "law of effect" (Thorndike 1901). This states, in essence, that behaviors followed by satisfying consequences will tend to be repeated and those associated with undesirable results

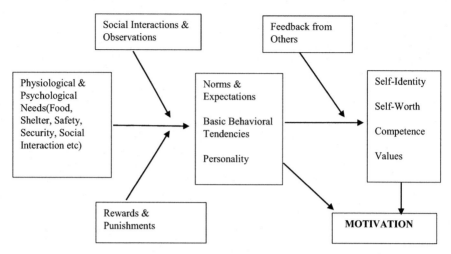

Fig. 1 Generalized needs-based model of motivation: Motivation results from a combination of essential drives, learning, and esteem-related processes

will tend to diminish in frequency. Desirable consequences increase the frequency of a behavior, while undesirable consequences decrease the frequency of behavior. Thus, given a set of physiological and psychological needs, human behavior can be shaped through associating specific behaviors with the satisfaction or denial of various needs. This is referred to as *conditioning*, or *reinforcement,* and it can take numerous forms (Skinner 1938).

What is traditionally referred to as *positive reinforcement* occurs when a behavior becomes associated with desirable outcomes (or rewards). If a person is hungry and they receive some tasty food as a result of a certain behavior, that behavior will be more likely to occur in the future. Similarly, emotional experiences can also reinforce behavior: If a behavior results in positive feedback from others, such as a feeling of social acceptance and belonging, that behavior will be more likely to be repeated. Behavior is also encouraged if it eliminates or reduces the impact of some negative stimulus. For example, if someone feels anxious and they drink a glass of wine and the feeling of anxiety goes away, they will be more likely to drink wine in the future, especially if they are feeling anxious. This is termed (somewhat confusingly) *negative reinforcement* because the behavior is negating, or removing, a negative stimulus. It still, however, encourages the same behavior to occur in the future. Therefore, it is a source of motivation or reinforcement.

Certain consequences, in contrast, tend to reduce the frequency of a behavior: These are termed punishments. Again, punishments can be both positive and negative in nature. A behavior might result in physical pain or some other unpleasant emotion such as fear; this is (again counter-intuitively) *positive punishment*. Positive punishment is a painful physical or mental experience that is associated with a behavior, spanking or scolding for example, which has the effect of reducing the behavior in the future. Such punishments are termed as positive because they add an undesirable association to a behavior. In contrast, *negative punishment* also reduces associated behaviors, but it associates the behavior with the loss, or removal of, positive reinforcers. For example, if a child's bad behavior is associated with losing access to a valued toy or not being given cake after dinner, it is termed as negative punishment. It is still punishment, because it reduces the likelihood of a behavior occurring in the future. However, in the case of positive punishment, a behavior results in a negative consequence that would not have existed before. In the case of negative punishment, a behavior results in the loss of some previously valued, or rewarding, experience. In either case, the associated behavior will be less likely to occur in the future. Hence the label *punishment*.

It is worth noting in this context, that the type of reinforcement associated with a specific behavior can change over time. Someone might begin using drugs, for example, because it provides them with a feeling of elation, a high, which is a *positive reinforcement*. Later, if they become addicted, they might be motivated more by the desire to escape from the physical discomfort associated with withdrawal. This is a *negative reinforcement*, but still an incentive to continue using. Eventually, if they were to arrive at the point where they lost their home or wife or children because of their drug use, this would be a type of *punishment* (negative punishment). They are losing something that they value, therefore they are more motivated to stop using.

Considering the relation of risk perception to conditioning and motivation, it is important to also consider the concept of immediacy: If a punishment is expected to occur in the future it will be strongly discounted in motivational force when compared to rewards that are expected immediately (Skinner 1953). Of course, there are many ways in which expected future costs or rewards might influence behavior: The size of the reward/cost; perceived likelihood of the outcome; current appetitive state; and individual differences, all play a role in such situations. Nevertheless, with all other factors remaining constant, there is a strong overall tendency to devalue future rewards and risks in comparison to currently available rewards or costs. This concept is discussed at length in a separate contribution of this volume entitled *temporal discounting of future risks*.

3.2 Social Learning

Although most early research on learning focused on the direct effect of rewards and punishments on behavior, more recently, the understanding that relatedness and social contact are central to human motivation, has led psychologists to focus more on the effects of social context, and how human behaviors are shaped by the behaviors of others within their social group. Bandura et al. (1961) identified these processes as *social learning*. A key finding from social learning research is the concept of *modeling*, that behaviors can be learned through observation alone. People, especially children, are keen observers of others, and they tend to imitate behaviors that they observe as rewarding for other people. The observer does not need to have a direct experience of being rewarded for a particular behavior themselves in order to be motivated to engage in that behavior (Bandura 1977). They merely need to observe the behavior in others and perceive it to be associated with some desirable outcome such as, say, physical pleasure or social acceptance. Thus, given the importance that humans place on social relatedness and acceptance, if behaviors are portrayed or interpreted as normative for a social group, the desire to fit into that social group can in itself become a strong motivator to engage in those behaviors (Erbaydar et al. 2005).

Through such social learning processes, humans absorb, largely unconsciously, wide ranges of behaviors and cognitive patterns which, over time, become engrained in their understanding of who they are, and what is normal (Erikson 1959; Quinn 2003). Considered from this perspective, the vast majority of day-to-day human behavior is not motivated by cognitive evaluations, but by fundamental, survival-based, tendencies for human beings to learn from and fit into their social surroundings. When deep-seated, culturally learned, normative behavior and cognitive tendencies are challenged by new information, as often as not, an array of defense mechanism are employed to reframe or reinterpret such new information in ways which are less threatening (Festinger 1957). This concept is discussed further in the section titled *cognitive dissonance*.

3.3   Social Influences on Risk Perception

Specifically considering how social and cultural learning processes relate to the perception of risk, Kasperson et al. (1988) has described a series of processes that lead to the social amplification (or, conversely, attenuation) of risk. Kasperson argues that the perception of risk is not, for the public at large, based upon a mathematical assessment of the probabilities and magnitudes of potential events. Instead, risk perception results from a combination of intuitive biases, personal interests, and cultural values. Individuals and groups through their psychological and cultural reactions to risk-related stimuli create secondary social and economic effects which ripple throughout the rest of society often causing the public to either greatly overestimate or underestimate the risks involved in certain behaviors or events.

Essentially Kasperson suggests that risk perception, and social learning in general, tends to have a kind of snowballing effect. People's emotional reactions to events, as well as the observed reactions of other people can cause chain-reaction-like effects that either increase or decrease the societal perception of and reaction to risk. Traditional, strictly analytical, risk analyses neglect such social effects. Thus, their results often differ greatly from how the public perceives the severity of different risks. One example of such social amplification processes is the perception of risk from terror attacks: Americans often rate the risk of terror attacks as a great threat to their safety, when in fact they are about 2000 times more likely to die in an automobile accident than a terrorist attack. The news coverage and emotional shock involved in terrorist attacks causes the actual risk involved to be greatly overrated compared to using a product that is a normal part of day-to-day life such as motor vehicles. Likewise, the risks involved in using other products that are deeply embedded in many cultures, such as alcohol and tobacco, are often grossly under-perceived due to their normalization.

4 Cognitive Models of Motivation

4.1 Equity Theory

Adams' Equity Theory (1963) describes motivational tendencies related to the perceived fairness of a situation. Individuals tend to evaluate the effort put into an activity in relation to what they receive, or expect to receive, in return. Essentially, the individual desires an equitable, or balanced, relationship between their effort expended and what they receive in return. When there is an imbalance, or effort begins to outweigh rewards he becomes de-motivated. Equity theory posits that these perceptions of fairness are rooted largely in how the individual views his own situation relative to others'. If he perceives others to be receiving greater benefits in relation to their efforts, for example, if a student sees classmates continually receiving better marks while putting in the same or less study time, he will be less motivated to study. Optimal motivation, thus, occurs when individuals perceive their situation to be equitable; that they are being treated fairly and receiving appropriate recognition or other compensation for their efforts.

4.2 Expectancy

Expectancy Theory (Vroom 1964) proposes that the individual weighs expected rewards vs. desired results. The individual makes decisions by estimating how well the expected results of a behavior match with desired results. The *valence*, or degree of desirability, of an outcome is the first element of this evaluation. Potential outcomes are evaluated in terms of how desirable or undesirable they are. The individual also evaluates *instrumentality,* or their perceived ability to achieve an outcome. Given these variables, *expectancy* is estimated: The individual forms a subjective impression how likely it is that a specific action will lead to various outcomes, and those outcomes are weighted by their relative desirability. Winning the lottery, for example, is a very desirable outcome, however, its likelihood is quite low, but also the relative cost of a lottery ticket is low. Given the high level of desirability, many people are still motivated to buy lottery tickets despite the low possibility of winning. Expectancy theory, thus, suggests a calculus involving the desirability, achievability and costs or risks involved when making decisions.

4.3 Social Cognitive Theory

Later in his career, Bandura (1986), expanded on his theory of social learning to include more cognitive factors. His newer Social Cognitive Theory (SCT) thus includes consideration of the moderating and self-regulatory capacities involved in cognitive evaluations. Similar to expectancy theory, Bandura suggests that actions are evaluated based upon the desirability and likelihood of expected outcomes. SCT, however, specifically emphasizes the role that social modeling plays in such evaluations. Cognitive evaluations are based on standards, or benchmarks, that are shaped through observing and interacting with others. These standards guide the manner in which individuals value rewards and evaluate potential behaviors. Bandura particularly emphasizes three cognitive factors involved in motivation: *Self-efficacy;* do they feel that they can effectively perform the action? *Feedback*; what kind of response do they receive, or expect to receive, when they perform the action? And, *environmental context*; what environmental factors are present that either encourage or discourage that behavior? Thus, similar to expectancy theory, social cognitive theory argues that the individual weighs several factors against each in making decisions, but Bandura places special emphasis on the anchoring role of social standards and socio-environmental context in these evaluations.

5 Conscious and Unconscious Processing

5.1 Psychodynamic Theory

In contrast to the idea of motivation being either strictly rational or based upon instinct, Freud (1923) proposed a more dynamic, multi-layered structure of the human psyche. Freud argued, similar to other needs theorists that the root of all human motivation lies in evolutionarily-based psychological and physiological drives, but he also asserted that such instinctual drives are engaged in constant interplay with other aspects of the mind which are oriented towards the outside world and fitting into the social environment. Freud termed the instinctual part of human nature the "id". When born, he argued, a child possesses only the id; the set of drives and wants that allow it to live and feel satiated. This id operates, in Freud's terms, according to the "pleasure principle": It merely wants to feel good, to satisfy its' needs. The id is essentially unconscious. Though the conscious mind may be aware of the id's desires and wants, it cannot negate them. The conscious mind instead, over time, develops an understanding of how to satisfy the id within its' existing physical and social constraints. What Freud terms the "ego", or the self, is a mechanism that develops over time which enables the individual to satisfy his needs. People learn the necessary skills and social protocols to get what they want and need within their physical and social environment. Freud referred to this as the "reality principle". The ego, or self, must balance the unconscious desires and needs of the id with the external constraints of living amongst other people in a physical world. Thus, in Freud's view humans possess the ability to rationally evaluate costs and benefits as many cognitive theories propose. However, such rationality is essentially beholden to unconscious urges which, at many times, contradict the self's rational evaluations as well as society's moral codes. In other words, Freud argued that humans can behave rationally at times, however, at bottom they are driven by instinct.

5.2   Fast and Slow Thinking

More recently, Nobel Prize winner Daniel Kahneman (2011) has provided extensive evidence for the various ways in which human thought processes are affected by unconscious biases as opposed to being strictly rational evaluations. Essentially, Kahneman concludes that there are two modes of thought that humans generally engage in: Type 1, or "Fast" thinking, and type 2 or "Slow" thinking. Fast thinking (also sometimes called "hot" cognition) is instinctive, stereotypic, and emotional; while slow thinking (or "cold" cognition) is logical, deliberative, effortful, and relatively infrequent. Kahneman has found that much of human cognition is guided by "heuristics", or mental shortcuts which circumvent logic, although often the individual believes that they are being rational when engaging in such thinking.

Many such heuristics have been experimentally established. Some that are particularly relevant to the evaluation of risk are: A general tendency towards optimism, which includes a belief that we have control over our lives, as well as a strong bias towards considering only evidence that we have experienced directly. In other words, when evaluating risk, individuals will tend to consider data that they have gathered personally: If an individual has positive associations with a product, but has not personally experienced negative consequences of its' use, he will tend to weigh his own positive personal experiences much more heavily than abstract potential downsides. "Framing" of information is also a key factor in how people make judgments. For example, if one states: "90% of consumers who use this product experience no ill effects"; instead of "10% of consumers who used this product became ill", people will tend to judge the risks as less severe. Similarly, Kahneman has established an "availability" heuristic, which demonstrates a human tendency to weight readily available (i.e. oft repeated) information especially heavily in decision making. Thus, if someone consistently hears of the benefits from using a product, but only occasionally hears of any negative repercussions, they will tend to focus more on the readily accessible (oft-repeated) information.

6   Self-Understanding and Motivation

Psychologists have gradually been developing an understanding of the importance of personal identity, or a sense of oneself and how one fits into the broader society, in motivation (Erikson 1959). Humans seem to have an innate desire to make sense of their existence and do this by creating internal stories or narratives (McAdams 2001) that provide context and meaning to their day-to-day existence and the activities that they find themselves engaged in (Quinn 2003). As has been discussed extensively to this point, humans engage in behaviors for a multitude of reasons, many of which are not strictly rational. The individual, however, generally wants to feel good about himself. He wants to feel that his behaviors make sense and are justified. This allows him to maintain a positive sense of self, which is important for maintaining future engagement with the world. Thus, there is a core motivation for individuals to portray themselves internally, in their own personal narratives, as well as externally, in how they present themselves to other people in a rationally consistent and meaningful way. Reminiscent of Kahneman's bias towards optimism, people are generally driven towards believing that they are correct and justified in what they do.

6.1   Cognitive Dissonance

A correlate of this desire for consistency is the well-established tendency towards cognitive dissonance reduction (Festinger 1957). Essentially, when the individual experiences inconsistency, such as having contradictory beliefs or inconsistent patterns of thought and behavior, he experiences anxiety, or discomfort, and is motivated to eliminate the inconsistency. This, termed *dissonance reduction*, can be accomplished by either changing one's behavior or changing one's cognitions. For example, if someone learns that a product they have been using is potentially harmful, they could stop using it, or they could alter that cognition by saying to themselves that they and their friends have been using the product for a long time and have seen no ill-effects, therefore it must be fine. They might even attribute the information to some kind of left-wing conspiracy to harm their preferred brand, and thus become even more loyal to the product. Such entrenchment of behavior in the face of threat has been demonstrated extensively in research related to Terror Management Theory (Greenberg et al. 1997). Specifically, in the face of threat, people tend to defend themselves psychologically by strengthening their association with key aspects of their identity, such as political beliefs or well established behaviors. Threatened people express greater levels of loyalty to social groups, ideas, and norms that they identify with. Thus, especially in the case of well-established behaviors or social norms, perceived threats could actually increase the individual's motivation to engage in risky behaviors (Fig. 2).

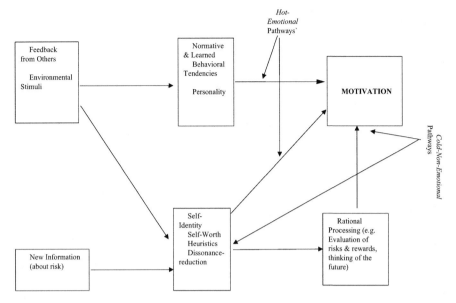

Fig. 2 Simplified model illustrating multiple processing pathways. Information first passes through the individual's self-structures and is subject to dissonance reduction. When in a non-aroused state, rational structures can become engaged and influence motivation. Most times, especially during emotional arousal, these rational pathways are bypassed in favor of well-rehearsed behavioral strategies and self-promotion/protection

7 Personality Factors and Individual Differences in Motivation

Decades of research has shown that, across cultures, individuals tend to differ across a relatively small number of personality traits which are stable throughout the lifespan. Eysenck (1952) first identified two essential dimensions to personality: Extraversion vs. introversion; a person's tendency to be outgoing, sociable and energetic as opposed to reserved and reflective, and neuroticism vs. stability; a person's tendency to be sensitive, nervous, and prone to negative emotions, as opposed to being emotionally stable and calm. Starting with Tupes and Christal (1961) a number of researchers have expanded the number of personality dimensions to five, often referred to as the "Big Five". In addition to Eysenck's dimensions of extraversion and neuroticism, the big five also includes openness, conscientiousness, and agreeableness. Openness is the degree to which the individual is open to new experiences, curious about new ideas and creative, as opposed to cautious, pragmatic, and consistent. Conscientiousness is the degree to which the individual is organized, self-disciplined, and dutiful as opposed flexible, spontaneous, and possibly unreliable. Finally, agreeableness is the tendency to be cooperative, compassionate, and helpful, as opposed to competitive, mistrustful, and antagonistic towards others. Differences in personality can influence how risk is perceived.

7.1 Individual/Personality Differences in Risky Behavior

Generally, research has shown that young adults who engage in risky behaviors share a number of traits: They are non-traditional, and tend not to be harm-avoidant. They are less self-controlled and less careful. (Caspi et al. 1997). Additionally, youths who engage in multiple risky behaviors tend to be more aggressive than those engaging in only one type of risky behavior. Interestingly, such differences in personality and behavior appear to have roots in early childhood, if not genetics. "Under-controlled children", meaning those who had difficulty sitting still, or, were impulsive, irritable, and out of control, at age 3, were more likely to engage in risky behaviors at age 21 (Caspi et al. 1997). Similarly, Zuckerman and Kuhlman (2000) found that risky behaviors such as binge drinking, smoking, drug use and risky sex tend to be interrelated: Those that engage in one risky behavior are more likely to engage in others. Risky behaviors also closely relate to personality traits such as impulsivity and aggression/hostility.

There are, however, contradictory findings with regard to sociability. Zuckerman and Caspi found opposite relationships in regard to sociability and risky behaviors. Likely this difference stems from differences between the contexts of the studies. One study (Caspi) using a community sample found that greater sociability led to less drinking, while the other (Zuckerman) which sampled students at a university with a strong drinking culture found sociability to relate to higher levels of binge drinking. This difference can probably be interpreted in terms of a general desire for social acceptance: In contexts where a majority of people engage in risky behaviors, people will be more likely to engage in those behaviors. Although risky behaviors might be frowned upon by the general public, context can play a large role in how individuals, especially highly sociable individuals relate to such risk.

7.2 Individual Differences in Assessing the Future

The perceived delay of potential costs or benefits is also important in risk assessment. Generally, the level of motivation associated with an expected reward or punishment decreases with the amount of time assumed to fall in between a behavior and its' potential reward or punishment. Studies, however, also point to individual differences in the tendency for discounting the future. Generally, those with higher levels of extraversion show a preference for immediate gratification. Those with addictive tendencies such as heavy drinkers and drug users also tend to place less weight on future consequences (Ainslie and Monterosso 2003). In contrast, those with higher IQs, or greater cognitive capacity, tend to value future consequences more highly (Hirsh et al. 2010).

Situational factors, such as emotional state, also play a role in the degree to which people consider future costs or benefits. During states of emotional arousal, for example when viewing photos of attractive women, or after winning a game, people tend towards pursuing immediate gratification and disregarding future consequences. This is especially true of those high in extraversion (Wilson and Daly 2004).

7.3 Lack of Motivation

Patients exhibiting clinically low levels of motivation generally have an altered perception of how effort relates to reward (Gard et al. 2014). Essentially, those who show abnormal lack of motivation tend to see the effort involved in pursuing any particular goal as far outweighing any possible benefits involved; effort is overvalued while rewards are undervalued. As discussed in the previous section on cognitive factors, similar thought processes probably relate to de-motivation even in non-clinical populations. When individuals feel ineffective at performing a task; when they lack self-efficacy or feelings of competence, they are less motivated. Also, when the individual feels as their situation is unfair, or they are not receiving appropriate rewards for the effort that they expend, they are less motivated. Similarly, when individuals perceive environmental barriers or social impediments to effectively performing an action they will be less motivated.

8 Motivation and Risk Perception

Although the topic is too complex to sum up neatly, several broad conclusions can be arrived at with regard to motivation and risk perception.

8.1 Human Thinking Is Generally Based on Shortcuts

In general, humans tend to focus on the ideas/associations that are most readily accessible. Those ideas, good or bad, that have been repeated often and those that have been introduced recently will be recalled most readily (Kahneman 2011). People also tend to prefer and have a positive bias towards what is familiar and deeply embedded within their social environment (Quinn 2003). Emotional state is also important, when people are experiencing strong emotions they will tend not to engage in rational assessments (Kahnemann 2011) and they will be more likely to choose products based on superficial qualities or previous patterns. Similarly, there is a tendency for people to overvalue the present, weighing current rewards much more highly than future costs. This tendency is especially strong during times of high emotional arousal as well as for those with extraverted personalities (Hirsh et al. 2010).

8.2   Humans Want to Feel Socially Connected and Capable

Belonging and relatedness are powerful motivators (Deci and Ryan 2000). Humans have a basic need to feel that they are a part of a group and that they are socially connected. When they feel ostracized or that their social relationships are at risk, it is interpreted emotionally as a threat to their very existence (Greenberg et al. 1997). Conversely, when individuals feel that they are accepted and that their position as part of a valued group is secure, they feel relaxed and empowered (Ryan and Deci 2000). Thus, given the choice of doing something that is socially normative and that will make the individual feel more connected to desirable others, the individual is strongly motivated to devalue any risks that might be associated with that behavior. Similarly, humans want to feel competent, and that their actions are freely chosen (Deci and Ryan 2000). If they or their social group are engaging in certain behaviors or consuming certain products, they are often motivated to do the same and to protect their self-image by devaluing the risks and overvaluing the benefits associated with those behaviors.

8.3   People Want to Feel that They Are Consistent and Correct

People have a basic need for cognitive consistency; they want to be able to consider themselves to be rational and sensible (Festinger 1957). Generally, people will be motivated to choose products whose perceived benefits far outweigh any potential risks (Vroom 1964). However, given conflicting evidence, humans generally prefer information that allows them to feel competent and consistent (Ryan and Deci 2000) and they are biased towards filtering information in ways that allow them to feel they are not making poor decisions (Asch 1951). Finally, when people are threatened with a high level of risk, they tend to retreat towards the safety of their cultural and social norms (Greenberg et al. 1997). Oftentimes the most salient risk or benefit is not so much inherent in the product itself but how that product relates to their important relationships and their social embeddedness. The perception of serious risk makes people even more motivated to conform to social norms, and less likely to engage in strictly rational evaluations.

In the end, humans do have the capability of performing rational evaluations and carefully assessing the costs and benefits associated with products. Most day-to-day decisions, however, are based upon less effortful mental shortcuts which allow them to maintain their self-image while efficiently navigating their physical and social worlds.

References

Adams, J. S. (1963). Toward an understanding of inequity. *Journal of Abnormal and Social Psychology, 67*, 422–436.

Ainslie, G., & Monterosso, J. (2003). Hyperbolic discounting as a factor in addiction: A critical analysis. In R. Vuchinich & N. Heather (Eds.), *Choice, behavioral economics and addiction*. Oxford: Pergamon.

Alderfer, C. P. (1969). An empirical test of a new theory of human needs. *Organizational Behavior and Performance, 4*(2), 142–175.

Asch, S. E. (1951). Effects of group pressure upon the modification and distortion of judgements. In H. Guetzkow (Ed.), *Groups, leadership and men*. Pittsburgh: Carnegie Press.

Bandura, A. (1977). *Social learning theory*. Englewood Cliffs, NJ: Prentice Hall.

Bandura, A. (1986). *Social foundations of thought and action: A social cognitive theory*. Saddle River, NJ: Prentice-Hall.

Bandura, A., Ross, D., & Ross, S. A. (1961). Transmission of aggression through the imitation of aggressive models. *Journal of Abnormal and Social Psychology, 63*, 575–582.

Bowlby, J. (1988). *A secure base: Parent-child attachment and healthy human development*. London: Routledge.

Caspi, A., et al. (1997). Personality differences predict health-risk behaviors in young adulthood: Evidence from a longitudinal study. *Journal of Personality and Social Psychology, 73*, 1052–1063.

Deci, E. L., & Ryan, R. M. (2000). The 'what' and 'why' of goal pursuits: Human needs and the self-determination of behavior. *Psychological Inquiry, 11*, 227–268.

Erbaydar, T., Lawrence, S., Dagli, E., Hayran, O., & Collishaw, N. E. (2005). Influence of social environment in smoking among adolescents in Turkey. *European Journal of Public Health, 15*, 404–410.

Erikson, E. H. (1959). *Identity and the life cycle*. New York: Norton.

Eysenck, H. J. (1952). *The scientific study of personality*. London: Routledge.

Festinger, L. (1957). *A theory of cognitive dissonance*. Palo Alto: Stanford University Press.

Freud, S. (1923/1960). *The ego and the id* (trans. J. Strachey). New York: Norton.

Gard, D. E., Sanchez, A. H., et al. (2014). Do people with schizophrenia have difficulty anticipating pleasure, engaging in effortful behavior, or both? *Journal of Abnormal Psychology, 123*, 771–782.

Greenberg, J., Solomon, S., & Pyszczynski, T. (1997). Terror management theory of self-esteem and cultural worldviews: Empirical assessments and conceptual refinements. In M. P. Zanna (Ed.), *Advances in experimental social psychology* (Vol. 29, pp. 61–139). San Diego: Academic Press.

Hirsh, J. B., et al. (2010). Positive mood effects on delay discounting. *Emotion, 10*, 717–721.

James, W. (1890). *The principles of psychology*. New York: Holt.

Kahneman, D. (2011). *Thinking, fast and slow*. New York: Farrar Straus and Giroux.

Kasperson, R. E., et al. (1988). The social amplification of risk: A conceptual framework. *Risk Analysis, 8*(2), 177–187.

Maslow, A. H. (1943). A theory of human motivation. *Psychological Review, 50*(4), 370–396.

McAdams, D. P. (2001). The psychology of life stories. *Review of General Psychology, 5*, 100–122.

McDougall, W. (1912). *Psychology: The study of behaviour*. London: Williams and Norgate.

Panksepp, J. (2005). Affective consciousness: Core emotional feelings in animals and humans. *Consciousness and Cognition, 14*, 30–80.

Quinn, N. (2003). Cultural selves. *Annals of the New York Academy of Sciences, 1001*, 145–176.

Ryan, R. M., & Deci, E. L. (2000). Intrinsic and extrinsic motivations: Classic definitions and new directions. *Contemporary Educational Psychology, 25*, 54–67.

Schore, A. N. (1994). *Affect regulation and the origin of the self: The neurobiology of emotional development*. Hillsdale, NJ: Erlbaum.

Skinner, B. F. (1938). *The behavior of organisms*. New York: Appleton-Century.

Skinner, B. F. (1953). *Science and human behavior*. New York: Macmillan.

Thorndike, E. L. (1901). Animal intelligence: An experimental study of the associative processes in animals. *Psychological Review Monograph Supplement, 2*, 1–109.

Tupes, E. C., & Christal, R. E. (1961). Recurrent personality factors based on trait ratings. Technical Report ASD-TR-61-97. Personnel Laboratory, Air Force Systems Command. Lackland, TX.

Vroom, V. H. (1964). *Work and motivation*. New York: Wiley.

Wilson, M., & Daly, M. (2004). Do pretty women inspire men to discount the future? *Procedures of the Royal Society of London, 271*, S177–S179.

Wilson, T. D., & Lassiter, G. D. (1982). Increasing intrinsic interest with superfluous external constraints. *Journal of Personality and Social Psychology, 42*, 811–819.

Zuckerman, M., & Kuhlman, D. M. (2000). Personality and risk-taking: Common biosocial factors. *Journal of Personality, 68*, 999–1029.

Marketing and Market Research

Burak Tunca

1 What Is Marketing and Market Research?

Business history abounds with stories of successes and failures. There are many brands and products that remained relevant to customers over time and across international markets, as well as iconic companies that have disappeared from the marketplace. Although there are several reasons as to why businesses fail, in many cases the culprit is the inability to identify and meet needs and wants of the market, or simply, failures in marketing and market research.

The American Marketing Association formally defines marketing as "the activity, set of institutions, and processes for creating, communicating, delivering, and exchanging offerings that have value for customers, clients, partners, and society at large" (AMA 2016). Marketing thus represents a confluence of different actors involved in exchange processes. The objective of businesses is to deliver sought after offerings to the exchange and to obtain desired responses (e.g., positive judgments and feelings) from other parties (Kotler and Keller 2016). In other words, for businesses, marketing needs to managed. Marketing management can be defined as "the art and science of choosing target markets and getting, keeping, and growing customers through creating, delivering, and communicating superior customer value" (Kotler and Keller 2016, p. 27).

How can marketers identify and deliver the offerings customers need and want? This crucial information is generally provided to the marketing managers through a process called market research. Market research can be defined as "the systematic gathering and interpretation of information about individuals or organizations using the statistical and analytical methods and techniques of the applied social sciences to gain insight or support decision making" (Phillips 2007, p. 38). This definition

B. Tunca (✉)
School of Business and Law, University of Agder, Post Box 422, Kristiansand, Norway
e-mail: burak.tunca@uia.no

© Springer International Publishing AG 2017
G. Emilien et al. (eds.), *Consumer Perception of Product Risks and Benefits*,
DOI 10.1007/978-3-319-50530-5_21

highlights the two major aspects of market research: it is a function and it is a process.

First, market research serves the function of providing marketing intelligence to the managers for effective decision making. Management can use this intelligence for planning (e.g., assessing the environment or determining opportunities), problem-solving (e.g., decisions regarding marketing activities), or control (e.g., monitoring the status, Churchill and Iacobucci 2005). Second, market research is a dynamic process that consists the steps of problem formulation, research design, sampling, data collection, data analysis, and market research report.

Note that "market research" and "marketing research" are two terms that generally create confusion. Hunt (1976) makes the distinction that marketing research is concerned with expanding our knowledge of marketing (e.g., developing new theories), whereas market research is concerned with solving marketing related problems of companies. To maintain consistency, I use the term "market research" throughout this contribution. Nevertheless, the topics presented here are equally relevant in both market and marketing research applications.

The objective of this contribution is to familiarize the readers with emerging issues in marketing and market research. Most of the topics presented here could easily be the subject of an entire contribution or article; I therefore only introduce the main ideas and most widely known publications for each topic. Interested readers are encouraged to follow the references for more thorough information.

2 Marketing and the Contemporary Issues

Marketing is highly susceptible to the rapidly changing environment. Kotler and Keller (2016) identify three transformative forces that shape marketing management today: technology, globalization, and social responsibility.

First, technology, particularly advancements in mobile phones and the Internet, introduced new challenges and opportunities for marketers. Consumers are increasingly spending more time online, mostly using smart phones and tablets, where they receive marketing campaigns, communicate with brands, and make purchases (Winer and Dhar 2011). Second, rapid globalization, especially in the form of advanced transportation and communication, allowed companies to penetrate into foreign markets and allowed customers to make purchases globally. And third, marketers are increasingly being called to respond to ethical issues, sustainability, and social responsibility in their operations (Kotler and Keller 2016).

These transformative forces gave rise to new consumer and company capabilities (Kotler and Keller 2016). For example, consumers can quickly get in touch with companies via social media, compare competing products and prices more easily over the Internet, rapidly obtain information about the experiences of other consumers with a company, and customize and co-create products and services (Winer and Dhar 2011). Put simply, consumers are more powerful.

Companies also acquired new capabilities. For example, marketers can get richer information about markets, customers, and competitors from the Internet, augment customer-brand relationships over social media platforms, reach the target market on mobile phones, benefit from online brand communities, and supply offerings and marketing promotions tailored to specific customer groups (Kotler and Keller 2016).

These new marketing realities reshaped fundamental philosophies of marketing. Kotler and Keller (2016) point out that marketing managers are moving forward to the concept of the holistic marketing concept from the marketing concept, and the traditional four Ps of marketing (i.e., product, price, place, and promotion) are being updated with new variables.

2.1 From the Marketing Concept to the Holistic Marketing Concept

The marketing concept, which holds that the key to marketing success is delivering superior value to the target market, has been the dominating marketing philosophy since the 1950s (Kotler and Keller 2016). Prior to the marketing concept, companies embraced other philosophies such as the product concept (i.e., the key is producing the best product) and the selling concept (i.e., the key is persuading customers to buy the products). With its focus on customer satisfaction, the marketing concept quickly replaced the product and selling dominant perspectives.

The transformative forces of the twenty-first century gave rise to a new conceptualization of marketing activities called the holistic marketing concept (Kotler and Keller 2016). As the name suggests, the holistic marketing concept recognizes the necessity of a broad, integrated perspective on marketing programs, processes, and activities. Four components characterize holistic marketing: (1) relationship marketing, (2) integrated marketing, (3) internal marketing, and (4) performance marketing (Kotler and Keller 2016).

First, relationship marketing aims to develop mutually satisfying, enduring relationships with the stakeholders of the company (e.g., customers, employees, business partners, shareholders, etc.). From the relationship marketing perspective, these long-term relationships create a valuable asset for the company called a marketing network. Thus, stronger the marketing network, the higher the profits.

Second, integrated marketing aims to create value form marketing activities as a whole, such that all marketing activities are designed and implemented as a part of an integrated system. Integrated marketing also requires integrated communication and channel strategies.

Third, internal marketing aims to ensure that appropriate marketing principles are adopted not only in the marketing department, but also throughout the organization. Internal marketing recognizes that all departments in the organization should understand the company's marketing orientation and cooperate to deliver superior value to the customers. This requires significant commitment and involvement from the senior management.

Last, performance marketing aims to understand returns on marketing activities, both financially and nonfinancially. Marketers are increasingly assessing financial returns through intangible assets such as brand equity, customer base, and relationships. Furthermore, in accord with the greater customer focus on social responsibility, marketers are increasingly considering the ethical, social, and environmental impacts of their marketing activities.

2.2 The Updated Four Ps and the Four As

Traditionally, the marketing mix (or marketing tactics) has been conceptualized through the famous four Ps, that is, *product* (the goods and services offered by the company), *price* (the financial value of the goods and services), *place* (channels where the goods and services are available), and *promotion* (activities designed to promote the goods and services). In the face of new marketing realities and the holistic marketing concept, Kotler and Keller (2016) introduced an updated version of the four Ps, which incorporates people, processes, programs, and performance.

First, the *people* concept recognizes the importance of employees for marketing success, thereby reflecting the internal marketing component of the holistic marketing concept. It also suggests that viewing consumers as people and paying attention to their lives more broadly is valuable for marketers. Second, the *processes* concept reflects the value of establishing processes to enhance long term relationships with the stakeholders of the company, thereby corresponding to the relationship marketing component of the holistic marketing concept. Third, the *programs* concept reflects the company's integrated marketing activities (online and offline) directed at the consumers. Last, the *performance* concept reflects financial and nonfinancial implications of the marketing activities, as in the performance marketing component of the holistic marketing concept.

In addition to the updated four Ps, Sheth and Sisodia (2012) presents a novel, customer-oriented framework that outlines the four As of marketing, namely, acceptability, affordability, accessibility, and awareness.

Acceptability refers to the extent to which a company's offerings meet or exceed customer needs and expectations. The two dimensions of acceptability are functional acceptability (objective performance attributes of the offering) and psychological acceptability (subjective image attributes of the offering).

Affordability refers to the extent to which customers can afford the price of an offering. Affordability also has two dimensions: economic affordability (ability to pay) and psychological affordability (willingness to pay).

Accessibility refers to the extent to which customers can easily acquire an offering. The two dimensions of accessibility are availability (the company supplies match the customer demand) and convenience (customers can reach the offering easily).

Awareness, finally, refers to the extent to which customers are informed about the attributes and benefits of a product, such that this awareness persuades them to try the offering or continue buying it. Product knowledge and brand awareness are the two dimensions of awareness.

3   Market Research Process and the Contemporary Issues

Market research is not a static entity, but a dynamic process that consists of sequential steps. Market research process begins with problem formulation, proceeds with research design, sampling, data collection, data analysis, and ends with a market research report. In reality, however, researchers do not follow this order in a lockstep fashion, but rather go back and forth between steps as they refine the decisions made in each step (Churchill and Iacobucci 2005).

3.1   Formulating Research Problems

The first step of market research process is concerned with research problem formulation. This is a crucial step in the process, because, as we will see in the subsequent sections, most of the decisions made in the rest of the process are highly dependent on the research problem at hand. Put simply, the market research process will be hampered without a clearly formulated research problem.

The nature of research problems is generally different among marketing academics and practitioners. Marketing academics aim at developing new knowledge and making contributions to marketing theory. For example, recent special issues of esteemed marketing journals would give a general idea about research problems marketing academics are currently interested in. Marketing practitioners, on the other hand, aim at assisting managerial decision making by findings solutions to marketing problems or identifying opportunities for the company. For example, what are the customer perceptions of our new product packaging? Or, would our product sell in a new target market? Such problems and opportunities may arise from unanticipated changes in the internal and external business environment (e.g., technological or societal changes), planned changes (e.g., introduction of a new product), or ideas that emerge by chance (e.g., from a customer feedback; Churchill and Iacobucci 2005).

When formulating problems, researchers are advised to delay research until the problem at hand is clearly defined (Brown et al. 2014). To achieve this objective, researchers should first understand the problem. Meetings and discussions with clients and decision makers are essential components of this step. Such meetings not only enable researchers to obtain background information about the problem and capture the problem from the decision maker's perspective, but also augment engagement of the client in the overall market research process and establish client's expectations from the research (Brown et al. 2014; Malhotra 2015). The meetings and discussions with decision makers can be structured by conducting a problem audit, which can identify underlying causes of the problem at hand by examining the origin and the nature of the problem and establishing alternative courses of action, preferably with a team consisting of the market researchers and members from the management (Malhotra 2015). Problem audits can be supplemented with secondary data and exploratory research (e.g., focus groups or interviews with industry experts).

Additionally, to better understand the problem, researchers should also comprehend the organization and the industry, or in other words, the environmental context of the problem. To accomplish this task, researchers should take into account past information and forecasts (for the organization and the industry), organizational resources and constraints, organizational objectives, buyer behavior, legal and economic environment, and finally the marketing and technological skills of the organization (Malhotra 2015).

After soliciting information from decision makers and examining the environmental context to understand the problem, researchers should formulate the problem. At this step, it is important to distinguish between management decision problems and market research problems. While management decision problems are action-oriented and aimed at what the decision maker needs to do (e.g., should we introduce a new product?), market research problems are information-oriented and aimed at providing the information to assist decision-making (e.g., what are the consumer preferences for a new product?; Malhotra 2015). These two problems are, however, strongly interrelated. In other words, the market research problem can be seen as a restatement of the management decision problem from the researcher's viewpoint (Brown et al. 2014). The market research problem should not only be closely linked to the management decision problem, but also guide the overall research project (Malhotra 2015).

When defining market research problems, researchers face the challenge of defining the problem very broadly (i.e., failing to define a specific problem to be addressed) or very narrowly (i.e., failing to consider alternative approaches to the problem). Recognizing the shortcomings of overly broad or narrow research problems, Malhotra (2015) suggests that the market research problem should encompass a broad statement, which provides a general description of the problem, and specific components, which guides the subsequent steps of the research project. To illustrate, a broad statement would be "what are the purchase intentions of customers for a new product?", and the corresponding specific components to this broad statement would be "who are our customers?" and "what is the level of brand loyalty among customers?". The overall problem formulation process is summarized in Fig. 1.

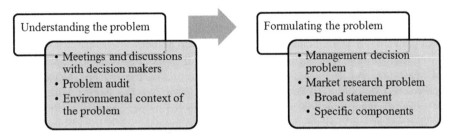

Fig. 1 The problem formulation process (adapted from Malhotra 2015)

3.2   Research Design

Once a clear market research problem is formulated, the next step is to select the appropriate research design to address this problem. Research design can be viewed as an action plan that guides researcher's decisions in the subsequent sampling and data collection steps. Research designs generally serve the objectives of three types of research: (1) *exploratory*, when the objective is to provide insights into understanding a problem or to uncover novel ideas, (2) *descriptive*, when the objective is to describe a phenomenon, and (3) *causal*, when the objective is to establish cause-and-effect relationships (Churchill and Iacobucci 2005; Malhotra 2015). Because different designs serve the purposes of different problems, the selection of research design should be solely guided by the research problem.

3.2.1   Exploratory Research Designs

Exploratory research is appropriate when there is little known about the problem at hand. Exploratory research may allow researchers to gain insight into a problem that is not clearly defined, thereby facilitating the formulation of more precise research problems to be examined via more conclusive (descriptive or causal) research designs. A major characteristic of exploratory research is its flexibility in the choice of research methods. Exploratory studies are not strictly structured, and researchers often use secondary data (e.g., literature reviews and data mining) or qualitative research methods based on small samples. The most common qualitative exploratory studies include focus groups, depth interviews, and projective techniques (Malhotra 2015). A contemporary development in qualitative research methods is *netnography* (Kozinets 2002).

First, in a focus group, a small, homogenous group of prescreened respondents (8–12 individuals) come together to discuss some topic of interest with a (trained) moderator in an unstructured, conversational manner (Malhotra 2015; Churchill and Iacobucci 2005). For example, a fast food company can conduct a focus group to explore what customers think about the quality of their products. Focus group is one of the most widely used qualitative market research techniques. The popularity of the method stems from the unexpected findings that emerge from the dynamic, free-flowing discussions within the group (Malhotra 2015). Thus, focus groups can provide valuable insights into the unclear problem at hand.

A detailed moderator's guide, which outlines the discussion topics, the sequence of questions, and the allocated time, should be prepared before the focus group interview (Malhotra 2015). A typical focus group session begins with a 5–10 minutes of introduction period, during which the moderator presents the topic of discussion and explains how and why the discussions are being observed and recorded. Afterwards, the moderator facilitates the beginning of a discussion by asking a general question about the topic. This general question is followed by specific questions to the specific members of the group. Once the discussion permeates the focus group, the moderator recedes to the background, occasionally nudging the dynamic discussion to follow the moderator's guide (Churchill and Iacobucci 2005).

Given the advancements in communication technologies, focus groups are increasingly taking place online. The online focus groups members can be located anywhere in the world and participate in the discussion over the Internet, yielding immense time and cost benefits. Despite its convenience, online focus groups may not replicate the traditional version because the digital communication may inhibit the synergy that is created when members meet in person (Brown et al. 2014). Online focus groups tend to have fewer members (e.g., 4–6), since too many respondents may cause confusion during the online discussions (Malhotra 2015).

Second, exploratory studies can be conducted through depth interviews. Depth interviews are similar to focus groups; the main difference is that while focus groups are conducted in groups of respondents, depth interviews are conducted with a single respondent. Analogous to focus groups, depth interviews are flexible and mostly unstructured. The main objective of depth interviews is to obtain information from individuals knowledgeable about the topic of research, which could include current customers, members of the target market, managers and decision makers, employees, industry experts, etc. (Brown et al. 2014). Given the strengths in gathering rich and detailed information, depth interviews are suitable for exploratory research.

Third, projective techniques are often used in exploratory research. Projective techniques are different than focus groups and depth interviews, because while the research topic is introduced to the respondents in the latter methods, the purpose of the research is generally disguised in projective techniques (Malhotra 2015). Hence, in this method, respondents are encouraged to reveal their underlying beliefs, motivations, feelings, thoughts, or behaviors regarding the research topic indirectly, by describing or structuring various ambiguous stimuli (Brown et al. 2014). The main assumption here is that individuals project their internal states while trying to make sense of the given ambiguous situations.

The most common projective techniques include: (1) *word association*, in which respondents react to a list of words with the first word that comes to their mind, (2) *sentence completion*, in which respondents are given incomplete sentences and asked to complete them, (3) *storytelling*, in which respondents are asked to tell a story about a drawing, photograph, picture, or cartoon, and (4) *roleplaying*, in which respondents are asked to play the role of a person in a given scenario (Brown et al. 2014).

An important contemporary development in qualitative research methods that is applicable to exploratory research is *netnography*, which refers to the application of ethnography (the scientific study of social groups) to understand consumer culture (shared beliefs, artifacts, and practices) in online communities (Kozinets 2002). Online (also called virtual) communities refer to cross-consumer communication groups formed in the Internet, for example in social media, blogs, forums, newsgroups, etc., in which the participants exchange ideas, share information, and build communities about market-oriented topics (Kozinets 2002). Such online communities are rich and vibrant sources of consumer data (including conversations, images, videos, audio recordings, avatars, etc.), and researchers can use netnography to tap into these sources in an unobtrusive and covert manner. This is possible because, unlike the other ethnographic methods or qualitative techniques (e.g., interviews or focus groups), netnography does not rely on participant-researcher interaction, rendering it a suitable method for investigating sensitive research topics (Kozinets 2002).

In conducting a netnography, Kozinets (2002) suggests following five methodological steps. In the first step, *entrée*, researchers identify relevant online communities based on the formulated research questions, the number of discrete members, the amount of activity, and availability of qualitatively rich data in the online community. The second step pertains to *data collection*. Two major types of data are generated in netnography: (1) the data obtained directly from the between-member communications in the online community (e.g., via post and discussions), and (2) the data produced by the researchers' own reflections about the online community (e.g., via field notes). Although researchers can be active participants in the online community, it should be noted that, contrasting ethnography, researchers can also conduct netnography only through observation, without generating personal reflections (Kozinets 2002). In the third step, *interpretation*, the classified and coded data is interpreted, mainly with respect to the conventional standards of qualitative data analysis. Given that netnography is restricted to the study of specific communities, the reliability and generalizability of the findings can be enhanced with corroborating evidence, for example by analyzing data obtained by other research methods.

Kozinets (2002) also draws attention to the *ethical considerations* step in netnography, recommending that researchers should disclose their presence in the online community, obtain informed consent from the members and safeguard their anonymity, cogitate whether the medium is a private or a public platform, and solicit feedback from the community members. Feedback seeking is called *member check*, and it is the final step of the netnography research process.

3.2.2 Descriptive Research Designs

Descriptive research is used when the objective is to describe characteristics of relevant groups (e.g., understanding demographics of a target market), to determine the proportion of people who behave in a certain way (e.g., the size of customers shopping at the farmer's market), or to make specific predictions (e.g., how much are customers willing to pay for the new product?; Brown et al. 2014). Thus, unlike flexible exploratory research, descriptive research is guided by predefined research problems. Surveys, longitudinal analysis, and observations are the most commonly used descriptive research methods (Malhotra 2015).

First, surveys are structured questionnaires that are administered to a specific sample from a population, designed to elicit information from respondents regarding their behavior, motivations, intentions, attitudes, demographics, and lifestyle (Malhotra 2015). Surveys are cross-sectional designs, that is, the data is collected at a single point in time from a representative sample of a specific population (Churchill and Iacobucci 2005). The survey questionnaires can be administered via telephone, mail, e-mail, web page, or personal interview. Malhotra (2015) suggests that response rates for surveys can be improved by giving an initial notification about the survey, providing incentives, and making follow-up contacts with the respondents.

Second, in longitudinal analysis, a fixed set of variables are measured repeatedly using the same group of respondents, in order to capture the changes taking place over time (Malhotra 2015). Topics that are relevant to longitudinal designs are, for example, the long-term effect of price promotions or long-term changes in the brand equity (Churchill and Iacobucci 2005). Longitudinal designs are implemented using panels, which refer to a sample of respondents who are committed to provide information to the researchers about a topic at specified intervals (Malhotra 2015).

Third, through observations, researchers can obtain information about the research topic by observing and recording respondents' behavioral patterns (Malhotra 2015). Observational techniques can capture the information that respondents are unaware of or not willing to communicate (Churchill and Iacobucci 2005). For example, in a survey, consumers may indicate that they spend equally on fresh and frozen food; however, simply observing consumers' behavior in the supermarket may reveal a different pattern.

Observations can be *personal* (i.e., data is collected by a trained observer) or *mechanical* (i.e., data is collected by special devices, such as traffic counters, optical scanners, or eye-tracking and voice pitch analysis tools), and observations can take place in the field or in the labs (Churchill and Iacobucci 2005; Malhotra 2015). Although observational designs minimize interviewer biases and eliminate errors in self-reported behavior, observations do not provide insight into the underlying motivations of a behavior and can only be used to examine frequent behaviors of short duration (Malhotra 2015). Furthermore, unstructured observations can also be used for exploratory research purposes (Brown et al. 2014).

3.2.3 Causal Research Designs

The objective of causal research is establishing cause-and-effect relationships. Similar to descriptive research, causal research is based on specific problems; unlike descriptive research, which can describe groups or inform about associations between variables, causal research is concerned with causality, that is, the extent to which the occurrence of a variable increases the probability of the occurrence of another variable (Malhotra 2015). There are three basic types of evidence for causality: (1) concomitant variation, (2) time order of variables, and (3) elimination of alternative explanations (Churchill and Iacobucci 2005).

Concomitant variation refers to the extent to which two variables (say the cause, X, and the effect Y) vary together (correlate) in the way predicted by the research hypothesis (Churchill and Iacobucci 2005). Concomitant variation provides support for causality, but does not prove it: for example, a third variable may be the causal factor for both X and Y (Churchill and Iacobucci 2005; Malhotra 2015). The time order of variables principle states that, if X causes Y, the occurrence of X should precede the occurrence of Y, and the elimination of alternative hypothesis principle states that, researchers should control for other possible causal factors to establish that it *is* X, not another variable, that causes Y (Churchill and Iacobucci 2005). These three types of evidence for causality can be obtained from experimentation, which is the most common method of causal research.

In an experiment, the researcher manipulates and controls one or more independent variables and observes the effect of this manipulation on the dependent variable (Churchill and Iacobucci 2005). To illustrate, if we are testing a hypothesis of "X causes Y" (e.g., new packaging increases attitudes toward the product), the researcher can manipulate the levels of X (e.g., X present or absent; product with and without new packaging) and observe the variation in Y (change in attitudes toward the product). There are two types of experiments: field experiments, which are conducted in natural settings (e.g., actual market conditions), and laboratory experiments, which are conducted in artificial settings in which the researcher constructs the special conditions (Malhotra 2015).

A key aspect of experimentation that sets it apart from other designs is the random assignment of participants to experimental and control groups. Random assignment attempts to minimize the influence of other variables by distributing them equally across different groups (Malhotra 2015). While experimental groups are exposed to the manipulated independent variable, the control group is not, thereby providing a point of comparison when investigating the effects of manipulated independent variables on the dependent variable (Malhotra 2015).

Two types of validity, namely internal and external validity, are crucial in experimentation. Internal validity is concerned with the extent to which we can attribute the observed effects to experimental manipulations (and not to other factors), whereas external validity is concerned with the extent to which the observed effects can be generalized to other populations, contexts, times, or stimuli (Churchill and Iacobucci 2005; Malhotra 2015). While laboratory experiments have

Table 1 An overview of research designs in market research

Research design	Main purpose	Methods
Exploratory	– To provide insights into understanding a problem – To uncover novel ideas	– Secondary data – Qualitative methods – Unstructured observations
Descriptive	– To describe characteristics of groups – To determine the proportion of people who behave in a certain way – To make specific predictions	– Surveys – Longitudinal analysis – Observations
Causal	– To establish cause-and-effect relationships	– Experiments

relatively high levels of internal validity, field experiments have relatively high levels of external validity (Brown et al. 2014).

Researchers tend to interpret findings from descriptive research designs (e.g., cross-sectional surveys) as implications of causal relationships; however, this is a fallacy and should be avoided. Descriptive studies fail to provide evidence of causality with respect to concomitant variation, time order, and elimination of alternative explanations (Churchill and Iacobucci 2005). Relative to other research designs, experiments may be more time consuming and costly; moreover, administration of experiments tend to be more complicated than other designs (Malhotra 2015). To sum, Table 1 presents an overview of market research designs.

3.3 Sampling and Data Collection

Necessary data for the research can be obtained from primary and secondary sources. In short, *primary data* refers to the novel data collected by the researcher, whereas *secondary data* refers to the already existing data. Although researchers have an inclination towards obtaining primary data, Churchill and Iacobucci (2005) suggest that researchers should not underestimate the amount and quality of the secondary data already available for research purposes. There are several advantages of secondary data over primary data, such as economies of time and cost; nonetheless secondary data may not fit the research problem at hand well and may have questionable accuracy (Churchill and Iacobucci 2005). Although secondary data may not provide the complete solution to the research problem, it could be used for exploratory purposes, as a valuable supplement to the further investigations of the problem with primary data. Primary data is obtained via research designs that are tailored to a particular research problem, and is therefore more frequently used by market researchers.

After the problem is formulated and the research design is determined, researchers make decisions regarding the sample that will be used in the research.

Sampling is a five-steps process (Malhotra 2015). In the first step, researchers define the target population, which includes all individuals or objects that meet the criteria sought by the researcher. In the second step, researchers identify the sampling frame, which provides a list or guidelines for sampling from the target population. In the third step, researchers select a sampling technique, which consists of nonprobability sampling (based on researcher's judgment, e.g., convenience, judgment, snowball, or quota sampling) and probability sampling (based on chance, e.g., simple random, systematic, stratified, or cluster sampling). In the fourth step, researchers determine the sample size (i.e., how many elements will be included in the study?). In the fifth and final step, researchers execute the sampling process, which requires a detailed description as to how the sampling decisions were made (Malhotra 2015). Once the sampling process is completed, researchers proceed to data collection.

In the data collection stage, researchers should be aware of errors that can bias the research findings. There are five types of error associated with data collection (Brown et al. 2014):

1. *Sampling error* refers to the discrepancy between results from the sample and the population. Sampling error is less troublesome than the other types of errors; it can be reduced by increasing the sample size and can be examined through the margin of sampling error statistic.
2. *Noncoverage error* refers to the failure of excluding qualified elements of a defined population in the sampling frame. Given that noncoverage error is a sampling frame problem, it can be reduced by improving the quality of the sampling frame.
3. *Nonresponse error* refers to the failure to obtain information from some elements of the sample. Nonresponse error becomes a potential problem for a study when there is a systematic difference between respondents and nonrespondents. Nonresponse error can be diagnosed by identifying and contacting a sample of nonrespondents, by comparing respondent demographics with the population demographics, or by comparing the results of early responders with late responders.
4. *Response error* occurs when respondents provide inaccurate answers to questions. Response error may arise from researcher's faults in preparing the research instrument (e.g., problems with wording of items), or from respondent's inability or reluctance in providing answers.
5. *Office error* refers to the errors that arise when editing, coding, or analyzing data.

Some of the contemporary discussions in sampling and data collection pertain to *crowdsourcing*, which facilitates data collection over the Internet, *statistical power*, which guides researchers in sample size decisions, and *indirect measures*, which may reduce response errors in measuring consumer attitudes.

3.3.1 Crowdsourcing

The Internet provides easy access to diverse groups of the population and thus poses new sampling and data collection opportunities to market researchers. Recently, utilizing *crowdsourcing* has been a popular method for data collection. Crowdsourcing simply refers to outsourcing a job or a service from the participants of online platforms that facilitate the exchange between the job suppliers and the workers. On such online platforms, the job suppliers post a task (e.g., an online survey) with a compensation that generally varies based on task complexity, and then solicit inputs from workers that are eligible for the task. Currently the most popular crowdsourcing platform is Amazon's Mechanical Turk (MTurk), which provide access to a participant pool available for conducting research that is diverse with respect to age, education, income, social class, and nationality (Buhrmester et al. 2011).

Web-based crowdsourcing has several advantages over traditional methods of sampling and data collection: (1) participants in crowdsourcing platforms are demographically diverse, thus researchers can conduct research beyond undergraduate student samples and even investigate specialized samples, (2) data collection is quick and inexpensive, (3) experimenter related biases are eliminated, (4) - computer-based designs can be easily replicated by other researchers, and (5) reliability of the data is generally equivalent to the traditional methods (Buhrmester et al. 2011; Birnbaum 2004).

Researchers should be aware that participation rate in crowdsourcing depends on compensation level and time commitment (Buhrmester et al. 2011), and web-based designs may be susceptible to multiple submissions and response biases (for remedies of these shortcomings, see Birnbaum 2004). Nevertheless, the advantages of crowdsourcing clearly outweigh its weaknesses, and when coupled with rigorously designed studies, it becomes a valuable source of data for researchers.

3.3.2 Statistical Power

A crucial tenet of quantitative research designs (e.g., surveys and experiments) pertains to sample size. Prior to data collection, researchers must determine the sample size necessary to detect the hypothesized effects in their study. This sample size decision is linked to the concept of *statistical power*, which refers to the probability that a statistical test will correctly reject a false null hypothesis (Cohen 1992). Or, in other words, if a study is under-powered, statistical tests may fail to produce meaningful results when there was actually an effect to be detected (i.e., the Type II error).

Statistical power is a function of three factors: sample size, effect size, and the significance criterion. Thus, when determining the necessary sample size, researchers should take desired power, effect size, and the significance criterion into consideration. First, researchers can set the desired power at the recommended

80% level (Cohen 1992) or select a higher power level if necessary. Second, the effect size (i.e., the magnitude of the hypothesized effect) can be determined based on the researcher's expectations or the previous studies that tested similar hypotheses. Finally, researchers can use the conventional 5% significance criterion, or set another appropriate significance level based on their study. Larger sample sizes, larger effect sizes, and increased significance levels are associated with higher statistical power.

Statistical power analysis is not a contemporary issue; the importance of power analysis has been highlighted for decades. Nevertheless, researchers continue to neglect conducting power analysis in their studies. Power analyses are crucial, because it forces researchers to consider the effect sizes (i.e., the magnitude of differences) they want to detect in the study. For example, consider a researcher who will conduct an experiment to examine the effect of a new product packaging on consumers' willingness-to-pay, anticipating that the respondents in the experimental (new packaging) condition will be willing to pay more for the product than the respondents in the control group. How big of a difference between the groups is meaningful for the research purposes? The researcher's effect size estimates will determine the necessary sample size in this example.

There are free computer programs dedicated to statistical power analysis (e.g., G*Power; Faul et al. 2007) which can be used for determining sample size based on different statistical tests. Power analyses, when conducted, should be reported in detail.

3.3.3 Indirect Measures of Attitudes

Investigating attitudes has always been challenging, for individuals tend to give socially desirable responses to self-report questions or sometimes they lack introspective access to their true attitudes. For instance, consumers may not reveal their attitudes toward drinking or smoking accurately when asked about it in a direct fashion that allows them to deliberate on their responses. This limitation may give rise to response errors in attitude research.

Social psychologists conceptualized that individuals hold two types of attitudes: *explicit attitudes*, which refer to the deliberately formed verbal judgments about objects, and *implicit attitudes*, which refer to the spontaneous and automatic responses to objects (Greenwald and Banaji 1995). While explicit attitudes are measured directly via verbal self-report statements, implicit attitudes are measured indirectly via computer-aided tests that evaluate automatic associations in memory.

Currently, the most popular measure of implicit attitudes is the Implicit Association Test (IAT, Greenwald et al. 1998). The IAT is a computerized task in which the respondent is presented with target-concepts (e.g., young people–old people) and attribute dimensions (e.g., good–bad), and throughout the test the respondent categorizes pairs of target-concepts and attributes (e.g., young people—good, old people—bad; young people—bad, old people—good). The IAT then evaluates the automatic associations between target-concepts and attributes based on the response latencies, that is, how quickly the respondent categorizes the association under investigation (e.g., quicker responses to the old people—bad pair indicates stronger negative automatic attitudes toward old people).

The IAT can also be used to measure individuals' attitudes toward themselves (i.e., self-esteem). Self-esteem has long been a central construct in consumer research, given the individuals' tendencies to enhance their self-concepts with material possessions. Analogous to the distinction between explicit and implicit attitudes toward objects, individuals' self-evaluations also take two forms: *explicit self-esteem*, which represents deliberate and reflective self-evaluations, and *implicit self-esteem*, which represents automatic and uncontrolled self-evaluations (Greenwald and Banaji 1995). Consumer researchers have long relied on explicit self-esteem, which assessed self-evaluations directly through self-report measures with self-evaluative statements (e.g., "I am satisfied with myself"). Self-report measures of self-esteem are, however, susceptible to individuals' socially desirable responses or other biases arising from self-presentational motives. Thus, both implicit and explicit self-esteem should be taken into consideration when self-esteem construct is investigated. IAT can assess implicit self-esteem by measuring the response latencies on the self-related words (e.g., I, me, myself) and positive attributes (e.g., good, warm) categorization. In addition to IAT, name-letter liking (positivity towards name initials) can also be used as a measure of implicit self-esteem (Greenwald and Banaji 1995).

Implicit measures are consequential for market research, because, although the majority of research is based on the assumption that consumers make deliberate, thoughtful decisions, consumers also have internal, uncontrolled motivations and goals that could be activated automatically without the individual's awareness of the initiation or operation of the process (Bargh 2002). Thus, researchers should be aware that both controlled and automatic processes influence consumption behaviors. In other words, both explicit and implicit attitudes may be activated by environmental cues and in turn exert influence on behavior.

3.4 Data Analysis

Once the studies are designed based on the research problem and relevant qualitative or quantitative data are collected, the next step pertains to the analysis of the data. The data analysis stage is central to the market research process, for researchers have to extract meaning out of the cluttered raw data using the methodologies appropriate for the research question and the type of data at hand.

Regardless of the type of data collected (i.e., qualitative or quantitative), the data analysis stage begins with some pre-analysis procedures. The aim of these procedures is to ensure the quality of the raw data for the subsequent analyses and interpretation, because imperfections in the raw data may confound the results. For qualitative methods, data analysis generally begins with transcribing (if necessary) and coding. Coding is the process of transforming qualitative observations into quantitative measures (Churchill and Iacobucci 2005). Coding allows researchers to capture summative, more general attributes from verbal or visual data. For example, imagine a group of researchers who conducted a focus group with customers to understand the important attributes of their cars. A relevant code for this research would be "safety". Thus, researchers can examine the interview transcript and code the sentences that indicate safety (e.g., "number of airbags is important for me" would be coded as "safety"). Interpretations then can be made based on the patterns and frequencies of these codes. To improve the reliability of coding, researchers are recommended to train multiple coders and evaluate the amount of agreement between the coders (Churchill and Iacobucci 2005).

Similarly, for quantitative methods, data analysis stage begins with screening the dataset for imperfections such as erroneous data patterns, data entry errors, outliers, and missing values. Such flaws in the dataset may pose threats to the validity of the conclusions drawn from statistical data analyses. When data is entered into a statistical data analysis software, a codebook that provides information on how each item was coded into the software should be prepared (Churchill and Iacobucci 2005). Subsequently, the data can be presented in the form of various graphs, tables, and descriptive statistics. If necessary, the data can be analyzed further with the appropriate type of inferential statistics (e.g., between-group comparisons, regression analysis, conjoint analysis, etc.; Churchill and Iacobucci 2005). Preparing a data analysis plan that outlines primary and secondary variables (or other data), and documents a detailed explanation of the procedures for conducting the statistical analysis can further assist researchers.

Contemporary issues in data analysis pertain to the analysis of data collected from different cultural contexts, statistical mediation and moderation analysis, and the use of confidence intervals and effect sizes.

3.4.1   Analysis of Cross-Cultural Data

As a result of globalization and rapid growth of world trade, market research is increasingly taking place across borders. For decision makers in multinational companies, market research serves the crucial function of providing information about consumers in foreign markets. For marketing academics, market research enables testing and developing theories in diverse cultural contexts. Consequently, marketing practitioners and academics frequently work with data collected in more than one country.

Analysis of cross-cultural data, however, poses a measurement invariance (or equivalence) challenge, especially when collected via survey methods. Measurement invariance refers to the assumption that a measurement instrument performs similarly (i.e., measures the same attribute) when making comparisons, for example between cultural groups, time points, or any other categories (Davidov et al. 2014). Thus, the validity of cross-cultural comparisons is dependent on an invariant measurement instrument that is understood and interpreted similarly by respondents in different groups. Lack of invariance may indicate that the observed results are products of statistical confounds rather than true differences, which poses a substantial threat to the conclusions of any comparative study.

Measurement invariance encompasses both theoretical and statistical elements. A statistically sound measurement instrument requires, first of all, theoretical constructs that are comparable between groups at the conceptual level. Accordingly, when conducting research across cultures (or other groups), researchers must ensure that the theoretical constructs under investigation do not have culture- or group-specific meanings. For example, prior market research suggested that the concept of service quality might have different meanings across cultures and the measures for this construct should therefore be adapted to the study context (Carrillat et al. 2007). To avoid anomalies arising from incomparable theoretical constructs across groups, researchers should scrutinize the conceptual connotations of the constructs, preferably through expert opinions and focus groups, and also pay attention to the instrument translations to prevent potential item-level biases (Davidov et al. 2014).

In the current section, we are concerned with the statistical comparability of measurement instruments at the data analysis phase (e.g., comparison of mean scores or regression parameters across groups). Statistical considerations in measurement invariance mainly pertain to the between-groups comparability of empirical qualities of measurement models (theoretical constructs and their corresponding observed variables) when researchers collect data from at least two different groups using the same instrument. Multigroup Confirmatory Factor Analysis (MGCFA), which will be briefly introduced here, is currently the most widely adopted statistical method to test for measurement invariance (Davidov et al. 2014; Steenkamp and Baumgartner 1998).

MGCFA is a sequential testing method, which begins by a comparison of the overall structure of the measurement models across groups (without imposing any restrictions on the models), and proceeds by adding constraints on the model (e.g., restricting factor loadings and mean scores of the constructs to equality across groups). Additional constraints to some degree worsen the model fit obtained in the unconstrained model; accordingly, MGCFA establishes measurement invariance by comparing the discrepancies in the fit of the constrained and unconstrained models (larger discrepancies indicate violation of invariance). The sequential steps of conducting measurement invariance analysis using MGCFA are explained comprehensively in Steenkamp and Baumgartner (1998). MGCFA can be implemented with dedicated statistical packages (e.g., Lisrel, AMOS, or Mplus). It should also be noted here that there are various statistical approaches available to scrutinize which specific items are biased in a measurement model (see, van de Vijver and Leung 2011).

Measurement invariance is also sensitive to the method of data collection. As discussed earlier, survey methods, in which the same questionnaire is administered to the members of different groups, are most susceptible to measurement noninvariance. On the other hand, computer-aided methods (e.g., IAT and eye-tracking) are potentially less vulnerable to bias and can therefore yield more accurate between-group comparisons. Researchers should consider employing different data collection techniques when conducting cross-cultural market research.

3.4.2   Statistical Mediation and Moderation Analyses

Mediation and moderation models enable researchers to further explicate observed relationships between constructs. Consider the simple association between consumers' attitudes toward an advertisement and their purchase intentions for the brand. Through mediation models, researchers can identify other constructs that mediate this relationship, and thereby clarify how or why this relationship occurs (Baron and Kenny 1986). For example, attitudes toward the brand can be modelled as a mediating variable in the example above: consumers' attitudes toward the ad enhance their attitudes toward the brand, which in turn increase purchase intentions for the brand.

Moderation models, on the other hand, examine the *when* question, and therefore aim at uncovering the boundary conditions of observed relationships. Moderating variables elucidate under what circumstances, for which types of products, for which consumers, in which cultures, etc., the relationship occurs (or does not occur). In our advertisement—purchase intention example, we can postulate that the strength of this association is contingent on consumer's level of involvement with the product, such that the influence of attitudes toward the advertisement on purchase intentions will be stronger for consumers with high (versus low) levels of product involvement. After developing conceptual models that explain how mediators or moderators are related to the problem at hand, researchers analyze statistical models based on collected data to determine those mediation or moderation effects.

In testing statistical mediation, a contemporary development has been the introduction of alternatives to the long dominant Baron and Kenny (1986) approach. The Baron and Kenny approach is based on hierarchical multiple regression analyses, and its central tenet is that a statistically significant association between two variables will be will be largely reduced in magnitude (and even become nonsignificant) when the mediator is entered into the model, suggesting that the mediator accounts for the given relationship. The reduction in the main effect and the significance of the indirect model (i.e., the effect that is transferred through the mediator) are then tested with a method known as the Sobel test, which is criticized to be a conservative test with low power and high reliance on normal distribution of the indirect effects (Hayes 2013). These limitations impeded the use of the Sobel test and gave rise to alternative methods to test for indirect effects in mediation models.

Recently, bootstrapping approach to mediation (Hayes 2013; Shrout and Bolger 2002) has gained popularity among researchers. Bootstrapping is a resampling technique, in which the statistics of interest are computed based on large numbers (e.g., 5000 or 10000) of resamples that are generated from the original sample with replacement. For example, if we have an original sample of five observations (e.g.,

7, 4, 6, 9, 2), some bootstrap samples (with replacement) would appear as: (6, 4, 2, 2, 9), (4, 7, 4, 9, 9), (2, 4, 7, 9, 2), etc.

When testing for mediation, an indirect effect for each bootstrap sample is computed, and then based on the total number of bootstrap samples (e.g., 5000 or 10000), a confidence interval (typically at the 95% level) for the indirect effect is generated. The mediation effect is established when the confidence interval for the indirect effect excludes zero. Bootstrapping approach is not bounded with the assumption of normal distribution of the indirect effect, and therefore yields more accurate estimates than the Sobel test (Hayes 2013). Although initially bootstrapping was deemed appropriate in small samples (Shrout and Bolger 2002), a recent simulation study (Koopman et al. 2015) reported that using bootstrapping in small samples may lead to inflated Type I error rates (i.e., finding more than $\alpha\%$ false significant indirect effects).

Although rigorous statistical analyses are consequential in testing for mediation effects, researchers should be cautious in presenting statistically significant mediation effects as a proof of their conceptual (theoretical) mediation model. As explicated in Fiedler et al. (2011), a statistically supported model, especially in a cross-sectional design, may not reveal the true mediator, but instead may correspond to a spurious mediator (a variable that is highly correlated with the true mediator) or a correlate (an alternative) of the independent or the dependent variable. Examining alternative theoretical models and employing different designs (e.g., experimental or longitudinal) are therefore imperative in mediation-based designs. When reporting results of mediation analysis, researchers are also recommended to refrain from making cogent claims about "establishing causal mechanisms" or "revealing underlying processes" (Fiedler et al. 2011).

A contemporary issue in testing statistical moderation pertains to the treatment of moderator variables that are measured as a continuous scale. In such occasions, a common yet flawed procedure was to discretize the continuous variable into groups, for example based on the median score of the variable (hence called median-split), and then to conduct an Analysis of Variance (ANOVA) based on the categorical variables. There is now a consensus that the discretization of continuous variables may result in reduced statistical power, loss of information, and false significant findings, and thus should be avoided (e.g., Fitzsimons 2008). Instead, researchers are recommended to use the continuous variables without transformation in statistical moderation analysis. A common approach to analyzing moderation with continuous variables is the pick-a-point (also called simple slopes) technique (Aiken and West 1991), in which the conditional effect of an independent variable on a dependent variable is examined at high and low values of the moderator (e.g., $+/- 1SD$ from the mean). A major limitation of this approach is that such arbitrarily selected points do not correspond to theoretically meaningful values on the scale; moreover, depending on the sample distribution, those the selected values may be outside the range of the observed data, thereby making the analysis sample specific (Hayes 2013).

Researchers can overcome the limitations of the pick-a-point approach by implementing the Johnson–Neyman method (Johnson and Neyman 1936) in their moderation analyses. The Johnson-Neyman method tests the conditional effect of an independent variable on a dependent variable at all values of the continuous moderator, and returns a "region of significance" within which this conditional effect differs from zero at a specified significance level (e.g., $p < 0.05$). Because the method is not bounded by arbitrarily selected values, researchers can examine moderation at specific values selected with guidance from theory, or explore the entire range of values to accurately identify the points at which moderation occurs. For example, if we hypothesize age as a moderator (e.g., the relationship between brand heritage and brand attitudes will be stronger among older consumers), we can reveal at what specific age the relationship becomes significant (e.g., for respondents above 44 years old brand heritage significantly influences brand attitudes).

The Johnson–Neyman analysis is not a new development, but it has only recently been integrated into the mainstream statistical analysis programs (e.g., PROCESS Macro for SPSS and SAS, Hayes 2013), which propelled its use in moderation analyses.

3.4.3   Confidence Intervals and Effect Sizes

Null hypothesis significance testing (NHST) is still the most common method for making inferences from statistical tests. In NHST, significance levels (p-values) obtained from statistical analyses are used make judgments about the level of support (or no support) for the study hypothesis (e.g., null hypothesis is rejected, or alternative hypothesis accepted, when $p < 0.05$). Cumming (2012, p. 27) explains the meaning of the p-value with a neat example. Consider the two following probabilities: (1) the probability of obtaining such results from our study, if our hypothesis is true, and (2) the probability that our hypothesis is true, if we've obtained such results from our study. Although researchers tend to interpret the p-value as in the latter statement, the first statement is the correct one. Thus, the p-value provides us the conditional probability of the data, not the hypothesis (Kline 2004).

NHST suffers from various drawbacks that should be recognized by researchers. Some of these drawbacks, as outlined in Cummings (2012) and Kline (2004), include: (1) p-values are sensitive to sample size, thus, in sufficiently large samples any relationship may appear significant and in small samples existing effects may not emerge, (2) NHST gives rise to dichotomous interpretations of the results (i.e., hypothesis is supported or not), and (3) p-values do not inform researchers about the probability of replications. Despite such criticisms, NHST remains as a prevalent method for statistical inference. Researchers can, however, improve the rigor of their analysis by supplementing p-values with confidence intervals and effects sizes.

Confidence intervals can render statistical results more informative by providing interval estimates along with point estimates. While the mean score of a measure obtained from a sample (e.g., $M = 14$) is a point estimate of the population mean, a confidence interval (CI) provides the interval estimate (e.g., 95% CI for the

M [10, 18]), which informs us about the precision or accuracy of the point estimate (Cumming 2012). Thus, narrower interval estimates indicate more precise point estimates. Although it is possible to use other values, conventionally confidence intervals are evaluated at the 95% level. For example, a 95% confidence interval for a sample mean can be interpreted as follows: when the analysis is replicated with multiple samples from the same population, in the long run, 95% of the confidence intervals will include the true population mean and 5% will not (Cumming 2012). However, note that interpreting a single confidence interval as "we are 95% confident that the true population mean is between value X and value Y" is incorrect, because we might simply have obtained a confidence interval from the 5% group that does not capture the true population mean. We can therefore only talk about the long run probabilities of confidence intervals.

Confidence intervals, which provide a range for estimates, are more informative about precision and accuracy than single point estimates, and thus can allow researchers to steer away from the dichotomous thinking encouraged in NHST (Cumming 2012). Furthermore, confidence intervals become beneficial when evaluating multiple studies with the same conditions, as they reveal a range of possible results based on multiple confidence intervals, and thereby encourage replication of results (Kline 2004). Researchers are therefore recommended to report confidence intervals for primary results whenever possible.

An effect size refers to the magnitude of the phenomenon under investigation (Cohen 1992). While a p-value only informs about the probability of the data and presents a "reject or no reject" decision to the researcher, effect size informs about how large the magnitude of the effect is. Intuitively, the larger the effects are, the more substantial are the findings for research and practice. In sufficiently large samples, trivial effects may emerge as significant. Researchers therefore should evaluate and report effect sizes together with p-values.

There are various effect size indexes for different statistical analysis, and those effect size indexes are generally interpreted as small, medium, or large (see, Cohen 1992). For example, for the simple correlation coefficient (Pearson's r) between two variables, 0.10, 0.30, and 0.50 correspond to small, medium, and large effect sizes, respectively. For between-group comparisons, Cohen's d is a common index of effect size (0.20 for small, 0.50 for medium, and 0.80 for large effects). In addition to reporting effect sizes, researchers should also report the accompanying confidence interval for the effect size, because the confidence interval provides the range of possible effect sizes in the population (Kline 2004). This information, for example, would be useful for other researchers when designing studies on a similar topic.

The usefulness of effect sizes and confidence intervals could best be understood through meta-analysis. With meta-analysis, researchers can combine results from different studies on similar questions and make general conclusions based on the combined evidence (Cumming 2012). Meta-analysis is grounded upon effect sizes and confidence intervals, because p-values alone do not inform us about the range of estimates and magnitude of effects. Thus, reporting effect sizes and confidence intervals are vital for future meta-analyses that aim to synthesize the literature.

Understanding effect sizes and confidence intervals encourages replication and meta-analytical thinking (Kline 2004). In this way, researchers evaluate evidence based on magnitudes rather than the frequencies of rejected hypotheses.

3.5 Reporting Market Research

The final step of market research pertains to reporting the research findings. Marketing academics communicate their findings through scientific publication outlets such as journals and books; their audience is generally the other scholars and the reports are judged based on their scientific merit. Marketing practitioners, however, report their results to executives or managers who are usually more interested in the qualitative conclusions of the report than the technical details of research. Regardless of the type of audience, market research reports should be complete, accurate, and clearly written (Brown et al. 2014). Complete reports provide all necessary information to the reader while omitting irrelevant information; accurate reports present correct information with a logical line of reasoning; clearly written reports are well organized with precise expressions (Brown et al. 2014).

A vital aspect of market research reports is the *executive summary*. Most executives would like to obtain the essential information about the results, conclusions, and recommendations as quickly and as briefly as possible. The executive summary should therefore be prepared meticulously. The executive summary should state who authorized the research, outline the specific research questions or hypotheses that guided the research, explain how the data were collected, and present, often in a bullet format, the key findings, conclusions, and recommendations (Brown et al. 2014; Churchill and Iacobucci 2005).

In addition to the written report, market research results are often presented with an oral report. When preparing the oral report, researchers should take into consideration the level of knowledge and involvement of the audience (Brown et al. 2014). In presenting the oral report, researchers can present the key results and conclusions at the end of the presentation or immediately after the introduction (purpose and main objectives). The former method allows researchers to build a logical case through sequential presenting of the supporting evidence; the latter method tends to engage the managers in the results early in the presentation and allows them to evaluate the supporting evidence in light of the key findings (Churchill and Iacobucci 2005).

References

Aiken, L. S., & West, S. G. (1991). *Multiple regression: Testing and interpreting interactions.* Newbury, CA: Sage.

AMA. (2016). *Definition of marketing.* Accessed March 23, 2016, from https://www.ama.org/AboutAMA/Pages/Definition-of-Marketing.aspx

Bargh, J. A. (2002). Losing consciousness: Automatic influences on consumer judgment, behavior, and motivation. *Journal of Consumer Research, 29*(2), 280–285.

Baron, R. M., & Kenny, D. A. (1986). The moderator–mediator variable distinction in social psychological research: Conceptual, strategic, and statistical considerations. *Journal of Personality and Social Psychology, 51*(6), 1173–1182.

Birnbaum, M. H. (2004). Human research and data collection via the Internet. *Annual Review of Psychology, 55*(1), 803–832. doi:10.1146/annurev.psych.55.090902.141601. Accessed March 23, 2016.

Brown, T. J., Suter, T. A., & Churchill, G. A. (2014). *Basic marketing research: Customer insights and managerial action* (8th ed.). Stamford, CT: Cengage Learning.

Buhrmester, M., Kwang, T., & Gosling, S. D. (2011). Amazon's Mechanical Turk: A new source of inexpensive, yet high-quality, data? *Perspectives on Psychological Science, 6*(1), 3–5. doi:10.1177/1745691610393980. Accessed March 23, 2016.

Carrillat, F. A., Jaramillo, F., & Mulki, J. P. (2007). The validity of the SERVQUAL and SERVPERF scales: A meta-analytic view of 17 years of research across five continents. *International Journal of Service Industry Management, 18*(5), 472–490.

Churchill, G. A., & Iacobucci, D. (2005). *Marketing research: Methodological foundations* (9th ed.). Ohio: Thomson South-Western.

Cohen, J. (1992). A power primer. *Psychological Bulletin, 112*(1), 155–159.

Cumming, G. (2012). *Understanding the new statistics: Effect sizes, confidence intervals, and meta-analysis.* New York, NY: Routledge.

Davidov, E., Meuleman, B., Cieciuch, J., Schmidt, P., & Billiet, J. (2014). Measurement equivalence in cross-national research. *Annual Review of Sociology, 40*(1), 55–75.

Faul, F., Erdfelder, E., Albert-Georg, L., & Buchner, A. (2007). G*Power 3: A flexible statistical power analysis program for the social, behavioral, and biomedical sciences. *Behavior Research Methods, 39*(2), 175–191.

Fiedler, K., Schott, M., & Meiser, T. (2011). What mediation analysis can (not) do. *Journal of Experimental Social Psychology, 47*(6), 1231–1236.

Fitzsimons, G. J. (2008). Editorial: Death to dichotomizing. *Journal of Consumer Research, 35*(1), 5–8.

Greenwald, A. G., & Banaji, M. R. (1995). Implicit social cognition: Attitudes, self-esteem, and stereotypes. *Psychological Review, 102*(1), 4–27.

Greenwald, A. G., McGhee, D. E., & Schwartz, J. L. K. (1998). Measuring individual differences in implicit cognition: The implicit association test. *Journal of Personality and Social Psychology, 74*(6), 1464–1480. doi:10.1037/0022-3514.74.6.1464.

Hayes, A. F. (2013). *Introduction to mediation, moderation, and conditional process analysis: A regression-based approach.* New York, NY: Guilford Press.

Hunt, S. D. (1976). *Marketing theory: Conceptual foundations of research in marketing.* Columbus, OH: Grid.

Johnson, P. O., & Neyman, J. (1936). Tests of certain linear hypotheses and their application to some educational problems. *Statistical Research Memoirs, 1*, 57–93.

Kline, R. B. (2004). *Beyond significance testing: Reforming data analysis methods in behavioral research.* Washington, DC: American Psychological Association.

Koopman, J., Howe, M., Hollenbeck, J. R., & Sin, H.-P. (2015). Small sample mediation testing: Misplaced confidence in bootstrapped confidence intervals. *Journal of Applied Psychology, 100*(1), 194–202.

Kotler, P., & Keller, K. L. (2016). *Marketing management* (15th ed.). Essex: Pearson.

Kozinets, R. V. (2002). The field behind the screen: Using netnography for marketing research in online communities. *Journal of Marketing Research, 39*(1), 61–72.

Malhotra, N. K. (2015). *Essentials of marketing research: A hands-on orientation.* Essex: Pearson.

Phillips, A. (2007). What is market research? In M. V. Hamersveld & C. de Bont (Eds.), *Market research handbook* (pp. 37–60). West Sussex: Wiley.

Sheth, J. N., & Sisodia, R. (2012). *The 4 A's of marketing: Creating value for customer, company and society*. New York, NY: Routledge.

Shrout, P. E., & Bolger, N. (2002). Mediation in experimental and nonexperimental studies: New procedures and recommendations. *Psychological Methods, 7*(4), 422–445.

Steenkamp, J.-B. E. M., & Baumgartner, H. (1998). Assessing measurement invariance in cross-national consumer research. *Journal of Consumer Research, 25*(1), 78–107. doi:10.1086/209528.

van de Vijver, F., & Leung, K. (2011). Equivalence and bias: A review of concepts, models, and data analytic procedures. In D. Matsumoto & F. van de Vijver (Eds.), *Cross-cultural research methods in psychology*. New York, NY: Cambridge University Press.

Winer, R. S., & Dhar, R. (2011). *Marketing management* (4th ed.). New Jersey: Pearson.

Consumer Behavior Research Methods

Polymeros Chrysochou

1 Foundations in Consumer Behavior Research Methods

The history of consumer behavior research is largely intertwined with the history of marketing thought (Sheth 1985), and thus each marketing era has had an effect on consumer behavior research. In the early years of the development of the discipline, consumer behavior research methods focused on sampling, collecting data, and analytical techniques (Clow and James 2013). The primary goal of marketing research at that time was to measure phenomena and consumer characteristics. Researchers also focused on measuring opinions, perceptions, preferences, attitudes, personalities, and lifestyles.

The development in computing in the 1970s made data collection and data analysis simpler and faster, which shifted the focus of consumer research on the analytical methods. In this era the focus was in better understanding the market, the consumer, and the decision process. In early 2000s the focus shifted from data analysis to finding the actual meaning behind the data, in order to provide further support in marketing decisions. The focus on research was into providing insights behind consumer choices, and how the results could provide support on marketing strategies and tactics (Clow and James 2013).

The latest phase is characterized by more developments. New forms of data (e.g. big data, internet, social media) have become available, which have given rise to exploring phenomena related to relationship between firms and consumers (e.g. word-of-mouth, engagement), and further exploring reasons behind consumer

P. Chrysochou (✉)
Department of Business Administration, Aarhus School of Business and Social Sciences, Bartholins Alle 10, 8000 Aarhus, Denmark

Ehrenberg-Bass Institute for Marketing Science, School of Marketing, University of South Australia, Adelaide, SA, Australia
e-mail: polyc@mgmt.au.dk; polymeros.chrysochou@marketingscience.info

© Springer International Publishing AG 2017

G. Emilien et al. (eds.), *Consumer Perception of Product Risks and Benefits*,
DOI 10.1007/978-3-319-50530-5_22

choices and behaviors. In addition, emphasis has been put on challenging and improving the internal and external validity of the studies, with several advancements being made in the field of consumer behavior research.

2   Steps in the Design of Research Projects

Each consumer behavior research project may have its own challenges and approach. However, in the design of any research project researchers follow the same general steps: research objectives; research design; sampling plan; data collection; data analysis; and reporting (Fig. 1).

- *Research objectives*: Prior to conducting any research project, the researcher needs to carefully consider the objectives. This step also includes the development of research questions and hypotheses, supported by theory and earlier research in the field.
- *Research design*: In the research design phase the researcher is required to make considerations on which research method will be more appropriate to answer the research questions and hypotheses set.
- *Sampling*: In this step the researcher makes considerations on the participants and how they will be approached. It is essential in this process to define the population from which the sample is drawn.
- *Data collection*: During data collection the researcher enters the field and collects the data. This is the most exciting step for the researcher, but also time consuming.
- *Data analysis*: Once the data have been collected, the researcher analyses the data in order to test the hypotheses and answer the research questions. The nature of the data (i.e. text, numerical) defines the analytical approach that the research can follow.
- *Reporting*: The final step in this process is to prepare a report and present the research findings to the research community and the interested stakeholders.

An important consideration in the overall process of the research design is ethical issues that may arise. Such ethical issues may relate to data collection (e.g. protect participants and respecting their privacy, acquiring an informed

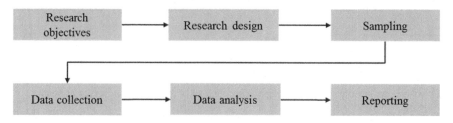

Fig. 1 Steps in the design of research projects

consent from participants), data analysis (e.g. avoid deliberate misinterpretation of the results or misuse of a data analysis method), or even when reporting the results (e.g. authorship and proper acknowledgement). Several organizations provide standards and codes of conduct (e.g. ESOMAR or American Marketing Association). Nevertheless, such ethical issues are best resolved by all involved the stakeholders behaving honorably.

2.1 Primary Versus Secondary Consumer Behavior Research

Data is the backbone of consumer behavior research. Any phenomenon studied within the field of consumer behavior requires researchers to analyze data. Depending on their source, data can be either *primary* or *secondary* (Malhotra et al. 2012).

- *Primary data* are collected directly from researchers for the purposes of their research objectives and have full control of what the data measure.
- *Secondary data* are data previously collected for other purposes and researchers use them for the purpose of their research objective.

Secondary data can be distinguished into *internal* and *external* (Malhotra et al. 2012). Internal data include information that has been collected within firms, such as customer and sales databases. External data are data generated outside the firm, such as from government sources, non-governmental organizations, syndicated services and social media. Sources of secondary data are Eurostat (http://ec.europa.eu/eurostat), Euromonitor (www.euromonitor.com), and national census data and statistics services. One useful website that provides links and sources to useful secondary data is SecondaryData.com (www.secondarydata.com).

The source of data is what distinguishes to a large extend consumer behavior research into *primary* and *secondary research*.

- *Primary research* is research that uses mainly primary data, and requires researchers to use research methods, such as focus groups, surveys and observations, that are specifically developed to answer the objectives of their study.
- *Secondary research* is research that has been conducted previously by others. In other words, any research that uses sources and data that are already available is called secondary research.

Conducting "original" research is not necessary connected with the use of primary data. Instead it is often recommended to search for and use secondary data prior to conducing any primary research (Malhotra et al. 2012). Primary research has the advantage of researchers tailoring to their own needs, while secondary research may not be able to answer all questions posed by researchers. The need to conduct primary research may also arise by the need to have more up-to-date data, and also data that come from the desired population. On the other hand, secondary research may use data that are outdated and come from samples that do not belong to the desired population. This overall, brings in another challenge to researchers when using secondary data since the overall reliability may be questioned. Thus, primary research has the advantage that the researcher can ensure the reliability of the data used. Primary research requires also more time and resources, and thus secondary research may be preferred if no time or limited resources are available.

3   Primary Research Methods

The choice of a primary research method mainly depends on whether the study attempts to measure behavior or explore opinions (e.g. attitudes, perceptions, beliefs). If the study attempts to measure opinions and the aim is to get a deep understanding of the phenomenon, methods such as focus groups and in-depth interviews could be used. If the aim is more to get an overview and not explore in-depth the phenomenon, then survey methods should be preferred. If the study attempts to measure behavior and the behavior can be assessed in its natural environment, then appropriate methods are observations, ethnography and panel data. If the behavior cannot be assessed in its natural environment then experiments and physiological measures could be used instead.

Primary research methods can be *qualitative* or *quantitative* in nature. **Qualitative research** aims to provide insight and in-depth understanding of the problem, while **quantitative research** aims to quantify the data by applying some form of statistical analysis (Malhotra et al. 2012). The qualitative methods discussed in this contribution are: focus groups, in-depth interviews, observations, ethnography, and projective techniques. The quantitative methods are: surveys, experiments, physiological measures, and panel and scanner data.

Qualitative and quantitative methods have several differences, thus serving different purposes and research needs. Table 1 provides a summary of these differences. In relation to the purpose of research, qualitative methods aim to explore and gain a deeper understanding of the phenomenon under investigation, whereas quantitative methods aim to test hypotheses, make predictions and generalize results to the population of interest. In qualitative methods the sample is small and data are generally unstructured, whereas in quantitative methods the sample is rather big and can be representative of the population, and data are mainly structured. Finally, qualitative methods do not aim to generalize to the population, whereas quantitative methods are more proper when generalizability is a necessity of the research objective.

Table 1 Comparison of qualitative and quantitative methods

	Qualitative methods	Quantitative methods
Purpose	To explore and gain a deep understanding of phenomena	To test hypotheses, make predictions and generalize results to the population of interest
Sample	Small number, usually non-representative cases	Large number, usually representative cases
Data	Qualitative (i.e. verbal responses, text), unstructured	Quantitative (i.e. numbers), structured
Analysis	Non-statistical, aim to identify patterns, features, themes	Statistical, aim to identify statistical relationships
Generalizability	Findings are less generalizable	Aim is to produce result that are generalizable
Examples	In-depth interviews, focus groups, observations	Surveys, experiments

Source: Adapted by Malhotra et al. (2012) and Johnson and Christensen (2012)

3.1 Qualitative Methods

3.1.1 Focus Groups

A focus group is a popular qualitative method in which a group of participants discusses on a topic of interest to the researcher (Krueger and Casey 2009). Participants can be asked about their perceptions, feelings, beliefs, and ideas about a brand, product or service. A focus group is usually used when the objective is to explore consumer views on new product concepts (e.g. new forms of packaging, product variants, new brands), and explore ways to increase consumer acceptance. A focus group is preferred when the objective is to get a deeper understand of the phenomenon under investigation. What makes this method unique is that it allows participants to interact and be influenced with each other, which results in generation of rich data and provides a more natural environment to participants.

Below are issues that should be considered in preparation of a focus group (Krueger and Casey 2009; Bryman 2012):

- **Participants**: Participants should be recruited with the objective that they can provide rich information about the topic. Participants should be comfortable to talk to each other, and power differentials should be avoided. If the topic of interest requires participation of consumers with diverse background it is preferable to have separate focus groups (e.g. men versus women), unless to objective of the study requires such interaction.
- **Number**: Three to four focus groups are usually recommended for each type of participant.
- **Size**: The group should be large enough to generate discussion, but not large enough as it may make some participants to be left out.
- **Length**: The ideal time that a focus group should last is between 60 and 90 min. If a focus group lasts more participants get fatigued and the group productivity is reduced.

- *Environment*: A focus group should take place in a comfortable environment where participants feel safe and free to talk. Participants should be seated in a way that they can see each other and are not distracted.
- *Moderator*: The moderator should be skillful and have experience in conducting a focus group. The moderator should make participants feel comfortable, control the dominant participants, make sure that the discussion does not go off-track, and manage the flow of the discussion.
- *Equipment*: A focus group is usually audio-recorded. However, it can also be video-taped when emotional reactions and body movements are the focus of the analysis. A focus group may also be conducted in a room with a one-way mirror in order to allow external observers follow the discussion without any interruption.
- *Discussion guide*: An essential element in the planning of a focus group is the discussion guide. A discussion guide contains questions and the time that the moderator needs to assign in each one. The development of the questions is challenging and should be made carefully so that they address the topic, are easy to answer, elicit information and generate discussion.

The above issues are essential in the preparation of a focus group and the researcher should make these considerations and write them down in a *research protocol*, together with required resources and budget estimates. It should be mentioned that focus groups is not a cheap research method, especially when considering the costs per participant.

After conducting the focus groups the hard task of analysis takes place. Different types of analysis are used, such as memory-based, note-based, tape-based and transcript-based (Krueger and Casey 2009), with the latter type being the most common. Overall, the analysis of the transcripts should be systematic, sequential, verifiable and continuous. Plenty of software options are available (e.g. NVivo, MAXQDA, ATLAS.ti) that can assist the researcher in the analysis of the transcripts, with some allowing the analysis of audio or video as well.

Overall, a focus group can be a powerful research method. When well executed, a focus group can provide the researcher with very rich data, as long as participants are engaged fully. However, the researcher should be aware that focus groups should not be used as a process to getting people reach a consensus or as a test of knowledge. Finally, focus groups do not provide statistical data and should not be used as a method to project to the population.

3.1.2 In-depth Interviews

An in-depth interview is a qualitative method that involves conducting intensive individual interviews with a small number of respondents to explore their perspectives on a topic of interest to the researcher (Boyce and Neale 2006). In-depth interviews are appropriate when the researcher wants to gain a deeper insight about the respondents' evaluations on the topic under investigation. The method allows the researcher to produce very precise and specific answers from the respondents, which other forms of qualitative methods (e.g. focus groups) and quantitative methods cannot encompass.

The advantage of in-depth interviews is that it allows respondents to provide their answers and views in peace, without time restriction, and to further elaborate on their answers without being influenced by the opinions of other respondents. In-depth interviews should be used in place of focus groups when the topic under investigation is controversial, sensitive or tabooed, and thus the risk of social desirability bias high. It is also preferred when participants are hard to gather to a focus group (e.g. key-informants that live in different locations or participants with busy schedules). In-depth interviews differ from survey interviews in that they are less structured, thus they allow the researcher to be more flexible during the actual interview (e.g. ask additional questions, deviate from the interview guide).

Kvale (1996) identifies seven stages of conducting in-depth interviews:

1. *Thematizing*: During the thematizing the researcher needs to think through the goals and the primary questions of the study that will help guide the subsequent decisions that must be made. The research needs to clarify the purpose of the interviews and the topic to be investigated, and make a careful planning.
2. *Designing*: At this stage the researcher should develop an overview of the entire project before the interviewing begins. Decisions should be made on issues such as selection of participants, sampling, interview guide, ethics, transcripts and analysis, reporting, and available funds.
3. *Interviewing*: At this stage the actual interviews take place. Apart from the participant, the interviewer is an instrument to this process, and thus factors like fatigue, personality, knowledge, skill, training and experience, may affect the process of the interview.
4. *Transcribing*: Transcribing involves the preparation of material from the interview for analysis. At this stage the interviews are being transcribed verbatim, together with additional notes that the researcher may have created.
5. *Analyzing*: At this stage the transcripts are analyzed in order to determine the meaning of the information gathered in the interviews. Methods for analyzing vary widely and the choice depends on the purpose of the study, the nature of the material, and available time and resources. Similar to the analysis of focus group interviews, computer software is available that assist this process.
6. *Verifying*: At this stage the researcher needs to account for issues of *reliability* (consistency of the findings), *validity* (if the study investigates what the researcher aims to investigate), and *generalizability* (whether the findings can be generalized to the population).
7. *Reporting*: In the final stage of reporting the researcher communicates and reports the findings of the study. The report must (a) be in a form that meets scientific criteria, (b) meet ethical consideration (e.g. confidentiality), and (c) be readable and usable.
8. In-depth interviews can produce rich data and provide an in-depth insight of the phenomenon under investigation. However, the researcher should be aware that

the method is time- and labor-intensive, and requires skillful and well-trained interviewers. In addition, given the small sample results from in-depth interviews are very hard to generalize.

3.1.3   Observation

Observation is the systematic description of events, behaviors, and artifacts in the social setting chosen for study (Marshall and Rossman 2014). As a method, observation involves collecting impressions of the world using one's senses in a systematic and purposeful way to learn about a phenomenon of interest to the researcher. Observation can be used by both qualitative and quantitative researchers, although it is most commonly used in anthropological fieldwork. More quantitative observation is often referred to as systematic or structured observation, whereas more qualitative approaches include naturalistic observation, non-structured observation, and participant observation (McKechnie 2008). This section mainly focuses on observation as a qualitative method.

Observations can take place in a laboratory setting, although typically take place in a natural setting. This allows the researcher to explore the phenomenon while it occurs in the real world. Usually the researcher takes part in everyday activities related to the phenomenon, observing directly the events that take place (*participant observation*). However, in pure observations the researcher is removed from the actions and behaviors, so that s/he does not influence them (DeWalt et al. 1998). According to Jorgensen (1989), participant observation is appropriate when:

(a) Little is known about the phenomenon (e.g. a newly formed group);
(b) There are important differences between the views of insiders as opposed to outsiders (ethnic groups or subcultures);
(c) The phenomenon is somehow obscured from the view of outsiders (e.g. family life);
(d) The phenomenon is hidden from public view (e.g. crime and deviance).

Observations are exploratory in nature and involve a variety of data collection methods, such as text, field notes, audio and video recordings. The aim of observations is to explore unforeseen phenomena and give reasoning to them following an inductive approach. To conduct an observation the researcher may follow three types of processes (Kawulich 2005):

1. *Descriptive observation*: At this stage the researcher observes everything assuming no prior knowledge of the phenomenon or theoretical interpretation.
2. *Focused observation*: This type of observation emphasizes the collection of additional data (e.g. interviews) and the participants' insights provide guidelines to the researcher on what to observer.
3. *Selective observation*: As a final stage, the researcher focuses on different types of activities to help delineate the differences in those activities.

Observations allow the researcher to explore phenomena from the backstage, as they occur in real life without participants being obstructed, and allow the researcher to describe them in depth. The method is powerful when combined with other methods, such as interviewing, and is well suited to the study of social processes over time (McKechnie 2008). Finally, observations are well suited both for *theory generation* (e.g. discover new concepts, build a novel conceptual framework and propositions) and *theory verification* (e.g. test and validate an existing theory).

On the other hand, observations have several methodological problems. As a method is challenging, as it may be hard to get access to the content of interest to study (e.g. getting permission to collect data and earn trust of the observant). There is a high risk that the observer may interfere with the observed phenomenon, and thus his/her overall presence may introduce bias and to some extend threaten the trustworthiness of the data collected. Additional observer bias may be introduced, since the person who observes is the same who interprets, reducing subjectivity in the interpretation of the phenomenon. Finally, observations are time consuming and resource demanding, and depend strongly on the skills of the observer.

3.1.4   Ethnography

Ethnography combines two ancient Greek words: "ἔθνος" (ethnos: tribe, nation, people) and "γράφω" (grapho: I write). Ethnography is therefore the work of describing a culture (Spradley 1979). In their manifesto for ethnography, Willis and Trondman (2000) refer to ethnography as the "disciplined and deliberate witness-cum-recording of human events". Thus an ethnographer aims to write and describe people and cultures, through immersion for a long-term period with the culture. An ethnographer describes in-depth a variety of cultural aspects, such as language use, rituals, ceremonies, relationships, and artifacts. Although for some researchers ethnography and participant observations are indistinguishable, ethnography has an additional meaning in that it refers to both a method of research and the written product of that research (Bryman 2012).

Ethnographic research takes place in the native environment to see how people behave. For example, in a study that examined how consumer responses to television advertising texts are influenced by everyday social interactions and media technology use, the researchers conducted an ethnographic study in participants' homes (Jayasinghe and Ritson 2013). Such naturalistic approach is an advantage compared to controlled conditions that may create biased responses. Ethnographers engage in participant observation and field interviewing. In addition, they may augment field observation through other forms of methods, such as archival research, interviews and questionnaires. An ethnographic research can have a number of the following features (Atkinson and Hammersley 1994):

(a) It explores social phenomena, rather than testing hypotheses;
(b) Uses unstructured data;

(c) Investigates a small number of cases; and

(d) Involves the interpretation of the meanings and functions of behavior through verbal description rather than statistical interpretation.

Ethnographic research requires fieldwork. In the field, basic anthropological concepts, data collection methods and techniques (e.g. participants observations, interviewing, questionnaires), and analysis are the fundamental elements of ethnography (Fetterman 2010). To conduct an ethnographic study, similar steps described by Kvale (1996) for in-depth interviews (see above) apply as well.

With the introduction of online communities an adapted form of ethnographic research has emerged known as *netnography* (Kozinets 2002). Netnography as a method is faster, simpler and less expensive than traditional ethnography. Netnography has been used to provide information on the symbolism, meanings, and consumption patterns of online consumer groups. Netnography has been used in identifying coping strategies brides employ in managing the cross-cultural ambivalence (Nelson and Otnes 2005).

Ethnography as a method has several advantages. It can provide context for behaviors, accounting for complexity and interrelationships among group interactions. Ethnography can provide in-depth understanding of the phenomenon and open up qualities of group experience in a way that other research methods cannot. Ethnography is suitable in exploring why behaviors occur rather than just observing them. Finally, it has the power to highlight and uncover notions that are taken for granted and confront them. Ethnography has also challenges. As a method is time consuming, cumbersome and can be rather expensive. The time commitment that the ethnographer needs to put during the fieldwork and in the writing process is immense (months/years). It further takes time to build trust with informants in order to facilitate full and honest discourse. The ethnographer needs to be well-trained and skilled, and be as unobstructive as possible to avoid influencing participants' behavior. The ethnographer needs to be aware of such bias, which may also impact data collection and interpretation. Finally, as any qualitative method, the generalizability of the findings is always questionable.

3.1.5 Projective Techniques

All the above methods require participants to directly provide answer to the phenomenon of interest to the researcher. In certain occasions there is reason a researcher to expect that by using a direct method social desirability bias (i.e. bias caused from respondents answering based on what is expected to be correct or socially acceptable) may be high. This phenomenon occurs often is consumer behavior research, especially when the topic being investigated is sensitive or hard for participants to articulate their feelings, beliefs, attitudes or motivation. In such occasions *projective techniques* are preferred.

Projective techniques are techniques that use vague, ambiguous, unstructured stimuli or situations and by giving the situation some structure participants "project" their personality, attitude, opinion, and self-concept (Clow and James 2013). Projective techniques allow participants to uncover feelings, beliefs, attitudes and motivation that many find difficult to articulate (Donoghue 2000). For example, using projective techniques Cotte and Latour (2009) explored the meaning of online gambling consumption to consumers.

In consumer behavior research projective techniques may be classified into five types based on the response type required by participants: association, completion, construction, expressive and choice ordering.

- *Association*: In association techniques participants are presented with a stimulus and respond by indicating the first word(s), image(s) or thought(s) that comes to their minds. A common association technique is word association tasks in which respondents are presented with a list of words and are asked to report what comes to their mind. Such techniques have been used by researchers in exploring consumer associations with brands and products (Krishnan 1996).
- *Construction*: In construction techniques participants are presented a stimulus and are asked to construct a story or a picture (Donoghue 2000). A common construction technique is the Thematic Apperception Test (TAT) in which respondents are shown pictures of ambiguous social situations and are asked to tell a story concerning the characters in each picture (Lilienfeld et al. 2000).
- *Completion*: In completion techniques participants are given an incomplete sentence, story or conversation, and are asked to finish it. A common completion technique is sentence completion tests in which participants are provided with an incomplete sentence (e.g. "A person who collects stamps is. . .") and are asked to complete it. Such techniques are often used in brand mapping (Donoghue 2000).
- *Expressive*: In expressive techniques participants are asked to role-play, act, draw or paint a specific concept or situation (Donoghue 2000). Common expressive techniques are role-playing and third-person techniques. In a role-playing task a respondent is asked to play the role or assume the behavior of someone else, while in the third person task a respondent will be asked to relate the feelings or attitudes of a third person such as a friend, neighbor, etc. in a given situation (Malhotra et al. 2012). The main assumption behind these techniques is that participants will project their own feelings and beliefs into the role.
- *Choice ordering*: In choice ordering techniques participants are asked to explain why certain things are most important or least important, or to "rank" or "order" or "categorize" certain factors associated with a product, brand or service (Donoghue 2000).

Projective techniques have several advantages. First, they allow respondents to express their feelings in an indirect way which oftentimes is hard for them to articulate and verbalize. Second, they allow participants to provide their initial thoughts intuitively, thus minimizing social desirability bias. Finally, the methods used are more creative and compared to mainstream research methods, respondents seem to like more (Catterall and Ibbotson 2000). In regards to disadvantages, projective techniques result in data that are rather complex and require skillful researchers in interpreting them correctly. In addition, questions are often raised in relation to their degree of reliability and validity. Finally, projective techniques require more time and may be more expensive compared to direct methods.

3.2 Quantitative Methods

3.2.1 Survey Research

Survey research involves the collection of information from a sample of individuals through their responses to questions (Check and Schutt 2011). The aim of survey research is to study the characteristics of a target population, and understand their attitudes, perceptions, motives, beliefs and, in general, collect their opinions to a phenomenon of interest to the researcher. Survey research combines sampling, designing questions, and data collection. Decisions in relation to these aspects will subsequently affect precision, accuracy and credibility of the research study (Fowler Jr 2013).

(a) **Sampling**: Sampling is the methodology that is used to select the participants of the study. Decisions that need to be made relate to how participants will be reached (i.e. following a probabilistic or a non-probabilistic method), what should be the appropriate size, and what medium will be used to administer the survey (e.g. written, verbal). These decisions affect representativeness of the sample, and consequently generalizability of the results.

(b) **Designing questions**: This task involves decisions related to choosing the questions that will form the final questionnaire. Decisions should be made on what questions to ask, how to best word questions, and how to arrange the questionnaire. The aim is to ensure that respondents clearly understand and easily answer to all questions, and that the data collected are able to be analyzed with proper statistical techniques. Researchers should always aim at employing questions and scales that have already been validated and used in earlier research, unless is necessary to develop them on their own.

(c) **Data collection**: At this stage the required information is being gathered. Data collection can be conducted with an interviewer (through personal or telephone interviews) or be self-administered (i.e. respondents complete the questionnaire on their one). Another distinction is whether data collection is computer-assisted or paper-based. A combination of the above methods makes some frequently used interviewing techniques, such as computer-assisted personal interviews (CAPI) and computer-assisted telephone interviews (CATI). The growing penetration of the internet and the development of online survey tools (e.g. Qualtrics, SurveyXact) have increased the popularity of computer-assisted methods.

Survey research is mainly conducted with the use of questionnaires. The design of a questionnaire has a major impact on respondents' level of understanding, involvement and completion rate. It is therefore important that researchers carefully

Table 2 Comparative evaluation of survey methods

	Email	Online	Telephone CATI	Home and workplace	Street surveys	CAPI	Postal
Task factors							
Flexibility of data collection	*	****	****	*****	*****	****	*
Diversity of questions	***	****	*	*****	*****	*****	***
Use of physical stimuli	*	***	*	****	*****	*****	***
Sample control	*	**	****	****	****	***	*
Quantity of data	***	****	**	***	***	***	**
Response rate	*	**	***	*****	****	*****	*
Situational factors							
Control of data collection environment	*	*	***	****	*****	*****	*
Control of field force	*****	*****	***	*	***	***	*****
Potential for interviewer bias	None	None	***	*****	*****	*	None
Potential to probe participants	*	*	*	*****	***	***	*
Potential to build rapport	*	*	***	*****	****	****	*
Speed	*****	*****	*****	****	***	****	*
Low cost	*****	*****	***	*	**	**	***
Participant factors							
Perceived participant anonymity	***	*****	***	*	*	*	*****
Social desirability	*****	*****	***	**	*	****	*****
Obtaining sensitive information	***	***	*	*****	*	***	***
Low incidence rate	***	*****	*****	*	*	*	***
Participant control	*****	****	**	*	*	*	*****

Source: Malhotra et al. (2012)
Key: *, low; **, moderate to low; ***, moderate; ****, moderate to high; *****, high

design questionnaires when considering the aspects presented above. One important and final step in the questionnaire design process is pre-testing the questionnaire. Pretest is conducted with a small number of participants or colleagues and aims at identifying potential problems in the questionnaire in relation to the wording, the sequence and format of the questions. Pre-test also allows evaluating the nature of the data that will be collected.

The selection of the appropriate method to conduct a survey strongly depends on the situation the researcher has to deal with, taking into consideration strengths and weaknesses of each method. Table 2 provides a comparison of different survey methods on a list of issues. Malhotra et al. (2012) categorize these issues into three factors: **task** (issues that relate to the nature of the design of questionnaire and the objective of the study), **situational** (issues that relate to the actual interview) and **participant** (issues that relate to participants).

Surveys can be conducted only once at a given point in time (*cross-sectional*) or repeatedly over time (*longitudinal*). Longitudinal surveys have the advantage of observing consistency, as an indicator of external validity, and patterns in the phenomenon studied. They further allow measuring development of the phenomenon over time.

Survey research has several advantages. It can obtain opinions from a relatively big sample within a small amount of time and at low cost per participant. It is relatively easy to administer and develop, and allows the researcher to be flexible in the type and number of questions used. Survey research is also more suitable for reaching generalizations in a phenomenon that is being studied. For several qualitative studies, survey is a method of empirical validation of the theoretical phenomenon that has been observed. However, it is important to note that survey research, unless being a census, produces estimates and not exact measurements of the population.

Survey research has several weaknesses that the researcher needs to carefully take into consideration. One of the most important weaknesses is that surveys are vulnerable to bias. Bias can take several forms: *sampling bias* (i.e. not proper sampling has been method has been used), *measurement bias* (i.e. the wording or order of the questions may bias the answers), *response bias* (i.e. participants may be prone to not giving the correct answer), *researcher bias* (i.e. bias introduced by the researcher subjective views and decisions during all steps, including the analysis of the data). Survey research is appropriate to collect opinions, but not always appropriate to explore behavior, especially in phenomena that the respondent may have poor recall of the behavior, or may be sensitive to report it.

3.2.2 Experiments

Experiments consist a research method for establishing cause-and-effect relationships (Malhotra et al. 2012). Causality means that the occurrence of one event (independent variable) will have a cause on another event (dependent variable). Experiments can take place in the laboratory (*laboratory experiments*) or in the field (*field experiments*). In field experiments participants are observed, often without being aware, thus they avoid response bias. In addition, field experiments avoid confounding factors that lab experiments may introduce (e.g. distractions, unnatural setting), but at the same time confounding factors (e.g. light or temperature) cannot be controlled in the same way as a research can in lab experiments.

In the design of experiments certain components needs to be taken into consideration:

- **Dependent variable**: The dependent variable is what the researcher aims to measure and is the outcome variable of the experiment.

- *Independent variable*: The independent variable is what the researcher manipulates or changes in an experiment, and is assumed to have an impact on the dependent variable.
- *Extraneous variable*: Extraneous variable is any variable other than the independent, that may affect the dependent variable. Such a variable may confound the results of the experiments.
- *Treatment*: Treatment is the manipulation of the independent variable.
- *Treatment group*: A group of participants that is exposed to the treatment (e.g. a group in which a new drug is being tested).
- *Control group*: A group of participants that is not exposed to the treatment (e.g. a group that receives no drug, or receives a placebo).

Experimental designs can be classified into pre-experimental, true experimental, quasi-experimental and statistical designs (Malhotra et al. 2012). Pre-experimental designs are characterized by the absence of randomization procedures. True experimental designs are characterized by randomization, and the researcher randomly assigns participants and treatments to experimental groups. Quasi-experimental designs are used when true experimentation cannot be used, and the researcher is unable to achieve full manipulation of scheduling or allocation of treatments to participants.

Experiments have several advantages to other methods. They allow researchers to have a great level of control over the variables (independent and extraneous), thus allowing them to obtain more accurate results. The manipulation of the independent variable further ensures that the obtained result is due to the treatment. Experiments can also be repeated across different points of time or several groups, thus allowing researchers to be more confident of their findings.

Experiments have also weaknesses. Several extraneous variables that may not be aware to the researchers may confound the results. This means that researchers need to be aware of all confounding factors and control for them. Experiments are not suitable for any occasion. For example, some independent variables may not be able to manipulate (e.g. due to ethical reasons) and thus another method may be more suitable. Finally, experiments are sensitive to response bias and are subject to human error, issues that may distort the reliability of the findings.

3.2.3 Physiological Measures

Modern consumer behavior shows that consumers make more automatic decisions without making any conscious effort (Dijksterhuis and Bargh 2001). Consumers are thus not as rational as traditional theories have thought (Kahneman 2003). For example, a growing number of research shows that consumer decisions are more emotional than rational (Damasio 1994). In light of such discoveries, researchers are skeptical when using self-reported measures to explore consumer processes and related phenomena, and therefore *physiological measures* are preferred instead.

Physiological measures assess how the human body functions and reacts to certain external stimuli that the researcher is interested in exploring. They can be simple measures, such as heart rate, to more complicated ones, such as brain functions. Physiological measures that are used often in consumer behavior research are eye-tracking, facial electromyography (EMG), electrodermal activity (EDA), electroencephalography (EEG). A description of these measures follows.

- *Eye-tracking*: Eye-tracking involves the study of eye-movements to assess visual attention (Duchowski 2007). Using devices called eye-trackers consumers' eye movements and eye positions are recorded in order to understand where consumers look and how they navigate (i.e. analyzing visual paths). Eye-tracking has several applications in consumer behavior research, with several applications in product and website design, and advertising.
- *Electrodermal activity (EDA)*: EDA describes variation in the electrical characteristics of the skin. EDA is used as a measure to study emotional reaction (Huston et al. 2015). One of the traditional and most common EDA measure is skin conductance (SC) that is considered a sensitive measure of arousal and a good indicator of the intensity of emotion. The method is considered cheap and easy to conduct, and is often complemented with additional physiological measures of emotional reaction (e.g. EMG).
- *Facial electromyography (EMG)*: Facial EMG is used to measure responses associated with emotional valence (Huston et al. 2015). EMG records facial muscle movements (mainly the corrugator supercili, zygomaticus major, and orbicularis occuli), that reflect the conscious and subconscious expression of emotions. Facial EMG and EDA are often conjointly used in assessing consumer emotional reactions to advertising, packaging, and other marketing stimuli.
- *Electroencephalography (EEG)*: EEG is a method to record electrical activity of the brain (Niedermeyer and da Silva 2005). Human brains react subconsciously to external events and recording these reactions help researchers understand consumers' behavior. EEG is thus used to assess how consumers respond to marketing stimuli (e.g. advertisements, commercials, packaging). In marketing terms, the growing use of EEG has been the focus of what is known as *neuromarketing* (Morin 2011).

Physiological measures have several advantages. They are considered as more objective measures of consumer reactions (either being cognitive or emotional), and remove potential interviewer bias. Physiological data are also more accurate, especially for studying phenomena that are hard to articulate with other methods. However, physiological measures have certain challenges and weaknesses. They require the use of special and rather expensive equipment that require researchers to be skillful in their use. Most of these measures are assessed in conditional settings being also obstructive to participants, thus response bias may be rather high. Finally, physiological responses do not always have clear theoretical explanations, and thus are prone to yielding ambiguous data. This is important issue for consideration, especially when physiological measures are used as proxies of behavior that the researcher is interested in studying.

3.2.4   Panel and Scanner Data

Panel data are observations of the same individuals over a period of time. They are usually obtained either from households/consumers or companies. Panel data record mainly purchases over time that are registered either in the store, through scanners at the cash register, or at home, through households registering their purchases with home scanners or other forms of methods (e.g. collecting the receipts; registering purchases online). The former is known as *scanner data* and are mainly collected by retailers who own loyalty programs and registered purchases of their members. The latter is known as *household panel data* and are mainly collected by firms specializing in this type of data collection, such as Nielsen (www.nielsen.com) and GFK (www.gfk.com).

The two types of data are collected with different methodologies, and thus provide different abilities to researchers. Scanner data record transactions that occur in-store from consumers whose profile is usually not known (unless they are members of a loyalty program), whereas household panel data record purchases only from a selected number of households whose profile is known. Scanner data only record purchases in specific stores, whereas household panel data record purchases across all types of stores. The bottom line is that both types of data provide information that can answer different research questions and if combined can help in analyzing and understanding better consumer purchase behavior.

Panel and scanner data allow for calculating certain measures of brand performance that are very useful for marketing managers that aim at developing their brands (Sharp 2010).

- *Market share*: The number of purchases attributes to a specific brand, expressed as a percent of the total purchases in product category.
- *Penetration*: The number of households buying a given brand at least once within a given time period, expressed as a percent of the total number of households that are members of the panel.
- *Purchase frequency*: The average number of times that a brand was purchased from its buyers brand within a given time period.

The power of panel and scanner data is that they allow for recording purchase behavior. At the same time, behavior can be linked with other forms of individual data (e.g. socio-demographics, attitudes, media consumption) and store-related data (e.g. promotions, in-store advertising). This provides a powerful tool to researchers who wish not only to explore purchase behavior, but link external variables to explore what influences such behavior (e.g. attitudes, socio-demographics). Such data allow the investigation of phenomena that are hard to conduct with other methods, such as the impact of advertising and in-store promotions on sales.

Panel and scanner data have further the advantage of recording information over time that is useful for observing and analyzing various behavioral phenomena (e.g. calculating market shares, observing behavioral loyalty and brand switching behavior, estimating effectiveness of promotions) and also to forecast them (e.g. forecasting sales and market shares). The advantage of panel and scanner data over other forms of data is that they are more accurate as they eliminate response and recall bias. Of course, members of the panel may not be representative of the population and may produce response bias, especially because members of the panel may be "trained" and not act natural. On the other hand, panel and scanner data require a big investment from firms to collect, are rather expensive and are hard to acquire. Finally, they are complex to analyze, thus requiring skills from researchers.

4   An Evaluation of Consumer Behavior Research Methods

Every method described above has strengths and weaknesses, and researchers should be aware of them prior to selecting a method. Consumer behavior research requires a big investment of resources in regards to money and time. These issues need to be carefully considered by researchers as well. However, consumer behavior research can provide recommendations to marketing managers and practitioners that may save them from costs attributed to wrong decisions.

Knowing which research method is the right one to conduct is not enough. Each research method requires specific skills and knowledge that require training and practice. In addition, each method is useful as long as it is conducted in proper terms, acknowledging their limits. On top of the choice of method, most answers to a phenomenon under investigation require personal judgment and experience. Thus, results always have a level of subjectivity introduced from researcher bias, and such bias needs to be taken into consideration as well.

Social and real life phenomena that consumer behavior research deals with are rather complex and hard to explain or analyze. Consumer behavior research methods do not always aim at making accurate predictions of such phenomena, but focus mostly at explaining and providing reasoning behind such phenomena. If the aim is to make a prediction, then such predictions come with an error and the aim of the research method is to minimize that error. It is important to keep in mind that statistical significance (i.e. minimizing the error) should not be the only target to the researcher. Instead, researchers should focus on the actual size of the effect and the overall importance of their findings.

One last point is the issue of complexity of the research method. Several consumer behavior research methods may be too complex or sophisticated, which may sound too "cool" or "novel". However, this should not mean that a simple or "old fashioned" method should not be preferred. On the opposite, a simple research method may provide the same answer to the research objective and, oftentimes, may require fewer resources.

5 Improving Quality in Consumer Behavior Research Methods

Methods in consumer behavior research have been dominated by cross sectional surveys, longitudinal and experimental research designs. Cross sectional surveys are the most common used design because of the ease in operationalization and interpretation of data, but also because they allow efficient measurement of several types of variables. However, such designs suffer from certain biases, such as social desirability and common method bias. In addition, they have been heavily criticized on their external validity and overall generalizability.

A solution to addressing these limitations and minimize the impact of such biases is through the use of longitudinal studies and experimental designs. It is therefore recommended to prefer these designs over cross sectional ones, when appropriate. In addition, another recommended avenue is through the use of mixed design studies that allows for further validation and external validity of the research findings. Finally, despite early suggestions on the importance of replications in consumer behavior research (Kollat et al. 1970), replications do not attract much attention and in fact should be practiced more often since they allow for improving external validity and find conditions under which an effect may exist. In this respect, replications should further be extended and be employed with different methods whenever feasible.

References

Atkinson, P., & Hammersley, M. (1994). Ethnography and participant observation. *Handbook of Qualitative Research, 1*(23), 248–261.

Boyce, C., & Neale, P. (2006). *Conducting in-depth interviews: A guide for designing and conducting in-depth interviews for evaluation input.* Watertown, MA: Pathfinder International.

Bryman, A. (2012). *Social research methods.* New York, NY: Oxford University Press.

Catterall, M., & Ibbotson, P. (2000). Using projective techniques in education research. *British Educational Research Journal, 26*(2), 245–256.

Check, J., & Schutt, R. K. (2011). *Research methods in education.* Thousand Oaks, CA: Sage Publications.

Clow, K. E., & James, K. E. (2013). *Essentials of marketing research: Putting research into practice.* Thousand Oaks, CA: Sage Publications.

Cotte, J., & Latour, K. A. (2009). Blackjack in the kitchen: Understanding online versus casino gambling. *Journal of Consumer Research, 35*(5), 742–758.

Damasio, A. (1994). *Descartes' error: Emotion, reason and the human brain.* New York, NY: Quill.

DeWalt, K., DeWalt, B., & Wayland, C. (1998). Participant observation. In H. Bernard (Ed.), *Handbook of methods in cultural anthropology* (pp. 259–300). Walnut Creek, CA: AltaMira Press.

Dijksterhuis, A., & Bargh, J. A. (2001). The perception-behavior expressway: Automatic effects of social perception on social behavior. *Advances in Experimental Social Psychology, 33*, 1–40.

Donoghue, S. (2000). Projective techniques in consumer research. *Journal of Family Ecology and Consumer Sciences, 28*, 47–53.

Duchowski, A. (2007). *Eye tracking methodology: Theory and practice*. London: Springer.

Fetterman, D. M. (2010). *Ethnography: Step-by-step* (3rd ed.). Thousand Oaks, CA: Sage Publications.

Fowler Jr., F. J. (2013). *Survey research methods*. Thousand Oaks, CA: Sage Publications.

Huston, J. P., Nadal, M., Mora, F., Agnati, L. F., & Conde, C. J. C. (2015). *Art, aesthetics, and the brain*. Oxford: Oxford University Press.

Jayasinghe, L., & Ritson, M. (2013). Everyday advertising context: An ethnography of advertising response in the family living room. *Journal of Consumer Research, 40*(1), 104–121.

Johnson, B., & Christensen, L. (2012). *Educational research: Quantitative, qualitative, and mixed approaches* (4th ed.). Thousand Oaks, CA: Sage Publications.

Jorgensen, D. L. (1989). *Participant observation: A methodology for human studies*. Newbury Park, CA: Sage Publications.

Kahneman, D. (2003). Maps of bounded rationality: Psychology for behavioral economics. *American Economic Review, 95*(3), 1449–1475.

Kawulich, B. B. (2005). Participant observation as a data collection method. *Forum: Qualitative Social Research, 6*(2), art. 43.

Kollat, D. T., Engel, J. F., & Blackwell, R. D. (1970). Current problems in consumer behavior research. *Journal of Marketing Research*, 327–332.

Kozinets, R. V. (2002). The field behind the screen: Using netnography for marketing research in online communities. *Journal of Marketing Research, 39*(1), 61–72.

Krishnan, H. S. (1996). Characteristics of memory associations: A consumer-based brand equity perspective. *International Journal of Research in Marketing, 13*(4), 389–405.

Krueger, R. A., & Casey, M. A. (2009). *Focus groups: A practical guide for applied research*. Thousand Oaks, CA: Sage Publications.

Kvale, S. (1996). *InterViews: An introduction to qualitative research interviewing*. Thousand Oaks, CA: Sage Publications.

Lilienfeld, S. O., Wood, J. M., & Garb, H. N. (2000). The scientific status of projective techniques. *Psychological Science in the Public Interest, 1*(2), 27–66.

Malhotra, N. K., Birks, D. F., & Wills, P. (2012). *Marketing research: An applied approach* (4th ed.). Harlow: Pearson Education Limited.

Marshall, C., & Rossman, G. B. (2014). *Designing qualitative research* (5th ed.). Thousand Oaks, CA: Sage Publications.

McKechnie, L. E. F. (2008). Observational Research. In L. M. Given (Ed.), *The Sage encyclopedia of qualitative research methods*. Thousand Oaks, CA: Sage Publications.

Morin, C. (2011). Neuromarketing: The new science of consumer behavior. *Society, 48*(2), 131–135.

Nelson, M. R., & Otnes, C. C. (2005). Exploring cross-cultural ambivalence: A netnography of intercultural wedding message boards. *Journal of Business Research, 58*(1), 89–95.

Niedermeyer, E., & da Silva, F. L. (2005). *Electroencephalography: Basic principles, clinical applications, and related fields*. Philadelphia, PA: Lippincott Williams & Wilkins.

Sharp, B. (2010). *How brands grow: What marketers don't know*. Oxford: Oxford University Press.

Sheth, J. N. (1985). History of consumer behavior: A marketing perspective. In C. T. Han & J. N. Sheth (Eds.), *Historical perspectives in consumer behavior: ACR Singapore conference, Singapore* (pp. 5–7).

Spradley, J. (1979). *The ethnographic interview*. New York, NY: Holt, Rinehart and Winston.

Willis, P., & Trondman, M. (2000). Manifesto for "ethnography". *Ethnography, 1*(1), 5–16.

Use, Abuse and Misuse

Michel Bourin and Abdeslam Chagraoui

1 Definition of Product Misuse and Abuse

There are many ways of understanding: use, misuse and abuse. For example, misuse and abuse of prescription drugs are the intentional or unintentional use of medications without a prescription, in a way other than prescribed, such as wanting to experience improved physical and mental condition, or exceeding the prescription instructions without medical supervision. For some people, taking prescription drugs is a way of coping with stressful situations or peer pressure and potentially leads to using drugs to deal with feelings. These conditions could result in increased frequency and/or taking larger amounts of drugs resulting in abuse.

Prescription drugs are misused and abused more often than any other drugs, except for marijuana and alcohol. Misconceptions about the safety and increasing availability of prescription drugs as well as misunderstanding of their adverse effects result in increased misuse and abuse. Indeed, emergency department visits and treatment admissions involving prescription drug abuse or misuse have risen significantly in recent years. A recent study reported that more than 20% of emergency admissions and visits were related to prescription drug misuse and illicit drug use. In some areas prescription, drug abuse is overtaking illicit drug use. Other adverse outcomes that may result from prescription drug misuse and abuse include the risk of suicide and even death among drug-dependent individuals. Moreover, more deaths involving overdose have been reported due to prescription drugs than to illicit drugs (Control and Prevention 2011). The elderly may be vulnerable to major falls with increased risk of bone fracture and, for some, intravenous drug use

M. Bourin (✉)
Nantes University, 98, rue Joseph Blanchart, 44100 Nantes, France
e-mail: Michel.bourin@univ-nantes.fr

A. Chagraoui
Faculty of Medicine, University of Rouen, 22 bd Gambetta, 76183 Rouen Cedex 1, France

increases the risk of blood-borne virus infections, especially HIV and hepatitis, leading to the infection of needle sharers (Nutt et al. 2007). The three misused or abused types of legal drugs that people most commonly become addicted to, are opioid analgesics, psychotropics, and over-the-counter medications. This paradigm could be extended not only to the use, misuse, and abuse of alcohol and tobacco but also to illegal drugs such as cannabis, cocaine, ecstasy amphetamines and illegal opioids. It is also possible to associate other addictions such as food, compulsive shopping, Internet, gaming, sex, and abuse. We enter a broad spectrum of mood disorders.

One of the significant difficulties in promulgating information regarding use, misuse, and abuse, is the lack of consensus on terminology and an understanding of the proper use of terminology among clinicians, patients, pharmacists, insurers, diagnostic coding agencies, medical societies, regulators, government agencies, and pharmaceutical manufacturers. While inaccurate, more than half of family physicians believe that the use of long-acting opioids for patients with moderate to severe chronic non-malignant pain leads to addiction.

To enable a coherent approach to the problems related to the non-medical use of medications, here are some definitions that might be helpful (Table 1).

Lessenger and Feinberg (2008) provide the following list of use and abuse trends to help physicians identify prescription abuse:

Use of prescription drugs falls into these categories:

- For legitimate, prescribed medical treatment; for example, methamphetamines for narcolepsy and opiates for severe trauma.
- As an additional drug to use when the drug of choice is unavailable on the streets.
- As a booster for a more intense high.
- As an alternative addictive drug when their drug of choice has been eliminated from use by drug testing.
- As an alternative addictive drug prescribed by physicians; for example, amphetamines in diet clinics; these prescriptions may be issued either naively by the physician or for profit.

According to The Drug Abuse Warning Network (DAWN) (Hughes et al. 2007) which is a public health surveillance system that monitors drug-related hospital emergency department visits in order to report on the impact of drug use, misuse, and abuse in metropolitan areas and across the USA; people who abuse prescription drugs tend to:

- Be white.
- Be younger (when stimulants are the drug of choice).
- Use opiates.
- Be women; women tend to use tranquilizers and sedatives.
- Mix their medications with alcohol.
- Use prescription drugs and drugs that are safe and effective for use by the general public without a prescription, defined as over-the-counter (OTC)

Table 1 List of some definitions (based on medication use)

Terms	Definitions
Abuse	This is an intentional, maladaptive pattern of use of a medication (whether legitimately prescribed or not) (Savage 2016)
Dependence	Dependence involves adaptive changes occurring due to repeated drug use and is frequently motivated by the nature of drug experiences
Addiction	Addiction is a compulsive behavior involving exogenous psychoactive substances. Taking the substance may produce an initial feeling of enjoyment, but when repeated, it becomes irresistibly compulsive and can cause social and professional dysfunction. These social factors may also be the underlying causes for drug addiction
Chemical coping	Chemical coping is a working definition that describes patients' intake of opioids on a scale that spans the range between normal nonaddictive opioid use for pain all the way to opioid addiction
Diversion	Redirection of a prescription drug from its lawful purpose to illicit use; can be done with criminal intent
Drug poisoning	Exposure to natural or synthetic substances that has an undesirable effect, often fatal; includes drug overdoses resulting from misuse or abuse. In the U.S., drug overdose deaths were second only to motor vehicle crash deaths among leading causes of unintentional injury or death in 2007
Misuse (noncompliant use)	The intentional or unintentional use of a prescribed medication in a manner that is contrary to directions, regardless of whether a harmful outcome occurs. Misuse can be grouped into several categories
Non-medical use	Intentional or unintentional use of legitimately prescribed medication in an unprescribed manner for its psychic effect (either experimentation or recreationally), deciding to increase the dose of one's own medication, unknowingly taking a larger dose than directed, engaging in a suicidal attempt or gesture, and inadvertent poisoning
Pharming	Coined by teenagers, "pharming" is the term used to describe raiding the medicine closet for prescription medicines, popularly known as "pilz" (Levine 2007)
Physical dependence	A state of adaptation manifested by a drug class-specific withdrawal syndrome that occurs by abrupt cessation of a drug, rapid dose reduction (Raith and Hochhaus 2004)
Prescription medications	Pharmaceuticals dispensed by a pharmacist on the presentation of a prescription written by a physician, dentist, or other health care provider who is legally authorized to write prescriptions
Pseudoaddiction	Occurs when patients with inadequately treated pain exhibit drug-seeking behavior similar to that of addiction. This behavior resolves with reasonable dose increases as opposed to "out of control" or "compulsive" use reflecting addictive drug-seeking behavior which remains the same or worsens
Self-medication	Use of a drug without consulting a health care professional to alleviate stressors or disorders such as depression and anxiety
Substance use disorder (SUD)	A condition involving the intoxication, withdrawal, abuse or dependence upon, a substance with defined abuse or dependence potential, including alcohol, meeting the criteria for clinical diagnosis delineated by the current Diagnostic and Statistical Manual (DSM) and/or the current International Classification of Diseases (ICD)

(continued)

Table 1 (continued)

Terms	Definitions
Tolerance	A state of adaptation in which exposure to a given dose of a drug induces changes that result in diminution of one or more of the drug's effects over time. It leads more often to markedly increase the dose to obtain the same effect. It is very common with all benzodiazepine drugs
Withdrawal	A variety of unpleasant symptoms (e.g., difficulty concentrating, irritability, anxiety, anger, depressed mood, sleep disturbance, and craving) that occur after use of an addictive drug is reduced or stopped. Withdrawal symptoms are thought to increase the risk for relapse, because the subject experiences a bad feeling which is rapidly corrected with consumption of the drug

drugs. These drugs are often found on display shelves in pharmacies with easy access to consumers, but may also be found in non-pharmacy outlets, such as grocery stores, convenience marts and large discount retailers. In the U.S., there are more than 80 classes of OTC drugs, ranging from allergy medicines to pain relievers to weight loss products. OTC medications in conjunction with alcohol may be a vehicle for suicide.

- Obtain the prescription medication by prescription from their physicians or dentists, as gifts from friends, or purchase them on the black market.

2 Use, Misuse and Abuse of Medicines

2.1 Use, Misuse and Abuse of Opioids and Psychoactive Medications

In the mid-nineteenth century, it was the custom for physicians to frequently prescribe morphine and other opium preparations. By the end of the century, many medical doctors had come to recognize that chronic use of morphine was a disorder.

Misuse of opioids is far more common than heroin use (Brady et al. 2016). As is true for heroin, nonmedical use of opioids other than heroin is predominantly a problem of young adults (Cicero et al. 2014). Opioid dependence rarely results from a temporary prescription of opioids for treatment of acute pain or pain due to terminal illness. Opioids are a mainstay in the treatment of pain with cancer, surgery and trauma; however, they remain controversial when used out of this pathological context. Abuse of prescription opioids results from the combination of several factors and leads to the subsequent resurgence of heroin use among opioid addicts.

In the United States, there is a dramatic increase in abuse of prescription opioids (Brady et al. 2016).

Indeed, prescription opioids represent the second-most abused class of drug behind marijuana; since 2007, 12.5 million Americans have reported using a prescription opioid analgesic for non-medical purposes, a large number of whom fulfil the diagnostic criteria for abuse or dependence.

According to The World Health Organization, chronic pain increases the likelihood of depression, anxiety and difficulty working (Currie and Wang 2005). Chronic pain is well recognized as a public health problem which justifies the active treatment of pain.

Furthermore, it should be noted that, in the United States, increasing the availability of opioids has contributed to a significant increase in the number of opioid prescriptions from 76 million in 1991 to nearly 207 million in 2013.

Moreover, purchasing medications including opioids from online pharmacies has contributed significantly to the diversion of prescription medications. So that someone desiring prescription medications could simply order them online, bypassing legal and regulatory provisions that may be a source of potential adverse medical consequences such as substance abuse or addiction.

More surprisingly, some elderly are involved in the sale of their prescribed opioids as a part-time way of earning extra money (Manchikanti 2006).

In some countries, illicit use of prescription opioids is exceeding consumption of cocaine or other drugs with similar effects. Buprenorphine and methadone are the two most important abused opioids in Europe or France, whereas oxycodone and hydrocodone are the most widely abused in the USA (Casati et al. 2012).

It is noteworthy that the opioid hydrocodone has an extended-release formulation. Indeed, to provide an efficient way of ingesting large quantities of opioids, the pill can be easily crushed, snorted or dissolved by bypassing its extended-release form, thereby increasing the potential exposure of abuse and overdose because of its availability at higher dosages.

Opioid prescription is becoming a major concern in the teenage population. Indeed, between 1991 and 2001, use of opioids among students in 8th, 10th, and 12th grades was up 173% rising to almost 7 million in 2010.

Furthermore, it should also be pointed out that among nonopioid prescription drugs that are misused, sedatives and anxiolytics are associated with illicit drug use. To take up these challenges, it is critically important that the prescription of opioid analgesics is thoroughly understood by clinicians so as to master their prescribing practice to minimize harm while reaping the benefits regarding safety and efficiency for the patient.

2.2 OTC Medications

OTC medication abuse has been identified in many countries (McAvoy et al. 2011) and although implicated products vary, five key groups have emerged: codeine-based (especially compound analgesic) medicines, cough products (particularly dextromethorphan), sedative antihistamines, decongestants, and laxatives. No clear patterns relating to those affected or their experiences have been identified, and they may represent a hard-to-reach group, which coupled with heterogeneous data, makes estimating the scale of abuse problematic. Associated harm included direct physiological or psychological harm (e.g., opiate addiction), injury from another ingredient (e.g., ibuprofen-related gastric bleeding) and associated social and economic problems. Strategies and interventions include limiting supplies, raising public and professional awareness and using existing services and Internet support groups, although associated evaluations are lacking. Terminological variations have been identified (Cooper 2013).

2.3 Universal Challenge

Physicians must be able to prescribe safely and efficiently scheduled drugs and, at the same time, must identify and manage misuse and abuse in their practices. Ethics drive physicians to prescribe, but fear of sanctions may affect physician prescribing behaviors, which might compromise the quality of care. The problem cannot be ignored because abusers often face complications, such as psychiatric and behavioral problems, suicidal ideation, addiction and dependence, adverse effects, societal damage, social and family dysfunctions, suicidal ideation, criminal consequences, and overdoses.

The universal challenge is to control adequately conflict while identifying and managing high-risk situations and possibly treating addictions resulting from the balance of public health priorities against individual pain and suffering.

2.4 Prevalence of Misuse and Abuse

Keep in mind that prevalence of prescription use, misuse, and abuse varies among clinical settings and by definition of misuse or abuse. True prevalence is unknown but appears to be increasing.

2.4.1 Teens

Adolescents are at high risk. Substance use before age 18 years is associated with an eightfold likelihood of developing substance dependence in adulthood (Mars et al. 2014). While illicit drug abuse is declining in this group prescription drug abuse is climbing.

- Teens say prescription drugs are easier to obtain than illicit drugs and 52% believe prescription narcotics are available everywhere (Rogers and Copley 2009).

Table 2 Non-medical use
and abuse of commonly
prescribed medications (After
Riggs 2008)

Types of medications	Percentage
Stimulants	54
Pain medications	26
Sedatives or anxiolytics	19
Sleep medications	14

- College campuses are especially high-risk environments for the non-medical abuse and diversion of prescription medications; 9.4% of students abuse pain medications prescribed to them, and 13.4% of students have been approached to divert their pain medication.
- Peer pressure is one of the reasons why teens abuse medication. Listed below are some drugs obtained this way (Riggs 2008) (Table 2).

2.4.2 Women

Women represent a large and growing population of prescription abusers and have a higher risk than men based on biological differences, more psychiatric problems (depression, anxiety), and higher rates of physical, emotional or sexual abuse (Green et al. 2009). Adolescent girls and women use drugs to cope with stressful situations while men tend to use alcohol. Women are more likely than men to be prescribed a drug with abuse potential, such as narcotics or anti-anxiety medications (Manchikanti 2006). Prevention and intervention efforts with a gender-specific approach are warranted.

2.4.3 Elderly

The elderly are very susceptible to pain medication misuse/abuse. The elderly makeup 13% of the total population but receive one-third of all prescribed medications (Manchikanti 2006). The elderly tend to have more chronic, long-term pain issues, tend to use multiple medications due to other comorbid medical conditions (especially dietary supplements and OTC medications), and may be experiencing waning cognition, making them susceptible to unintentional misuse or abuse. Drug metabolism changes with age, predisposing the elderly to more toxic effects of all medications. Chronic pain is by far the most common reason for nonmedical use of prescription pain medications later in life. The age range most at risk appears to be 50–64 years, which does not correspond to the peak of chronic pain in the elderly, which is age 65 years. Physicians treating older adults should be aware of these trends.

2.4.4 Hospitalizations

From 1999 to 2006, the number of people hospitalized for prescription drug overdose increased 37% in the US (DuPont 2010).

2.4.5 Deaths

Deaths from unintentional drug overdoses have been rising steeply since 1990; rates have increased roughly fivefold in US (Centers for disease control and prevention 2010). In 2007, there were 27,658 unintentional drug overdose deaths in the United States. The number involving opioid analgesics was almost twice as high as for cocaine and five times higher than for heroin. Overdose deaths have now overtaken the annual number of motor vehicle crash fatalities in 16 states and are more than double the annual number of murders nationwide (DuPont 2010). Clearly, there is a widespread problem of epidemic proportions. Prescription opioid abuse is a major public health issue. The 2010 National Survey on Drug Use and Health estimated that 35 million American (13.7%) adults aged 12 years and older had used a pain killer non-medically at least once in their lifetime. This is an 18% increase since 2002. In November 2011, the National Morbidity and Mortality Weekly Report reported 36,450 deaths from medical drug overdoses in 2008 (MMWR 2011).

2.5 Prescriber's Role

Primary care providers have an important role in the identification of prescription drug abuse as 70% of Americans visit their primary care doctor at least once every 2 years (Riggs 2008). In any prescription pain reliever abuse situation there are at minimal two parties involved:

(1) the physician who either knowingly or naively prescribes pain relievers to a person who is faking pain, (2) the person who fakes or exaggerates pain to get a prescription. Since it's hard to control patient behavior, one key solution to this epidemic lies with the prescriber. Primary care physicians are well poised to recognize substance use in their patients and to take steps to address the issue before use escalates. However, <40% of physicians receive training in medical school to identify prescription drug abuse or recognize the warning signs of drug diversion. Nationally, more than 40% of primary care physicians report difficulty in discussing the possibility of prescription medication abuse with patients and more than 90% fail to detect symptoms of substance abuse (Crozier et al. 2010). Lack of knowledge regarding the artfulness of prescription abuse puts control into the patient's hands. Professionals who prescribe or work around controlled substances are also at risk of abusing readily available medications. Unfortunately, some prescribers contribute to the problem by dealing or by personal addiction (Table 3).

Table 3 Prescriber involvement in prescription abuse (after The American College of Preventive Medicine)

Category	Types of involvement
Deficient (Dated Practitioner)	Too busy to keep up with Continuing Medical Education
	Unaware of controlled drug categories
Deficient (Dated Practitioner) Duped	Only aware of a few treatments or medications for pain
	Prescribes for friends or family without a patient record
	Unaware of symptoms of addiction
	Remains isolated from peers
	Only education is from drug representatives
	Always assumes the best about his patients and is gullible
	Leaves script pads lying around
Duped Deliberate (Dealing)	Falls for hydrophilic medicine excuse—fell into the toilet or sink
	Patients only want specific medications (i.e., Oxycontin or Percocet)
	Co-dependent—cannot tell patients "NO" when they ask for narcotics
	Practitioner becomes a mercenary
	Sells drugs for money, sex, street drugs, etc.
Deliberate (Dealing) Drug Dependent (Addict)	Office becomes a pill factory—full of drug seekers
	Prescribes for known addicts who will likely sell drugs to others
	Starts by taking controlled drug samples
	Asks staff to pick up medications in their names
Drug Dependent (Addict)	Uses another prescribers' Drug Enforcement Administration
	Calls in scripts in names of family members or fictitious patients and picks them up himself

2.6 Physician Strategies

All physicians treating patients with opioids or other medicines with addict potential should be evaluating and re-evaluating patients on an ongoing basis for the risk of tolerance, misuse, abuse, and addiction. Physicians need to learn how to assess the risk of addiction and aberrant drug-related behavior to protect patients at-risk from developing dependence and to better treat patients who may be at lower risk.

Physicians must encourage the patient to become an active and engaged actor in part of their treatment process and improve the correct use of drugs based on scientific studies. This helps maintain patients' motivation.

Patients may not understand the effects of combining drugs. For example, some drugs may potentiate others and so they can cause life-threatening side effects or can lead to addiction and chronic adverse effects.

The challenge for the physician is to help patients managing, for example the stressors without the use of chemicals or delivering brief periods of appropriate medicinal treatments.

The question must be asked: Why do some people become addicted, while others do not?

Although some drugs are more addictive than others, only certain people using drugs are subject to becoming addicted taking these drugs. Indeed, no single factor can predict whether or not a person will become addicted to drugs. Risk for addiction is influenced by a person's biology, social environment, emotional states, and age or stage of development. The more risk factors an individual has, the greater the chance that taking drugs can lead to addiction (Strobbe 2014). Note that few, if anyone, begin drug use with the intent to become an addict. Addiction is an unintended but treatable complication of prescribed or non-prescribed use of a drug that has abuse potential.

Physicians are legally responsible for prescribing scheduled drugs, hence; should be familiar with federal and state prescribing laws. Remember the most stringent law takes precedence, whether by the state or by the Federal government. The majority of states have Prescription Drug Monitoring Program (PDMPs) requirements to help curb abuse. It is particularly necessary to take action when catastrophic use—involvement of illegal activity—of a controlled substance places a patient in immediate harm.

2.7   Doctor/Patient Conversations

Many physicians have difficulty discussing critical issues with patients. A report finds that over 40% of physicians have difficulty discussing substance abuse, including abuse of prescription drugs, with their patients compared with <20% having difficulty discussing depression (National Institute on Drug Abuse. Research Report. Prescription drugs—abuse and addiction. http://www.nida.nih.gov/PDF/RRPrescription). Some conversations will be needed just to convince patients to take their medication; other conversations will focus on taking medication properly, and still others on the touchy subject of abuse.

Unfortunately, the addicted person tends to deny responsibility for the uncritical use of psychoactive substances. Thus, devolving responsibility for his own behavior problems on others, this could be a serious obstacle along the road to recovery. Therein lies both the difficulty and the key for the clinician.

For most patients the terms opioid and narcotic can have a chilling effect on a patient's willingness to accept and adhere to pain treatment. Patients often fear long-term outcomes, such as addiction with strong pain relievers.

3   Use, Misuse and Abuse of Consumers Products

3.1   Tobacco and Nicotine

The act of smoking and addiction to nicotine lead to dependency on cigarettes (Benowitz 2010). The development of tobacco addiction is accompanied by the development of tolerance such that over time, progressively larger doses of nicotine produce relatively weak effects compared to when smoking began. Corresponding to the development of tolerance is an escalation in dose intake that may be necessary to achieve the results initially obtained by lower doses (Benowitz 2010). Tolerance is often accompanied by the development of physiological dependence such that abrupt termination of nicotine intake is accompanied by the onset of withdrawal signs and symptoms termed a withdrawal syndrome (Benowitz 2010).

Every year about 40% of smokers attempt to quit (Cahill et al. 2015). Despite the desire of many smokers to cease consumption, only 3% of attempts are successful this is likely due to the highly addictive properties of nicotine (Jha et al. 2006). If some can quit smoking, this usually occurs after many attempts. However, smoking substantially increases the risks of premature mortality (Boyle 1997). The physicochemical properties of nicotine seem to play a significant role in the consumption of tobacco. Indeed, delivery of nicotine in a free-base form has a significant physiological impact and thereby, seems to be a critical determinant of continued nicotine-seeking behavior (Le Foll and Goldberg 2009).

These chemical changes may be a factor in determining the nicotine-seeking behavior that indirectly influences a smoker's perception, leading to its continuing use. Besides, the psychopharmacological effects of nicotine result in alteration of mood and modulation of cognition, thereby favoring addiction (Hughes 2006).

So, to reduce the addictive nature of nicotine, we must develop preventive actions and thus reduce the morbidity and mortality associated with tobacco use.

The gender gap in smoking is different between adults and adolescents (Table 2). According to, Warren et al., overall, unlike men who are four times more likely than women to smoke, boys are only twice as likely as girls to smoke (Warren et al. 2006).

Concerning prevalence of cigarette use among adults and adolescents, the proportion of men who smoke is 42% while that of women is 11%. Among adolescents, 55% of boys smoke cigarettes, whereas 39% of girls smoke cigarettes (Christofides 2003).

To prevent an intensification of the current tobacco epidemic in the coming decades, serious attention must be focused on women and young children, who are particularly vulnerable targets for tobacco marketing strategies.

The effects of nicotine on different organ systems depend upon the dose and speed of administration including relaxation of skeletal muscles, stimulation of the heart rate and nausea.

It is noteworthy that the high prevalence of psychiatric comorbidity is associated with smoking. In fact, 7% of nicotine-dependent individuals have a comorbid psychiatric disorder (Grant et al. 2004). In some individuals, nicotine use is often associated with neuropsychiatric disorders such as depression, anxiety or other mood disorders (Grant et al. 2004). Nicotine dependence is considered a psychiatric disorder. It is manifested by compulsive drug-taking and withdrawal when abruptly stopping smoking.

Although there is a medical need for pharmacotherapies, currently available treatments, even if shown to be somewhat effective, are not effective for all individuals. Several therapeutic approaches are being developed. This is the challenge of emerging research (Herman and Sofuoglu 2010).

However, functional brain imaging may facilitate our understanding of the neuronal circuits underlying brain function associated with smoking to identify the molecular targets involved in acute and chronic effects of nicotine and tobacco addiction (Benowitz 2009).

Most of 95% of smokers who quit tobacco smoking do so without any formal treatment (Garvey et al. 1989). Quitting smoking significantly reduces the risk of tobacco-related morbidity and mortality, yet there is a high rate of relapse amongst smokers who try to quit (Gilpin et al. 1997). Phenotypic biomarkers have the potential to improve smoking cessation outcomes by identifying the best available treatment for an individual smoker. The nicotine metabolite ratio (NMR) is a reliable and stable phenotypic measure of nicotine metabolism that can guide smoking cessation treatment among smokers who wish to quit (Allenby et al. 2016). The NMR accounts for sources of variation in nicotine metabolism including genotype and other biological and environmental factors such as estrogen levels, alcohol use, body mass index, or menthol exposure are of interest. Clinical trials have validated the NMR as a biomarker to predict therapeutic response to different pharmacotherapies for smoking cessation (Allenby et al. 2016). Current evidence supports the use of nicotine replacement therapy for slow metabolizers, and non-nicotine treatments such as varenicline for normal metabolizers. Several effective pharmacotherapies are available to treat tobacco dependence. However, the long-term effectiveness of these treatments has been limited because the majority of smokers who attempt to stop smoking eventually relapse (Benowitz 2009). Approaching the treatment of tobacco use and dependence as a chronic disease and the development of innovative drug therapies offers new hope for the treatment of tobacco-dependent patients. Combination bupropion and varenicline displayed greater efficacy in smoking cessation than varenicline monotherapy, though further safety analysis is warranted to rule out additive psychiatric adverse effects (Vogeler et al. 2016).

3.2 Alcohol

While the prescription of psychotropic drugs is becoming more and more subject to state regulation and drugs are only provided after full professional evaluation in a medical or therapeutic context, alcohol on the other hand, as well as being an important economic commodity, remains easily accessible.

Moreover, alcohol conveys two contradictory messages; one associated with well-being and the other clearly contributes to major social and health problems. The anchoring of alcoholism in our societies stems from its wide availability, its price, and its legality. Nowadays there is little primary alcoholism i.e., consumption of alcoholic beverages instead of water. This kind of alcoholism was very common when people began work at a very young age notably in the country-side (Winokur and Clayton 1967). Secondary alcoholism which is often a "self-treatment" for anxiety, mainly panic disorder and social anxiety previously called social anxiety (Terlecki and Buckner 2015). Around 20% of bipolar patients have high of alcohol consumption (Pringuey et al. 2014).

Moderate acute alcohol intake has a sedative, muscle relaxing and stress reduction activity (Zimmermann et al. 2007). Furthermore, to improve motor performance, cognitive and information-processing tests under the influence of alcohol reflect physiological excitation.

Other effects could also be mentioned including decrease of negative mood states, as well as increased talkativeness; Alcohol tends to trigger stronger feelings of euphoria and well-being and removes inhibitions. These symptoms increase the probability of repeated alcohol consumption and, therefore, create the right conditions for developing excessive intake.

After acute alcohol consumption, ethanol readily and rapidly passes the blood-brain barrier. There are many ways in which it interacts with several neurotransmitter systems and thereby modulates individual vulnerability to developing alcohol dependence. The risk of increased alcohol consumption and the development of alcohol-related problems are probably linked to the anxiolytic effect of alcohol and may affect the ability of decision-making after alcohol consumption. It is thus difficult for subjects to assess the level and gravity of situations. Decreased glucose metabolism has been shown in the whole brain following acute ethanol consumption, particularly at higher doses. This may reflect a lower activity of the cerebral cortex that is likely due to the sedative effect induced by ethanol (Hendler et al. 2013). An animal model has shown that consumption of high doses of ethanol in adolescence decreases sensitivity to the sedative effects of acute alcohol consumption (Crews et al. 2007). This can have serious consequences, as this period of life is critical for cortical development. It is thus easy to understand the brain damage that might result from alcohol intake. So, adolescents are more vulnerable to neurotoxicity induced by high doses of ethanol (Crews et al. 2007). Chronic alcohol use results in the development of tolerance. This is due to neuroadaptive changes in the brain that can cause withdrawal symptoms caused by abruptly stopping substance use. These changes are intended to maintain homeostasis between excitatory and inhibitory brain functions and counteract the acute effects of alcohol abuse. When high-dose ethanol is abruptly discontinued, this may lead to severe disturbance of homeostasis and may have a clinical impact resulting in psycho-vegetative withdrawal.

In people who are more stressed or more anxious, drugs, such as benzodiazepines are frequently abused in association with alcohol. The goal of this combination is to improve the effectiveness of primary substance and to attenuate their adverse effects.

Drug and alcohol addictions are widespread among cocaine-dependent individuals. This association has adverse consequences by producing toxic psychoactive metabolites such as cocaethylene. Moreover, the hepatic effects of alcohol alter drug metabolism which explains poorer treatment outcome (Pennings et al. 2002).

3.3 Illicit Drugs: Marijuana

Cannabinoids are constituents of the marijuana plant (cannabis sativa plant). The main psychoactive ingredient is delta-9-tetrahydrocannabinol, known as THC. Its action has been known for centuries due to its recreational and medicinal properties. It's most common mode of use is smoking.

Marijuana is one of the most commonly used and abused illicit drugs worldwide. Recent years have seen significant advances in understanding the mechanisms of cannabinoid-induced behavioral and biochemical alterations. Recent research indicates the existence of endogenous cannabinoids in the human body. These are substances that act like marijuana, called marijuana-like substances and represent an endocannabinoid physiological control system.

Marijuana effects vary based on individual factors and are produced by binding to the brain's specific receptors called cannabinoid receptors (Costa 2016). The functioning of specific areas of the brain is preferentially affected; this is related to the fact that these areas have high concentrations of cannabinoid receptors. These specific areas include the hippocampus, the cerebellum, the basal ganglia, and the cerebral cortex. The hippocampus is known to play a critical role in certain types of learning. It is thus not surprising that THC interferes with learning and memory. Thus, through its action on the limbic system, THC could interfere with recognition memory more than discrimination learning (Aigner 1988).

THC affects the cerebellum whose crucial role is to coordinate all body movements. In addition, it affects the basal ganglion which is involved in movement control. This results in slower reaction times, distorted perceptions and impaired coordination.

Marijuana may also cause mental disorders. Indeed, it has been shown that early marijuana use increases risk of developing psychosis.

Estimates indicate that 27.0 million Americans aged 12 or older were current illicit drug users (Samsha: Behavioral Health Trends in the United States). Indeed, 22.2 million people aged 12 or older reported using marijuana during the month before the survey interview (Samsha: Behavioral Health Trends in the United States) (Fig. 1). Marijuana adversely impacts brain development of adolescents and may also affect their likelihood of consuming other drugs as they move through childhood. Long-term marijuana abuse can lead to addiction. Indeed, after an

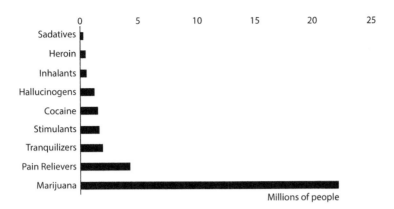

Fig. 1 Numbers of past month illicit drug users among people aged 12 or older: 2014. Behavioral. Health trends in the United States: Results from the 2014 National Survey on Drug Use and Health (http://www.samhsa.gov/data/sites/default/files/NSDUH-FRR1-2014/NSDUH-FRR1-2014.htm accessed, 12 March, 2016

extended period of continuous use, stopping suddenly leads to behavioral disorders and compulsive drug-seeking behaviors. Withdrawal symptoms result in depressed mood, irritability, anxiety, sleeplessness, difficulty concentrating and drug craving.

Intensive use of high-potency cannabis increases the risk of developing psychosis. Studies indicate a possible link between marijuana use and some psychiatric disorders such as schizophrenia or related disorders (Kelley et al. 2016). The intoxicating properties of marijuana have been described as similar to those of moderate alcohol intoxication. The principal salient features of such intoxication are the induction of subjective states of relaxation and euphoria. However, aversive aspects of marijuana use have also been reported, and these effects are similar to the unpleasant subjective states following alcohol intake (nausea, vertigo and dysarthria). Many regular marijuana users have reported that their first experience with the drug was indeed unpleasant.

Acute and chronic marijuana use may cause undesirable effects on cognitive process and perception, mainly regarding object size and perception of object distance. Marijuana smoking is reported to impair accurate color discrimination, to increase visual reaction time and sensitivity to light (Kiplinger et al. 1971). A particularly severe behavioral impairment associated with marijuana smoking is a decrease in the accurate detection of light stimuli in the peripheral visual field. This last point results in enhanced risk of automobile accidents following recent marijuana consumption (Hartman and Huestis 2013).

Many studies have shown that marijuana use may lead to a distortion of sense of time which may also be a factor associated with increased risk of automobile accidents (Hartman and Huestis 2013). There is also considerable evidence that marijuana use can adversely affect aircraft pilot performance.

Smoking marijuana produces impairment in performance of complex cognitive tasks. Frequent smokers had significantly more difficulty compensating for tracking errors in critical tracking tests than occasional smokers, 1.5 h after smoking. Occasional smokers especially were subject to divided attention and their performance declined significantly with session group effects for tracking error, hits, false alarms and reaction time (Desrosiers et al. 2015).

3.4 Foods and Beverages

Regular consumption of energy dense foods can have a significant impact on the function of the brain and is reflected in neural changes. Foods of abuse are known to act on systems in the brain in a similar way to drugs of abuse including the dopaminergic and opioidergic systems (Koob and Volkow 2010). Interaction of genetic and biological factors can be involved with environmental factors and contribute significantly to abnormal behavior in which food intake gets out of control leading to addiction and corresponding metabolic syndrome.

In the same way as for drugs, food, mainly very palatable and highly nutritious food, can be addictive. Indeed, food and drugs of abuse may use similar brain pathways, including the dopaminergic system (Koob and Volkow 2010). This results in loss of control over behavior and can lead to excess food consumption in the absence of metabolic need. This could result in distortion and fluctuation in body size and elevated body mass index which would consequently account for the increasing obesity epidemic and the corresponding metabolic syndrome (Gearhardt et al. 2011), which is not without significant public health problems that are among the leading causes of death in the United States. However, food addiction does not explain all obesity.

Eating disorders commonly start during adolescence or young adulthood, corresponding to a vulnerable period because the biological maturation process is still underway.

Factors that initiate and maintain excessive food intake are similar to those of drug addiction. Indeed, modern brain-imaging techniques, such as functional magnetic resonance imaging (fMRI) have shown that foods induce potent stimulation of brain reward circuits, in the same way as substances of abuse (Kelley et al. 2005). This could suggest a likely overlap in the biology of neurotransmitters across those disorders. Several neurotransmitters seem to play a significant role in the cognitive and emotional modulation of food, in particular, serotonin. Indeed, Neurotransmitter receptor imaging studies have shown the involvement of some serotonin subtype receptors in the modulation of mood, impulse control, feeding, and anxiety. 5-HT1A subtype receptor appears to play a part in food reward modulation. Some neurobiological effects of dopamine have been associated with conditioning and control of foods of abuse. Indeed, food and food cues have been reported to result in increased dopamine release resulting in repeated stimulation of the dopaminergic reward. This process leads to a situation of neurobiological adaptation that results in compulsive behavior. Some neuropeptides can regulate food intake interacting with the dopamine system in the ventral tegmental area (VTA). The dopaminergic neurons in the VTA project to the nucleus accumbens (NAc), prefrontal and limbic regions which are part of the brain reward system involved in substance abuse (Volkow et al. 2012).

4 Pathological Behavior

4.1 Gambling Disorder

Whereas gambling represents a harmless form of entertainment for most consumers, it can become dysfunctional in a minority. In these individuals, the negative consequences are severe and include financial debt, bankruptcy, family dissolution and criminal behavior. The reclassification of gambling disorder within the Diagnostic and Statistical Manual of Mental Disorders, 5th Edition (DSM-5) addictions category marks a significant step for addiction science.

Gambling addiction creates an irresistible, recurrent and persistent urge to gamble, so that the addicted person is unable to take control over the decision to stop gambling. Even though gambling is unlikely to exert damaging effects on the brain, gambling disorder could cause severe negative consequences and lead to social impairment and cognitive sequelae and may provide insights into addictive vulnerabilities.

One of the most significant changes to the gambling environment has been the increased availability of Internet gambling. Indeed, Internet gambling is the fastest growing segment of the gambling industry. Globally, the largest online gambling product is wagering, accounting for 53% of the online gambling market, followed by casino games (including slot machines/pokies/electronic gaming machines, 25.4%), poker (14.2%), and bingo (7.4%).

Moreover, very easy access to online gambling has attracted a growing number of young people, which, unfortunately, is not without social consequences in this population group. Thus, inevitably problems with gambling have a serious impact on professional life as well and must be considered as serious addictions.

4.2 Internet Addiction

Research on Internet addiction disorder indicates rates may range from 1.5 to 8.2% of Europeans and Americans (Weinstein and Lejoyeux 2010) whereas other studies have estimated the prevalence as 9–13.5% among Canadian youth (MacLaren and Best 2010) Men appear to be more addicted to this behavior than women. The virtual world offered by the internet produces the illusion of leaving one's worries behind and forgetting one's problems.

There seems to be high comorbidity with Internet addiction and some psychiatric disorders such as affective and anxiety disorders. Indeed, in some patients, obsessive-compulsive behaviors have been highlighted before Internet addiction (Cho et al. 2013).

Internet addiction can be assessed using a validated test and a reliable measure. The assessment concerns the extent of a patient's involvement with a computer. Addictive behavior is classified regarding mild, moderate and severe impairment (Widyanto and McMurran 2004). Risk Factors associated with Internet addiction are social, psychological and biological. This concerns introverted individuals who have difficulty communicating and dealing with others and tend to use online communication that seems safer and easier to them. Using this method of communication allows communication among parties who might otherwise not have been able to communicate at all. This type of communication has thus become a substitute for the missing social connection in their lives; thus contributing to the development of Internet addiction.

In some individuals, addiction to internet prevails with no previously known medical conditions while others suffer from prior psychological or psychiatric problems such as anxiety, depression, obsessive-compulsive disorder, or substance abuse.

Through functional magnetic resonance image (fMRI) and electroencephalography (EEG), studies investigating the brain, have shown biological modifications associated with Internet addictions. These biological changes result in cognitive changes (Liu et al. 2010).

In anatomical terms, gaming cues activate the dorsolateral prefrontal cortex (DLPFC), nucleus accumbens, and dorsal striatum in individuals with internet gaming disorder (IGD). This reinforces the hypothesis that online gameplay induces dopamine release in the brain reward circuitry (Sun et al. 2012). Moreover, it seems that behaviors in pathologic gamblers may involve dopamine neurons in the mesolimbic system (Bechara 2003). Furthermore, it was suggested that video game play was associated with impairment of the release of the dopamine. This dopaminergic imbalance can be redressed by increasing dopamine release within the brain reward system that can reduce negative emotions due to withdrawal symptom and reduce craving for addictive behavior. As with the obsessive compulsive disorder and pathological gambling internet gaming disorder is marked by repetitive thoughts and behavior. These behaviors are associated with increased impulsivity. Serotonin appears to play a significant role in depressive mood and anxiety as well as in impulsivity (Lesch and Merschdorf 2000).

4.3 Sex Addiction

According to the Advancement of Sexual Health (SASH) definition «sex addiction is a persistent and escalating pattern or patterns of sexual behaviors acted out despite increasingly negative consequences to self or others» (Herkov 2016).

Indeed, sex addicts, despite the adverse effects that sex addiction can lead to and the physical, mental or emotional and adverse consequences on their personal and professional lives are constantly prey to an irresistible sexual desire as sex addiction becomes the central element of an individual's thinking process.

Sex addiction could be considered as behavior that will relieve an emotional distress; providing a feeling of comfort, addiction becomes the only source of the individual's well-being.

The medical question that remains controversial is whether sex addiction should be regarded as the symptomatology of other disorders or should be considered as a primary behavioral disorder (Grant et al. 2014).

4.4 Compulsive Buying

Pathological buying, compulsive buying, buying addiction and monomania are different terminologies describing the same phenomenon in which individuals are preoccupied with shopping, suffer from recurrent buying impulses or episodes and lose control over their buying behavior. The behavioral excess is related to adverse consequences such as marked distress, social and occupational problems, delinquency or financial bankruptcy. Estimates of prevalence deriving from studies in the US and Germany range from 5.8 to 8% (Mueller et al. 2010).

5 Economic Burden

Close to half a trillion U.S. dollars are spent on expenses associated with medical, economic, social, and the criminal impact caused by the use and abuse of addictive substances. In 2002, abuse of prescription drugs cost nearly $181 billion (Whiteford et al. 2015). A significant amount of these dollars are attributed to opioid abuse. The average total cost per patient of health care for opioid abusers was $15,884 compared with $1830 for nonabusers, a difference of $14,054 per patient. These costs include substance abuse treatment and comorbidity costs such as pancreatitis or hepatitis. The immeasurable indirect costs include drug theft, the commission of crimes to support addiction, doctor shopping, loss of productivity and wages, and the administration of law enforcement (Meyer et al. 2014).

Between 2002 and 2007, the nonmedical use of prescription pain relievers grew from 11.0 to 12.5 million people in the United States. Societal costs attributable to prescription opioid abuse were estimated at $55.7 billion in 2007. A total of 23 studies (183 unique citations identified, 54 articles subjected to full text review) were included in this review and analysis.

Findings from the review demonstrated that rates of opioid overdose-related deaths ranged from 5528 deaths in 2002 to 14,800 in 2008. Furthermore, overdose reportedly results in 830,652 years of potential life lost before age 65. Opioid abusers were more likely to utilize medical services, such as emergency department, outpatient physician visits, and inpatient hospital stays, relative to non-abusers. When compared to a matched control group (non-abusers), mean annual excess health care costs for opioid abusers with private insurance ranged from $14,054 to $20,546. Similarly, the mean annual excess health care costs for opioid abusers with Medicaid ranged from $5874 to $15,183. The issue of opioid abuse has significant clinical and economic consequences for patients, health care providers, commercial and government payers, and society as a whole.

In 2010, mental and substance use disorders accounted for 183.9 million DALYs (95% UI 153.5–216.7 million), or 7.4% (6.2–8.6) of all DALYs worldwide. Such disorders accounted for 8.6 million YLLs [6.5–12.1 million; 0.5% (0.4–0.7) of all YLLs] and 175.3 million YLDs [144.5–207.8 million; 22.9% (18.6–27.2) of all YLDs]. Mental and substance use disorders were the leading cause of YLDs worldwide. Depressive disorders accounted for 40.5% (31.7–49.2) of DALYs caused by mental and substance use disorders, with anxiety disorders accounting for 14.6% (11.2–18.4), illicit drug use disorders for 10.9% (8.9–13.2), alcohol use disorders for 9.6% (7.7–11.8), schizophrenia for 7.4% (5.0–9.8), bipolar disorder for 7.0% (4.4–10.3), pervasive developmental disorders for 4.2% (3.2–5.3), childhood behavioral disorders for 3.4% (2.2–4.7), and eating disorders for 1.2% (0.9–1.5). DALYs varied by age and sex, with the highest proportion of total DALYs occurring in people aged 10–29 years. The burden of mental and substance use disorders increased by 37.6% between 1990 and 2010, which for most disorders was driven by population growth and aging (Whiteford et al. 2013) (Table 4).

Table 4 Proportion of disability-adjusted life years (DALYs), of years lived with disability (YLDs) and of years of life lost (YLLs) explained by each mental and substance use disorder group in 2010

Mental and substance use disorders	DALYs (%)	YLDs (%)	YLLs (%)
Depression disorders	40.5	42.5	
Anxiety disorders	14.6	15.3	
Schizophrenia	9.6	7.4	7.1
Bipolar disorder	7.0	7.4	
Eating disorders	1.2	1.1	2.4
Childhood behavioral disorders	3.4	3.5	
Pervasive developmental disorders	4.2	4.4	
Idiopathic intellectual disability	0.6	0.6	
Alcohol use disorders	9.6	7.9	44.4
Drug use disorders	10.9	9.4	41.7
Other mental disorders	0.8	0.6	4.3

6   Regulatory Initiatives

A regulatory framework is crucial to ensure that consumer products are right to their labelling (not misbranded), or there is no assurance that the products are as advertised. Concerning foods and drugs, claims such as 'fresh', 'reduced sodium', and 'faster acting' must be supportable with data to the satisfaction of the regulatory agency.

With a prescription drug abuse epidemic so large and so widespread, federal, state, and local governments, as well as professional associations and pharmaceutical companies have attempted to provide solutions using tools such as:

- FDA approval of drugs as safe and efficacious with precautionary "black box" warnings on drugs to alert and educate health care practitioners and the public regarding the abuse potential of various medications.
- FDA initiatives including its "Safe Use Initiative" to reduce preventable harm by identifying specific, preventable medication risks and developing, implementing and evaluating cross-sector interventions with partners who are committed to safe medication use.
- Drug schedules were adopted in 1970 when the Controlled Substance Act was passed by Congress to regulate the manufacture, deportation, possession, use, and distribution of drugs that have a potential for abuse. Drugs fall into five classifications or schedules. The DEA has a published list at http://www.justice.gov/dea/pubs/scheduling.html
- Refill limits allow physicians to monitor a patient's disease course periodically, particularly during long-term therapy as an aid to detection of tolerance, drug interactions, compliance, misuse or abuse.
- State laws governed by oversight boards, license, disciplinary actions, and/or sanctions focus on the problem of prescription abuse.
- Internet control by increased DEA monitoring of Internet prescription drug sales. Weak "online consultations" and no prescription requirements, or faxing of prescriptions which can easily be forged, makes these sites targets for drug diversion.
- Prescription drug monitoring programs collect information to be shared with law enforcement agencies, health care and regulatory agencies, and practitioners to help identify inappropriate or illegal use of controlled prescription drugs. In some cases, PDMs create fear in the prescriber community regarding sanctions, which can lead to under treatment of pain. Nevertheless, many states find success with these types of programs noted by the reduced rated of drug diversion.
- Abuse deterrent formulations are newer compounds with altered pharmacokinetic profiles that make it difficult to extract the active ingredient out of a controlled drug rendering it useless for alternate routes of administration such as injection, snorting, or smoking.

7 Perspectives and Recommendations

When most people hear the word "addiction," they think of dependence on substance, such as drugs or alcohol. And for good reason: According to the U.S. Substance Abuse and Mental Health Services Administration (SAMHSA), an estimated 23.1 million Americans aged 12 years or older have a significant problem with alcohol or drugs.

But uppers, downers, and other commonly abused substances aren't the only things Americans are addicted to. In fact, just substitute the word "behavior" for "substance," and you open up the definition of addiction to all kinds of dependencies, some of which may surprise you.

Whether its sex, internet, or bungee jumping, desire to experience that "high" becomes so intense that the addict loses control and seeks the activity despite all negative consequences.

There is a broad range of vulnerability profiles that could otherwise trigger drug abuse. Among the vulnerability factors that are capable of influencing the preference for some drugs, it could mention the level of impulsivity or compulsivity. Some people may also exhibit concurrent substance use and mental health disorders.

Given the fact that any drug can induce dependence, the public people should be informed about the potential harm associated with any drug of potential abuse and subsequent threats concerning public health.

The public must keep in mind that a drug is not a harmless product despite the benefits it provides if recommendations for use are not followed: compliance with prescribed doses, taking into account the appropriate dosage in a specific context, taking the right dosage, at the right time and for the right duration, not long enough, not at all, drug use in combination with alcoholic beverages, or any other drug or natural health products is not recommended, some drugs are contraindicated in patients who are hypersensitive to the drug or any of its ingredients. Not adhering to these recommendations may increase the probability of producing long-term addiction and hence taking certain types of medicinal products.

8 Research Areas and Prevention

8.1 Trajectories

The purpose of this brief paragraph is to afford an idea of the state of knowledge about addiction trajectories. The idea here is not to conduct an exhaustive critical survey of the scientific literature. The notion of trajectory refers to the idea that persons with a given condition will develop through a series of phases, each of which has a certain number of attributes distinguishing it from the next. These steps succeed each other in time, but are not necessarily linear: individuals may "skip" a phase, go back to a phase and get caught in loops. Etymologically speaking; however, the notion of phase refers to a crossing, a journey, and the idea is to go, in steps, from one state to the next. Addiction experts have also used the terms "career", "life cycle of addiction" and "natural history of addiction". The "path" most often studied in this field is as follows: consumption starts, and then evolves towards substance abuse or dependence, followed by treatment, the expected effects of which are an end to or control of the abuse and an attenuation or disappearance of its harmful consequences. Frykholm (1979) suggests three phases of disengagement: ambivalence (impulsive attempts followed by relapses), treatment (serious efforts to abstain) and emancipation when the individual definitely wants to be free of drugs and therapists. Castel (1994) speaks of a temporal, six-stage path: (1) initiation or experimentation, (2) escalation, (3) maintenance, (4) a dysfunctional period, (5) cessation, (6) the duration of the former addict. The work of Hser's team will serve as a departure point since those authors conducted a survey of the literature on each of the phases before reporting the findings of their own analyzes and because they have systematically observed the differences between men and women. However, there are certain limits to this approach: the findings are based on a relatively homogeneous sample of 546 opiate users enrolled in methadone treatment programs in four counties in California. The data were gathered from a retrospective longitudinal estimate (structured interviews), and the study was conducted in the late 1980s. For this reason, using this basic description, which provides the most widely validated data, we present more recent or more focused studies to reveal more contemporary observations or trends. However, it should be noted at the outset that these five phases merely refer to the trajectory most often studied. This represents only one of the possible ways in which the steps can be linked since it reflects only one of the possible outcomes of each of the phases examined. For a fuller understanding of trajectories, it must be understood that some outcomes are possible for each phase, including cessation of consumption or avoiding the transition to abuse or dependence. For example, after being introduced to a substance, some consumers will stop using it while others will continue using without experiencing any problems, and a minority will be exposed to lethal consequences (accident under the influence of drugs, suicide, and infection with a terminal disease). Moderate drinkers, for example, are also likely to know or experience the problems associated with drinking. Recent studies on intoxication (five or more drinks on a single occasion) show that intoxication episodes are mostly reported by moderate drinkers (14 drinks or less per week) and that moderate drinkers may represent as much as one-third of all drinkers who report having alcohol problems (Demers and Quesnel Vallée 1998). The purpose of primary and secondary prevention is to influence the course of the trajectory toward cessation or control of drinking and to avoid the transition to substance abuse. A certain number of users will become abusers or dependents. Once dependence has started, treatment and rehabilitation are the outcomes most often studied. Spontaneous remission and death are also two possible outcomes. The purpose of the harm reduction approach is to offset the negative consequences of excessive use. Following this way we took as example addiction to gambling and internet.

Many factors can contribute to a gambling addiction, including desperation for money, the desire to experience thrills and highs, the social status associated with being a successful gambler, and the entertaining atmosphere of the mainstream gambling scene. Unfortunately, once a gambling addiction takes hold, breaking the cycle is difficult. Severe addictions can take hold when someone feels desperate financially and wants to make back what they have lost. Once the person finally wins, while they may end up collecting a massive amount of money from that win, it is rarely enough to cover what has already been lost.

Internet addiction results in personal, family, academic, financial, and occupational problems that are characteristic of other addictions. Impairments of real life relationships are disrupted as a result of excessive use of the Internet. Individuals suffering from Internet addiction spend more time in solitary seclusion, spend less time with real people in their lives, and are often viewed as socially awkward. Arguments may result due to the volume of time spent on-line. Those suffering from Internet addiction may attempt to conceal the amount of time spent on-line, leading her or him to withdraw and isolate her- or himself from society.

8.2   Knowing the Risks

Communicating risk is a key public health strategy. The implicit assumptions are that the public interprets risk information in a logical fashion and adopts behavioral changes to reduce risk. Risk perception is a rational knowledge of a population increased probability of been affected by an undesirable event. Does knowledge of probability affect our attraction or repulsion for behavior? Our brain is much more affected by our positive or negative emotional experiences towards a behavior. As our understanding for how best to interrupt the destructive course of substance abuse problems has grown, the parallel process of preparing treatment professionals has also been developing. Addiction specialties have recently emerged in medicine, nursing, and other allied health and human service professions. The primary caregivers, however, have traditionally been counsellors who specialize in chemical dependency treatment. Historically, those counsellors have been trained in specialty training programs often developed by treatment agencies rather than in academic institutions. Today, due to a variety of policy and economic factors, the preparation of substance abuse counsellors is being undertaken by colleges in cooperation with treatment agencies, where classroom and field training experiences are being integrated into competency-based instructional programs.

8.3   Prevention

What are the harms from which preventive programs seek to save youth? Parents and other adult's worries about youthful drug use often have more to do with potential harm to the youth's future career or social and personal development than with damage to health. Use of the drug may substitute for other activities more desired by adults. By example, the young drinker may be victimized by his or her drinking companions. Reflecting laws against purchase and use by youth, even of substances like alcohol or tobacco which are legal for adults, the main worry may be about being arrested and the potential blot on the youth's record that this would entail.

Prevention approaches can be classified on a number of dimensions: according to the goal of the particular program (e.g., preventing use, preventing harm, preventing stigma); the strategy (e.g., deterrence, education/persuasion, regulation); the institutional base (e.g., the schools, the courts, the community, the family, and the media); or the target population (e.g., youth in general, high-risk youth, heavy users). A classic typology in alcohol problems prevention focuses on the program goals, distinguishing between interventions aimed at the "phase of choice" (whether or not there is drinking), those aimed at the "phase of use" (shaping the pattern of drinking), or at the "phase of consequences" (avoiding harm from a given drinking pattern) (Moore and Gerstein 1981). In the context of youthful drug use, the last two of these goals are commonly combined in current discussions under the rubric of "harm reduction." Usually, the "phase of choice" is divided in current discussions of two types, by target population: nonusers are subdivided into "high-risk youth," who are contemplating drug use or are expected to be doing so, and other non-using youth.

The resulting typology of approaches resembles the split between "primary", "secondary," and "tertiary" prevention which has been conventional in the public health field. In a recent publication, propose a new terminology for much the same three types, based on a classification system. Universal prevention programs are those that target entirely with messages of preventing or, at least, delaying use. These are blanket programs, designed to target a large group of people, some of whom may not have individual risk factors for use. Selective prevention programs target subgroups considered at high risk for substance use or abuse (e.g., children from low-income families, or with a poor academic record), but yet show no signs of involvement. These subgroups are considered at higher risk than others, and the programs are usually intended to delay or prevent abuse by reducing risk factors and increasing protective factors. Indicated prevention programs are designed to prevent abuse among those who already use substances and show early signs of misuse or show signs of other serious problems or mood disorders that increase their risks of developing a substance abuse problem.

Acknowledgments The authors are grateful to Nikki Sabourin-Gibbs, Rouen University Hospital, for the writing assistance and review of the manuscript in English.

References

Aigner, T. G. (1988). Delta-9-tetrahydrocannabinol impairs visual recognition memory but not discrimination learning in rhesus monkeys. *Psychopharmacology (Berlin), 95*(4), 507–511.

Allenby, C. E., Boylan, K. A., Lerman, C., & Falcone, M. (2016). Precision medicine for tobacco dependence: Development and validation of the nicotine metabolite ratio. *Journal of Neuroimmune Pharmacology, 11*(3), 471–483.

Bechara, A. (2003). Risky business: Emotion, decision-making, and addiction. *Journal of Gambling Studies, 19*(1), 23–51.

Benowitz, N. L. (2009). Pharmacology of nicotine: Addiction, smoking-induced disease, and therapeutics. *Annual Review of Pharmacology and Toxicology, 49*, 57–71.

Benowitz, N. L. (2010). Nicotine addiction. *The New England Journal of Medicine, 362*(24), 2295–2303.

Boyle, P. (1997). Cancer, cigarette smoking and premature death in Europe: A review including the Recommendations of European Cancer Experts Consensus Meeting, Helsinki, October 1996. *Lung Cancer, 17*(1), 1–60.

Brady, K. T., McCauley, J. L., & Back, S. E. (2016). Prescription opioid misuse, abuse, and treatment in the United States: An update. *The American Journal of Psychiatry, 173*(1), 18–26.

Cahill, K., Hartmann-Boyce, J., & Perera, R. (2015, May 18). Incentives for smoking cessation. *Cochrane Database of Systematic Reviews, 5*, CD004307. doi:10.1002/14651858.CD004307.pub5.

Casati, A., Sedefov, R., & Pfeiffer-Gerschel, T. (2012). Misuse of medicines in the European Union: A systematic review of the literature. *European Addiction Research, 18*(5), 228–245.

Castel, R. (1994). Les sorties de la toxicomanie. In A. Ogian & P. Mignon (Eds.), *La demande sociale de drogue* (pp. 23–30). Paris: La Documentation Française.

Centers for Disease Control and Prevention (CDC). (2010, July). *Unintentional drug poisoning in the United States.* http://www.cdc.gov/HomeandRecreationalSafety/pdf/poison-issue-brief

Cho, S. M., Sung, M. J., Shin, K. M., Lim, K. Y., & Shin, Y. M. (2013). Does psychopathology in childhood predict internet addiction in male adolescents ? *Child Psychiatry and Human Development, 44*(4), 549–555.

Christofides, N. (2003). *Tobacco control and sustainable development in Africa.* In INWAT workshop presentations from the 12th world conference on tobacco or health, November 24, 2007.

Cicero, T. J., Ellis, M. S., Surratt, H. L., & Kurtz, S. P. (2014). The changing face of heroin use in the United States: A retrospective analysis of the past 50 years. *JAMA Psychiatry, 71*(7), 821–826.

Control and Prevention. (2011). Vital signs: Overdoses of prescription opioid pain relievers—United States, 1999–2008. *MMWR: Morbidity and Mortality Weekly Report, 60*, 1487–1492.

Cooper, R. J. (2013). Over-the-counter medicine abuse—A review of the literature. *Journal of Substance Use, 18*(2), 82–107.

Costa, M. A. (2016). The endocannabinoid system: An emergent player in human placentation. *Reproductive Toxicology, 61*, 58–67.

Crews, F., He, J., & Hodge, C. (2007). Adolescent cortical development: A critical period of vulnerability for addiction. *Pharmacology, Biochemistry, and Behavior, 86*(2), 189–199.

Crozier, M. K., McMillan, S., Hudson, S., & Jones, S. (2010). The Eastern North Carolina opioid prescriber's project: A model continuing medical education workshop. *Journal of Opioid Management, 6*, 359–364.

Currie, S. R., & Wang, J. (2005). More data on major depression as an antecedent risk factor for first onset of chronic back pain. *Psychological Medicine, 35*(9), 1275–1282.

Demers, A., & Quesnel Vallée, A. (1998). *L'intoxication à l'alcool.* Montréal: Comité permanent de lutte à la toxicomanie (CPLT), Gouvernement du Québec.

Desrosiers, N. A., Ramaekers, J. G., Chauchard, E., Gorelick, D. A., & Huestis, M. A. (2015). Smoked cannabis' psychomotor and neurocognitive effects in occasional and frequent smokers. *Journal of Analytical Toxicology, 39*(4), 251–261.

DuPont, R. L. (2010). Prescription drug abuse: An epidemic dilemma. *Journal of Psychoactive Drugs, 42*(2), 127–132.

Frykholm BTermination of the drug career (1979). An interview study of 58 ex-addicts. Acta Psychiatrica Scandinavica 59(4):370-380.

Garvey, A. J., Heinold, J. W., & Rosner, B. (1989). Self-help approaches to smoking cessation: A report from the normative aging study. *Addictive Behaviors, 14*(1), 23–33.

Gearhardt, A. N., White, M. A., & Potenza, M. N. (2011). Binge eating disorder and food addiction. *Current Drug Abuse Reviews, 4*(3), 201–207.

Gilpin, E. A., Pierce, J. P., & Farkas, A. J. (1997). Duration of smoking abstinence and success in quitting. *Journal of the National Cancer Institute, 89*(8), 572–776.

Grant, B. F., Hasin, D. S., Chou, S. P., Stinson, F. S., & Dawson, D. A. (2004). Nicotine dependence and psychiatric disorders in the United States: Results from the national epidemiologic survey on alcohol and related conditions. *Archives of General Psychiatry, 61*(11), 1107–1015.

Grant, J. E., Atmaca, M., Fineberg, N. A., Fontenelle, L. F., Matsunaga, H., Janardhan Reddy, Y. C., Simpson, H. B., Thomsen, P. H., van den Heuvel, O. A., Veale, D., Woods, D. W., & Stein, D. J. (2014). Impulse control disorders and "behavioural addictions" in the ICD-11. *World Psychiatry, 13*(2), 125–127.

Green, T. C., Grimes Serrano, J. M., Licari, A., Budman, S. H., & Butler, S. F. (2009). Women who abuse prescription opioids: Findings from the Addiction Severity Index-Multimedia Version Connect prescription opioid database. *Drug and Alcohol Dependence, 103*(1–2), 65–73.

Hartman, R. L., & Huestis, M. A. (2013). Cannabis effects on driving skills. *Clinical Chemistry, 59* (3), 478–492.

Hendler, R. A., Ramchandani, V. A., Gilman, J., & Hommer, D. W. (2013). Stimulant and sedative effects of alcohol. *Current Topics in Behavioral Neurosciences, 13*, 489–509.

Herman, A. I., & Sofuoglu, M. (2010). Comparison of available treatments for tobacco addiction. *Current Psychiatry Reports, 12*(5), 433–440.

Herkov, M. (2016). Visited, mars 12, 2016, from http://psychcentral.com/lib/what-is-sexual-addiction/

Hughes, A. A., Bogdan, G. M., & Dart, R. C. (2007). Active surveillance of abused and misused prescription opioids using poison center data: A pilot study and descriptive comparison. *Clinical Toxicology, 45*(2), 141–151.

Hughes, J. R. (2006). Clinical significance of tobacco withdrawal. *Nicotine Tobacco Research, 8* (2), 153–156.

Jha, P., Chaloupka, F. J., Moore, J., Gajalakshmi, V., Gupta, P. C., Peck, R., Asma, S., & Zatonski, W. (2006). Tobacco addiction. In: D. T. Jamison, J. G. Breman, A. R. Measham, G. Alleyne, M. Claeson, D. B. Evans, P. Jha, A. Mills, & P. Musgrove (Eds.), Disease control priorities in developing countries, 2nd ed. Washington, DC: World Bank. Chapter 46. PMID.

Kelley, A. E., Schiltz, C. A., & Landry, C. F. (2005). Neural systems recruited by drug- and food-related cues: Studies of gene activation in corticolimbic regions. *Physiology and Behavior, 86* (1–2), 11–14.

Kelley, M. E., Wan, C. R., Broussard, B., Crisafio, A., Cristofaro, S., Johnson, S., Reed, T. A., Amar, P., Kaslow, N. J., Walker, E. F., & Compton, M. T. (2016). Marijuana use in the immediate 5-year premorbid period is associated with increased risk of onset of schizophrenia and related psychotic disorders. *Schizophrenia Research, 171*(1–3), 62–67.

Kiplinger, G. F., Manno, J. E., Rodda, B. E., & Forney, R. B. (1971). Dose-response analysis of the effects of tetrahydrocannabinol in man. *Clinical Pharmacology and Therapeutics, 12*(4), 650–657.

Koob, G. F., & Volkow, N. D. (2010). Neurocircuitry of addiction. *Neuropsychopharmacology, 35*(1), 217–238.

Le Foll, B., & Goldberg, S. R. (2009). Effects of nicotine in experimental animals and humans: An update on addictive properties. *Handbook of Experimental Pharmacology, 192*, 335–367.

Lesch, K. P., & Merschdorf, U. (2000). Impulsivity, aggression, and serotonin: A molecular psychobiological perspective. *Behavioral Sciences and the Law, 18*(5), 581–604.

Lessenger, J. E., & Feinberg, S. D. (2008). Abuse of prescription and over-the-counter medications. *Journal of the American Board of Family Medicine, 21*(1), 45–54.

Levine, D. A. (2007). "Pharming": The abuse of prescription and over-the-counter drugs in teens. *Current Opinion in Pediatrics, 19*(3), 270–274.

Liu, J., Gao, X. P., Osunde, I., Li, X., Zhou, S. K., Zheng, H. R., & Li, L. J. (2010). Increased regional homogeneity in internet addiction disorder: A resting state functional magnetic resonance imaging study. *Chinese Medical Journal, 123*(14), 1904–1908.

MacLaren, V. V., & Best, L. A. (2010). Multiple addictive behaviors in young adults: Student norms for the Shorter PROMIS Questionnaire. *Addictive Behaviors, 35*(3), 252–255.

Manchikanti, L. (2006). Prescription drug abuse: What is being done to address this new drug epidemic? Testimony before the Subcommittee on criminal justice, drug policy and human resources. *Pain Physician, 9*(4), 287–321.

Mars, B., Heron, J., Crane, C., Hawton, K., Lewis, G., Macleod, J., Tilling, K., & Gunnell, D. (2014, October 21). Clinical and social outcomes of adolescent self harm: Population based birth cohort study. *BMJ, 349*, g5954. doi:10.1136/bmj.g5954.

McAvoy, B. R., Dobbin, M. D., & Tobin, C. L. (2011). Over-the-counter codeine analgesic misuse and harm: Characteristics of cases in Australia and New Zealand. *The New Zealand Medical Journal, 124*(1346), 29–33.

Meyer, R., Patel, A. M., Rattana, S. K., Quock, T. P., & Mody, S. H. (2014). Prescription opioid abuse: A literature review of the clinical and economic burden in the United States. *Population Health Management, 17*(6), 372–387.

MMWR. (2011). *Vital signs: Overdoses of prescription opioid pain relievers—United States, 1999–2008* (pp. 1487–1492).

Moore, M. H., & Gerstein, D. R. (1981). *Alcohol and public policy: Beyond the shadow of prohibition. National Research Council (US) panel on alternative policies affecting the prevention of alcohol abuse and alcoholism.* Washington, DC: National Academies Press (US).

Mueller, A., Mitchell, J. E., Crosby, R. D., Gefeller, O., Faber, R. J., Martin, A., Bleich, S., Glaesmer, H., Exner, C., & de Zwaan, M. (2010). Estimated prevalence of compulsive buying in Germany and its association with sociodemographic characteristics and depressive symptoms. *Psychiatry Research, 180*(2–3), 137–142.

National Institute on Drug Abuse. (2016). *Research report. Prescription drugs—Abuse an addiction.* http://www.nida.nih.gov/PDF/RRPrescription

Nutt, D., King, L. A., Saulsbury, W., & Blakemore, C. (2007). Development of a rational scale to assess the harm of drugs of potential misuse. *Lancet, 369*(9566), 1047–1053.

Pennings, E. J., Leccese, A. P., & Wolff, F. A. (2002). Effects of concurrent use of alcohol and cocaine. *Addiction, 97*(7), 773–783.

Pringuey, D., Cherikh, F., Lunacek, S., Giordana, B., Fakra, E., Belzeaux, R., Adida, M., & Azorin, J. M. (2014). Comorbidity of affective disorders and alcohol use disorder. *Encephale, 40*(Suppl 3), S3–S7.

Riggs, P. (2008). Non-medical use and abuse of commonly prescribed medications. *Current Medical Research and Opinion, 24*(3), 869–677.

Raith, K., & Hochhaus, G. (2004). Drugs used in the treatment of opioid tolerance and physical dependence: A review. *International Journal of Clinical Pharmacology and Therapeutics, 42*(4), 191–203.

Rogers, P. D., & Copley, L. (2009). The nonmedical use of prescription drugs by adolescents. *Adolescent Medicine: State of the Art Reviews, 20*(1), 1–8.

Samhsa: Behavioral health trends in the United States: Results from the 2014 National Survey on Drug Use and Health (p. 4). Accessed December 12, 2015, from http://www.samhsa.gov/data/sites/default/files/NSDUH-FRR1-2014/NSDUH-FRR1-2014.pdf

Savage, C. L. (2016). Substance use and substance abuse—What's in a name? *Journal of Addictions Nursing, 27*(1), 47–50.

Strobbe, S. (2014). Prevention and screening, brief intervention, and referral to treatment for substance use in primary care. *Primary Care, 41*(2), 185–213.

Sun, Y., Ying, H., Seetohul, R. M., Xuemei, W., Ya, Z., Qian, L., Guoqing, X., & Ye, S. (2012). Brain fMRI study of crave induced by cue pictures in online game addicts (male adolescents). *Behavioural Brain Research, 233*(2), 563–576.

Terlecki, M. A., & Buckner, J. D. (2015). Social anxiety and heavy situational drinking: Coping and conformity motives as multiple mediators. *Addictive Behaviors, 40*, 77–83.

Vogeler, T., McClain, C., & Evoy, K. E. (2016). Combination bupropion SR and varenicline for smoking cessation: A systematic review. *The American Journal of Drug and Alcohol Abuse, 42* (2), 129–139.

Volkow, N. D., Wang, G. J., Fowler, J. S., Tomasi, D., & Baler, R. (2012). Food and drug reward: Overlapping circuits in human obesity and addiction. *Brain Imaging in Behavioral Neuroscience, 11*, 1–24. Berlin, Heidelberg: Springer.

Warren, C. W., Jones, N. R., Eriksen, M. P., Asma, S., & Global Tobacco Surveillance System (GTSS) collaborative group. (2006). Patterns of global tobacco use in young people and implications for future chronic disease burden in adults. *Lancet, 367*(9512), 749–753.

Weinstein, A., & Lejoyeux, M. (2010). Internet addiction or excessive internet use. *The American Journal of Drug and Alcohol Abuse, 36*(5), 277–283.

Whiteford, H. A., Degenhardt, L., Rehm, J., Baxter, A. J., Ferrari, A. J., Erskine, H. E., Charlson, F. J., Norman, R. E., Flaxman, A. D., Johns, N., Burstein, R., Murray, C. J., & Vos, T. (2013). Global burden of disease attributable to mental and substance use disorders: Findings from the Global Burden of Disease Study 2010. *Lancet, 382*(9904), 1575–1586.

Whiteford, H. A., Ferrari, A. J., Degenhardt, L., Feigin, V., & Vos, T. (2015, February 6). The global burden of mental, neurological and substance use disorders: An analysis from the Global Burden of Disease Study 2010. *PLoS One, 10*(2), e0116820. doi:10.1371/journal.pone.0116820.eCollection.

Widyanto, L., & McMurran, M. (2004). The psychometric properties of the internet addiction test. *Cyberpsychology and Behavior, 7*(4), 443–450.

Winokur, G., & Clayton, P. (1967). Family history studies. II. Sex differences and alcoholism in primary affective illness. *The British Journal of Psychiatry, 113*(502), 973–979.

Zimmermann, U. S., Blomeyer, D., Laucht, M., & Mann, K. F. (2007). How gene-stress-behavior interactions can promote adolescent alcohol use: The roles of predrinking allostatic load and childhood behavior disorders. *Pharmacology, Biochemistry, and Behavior, 86*(2), 246–262.

Consumer Behavior in Subpopulations

Qing Wang and Naina Narain

1 An Overview of Research on Consumer Behavior in Special and Subpopulation

1.1 Special and Subpopulations

Some of the most enduring issues in consumer behavior pertain to special or subpopulations. Special or subpopulations are defined as those segments that lie outside the traditional focus for consumer research (Corfman and Roedder John 1998). Children, elderly consumers, specific generations and ethnic groups are examples of special populations. Understanding the unique characteristics of these special populations is particularly important for government organizations and businesses, as a product, promotional method, distribution channel or pricing strategy may be correct for the majority of consumers but could be misconstrued or even lead to misuse in a special population, putting these people at risk or even harm.

The list of special populations can be rather extensive—low literacy individuals, mentally ill patients, children/youth/adolescents, elderly, institutionalized (prison, hospital, retirement/nursing home), migrants, ethnic minorities, homeless people, HIV patients and drug addicts are all amongst members of special populations who face some type of discrimination and prejudice due to social barriers (Faugier and Sergeant 1997). For various reasons, they are hidden from the general public. As a result, limited access to information regarding their behavior has led to a substantial gap in knowledge regarding their needs.

Q. Wang (✉)
Warwick Business School, The University of Warwick, Coventry CV4 7AL, UK
e-mail: Qing.Wang@wbs.ac.uk

N. Narain
University of Warwick, Coventry, UK

© Springer International Publishing AG 2017   459
G. Emilien et al. (eds.), *Consumer Perception of Product Risks and Benefits*,
DOI 10.1007/978-3-319-50530-5_24

Through a broader lens, special populations are defined as small subgroups of the population that are considered unique and not commonly visible (Sell and Petrulio 1996). Sudman and Kalton (1986) define a special population as a small subgroup of a population of interest to a researcher. Identifying members of certain special populations can be time consuming and costly. In recent years, special populations being surveyed (Sudman and Kalton 1986) have included (a) ethnic groups such as black Africans, Hispanics, Cubans, (b) people with salaries either above or below a certain amount, (c) employees in specific industries, and (d) users of a specific service or product.

1.2   Sampling Techniques

The challenges of studying special populations or 'hidden populations' derive from two characteristics as outlined by Heckathorn (1997). Firstly, no sampling frame exists which implies that the size of the population is unknown. Secondly, there is a threatening trait that characterizes its members which leads to privacy concerns. As a result, the sample may refuse to cooperate or give unreliable information to protect their privacy and interests.

To overcome difficulties in sampling special populations, three methods have been applied: chain referral sampling, particularly snowball sampling (Penrod et al. 2003), key informant sampling, and targeted sampling (Heckathorn 1997). Next, a brief description of each of these sampling techniques is provided.

1.2.1   Snowball Sampling

One of the best-known methods is snowball sampling, originally suggested by Goodman (1961). It is a sampling technique whereby initial contacts chosen randomly provide the names of other members who fulfil the inclusion criteria. Each subject who agrees to participate is then asked for a specific number of additional names. This process continues until the desired size of the sample is reached (Penrod et al. 2003). However, there are several problems that afflict chain-referral samples. Firstly, inferences made about members found by tracing chains relies mainly on the initial sample and is never random or without bias. Secondly, these chain-referral samples are more biased towards those subjects who agree to cooperate (Heckathorn 1997). Thirdly, the issue of 'masking' arises in populations with strong privacy concerns, whereby participants protect their friends by not referring them. Lastly, because these referrals occur based on the network of subjects, those who have larger personal networks tend to be oversampled leaving the relatively isolated members excluded from the research. The main argument made by Erickson (1979) is that this method is unable to produce claims that are unbiased. Erickson suggests that these problems can be resolved by building in 'added incentives'. As a result, two additional sampling methods were developed to tackle some of these problems.

1.2.2   Key Informant Sampling

Deaux and Callaghan (1985) developed a method to resolve the selection and response bias problems by selecting informative respondents and asking them about others' behavior, rather than their own. For example, a researcher might ask public health officials about drug use behavior. However, there are risks associated with this method dependent on the context. In the case where the informants are professionals, their professional orientation might bias their response: counselors might exaggerate their client's difficulties (Heckathorn 1997). Also, these key informants might not have the detailed knowledge about others especially if it is extremely personal. Therefore, the key informant approach is not effective in acquiring highly detailed and personal information.

1.2.3   Targeted Sampling

To account for the under-sampling produced by traditional methods, Watters and Biernacki (1989) have developed targeted sampling dependent on ethnographic mapping. There are two steps involved in this model to respond to the deficiencies of chain-referral methods: First, to map the special population based on the degree of penetration into the local networks; and, second, ensure that respondents are from different areas and include subgroups in the final sample. Ethnographic mapping is used in order to identify a predetermined number of respondents at the sites. However, this method of targeted sampling is limited by the effects of the time of day when researchers gather participants, which location they operate in and the strategies they use (Heckathorn 1997).

Acknowledging the limitations of the targeted approach, there have been several modifications to chain-referral methodologies. This is due to the increasing recognition of the power of social networks. The popular six degrees of separation theory (Karinthy 1929), where every individual is indirectly associated with every other individual through approximately six intermediaries, stresses the value of referrals. This implies that even members that are isolated or 'hidden' can be reached via chain referral methods.

Despite numerous refinements to these techniques, including the more recently identified Respondent-Driven Sampling (Schonlau and Liebau 2012), the central question remains unresolved, that is, "how to draw a random (initial) sample?" as highlighted by Spreen (1992). Concerns about special populations in terms of how to reach, understand, and influence their behavior have become even more important with the use of digital technology that permeates every stage of the consumer decision process. Social media networks provide new communication channels for special populations, which represents both new challenges and opportunities for researchers.

Against this background, Langer and Beckman (2005) suggest that netnography is a suitable methodology for sampling special populations because it allows the researcher to gain detailed information about the members in an unobtrusive and covert manner. As a result, netnography as a promising approach for studying special populations is discussed and a case study using netnography is presented.

1.3   Netnography

Netnography is "a qualitative research methodology that adapts ethnographic research techniques to study the cultures and communities that are emerging through computer-mediated communication" (Kozinets 2002, p. 62). Ethnographic research holds that individuals mentally construct multiple realities. It is therefore "appropriate to view the research domain as being a social construction relative to the situation" (Travis 1999, p. 1043). Langer and Beckman (2005) studied customers of cosmetic surgery as a special population, based on the assumption that those who consider cosmetic surgery are less likely to talk about it publicly. This qualifies them as a special or 'hidden' population. They argue that analyzing public online communications between special populations is both legitimate and ethical. However, the guidelines for this methodology should be context specific and researchers should be constantly aware of the privacy rights of the sample (Hill 1995).

In summary, ethnographic research is commended for providing in-depth insights into social and cultural communities, as well as the underlying needs, desires, and motives of participants (Kozinets 2002). Netnography has the benefits of being faster, simpler, economical, unobtrusive and providing continual access in comparison with other qualitative research methods (Kozinets 2002; Parsons and Maclaran 2009). The aim is to identify the types of groups or communities formed around the brand and the leading themes emerging from the social interactions.

Social network analysts have identified two ways to interpret behavior: one that focuses on structure and the other on both structure and actor-diversity (Doreian 2001). In the former, the pattern of relations in a network reflects the social identity of the individuals, their underlying preferences and characteristics. Whilst in the latter the network is viewed as a channel for the exertion of influence where an individual's position in the network determines the information accessible to that person and whom he or she may influence (Watts 2003). Thus, a person's social identity depends on not just which group he/she may belong to but also on their position to influence the groups.

Social network analysis technique is a method to visualize the structure of a particular network. It is a powerful tool to help marketers identify points of interest for their customers such as clusters and other structural characteristics that would not be obvious in statistical data otherwise (Newman and Girvan 2004). Developed in the 1960s, it was an interdisciplinary methodology for research in social psychology. In the 1970s with the rapid advancements of formal analyzing techniques, it became an attractive tool for marketers, economists and engineers. Today, online communities are created around every conceivable topic. As a result, social network analysis has become an increasingly popular tool for online social network research.

Specifically, Gephi is an open-source network analysis and interactive visualization platform. It can display large networks in real-time and can speed up the exploration using a 3D render engine. It offers the possibility to understand structure transition or the flow of information in networks (Moody 2005). Although the core of this software is functional, the development of new features focusing on filters, statistics and tools is required.

Some of its most attractive features are its support of many different native graph formats, real-time interactive features, and easy-to-use interface. Most importantly, it has many supporting features built for dynamic network analysis that incorporate functions such as live filtering, a combination of static and dynamic metrics, a multitude of layouts, and a timeline component that can generate various longitudinal reports. It is therefore selected as the social network analysis tool for the case study presented in this contribution.

2 A Case Study on the Social Media Usage Behavior of the Millennial Generation

In this case study, the millennial generation is selected as a special subpopulation due to its unique characteristics in social media usage. It takes a broader lens, as proposed by Sell and Petrulio (1996) and Sudman and Kalton (1986) who define a special population as a small subgroup of a population of interest to a researcher. In this case, the millennial generation is studied as active users of a specific service or product, namely a social media network.

Millennials are leading a generational shift in the concepts of status and money, the likes of which have not been seen since the 1960s (Eastman et al. 2014). Whilst each new generation differs in values, characteristics, and behavior, this has been greatly exacerbated for millennials by technological developments over the past three decades, resulting in an attitude that technological accessibility and interconnectivity are essential. Given the importance of social media for the millennial generation, it is crucial for brands to transform their deep-rooted marketing traditions, and to position themselves to cater for the millennial consumers. This will require a greater understanding of the millennial generation.

According to Howe et al. (2000), the population was comprised of five generations with the following birth dates: The G. I. Generation (1901–1924), the Silent Generation (1925–1942), the Boom Generation (1945–1960), Generation X (1961–1981), and the Millennial Generation (1982–2002). Based on the calculation of Lancaster and Stillman (2002), the American Millennial Generation, raised by the Baby Boomers, was approximately more than 75 million in size and was heralded as a generation with high purchasing power in comparison to previous generations (Henrie and Tayor 2009).

A recent report (Woodward 2016) found that millennials show distinct differences with other demographic groups. They are much more likely to look outside the family base for influence and opinions. Compared to Generation X-ers, Boomers and Silents, they are much more likely to listen to the views of friends and colleagues, as well as strangers, reflecting a willingness to take account of online reviews and social media interaction. They are skeptical of conventional advertising or marketing experts, but are highly influenced by celebrities, particularly those who are active on social media.

In addition, the millennials show a greater willingness to influence others as well as being prone to influence from their peers. Millennials are the most brand-sensitive and socially aware generation due to the need for forming self- and social-identity and are willing to share their brand preferences over social media or online (Parment 2014; Kim and Jang 2014). In other words, the millennial generation is a digitally-empowered generation for whom the practical use of mobile technology, combined with social media, is second nature to them and an inseparable part of their purchasing process. Therefore, in order to reach this generation, brands and retailers are facing the challenge of continuous innovation providing omni-channel connectivity with this consumer group and to assess the influences and sources of information that inform those brand choices (Fromm and Garton 2013).

This generation, known for being 'digital natives', exhibits markedly different consumption habits to those of their predecessors through their extensive use of social media (Mangold and Smith 2012). Therefore this case study addresses two key issues based on the original research findings of the millennial generation: (a) The types of needs satisfied by the use of social media; and, (b) the effect of social media on perceived brand value.

2.1 Types of Needs Satisfied by Social Media

Millennials are three times as likely as other generations to use social media as a pre-purchase research tool. A recent study (Market Strategies International 2014) showed that millennial shoppers are using multiple social media channels for specific purposes. For instance, millennials are much more likely than other generations to use YouTube for learning about products, Twitter for expressing opinions about products and Instagram for posting photographs about products. They are fundamentally different from other generations in that they are more engaged, more vocal and more visual. They are not merely passive readers—they post, pin, view and blog and they are willing to experiment and move to the next innovation in social media. This finding indicates that the millennials are highly advanced and sophisticated in using social media in terms of meeting different type of needs, e.g., utilitarian need in learning about product information on YouTube, symbolic need in expressing their opinion on Twitter and hedonic need in posting photographs on Instagram. Understanding their social media attitude and behavior has significant implications for brand marketers. However, there is little research into exactly how, where and why Millennials conduct their information search. Therefore this research proposes that:

Proposition 1 *The millennials are sophisticated in their attitude and behavior towards social media usage and are seeking to meet different types of needs, including utilitarian, symbolic and hedonic, through social media use.*

2.2 Major Influencers

Millennials view social media comments as more transparent and blogs as usually more objective and credible than traditional advertising. Three-quarters of millennials trust family and friends most when researching products or services and are heavily influenced by celebrities as their fans (Market Strategies International 2014). Eastman et al. (2014) use social comparison theory (Festinger 1954) to explain the influence of celebrities on the millennials and suggest that social comparison has become an even stronger 'driver' for the millennial generation as a result of the proliferation of social media and the lack of independent decision making.

Proposition 2 *Celebrities with a large fan base on social media are highly influential to the millennial generation.*

2.3 Effect of Social Media on Perceived Brand Value

The integration of social media and brands provides huge potential for the millennials in their social identity building. This is because brands epitomize consumption and help build socially desirable identities (Kapferer and Bastien 2012; Brown et al. 2003; Han et al. 2010), whilst multiple social media channels provide potential for communicating desirable self-image and social identity widely and instantaneously. Millennials are more consumption oriented than other generations as a result of the proliferation of communication technologies and prone to status-seeking consumption, in particular through branded products. This focus on consumption and self-expression can be explained using consumer culture theory, in that, as traditional societal structures disintegrate, identity construction through consumption becomes prevalent. These consumers are assuming dominance in the marketing and branding sphere by producing their own cultural identities rather than being dictated to (Firat and Venkatesh 1995), removing the element of control that brands once had—an element that has traditionally been imperative to luxury brand management. Therefore it is proposed that:

Proposition 3 *The integration of brands and social media enhances the ability of millennials to create and communicate self-identity.*

For brands, social media facilitates customer service, public relations, consumer education, and a closer client relationship (Kapferer 2015; Okonkwo 2010). For consumers, social media allows high levels of interaction and engagement with like-minded consumers, increases the desirability of the brands, and has a significant impact on the purchase decision process. Little empirical research has been carried out to understand the effect of social media on the perceived value of brands.

These millennial shoppers want a seamless, digitally enabled, multi-channel experience (Remy et al. 2015). They have exhibited a shift in values, behaviors, attitudes and interests as a result of the birth of the Internet and the vast technological advancements of the past 20 years (Okonkwo 2010). They have become time-poor and are therefore early adopters of technology as this facilitates their day-to-day life (Watson 2015). Furthermore, they are empowered, independent, and vocal about their opinions through social networking platforms. Therefore, it is proposed that:

Proposition 4 *Millennial consumers value brands based on the extent they can engage with the brand to enhance their social identity and provide a multi-sensory experience.*

Next, an exploratory study using netnography is presented to demonstrate the effectiveness of the method in studying a special population and to provide preliminary empirical evidence for the propositions. In this case the netnography method has been applied to the Twitter online community for Tom Ford. The subjects, i.e., millennials, are in their formative years of self-identity construction and exhibit social negotiations within online communities (Atkin 2004; Muniz and O'Guinn 2001). This lends itself to the netnography approach to acquire comprehensive information concerning the subjects' behavior in the digital environment.

2.4 A Social Network Analysis of Tom Ford

2.4.1 Brand Image and Positioning of Tom Ford

Tom Ford is an American fashion designer and film director. He gained fame as the creative director at Gucci and Yves Saint Laurent. In 2006, after leaving Gucci, Ford launched a line of menswear, beauty, eyewear and accessories, named after him. Despite being a new brand, Tom Ford has acquired an exclusive and luxury image due to Ford's history as creative designer with luxury brand Gucci as well as his immaculate and exquisite lifestyle personified in the brand.

The evidence suggests that Tom Ford has a promising future as a truly luxury brand. However, unlike the traditional luxury brand, Tom Ford has been created in the era of digital technology with the millennial generation as the main customer base who has twice as much spending power and willingness to spend on luxury items as their parents' generation (Jing Daily 2014). This means that Tom Ford has to engage with the millennial generation on social media in a novel and creative manner to capture the interest and imagination of the young and digital savvy consumers. Indeed, compared to other luxury brands, Tom Ford has been extremely active on social media.

The brand generated huge publicity and is favored by younger generation celebrity clientele. Tom Ford targets millennial customers who aspire to be vividly outstanding and glamorously sexy, as one of Tom Ford's advertisement agencies, Conversation Agency stated, the goal of Tom Ford is to strengthen and expand the brand's influence with a sleek and unique way to engage a younger, more tech-savvy generation. Therefore this study examines the effect of the Tom Ford social media strategy by taking a snapshot of conversations on Twitter associated with Tom Ford during a 7-day period in February 2016 using social network analysis.

2.4.2   Procedure

The traditional sampling methods have their limitations as discussed earlier. Therefore, this case study provides an alternative way of sampling the target populations through social network analysis of online communities by selecting topics or brands that are particular interesting to the target population.

Using the Twitter Application Programming Interface (API) and searching for the specific keyword #tomford, which acts as the mediation device, 3071 tweets were extracted during the course of 1 week in February 2016. First, to prepare the data in a format ready for analysis using Gephi software, Google Refine was used to extract mentions and hashtag and arranged the downloaded data into a two-column format: Screen name in the first column and hashtag or mention in the second column tweeted by that user. This file was then downloaded as CSV ready for Gephi.

A graph was generated using Gephi, which shows the structure of the Tom Ford online community on Twitter during the selected period. Each hashtag (#) or mention (@) represents a node and the connections or interactions between nodes are lines, which represent edges. This shows which players are important in the network. The network identified here is dense and complex because there are many tweets on a daily basis and different communities discuss different topics. The graph type selected at the start of the analysis was 'Direct' which implies that the interaction between two nodes is directed; the user is directing his tweet to the account mentioned or contributing to the discussion over the #tomford.

The traditional sampling methods as described have their limitations as discussed earlier. Therefore, this case study is not to demonstrate the use of these traditional sampling methods. Instead, it provides an alternative way of getting access to the target populations through social network analysis of online communities around a specific topic or brand.

2.4.3   Analysis and Results

Main Themes and Celebrity Influence
As shown in Fig. 1, the size of the label is based on the number of connections of a particular node—the larger the size of the label displayed, the higher number of connections it has, and the greater the degree of centrality of the node, which indicates the influential power of that node. The labels with @ are twitter accounts and the labels with # are themes. In this case, the twitter accounts with the highest number of interactions include Swatchandreview, Dimondonyc, Time, and Arianagrande. The themes with highest number of interactions include Drake, Champagnepapi, Giveaway, Blacktie, Style, Fashion, and Sohappy. Next, the most influential twitters and themes were analyzed.

The main themes—#drake and #champagnepapi: Millennials are known to associate themselves with Drake because of his song lyrics. Rap Genius released statistics showing that Drake, the hip hop star, not only topped the Most Artist Views category but also the Most Song Views for *Know Yourself.* Therefore, he is known to express his feelings explicitly in his songs and refers to social media, new taxi services like Uber and self-obsession, which are timely and culturally relevant issues. During this period the tweets were extracted, Tom Ford had recently launched a new line of lipstick products named after Drake's Instagram name, champagnepapi. This strategy generated huge online interest for the new product

Fig. 1 Structure of Tom Ford online community on Twitter (Authors own illustration; for illustration purpose only)

among millennial consumers as indicated in the graph by the size of the labels of Drake and Champagnepapi.

The main bloggers—@dimondonyc is the Twitter handle for a social media blogger known as DiMondo. His association with Tom Ford was due to his social media posts of every black tie event that he attends where he wears only Tom Ford. Fashion bloggers have enormous influence on the millennial consumers who are fashion conscious but skeptical about mainstream advertising. The blogger has been referred to as the 'most photographed face in NYC and has a following of over 50,000 on Instagram. Although his Twitter fan-base is of a modest 5394 followers, his influence on millennials on Instagram transfers to the conversation on Twitter. He embodies a style of sophistication and high fashion which are supported by the hashtags #blacktie, #tux, #style, #crystal that are frequent terms used in tweets directed to him.

The results provide preliminary evidence to support research Propositions 1 and 2—that millennial consumers are active and sophisticated in social media usage and are more influenced by celebrities who have a large social media fan-base than traditional advertising.

Online Community and Self-Identity Building

Next, the research proposes that millennial consumers are susceptible to reference group influences and they form communities on social media for self-expression and self-identity building using luxury brands. In this study, modularity is used as a measurement to assess if the network built around Tom Ford can be divided into smaller clusters, or modules, in order to find community structure for Tom Ford. High modularity indicates that a network has a higher rate of intra-relative to inter-module edges (Newman and Girvan 2004). Specifically, a modularity algorithm called the Louvain method, developed by Blondel et al. (2008) in Gephi is applied in this research to find communities in the network. A modularity attribute has been applied to the nodes of the network, which distinguishes them by color; mentions and hashtags belonging to the same color can be identified as a particular community. The resulting value of 0.639 is moderately high and suggests that there are 190 communities with distinct characteristics. The modularity is calculated based on the algorithm created by Blondel et al. (2008), which looks for the nodes that are more densely connected together than to the rest of the network. It is the fraction of the edges that lie in the identified groups minus the expected fraction if the edges were randomly distributed. The value lies in the range of $[-1/2,1]$. In this case, it shows which hashtags and mentions are more densely connected between each other. This network has a relatively high modularity of 0.639 indicating dense connections within modules but sparse connections between nodes of different modules.

The results indicate that the Tom Ford network appears to create a majority of subgroups that are divided around celebrity clientele (e.g., Drake) and are aligned closely with famous personalities whom the millennial population closely associates with on social media sites. The Other clusters appear to encompass the sphere of influence or affinity between Tom Ford's product information and Mr. Ford himself. This finding is consistent with research Propositions 3 and 4—that the millennial consumers use social media to identify with similar others in the reference group and to construct self-identity through association with the reference group on social media. However, the large amount of small communities makes it less influential, less visible hence less effective in achieving self-expression and self-identity building. To increase the influence of the brand community, luxury brands like Tom Ford should focus on driving marketing efforts towards generating larger communities with topics that influence the millennial customer like #drake and #dimondo.

3 Conclusions and Implications for Consumer Behavior in Special and Subpopulations

Some of the most enduring issues in consumer behavior pertain to special and subpopulations. Specifically, difficulties in sampling have restricted access to information regarding their behavior. This has led to a substantial gap in knowledge regarding their needs due to the lack of effective research techniques. Concerns about special populations in terms of how to reach, understand, and influence their behavior have become even more important with the use of digital technology that permeates every stage of the consumer decision process.

Therefore, in this contribution, firstly, an overview of research on consumer behavior in special populations is provided. Three sampling techniques tradition-ally used to study special populations are described and their limitations are examined. Next, a promising approach, i.e., netnography, as a suitable methodol-ogy for sampling special populations is discussed. It has the advantage of allowing the researcher to gain detailed information about the members in an unobtrusive and covert manner.

To demonstrate the effectiveness of netnography as a social network analysis tool, an in-depth and detailed case study of the millennial generation on their social media usage behavior is presented. In selecting the millennial generation as a special population, the authors take a broader lens, as proposed by Sudman and Kalton (1986) who define special populations as a small subgroup of a population of interest to a researcher. This case study addresses two key issues based on original research findings of the millennial generation: (a) the types of needs satisfied by the use of social media and (b) the effect of social media on perceived brand value. It presents an exploratory study of the millennial consumer's social media usage behavior regarding the brand Tom Ford.

The case study using data from social media has revealed preliminary evidence to support the main research propositions. Specifically, it is found that: (1) Millen-nials are sophisticated in their attitude and behavior towards social media usage and are seeking to meet different types of needs including utilitarian, symbolic and hedonic through social media; (2) celebrities with a large fan base on social media are highly influential to the millennial generation; (3) the integration of luxury brands and social media enhances the ability of millennials to create and communicate self-identity; and, (4) millennial consumers value luxury brands based on the extent the brands can engage with them, enhance their social identity and provide a multi-sensory experience.

The findings indicate that the digital generations want an all-encompassing, immersive digital experience in terms of channel, communications, and service. Brands have lost a total control over their traditional exclusive image. Instead, their brand image is, to a large extent, co-created through engaging with the millennial consumers on social networks. This case study demonstrates how the netnography approach can be used to examine specific research questions in a real research setting. It provides evidence of the effectiveness of netnography in studying consumer behavior in special populations. The findings of this contribution have significant implications for researchers hoping to communicate and engage with a special population. Finally, it is important to note that the case study presented in this contribution is only a manifestation of the challenges facing researchers and demonstrates how using innovative methods such as netnography may help solve the problem. However, it is important to note that this is only suitable for studying a subpopulation that are technical advanced in using digital media. Therefore, depending on the type of subgroups, conventional and low-tech methods such as observation and traditional ethnographic approach may still be important.

References

Atkin, D. (2004). *The culting of brands: Turn your customers into true believers*. New York, NY: Penguin.

Blondel, V. D., Guillaume, J. L., Lambiotte, R., & Lefebvre, E. (2008). Fast unfolding of communities in large networks. *Journal of Statistical Mechanics: Theory and Experiment*, P10008.

Brown, S., Kozinets, R. V., & Sherry Jr., J. F. (2003). Teaching old brands new tricks: Retro branding and the revival of brand meaning. *Journal of Marketing, 67*(3), 19–33.

Corfman, K., & Roedder John, D. (1998). Special session summary consumer research with special populations: Issues, problems, and solutions. *Asia Pacific Advances in Consumer Research, 3*, 92–93.

Deaux, E., & Callaghan, J. W. (1985, June). Key informant versus self-report estimates of health behavior. *Evaluation Review, 9*(3), 365–368.

Doreian. (2001). Causality in social network analysis. *Sociological Methods and Research, 30*(1), 81–114.

Eastman, J. K., Bock, D. E., & Larsen, L. (2014). *Millennial money matters: The impact of perceived knowledge and perceived risk on retirement investment decisions*. In AMA 2014 summer marketing educators conference.

Erickson, B. H. (1979). Some problems of inference from chain data. *Sociological Methodology, 10*, 276–302.

Faugier, J., & Sargeant, M. (1997). Sampling hard to reach populations. *Journal of Advanced Nursing, 26*(4), 790–797.

Festinger, L. (1954). A theory of social comparison processes. *Human Relations, 7*(2), 117–140.

Firat, A. F., & Venkatesh, A. (1995). Liberatory postmodernism and the reenchantment of consumption. *Journal of Consumer Research, 22*(3), 239–267.

Fromm, J., & Garton, C. (2013). *Marketing to millennials: Reach the largest and most influential generation of consumers ever*. Chicago, IL: American Marketing Association.

Goodman, L. A. (1961). Snowball sampling. *The Annals of Mathematical Statistics, 32*(1), 148–170.

Han, Y. J., Nunes, J. C., & Drèze, X. (*2010*). Signaling status with luxury goods: The role of brand prominence. *Journal of Marketing, 74*(4), 15–30.

Heckathorn, D. D. (1997). Respondent-driven sampling: A new approach to the study of hidden populations. *Social Problems, 4*(2), 174–199.

Henrie, K. M., & Tayor, D. C. (2009). Use of persuasion knowledge by the millennial generation. *Young Consumer, 10*(1), 71–81.

Hill, R. P. (1995). Researching sensitive topics in marketing: The special case of vulnerable populations. *Journal of Public Policy & Marketing, 14*(1), 143–148.

Howe, N., Strauss, W., & Matson, R. J. (2000). *Millennials rising: The next great generation*. New York, NY: Vintage Books.

Jing Daily. (2014, February 28). *Jing Daily's China luxury brief*.

Kapferer, J. N., & Bastien, V. (2012). *The luxury strategy: Break the rules of marketing to build luxury brands* (2nd ed.). Great Britain and USA: Kogan Page.

Kapferer, J. N. (2015). *How luxury brands can grow yet remain rare*. UK and USA: Kogan Page.

Karinthy, F. (1929). Chains. In *Everything is different*. Budapest: Atheneum Press.

Kim, D., & Jang, S. (2014). Motivational drivers for status consumption: A study of Generation Y consumers. *International Journal of Hospitality Management, 38*, 39–47.

Kozinets, R. V. (2002). The field behind the screen: Using netnography for marketing research in online communities. *Journal of Marketing Research, 39*(1), 61–72.

Lancaster, L. C., & Stillman, D. (2002). *When generations collide. Who they are. Why they clash. How to solve the generational puzzle at work*. New York, NY: Collins Business.

Langer, R., & Beckman, S. C. (2005). Sensitive research topics: Netnography revisited. *Qualitative Market Research: An International Journal, 8*(2), 189–203.

Mangold, G., & Smith, K. (2012). Selling to millennials with online reviews. *Business Horizons, 55*(2), 141–153.

Market Strategies International. (2014, June 10). *Market strategies study: Millennial shoppers trust social media more but diversify beyond Facebook*.

Moody, M. B.-d. (2005). Dynamic network visualization. *American Journal of Sociology, 110*(4), 1206–1241.

Muniz, A. M., & O'Guinn, T. C. (2001). Brand community. *Journal of Consumer Research, 27*(4), 412–432.

Newman, M. E. J., & Girvan, M. (2004). Finding and evaluating community structure in networks. *Physical Review E, 69*(2).

Okonkwo, U. (2010). *Luxury online: Styles, systems, strategies*. UK and USA: Palgrave Macmillan.

Parment, A. (2014). *Marketing to the 90s generation: Global data on society, consumption, and identity*. New York, NY: Palgrave Macmillan.

Parsons, E., & Maclaran, P. (2009). *Contemporary issues in marketing and consumer behaviour*. Oxford: Butterworth-Heinemann.

Penrod, J., Preston, D. B., Cain, R. E., & Starks, M. T. (2003). A discussion of chain referral as a method of sampling hard-to-reach populations. *Journal of Transcultural Nursing, 14*(2), 100–107.

Remy, N., Catena, M., & Durand-Servoingt, B. (2015, July). *Digital inside: Get wired for the ultimate luxury experience*. McKinsey & Company.

Schonlau, M., & Liebau, E. (2012). Respondent-driven sampling. *Stata Journal, 12*(1), 72–93.

Sell, R. L., & Petrulio, C. (1996). Sampling homosexuals, bisexuals, gays, and lesbians for public health research: A review of the literature from 1990 to 1992. *Journal of Homosexuality, 30*, 31–47.

Spreen, M. (1992). Rare populations, hidden populations, and link-tracing designs: What and why? *Bulletin of Sociological Methodology, 36*, 34–58.

Sudman, S., & Kalton, G. (1986). New developments in the sampling of special populations. *Annual Review of Sociology, 12*, 401–429.

Travis, J. (1999). *Exploring the constructs of evaluative criteria for interpretivist research.* In Proceedings for the 10th Australasian conference on information systems. Accessed online August 15, 2016.

Watts, D. J. (2003). *Six degrees: The science of a connected age.* New York, NY: Norton.

Watson, S. (2015, June 4). *Digitas LBi—Connected commerce.* London: Net-A-Porter—The Net Set.

Watters, J. K., & Biernacki, P. (1989). Targeted sampling: Options for the study of hidden populations. *Social Problems, 36*(4), 416–430.

Woodward, R. (2016, March). The millennial consumer—Who are they? *Management Briefing.*

Part IV
Regulation and Responsibility

Regulatory Prospective for Medicinal Products

Louis A. Morris

1 Risk Communication for Prescription Medical Products

The current contribution focuses on the US regulation of medical products. Over the years, the US Food and Drug Administration (FDA) has developed a sophisticated regulatory scheme to enable truthful communication of product risks and benefits. This scheme can serve as a model for other products that must convey risks as well as benefits in their communications.

Medical products, specifically prescription drugs, are unique and serve as the focus of this contribution. Compared to other consumer products, the margin for safe use of prescription drugs is often razor thin and there is a precise calculus that must be undertaken to determine whether a drug is safe to use. This calculus is defined by the benefit to risk equation: the benefits must outweigh the risks for a product to be considered safe. What makes the analysis unique is the large number of risks that must be continually discovered and assessed, and compared to benefits that are also continually discovered and assessed, over the life cycle of the product's use.

1.1 Risk-Benefit Communication

The communication of prescription drug risks and benefits is delivered in two fashions. First, the risks and benefits of these products are summarized in the products label. The label outlines the conditions under which the product can be safely used. Only people with the specific diagnoses outlined in the product label,

L.A. Morris (✉)
Louis A Morris & Associates, Inc. 8 Norman Court, Dix Hills, NY 11746, USA
e-mail: lmorris@optnline.net

© Springer International Publishing AG 2017
G. Emilien et al. (eds.), *Consumer Perception of Product Risks and Benefits*,
DOI 10.1007/978-3-319-50530-5_25

who do not have specified contraindications and who take described precautions, can safely use the product. Further, if adverse events occur, product users are informed to take preventive or remediate actions and seek medical help at the first sign of trouble. The second channel of communication is through product promotional vehicles such as paid advertisements, personal sales, public relations activities and promotional materials distributed by the manufacturer. Education information may be viewed either as product label information or as promotional information depending on how it is presented and delivered.

The majority of risk communication (in terms of money spent and frequency of interdiction) is promotional in nature; targeting health professionals who prescribe and dispense the medications. In the United States and New Zealand, promotional information, in terms of print and televised commercials, can also be directed at patients and consumers. In addition to promotional information, there is a sizeable amount of effort in many countries directed at educating patients with printed information about prescription medicines. For the purpose of this contribution, we focus on consumer receipt of risk-benefit information.

There are multiple forms of patient educational materials; some of which is approved by governmental agencies (e.g., patient package inserts, mediation guides, patient information leaflets) and some are commercially available and provided by private sector groups (e.g., consumer medication information) or commercial brochures provided by the pharmaceutical company for the benefit of the patient (i.e., regulated as promotional information). Generally, these patient educational sources of patient information are summarization of the professional package insert; with additional information to explain complex medical concepts or provide information relevant to patients that are assumed to be known and understood by health care professionals, as such are considered unnecessary in professional information.

To assure that product use is safe, it is essential that all the educational and promotional information accompanying medical product is the "truthful". The simple principle; one must tell the truth; takes on important meaning for medical products as misinformation or deceptive communications can lead to incorrect use and to preventable harm. Ethical and legal criteria have been established to prevent such miscommunication and government agencies continually monitor new and existing medical product communications to assure accurate and truthful communication.

The WHO "Ethical Criteria for Medicinal Drug Promotion" specifies that "all promotion-making claims concerning medicinal drugs should be reliable, accurate, truthful informative, balanced, up-to-date, capable of substantiation and in good taste. They should not contain misleading or unverifiable statements or omissions likely to induce medically unjustifiable drug use or to give rise to undue risks" (WHO 1988).

In Europe, the European Union (EU) member states have adopted principles that follow the EU (2001) directive that specifies that "member States shall prohibit any advertising of a medicinal product in respect of which a marketing authorization has not been granted in accordance with Community law". The directive specifies that all parts of the advertising of a medicinal product must comply with the particulars listed in the summary of product characteristics (a summary of product information that serves as the basis of the approved label) and that the advertising of a medicinal product: "shall encourage the rational use of the medicinal product, by presenting it objectively and without exaggerating its properties [and it] shall not be misleading."

Similarly, in the United States (US) the Food Drug and Cosmetic Act (FDCA) dictates the legal requirements for the approval and marketing of drugs and medical devices. This law specifies that all labels and advertisements for prescription medication cannot be false or misleading and must provide "adequate directions for use" so that product users are not misled by the labeling or advertising for the product.

Although the principle; one must tell the truth; seems simple; what constitutes the "truth" becomes more complicated when one reviews product claims (i.e., explicit or implied statements about the product or its effects). What constitutes miscommunication is further specified in laws, regulations, and in research relating to risk communication.

2 False or Misleading Labeling or Advertising

The focus of this section is the United States, although other countries have similar regulatory schema. According to the FDCA; a drug shall be deemed to be misbranded (an illegal act) if "its labeling is false or misleading in any particular" (Section 353 (a)). It is illegal to misbrand any drug released into interstate commerce [FD&C Act, sec. 301(b); 21 U.S.C. 331(b)].

The FDAC (section 201 (n)) states:

> "If an article is alleged to be misbranded because the labeling or advertising is misleading, then in determining whether the labeling or advertising is misleading there shall be taken into account (among other things) not only representations made or suggested by statement, word, design, device, or any combination thereof, but also the extent to which the labeling or advertising *fails to reveal facts material in the light of such representations* or material with respect to consequences which may result from the use of the article to which the labeling or advertising relates under the conditions of use prescribed in the labeling or advertising thereof or under such conditions of use as are customary or usual." Therefore, all of the important information necessary to make a labeling or advertising claim must be sufficiently complete (i.e., all of the "material facts" disclosed) so that reasonable members of the audience correctly understand the statements made and the consequences of use of the product.

The consideration of what constitutes "misleading" labeling has been most fully discussed by the FDA in relation to reviewing advertisements and promotional labeling. A FDA Guidance [Presenting Risk Information in Prescription Drug and Medical Device Promotion, May 2009] notes four important aspects of how FDA determines whether labeling or advertising information is considered false or

misleading that have implications for risk communication.
First, the Guidance states that:

> "When FDA evaluates the risk communication in a promotional piece, FDA looks not just at specific risk-related statements, but at the *net impression*—i.e., the message communicated by all elements of the piece as a whole. The purpose of the evaluation is to determine whether the piece *as a whole* conveys an accurate and non-misleading impression of the benefits and risks of the promoted product." Thus, FDA maintains that "[a] promotional communication that conveys a deceptive net impression of the product could be misleading, even if specific individual claims or presentations are not misleading."

Second, the FDA's analysis of labeling or advertising is based upon whether the impressions gained from the piece are likely to mislead a "reasonable consumer." The *reasonable consumer standard* used by FDA in evaluating promotional materials is adopted from the US Federal Trade Commission (FTC). According to the FTC, promotional communications are examined from the perspective of a "consumer acting reasonably in the circumstances." If the material is directed primarily to a particular audience, the FTC examines reasonableness from the perspective of that audience. Similarly, when applying the reasonable consumer standard, FDA, "takes into account the different levels of expertise of lay consumers and healthcare professionals. Due to their training and experience, healthcare professionals develop a level of knowledge related to scientific concepts and medical conditions and products that lay consumers do not possess. FDA takes this difference in knowledge and experience into account when assessing promotional materials directed at healthcare professionals versus those directed at lay audiences." However, FDA notes that "research has shown that experts [in this case healthcare professionals] are subject to the same cognitive biases and processing limitations as non-experts."

Third, is consideration of the extent to which an audience is misled. Not all members of an audience (or even a majority of the audience) have to be misled for a piece to be considered misleading. A labeling piece is considered misleading even if only a percentage of the audience is deceived by its message. There can be multiple interpretations of a claim (i.e., labeling or promotional statement) that are all considered reasonable. In fact, the FTC maintains that a statement can be considered deceptive even if it is a "secondary" interpretation and the primary interpretation is accurate. The FDA also maintains that there can be more than one interpretation of a claim and "when a seller's representation conveys more than one meaning to reasonable consumers, one of which is false, the seller is liable for the misleading interpretation".

Fourth, the FDA Guidance, and regulations upon which it is based, describe the types of promotional material that constitute false or misleading claims. Among the concepts underlying FDA law and regulations is the idea that drug companies have a requirement to provide an accurate and through description of the risks of the medicines they market in a balanced fashion. Section 502(n) of the FDC Act requires companies to present a "true statement" of information in brief summary relating to side effects, contraindications, and effectiveness. FDA regulations specify that an advertisement does not satisfy the requirement of providing a "true statement" of information if (among other reasons):

(i) It is false or misleading with respect to side effects, contraindications, or effectiveness; or
(ii) It fails to present a fair balance between information relating to side effects and contraindications, or
(iii) It fails to reveal facts "material in the light of its representations or material with respect to consequences that may result from the use of the drug as recommended or suggested" in the promotional material (21 CFR 202.1) (e) (5) (i, ii, iii).

Thus, the failure to disclose important facts that prevent a reasonable physician from accurately comprehending the statements made (i.e., failure to reveal material facts) constitutes false or misleading information.

2.1 Adequacy of Risk Communication: the Fertilizer Theory of Risk Communication

The basic tenet that drug communications must provide "adequate" directions for using the product necessitates consideration of what is the purpose of the risk communication (i.e., adequate for what purpose?). For a physician audience, the purpose of the communication is fairly straight forward; to permit the physician to receive all of the information necessary to make a proper prescribing decision and to provide the patient with counseling information necessary to monitor treatment and take necessary precautions or follow up actions. Labels for prescription drugs directed to health professionals are often 30 or more pages long with exhaustive risk communication details outlining warning, precautions, contraindications and adverse drug reactions.

For patients, the adequacy of risk communication is more difficult to judge. In general, there are three reasons for providing patients with information about their medication: *Consent, Avoidance and Monitoring.*

Consent: for certain drugs, such as birth control pills and vaccines, where patients are relatively healthy and taking medicines to prevent a disease or condition, an important aspect of patient information is to provide sufficient information about the products' risks and benefits so that the patient can provide "consent" (i.e., make an informed decision) about accepting the treatment.

Avoidance: for other drugs, where there are certain people who should not take the medicine (contraindications) or people need to use precautions while using the drug, the purpose of the information to help people "avoid" adverse outcomes.

Monitoring: for certain drugs, where there are adverse reactions that modify the risk-benefit equation determining whether the drug should continue to be used, drug information is necessary to "monitor" treatment so that the patient can seek medical help as soon as possible to avoid negative consequences of drug use.

To some extent, adequate risk communication for all drugs requires information about consent, avoidance and monitoring. However, the extent to which these three "purposes" need to be fulfilled varies with the type of drug and conditions of use for that medicine. The varying drivers of the content of patient information are (by analogy) similar to the varying ingredients for plant fertilizer—where the combination of the three basic ingredients [nitrogen, phosphorus, and potassium (potash)] is selected based on the desired results from the product's use (leaf growth, root growth, or flower color and size). Thus, the "fertilizer theory" of patient information has been proposed to connote that the "purpose" of patient information varies depending on the desired effects (consent, avoidance or monitoring) sought for the product. Drafters of patient risk communication must decide the extent to which each of the three purposes exist for each individual drug and tailor the risk communication document for those particular purposes. If consent is a major driver of the document; explanation of all major risks and benefits is a key communication objective. However, if avoidance or monitoring is a key driver, focus on who should not use the medicine, what activities, foods or other drugs to shun or how to identify certain physical reactions and identify them as side effects is the main communication objective. With these three purposes in mind; risk communication documents are composed with each purpose emphasized or moderated as necessary for that particular medicine.

2.2   Elements of an Adequate Warning

For those risks which must be communicated, adequate communication is essential. There are various definitions of risk, for some, risk is simply the probability that an event will occur and one must characterize the nature of the event to fully explain how that factor will be understood. For others, risk is the chance that a person will be harmed or experience an adverse health effect if exposed to a hazard. For still others, risk is described as the combination of the probability of occurrence of harm and the severity of that harm.

To fully characterize risks, efforts must be made to decrease the uncertainty regarding the factors that influence the nature, severity and likelihood with which a hazard can occur. To fully describe these risks, the WHO suggests a tiered approach to risk discovery and analysis. According to WHO (2008), risk assessments have included four principal components: *hazard identification*, or the identification of the type and nature of adverse effects that an agent has the inherent capacity to cause; *hazard characterization*, or the qualitative and, wherever possible, quantitative description of the inherent property of the agent of concern; *exposure assessment*, or the assessment of the magnitude of likely human exposures of an individual or a population to that agent; and *risk characterization*, or the qualitative and, wherever possible, quantitative determination of the probability of occurrence of adverse effects of the agent under defined exposure conditions.

Communicating this information requires selecting the essential aspects of the characterized hazard that are most meaningful and actionable. Weinstein (1999) suggests that decisions about personal risks require, at a minimum, information about the nature and likelihood of potential ill effects, information about the risk factors that modify one's susceptibility, and information about the ease or difficulty of avoiding harm.

Focusing on Medical Devices and relying on human factors psychology, FDA (2001) has noted that there are four elements of a complete warning:

- **A signal word (WARNING, CAUTION)** to alert the reader that what follows is important hazard information. A symbol or icon may emphasize the effect of the signal word. Additional enhancement, such as bolding, larger type, underlining, italics, or color may help the information stand out from the rest of the text. However, studies have demonstrated that a large difference in font size between the signal word and the text may de-emphasize the importance of the text and therefore reduce the likelihood that the text will be read.
- **A hazard avoidance directive** in the form: "**Do Not, Never, Avoid. . .**" (or **Do**, if more appropriate) followed by the action to avoid (or perform). The objective of this directive is to give clear instructions to the user on how to avoid the hazard.
- **A clear statement of the nature of the hazard** associated with the warning (e.g., allergic reaction to material), or precaution (e.g., loss of motor control) that characterizes the severity and the likelihood, and
- The **consequences**, specifying the serious adverse events, potential safety hazards and

  limitations in device use that result if users do not follow instructions. The purpose is to give them a clear idea of the risk, which is likely to increase compliance. Hazard alert research has shown that this element has a significant effect on readers. If the consequences are not included, the alert is likely to be less effective.

In addition; drug communications often require information on the likelihood of an adverse event occurring and information on how to identify an adverse event.

2.3   Adequate Communication

Unfortunately, the full description of pharmaceutical product risks presents a major dilemma for communicators. Examining the product labeling for most pharmaceutical products indicates that there are multiple adverse events that must be included in a warning message. Product labels may include hundreds of warnings, precautions, contraindications and adverse reactions. Limiting to only the most serious adverse events noted in the warning/precautions sections may still result in listing ten or more adverse reactions. Clearly, it is possible for patients to gain access to and read the professional product labels to gain a fuller understanding of the risks of a product. However, most patient information sources limit the amount of information to 3–5 pages.

Limiting patient information is likely essential for most readers. Information (or sensory) overload presents a formable problem for communicators. Limitations of our ability to attend to and process information presented in the environment makes the communication of any specific piece of information probabilistic. Unsworth and Engle (2007) suggest that this limitation is due to working memory restriction arising from two components: (1) limitation in our ability to pay attention to multiple stimuli in a specific time period (primary memory) and a reduced likelihood that we search for specific cues (information) in the existing environment (secondary memory). Like the excess of incoming information that might confront a pedestrian on a crowded city street, information overload forces one to be selective in the information received and retained. Large amounts of information can also inhibit information search as people may decide that there is already too much information to process; when reading, they may ignore information or skim over important details in an effort to manage the information environment and control what is being processed.

To make information more readable, and more likely to be read, most patient formation materials are usually limited to about one to three pages in length. Risk information is summarized and only the most important information is presented.

While the length of patient information has been set by convention, the contents of what characterizes successful risk communication are more controversial. In 1996, pursuant to US law, a private sector group developed criteria for the provision of useful prescription drug for patients (Keystone Report 1996). These criteria were accepted by the US government and establish the desired elements for acceptable patient information. The criteria established stated that prescription drug information had to be:

– scientifically accurate
– unbiased in content and tone
– sufficiently specific and comprehensive
– presented in an understandable and legible format that is readily comprehensible to consumers
– timely and up-to-date
– useful; that is, enables the consumer to use the medicine properly and appropriately, receive the maximum benefit, and avoid harm.

To measure progress toward meeting goals to present useful information to patients, FDA sponsored surveys that operationalized these criteria and sampled patient information for a few drugs in nationwide surveys (Kimberlin and Winterstein 2008). The most recent survey found that, for the most part (80% or more of the leaflets), the risk information sections of patient information met acceptability criteria and would be considered useful. Although, this finding (the acceptability of risk information presentation) is frequently debated in court for specific drugs in product liability lawsuits, the majority of drug-risk information provided to patients, according to the government-accepted criteria, is considered "useful."

3   Truthfulness of Individual Product Claims

Global proclamations about the "usefulness" of patient information do not necessarily predict whether specific risk communication documents or specific claims within these documents are adequate or "truthful." To determine whether a specific claim is truthful, a more microscopic examination of the claims made is necessary. In this instance, a two-part analysis is needed to determine whether the claim made is: (1) substantiated by sufficient data and (2) whether the information is communicated fully and correctly.

3.1   Substantiation

Substantiation refers to the evidence presented to support claims made in communication vehicles. The amount and nature of substantiation needed varies with the type of claim that is made about the product. We can categorize claims into three types that vary in terms of the type of evidence necessary for a consumer to verify its veracity: search claims, experience claims, and credence claims (Ford et al. 1988).

Search claims are those claims that can be accurately evaluated prior to purchase using prior knowledge, direct product inspection, reasonable effort, and normal channels of information acquisition, such as newspaper articles. With the internet, much more product information is available and consumers can determine the accuracy of a larger number of product claims. If a drug tablet is claimed to be easy to swallow, inspection of the size of the tablet may verify or disqualify this claim.

Experience claims can be accurately evaluated only after the product has been purchased and used for a period of time. If a drug promises fast pain relief, taking the product while experiencing pain can lead to an estimate of time to relief.

Credence claims are those that cannot be accurately evaluated even after the product is used because of the consumer's lack of technical expertise or because the cost of obtaining sufficient accurate information to check the veracity of the claim is higher than its expected value. Such claims can be verified by experts. Clinical trial claims of a product benefits or lack of side effects would be considered credence claims. In this instance, experts are needed to review product data and assure that there is sufficient evidence to support these claims.

In the US, the FDA requires "substantial evidence" which is currently defined as "data from one adequate and well-controlled clinical investigation and confirmatory evidence." Thus, to make a clinical claim of benefit or lack of risk, companies need to conduct a well designed clinical study; and have additional corroborative evidence, to support the claim [Section 115(a) FDAC]. FDA staff reviews such product claims in promotional materials and object to claims (and ask for their discontinuation) that are derived from inadequate studies or whose results are misinterpreted.

3.2 Explicit and Implied Claim Communication

The second aspect of claim review is the analysis of what is actually communicated by product information. The process of communication involves not only the presentation of information, but importantly the active processing of that information by the consumer. To comprehend a document or promotional piece, a consumer processes the presented information and "constructs" the meaning conveyed by the piece (Graesser et al. 1994). Meaning construction necessitates the use of "inferences" by the consumer to interpret or "fill in" aspects of the communication that are not fully communicated so that the communication is processed or understood in terms that the consumer can understand. Meaning construction involves three processes; (1) the application of the reader's goal in reading the document (how deeply does the reader process and understand the concepts conveyed; what meaning is extracted from the presented information); (2) the assumption that there is a coherent message presented in the document; that the words and phrases are conceptually related (local coherence) and that the overall meaning of the document is consistently related to the individual parts of the document (global coherence); and (3) inference making in order for the reader to explain the underlying assumptions and meaning conveyed by the presented claims. The process of constructing meaning indicates that promotional claims may convey meaning that goes beyond the precise claims presented in promotional material. To understand product claims, inferences are needed to maintain local and global coherence. As such, product claims may have both explicit and implied meanings.

Thus, to understand what is communicated in labeling and advertising, the perspective of the reader must be taking into account in terms of how the consumer processes the information and makes decisions based on the presented facts.

3.3 Heuristics and Biases

Information processing involves a series of steps in which the consumer must be exposed to information, attend to relevant material, extract and interpret its meaning, and use the information in making product decisions. At each step in this process, there are pitfalls where the consumers ability to successfully complete the steps can be mitigated by features of the presented information or biases in the manner in which the information is processed. In this section, we present a variety of information processing biases that can interfere with adequate and truthful communication.

Human information processing is hindered by a number of heuristics and biases that result from how information is processed. Heuristics are efficient cognitive processes, conscious or unconscious, that ignore part of the information available when we make decisions. Because using heuristics saves effort, the classical view has been that heuristic decisions lead to more errors than do "rational" decisions as defined by logic or statistical models. However, for many decisions, heuristics may lead to efficient and equally correct decisions (Gigerenzer and Gaissmaier 2011). On the other hand, heuristics do lead individuals to ignore potentially important information that should be considered and biases may lead people to focus on inconsequential information or process information in an unfair fashion.

Our information processing system was not built to notice and process the huge number of stimuli that can potentially influence our decisions. As such, much of the potential information impacting our sensory system is ignored or analyzed in a cursory fashion as we focus only on those aspects of the environment (in this case a document) that we perceive as most necessary and engage only a cursory review of other parts of the material. Even brief information, such as a one-page leaflet or short advertisement, may not be fully processed because of immediate concerns of reader is captured by other demands. Longer forms of information may require too much time to read. This lack of time and resources may inhibit the communication of important information.

However, even if the information is read fully, the way information is processed can lead to mistakes, as heuristics and biases influence how the information is processed, and ultimately influence decisions about use of the drug. Tversky and Kahneman (1974) first discussed this phenomenon by noting several of the mistakes people make when forming judgments involving probabilities. They described a number of heuristics that lead to misjudgments. For example, tendencies for people to misjudge stimuli because they are not perceived to be typical of members of a certain class (e.g., a drug is not likely to cause serious harm because it treats facial acne (the representativeness heuristic); tendencies for people to misjudge the likelihood that an event will occur due to how easily people can recall the occurrence of an event (e.g., a vaccine will cause a serious side effect because news media have been reporting on a case of a famous person having that side effect) (the availability heuristic), and the tendency for people to under (or over) estimate the probability of an event because of initial beliefs about the likelihood of the event (e.g., a drug is unlikely to cause a side effect because a doctor says the drug is safe) (anchoring and adjustment bias).

Numerous additional biases have been discussed in the literature (Stanovich and West 2008; Gigerenzer and Gaissmaier 2011). Although cognitive ability does correlate with the tendency to avoid some biases and lead to consideration of a greater number of factors that can reasonably influence a decision, cognitive ability does not necessarily mean that cognitive biases are not influential) (i.e., even smart people are subject to cognitive biases). Of particular interest in medical decision making are biases that influence beliefs about the potential for personal harm.

Judgments regarding pharmaceutical risks can be strongly influenced by the "emotionality" of presented information (the degree to which the presented information elicits an emotional response). For example; the degree to which a product outcome (e.g., nuclear explosion versus a skiing accident) engenders "dread" (a strong negative emotional reaction) influences our perception of risk (Slovic 1987). Slovic et al. (2004) have termed this aspect of risk judgments the "affective heuristic." According to Slovic, risk is processed both emotionally and analytically and influences our judgments in two different fashions. Risk as "feeling" refers to individuals' fast, instinctive, and intuitive reactions to danger. Risk as "analysis" brings logic, reason, and scientific deliberation to bear on risk management. Reliance on risk as feelings is described with "the affect heuristic."

The affective heuristic impacts how people perceive and evaluate risk. It may also be considered a general means of making decisions. Many researchers have emphasized the distinction between these two types of emotional and cognitive processes: those executed quickly with little conscious deliberation and those that are slower and more reflective. Stanovich and West (2000) called these "System 1" and "System 2" processes, respectively. System 1 processes occur spontaneously and do not require or consume much attention; they occur instantly and effortlessly and is unaffected by intellect, alertness, motivation or the difficulty of the problem being attempted at the time. Conversely, System 2 processes involve mental operations requiring effort, motivation, concentration, and the execution of learned rules. These system 2 processes are generally referred to as "cognitive deliberation" (Frederick 2005).

System 1 and System 2 are active, to some extent, in most decisions involving risk. However, there are differences among individuals in terms of the extent to which, System I decisions are over-ridden by System 2 deliberations. Recently, researchers have discovered distinct neural correlates to how certain types of biases, especially those with emotional overtones, influence human decision making. For example, risky choices are susceptible to the manner in which options are presented. This is demonstrated by the "framing effect".

The framing effect demonstrates that how a choice is presented; in terms of benefits (85% of the people taking this drug will live) or losses (15% will die) influences decision making. People are more likely to select the option framed as a gain than when the same option is framed as a loss. This clearly violates assumptions of human rationality when presented with a risky option.

Recently, scientists have investigated neural correlates of risky decisions and framing effects. De Martino et al. (2006) found that the framing effect was specifically associated with amygdala activity, (a section of the mid-brain responsible for processing emotional responses) suggesting a key role for an emotional system in mediating decision biases. Moreover, across individuals, orbital and medial prefrontal cortex activity (sections of the brain involved with rational processing) predicted a reduced susceptibility to the framing effect. This finding highlights the importance of incorporating emotional processes within models of human choice and suggests how the brain may modulate the effect of these biasing influences to approximate rationality.

Decision making under risk may depend on partially separate neural systems for dealing with potential losses and potential gains. Although the amygdala may be important for processing initial responses in decisions concerning potential losses, it is not the only neural structures that influence decision making under risk. We may undertake additional strategies to simplify our decisions (e.g., do what the doctor suggests). However, research does suggest that decision making involving potential losses is more emotionally driven, and more instantaneously provided than decision making involving potential gains.

4 Strategy for Presenting Information

The finding that there are distinct neural systems for processing risk information in terms of gains and losses suggest that drafting risk information for patients needs to incorporate both emotional and cognitive perspectives. The facts about the benefits and risks of drugs, gleamed from premarket, especially clinical trial data, and updated by post-marketing surveillance information should be used to define the content of patient information. However, the style of presentation; whether the informational tone is stark or reassuring, vivid and concrete or abstractly summarized; providing precise directions and complete description of the consequences of adverse events or broadly summarized information about what adverse events may occur, needs to be weighted and balanced by knowledge of how it will be processed. Depending on the goal of the drafter in presenting information, information can be crafted to maximize the intended use of the presented information.

Earlier we suggested three goals of patient information: consent, avoidance and monitoring. When drafting patient information; information pertinent to each goal should be presented to address the cognitive/emotional processes with which the information will be subjected.

For consent information, the goal is careful consideration of risks as well as benefits to achieve a thoughtful decision. This is a cognitive process where the reader needs to understand potential harms (taking into account their nature, severity and probability) and weight these risks against the potential benefits (taking into account the nature, prognosis and course of the treated disease). This process necessitates cognitive reflection and thoughtful consideration. Emotional reactions can interfere with this thoughtful deliberation. Therefore, language that engenders emotional processing needs to be minimized or at least countered with information that will engender reflective thought. Although, some people will react emotionally to risk information regardless of how the information is presented, presenting risk information in a balanced fashion (risks as well as benefits), phrased as scientifically objectively as possible, would enable thoughtful consideration. Risk likelihood, in terms of gain or losses, needs to be presented in a neutral fashion; perhaps presenting both methods of interpretation (stating risk in terms of both gains and losses).

For avoidance information, the objective is more emotionally laden. Here, we wish to allow people not only to recognize threats, but to act affirmatively to steer clear of these possible harms. To achieve the goal of presenting avoidance information, we need to motivate people to behave in accordance with the directions provided. Certain people must avoid taking contraindicated drugs. Other people must avoid certain activities (e.g., driving a car) or certain foods or drugs that can dangerously interact with taken medicines. To make these warnings salient, emotional language; such as vivid descriptions of the negative consequences of use, may be helpful to encourage desired action. Not only can emotional language help motivate precautionary action, emotional language can also help people remember desired directions.

The amygdala, which is central to emotional processing, is linked to memory processing in the hippocampus, which is central to the formulation of memories. These neural systems interact in subtle but important ways in the encoding and the storage of memories (Phelps 2006). Thus, emotionally processed information can aid people to engage in desired activities at the time preventive action is needed.

For monitoring functions, the key aspect of behavior is recognition and taking desired actions. The behavior required is simple, telling the doctor about the occurrence of an adverse event. Here, the key goal of presenting information is to elicit and maintain memory for certain physiological signs and symptoms. However, progress toward this goal can be disrupted if the consumer does not remember the effect to be reported or if the consumer does not view the effect as caused by the drug. Thus, there are two major cognitive issues related to this type of processing. First, the patient must recognize the pattern of events that constitute a threat. Second, patients need to be able to correctly attribute the cause of these events to trigger reporting the effect to the doctor (i.e., a momentary effect, such as fatigue or headache, can be attributed to some other aspect of the environment or personal history (lack of sleep) as opposed to the effects of a drug).

This type of pattern recognition involves a hierarchical process in which symptoms are processed from either a top-down process (individual events are expected, identified and immediately perceived as side effects) or a bottom-up process (information is gathered and eventually sufficient evidence is available to trigger recognition of the pattern as a side effect) (Bar 2003). Having a salient memory of taking the medication and being aware that recognized pattern of physiological outcomes is a side effect to be reported to the physician is most immediately driven by top-down information processing. To meet the monitoring goal, information should be presented in a fashion to foster top-down processing. Detailing easily identified physical reactions; "chunked" (or organized) to be consistent with physical effects, should engage top-down processing.

Unfortunately, remembering negative events can stimulate high levels of false memory, relative to remembering neutral events (Brainerd et al. 2008). Therefore, emotionally-laden descriptions can interfere with correct recognition and attribution of side effects. Presenting possible side effects with sufficient information of enable recognition in a neutrally phrased fashion should best meet the monitoring goals.

4.1   Absolute and Relative Risk

To fully communicate risk, information needs to be presented not only about the nature and severity of possible side effects; it also involves that presentation of information about the frequency of those events. Unfortunately, evidence indicates that patients often have a very poor understanding of probabilistic or quantitative risk information (Lloyd 2001).

As reviewed above, experimental evidence suggests that people use simplifying heuristics in risk perception and decision making. Rather than rely on frequency numbers, which are difficult to understand, people may rely on the vividness with which an example can be brought to mind (e.g., if a public figure suffered a similar effect). For example, Gigerenzer (2004) found that people tend to fear, low-probability, high-consequence events (dreaded risks, such as the terrorist attack on September 11, 2001). Analyzing data from the U.S. Department of Transportation for the 3 months following September 11, Gigerenzer found that the number of Americans who lost their lives while driving a car, to avoiding the risk of flying, was higher than the total number of passengers killed on the four fatal flights.

In addition to the dread risk bias, people often judge themselves to be at lower risk for various negative life events than their peers. The magnitude of this "optimistic bias" may be related whether people judge their own risk relative to that of an average peer (make comparative risk judgments) or judge their own and an average peer's risk separately (make absolute risk judgments) (Price et al. 2002).

To avoid these problems, several studies have sought to understand the most effective method of conveying the probability when presenting risk information to patients. Knapp et al. (2004) investigated whether side effect rates using numerical information (e.g., 1% rate) or verbal descriptors (e.g., "common" or "rare" side effects) produced unbiased estimates. As might be expected, numerical information produced the most precise estimates of side effect rate. However, patients may not be able to gain a perspective to fully understand the meaning of numerical risk presentations because of low levels of numeracy. Numeracy is an element of health literacy that refers to the ability to understand numbers (Peters 2007).

Edwards et al. (2002) suggest that using pictorials can help people understand complex risk frequency information. However, they caution that it is important to present this risk information in the proper perspective, so that patients can understand the relative and absolute value of the risk information. As shown above, different methods of presenting probability information can bias decision making or mislead the audience. For instance, the *absolute risk* a severe side effect is calculated by dividing the number of people who get the side effect by the number taking the drug. Thus, three people in 10,000 may get a severe side effect. This, can lead to the belief that this is a relative rare side effect. However, presenting risk in terms of its relative sense can lead to the opposite conclusion. The relative risk is calculated by dividing the decrease in morbidity or mortality by the baseline rate. Thus, if the baseline rate is rare (3 people in 100,000) the same side effect can present a tenfold risk increase (3 in 10,000 compared to 3 in 100,000) on a relative basis. To be fair, both relative and absolute risk information may need to be presented so that a reader can gain an accurate perspective on the likelihood of an adverse event.

Although such explicit risk presentations are desirable; such detailed descriptions must be reserved for the most essential communications. The sheer volume of risk information necessary to communicate requires that most risk presentations summarize details. Frequency descriptors (e.g., common, rare) are often used so that a range of side effects can be easily communicated; numerical presentations, pictorials and discussions of absolute and relative risk are reserved for only the most severe and consequential side effects.

5 Conclusion

When a medical product is used, it is not only the physical entity (e.g., a pill) that is presented; it is the information that surrounds its use that is subject to analysis. Just as medicines need to be pure and of high quality; information needs to be truthful and thorough for the drug to have its intended effect. Presenting truthful risk information is necessary to engender safe drug use. However, what constitutes "the truth" is not a simple issue. Human information processing limitations limit the amount of information that can be successfully presented and biases and heuristics used in processing influence what is communicated.

Presenting sufficient information so that all of the necessary material facts about a drug's risks are presented requires analysis of the goals of the communication and the manner in which the information is processed by the recipient of the message. Tradeoffs must be made so that the information will be truthfully communicated and will be sufficient for the intended purpose. Understanding both why the information is presented in terms of its goal (consent, avoidance and/or monitoring) and the information system to be used (emotionality and/or cognitive reflection) can aid in constructing adequate directions for use and in analyzing the degree to which the information is truthful or deceptive.

References

Bar, M. A. (2003). Cortical mechanism for triggering top-down facilitation in visual object recognition. *Journal of Cognitive Neuroscience, 15*(4), 600–609.

Brainerd, C., Stein, L., Silveira, R., Rohenkohl, G., & Reyna, V. (2008). How does negative emotion cause false memories? *Psychological Science, 19*(9), 919–925. Accessed October 15, 2015, from http://lab4.psico.unimib.it/nettuno/forum3/free_download/negative_emotions_401.pdf

De Martino, D., Kumaran, D., Seymour, B., & Dolan, R. (2006, August 4). Frames, biases, and rational decision-making in the human brain. *Science, 313*(5787), 684–687. Accessed October 1, 2015, from http://www.ncbi.nlm.nih.gov/pmc/articles/PMC2631940/

Edwards, A., Elwyn, G., & Mulley, A. (2002, April 6). Explaining risks: Turning numerical data into meaningful pictures. *BMJ, 324*(7341), 827–830. Accessed October 22, 2015, from http://www.ncbi.nlm.nih.gov/pmc/articles/PMC1122766/

EU. (2001). Directive 2001/83/EC of The European Parliament and of the Council of 6 November 2001 on the Community code relating to medicinal products for human use (OJ L 311, 28.11.2001, p. 67). Accessed October 1, 2015, from http://ec.europa.eu/health/files/eudralex/vol-1/dir_2001_83_cons2009/2001_83_cons2009_en.pdf

FDA. (2001). *Guidance on medical device patient labeling; Final guidance for industry and FDA reviewers.* Accessed September 17, 2015, from http://www.fda.gov/downloads/MedicalDevices/DeviceRegulationandGuidance/GuidanceDocuments/ucm070801.pdf (Appendix E)

Ford, G., Smith, D., & Swasy, J. (1988). An empirical test of the search, experience and credence attributes framework. *Advances in Consumer Research* (15), 239–244. Accessed September 23, 2015, from http://www.acrwebsite.org/search/view-conference-proceedings.aspx?Id=6817

Frederick, S. (2005, Autumn). Cognitive reflection and decision making. *Journal of Economic Perspectives, 19*(4), 25–42. Accessed October 15, 2015, from http://www.law.yale.edu/documents/pdf/LEO/Frederick_CognitiveReflectionandDecisionMaking.pdf

Gigerenzer, G. (2004) Dread risk, September 11, and fatal traffic accidents. *Psychological Science, 15*(4), 286–287. Accessed October 22, 2015, from http://pubman.mpdl.mpg.de/pubman/item/escidoc:2101348/component/escidoc:2101347/GG_Dread_2004.pdf

Gigerenzer, G., & Gaissmaier, W. (2011). Heuristic decision making. *Annual Review of Psychology, 62*, 451–482. Accessed October 12, 2015, from http://pubman.mpdl.mpg.de/pubman/item/escidoc:2099042/component/escidoc:2099041/GG_Heuristic_2011.pdf

Graesser, A., Singer, M., & Trabasso, T. (1994). Constructing inferences during narrative text comprehension. *Psychological Review, 101*(3), 371–395.

Keystone report. (1996). *Action plan for the provision of useful prescription medicine information.* In Steering Committee for the collaborative development of a long-range action plan for the provision of useful prescription medicine information. Accessed September 17, 2015 http://www.fda.gov/downloads/aboutfda/centersoffices/cder/reportsbudgets/ucm163793.pdf

Kimberlin, C, & Winterstein, A. (2008). *Expert and consumer evaluation of consumer medication information-2008* (Final Report). Food and Drug Administration. Accessed September 17, 2015, from http://www.fda.gov/downloads/AboutFDA/CentersOffices/OfficeofMedicalProductsandTobacco/CDER/ReportsBudgets/UCM163783.pdf

Knapp, P., Raynor, D., & Berry, D. (2004). Comparison of two methods of presenting risk information to patients about the side effects of medicines. *Quality and Safety in Health Care, 13*, 176–180. Accessed October 22, 2015, from http://www.ncbi.nlm.nih.gov/pmc/articles/PMC1743828/pdf/v013p00176.pdf

Lloyd, A. (2001). The extent of patients' understanding of the risk of treatments. *Quality in Health Care, 10*(Suppl I), 14–18. Accessed October 22, 2015, from http://www.ncbi.nlm.nih.gov/pmc/articles/PMC1765734/pdf/v010p00i14.pdf

Peters, E. (2007, May). Numeracy skill and the communication, comprehension, and use of risk-benefit information. *Health Affairs, 26*(3), 741–748. Accessed October 22, 2015, from http://content.healthaffairs.org/content/26/3/741.long

Phelps, E. (2006). Emotion and cognition: Insights from studies of the human Amygdala. *Annual Review of Psychology, 57*, 27–53.

Price, P., Pentecost, H., & Voth, R. (2002). Perceived event frequency and the optimistic bias: Evidence for a two-process model of personal risk judgments. *Journal of Experimental Social Psychology, 38*, 242–252. Accessed October 22, 2015, from http://heatherlench.com/wp-content/uploads/2006/08/frequency-and-optimism1.pdf

Slovic, P. (1987). Perception of risk. *Science, 236*, 280–285.

Slovic, P., Finucane, M., Peters, E., & MacGregor, D. (2004). Risk as analysis and risk as feelings: Some thoughts about affect, reason, risk, and rationality. *Risk Analysis, 24*(2). Accessed

October 1, 2015, from http://www.paul-hadrien.info/backup/LSE/IS%20490/risk%20as%
20analysis%20and%20as%20feelings-slovic.pdf

Stanovich, K. E., & West, R. F. (2000). Individual differences in reasoning: Implications for the
rationality debate. *Behavioral and Brain Sciences, 23*, 645–726.

Stanovich K., & West, R. (2008). On the relative independence of thinking biases and cognitive
ability. *Journal of Personality and Social Psychology, 94*(4), 672–695. Accessed October
15, 2015, from http://www.keithstanovich.com/Site/Research_on_Reasoning_files/JPSP08.
pdf

Tversky, A., & Kahneman, D. (1974). Judgment under uncertainty: Heuristics and biases. *Science,
New Series, 185*(4157), 1124–1131. Accessed October 1, 2015, from http://psiexp.ss.uci.edu/
research/teaching/Tversky_Kahneman_1974.pdf

Unsworth, N., & Engle, R. (2007). The nature of individual differences in working memory
capacity: Active maintenance in primary memory and controlled search from secondary
memory. *Psychological Review, 114*(1), 104–132.

Weinstein, N. (1999). What does it mean to understand a risk? Evaluating risk comprehension.
Journal of the National Cancer Institute Monographs, 25, 15–20.

WHO. (1988). *Ethical criteria for medicinal drug promotion.* http://apps.who.int/medicinedocs/
documents/whozip08e/whozip08e.pdf

WHO. (2008). *Part 1: Guidance document on characterizing and communicating uncertainty in
exposure assessment.* Harmonization Project Document No. 6. Accessed September 17, 2015,
from http://www.who.int/ipcs/methods/harmonization/areas/uncertainty%20.pdf

Regulations of Consumer Products

Zahra Meghani

1 Introduction

The regulation of consumer products in the United States (US), the European Union (EU) and Japan varies considerably depending on the category of products. This chapter provides a brief overview of the regulatory framework of the three regions, but because the class of consumer products is very large, it focuses on the regulation of genetically modified (GM) food. It is argued that the US, the EU, and Japan should revise their risk assessment protocol for GM food, providing opportunities for substantive public involvement in the process of assessing their risk.

In the United States of America, the Consumer Product Safety Commission (CPSC) is responsible for protecting the population from risk of injury or death associated with the use of consumer products (CPSC n.d.). The safety standards for goods such as toys, cribs, power tools, cigarette lighters, and household chemicals are under the purview of the CPSC.

The Federal Food, Drug, and Cosmetic Act (FFDCA) comprises of a set of laws that authorizes the US' Food and Drug Administration (FDA) to oversee the safety of food, drugs, and cosmetics. The agency also has regulatory authority over dietary supplements, bottled water, food additives, infant formulas and tobacco products. The US Department of Agriculture (USDA) has the primary responsibility of ensuring the safety and labeling of traditional (non-game) meats, poultry, and some egg products.

The FDA regulates brand name and generic prescription medications and it is responsible for ensuring the safety of non-prescription drugs used by humans. The category of biologics (such as vaccines, blood and blood products, cellular and gene therapy products, tissue and tissue products, and allergenics) is under the purview

Z. Meghani (✉)
Philosophy Department, University of Rhode Island, Kingston, RI 02881, USA
e-mail: meghaniz@uri.edu

© Springer International Publishing AG 2017
G. Emilien et al. (eds.), *Consumer Perception of Product Risks and Benefits*,
DOI 10.1007/978-3-319-50530-5_26

of the FDA, but the USDA regulates veterinary vaccines and other types of veterinary biologics. Medical devices, ranging from simple products like tongue depressors to complex technological products like heart pacemakers, are regulated by the FDA. Electronic devices that emit radiation (such as microwave ovens, X-ray equipment, laser products, and sunlamps) are also the responsibility of the agency (FDA 2016b).

In the European Union, consumer products are subject to the General Product Safety Directive (GPSD) 2001/95/EC unless there are European safety regulations that govern specific kinds of products (EC 2016a). The GPSD supplements the provisions of sector legislation that do not cover issues such as manufacturers' responsibilities and the scope of the power of regulatory authorities. The GPSD does not extend to pharmaceuticals, medical devices or cosmetics, all of which are covered under separate legislation.

According to the GPSD, a safe product is one that is in compliance with the safety provisions of the EU or the EU member states. When there are no applicable regulations or EU standards, then "national standards, Commission recommendations, codes of practices" are used (EC 2016a).

Food products are regulated under EC No 178/2002, which establishes the general principles and food law requirements for the EU region. The General Food Law created a comprehensive and coherent framework for the creation of food and feed regulations at the EU level and within individual states. The aim of the law was to establish standards and procedures for food products with the end of protecting human life and consumer interests, while facilitating trade in food products in the EU and internationally (EC 2016b). The law also created the European Food Safety Authority (EFSA), an autonomous agency that provides scientific advice and support to the EU (more on this later).

The regulatory system for medication in the EU comprises of the European Medicines Agency (EMA), the European Commission (EC), and medicine regulatory authorities of the 31 European Economic Area member states (EMA n.d.). The EU member states are obligated by EU legislation to abide by the same rules and requirements with respect to safety and approval of drugs. Only approved pharmaceutical products can be sold in the marketplace in the EU. Manufacturers or distributors of pharmaceutical products must secure authorization before bringing their products to the EU market. Sponsors of pharmaceutical products have three possible routes for securing authorization. If they use the centralized procedure, then they only have to submit an application to the EMA, which will conduct its assessment and recommend whether it should be permitted in the EU market as a whole. Its recommendation carries weight with EU states. This form of authorization is required for certain kinds of pharmaceutical products and the majority of innovative medicines are authorized through this process. But most pharmaceutical products are assessed and authorized by the national competent authorities of member EU states.

In Japan, the Consumer Affairs Agency (CAA) is charged with the responsibility of protecting and enhancing consumer benefits. Its remit includes labelling and safety of products and trade issues (CAA n.d.). The agency has a variety of responsibilities including evaluating and developing consumer policies. It also aims to prevent harm to consumers and create conditions enabling them to make informed choices. The CAA has established a system for consumers to collectively seek redress for damage from products. The agency is governed by the *Household Goods Quality Labeling Law* and it provides support to local government agencies about consumer affairs (CAA n.d.). The law applies to a variety of products, including textiles, plastic products, electrical appliances, and other manufactured items.

"The Law Concerning Standardization, etc. of Agricultural and Forestry Products" (known as "JAS Law") is responsible for the standards of production and quality of food products and drinks (MAFF 2007). The Ministry of Agriculture, Forestry and Fisheries (MAFF) enforces it. The law allows consumers to make informed food choices by providing them with information about the food products' ingredients and origin. The JAS Law has two food labelling systems; voluntary and mandatory (Godo 2015). Under the latter system, labels of food products must provide certain essential information about the food. The voluntary food labelling system provides assurance to consumers that the food meets certain MAFF standards (Godo 2015) (more on this below).

The Pharmaceuticals and Medical Devices Agency (PMDA) collaborates with Japan's Ministry of Health, Labor and Welfare (MHLW) (PMDA n.d.). The PMDA is responsible for protecting public health by ensuring the safety, efficacy and quality of pharmaceuticals products. It conducts scientific reviews of pharmaceutical products and medical devices and monitors their safety once they enter the market. The PMDA provides compensation to persons who have suffered an adverse drug reaction or infection from a pharmaceutical or biological product.

2 Three Different Approaches to Regulating GM Food

2.1 The US' Food Regulatory System

The USDA is responsible for the safety of poultry and meat. The US' Environmental Protection Agency (EPA) regulates pesticides and decides on the acceptable level of pesticide residue limits for food. Both agencies work in conjunction with the FDA. The FDA claims to conduct purely scientific risk assessments (Meghani and Kuzma 2011; Meghani 2014). It also engages in risk management of the products that fall under its jurisdiction and it is responsible for risk communication to the public.

The FDA was established by the Federal Food, Drug, and Cosmetic Act (FFDCA) in 1938 (Barley 2007). The Act was a response to the disaster caused by the marketing of diethylene glycol for treatment of streptococcal infections in children by the drug company Massengill. It had been selling the drug without conducting any safety test (Barley 2007), resulting in numerous fatalities. Thus, the

FDA was created to ensure that drug and food industries did not harm public health in their quest for profit [for a historical account of the roots of risk assessment in toxicology see, for instance, Hutt (2000) and Zachmann (2014)].

The FFDCA stipulated that drugs had to be labeled with sufficient directions for their safe use and new drugs could only be marketed following approval by the FDA; the agency would give its approval only if the manufacturer was able to provide evidence of the safety of the drug (FDA 2012). The Act also barred unsubstantiated claims about the therapeutic efficacy of drugs. In addition, the Act established food standards that were legally enforceable and it addressed the problem of "abuses in food packaging and quality" (FDA 2012).

In 1962, President John Kennedy signed the *Kefauver-Harris Drug Amendments*, which were a response to the thalidomide disaster. The *Amendments* expanded the scope of the regulatory authority of the FDA. As a result of the *Amendments*, drug manufacturers have to provide evidence to the agency of the efficaciousness of their products before marketing them and report serious side effects once they are on the market (FDA 2016a). The evidence of efficaciousness has to take the form of adequate and well-controlled studies conducted by qualified experts, and informed consent must be obtained from human research subjects (FDA 2016a).

Today, the FDA defines its mission as follows (FDA 2015a):

> FDA is responsible for protecting the public health by assuring the safety, efficacy and security of human and veterinary drugs, biological products, medical devices, our nation's food supply, cosmetics, and products that emit radiation. FDA is also responsible for advancing the public health by helping to speed innovations that make medicines more effective, safer, and more affordable and by helping the public get the accurate, science-based information they need to use medicines and foods to maintain and improve their health.

The agency's mission statement assumes that its duty of fostering public health requires that it serves the industry interests by speeding innovations and allowing new products to enter the market.

2.1.1 The US' Regulatory Oversight of GM Foods

The USDA, the EPA, and the FDA are charged with regulating genetically modified organisms (GMOs). The EPA is responsible for GM microbial pesticides. Specifically, the agency regulates the use of "bacteria, fungi, viruses, protozoa, or algae, whose DNA has been modified to express pesticidal properties" (EPA 2015b). As of December 2015, the EPA had registered eight GM microbial pesticides (EPA 2015b). The responsibility for protecting American agriculture against pests and diseases falls on Animal and Plant Health Inspection Service (APHIS), which is part of the USDA. The field testing of GM plants is regulated by APHIS and it also approves and licenses "veterinary biological substances, including animal vaccines, that may be the products of biotechnology" (EPA 2015b). The USDA also regulates herbicide-tolerant (GM) crops; those crops are not regulated by the EPA because they do not produce pesticides (EPA 2015b). It is the responsibility of the FDA to perform the risk assessment of GM food products, including genetically engineered (GE) animals that are to be used as food (more on this later).

In 1986, the Office of Science and Technology Policy (OSTP) issued the foundational policy document regulating GMOs. The OSTP's policy paper, "Coordinated Framework on the Regulation of Biotechnology" (CFRB), announced that for regulatory purposes no distinction should be made between GM food and their non-GM counterparts. President Reagan's administration justified the policy on the grounds that it would serve US interests by allowing the nation to establish supremacy over other countries in GM food development and trade (FR 1984, 49; Levidow et al. 2007). The OSTP also claimed that if the FDA differentiated between GM food and their conventional counterparts solely on the basis of the process of manufacture, the agency would be acting in an irrational and unscientific manner (FR 1984, p. 50880).

The CFRB has made it easy for GM food manufacturers to introduce their products to the marketplace because it mandated that GM food be governed by the same laws and regulations as those that applied to non-biotech food (FR 1984, p. 50878). GM food producers do not have to meet any additional or different regulatory criteria (Millstone et al. 1999). GM food also do not have to be identical to their conventional counterparts; they only have to be "substantially equivalent" to them with respect to their chemical composition (Levidow et al. 2007). The FDA's decision to consider GM food to be the same as their conventional counterparts [and not a novel chemical compound (such as a pharmaceutical, pesticide or a pesticide)] means that GM food sponsors do not have to perform complicated, high cost toxicological tests to identify the acceptable daily intake (ADI) for novel food products (Millstone et al. 1999). The ADI classification would have drastically cut the sale potential of GM food because the FDA stipulates that the ADI of any novel chemical compound should not comprise more than 1% of the human diet (Millstone et al. 1999). GM food products also cannot be labelled as "genetically modified".

In January 2009, 23 years after the CFRB was issued by the OSTP, the FDA issued the "Guidance for Industry Regulation of Genetically Engineered Animals Containing Heritable Recombinant DNA Constructs Final Guidance" (henceforth referred to as *Guidance* 2009). The policy document describes the FDA's regulatory approach to GM animal that are to be used as food. The FDA categorizes GE animals as new animal drugs (more on that later) *and* as GM food (*Guidance* 2009). The dual classification means that GE animals will be regulated simultaneously by different regulatory regimes (Meghani 2014). The agency has tried to justify its food safety standard for assessing GE animals as GM food on the grounds that it is consistent with the standard used by the Codex Alimentarius of the World Health Organization (WHO) (Meghani 2014). Like the CFRB, the WHO's 2008 "Guideline for the Conduct of Food Safety Assessment of Foods Derived from Recombinant-DNA Animals" requires that GE entities (that are to be used as GM food) should be substantially equivalent to their conventional counterparts in terms of their composition and key nutrients. [The FDA *Guidance*

(2009) does not employ the term "substantially equivalent;" however it describes that standard and refers to the WHO's *Guidance* 2008, which uses that language (Meghani 2014)].

GE animals are also treated by the *Guidance* as *new* animal *drugs*. The FDA justified its decision to consider GE animals as drugs by evoking the FFDCA, which categorizes as a drug any non-food article that aims "to affect the structure or any function of the body of man or other animals" (Guidance 2009, p. 5). The agency classified GE animals as *new* animal drugs because the composition of GE animals as pharmaceutical products is not yet recognized by scientific experts as efficacious and safe if used in the manner recommended (Guidance 2009). So, as a rule, GE animals (as new animal drugs) have to receive premarket approval from the FDA. The FDA's Center for Veterinary Medicine (CVM) evaluates the New Animal Drug Application filed by the developers of GE animals. In November 2015, the FDA approved the first GE animal—a GE salmon—for introduction into the US market as food (FDA 2015b).

In 2012, approximately 69.5 million hectares of GM crops were cultivated on US farmland. Corn (maize) and soybean constitute the vast majority of the cultivated GM crops (Dunwell 2014). Approximately 90% of corn and an estimated 95% of soybean in the US was genetically modified (Dunwell 2014).

The US' regulatory attitude towards GM food stands in contrast to the EU's conservative stance on the food biotechnology.

3   The EU'S Food Regulatory System

The European Food Safety Authority (EFSA) is funded by the EU, but it functions autonomously of the member states of the EU, and the European legislative and executive institutions (e.g., Commission, Council, Parliament) (EFSA n.d.). The agency was established in 2002 in the wake of a number of serious food safety failures in Europe during the late 1990s that alarmed the public and called into question the effectiveness of food regulatory agencies (Devos et al. 2014; EFSA n. d.). Thus, the EU created the agency with the aim of ensuring the safety of the food supply and restoring public confidence in the EU food safety system (EFSA 2009). It was decided that the same agency would not have the responsibility of ensuring the safety of the food supply *and* sponsoring the food industry (Millstone 2010).

The establishment of the EFSA was mandated by the General Food Law—Regulation 178/2002, which construes risk assessment as scientific activity that has no normative component (EC 2015b). The Regulation conceptualizes risk management as policy work that involves normative consideration (EFSA n.d.; see also EC 2016b). The EFSA (like the US' FDA) claims that it conducts scientific risk assessments of food products (EFSA n.d.). The EFSA reports are prepared by a panel of 19 scientific experts drawn from the research institutes, universities or risk assessment bodies of the EU (Devos et al. 2014). The agency issues an open call for scientific experts and then selects some of those who express interest in working with it. The members of the panel are required to declare any interest that falls within the purview of the EFSA and they must make a commitment to be objective (Devos et al. 2014).

The agency communicates the results of its risk assessments to the public and various agencies and states (EFSA n.d.). The EFSA reports and advice shape the EU's policies and legislation about food and feed safety, nutrition, animal health and welfare, plant protection and plant health. The agency also examines the effect of the food chain on plant biodiversity and animal habitats (EFSA n.d.). The EFSA has provided its scientific opinion on a variety of subjects, including Bovine Spongiform Encephalopathy (BSE), Salmonella, food additives, allergenic food ingredients, pesticides and genetically modified organisms (GMOs) (EFSA n.d.).

3.1 The EU's Regulatory Oversight of GM Foods

The EU defines GMOs as entities whose genetic material has been modified artificially using the techniques of modern biotechnology. Food or feed containing or consisting of GMOs or produced from GMOs are classified as "genetically modified (GM) food or feed" (EC 2016c). Unlike the US, the EU takes what it terms a "precautionary approach" to GMOs, requiring pre-market authorization for any GMO that is to be cultivated or enter the market within the EU and it requires post-market environmental monitoring of authorized GMOs, with the end of ensuring a high degree of protection of human and animal health and the environment (EC 2016c). Products containing GMOs have to be labelled as such (EC 2001).

The work of the EFSA is shaped by Regulation (EC) No 1829/2003, which establishes the protocol for decisions about the authorization of GM food and feed for market placement and the cultivation of GMO seed (EC 2015a). The entity sponsoring the GMO must submit its application to an EU member state, which then passes it to the EFSA. The application must contain safety studies and data. It must also include a monitoring plan, detection strategy and labelling proposal. The EFSA allows sponsoring entities to designate some of its submission as confidential business information.

Based on the information provided by the developer or sponsor of the GMO, the EFSA conducts its risk assessment and posts its report, giving the public a 1 month period to comment on it (EC 2015a). The EFSA does not make the decision whether a particular GM food should enter the marketplace because it construes that activity as 'risk management,' involving political, socio-ethical and economic considerations that lie beyond its scope. Risk management decisions, based on the reports prepared by the EFSA, are made by risk managers, such as the European Commission and EU Member States (Devos et al. 2014).

Once the European Commission receives the EFSA's risk assessment report, it has 3 months to make a decision regarding the authorization of the GMO. It must provide justification for its decision. Member states vote on the draft decision of the Commission under qualified majority rules. If the Standing Committee and the

Appeal Committee are unable to adopt the decision by qualified majority within a specified time period, it falls on the Commission to adopt the final decision (EC 2015a).

In March 2015, the EU issued Directive 2015/412 (EU 2015), which inserted Article 26b in Directive 2001/18/EC. The article permits member states to restrict or bar the cultivation of GMOs in all or some part of its territories on "compelling grounds," which include environmental policy objectives, town and country planning, land use, socioeconomic impacts, avoidance of GMO presence in other products, agricultural policy objectives and public policy (EU 2015). The Directive also stipulates that the restrictions must be consistent with EU law and qualify as reasoned and they must not discriminate between national and non-national products.

Prior to the implementation of Directive 2015/412, if a GM crop was authorized under EU law, then it was automatically authorized for use in all member states. Thus, in the case of GM maize Novartis BT176, the GM seed could be cultivated in the territories of any member state even though many states objected to its use (Dobbs 2015). Member states could only provisionally limit or ban its use in their territories if "they had new evidence that the organism concerned constitutes a risk to human health or the environment or in the case of an emergency" (EC 2015a).

In the wake of Directive 2015/412, 19 countries (constituting more than half of the EU member states) exercised their right to prohibit the cultivation of GMOs in their territories. The countries in question were Austria, Belgium (on behalf of the Wallonia region), Bulgaria, Croatia, Cyprus, Denmark, France, Germany, Greece, Hungary, Italy, Latvia, Lithuania, Luxembourg, Malta, the Netherlands, Poland, Slovenia and the U.K. (on behalf of Scotland, Wales and Northern Ireland) (Stearns 2015).

As of December 2015, multiple strains of GM cotton, GM maize, GM soybean, GM oilseed rape were authorized for use in the EU (EC n.d.). A strain of GM sugarbeet was also registered as authorized for use in the EU (EC n.d.). (The sponsors of the GMOs were Monsanto, Bayer, Dow AgriSciences, Syngenta, Pioneer, BASF, and KWS SAAT (EC n.d.). However, currently, the only GM plant cultivated in the EU is a GM maize. It is grown primarily in Spain and constitutes 30% of the land devoted in that country to the crop (USDA 2015).

The EU does not export any GE food or feed products, but it imports approximately 30 million metric tons of soybeans and an estimated 7 million metric tons of corn products; both are used primarily as feed for livestock and poultry (USDA 2015). GM soybeans and GM corn constitute 90% and less than 25% of the feed imported by the EU (USDA 2015). So, while many of the EU states have closed their doors to GM food, GM feed is imported into the region.

The EU's regulatory attitude towards GM food is not unique; Japan has a somewhat similar approach to the food biotechnology.

4 Japan's Food Regulatory System

In 2003, Japan enacted the Food Safety Basic Law (FSBL) as part of the reform of its food safety policy-making institutions following the detection of BSE in domestic cow herds (Millstone 2010). The FSBL's aim is to promote "policies to ensure food safety by establishing basic principles, by clarifying the responsibilities of the state, local governments and food-related business operators and the roles of consumers and establishing a basic direction for policy formulation, in order to ensure food safety" (MHLW 2003).

With the enactment of the FSBL, Japan introduced a new risk analysis approach to food safety regulation that was nominally modelled on the EU's EFSA (Millstone 2009). The approach entailed separating risk assessment from risk management and risk communication. Within Japan's new risk analysis paradigm, risk assessment has been construed as a purely scientific activity (as discussed earlier, both the EU and the USA claim that their risk evaluations of food, including GM food, are purely scientific). Risk management is conceptualized by Japan as the "implement[ation of] necessary measures based on risk assessment" (MHLW n.d.-b). Risk communication entails the "exchange [of] information and opinions among related people representing the people including public, government, and academia" (MHLW n.d.-b).

The Food Safety Commission (FSC) (created in 2003 by the FSBL) conducts risk assessment (MHLW n.d.-c) and it communicates about risks and dangers from food to stakeholders, including the public. Risk management is governed by the Food Sanitation Law (FSL) and other food laws. Among other things, the FSL covers the establishment of standards for food and additives (MHLW n.d.-b). The Ministry of Health, Labor and Welfare (MHLW) and the Ministry of Agriculture, Forestry and Fisheries (MAFF) are the government entities responsible for risk management (Millstone 2010). While Japan has separated risk assessment from risk management (see Fig. 1), Japanese ministers expect the FSC to provide scientific reports and policy advice, re-establishing a technocratic approach to science policy formulation (Millstone 2010). Such an approach is appealing to public officials involved in risk management for two reasons. First, it serves as strong insulation from challenges to their policy by the public on normative grounds because they can claim that their policies are scientific (read: factual), and thus, value neutral. Second, it shields them from public blame in the case of any food safety disasters (Millstone 2009).

4.1 Japan's Regulatory Oversight of Genetically Modified (GM) Foods

The evaluation of the safety of GM food is mandated by the FSL. The applications are submitted to MHLW, which then requests that the FSC evaluate them (MHLW

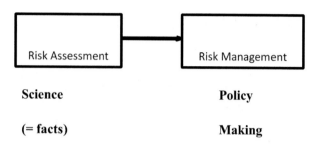

Fig. 1 Technocratic model of science policy formulation (Millstone 2010, p. 5)

n.d.-d) (for standards for assessing GM food see FSC 2004, *Standards for the Safety Assessment of Genetically Modified Foods (Seed Plants)*). The FSC's risk assessments are based on the data submitted the sponsor of the GM food. Developers and importers of GM food are obligated to request food safety approval (by genetic event) (Ebata et al. 2013). The FSC consults with scientists and gives the public the opportunity to provide its comments (Ebata et al. 2013). On the basis of the FSC's report, the MHLW decides whether to approve the GM food and then it notifies the public of its decision (MHLW n.d.-d).

Japanese GM food labelling regulations are stricter than those of the US but more lax than those of the EU (Ebata et al. 2013). The labeling system is part of the legal safety assessment system under the FSL and it is the responsibility of the MAFF and the MHLW. It is the latter agency's duty to publicize that a product has undergone the safety assessment. In compliance with the Japanese Agricultural Standards Law, the MAFF aims to allow consumers to make informed choices about the food they purchase.

In Japan, food products may be labelled "genetically modified," "genetically modified organisms not segregated," or "not genetically modified." Food products that are not genetically modified do not have to be identified as such. GM food products do have to be labelled, but there are some exceptions (more on this later).

The MHLW categorizes GM food into the two following categories (MHLW n.d.-a):

a. GM food whose compositional or nutritional values are significantly different from their conventional counterparts must be labelled as "genetically modified"; the label has to specify the nature of the difference between it and its conventional counterpart.
b. GM food whose compositional or nutritional values are considered to be substantially equivalent to their conventional counterparts.

The latter kind of GM food products are sub-classified for labelling purposes into the following two groups:

bi. GM foods in which the modified DNA or the resulting proteins remain even after it has been processed.
bii. Processed (GM) food (such as edible oils and soy sauce) in which the modified DNA or the resulting proteins cannot be detected after it has been processed

and the food is considered substantially equivalent to its conventional counterpart.

Thus, a food product such as soy sauce that has genetically modified raw material (in this case, GM soybeans) does not have to be labelled as "genetically modified" if the soy sauce (the end product) does not have the DNA characteristics of the GM soybeans and if the nutritional or compositional value of the soy sauce in question is substantially equivalent to its conventional counterpart (MHLW n.d.-a; Ebata et al. 2013). GM food in which the modified DNA or the resulting proteins remain even after they have been processed must be identified as "GMO" (MHLW n.d.-a; Ebata et al. 2013).

Food products are exempt from mandatory labelling if a GM food product is accidentally mixed with non-genetically modified food, provided that the former is no more than 5% of the total weigh of the final food product and documented effort was made to keep GM food separate from non GM food (Ebata et al. 2013). In addition, the labelling requirement only applies to the first three ingredients. So, a food product could contain genetically modified components but it would not have to be labelled "genetically modified" provided that its first three ingredients did not contain genetically modified component(s) that exceeded 5% of the weight of the (final) food product (Ebata et al. 2013).

Japan is a large scale importer of agricultural foods, including GM food products but they are not labelled as such if, following processing, the modified DNA or the resulting proteins do not remain. The vast majority of imported GM products are used as animal feed, but the food products from those animals are not labelled (Ebata et al. 2013). As of November 2015, 303 GM crops had been evaluated by the FSC, including two hundred and one strains of GM corn, twenty varieties of GM soybeans, three kinds of GM sugar beets, eight strains of GM potatoes, 20 kinds of GM canola, and one kind of GM papaya (MHLW 2015).

This section of the contribution has detailed the architecture of the GM food regulatory system of Japan, the EU, and the US. The agencies responsible for different aspects of the risk analysis process of GM food are identified in Table 1.

Table 1 A comparative overview of the food regulatory architecture of the US, the EU, and Japan

	USA	EU	Japan
Risk assessment	Food and Drug Administration (FDA), Environmental Protection Agency (EPA), United States Department of Agriculture (USDA)	European Food Safety Authority (EFSA)	Food Safety Commission (FSC)
Risk management	FDA, EPA, USDA	European Commission, Member States of European Union	Ministry of Health, Labour and Welfare (MHLW) and the Ministry of Agriculture, Forestry and Fisheries (MAFF)
Risk communication	FDA, EPA, USDA	EFSA	FSC

5　Evaluation of the Scientific Risk Assessment Model Used by the FDA, the EFSA, and the FSC

While there are substantial differences in the regulatory regimes for GM food of the US, the UK, and Japan, they are based on the same model of risk assessment. The US' FDA, the EU's EFSA, and Japan's FSC describe their risk assessments as scientific endeavors that are not influenced by any normative elements. Below, it is argued that conception of risk assessment is flawed.

5.1　Scientific Inquiry as a Normative Activity

First and foremost, any scientific inquiry that has significance for human well-being qualifies as a normative activity. Broadly speaking, such activities are ones about which normative judgments can be made, i.e., judgments that evoke ethical, political, cultural, or religious norms. Another way in which scientific inquiry qualifies as a normative activity is if it has consequences about which normative judgments can be made. For instance, the decision to investigate the etiology of a disease in terms of genetic factors rather than the interaction between environmental and genetic factors (because the latter project would be complicated and politically loaded) has ethical and political import. Moreover, that decision might have consequences that could have moral and political ramifications; potential strategies for preventing the disease might not be identified because the investigation of the etiology fails to take into account the complex interaction between the environment and genes responsible for the disease.

Third, scientific inquiry qualifies as a normative endeavor because investigators' decisions about study duration, subject selection criteria, and choice of clinical trial sites may be dictated by social considerations [see, for instance, Intemann and Melo-Martín (2010) analysis of an HPV vaccine study] and those choices could have ethical or political weight. Researchers' choice of methodology may be shaped by normative and pragmatic concerns that have ethical or political significance. In the US, for instance, animal scientists involved in the development and testing of new drugs primarily use male animals as research subjects (Rabin 2014). Within the epistemic community of animal scientists, female animals are not considered significantly different from males and they are regarded as undesirable research subjects because the hormonal fluctuations characterizing their reproductive cycle is viewed as a threat to "delicately calibrated experiments" (Rabin 2014). The choice of this gender-biased research methodology has serious moral implications; the drugs developed using it fail to take into account the relevant physiological differences between women and men, to the detriment of women patients.

There are other ways in which scientific inquiry qualifies as a normative enterprise. Scientific theories may be embedded with normative assumptions. For instance, theories might be laden with gendered assumptions about the behavior of the sexes [see, for instance, Owen's (2005) analysis of anthropological theories and Longino's (1990) analysis of neurobiology theories], and thus, research projects based on such theories have ethical and political significance and consequences.

5.2 Risk Assessment as a Normative Activity

Scientific risk assessment is a particular kind of scientific activity and like any scientific inquiry that has significance for human well-being it qualifies as a normative activity. The legal context within which regulatory agencies operate "make" their risk assessment activities normatively loaded. For example, in the US, the EPA (by virtue of the 1976 Toxic Substance Control Act) can only test chemicals if it has been provided with evidence of harm from them (Rich 2016). Thus, chemical companies engage in self-regulation with respect to the tens of thousands of chemicals that are available in the US market and the EPA has only placed restrictions on five chemicals (Rich 2016; see also NRC 2009). This state of affairs has significance and consequences that are both moral and political.

Uncertainty is an intrinsic aspect of every stage of risk assessment (NRC 2009), and in the face of uncertainty, regulatory agencies have to make assumptions (the US' EPA term for "assumptions" is "defaults") about evidence of risk and exposure. Those choices may have ethical or political significance. Moreover, when a regulatory agency presents to the public (or allows the public to remain under the misimpression that) a particular assumption is a fact rather than a supposition (among a range of competing assumptions), that act has moral and political import. Also, consider that risk assessors routinely omit chemicals from their risk assessment (or consider them only nominally) if there are not a sufficient number of reliable epidemiological or toxicological studies about them (NRC 2009). Such decisions have ethical and even political salience and, to state the obvious, normative consequences.

Risk assessment is generally conceptualized as a four stage (or part) process: hazard identification, dose (or exposure) response assessment, exposure assessment, and risk characterization (NRC 1994). During *hazard identification* risk assessors make the decision which factors they will construe as risks that they will examine (it is not possible for them to evaluate all possible risk factors). In deciding to consider some elements, but not others, as a risk that should be investigated, risk assessors make a choice that has normative weight and consequences. Moreover, the decision to consider potential hazards individually or in synergistic interactions (which is what occurs in reality) (NRC 1994) carries normative import. Hazard identification also involves characterizing the nature and strength of the evidence of causation (NRC 1994, p. 5). What constitutes relevant evidence and the amount of evidence that qualifies as necessary or sufficient for a particular conclusion may be a matter of scientific controversy, and it may have ethical or political consequences (Millstone 2015).

Dose (or exposure) response assessment involves conceptualizing the relationship between exposure and the incidence and severity of the adverse health effect (NRC 1994, p. 5). Characterizing that relationship entails consideration of elements that affect exposure-response relationships, such as intensity and pattern of exposure, age, and elements of life style. Consider that when risk assessors choose between competing models and scientifically plausible data to characterize the relationship between exposure and the adverse health effect (IOM 2001, p. 28), they may be making a decision that has moral or political dimensions. Thus, their decision may qualify as a normative one even if they choose models and data with the greatest support (assuming there are clear-cut grounds for making such a choice). Moreover, as hazards are usually different in kind and degree, a pragmatic decision to use the same (standard) method to assess different types of hazards is an ethical and political choice.

The failure to update dose-response methodology when substantial evidence has accumulated against the status quo methodology is a moral and political matter. For instance, risk assessments usually evaluate the impact of high doses of chemicals on subjects to identify the lowest observed adverse effect levels (LOAELs) and no observed adverse effect levels (NOAELs) (Birnbaum 2012, p. A143). In conjunction with other factors, they use LOAELS and NOAELS to estimate references doses, i.e., doses that are safe for humans. But that methodology has been shown to be flawed because some kinds of chemicals (such as industrial chemicals, plasticizers, pesticides, phytoestrogens, preservatives, detergents, flame retardants, and sunblock) have an effect at lower doses that is not inferable from their effect at higher doses (Birnbaum 2012, p. A143). So, the continued use of the standard methodology for risk assessment purposes is ethically significant. In addition, given that there is substantial evidence that different kinds of chemicals have effects that are "missed" if risk evaluations are predicated on the assumption that there is a linear response between dose and effect (Birnbaum 2012, p. A143), the failure of regulatory entities to use a methodology that entails investigating a range of dose responses, including nonlinear dose responses, is an ethical and political issue.

Given gaps in scientific knowledge, during exposure response assessment, risk assessors have to extrapolate from animal responses to human responses and from low exposure to high exposure. What constitutes low or high exposure may be a matter of scientific controversy and it may have ethical, political, economic or other kind of normative import. The extrapolation from animal responses to human responses involves contestable assumptions (see, for instance, Krimsky 2014) and it may have ethical or political consequences. Additionally, the decision to not take into consideration the variation among individuals in their response to the risk factor could result in significant underestimation of human risks (NRC 1994, p. 40) and that is an ethical and political matter.

Exposure assessment entails a "numerical estimate of exposure or dose" (EPA 2015a). It involves the determination of the severity, frequency, and duration of actual (or hypothetical) exposures of humans (to the elements construed as risk factors) (NRC 1994, p. 5). Identifying and modelling exposure pathways for individuals and groups is complicated and complex and usually involves a high degree of uncertainty (NRC 2009). For instance, the numerical estimates made by researchers about exposure to pesticide experienced by members of a community located near farms requires that researchers take into account multiple variables (such as age, work location, eating habits, activity level, etc.). As there will be significant degree of uncertainty about some of those factors, researchers will have to fill in gaps in their knowledge by making conjectures that could involve subjective or normative assumptions about individuals and groups, and thus their numerical estimates about their exposure to the pesticides would not be value-free.

Risk characterization combines the evaluation of exposure and response under various exposure conditions to estimate the likelihood of specific harm to individuals or populations who are exposed to the risk factor (NRC 1994, p. 5). This step is normatively loaded because the approximations required involve judgment calls that have ethical or political weight (the decisions themselves might be shaped by normative considerations). Moreover, as there is variability within populations and amongst populations, when, for pragmatic reasons, risk assessors do not or cannot take into account variability within populations or among groups and they choose to report risks as averages (IOM 2001, p. 27), their decision has moral and political salience. Consider that very young children's detoxification system is not as well developed as that of adults. So, the level of exposure to a particular chemical that is deemed by the relevant regulatory agency to be safe for all populations may not be safe for very young children (even if the uncertainty/safety factor of 10 is applied to the threshold dose) (Edginton and Ritter 2008).

6 Discussion

Given that any risk assessment that has to do with human well-being is fundamentally a normative activity, the US' FDA, the EU's EFSA, and Japan's FSA are not justified in claiming that their scientific risk assessments of GM food have no normative dimensions. In the interest of presenting to the public an accurate account of the nature of their work, the regulatory entities of the US, the EU, and Japan should acknowledge that their risk assessment of GM food involve normative choices. The failure of regulatory agencies to acknowledge the value laden nature of their work can be understood as an attempt to insulate or shield themselves from public scrutiny and engagement. But that is not acceptable because as regulatory agencies in liberal democracies, they are accountable to the public and must not attempt to evade that responsibility.

The refusal of regulatory entities to acknowledge the normative dimension of their work is also pernicious because it means that the polity is denied the opportunity to make ethical and political decisions about issues that affects it. That is unacceptable because it violates the fundamental principle which justifies the existence of the liberal democratic state. According to that principle, the liberal democratic state must respect the ability and the right of the people to engage in self-definition. In other words, the people's ability and right to make ethical and political decisions about matters that affect them must be respected by the liberal democratic state (Waldron 2012, pp. 195–196). Thus, the FDA, the EFSA, and FSC should create open, transparent processes to include effected constituencies in the dialogue, deliberations, and decision-making about which values should shape the risk evaluation of GM foods at every stage of the risk assessment process (see, for instance, Meghani and Kuzma 2011). Foreclosing the possibility of public involvement, specifically, informed, collaborative decision-making about normative issues, qualifies as deception and a betrayal of the public's trust and confidence in regulatory authorities and the liberal democratic state itself.

References

Barley, S. R. (2007). Corporations, democracy, and the public good. *Journal of Management Inquiry, 16*(3), 201–215.

Birnbaum, L. S. (2012). Environmental chemicals: evaluating low-dose effects. *Environmental Health Perspectives, 120*(4), A143–A144.

Consumer Affairs Agency (CAA), Government of Japan. (n.d.) *List of minister, state minister and parliamentary vice-minister*. Accessed May 3, 2016, from http://www.caa.go.jp/en/index.html

Devos, Y., Aguilera, J., Diveki, Z., Gomes, A., Liu, Y., Paoletti, C., du Jardin, P., Herman, L., Perry, J. N., & Waigmann, E. (2014). EFSA's scientific activities and achievements on the risk assessment of genetically modified organisms (GMOs) during its first decade of existence: Looking back and ahead. *Transgenic Research, 23*(1), 1–25.

Dobbs, M. (2015). *Choosing to go GM-free? The new EU Legal Framework for genetically modified crops*. EU Law Analysis (blog). Accessed May 3, 2016, from http://eulawanalysis123.blogspot.com/2015/03/choosing-to-go-gm-free-new-eu-legal.html

Dunwell, J. M. (2014). Genetically modified (GM) crops: European and transatlantic divisions. *Molecular Plant Pathology, 15*(2), 119–121.

Ebata, A., Punt, M., & Wesseler, J. (2013). For the approval process of GMOs: The Japanese case. *AgBioForum 16*, 2. Accessed May 3, 2016, from http://www.agbioforum.org/v16n2/v16n2a05-ebata.htm

Edginton, A., & Ritter, L. (2008). Predicting plasma concentrations of Bisphenol A in young children (<two years) following typical feeding schedules using a physiologically-based toxicokinetic model. *Environmental Health Perspectives*. doi:10.1289/ehp.0800073.

European Commission (EC). (n.d.). *Genetically modified organisms: EU register of authorised GMOs*. Accessed May 3, 2016, from http://ec.europa.eu/food/dyna/gm_register/index_en.cfm

European Commission (EC). (2001). *Regulating GM crops: EU countries' rights* (Directive 2001/18/EC). Accessed May 3, 2016, from http://eur-lex.europa.eu/legal-content/EN/TXT/?uri=URISERV%3Al28130

European Commission (EC). (2015a). *Fact sheet: Questions and answers on EU's policies on GMOs*. Accessed May 3, 2016, from http://europa.eu/rapid/press-release_MEMO-15-4778_en.htm

European Commission (EC). (2015b). *Food safety: Food: General food law*. Accessed May 3, 2016, from http://ec.europa.eu/food/safety/general_food_law/index_en.htm

European Commission (EC). (2016a). *Consumers: General product safety directive*. Accessed May 3, 2016, from http://ec.europa.eu/consumers/consumers_safety/product_safety_legislation/general_product_safety_directive/index_en.htm

European Commission (EC). (2016b). *Food safety: Food: Food law general principles*. Accessed May 3, 2016, from http://ec.europa.eu/food/safety/general_food_law/principles/index_en.htm

European Commission (EC). (2016c). *Plants: Genetically modified organisms*. Accessed May 3, 2016, from http://ec.europa.eu/food/plant/gmo/index_en.htm

European Food Safety Authority (EFSA). (n.d.). *About EFSA*. Accessed May 3, 2016, from http://www.efsa.europa.eu/en/aboutefsa

European Food Safety Authority (EFSA). (2009). *EFSA's approach on Public Consultations on scientific outputs*. Accessed May 3, 2016, from http://www.efsa.europa.eu/en/corporate/pub/consultationspolicy

European Medicines Agency (EMA). (n.d.). *About us*. Accessed May 3, 2016, from http://www.ema.europa.eu/ema/index.jsp?curl=pages/about_us/general/general_content_000235.jsp&mid=

European Union (EU). (2015). *Directive (EU) 2015/412 of the European Parliament and of the Council of 11 March 2015 amending Directive 2001/18/EC as regards the possibility for the Member States to restrict or prohibit the cultivation of genetically modified organisms (GMOs) in their territory*. Accessed May 3, 2016, from http://eur-lex.europa.eu/legal-content/EN/TXT/?uri=OJ:JOL_2015_068_R_0001

Federal Register (FR). (1984, December 31). 49, 10084.

Food Safety Commission (FSC) (of Japan). (2004). *Standards for the safety assessment of genetically modified foods (seed plants)*. Accessed May 3, 2016, from http://www.fsc.go.jp/english/standardsforriskassessment/gm_kijun_english.pdf

Godo, Y. (2015). *Food labeling regulations under the JAS Act*. Food and Fertilizer Technology Center (FFTC) Policy Platform. Accessed May 3, 2016, from http://ap.fftc.agnet.org/ap_db.php?id=384&print=1

Hutt, P. B. (2000). *A brief history of risk assessment*. FDA. Accessed May 3, 2016, from http://www.fda.gov/downloads/AboutFDA/WhatWeDo/History/OralHistories/SelectedOralHistoryTranscripts/UCM288761.pdf

Institute of Medicine (IOM). (2001). *Food safety policy, science, and risk assessment*. In Strengthening the connection: Workshop proceedings.

Intemann, K., & Melo-Martín, I. (2010). Social values and scientific evidence: The case of the HPV vaccines. *Biology and Philosophy, 25*(2), 203–213.

Krimsky, S. (2014). Low-dose toxicology: Narratives from the science-transcience interface. In S. Boudia & N. Jas (Eds.), *Powerless science? Science and politics in a toxic world* (pp. 234–253). New York, NY: Berghahn Books.

Levidow, L., Murphy, J., & Carr, S. (2007). Recasting "substantial equivalence": Transatlantic governance of GM food. *Science, Technology & Human Values, 32*(1), 26–64.

Longino, H. E. (1990). *Science as social knowledge*. Princeton, NJ: Princeton University Press.

Meghani, Z., & Kuzma, J. (2011). The "revolving door" between regulatory agencies and industry: a problem that requires reconceptualizing objectivity. *Journal of Agricultural and Environmental Ethics, 24*(6), 575–599.

Meghani, Z. (2014). Risk assessment of genetically modified food and neoliberalism: An argument for democratizing the regulatory review protocol of the Food and Drug Administration. *Journal of Agricultural and Environmental Ethics, 27*(6), 967–989.

Millstone, E., Brunner, E., & Mayer, S. (1999). Beyond 'substantial equivalence'. *Nature, 401*, 525–526.

Millstone, E. (2009). Science, risk and governance: Radical rhetorics and the realities of reform in food safety governance. *Research Policy, 38*(4), 624–636.

Millstone, E. (2010). *The evolution of risk assessment paradigms: In theory and in practice.* Accessed May 3, 2016, from http://pages.ucsd.edu/~aronatas/workshop/Millstone%20Paper% 2026April%202010.pdf

Millstone, E. (2015). *Why science is not enough for good policy.* Accessed May 3, 2016, from http://www.scidev.net/global/policy/opinion/science-good-policy-knowledge-sussex.html

Ministry of Agriculture, Forestry and Fisheries (MAFF). (2007). *JAS Law.* Accessed May 3, 2016, from http://www.maff.go.jp/e/jas/law.html

Ministry of Health, Labour and Welfare (MHLW). (n.d.-a). *Foods produced by recombinant DNA techniques.* Accessed May 3, 2016, from http://www.mhlw.go.jp/english/topics/foodsafety/ dna/

Ministry of Health, Labour and Welfare (MHLW). (n.d.-b). *Food safety information.* Accessed May 3, 2016, from http://www.mhlw.go.jp/english/topics/foodsafety/administration/index. html

Ministry of Health, Labour and Welfare (MHLW). (n.d.-c). *New measures for food safety: Risk analysis.* Accessed May 3, 2016, from http://www.mhlw.go.jp/english/topics/foodsafety/ administration/dl/02.pdf

Ministry of Health, Labour and Welfare (MHLW). (n.d.-d). *Procedure for safety assessment.* Accessed May 3, 2016, from http://www.mhlw.go.jp/english/topics/foodsafety/dna/01.html

Ministry of Health, Labour and Welfare (MHLW). (2003). *Food safety basic law, 2003.* Accessed May 3, 2016, from http://www.fsc.go.jp/sonota/fsb_law1807.pdf

Ministry of Health, Labour and Welfare (MHLW). (2015). *List of products that have undergone safety assessment.* Accessed May 3, 2016, from http://www.mhlw.go.jp/english/topics/ foodsafety/dna/

National Research Council (NRC). (1994). *Science and judgment in risk assessment.* Washington, DC: National Academy Press.

National Research Council (NRC). (2009). *Science and decisions: Advancing risk assessment.* Washington, DC: The National Academies Press. doi:10.17226/12209.

Office of Science, Technology Policy (OSTP). (1986). Coordinated framework for regulation of biotechnology. *Federal Register, 51*, 23302–23393.

Owen, L. (2005). *Distorting the past: Gender and the division of labor in the European Upper Paleolithic.* Tübingen: Kerns Verlag.

The Pharmaceuticals and Medical Devices Agency (PMDA). (n.d.). *Outline of PMDA: Who we are.* Accessed May 3, 2016, from http://www.pmda.go.jp/english/about-pmda/outline/0005. html

Rabin, R. C. (2014, May 14). Labs are told to start including a neglected variable: Females. *NYTimes.* Accessed May 3, 2016, from http://www.nytimes.com/2014/05/15/health/nih-tells-researchers-to-end-sex-bias-in-early-studies.html?_r=1

Rich, N. (2016, January 6). The lawyer who became DuPont's worst nightmare. *NYTimes.* Accessed May 3, 2016, from http://www.nytimes.com/2016/01/10/magazine/the-lawyer-who-became-duponts-worst-nightmare.html

Stearns, J. (2015, October 5). *Most EU countries to ban cultivation of 8 GMOs using new rules.* BloomburgBusiness. Accessed May 3, 2016, from http://www.bloomberg.com/news/articles/ 2015-10-05/most-eu-countries-to-ban-cultivation-of-8-gmos-using-new-rules

US Consumer Product Safety Commission (CPSC). (n.d.). *About CPSC.* Accessed May 3, 2016, from http://www.cpsc.gov/en/About-CPSC/

US Department of Agriculture (USDA). (2015). *GAIN Report Number: FR9174.*

US Environmental Protection Agency (EPA). (2015a). *Conducting a human health risk assessment.* Accessed May 3, 2016, from https://www.epa.gov/risk/conducting-a-human-health-risk-assessment

US Environmental Protection Agency (EPA). (2015b). *EPA's regulation of biotechnology for use in pest management.* Accessed May 3, 2016, from http://www.epa.gov/regulation-biotechnol ogy-under-tsca-and-fifra/epas-regulation-biotechnology-use-pest-management

US Food and Drug Administration (FDA). (2012). *About FDA: FDA history—Part II.* Accessed May 3, 2016, from *http://www.fda.gov/AboutFDA/WhatWeDo/History/Origin/ucm054826.htm*

US Food and Drug Administration (FDA). (2015a). *About FDA: What we do.* Accessed May 3, 2016, from http://www.fda.gov/AboutFDA/WhatWeDo/default.htm

US Food and Drug Administration (FDA). (2015b). *FDA has determined that the AquAdvantage salmon is as safe to eat as non-GE salmon.* Accessed May 3, 2016, from http://www.fda.gov/ForConsumers/ConsumerUpdates/ucm472487.htm

US Food and Drug Administration (FDA). (2009). *Guidance for industry regulation of genetically engineered animals containing heritable recombinant DNA constructs final guidance.* Accessed May 3, 2016, from http://www.fda.gov/downloads/%20AnimalVeterinary/GuidanceComplianceEnforcement/%20%20GuidanceforIndustry/UCM113903.pdf

US Food and Drug Administration (FDA). (2016a). *50 years: The Kefauver-Harris amendments.* Accessed May 3, 2016, from *http://www.fda.gov/Drugs/NewsEvents/ucm320924.htm*

US Food and Drug Administration (FDA). (2016b). *What does FDA regulate?* Accessed May 3, 2016, from http://www.fda.gov/AboutFDA/Transparency/Basics/ucm194879.htm

Waldron, J. (2012). Democracy. In D. Estlund (Ed.), *The Oxford handbook of political philosophy* (pp. 187–203). Oxford: Oxford University Press.

Zachmann, K. (2014). *Risk—A multidisciplinary introduction.* New York, NY: Springer International Publishing.

Manufacturer Responsibilities

Elizabeth Beard Goldsmith

1 Introduction

The world is rapidly changing. Consumers demand the latest products, pushing manufacturers to innovate and deliver fast. Rapid change brings with it the greater chance of mistakes in production, distribution, decision making, communication, and in the marketplace.

Manufacturers make products for sale or use. The manufacturing process can take place in households through hand-made crafts to immense global factories. Human labor, tools, machines and equipment, raw materials, chemicals, design and engineering may be involved. Manufacturing industries include aircraft, automobiles, clothing, computers, electrical equipment, heavy machinery, furniture, consumer electronics, paper, and refined petroleum products. Specialty applications can be to defense, energy, commercial marine, industrial, construction, medical, mining, and offshore oil and gas.

Many manufacturing companies have historic roots such as luxury United Kingdom coat maker Burberry's founded by Thomas Burberry in 1856. One of the buildings still used today dates from the 1880s and houses 45 looms, which pump out gabardine, with a handful of workers checking for cloth quality. The mill works 24 h a day with 75 people over three shifts. Finishing requires direct manual labor to produce 5000 trench coats a week. To satisfy the ultimate end user, the consumer, hand stitching is required. "Using swift, sure strokes, Amanda's strong fingers, one tipped with a thimble, push a needle through tough gabardine fabric.

"It is not enough that we do our best; sometimes we must do what is required." Winston Churchill, former British prime minister.

E.B. Goldsmith (✉)
Department of Retail, Merchandising and Product Development, College of Human Sciences, Florida State University, Tallahassee, FL 32306-1110, USA
e-mail: egoldsmith@fsu.edu

© Springer International Publishing AG 2017
G. Emilien et al. (eds.), *Consumer Perception of Product Risks and Benefits*,
DOI 10.1007/978-3-319-50530-5_27

Table 1 Top 20 countries/
regions by manufacturing
output

Rank	Country/Region	(Millions of $US)	Year
	World	11,917,240	2013
1	China	2,922,520	2013
	European Union	2,312,723	2013
2	United States	1,943,810	2013
	Eurozone	1,793,895	2013
3	Japan	904,590	2013
4	Germany	771,183	2014
5	South Korea	389,581	2014
6	India	325,246	2014
7	Italy	299,017	2014
8	France	283,663	2014
9	Russia	267,591	2014
10	United Kingdom	246,900	2014
11	Brazil	218,802	2014
12	Mexico	216,066	2014
13	Indonesia	186,743	2014
14	Spain	168,995	2014
15	Canada	162,074	2014
16	Turkey	126,344	2014
17	Switzerland	123,855	2014
18	Thailand	121,677	2014
19	Netherlands	96,953	2014
20	Australia	92,768	2014

Source: World Bank

After more than 20 years in Burberry's factory in Castleford, Yorkshire, she can stitch a collar in 8 min—and so neatly the eventual owner of the trench coat she is making will never notice her work. At most, the wearer may be vaguely aware that their coat snugly hugs their neck in a way a standard high-street raincoat never could" (Butler 2016, p. 1).

Manufacturers self-regulate in terms of quality control, and it is in their best interest to keep up with demographic trends, to be forward-looking and efficient in the use of resources, human and material. In some industries the word "fabricate" is used more often than manufacturing. Besides internal regulation, manufacturers are also subject to external review, standards and regulations set by various levels of governments.

To show how manufacturing is distributed internationally, Table 1 lists the top 20 countries (or areas) by value of manufacturing output in a given year. China tops the list followed by European countries, the United States, and Japan. A leading story in manufacturing output is the steady rise of exports coming from China. It is one of the most significant events in international trade in recent decades (Feenstra 2016). Major manufacturers in Asia are Samsung, Toyota, and Sony. In North America there are Ford, General Motors, Procter & Gamble, Raytheon, and Boeing. European examples are Siemens, Michelin, and Volkswagen Group. Some businesses compete with each other such as the airlines and automobile companies; others such as Google stand alone. "How much of the world is actually monopolistic? How much is truly competitive? It is hard to say because our common conversation about these matters is so confused. To the outside observer, all businesses can seem reasonably alike, so it is easy to perceive only small differences between them. But the reality is much more binary than that. There is an enormous difference between perfect competition and monopoly, and most businesses are much closer to one extreme than we commonly realize" (Thiel 2014, p. 1).

Small or medium sized manufacturers who wish to expand face the challenges of competing with large established firms. Issues include access to natural resources, economic conditions, financing construction of or the retro-fitting of existing buildings and equipping factories, training and paying labor, legal issues, and following government regulations.

2   Trust and Responsibility

"Consumer well-being (CWB) has long been of interest to scholars, managers, and public policy experts and continues to captivate academics and practitioners" (Pancer and Handelman 2012, p. 177). A large part of consumers' well-being lies in their ability to trust the products they use and the manufacturers who make them. When trust is violated, it is difficult to win back.

Trust can spring from many parts of the manufacturing process. Where water is used in manufacturing, the effect of manufacturing on water is a consumer issue because clean drinking water is essential to human life and sustainability. Possible contaminants, some of which come from industrial processes, include organic chemical contaminants such as synthetic and volatile organic chemicals, which can be by-products of petroleum production and other industrial processes. Other sources are pesticides and herbicides, which may come from industrial plants and production. Radioactive contaminants can come from mining activities as well as oil and gas production and from making products involving radioactive substances. Inorganic contaminants are found in salts and metals as a result of mining and oil and gas production. Finally, microbial contaminants such as bacteria and viruses can come from sewage treatment and industrial plants.

Water contamination can occur in springs, wells, reservoirs, oceans, rivers, lakes, streams, and holding ponds. In the United States, the Food and Drug Administration (FDA) regulations establish limits on contaminants in bottled water. The Environmental Protection Agency is involved in water and air quality regulations. Responsible manufacturers do their part by employing proper waste disposal to minimize the exposure of contaminants and chemicals to surrounding communities. In addition, some consumers are more vulnerable to contaminants in drinking water than is the general population. Examples are immune-compromised persons such as those with cancer undergoing chemotherapy, people with HIV/AIDS or other immune system disorders, infants, and the elderly.

Managers and facility designers should take full advantage of the latest technological and ecological solutions to meet consumer needs and regulatory compliance. They should also make sure, from the beginning, that there is trust and collaborative effort between researchers and developers (i.e., research tools, diagnostic tests) and manufacturers (Hill 2011). To be more specific about trust, "When introducing new measurements into the laboratory either as research tools or diagnostic tests, laboratories often rely on information supplied by the manufacturer to decide whether a commercial reagent kit is likely to be useful for a particular purpose" (Hill 2011, p. 93).

3   Social Responsibility

An academic leader in the field of Corporate Social Responsibility, David Glen Mick, declares that "the time for authoritative and constructive scholarship in consumption and well-being has arrived" (2008, p. 379). CSR seeks to benefit consumer welfare and improve quality of life for all human beings affected by consumption worldwide. It can be applied to a wide variety of industries including the highly competitive pharmaceutical industry (West and Dobson 2011).

Pancer and Handelman (2012) discuss Mick's work within the general context of consumer well-being. They conclude that incorporating more community-centered and contextually-bound criteria into the understanding of consumer well-being would yield new research insights. There are many measures and indices of consumer well-being. Most recent contributions to the literature redefine consumer well-being as "the alignment of individual and societal needs (i.e., physical, psychological, economics, social) as they relate to consumption" (Burroughs and Rindfleish 2011, p. 252).

CSR calls for a corporate mindshift or transformation providing needed changes for a more sustainable business model. A positive marketing message could be "doing well by doing good." It refers to improving society and the environment through best practices. These may include altruism, strategies, and ethics. Altruism refers to helping others such as giving back to communities through scholarships and philanthropic activities. Strategies refer to engaging in socially responsible activities including improved employment practices while increasing value to the firm. Ethics are principles of right or good conduct. They mean acting in ethical ways, having core principles or standards, acting with integrity, going beyond the minimal basics prescribed by regulations and laws. Management encourages employees to make ethical decisions by setting an example and management uses moral principles or values in deliberations.

Manufacturer responsibility to the public in food-safety cases is well-documented. In examining the supply chain, was something done wrong at the plant or in transportation from the field? Were sufficient sanitation and quality control steps in place? Illness from fresh produce and fast food restaurants serve as classic cases in business management, public health, communication, and marketing literature. Cases keep emerging. In 2015, many cases of illness from Chipolte restaurant food were reported at several locations in the United States. "E. Coli was traced to meals purchased in the metro Portland area and several counties in Washington from October 14–23, and at least 22 people were sickened" (E. Coli Leaves Chipotle Investors Skittish 2015, p. 5B). Chipolte executives went on television trying to reassure customers about quality control. A full page letter from Chipotle founder Steve Ells appeared in *USA Today* on December 16, 2015 (p. 5A). His last sentence stated "I'd like to take this opportunity to apologize on behalf of us at Chipotle, and to thank our loyal customers who have stood by us through this difficult time." To give another food safety example, in Northern India high levels of lead were found in instant-noodle packets from Nestle SA. In response "millions of packets were pulverized and burned in cement kilns, the company said" (Rana 2015, p. B9).

4 Customer Care

Attention to food safety is important to society. It is an example of customer care. Customer care is a subset of consumer well-being discussed in the last section about CSR with leading theorist David Glenn Mick. Within CSR exists Customer Relationship Management or CRM, which is an integrated information system wherein the fundamental unit of data collection is the consumer. For example, data could be collected on consumer satisfaction, the measure of whether or not a consumer's total consumption experience has met or exceeded his or her expectations. "Today, numerous measures and indices exist that account for different conceptualizations of consumer well-being. Contemporary models include the cost of living model, the consumption equity model. The quality model, the shopping model, the consumer/ product life cycle model, and the need satisfaction model" (Pancer and Handelman 2012, p. 178).

Another aspect of customer care is that in today's accelerated technology-forward manufacturing environment, it is difficult for the firm to know which parts to store for repairs and how much storage to devote to replacement parts. Another concern is what repairs to provide. The labor needed to handle complaints and to service replacements is expensive. As an example, a consumer, known to the author, had a famous name brand refrigerator made by a Korean company that broke down four times in the first 2 years of ownership. For the first three times the manufacturer replaced the part that kept breaking, but by the fourth time the manufacturer offered partial cash back or a replacement because that refrigerator model was no longer made. The company concluded that something far more than the part was not working, and it was costing them too much in time and effort to keep up with the repairs. The homeowners liked this solution because they had been inconvenienced by the repairs and paid for some of the labor costs. The moral of this story is that manufacturers should take care of their customers by providing solutions when things go wrong. Their jurisdiction extends beyond the factory or other place of manufacturing.

Flat screen televisions, laptops, cellphones, and small appliances are being constantly replaced. Should the manufacturer be responsible for providing services and parts for an appliance or electronic that is now completely out-of-date?

The underlying premise in customer care is that we want better lives not just for ourselves but for our children and future generations. We can discuss customer care product by product, industry by industry, or by economic or environmental impacts, up next.

5   Economic and Environmental Impacts

One of the most impactful industries on world economies and the environment is the car industry. Car safety is a concern for all of us; our lives depend on it. A famous advocate for car safety was Ralph Nader. His 1965 authoring of *Unsafe at Any Speed*, highlighted the need for better built cars and for consumers to use of seatbelts. It is hard to remember a time without seatbelts. The centerpiece of his book was the Chevrolet Corvair. "The automobile had been around for 70 years before Ralph Nader got general recognition of the fact that autos included unsafe design features and sometimes were ill-engineered," according to Aaker and Day (1982, p. 31). "A series of horrendous accidents caused by poorly manufactured cars led to a call for reform. Nader spoke out against industrial pollution and the abuse of corporate power not only in the car industry but also in the home repair industry, the food industry, and securities, to name a few. He testified extensively before Congress and still advocates on behalf of consumers, particularly regarding environmental concerns, and he founded consumer groups that are still active" (Goldsmith 2009, p. 54).

Besides Ralph Nader there are many other famous consumer advocates. Another American consumer advocate was biologist Rachel Carson, author of *Silent Spring*. She is often cited as the founder of the modern environmental movement, which has tangents such as the organic movement and slow-food movement. She exposed pollution problems and advocated for more use of natural pests or deterrents rather than chemicals.

In more recent times the discussion of economic and environmental impacts swirls around the concepts of sustainability which has many definitions. The most fundamental comes from the ancient Great Law of the Native American Iroquois people which states,

> 'In every deliberation, we must consider the impact on the seventh generation.' This philosophy ensured not only the continuity of the environment, but also was crucial to their survival as a cultural group, five tribes with a shared language … In 1954, R. Buckminster Fuller, the famous architect and theorist defined sustainability as: the conscious design of our total environment, in order to help make the Earth's finite resources

meet the needs of all of humanity without disrupting the ecological processes of the planet. In 1994, the United Nations defined sustainability as 'meeting the needs of the present, without sacrificing the needs of our future' (Goldsmith 2013, p. 1).

To be more specific, it can be said that "Sustainable behavior is a multidimensional concept that includes behaviors such as conservation of natural resources through efficient use, recycling, purchase and use of green products, and other behaviors that preserve the natural environment including air and water quality. One means of promoting these desirable behaviors is the use of social influence, that is, the influence that people have over other people. Social influence is how one person or group affects another's opinions, attitudes, emotions or behaviors" (Goldsmith 2015, p. 3). Social influence, the "who" behind consumer behavior and sustainability, can take place in-person or online or through other forms of media such as blogs and other platforms. It is harder to ignore or hide product defects than ever before because of online reviews.

A combination of social influence with economic and environmental impacts is illustrated in the following case study about Birkin handbags. These are high-end handbags that have become collectibles. Some have sold for over a $1 million. "Jane Birkin wants to put some distance between herself and one of the world's most coveted handbags. The British actress has asked Hermes International SCA to remove her name from its iconic crocodile-skin purse because of what she called the cruel methods used on farms that raise the reptiles for their pricey skins. 'I have asked Hermes to unbaptise the Birkin Croco until better practices in line with international norms can be put in place,' the 68-year-old Ms. Birkin said. Crocodile farms have become a target of the activist animal-rights group PETA ... The bag was first conceived when Ms. Birkin, seated next to then-Hermes chairman Jean-Louis Dumas on a plane in 1984, complained that she couldn't find a bag big enough to suit her. Mr. Dumas offered to create one that would be large enough for her to carry 'her house' but stylish enough for the brand to lend the bag its name. The Birkin became an instant classic." (Chow, Jason, July 30, 2015, "Birkin Asks Hermes to Take Her Name Off Crocodile Purse," *The Wall Street Journal*, p. B1).

Professor Jing Jian Xiao describes the interaction of different parts of market economies and how they impact consumers this way:

> Governments through economic policies affect consumer income, expenditure, debt, and asset. Businesses provide consumer opportunities to earn and spend money. Businesses or governments in different countries control mass media to frame and influence consumer spending and other economic behaviors. Advances in technologies, especially information technologies, change the world on the daily basis and provide consumers novel products and services that increase the comfort level of consumer life in many ways (Xiao 2015, p. 16).

A large worldwide industry, retailing, along with other supply chain industries are struggling to keep up with technological advances. The National Retail Federation *NRF Smart Brief* (Dec. 22, 2015) reported that over six out of ten retailers say they are planning to upgrade their merchandise planning systems within 2 years as twentieth century can't effectively address today's omni-channel environment. The global supply chain (global networks) of civil society also come into play, manufacturers have to be consistent, and if things go wrong criminal sanctions for trade union rights violations are possible (Connor and Haines 2015).

6 Product Quality

Marketers and manufacturers can make innocent or not so innocent mistakes. Quality control can be defined as the process which involves the review of all factors involved in production. For instance, a quality control manager for a food company may be in charge of overseeing that fruits and vegetables are being properly washed and sorted on a production line before they move to the canning process.

Collaborations on quality control involving engineers, managers, and statisticians fall under a type of decision making called "decision analysis," which involves problem evaluation and the development of possible solutions using Bayesian probabilities and optimization techniques leading to the highest expected utility (Fox 2015). Quality control is in place to reduce potential mistakes and in so doing protect consumers and the firm's reputation. Unfortunately, a company may not discover a product defect until the product is on the store shelves or in the case of cars, on the streets.

Product recalls are all too common, and recalls are found in many industries. Marketers can, however, intentionally release harmful products to their target market. This, of course, would be considered unethical. At issue is the intent and knowledge of the firm. Consumer perceptions of incidents such as these are also important, as bad events can mean disaster for the firm in terms of lost business, consumer boycotts, and bad publicity (Babin and Harris 2011, p. 307).

An example of failed quality control was a recall of almost 90,000 pounds of beef sent to Walmart by a supplier. The beef patties were suspected of being contaminated with extraneous wood materials (Walmart Supplier Recalls Beef Products 2016, p. 5B). Some retailers have their own laboratories to test private-label products as well as nationally manufactured products. They may "adhere to stricter ethical and environmental standards that go beyond existing government regulations" (Dunne et al. 2011, p. 212). In the United States, two agencies have the main responsibilities for food safety: the Food Safety and Inspection Service in the Department of Agriculture enforces regulations on meat and poultry and the Food and Drug Administration in the Department of Health and Human Services is responsible for all other food products (Xiao 2015).

7 Risk Communication

Examples have already been given about company communication to private individuals and to the public in general about failed or injurious products. Communication is a process in which participants create and share information. In this process a lot can go wrong. Misrepresentations could involve the advertising and sales promotion of a product that may give the consumer a false sense of security of the safety of a product or service that may draw attention away from the actual hazards of its use. Examples would be certain types of sports equipment or all-terrain vehicles (ATVs). In the United States, the Consumer Product Safety Commission is charged with protecting consumers from possible hazards associated with risks of injury from approximately 15,000 consumer products.

A product recall may be necessary or an outright ban or an issuing of a public alert about a design defect may be needed. Public alerts can be seen and heard in a variety of ways, such as TV and newspapers. For example, a pediatrician's waiting room may have posters about dangerous cribs or other infant equipment. Poor quality materials or shoddy workmanship may be involved or design flaws.

Technical communication research is a specialization area that may trace how messages move through society. The public finds out about oil spills and food-based illnesses through mass media, but there are other levels of discovery and discourse including the technical communication research literature and within companies and among regulators. Warranties and guarantees are subject to much care in their design. Notice the lengthy warnings given on television advertisements about the use of certain pharmaceutical drugs. Other than television advertisements from the company, where do consumers go for product advice? The first place for product or service information is the company website according to an IntelliResponse survey of 1000 consumers (Carey and Trap 6.2/2014). Sixty-eight percent of survey responders said this. So, it is important for communication from the company, including technical communication, to be accurately reported and updated on the company website. According to the same survey, the other sources for production information were social media (10%), in store (10%), phone call (6%), mobile app (4%), and other (2%).

To reduce the need for new product information and exposure to risk, consumers often fall into repetitive buying habits. When they repeat their consumption behaviors they are "following an internal script or schemata, a stereotyped sequence of actions or events about what they should do in a certain consumption situation" (Goldsmith 2015, p. 59).

8 Ethical Production and Design

When most people think of ethics (or morals), they think of rules for distinguishing between right and wrong, such as the Golden Rule ("Do unto others as you would have them do unto you"), a code of professional conduct like the Hippocratic Oath ("First of all, do no harm"), a religious creed like the Ten Commandments ("thou shalt not kill..."), or wise aphorisms like the sayings of Confucius. This is the most common way of defining 'ethics': norms for conduct that distinguish between acceptable and unacceptable behavior (Resnik 2015).

Effective production and design is based on ethics, sound reasoning, and rational decision making. Ethics are norms for conduct, guiding principles or standards. As mentioned earlier, the practice of ethics involves acting with integrity. These actions are applicable to consumers (using products properly) and to manufacturers. Ethical situations are complex often with differing perspectives and requiring critical thinking (Flynn and Goldsmith 2013). Critical thinking is "the application of good reasoning strategies to reasoning problems" (Bishop 2012). Seeking problem solutions require manufacturers and associated industries to analyze problems, develop a set of possible solutions, select from alternatives, and evaluate the outcomes once in place.

The Better Business Bureau (BBB) was established in 1912 in the United States to discourage dishonest business practices. It has a Code of Ethics which includes sections on education, truthfulness, honesty, integrity, courtesy, and sensibility. Manufacturers and manufacturers' associations follow similar codes of ethics to guide production. Processes are evaluated and defects or flaws in the supply chain removed. Better quality products, higher prices, or changes to warranties may result. Accelerating technology with more extensive data immediately available of sales, for example, has led to manufacturer feedback at a much faster and more expansive pace.

9 The Future of Manufacturer Responsibilities

The main manufacturer responsibility is to fulfill the promises they have made—that products work and are safe and live up to the brand reputation. However, as long as consumer products are made there will be mistakes, there will be injuries. An industry goal is to reduce the likelihood of defective or unsatisfactory products. This is the future for respected manufacturers: to hold on to their standards and ethics and after mishaps to regain reputations for quality products by putting more safeguards in place. When there are mishaps the question is who should bear the costs? An argument is that manufacturers have the research expertise and laboratories, the engineering and technical knowledge, and the budget to assess the risks of product use and to ensure that these products are safe. Consumers, the ultimate end-users, don't have the time, the know-how, or the laboratories to conduct research before using a product. They put their trust in companies and in manufacturers to ensure purity and safety and thus, the manufacturer bears the consequences of poor or shoddy goods and services. Retailers may conduct product tests in their own laboratories.

Exploring further, what does the future hold for manufacturers? That is a very big question since manufacturing underlies all consumer products that we need to live and thrive. Social, ecological, and technological trends provide some of the answers. With the global spread of the Internet and with it consumer complaints and reviews through social media being highly visible and the amount of email or other forms of exchanges within companies, it appears likely that manufacturers will be under more scrutiny in the future (Goldsmith 2015).

One takeaway from this contribution is that many manufacturers have historic roots such as the Burberry coat factory in the United Kingdom. However, not all manufacturing is factory-based—the Internet and the software industry has changed that as well as a recognition worldwide of the rise of start-ups and small, handcrafted businesses. Elements such as quality control, job management, data storage and record keeping are undergoing new methods and examinations. Examples of management integrity and organizational culture were given in this contribution. Reducing defects and recalls are goals. In future, expect improved quality assurance, changes in employment, and a higher standard in all industries.

In August (2015), the pharmaceutical and biosciences enterprise GlaxoSmithKline—which had announced plans 4 years ago to sell off its manufacturing plant and leave Memphis—announced plans instead to invest another $2 million to upgrade the infrastructure and equipment at its operation there, supporting nearly 300 jobs. These designated Manufacturing Communities demonstrate how a well-integrated manufacturing sector is critical to America's continued growth and prosperity (Jason Miller, Deputy Director of the National Economic Council at the White House, "Manufacturing Relies on the Strengths of American Communities" https://www.commerce.gov/news/blog/2015/12/22).

This is an American example from a government source. Worldwide examples are countless. They underscore many of the concepts in this contribution—the importance of manufacturing to the growth and prosperity of local and national economies. Consumers have ethical concerns or moral judgments about business practices that may influence their purchase behavior (Burke and Milberg 2015). Decision analysis involving collaborations within companies will lead to better problem solving and solutions, the highest expected utility (Fox 2015). Ultimately, manufacturers have the responsibility to produce consistent, high quality products that are useful to consumer following industry standards and sustainable principles and in so doing, provide jobs and bolster trade and the worldwide economy.

References

Aaker, D., & Day, G. (1982). *Consumerism: Search for the consumer interest* (4th ed.). New York, NY: Free Press.

Babin, B., & Harris, E. (2011). *CB2*. Mason, OH: South-Western Cengage Learning.

Bishop, M. (2012, May 22). *Thinking about critical thinking*. In Presentation, Florida State University.

Burke, S. J., & Milberg, S. (2015). The role of ethical concerns in consumer purchase behavior: Understanding alternative processes. *Advances in Consumer Research, 20*, 119–122.

Burroughs, J. E., & Rindfleish, A. (2011). What welfare? On the definition and domain of transformative consumer research and the foundational role of materialism. In D. G. Mick, S. Pettigrew, C. Pechmann, & J. L. Ozanne (Eds.), *Transformative consumer research for personal and collective well-being* (pp. 245–262). New York, NY: Taylor & Francis.

Butler, S. (2016, May 13). The hands behind the heritage: Inside the Burberry factory in Yorkshire. *The Guardian*, 1–4.

Carey, A. R., & Trap, P. (2014, June 2). Want product advice? *USA Today*.

Connor, T., & Haines, F. (2015). Networked regulation as a solution to human rights abuse in global supply chains? The case of trade union rights violations by Indonesian sports shoe manufacturers. *Theoretical Criminology, 17*(2), 197–214.

Dunne, P., Lusch, R., & Carver, J. (2011). *Retailing* (7th ed.). Mason, OH: South-Western Cengage Learning.

E. coli leaves chipotle investors skittish. (2015, February 3). Tallahassee Democrat, p. 5B.

Feenstra, R. (2016). *The international trade and investment program* (NBER Reporter, No. 1, p. 1).

Flynn, L. R., & Goldsmith, R. E. (2013). *Case studies for ethics in academic research in the social sciences*. London: Sage.

Fox, J. (2015). From "economic man" to behavioral economics. *Harvard Business Review, 93*(5), 78–85.

Goldsmith, E. (2009). *Consumer economics: Issues and behaviors* (2nd ed.). Upper Saddle River, NJ: Pearson [London: Routledge (3rd ed., in press)].

Goldsmith, E. (2013). *An exploration of sustainability, consumer behavior, and social influence*. In A White Paper circulated in Germany from the University of Bonn.

Goldsmith, E. B. (2015). *Social influence and sustainable consumption*. Switzerland: Springer.

Hill, R. (2011). Verification and validation: Whose responsibility, manufacturer or end user? *Annals of Clinical Biochemistry, 48*, 93–94.

Mick, D. G. (2008, October). Introduction: The moment and place for a special issue. *Journal of Consumer Research, 35*, 377–379.

Pancer, E., & Handelman, J. (2012). The evolution of consumer well-being. *Journal of Historical Research in Marketing, 4*(1), 177–189.

Rana, P. (2015, June 18). Nestle navigating India regulations. *The Wall Street Journal*, B9.

Resnik, D. B. (2015). *What is ethics in research & Why is it important?* Accessed August 15, 2016, from http://www.niehs.nih.gov/research/resources/bioethics/whatis.cfm

Thiel, P. (2014, September 13). Competition is for losers. *The Wall Street Journal*, C1–C2.

Walmart Supplier Recalls Beef Products. (2016, January 7). USA Today, p. 5B.

West, T., & Dobson, R. (2011). Corporate social responsibility in the pharmaceutical industry: A qualitative study. *CPI/RPC, 144*(5), 213–215.

Xiao, J. J. (2015). *Consumer economic wellbeing*. Switzerland: Springer.

Consumer Responsibilities

Sue L.T. McGregor

1 Introduction

"Consumer responsibility is an important counterpart to corporate responsibility" (Houde 2010, p. 110). After a discussion of what constitutes the consumer interest, and a brief contextual overview of the emergence of consumer rights, the discussion turns to how consumer responsibilities evolved as a construct in the early eighties. An in depth overview of the five basic consumer responsibilities is then provided. Based on the assumption that the consumer movement of the twenty-first century is about human rights and justice (as well as the interests of consumers relative to business), some scholars started to associate consumer rights with human rights, which provided a natural segue to the idea that consumer responsibilities can be linked with the emergent human responsibility movement. In particular, McGregor (1999, 2003) suggested that we cannot have consumer rights without human rights, and we cannot be responsible consumers unless we are responsible humans.

2 The Consumer Interest

The marketplace comprises three key players: businesses, governments, and consumers (including consumer organizations). The consumers' interest as participants in the marketplace can be readily compromised due (a) to the actions of businesses; (b) external contexts (social, economic, political and technological); (c) the nuances of the decision making process during consumer resource management activities; and, (d) people's values, attitudes, and belief systems. Consumer issues can also be

S.L.T. McGregor (✉)
Mount Saint Vincent University, 11565 Peggy's Cove Road, Seabright, NS B3Z 2Y1, Canada
e-mail: Sue.mcgregor@msvu.ca

© Springer International Publishing AG 2017   527
G. Emilien et al. (eds.), *Consumer Perception of Product Risks and Benefits*,
DOI 10.1007/978-3-319-50530-5_28

affected by (e) the (in)adequacy of consumer protection policies and consumer laws, and (f) the consumers' ability and propensity to organize and participate in self-advocacy (Bannister and Monsma 1982; McGregor 2012).

If the market economy does not function properly, it is said to have failed (i.e., marketplace failure). This failure can result in an imbalance of power between the consumer and business, resulting in a *consumer issue*. These issues can fall within the following eight problem areas: (a) economic security/interest (financial security and privacy, and contractual and transactional fairness); (b) health and personal safety; (c) information asymmetry; (d) education (consumer and general); (e) competition (availability, choice, price and quality of a range of goods and services); (f) representation in the policy process; (g) redress; and, (h) environmental concerns (McGregor 2012).

It is in the best interest of consumers (to their *benefit or advantage*) to have these consumer issues dealt with properly, if they are to hold their own against the power of the business sector, and some would say against the government sector (in the form of public services—transportation, health, schools). Not addressing these issues leads to situations not in the best interest of consumers (individuals or aggregate) because they have not received any benefits and/or are harmed or disadvantaged in some way (morally, personally, financially) (McGregor 2012). When the interest of consumers is compromised or threatened, it is the role of governments to step in and mediate and/or mitigate the situation. Consumer organizations also play an influential role in this process (Hilton 2009). In efforts to ensure the consumers' interest is respected and protected, that they maintain an advantage and gain benefits from market transactions, a globally recognized set of consumer rights has been developed, discussed in the next section.

3 Formalization of Consumer Rights

Historically, the formalization of consumer rights preceded consumer responsibilities by 20 years, when in fact consumer responsibilities should always precede consumer rights (Singh 2001). The International Organization of Consumer Unions (IOCU, founded in 1960) adopted President J. F. Kennedy's 1962 four consumer rights as the pillar of its policy and its *Charter of Consumer Rights*: safety, choice, voice, and information. As a point of information, IOCU changed its name to Consumers International (CI) in 1995, and has consultative status with the United Nations (Hilton 2009). In 1978, Anwar Fazal (Malaysia) became the first person from the Third World to be president of IOCU (1978–1984). As a result of the subsequent influence of Asian consumerism, IOCU had added four more consumer rights by 1979: the right to consumer education, redress, a healthy environment, and basic goods and services (satisfy human needs to ensure survival) (Fazal 2011; Hilton 2009).

In 1985, after a decade of heavy IOCU lobbying and influence, the United Nations adopted these eight consumer rights in its *United Nations Guidelines for*

Consumer Protection (UNCPG) (UN Resolution 39/248) (Hilton 2009; Johnson 2014; Malcolm 2013; United Nations 2003). These rights are clearly set out in *Section II: General Principles*, and in varying degrees of detail in *Section III: Guidelines*. Table 1 provides an overview of the eight consumer rights. The UN guidelines provide important legitimacy to the principles of consumer rights, and they assist countries in the development of their consumer protection policies, including legislation and other policy instruments. In 1999, the guidelines were updated with a new section on sustainable consumption and production (Section G) (United Nations 2003). Consumers International (2013) recently developed a set of further amendments to the guidelines, this time on the topic of access to knowledge, with financial services, data protection and privacy new areas of concern (currently under consideration at the United Nations).

4 Formalization of Consumer Responsibilities

When all is said and done, if people have rights, they also have responsibilities, *even* in their consumer role; every right (entitlement) implies a responsibility (obligation) (Schmidt 1997). The *United Nations Guidelines for Consumer Protection* is heavily grounded in consumer rights, with the one exception being sustainable consumption, which says all marketplace players share responsibility. Section F on consumer education *does* say consumers need to become conscious of their rights *and* responsibilities (United Nations 2003). That being said, non-Western consumer advocates and lobbyist have long taken issue with the individualistic and self-serving tenor of the Western-informed consumer ideology and consumer philosophy that hinges on *rights* (Hilton 2009). There must be a place for corresponding responsibilities.

Nearly 20 years after the concept of consumer rights was introduced by President Kennedy in 1962, Anwar Fazal (IOCU president) led the call to formalize corresponding consumer *responsibilities* (CI 2015; Fazal 1979, 1982; Hilton 2009). In the late seventies, he maintained that self-protection is the ultimate protection because consumers cannot assume others will protect them. Consumers must use their own competence and vigilance and initiate action *for* their protection; that action is best ensured from a responsibilities approach (Fazal 2011).

In that spirit, IOCU (1980) entrenched five consumer responsibilities in the early eighties: (a) solidarity, (b) critical awareness, (c) action and involvement, (d) environmental awareness, and (e) social concern (see Table 2). Despite IOCU having eight consumer rights but only five consumer responsibilities, Fazal (1982) claimed that the latter five principles "provide a framework for action as responsible consumers" (p. 3). Indeed, IOCU called them a *Charter for Consumer Action*, and Fazal characterized them as "a frame of reference for... consumer action" (1979, p. 2).

Fazal (1982) said consumers must fulfil these responsibilities if they wished to obtain benefits from consumer organizations. He also observed that "meeting these

Table 1 Eight consumer rights and corresponding consumer responsibilities

Consumers have the right to	Consumers have the responsibility to
Basic goods and services (satisfy basic needs) Be able to consume (have access to) basic goods and services (necessities that are essential for survival): adequate food, clothing, shelter, health care, education, public utilities, water, and sanitation; right to freedom, equality and adequate conditions of life	*Sustainably use basic goods and services* Use these essential goods and services appropriately and sustainably so others can meet their basic needs; if feasible, become vocal advocates for poverty reduction, equality, justice, equity, and adequate conditions of life
Safety Be protected against products, production processes and services that are hazardous to health, life, or well-being (this refers to responsible business behavior (good faith efforts to provide safe merchandise and services), government regulations, and international standards)	*Consume safely* Read and follow instructions on products and use and dispose of them as intended (includes proper maintenance); check the qualifications of service providers before the transaction; refuse and report shoddy merchandise or unqualified service providers, protect oneself and others; remain alert for future warnings; be aware of standards for product safety
Information Be given the facts needed to make an informed choice, and be protected against fraudulent, dishonest or misleading advertising, marketing, and labelling; clear and comprehensive contracts; privacy and data protection; consumers with communication-related disabilities have the right to receive any information in a format that meets their needs; information that facilitates ethical and sustainable consumption choices	*Become informed* Seek out, ask for, critique and discriminate between product and service information so one can make an informed and critical choice; keep abreast of innovations and changes in the marketplace; read contracts before signing; request information be presented in a format that meets one's needs; vigilantly protect personal data and information; encourage the provision of information about the ethics and sustainability of product sourcing and service delivery
Choice Be able to select from a range of products and services, offered at fair and competitive prices with an assurance of satisfactory quality; physical and/or virtual access to the marketplace; reliable after-market services; market conditions that provide consumers with sustainable and ethical choices (freedom to choose consciously and mindfully); corporate social responsibility	*Choose carefully and consciously* Research and compare a range of products and services before purchasing; demand fair and competitive prices and assurances of quality; make informed, independent decisions; ask for help; resist high pressures sales; make needs and desires known to businesses, governments and consumer organizations; promote and engage in sustainable consumption by expanding choice criteria to include 'labor behind the label' and environmental impact; gain an appreciation that consumption choices can have ethical and moral overtones
Be heard (voice and representation) Have consumer interests represented in the making and execution of government policy, and in the development of products and services; have the importance of the consumer in the economic process recognized; form independent consumer and other relevant groups or organizations and the opportunity for them to	*Make themselves heard* Make needs and expectations known to vendors, governments, and consumer organizations; appreciate what constitutes *the consumer interest* and consumer issues; form and/or join consumer associations and related groups to make one's voice heard and

(continued)

Table 1 (continued)

Consumers have the right to	Consumers have the responsibility to
present their views in decision-making processes affecting them and the consumer interest; intervene in capitalism	encourage others to do so; make one's opinions known; challenge the capitalistic system
Redress Complain if dissatisfied with product or service; receive a fair settlement of just claims, including compensation for misrepresentation, shoddy goods, or unsatisfactory services; timely and respectful redress; access to avenues to obtain redress and to seek assistance and advice	*Seek redress* Insist on a fair and reasonable deal if not satisfied with the purchase; keep records, receipts and warranties; seek redress and complain so sellers' practices can change, those at fault can be penalized, and those victimized can be compensated; do so in a timely, honest and respectful manner; report abusive or illegal business practices (i.e., complain if dissatisfied—make the effort)
Consumer education Have access to knowledge and skills that are needed be an informed consumer throughout one's life; be able to make confident decisions and choices about goods and services; access to education on the environmental, social and economic impacts of consumer choices; be able to function effectively in the marketplace; be advised that consumers have rights in the marketplace	*Seek consumer education* Seek out and avail oneself of education programs during one's lifetime; advocate for inclusion of consumer education in public school systems; inform oneself about goods and services to be purchased; continually ask questions and critique the marketplace; be aware of consumer rights and responsibilities and how to act on them; be an ethical consumer; anticipate and initiate changes in the marketplace
A healthy environment Freedom, equality and adequate conditions of life (live, work and leisure) in an environment that is non-threatening to the well-being of present and future generations; life with dignity that enhances quality of life for individuals and society; learn how to be an ethical and moral consumer and to consume sustainably; learn that corporations have social and ecological responsibilities	*Build a healthy environment* Help build a healthy environment by conserving natural resources and by choosing products and services that do not harm the environment (or other species), now or in the future (sustainable consumption); minimize damage and harm; respect power consumers have in the marketplace; appreciate the interconnectedness of the marketplace with the world; encourage corporate social responsibility (the highest levels of ethical conduct)

consumer responsibilities will require the synergetic cooperation of governments, socially responsible businesses, academics and media" (Fazal 2011, p. 3). While most documents that outline these responsibilities do so in a one or two pithy lines, the following text shares a much more detailed and nuanced profile of each responsibility (CI 2015; Fazal 1979, 1982, 2011; Johnson 2014; McGregor 2003; Singh 2001).

Table 2 Overview of InterAction Council's Universal Declaration of Human Responsibilities

InterAction Council's Universal Declaration of Human Responsibilities (1997)
Fundamental principles of humanity
• Act in a humane way (compassion and benevolence)
• Strive for the dignity and self-esteem of everyone
• Promote good and avoid evil in all things
• Accept responsibility for everyone in spirit of solidarity
Non-violence and respect for life
• Respect life of all humans
• Resolve disputes on all levels with non-violence and peaceful ways
• Protect environment and other species for present and future generations
Justice and solidarity
• Behave with integrity, honesty, and fairness
• Do not deprive people of their property
• Make serious effort to overcome poverty, malnutrition, ignorance and inequality
• Promote sustainable development in order to assure dignity, freedom, security and justice for all
• Avail self of education and meaningful work so one can develop one's talents through diligent endeavor
• Lend support to the needy, disadvantaged, disabled and discriminated
• Use all property and wealth responsibly
• Use economic and political power in the service of economic justice and the social order
Truthfulness and tolerance
• Speak and act truthfully
• Respect privacy and personal and professional confidentiality
• Develop and adhere to codes of ethics
• Hold politicians, public servants, business leaders, scientists, writers and artists accountable to ethical standards
• Responsibly use media to inform public and criticize social institutions, leading to a more just society
• Foster tolerance and mutual respect (value diversity and avoid prejudice and acts of discrimination)
Mutual respect and partnership
• Respect the responsibility of caring for people in personal relationships (show respect and understanding)
• Ensure that marriage guarantees security and mutual support (provide love, loyalty and forgiveness)
• Engage in sensible family planning
• Do not exploit, abuse or maltreat children or partner
• Parent/child relationships should reflect mutual love, respect, appreciation and concern
Must not destroy any of the responsibilities, rights and freedoms set forth in this Declaration and in the Universal Declaration of Human Rights of 1948

4.1 Solidarity and Collective Action

This aspect of consumer responsibility refers to people organizing to develop strength and influence so as to promote and protect their common interests. A responsible consumer is supposed to work with other consumers (solidarity) and take assertive action to lobby for the consumer interest and make the consumer voice heard by government and business. Cooperative efforts through the formation of citizens groups can better ensure that adequate attention is given to the consumer interest. Collective solidarity better ensures that consumers can counter the activities of powerful and influential business and government agencies. Solidarity as a responsibility means exhibiting honesty, integrity, fairness and striving to meet one's potential while not abusing power and wealth. A consumer society fosters individualism. Consumer responsibility is best achieved through active cooperation and solidarity among people, and through the will to subordinate one's own interests to the common good. Consumers need to acquire knowledge and critical awareness if they wish to confidently act to make their collective voices heard.

4.2 Critical Awareness

Responsible consumers will be critically aware of and question the goods and services they consume (including price and quality). Why and what is behind people consume should be just as important as what they consume. Critical awareness is a process of making sense of factors external to the current purchase scenario through an analysis of issues and information. This requires the ability to critically analyze issues, which entails the identification of underlying values, rules, and beliefs that made the consumer purchase an issue. This means not taking things at face value but understanding the root causes. In the process of identifying and analyzing consumer scenarios, people must also be aware of the context in which they occur. The context influences the direction of how a consumer issue develops as well as the effectiveness of a choice of action (see Miller 1993). If someone is *critically* aware, they analyze a situation for its merits and faults and then come to a justifiable decision or choice of action. If consumers are uncritical, they can be a combination of gullible, naive, trusting, unsuspecting, and ignorant, having little knowledge. Critical consumers will be able to distinguish between needs and wants, privileging the former.

4.3 Action and Involvement

Consumers who are responsible will assert themselves and take action rather than be passive. They will act confidently and forcefully to make their voices heard, especially in individual consumer transactions. Regarding the latter, being assertive means feeling self-assured, and speaking for oneself while not stepping on other people's toes. Consumers who assert themselves would respect others' boundaries and rights while protecting their own boundaries and rights. As long as consumers remain passive and are not assertive, they will continue to be exploited and taken advantage of in the marketplace. Exploiting someone means taking unfair advantage of their circumstances. To jumpstart involvement and action, consumers can start with themselves and then move onto others around them, and then onto their community, nation, and globally.

Inaction and lack of involvement are irresponsible because they give power to other actors in the marketplace, setting up the dynamic of exploitation and exclusion, whether it be from the economy, society or the polity. Assertive action and involvement entails people acting to ensure they (and others) get equitable treatment and a fair and just transaction. Making the marketplace accessible to everyone corresponds to equality (everyone treated the same), but ensuring that consumers are provided with the support they personally need to get a fair transaction represents equity.

4.4 Environmental Awareness

It is essential to exercise critical judgment regarding the pressure to purchase goods and services of all sorts and to assess their impact on the environment, social relationships and overall well-being. Ecologically responsible consumers will (a) understand the environmental consequences of their consumption patterns and (b) recognize their individual and social responsibility to conserve resources and protect the earth for future generations. The UN consumer protection guidelines (consumer rights) intentionally flagged consumers as responsible "for promoting public participation and debate on sustainable consumption, for informing consumers, and for working with Government and business towards sustainable consumption" (United Nations 2003, p. 8).

With environmental awareness, people would develop an active relationship with the environment while maintaining a critical attitude toward consuming. They would appreciate the interdependence between the environment and human activity, especially consumption. Environmentally aware consumers would also recognize the difference between individual and collective needs, personal wants and needs, and take a critical stance toward the social, economic and ethical aspects of consumption as they relate to the environment. Environmentally sensitive consumers would be aware of possible conflicts between their desire to own things and the destruction of the environment (Learn Quebec 2015).

4.5 Social Concern and Social Responsibility

This responsibility comprises (a) being sensitive to the impact of one's consumption on other citizens, especially disadvantaged or powerless groups, whether in the local, national or international community; and (b) taking into account individual concerns of consumers and the shared concerns of society at large. Purchasing power is real power. With sensitive consumption, people can be concerned for others and act in a socially responsible manner to help bring about a just and better world. Socially responsible consumers will be sensitive to the prevailing economic, social and political realities, and act accordingly. Being aware of the impact of one's consumption decisions on other citizens (social concern) and the environment will mean that decisions about whether or not to consume a good or service will be made using choice criteria that include: the impact on another's standard of living, working conditions, gender relations, moral and material interests, intellectual property, and social security (i.e., health, education and social welfare).

5 Matching Eight Consumer Rights with Corresponding Consumer Responsibilities

Tulsian and Tulsian (2003) explained that there are two types of consumer responsibility, (a) duties in relation to consumer rights, and (b) duties in relation to other consumers. Regarding the former, many governments, consumer organizations, and industry sectors eschew the Consumers International model of five consumer responsibilities (in effect, duties to other consumers). Instead, they contrast the eight consumer rights with their attendant consumer responsibilities, see Table 1.

This approach to consumer responsibilities seems to focus on individual consumer transactions in the marketplace, while Consumers International's approach (i.e., five consumer responsibilities) concerns people's larger obligations to the community, society, and the ecosystem. The latter involves solidarity, collective action, assertive consumers, critically aware consumers, and a deep awareness of the connections between consumption and environmental sustainability. These are macro concepts, relative to consumers entering each micro transaction with an acknowledged appreciation of their rights as consumers and their accountability for their actions (i.e., responsibilities). Both the macro and micro approach to consumer responsibilities have merit, in that each reinforces the imperative that rights imply responsibilities.

6 Linking Consumer Rights with Human Rights

This section briefly examines the premise that people cannot exercise their consumer rights if they do not have human rights. It serves as a segue to the final idea in this contribution—being a responsible consumer means being a responsible human (with inspiration from the burgeoning human responsibility movement). Fazal (1979, 2011) stated that he felt compelled to add an eighth consumer right, that of basic human needs, inspired by the International Labor Organization's promotion of the *basic needs* approach. This approach attempts to define the absolute minimum resources necessary for long-term physical well-being, usually in terms of consumption goods purchased by the consumer.

Fazal (1979) reasoned that people have the right to purchase and use basic goods and services necessary for their survival, including water, shelter, clothing, utilities, sanitation, education, and health care. People have a right to consume so they can better ensure freedom, equality, and adequate conditions of life. In his historical commentary on the global consumer movement, Hilton (2009) actually had a chapter titled *Choose Life: Consumer Rights Versus Human Rights*. He explained that Western leaders of the consumer movement favored rights (especially the right to choice) and were adamantly against Fazal's "attention to duties and responsibilities" (p. 201). Furthermore, Western advocates felt that a focus on basic needs, human rights, and consumer responsibilities took the issue too far from the narrowly conceived interests of consumers in the West, who privileged rights.

Nonetheless, Hilton (2009) recognized the import of the additional consumer right to basic human needs, characterizing it as an outlier, seemingly detached from the main system of ideas (i.e., the other seven consumer rights, see Table 1). He believed this outlier, with its focus on people having the right to consume essential goods and services pursuant to their basic survival, "better ensures the defense of those human rights set out in Articles 22–27 of the Universal Declaration [of Human Rights] (Hilton 2009, p. 193). These six articles deal with what the government should do to ensure employment and working conditions, social security, leisure, standards of living, education, moral and material interests/authorship, and arts and cultural enjoyment (United Nations 1948).

The following discussion is predicated on the assumption that we cannot have consumer rights without human rights, and draws mainly on McGregor's (1999, 2003, 2010) contributions to this idea. Human rights ensure against the denial of the full humanity of a person due to oppressive, prejudicial, discriminatory actions of their government (not corporations). Human rights are inalienable, meaning incapable of being surrendered or transferred. These rights apply to every single person on this earth simply because they are living on this earth.

As a caveat, this contribution is not concerned with whether corporations are respecting human rights. The state is supposed to protect human rights while corporations are supposed to respect them. "The responsibility to respect human rights is a global standard of expected conduct for all business enterprises wherever they operate. It exists independently of States' abilities and/or willingness to fulfil their own human rights obligations, and does not diminish those obligations. And it exists over and above compliance with national laws and regulations protecting human rights" (United Nations 2011, p. 14).

6.1 United Nations Declaration of Human Rights

The United Nations' (1948) Declaration of Human Rights comprises 30 articles organized around six themes: (a) born free and equal (2 articles, 1–2); (b) civil and political rights (next 19 articles, 3–21); (c) economic, social and cultural rights (next 8 articles, 22–27); (d) social and international context within to achieve rights;

that is, peace and human security (1 article, 28); (e) duties to protect rights and freedoms of *others* in the community (1 article, 29); and, (f) one last article (30), which says that no one can take any one of the rights out of context and use it as an excuse to violate other rights in the Declaration, and that every single person, group, organization, and government is responsible for making the Declaration *work*.

In more detail, *civil and political rights* refer to recognition under the law; a fair trial; freedom of movement in and out of a country; freedom from arbitrary arrest, detention or exile; and freedom from torture. They also include the rights to privacy, to have a family, to own property, to engage in free, conscious thought, public assembly, and participation in government. The *economic, social and cultural rights* pertain to: employment and working conditions, social security, leisure, standards of living, education, moral and material interests/authorship, and arts and cultural enjoyment (United Nations 1948).

6.2   Relating UN Human Rights to Consumer Rights

Even at first glance, there is potential tension between one's consumer rights and one's human rights. Consumer rights *assume* the existence of human rights. How can one exercise the consumer right to have a voice in the policy process if one cannot vote or is not allowed to participate in government? How can consumer groups form to collectively voice consumers' opinions if people do not have the rights to assemble in groups in public and express their opinions, form or join a union, or enjoy security of person? How can people demand the right to consumer education when the education system is such that people cannot afford to attend, live too far away or there are no schools at all? This lack of access to education leads to illiteracy and ignorance in the general sense, and in the marketplace in particular. Also, how can people exercise their consumer right to information if they cannot read, or they lack freedom from interference of their privacy?

To continue, how can people exercise their consumer rights to basic needs or to safe goods and services if they do not have access to public services, proper sanitation, safe drinking water, or adequate shelter and clothing, or to a standard of living adequate for health and well-being? How can people exercise their consumer right to make choices in the marketplace if they do not have equal pay, adequate incomes or steady employment (the right to work), cannot move freely within the country, do not have the right to own property, do not have free thought, and have no rest or leisure time. More thought provoking, how can people exercise their consumer right to redress if they are not recognized as a person under the law, do not have access to justice, the right to effective remedy under the law, and cannot express opinions in public? Human rights have to be in place in order for people to exercise their consumer rights.

There is also a real tension between consumers' rights and the rights of other humans; that is, sometimes one's rights as a consumer impinge on the rights of other humans living in the global family (and this is where responsibility kicks in). Of all of the consumer rights, the right to choice seems to be the one that impinges the most on the human rights of other people (Hilton 2009). In order to assure choice in the Northern markets, governments have implemented trade laws to facilitate cross border transactions and transnational corporations (TNCs) have set up business off shore so they can lessen the cost of the production process. Unfortunately, in too many cases, the goods that are available in the Northern markets are provided by slave labor, child labor, prison labor and sweatshops or in countries that allow the TNCs to forego adhering to pollution or ecological concerns and human rights in pursuit of profit. Worse yet, elitist governments are often bribed to turn their eyes the other way leading to situations where labor rights are abused in efforts to earn more profits. This practice leads to abhorrent working conditions, job insecurity, and low living standards (all human rights). Consumers in Northern countries have been socialized to want more and more things to consume but have not been socialized to appreciate the impact of their consumption choices on the human rights of other people; that is, they are not always responsible for their decisions (McGregor 2010).

7   Linking Consumer Responsibilities with Human Responsibilities

Fazal claimed that during the 1980s, a new consumer conscience developed, based on global thinking, environmentalism, human rights, cultural diversity, and responsibility for the future (as cited in Hilton 2009). This sentiment was a departure from the conventional wisdom that the consumer movement was about protecting the consumer interest from oppressive business power by formalizing consumer rights. Hilton (2009) concurred, claiming that IOCU's (1980) five consumer responsibilities pushed the consumer movement into issues of poverty reduction, global justice, and sustainability, away from the original core concern for the rights of consumers relative to business, grounded in Western values of individual economic rights rather than global solidarity and co-responsibility.

Without a sense of responsibility in the consumer arena, "individuals act as atoms, unencumbered by social responsibilities and duties, free of the obligation to account for their preferences and choices. They are never required to endure sacrifices for a superior goal, nor do their actions represent anybody but themselves. They need not defer to any collective majority" (Gabriel and Lang 1995, p. 175). This section connects consumer responsibilities with human responsibilities, drawing on the global movement for a United Nations Declaration of Human Responsibilities (see McGregor 2013).

7.1   InterAction Council's Declaration of Human Responsibilities

There is a burgeoning, if not well coordinated, global movement for a declaration of human responsibilities (McGregor 2013). For illustrative purposes, this contribution will draw on the seminal work that spearheaded and inspired most of the other initiatives, that being the InterAction Council (1997). The Council is a committee of former heads of states and governments. Their work on human responsibilities started in 1987 and culminated in 1997 with a document entitled *A Universal Declaration of Human Responsibilities*. The Council is convinced that their declaration represents a necessary extension of Article 29 of the UN Declaration of Human Right (1948): "(1) Everyone has duties to the community in which alone the free and full development of his personality is possible."

The intent was to have the InterAction Council's (1997) declaration adopted by the United Nations, thereby ensuring a balance between rights and responsibilities at the United Nations. It did not receive sufficient state support when discussed at the UN, so it was never put to a formal vote. The InterAction Council continues to reaffirm and promote the merit of the Declaration. In the meantime, the declaration has been instrumental in reinforcing the notion that human rights and human responsibilities are mutually complementary (McGregor 2013).

The declaration comprises 19 articles, divided into six main topics: (a) fundamental principles of humanity (4 articles); (b) non-violence and respect for life (3 articles); (c) justice and solidarity (4 articles); truthfulness and tolerance (4 articles); and, mutual respect and partnership (3 articles). As with Article 30 of the human rights declaration, the final article of the human responsibility declaration says that no one can take any one of the responsibilities out of context and use it as an excuse to violate other responsibilities in the Declaration, and that every single person, group, organization and government is responsible for making the Declaration *work* (InterAction Council 1997) (see Table 2).

In more detail, the principles of humanity relate to treating everyone in a humane way and to the notions of self-esteem, dignity, good over evil, and the Golden Rule (do unto others as you would have done to you). Non-violence and respect for life also encompass responsibilities related to acting in peaceful ways, and respecting intergenerational and ecological protection. Justice and solidarity include honesty, integrity, fairness, sustainability, meeting one's potential, and not abusing wealth and power. Truthfulness and tolerance embrace the principles of privacy, confidentiality, honesty, and a respect for diversity. These principles apply to all people, politicians, business, scientists, professionals, media, and religions. Finally, the responsibility of mutual respect and partnerships includes caring for others' well-being, and appreciating and being concerned for the welfare and safety of others, especially when it comes to children and spouses but also to all men and women in partnerships (InterAction Council 1997).

7.2   Relating Consumer Responsibilities to Human Responsibilities

This section will share a comparison of Consumer International's (2015) five consumer responsibilities with the InterAction Council's (1997) declaration of human responsibilities (see Table 3), drawing on McGregor (1999, 2003). The five consumer responsibilities recognized by Consumers International inherently reflect the human responsibilities suggested by the InterAction Council.

7.3   Solidarity and Collective Action

First, consumers have the responsibility to organize themselves and to develop collective strength and influence so they can promote and protect their interests, referred to by CI as solidarity. The InterAction Council also suggested solidarity as a human responsibility and meant by this honesty, integrity, fairness and to strive to meet one's potential while not abusing power and wealth. A responsible consumer is supposed to work with other consumers (solidarity) and take assertive action to lobby for the consumer interest and make the consumer voice heard by government and business. A parallel human responsibility is justice and solidarity, especially using one's power in the service of economic justice and social order.

This responsibility also parallels the fundamental principle of humanity: accept responsibility for everyone in the spirit of solidarity. If these organized consumers spoke on behalf of the rights of citizens in other countries affected by northern consumption, they could have an impact on other citizens including their family well-being and standard of living, working conditions and labor laws, education, access to education, and their right to organize. They would be acting like a responsible human.

7.4   Critical Awareness

Second, consumers have the responsibility to be critically aware of, and to question, their choices in the marketplace, and the marketplace itself. This involves respecting the corresponding human responsibility of trustfulness, especially responsible use of the media to criticize social institutions. This consumption responsibility can also be equated to the human responsibility of mutual respect and partnerships relating to caring for others' well-being, welfare and safety, augmented by critically aware consumption decisions. Also, critically aware consumers would expect truthfulness, tolerance and honesty in all human relations, especially consumer transactions. Critical awareness also parallels the fundamental principle of humanity: accept responsibility for everyone in the spirit of solidarity.

Table 3 Comparison of Consumers International's consumers responsibilities and the InterAction Council's human responsibilities

Consumers International's Consumer Responsibilities	InterAction Council's Human Responsibilities
Solidarity and collective action Organize with other consumers to develop the strength and influence to promote and protect the consumer interest (rights)	*Justice and solidarity* • Use power in service of economic justice and social order *Fundamental principles of humanity* • Accept responsibility for everyone in spirit of solidarity *Non-violence and respect for life* • Resolve disputes with non-violence
Critical awareness Be more alert, critically aware and question all goods and services (design, production, marketing and selling), and the consumer society	*Justice and solidarity* • Promote sustainable development • Make serious effort to overcome adversity • Use power responsibly • Use power in service of economic justice and social order *Fundamental principles of humanity* • Accept responsibility for everyone in spirit of solidarity *Truthfulness and tolerance* • Respect privacy and confidentiality • Responsibly use media to criticize social institutions • Hold politicians and business leaders accountable
Action and involvement Take assertive action to ensure a fair deal/transaction; act confidently to exert one's power and make one's voice heard; remaining passive means loss of power	*Justice and solidarity* • Behave with integrity, honesty and fairness • Use power in service of economic justice and social order • Use all wealth responsibly • Avail self of education *Truthfulness and tolerance* • Respect privacy and confidentiality • Speak and act truthfully • Foster mutual respect *Non-violence and respect for life* • Resolve disputes with non-violence
Environmental awareness Understand and be sensitive to the ecological consequences of consumption; recognize responsibility to conserve and to consume sustainably	*Non-violence and respect for life* • Protect environment and other species *Justice and solidarity* • Use all wealth responsibly

(continued)

Table 3 (continued)

Consumers International's Consumer Responsibilities	InterAction Council's Human Responsibilities
	• Promote sustainable development *Truthfulness and tolerance* • Hold politicians and business leaders accountable • Responsibly use media to criticize social institutions
Social concern and social responsibility Be aware of the impact of consumption on other citizens, especially the disadvantaged and powerless (want equitable distribution of resources); take into account individual consumer's concerns and shared concerns of society relative to prevailing economic and social realities	*Fundamental principles of humanity* • Act in a humane way • Accept responsibility for everyone in spirit of solidarity *Justice and solidarity* • Use power in service of economic justice and social order • Make serious effort to overcome adversity • Lend support to needy *Truthfulness and tolerance* • Adhere to code of ethics • Hold politicians and business leaders accountable • Responsibly use media to criticize social institutions

Part of being critically aware is being cognizant of the context in which consumer transactions occur. This parallels the human responsibility of no one taking any one of the responsibilities out of context to use it as an excuse to violate other responsibilities in the Declaration. As well, the human declaration holds that every single person, group, organization and government is responsible for making the Declaration *work*. Responsible consumers would be consciously aware of the evolving politics of the global marketplace, and would hold politicians and business leaders accountable.

7.5 Action and Involvement

Third, responsible consumers would take action and get involved, be assertive rather than passive, and make a concerted effort to make their voice heard. Three parallel human responsibilities would be (a) acting in peaceful ways while making one's voice heard, respecting privacy and confidentiality, and being honest; (b) holding business, government, the media and other consumers to this high standard; and, (c) resolving disputes using non-violence.

7.6 Environmental Awareness

Fourth, the consumer responsibility to exercise environmental awareness parallels the general human responsibilities to (a) act in a non-violent way and respect life, including ecological protection; (b) exercise justice and solidarity, which includes sustainability, and respect for intra and inter-generational ecological imperatives; and, (c) respect truthfulness and tolerance by way of holding politicians and business leaders accountable, and responsibly using the media to critique the state of the global market and society.

7.7 Social Concern and Responsibility

Finally, social concern deals with being aware of the impact of one's consumption decisions on other citizens. If consumers were responsible humans, they would moderate their consumption decisions by being concerned with the Golden Rule, and by holding all marketplace players accountable. They would respect justice, solidarity, diversity, other's well-being, their standard of living and their working conditions. The consumer social concern and social responsibility parallels the human responsibilities of fundamental principles of humanity, justice and solidarity, and truthfulness and tolerance.

8 Conclusion

There are deep connections between consumer rights and responsibilities, and even more compelling, between consumer and human rights and responsibilities. Whether they perceive it or not, Northern Consumers are powerful collective players in a powerful global marketplace. Such power demands accountability. Yes, their interests need to be protected but they must also step forward and embrace the responsibility imperative. Conversely, Southern consumers are often disadvantaged in the marketplace, relative to business and relative to Northern consumers. They are negatively impacted on many fronts, as is the environment. Their human rights need to be protected by way of other consumers behaving as responsible humans.

All humans have responsibilities to each other, especially when they enter their consumer role; however, many people do not see themselves as responsible humans when they consume. They think they have consumer rights and deserve to be protected from business but the consequences of any irresponsible choices echo across the world, spilling over onto other humans, species, and the environment. The notion of consumer responsibilities gains another dimension when correlated with human rights and responsibilities.

References

Bannister, R., & Monsma, C. (1982). *The classification of concepts in consumer education [Monograph 137]*. Cincinnati, OH: South-Western Publishing.

Consumers International. (2013). *Consumers International proposals for amendments to the UN guidelines for consumer protection*. Geneva: UNCTAD. Accessed December 30, 2015, from http://unctad.org/meetings/en/Contribution/IGE2013_UNGCP_CI_en.pdf

Consumers International. (2015). *Consumer rights*. Accessed December 30, 2015, from http://www.consumersinternational.org/who-we-are/consumer-rights/

Fazal, A. (1979, February 12). *A charter for consumer action*. In Keynote at the UNIDO/IOCU seminar, Ankara, Turkey. Accessed December 30, 2015, from http://www.anwarfazal.net/speech-Charter.php

Fazal, A. (1982). *The new consumer movement: Acceptance speech for Right Livelihood Award*. Accessed December 30, 2015, from http://www.rightlivelihood.org/fazal_speech.html

Fazal, A. (2011, March 17). *A vision for consumer empowerment* [Web log post]. Accessed December 30, 2015, from http://consumersinternational.blogspot.ca/2011/03/vision-for-consumer-empowerment.ht/ml. http://consumersinternational.blogspot.com/

Gabriel, Y., & Lang, T. (1995). *The unmanageable consumer*. Thousand Oaks, CA: Sage.

Hilton, M. (2009). *Prosperity for all: Consumer activism in an era of globalization*. Ithaca, NY: Cornell University Press.

Houde, M.-F. (2010). *Annual report on the OECD guidelines for multinational enterprises 2009: Consumer empowerment*. Paris: OECD.

InterAction Council. (1997). *A universal declaration of human responsibilities*. Berlin: InterAction Council. Accessed December 30, 2015, from http://www.interactioncouncil.org/sites/default/files/udhr.pdf

International Organization of Consumers Unions. (1980). *Consumer action in developing countries—A consumer action charter [Consumercraft 1]*. Penang: IOCU.

Johnson, M. (2014, May 23). *8 consumer rights and responsibilities: How to be protected* [Web log post]. Accessed December 30, 2015, from https://blog.udemy.com/consumer-rights-and-responsibilities/

Learn Quebec. (2015). *BAL: Environmental awareness and consumer rights and responsibilities*. Laval, QC: Learn Quebec. Accessed December 30, 2015, from http://www.learnquebec.ca/en/content/curriculum/bal/env_cons/

Malcolm, J. (Ed.). (2013). *Updating the UN guidelines for consumer protection for the digital age*. Kuala Lumpur: Consumers International.

McGregor, S. L. T. (1999). Globalizing consumer education: Shifting from individual consumer rights to collective, human responsibilities. In *Proceedings of the 19th international consumer studies and home economics research conference* (pp. 43–52). Belfast: Ulster University.

McGregor, S. L. T. (2003). Globalizing and humanizing consumer education: A new research agenda. *Journal of the Home Economics Institute of Australia, 10*(1), 2–9.

McGregor, S. L. T. (2010). *Consumer moral leadership*. Rotterdam: Sense Publishers.

McGregor, S. L. T. (2012). *Consumer interest research (CIR) primer for policy-making purposes*. Ottawa, ON: Industry Canada, Office of Consumer Affairs. Accessed December 30, 2015, from http://www.consultmcgregor.com/documents/research/S_McGregor_report_on_Consumer_Interest_Research_for_posting.pdf

McGregor, S. L. T. (2013). Human responsibility movement initiatives: A comparative analysis. *Factis Pax (Journal of Peace Education and Social Justice), 7*(1), 1–26. http://www.infactispax.org/volume7dot1/mcgr.pdf

Miller, K. (1993). Assisting our communities: Critical awareness and self-direction. *Community Services Catalyst, 23*(1). Accessed December 30, 2015, from https://scholar.lib.vt.edu/ejournals/CATALYST/V23N1/miller.html

Schmidt, H. (1997, April 20–22). A *universal declaration of human responsibilities*. Berlin: InterAction Council. Accessed December 30, 2015, from http://www.interactioncouncil.org/a-universal-declaration-of-human-responsibilities.

Singh, B. (2001). *Consumer education on consumer rights and responsibilities*. Petaling Jaya: Direct Selling Association of Malaysia. Accessed December 30, 2015, from http://www.ciroap.org/ce/doc/cons_edu_final.pdf

Tulsian, P. C., & Tulsian, S. D. (2003). *ISC Tulsian's commerce for class XI* (2nd ed.). Delhi: Ratna Sagar P. Ltd.

United Nations. (1948). *The universal declaration of human rights (A/RES/3/217A)*. Paris: United Nations. Accessed December 30, 2015, from http://www.un-documents.net/a3r217a.htm

United Nations. (2003). *United Nations guidelines for consumer protection (as expanded in 1999) (Resolution 39/248)*. New York, NY: United Nations Retrieved from http://www.un.org/esa/sustdev/publications/consumption_en.pdf.

United Nations. (2011). *Guiding principles on business and human rights (Res 17/4)*. New York, NY: Human Rights Council. Accessed December 30, 2015, from http://www.ohchr.org/Documents/Publications/GuidingPrinciplesBusinessHR_EN.pdf

Society and Policy Maker's Responsibilities

Jennifer Kuzma

1 Introduction

Products on the market are designed to fulfill the needs of the consumers of those products. Product developers design, produce, and test them for efficacy to fulfill their purpose and for safety to consumers under conditions of use. However, the public sector plays an important role in overseeing developers' activities in production methods, such as monitoring laboratory and manufacturing processes, and in reviewing safety studies, often before the product enters the market. In some cases, the public sector also has authority to ensure that post-market monitoring occurs and to pull products from the market should any problems occur. Public sector organizations may also test products on the market to verify producer claims or to ensure safety and quality. Finally, the public sector funds applied research and development (R&D) on products through grants or contracts. Definitions of what constitutes the "public sector" vary, but all include government at their core. Therefore, the focus in this contribution is on government organizations especially at the national level where many of the decisions are made.

The contribution starts with a broad framing of consumer product governance. First, it overviews the cycle of product development and articulates the ethical responsibilities of public actors in governance systems. Principle-based ethics will be used to categorize some of these responsibilities, including principles of beneficence, non-maleficence, autonomy, integrity, and fairness. Sometimes principles will conflict in making particular decisions about products, and ethical dilemmas will result. In addition, the role of government policy-makers can be limited by the law, political climate, or capacity. Thus, resolving dilemmas in policy-making

J. Kuzma (✉)
School of Public and International Affairs, North Carolina State University, Campus Box 7565, Raleigh, NC 27695-7565, USA
e-mail: jkuzma@ncsu.edu

© Springer International Publishing AG 2017   547
G. Emilien et al. (eds.), *Consumer Perception of Product Risks and Benefits*,
DOI 10.1007/978-3-319-50530-5_29

involves the balancing of multiple objectives and an analysis of tradeoffs. This moves the discussion from ethical principles to policy criteria by which product oversight can be evaluated. In this context, the contribution presents specific criteria that have been formulated for oversight systems of consumer products. Examples of the differences and tradeoffs among sets of oversight policy criteria will be discussed.

The above sections of the contribution take a "top-down" look at responsibilities in consumer product governance, but the question arises as to whether the broader ethical principles or policy criteria from a systems perspective match the desires and expectations of consumers. In this context, a review of research on risk perception and social psychology is reviewed to better understand the factors and values affecting consumer attitudes towards products. Then, consumer preferences for oversight of food products made with nanotechnology (nano-foods) or genetic modification (GM foods) is presented to highlight more specific factors important to consumers. Areas of concordance and mismatch between the U.S. system for reviewing consumer products and consumer desires will be discussed.

Finally, the ethical principles, policy-system criteria, and consumer desires will be used to suggest ways of moving forward for novel products. Newer models in the social science literature present some guidance in moving from contested to more collaborative climates for governance of consumer products, and one is reviewed to illustrate this shift. However, in closing, the limitations of what policy-makers can deliver from practical and political standpoints are acknowledged.

2   Product Governance Systems and the Roles of the Public Sector

Governance is a broader term than "regulation" and can include any part of a system that attends to watchful and responsible care (Kuzma 2006). Thus, it includes formal, regulatory policies and procedures, as well as voluntary programs and informal codes of conducts. Governance involves state and non-state actors with multiple perspectives and goals in making consumer products available to publics. Governance occurs throughout the consumer product development chain, from product research and development, safety and efficacy testing, manufacturing, and post-market monitoring. Typically, the public sector has played the biggest role in the testing or review of products in government regulatory systems, but also has responsibilities in other stages of product development.

Responsibilities of the public sector with regard to consumer products can be thought of in terms of ethical principles. Principles of bioethics have been used for medicinal products in clinical settings (Beauchamp and Childress 2001) and have also been applied to the development and deployment of agricultural and consumer products (Kuzma and Besley 2008; Thompson et al. 2007). These include autonomy, beneficence, nonmaleficence, justice, and integrity. Scholars have spent considerable effort in defining these principles which are only briefly defined below for the purposes of examining government responsibilities to consumers.

Autonomy is to be able to make decisions for oneself without controlling interferences, with adequate understanding, and free from personal limitation. Beneficence is the active promoting of good or reduction of harm, while nonmaleficence is more passively preventing or not inflicting harm. Justice broadly, involves the idea that like cases should be treated alike and employs the concept of fairness. Fairness has multiple dimensions including (1) outcome or distribution, (2) process (including citizen voice), (3) interpersonal treatment, and (4) access to information (Colquitt et al. 2005). Thus, justice can include fairness in the distribution of goods or in procedures. Finally, integrity is both a virtue and a principle to guide action. It requires consistent, honest and truthful actions free of hypocrisy.

Sometimes principles will conflict in making particular decisions about products and ethical dilemmas will result. In addition, the role of public policy-makers can be limited by the law, political climate, expertise, data, knowledge, or capacity. Thus, resolving dilemmas in policy-making involves the balancing of multiple objectives and an analysis of tradeoffs. Below, consumer product development is discussed in the context the public sector's role in governance with regard to these principles.

3 Research and Development

Initial use-inspired basic research for consumer products often originates in public-sector academic or government labs. During basic research, exact products are not necessarily conceptualized yet and thus conscience decisions to protect consumers are not necessarily a part of the equation. Yet, these organizations must protect human research subjects through their Institutional Review Boards, the local environments through Institutional Biosafety Committees and Environmental Health and Safety guidelines, and research animals through Animal Use and Care Committee guidelines. Autonomy in the pursuit of research is balanced with social needs to keep the research free from human, animal, or environmental harm (non-maleficence). Beneficence is also relevant in actively pursuing research for the good of humankind or the planet.

When the research becomes more applied and consumer products are envisioned, patents can be pursued and act as a revenue generation strategy for public sector organizations. Since passage of some key acts in the mid-1980s (i.e., Bayh-Dole and Stevenson-Wydler Acts), public-organizations can seek intellectual property protection, such as patents, on public-funded work and then license these patents to private companies. Broad licensing follows a more open innovation model whereby many companies would have the opportunity to use the technology to develop the product, whereas exclusive licensing would allow just one or a few to do so. Beneficence comes into play in what licensing schemes would do the most overall "good" for society. In some cases, exclusive licensing can lead to more rapid development of products given the greater chance of making profits due to the semi-monopoly on the technology patented. That could ultimately be beneficial to consumers. On the flip side, however, there are arguments that better innovation would come from more open platforms of technology development. Public sector obligations to consumers at this stage might include the careful examination of whether broad or exclusive licensing is in the best interest of not only their organization, but the public good.

Justice or fairness issues also come into play in choices to license a technology broadly or exclusively. Consumers most likely paid for the initial research leading to the product (e.g., through taxes going to government grants to universities or companies). Researchers in public organizations and their institutions could face the ethical dilemma of benefiting themselves as a "public good" versus repaying consumers downstream by business arrangements that promote lower prices for beneficial products. Pharmaceutical products illustrate the conflict. Discoverers of the precursors to key drugs in academe have choices whether to promote arrangements with companies that are more just or fair to patients who ultimately paid for the research.

4   Safety and Regulation

Many consumer products require regulatory safety testing by government prior to their sale on the market, while others do not. Drugs, pesticides, and food additives are regulated prior to market entry and call for extensive safety studies to be submitted to the Food and Drug Administration (FDA) (drugs and food additives) and the Environmental Protection Agency (EPA) (pesticides). Other products require no pre-market testing by government, such as dietary supplements, cosmetics, and toys; but the government does have authority to recall products if they are shown to be harmful once bought and used. Ethical principles and obligations of the public sector, especially government, are perhaps the greatest at this stage in product development as significant harm could come from products that are not safe. Furthermore, it is argued that in a democracy like the United States, consumers should have some voice and choice about products through labels or information about their safety and composition. On the other side, government also needs to ensure that products that could have great benefits are not unduly stifled or delayed by its regulatory efforts.

A key component of regulation, particularly in the United States, is to minimize direct risks to human health and the environment (non-maleficence) while promoting the economic and social well-being of societies (beneficence). United States regulatory review is based upon cost-benefit analysis or utilitarian points of view, as consumer products that are regulated are evaluated based upon "sound science"; that is their "science-based" impacts, such as health, environmental, and economic risks and benefits (White House 2011).

Ethical choices come into play in the weighing of risks and benefits to make decisions, and also in the burden of proof in a regulatory system. Some believe that formal government regulation must precede product entry into the marketplace and be based on comprehensive safety studies that strive to avoid type II errors (false negatives—or assumptions of no negative health effects when there are some). These viewpoints tend to be labeled as more precautious about product entry into the market. Others take the view that products can enter the market without substantial pre-market oversight, and safety studies and experience can accumulate while developers bring products to market. Goals in this view are to expedite product use and avoid type I errors (false positives—or assumptions of negative effects when there are none). These views are considered more promotional of industry and product entry.

However, ethical issues in oversight, and thus government obligations to consumers, transcend a minimizing of risk and maximization of benefit. They include accountability in a system—for example, procedural accountability or whether there is an appropriate framework for decisions which serves the public interest and resists the inappropriate influence of private interests (relating to ethical principles of fairness, autonomy to choose, and integrity); and substantive accountability, which seeks to ensure that the decisions are justifiable in terms of the public interest goals of the system (relating to beneficence and autonomy) (Ogus 2002). System accountability also involves people's rights to choose products based on their preferences, perhaps through government labeling programs, as well as the fair distribution of risks and benefits or costs (Kuzma and Besley 2008; Thompson et al. 2007).

The availability of information about the composition of products, safety studies, and decision-making processes is important for autonomy and informed consent. Governments have obligations in these regards as well, although they are often weighed by regulatory agencies against the current legal rights of companies to claim such information as confidential business information (Kuzma and Besley 2008).

Once products are out into the market, the government often mandates or supports post-market monitoring of potential adverse impacts. However, it depends on the law and regulatory statute as to whether this is a requirement for continued product approval. Pesticides require some post-marketing monitoring for adverse consequences in the environment so that they may be re-registered every 5 years; whereas chemicals used in manufacturing do not in the United States. The absence of post-market monitoring makes even more important the role of the government during initial regulatory approval. Without post-market monitoring, it can take many years for adverse events to be reported and linked to the cause through epidemiological studies. Even then, the results of such linkages are sometimes contested in the courts by the product developers. Thus, the initial regulatory approval might warrant more precaution when formal post-market monitoring is not in place so that non-maleficence is respected.

5   Ethical Dilemmas

The public's obligations to consumers involve many principles that will conflict. For example, if regulation is too stringent in its avoidance of maleficence, beneficial drugs may not be available to consumers or could become too pricey. If transparency is increased during regulatory review in order to respect autonomy, business might lose profit through have to share confidential business information (CBI), thus jobs could decline, and consumers could ultimately lose jobs (non-maleficence). Within cost-benefit analysis itself, the estimation and incorporation of non-monetary costs, like death, illness, or ecological damage, is value-laden, and thus utilitarian calculations of these are not without assumptions and ethical choices. How much is a life worth? Are the older less valuable than the young? How much is a bird worth, or a clean river?

Consumer products can also impact socioeconomic systems in unpredictable ways. For example, they could create or destroy jobs; or change cultures for better or worse. What are the government's responsibilities in estimating and considering these impacts? The role of the public sector is often limited by law or regulation. For example, the FDA has authority to label food only when there are substantial changes to composition that might affect safety or nutrition under the Federal Food Drug and Cosmetic Act (FDCA). Although most consumers want to see their food labeled with processing information, such as whether a food comes from genetically engineered organisms (GEOs) or not, FDA might not be able to do so without new laws from Congress. Furthermore, even if it could, would labeling benefit consumers' lives? Autonomy and non-maleficence could conflict: labeling would likely increase consumer autonomy, but also could make food more expensive, thus decreasing consumer well-being.

So then how should these ethical dimensions be considered in the obligations of governments to consumers? This question moves us into the realm of policy analysis, and from ethical criteria to policy criteria.

6   Principles of Good Oversight of Consumer Products

Policy analysis has ethical foundations in the valuation of criteria by which alternatives are judged. In policy analysis, first a problem is identified and then alternatives to remedy or address the problem constructed. Tradeoffs among alternatives are evaluated by the consistent application of criteria such as efficiency (e.g., cost-benefit ratios), efficacy (e.g., how well the alternative addressed the policy problem), equity or fairness (distribution of costs and benefits), procedural transparency or fairness (who has voice and choice), and flexibility (ability to change if warranted). Oversight policy as a subset of public policy likewise can be judged by criteria.

Two Contrasting Views on Criteria for Oversight

In United States, the White House published principles of oversight for emerging technologies (White House ETIPC 2011). These provide indications of the responsibilities of the public sector for oversight of consumer products and include scientific integrity, public participation, communication, benefits and costs, flexibility, risk assessment and risk management, coordination, and international cooperation. Notably, many stress the priority of "science-based" risks, benefits, and costs. Scientific integrity is described "based on the best available scientific evidence" and "adequate information", yet it also states that "to the extent feasible, purely scientific judgments should be separated from judgments of policy." This is problematic based on the view of many social science and risk analysis scholars who argue that there cannot be "purely scientific judgments".

In fact, it is impossible to be completely "science based" in a regulatory system, as science cannot tell us what to do. For example, we might know the dose response curve for the harm caused by a certain product based on exposures, but that does not tell us where to draw the line for an acceptable safety limit for that product. Even more often, we do not know that dose-response curve very well, or at all. This uncertainty leads to various interpretations of the data into which we bring our own world-views to bear. The science gives us a guide, but what should be regulated and what is safe are based on values, taking into consideration the benefits, controllability, familiarity and other features of the system in which the product is embedded.

It is also striking that these principles do not frame scientific integrity with principles of honesty, lack of hypocrisy, and judgments that minimize conflict of interest and bias. These issues have been prominent in multiple case studies of product oversight, leading to decreased trust, transparency, and sometimes skewed results or interpretations. For example, a meta-analysis of publications in the biomedical sciences found that the results of articles associated with industry sponsorship had a significant correlation with pro-industry conclusions and that industry sponsorship was also associated with restrictions on publication and data sharing (Bekelman et al. 2003).

These U.S. government principles do include procedural criteria like communication of the risks and benefits to the public and public participation. However, these are not given priority over other types of criteria such as the ability of business to profit through maintaining CBI, and are to be done "to the extent feasible and subject to valid constraints" (White House ETIPC 2011). The criteria do state that public participation is important for accountability, increasing trust, and better decisions. Typically in consumer product regulatory decisions, federal register notices with comment periods are the only window into the process for the public and the major way to participate.

It is only in the criteria of coordination where the word ethics arises, and then it is heavily qualified: "federal agencies should seek to coordinate…to address the breadth of issues, including health and safety, economic, environmental, and ethical issues (where applicable) associated with the commercialization of an emerging technology, in an effort to craft a coherent approach" (White House ETIPC 2011).

This illustrates that economic and direct health and environmental safety take precedence over ethics, although most scholars agree that ethics cannot be separated from these endeavors. The choice of endpoints for safety testing, the interpretation of data for sensitive subpopulations, whether a precautious or promotional choice is taken in the face of uncertainty, choice of value of life or illness and discount rate figures in cost-benefit analyses, and determining when there is enough information to make a decision are all choices of value judgements. In fact, the principles document itself makes plenty of value judgements in that the "benefits of regulation should justify the costs", the avoidance of "unjustifiably inhibiting innovation, stigmatizing new technologies, or creating trade barriers", and the "promotion of innovation while also advancing regulatory objectives."

The principles document has a neoliberal position on the role of government regulation for consumer products, with a promotional stance on technological development at its core. This is a worldview not shared by all U.S. citizens, especially groups previously disproportionately affected by risks of consumer products such as females and racial minorities. Work based on cultural theory shows that people who are relatively "egalitarian and communitarian", more often women and racial minorities, are naturally sensitive to environmental and technological risks and believe that regulating commercial activities to reduce risk is justified in order to reverse social inequality and constrain self-interest (Kahan et al. 2007). Those who are more "individualistic or hierarchical" (often white males) tend to dismiss claims of environmental risk and are more committed to the autonomy of markets.

Non-profit groups with different worldviews than the U.S. government science and technology policy leaders have also developed principles of oversight for products stemming from emerging technologies. For example, the International Center for Technology Assessment (ICTA), a NGO critical of nanotechnology and biotechnology product development, published a set of criteria much different than the White House. ICTA takes a strong stance on the role of government in consumer product regulation in principles of a precautionary foundation; mandatory nano-specific regulations; health and safety of the public and workers; environmental protection; transparency; public participation; inclusion of broader impacts; and manufacturer liability (ICTA 2012). The ideas of protection, precaution, and liability are prominent in contrast to the White House principles. Public participation is given higher standing as well in that "open, meaningful and full public participation at every level is essential." The report also calls for the consideration of broader impacts, such as ethical, social, and economic ones, with specific attention to ethical principle of justice for the distribution of economic costs and benefits.

In the ICTA principles, burdens are also placed on product developers to demonstrate safety as "responsible stewards". The group endorses precaution as defined in the Louisville Charter for Safer Chemicals, which was drafted in response to the release of toxic air pollutants in poorer African American communities: "When an activity raises threats of harm to human health or the environment, precautionary measures should be taken even if some cause and effect relationships are not fully established scientifically" (Myers et al. 2005).

In U.S. government chemical regulation, particularly under EPA's Toxic Substances Control Act, often the burden of proof is on the federal agency to demonstrate unreasonable harm or risk through showing causal linkages between products and illness. Yet risk science in the public sector is notoriously underfunded, and although industry does conduct some product safety testing, it is often to meet the minimal regulatory standards and comes with conflict of interests (COI) and a lack of trust. The Catch-22 is that agencies usually do not have enough risk science information to demonstrate unreasonable harm, and therefore, chemicals pass through into the market without comprehensive safety testing (Davies 2006).

In contrast to the U.S government approach and White House principles, the ICTA, places consumer and worker protection first by keeping the product off the market until risk science accumulates. Precaution is an ethical worldview, no less or more scientific than the opposite worldview of promotion (i.e., burden of proof on agency's to show risk so that innovation can proceed).

7 Academic Work on Multi-Criteria Assessment of Oversight

Policy analysis approaches that employ multiple criteria for evaluation of options and tradeoffs can help to incorporate various societal concerns in decision making about consumer products. Multi-criteria decision analysis (MCDA) is a multidisciplinary field of analysis that relies on the notion that no single outcome or metric can capture the appropriateness or effectiveness of a system. MCDA allows for integrating heterogeneous information and evolved from operations research and refers to a range of approaches in which multiple criteria are developed, ranked, and used to compare alternatives for decision making. For MCDA focusing on analyzing risk, general categories of criteria have been described, such as utility-based criteria (cost, risk-benefit comparisons, and other outcomes), rights-based criteria (whether people have consented to risk), and best available technology-based criteria (use of best technologies available to reduce risk) (Linkov et al. 2007).

Another approach draws upon the strengths of MCDA to engage not only with the technical risk, but also with the social and ethical dimensions of oversight systems. For example, criteria by which oversight systems for consumer products could be evaluated have been developed through the use of stakeholder and expert elicitation, and then applied to multiple case studies of oversight (Kuzma et al. 2009). Significant quantitative relationships among normative (ethical), empirical (evidence-based), and procedural criteria were found, suggesting the inseparability of science and values in oversight systems. In several of the cases, U.S. oversight was found to be strong in its empirical basis, but weaker in institutional or normative dimensions.

For example, the oversight of genetically modified (GM) food products was shown to have weak legal grounding, few opportunities for public input, and low transparency (Kuzma et al. 2009). It has been hypothesized that mistakes made in not involving and informing the public early in GM food decisions continue to affect the agricultural biotechnology industry today and fuel contemporary consumer opposition to GM foods. GM food oversight was also found to be highly flexible which can be viewed as a strength and weakness. For example, the more flexible an oversight system, the better it can keep pace with changes in technological advances, but this also means that regulation can be loosened or strengthened over time due to political pressure (Kuzma 2014). Recently, several GM crops have not been regulated prior to market entry as a result of this flexibility, and this also fuels skepticism about GM foods.

In summary, governments have to weigh multiple priorities in overseeing consumer products, especially promoting innovation while protecting public health and the environment, and ensuring legitimacy and transparency. Perhaps the best approach is to allow for consumers, the ultimate funders of government programs to have more autonomy in the choice of which criteria are important to them for product oversight. For example, for each broad category of consumer products, interested and affected parties (including stakeholders and citizens) can deliberate about a set of evaluative criteria to judge an oversight system or regulatory decision. If a particular criterion is more important than another in a specific context (e.g., informed consent versus beneficence in product use) it can be weighted more heavily than others through MCDA approaches. Cumulative scores for one system alternative in comparison to another can be generated. Using public participation to develop a set of criteria for oversight for consumer products would increase autonomy and allow end users to make their own choices about what is important to them.

In summary, the government's obligations to consumers arguably should be determined by consumers themselves in order to maximize autonomy, informed consent, beneficence and non-maleficence, and justice. Models of public participation to accomplish this exist in the social science literature (Rowe and Frewer 2000) and might be ultimately less expensive than the product litigation and regulatory challenges that would otherwise ensue. Frameworks for bringing science together with value-choices and including interested and affect parties will be discussed further in the next section.

8 Case Study: Consumer Preferences for Nano and GM Food Products

The above sections of the contribution take a "top-down" look at responsibilities in consumer product governance, but what are the desires and expectations of consumers? Below is a brief review of literature on factors important to shaping consumer perception and attitudes about emerging products. Then, a description of some of our research on U.S. preferences for oversight of foods derived from nanotechnology and genetic engineering (nanofood or GM food) is presented.

9 Consumer Attitudes and Perceptions

Consumer perceptions, attitudes, and preferences towards products have been studied across a range of topics and technologies, as well as by several disciplines including marketing, economics, risk perception, and social and behavioral psychology. Perception refers to how an individual or members of the public regard or feel about something that presents uncertain or ambiguous risks and benefits based on stimuli and information they receive from a variety of sources and how they interpret that stimuli and information through a variety of sensory, affective, cognitive, psychosocial, experiential, cultural, and mental processes. Attitude, by contrast, refers to the way in which an individual or the public is predisposed to act in a particular situation based on their perception (Pickens 2005). Preference in the context of this contribution relate to the way consumers prefer the public sector to act with regard to product governance.

The processes and factors that contribute to perceptions of risks and benefits for technologies and their products have been studied and interpreted to form different theories and frameworks. For example, the psychometric paradigm focuses on identifying aspects of product and the risk associated with it, such as its whether or not it is dreaded, catastrophic, uncertain, voluntary, and novel. These factors influence perceptions of that risk and product, and ultimately attitudes, or judgments and decisions about that risk (Fischhoff et al. 1978). This theory would suggest that the government obligations are to reduce some of the anxiety provoking factors associated with consumer products such as uncertainty, involuntary exposure, unfamiliarity, and catastrophic risk.

There are also several sociological and cultural frameworks that emphasize the role of social factors in consumer attitudes towards products. Trust and confidence in social networks (e.g., social groups, communities, extended families and friends) and societal systems (i.e., the market, the political system, the regulatory system, news media,) play an important role in perceptions of risk for products, especially when those risks are new, uncertain, or ambiguous. They also influence people's reactions or behaviors in response to risk (for example, lack of trust in industry's ability to handle risk is associated with greater levels of political activism

(Rohrmann and Renn 2000). The social amplification of risk framework (SARF) focuses on the importance of intermediaries through which individuals receive risk information (e.g., media, government, industry, advertising, social groups, etc.). These sources can either amplify or attenuate risk information (Kasperson et al. 1988).

The above theories and frameworks generally explain factors and mechanisms that cause different risks to be perceived differently across individuals, but they are limited in explaining why individuals' risk perceptions vary according to those factors. They account more for variance against types of technological products or risk rather than variance across individuals. In contrast, there is a body of work that focuses on the values that people hold as predictors of perceptions and attitudes towards products, technologies, and risks. Core values are relatively stable over the course of an individual's life and provide a basis for attitudes and decisions especially in the face of new information. Values can also play a significant role in whom or what institutions people trust. For example, the more closely aligned people's values are with those of institutions responsible for managing products and risk, the more trust they have in those institutions (Whitfield et al. 2009). In particular, this relates to the obligations of government in product oversight, in that in order to gain and maintain trust, government policies and actions need to match the values of a variety of consumers and stakeholders, not just a few.

A key theory related to values and their effects on perceptions and attitudes is the cultural cognition of risk. According to cultural theory, differences in risk perception arise from differences in individuals' views of the world and ways of living (Douglas and Wildavsky 1983). According to the cultural cognition of risk, worldviews can be classified according to two cross-cutting dimensions or axes, egalitarian versus hierarchical and communal versus individualistic. These have been tested for a variety of environmental, health, and technological risks. For example, Douglas and Wildavsky (1983) suggest that those people who hold more egalitarian-collectivist worldviews tend to advocate against social institutions that produce inequality, whereas people with individualistic-hierarchical worldview tend to gravitate towards private control of activities and defend those with power and authority. Egalitarian-collectivists are generally more concerned with environmental risk associated with technologies or products, whereas individualistic-hierarchical people are more dismissive of these risks.

The cultural cognition hypothesis explains mechanisms for how individuals form their beliefs about risks to match their worldviews. Mechanisms of translating cultural worldviews to risk perception include identity-protective cognition; biased assimilation and group polarization; cultural credibility; cultural availability; and cultural identity affirmation, which relate to believing, seeking, or paying attention to risk information that supports your own world view or is conveyed by people whose worldviews match yours (Kahan 2012). Cultural cognition theory suggests that the government overseers of consumer products should use a variety of worldviews as lenses for the regulation of consumer products. Typically, this has not been the case. Leaders and decision-makers (e.g., division directors in government or company executives whom interact with them) are disproportionately

Caucasian males, who on average have higher individualistic-hierarchical world-views and thus rate product and technological risks as lower (Kahan et al. 2007). An opening up of regulatory processes to a greater diversity of people and perspectives might remedy this inequity and increase procedural justice.

In our own work with nano and GM foods, the above theories and frameworks have been useful for explaining perceptions and attitudes towards these products. Aspects of these studies related to consumers preferences for public sector oversight of these food products are discussed below.

10   Consumer Preferences for Nano- and GM Foods

The application of novel technologies to food, such as biotechnology and nano-technology, continues to grow rapidly. Genetically engineered (GE) crops constitute over 85% of corn, soybeans, and cotton grown in the United States. Food made with genetically-modified ingredients (GM foods) make up an estimated 70% of processed foods. While food derived from nanotechnology (nano-food) is presently limited in the market, numerous companies are pursuing nano-food applications for release to consumer markets with a predicted value of over $20 billion. It is being used in nano-modification of seed and fertilizers and pesticides, for food 'fortification' and modification, and interactive 'smart' food, packaging and tracking. The nanofood market is expected to surge from $2.6 billion US dollars today to 7.0 bn. US dollars in 2015 and to 20.4 billion US dollars in 2020, and more than 1200 Companies around the world are today active in research and development (Helmut Kaiser Consultancy 2015). Given the strong prevalence and interest in GM and nano-food, our work aimed to understand consumer perceptions of the benefits and risks, and their desires for labeling and oversight.

In one study, we compared GM and nano food with choice experiments in a large survey across the U.S. public (Yue et al. 2015b). Nano-foods evoked less negative reactions, as nanotechnology involves manipulation of "matter" and GM involves manipulation of living organisms (even if the food is consumed without living tissue). GM also caused more reduction in willingness to purchase and a higher willingness to pay to avoid them than nanotechnology across all groups of people and benefits. However, in both cases, willingness to pay for nano and GM food was significantly low, and consumers would pay an 87 cent premium to avoid nanofoods and a 96 cent premium to avoid GM food (Table 1). For both nano and GM foods, benefits of safety were the most accepted, followed by nutrition, and then the environment, and finally taste. In the case of nano-foods, certain benefits of better nutrition or food safety trumped the negative effect of nanotechnology. However the benefits of nutrition and safety were not enough to overcome the price premium consumers would tolerate to avoid GM foods.

In another study, we conducted focus groups to further inquire about public attitudes towards nanofoods and also found there that safety and nutrition, especially for poor or the elderly, were viewed most favorably by the participants

Table 1 Willingness to pay for GM or nano food products

Attributes	Willingness-to-pay ($/lb rice)	95% confidence interval
Nonotechnology	−0.87	(−0.97. −0.76)
GM	−0.96	(−1.08, −0.84)
Nutrition	0.92	(0.81, 1.03)
Safety	0.98	(0.86, 1.10)
Environment	0.57	(0.48, 0.66)
Taste	0.56	(0.46, 0.66)

(Brown and Kuzma 2013). We identified "altruism" as a potentially new attitudinal factor for consumer preferences (Brown et al. 2015). One participant summed it up as: "It seems like the nutrition, the longer shelf life, the potential for helping to feed the world's hungry, helping to get food, more food, and more nutrition that will last longer as it is being distributed."

In this same study, we also found that the participants were skeptical of the system into which nanofood products would be deployed, and we identified "skepticism" as potentially another new consumer perception factor (Brown et al. 2015). Skepticism is different from distrust in that it does not necessarily question whether someone or something can or should be trusted, but rather it questions claims that are not ascribed to anything specifically. Trust is ascribed to an actor (whether individual or institutional), whereas skepticism is not necessarily placed in an actor. Skepticism is broader and often system-wide, involving a questioning about whether events or attributes will exist as multiple parties or institutions believe or state. Feelings of skepticism may relate to events, processes, systems, or multiple institutions that are questioned. The following quotes illustrate a system-wide skepticism without pointing to a particular agency or actor:

> I mean it's most things in this world, I don't care if it is food or what it is, revolves around dollars, people will bring new technology, that is what they see at the end of the road. They are not trying to make me be 200, they are trying to fatten somebody's wallet and fill the big corporation whatever that takes, and they are willing to do a try. This nanotechnology wasn't free to develop, that is pretty obvious, somebody is going to pay for it, and so they are looking for ways to sell it to us. But with all our knowledge, nobody has billboards up that say get your food at Cub because we have nanotechnology. They are just sliding it in on us.

The quote also illustrates the importance of informed consent and autonomy to consumers, without which skepticism arises.

From these studies, we suggested that government should encourage technological investments towards the societal challenges that are most important (beneficence) and address system-wide skepticism by increasing the integrity of the processes (autonomy, informed consent) for which it has control or influence. Paying attention to altruism and skepticism may guide more responsible development of food products derived from emerging technologies in the future.

The above analysis focused on factors important to consumers embedded in the systems or products, but just like cultural theory states, consumers do not all think alike. When examining the data from the same survey, we identified four consumer segments with regard to what influenced their choice of product (Yue et al. 2015b). The first group, "Price Oriented/Technology Adopters," mainly factored price into their decisions, tended to be male, and favored benefits of taste over safety and nutrition (23% of participants). The second, "Technology Adverse," tended to be more female and would not generally choose GM or nano food, unless the technology was designed to improve safety (19% of participants). Group 3 "Technology Accepters/Benefits Orientation" was younger and would accept most GM or nano foods as long as the benefit was not taste (40% of participants). Group 4, "Technology Rejectors" was also more female but would not accept GM or nano food under any benefit conditions (18% of participants). In total, it is noteworthy that over 80% of those surveyed accepted nano or GM food under some benefit and price conditions.

Our study suggests that the majority of consumers will not reject these technologies outright, but rather base their decisions on a complicated calculus of benefits, risks, trust, and world views. Policy and government choices must then incorporate a variety of perspectives and not disenfranchise certain groups. For example, technology rejectors might be satisfied if they are given autonomy to reject the technology, and there is one thing that the vast majority of consumers do want to see, and that is food product labeling. Across numerous studies, people consistently desire positive labeling of GM foods (e.g., "this product contains"), although current U.S. policy is voluntary labeling for both positive and negative labeling for GM food. In our own study (Yue et al. 2015a), we found that people would like to see both nano and GM foods positively labeled (mean of 4.1 for each respectively out of a 5-point Likert scale "strongly agree" that foods containing these ingredients should be labeled).

However, in defense of current U.S. policy, some have made the argument that consumers "want to see everything on a label" and that it is not practical. To address this comment, we asked consumers in our study to prioritize, out of a list of 15 items, what they would most like to see on a food product label and asked them to choose only 3 of the 15 (Fig. 1). Presence of GM came second only to pesticide use, and nanotechnology came fourth.

As of February 2016, Congress is considering a bill to ban states from making their own decisions about GM food labeling, as some versions of state bills are due to go into effect in summer 2016 that would require it. However, this approach might not be in the best interest of consumers as they give GM food labeling very high priority, and ultimately might not be in the best interest of the industry. To increase autonomy and informed consent, which are clearly priorities for consumers especially groups with foundational objections to technologies, the government might want to reconsider mandatory GM food labeling. On ethical grounds, one could argue that in a democracy like the US, the government might be obligated to do so.

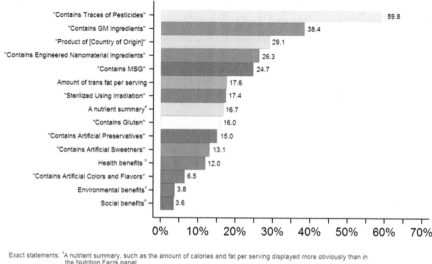

Exact statements: [a]A nutrient summary, such as the amount of calories and fat per serving displayed more obviously than in
the Nutrition Facts panel
[b]Health benefits such as "May reduce the risk of heart disease"
[c]Environmental benefits such as "Eco-friendly" or "Minimal Carbon Footprint"
[d]Social benefits such as "Fair Trade"

Fig. 1 Labeling priorities—selection percentage of top three choices

11 Moving Forward for New Products

"Sound science" should neither be ignored nor should it be the solitary basis for product decisions. Regulatory systems cannot be 100% based on science. Science cannot tell decision makers what to do, and values are always a part of setting safety standards and making other choices related to consumer products. So then whose values count? How do they count? Ethical principles, policy-system criteria, and consumer desires suggest ways of moving forward for new products. Currently, most product decisions are made between government agencies and the product developers, with little to no room for public or stakeholder input. Products go into the market, and most do no harm to consumers, but on the other hand, several need to be recalled after months or years of causing injury or illness, sometimes death. Consumers are willing to bear some uncertainty and risk about emerging products if the benefits are directed towards public good. Mistakes are bound to happen, but if the initial process of oversight was not fair or did not have integrity, skepticism and mistrust will increase. In a democracy, it is the obligation of the government to make decision-making processes fair to a range of perspectives, world views, and voices.

In order to do so, models in the social-science and policy-sciences literature present guidance in moving from contested to more collaborative climates for governance. One that has emerged recently and builds on several previous models is Responsible Research and Innovation (RRI). RRI has taken off in the European Union where it has been incorporated into EU policy for science, technology and innovation. The EU Commissioner, Maire Geoghegan-Quinn, in 2012 stated that "Research and innovation must respond to the needs and ambitions of society, reflect its values and be responsible ... *our duty as policy makers (is) to shape a governance framework that encourages responsible research and innovation.*" (Owen et al. 2012). A framework for RRI includes elements of anticipation, reflexivity, inclusion, and responsiveness which together embody the ethical principles, criteria, and consumer desires discussed in this contribution (Stilgoe et al. 2013). Each of these elements is briefly presented below.

Anticipation involves an early look at the promises and potential impacts that accompany consumer products far before they are to be released to the market. Intended and potentially-unintended impacts of products, including economic, social, environmental, and cultural ones are examined. It is a broader and earlier endeavor than the pre-market safety and risk assessments focused on direct health and environmental toxicity-testing that occupy most of U.S. decision making about products. Methodologies such as anticipatory governance, foresight, technology assessment, and scenario development are employed during upstream stages of product research and development to ask questions and explore possible implications that may otherwise remain hidden. Questions of what if, what is known, what is likely, what is plausible and what is possible are aimed to increase the resilience of innovation systems and socially-robust risk research before formal regulatory review.

Reflection strives to understand underlying purposes and motivations of product development, knowns and unknowns, uncertainties, areas of ignorance, assumptions, questions, and ethical dilemmas. Stilgoe et al. (2013) call for a "institutional reflexivity in governance", which puts the responsibility on institutions of practice, such as public-sector oversight, to hold "a mirror up to one's own activities, commitments and assumptions, being aware of the limits of knowledge and being mindful that a particular framing of an issue may not be universally held."

Inclusion involves a shift from top-down hierarchical decision-making to bottom-up and networked engagement. Deliberation brings new voices into governance of science and innovation through wider perspectives of public(s) and diverse stakeholders. It can help to reframe issues, identify areas of agreement and disagreement, and incorporate a wider array of knowledge and values. Consensus conferences, citizens' juries, deliberative mapping or polling, focus groups, and online forums are methods of upstream engagement that could be used to inform product regulatory decisions. At minimum, government advisory bodies should include lay persons as representatives, diverse experts with social science or humanities backgrounds, and a variety of stakeholders, in addition to the typical natural scientists and industry experts.

Responsiveness asks that the system of governance be open to modification in the face of changes in information, circumstances, technologies, and stakeholder and public values. Mechanisms for adaptive learning and capabilities to alter course or direction are critical, as well as openness and transparency. Flexible organizational cultures and arrangements can facilitate responsiveness. It also involves an honest recognition of the inability to fully predict outcomes from products entering the market, due to the fact there will always be uncertainty and a lack of full control. Post-market monitoring is essential with feedback loops in which diverse publics are re-engaged and science and value questions reconsidered.

To implement the framework of RRI and incorporate these four elements, Stilgoe et al. (2013) developed lines of questioning related to products, processes, and purposes of innovation. For example, the product line of question includes: will the risks and benefits be distributed? what other impacts can we anticipate? how might these change in the future? what don't we know about? and what might we never know about? The process line includes: how should standards be drawn up and applied? how should risks and benefits be defined and measured? who is taking part in these determinations? who will take responsibility if things go wrong? how do we know we are right? and what are the alternatives?

These questions, in addition to the ethical principles, policy criteria, and consumer desires discussed previously, can all provide guidance to policy-makers about ideal product governance for fulfilling ethical obligations. Barriers for implementation exist, however, and even with the best intentions, certain agencies will not be able to execute policies or procedures for inclusion, reflexivity, responsiveness, and anticipation. Some of those barriers are legal, like constraints of certain laws and regulations. Others have to do with capacity. For example, budgets of regulatory agencies involved in product governance like the Environmental Protection Agency, Food and Drug Administration, and Consumer Product Safety Commission are historically low. These barriers could be remedied by Congressional action in favorable political climates.

However, perhaps the greatest barrier is the bias that changes towards RRI will stifle innovation. This is speculative. It is just as likely that a RRI system could be designed that increases innovation by increasing the legitimacy and quality of oversight, through preventing mishaps, drawing upon local knowledge bases, fostering trust, reducing skepticism, and promoting products for public good. Experimentation with RRI on smaller scales might help with the design of systems that maximize both ethical obligations and promote socially responsible innovation. The first obligation of the public sector to consumers is then to provide the resources and venues for such experimentation.

References

Beauchamp, T. L., & Childress, J. F. (2001). *Principles of biomedical ethics*. Oxford: Oxford University Press.

Bekelman, J. E., Li, Y., & Gross, C. P. (2003). Scope and impact of financial conflicts of interest in biomedical research: A systematic review. *JAMA, 289*(4), 454–465.

Brown, J., & Kuzma, J. (2013). Hungry for information: Public attitudes toward food nanotechnology and labeling. *Review of Policy Research, 30*(5), 512–548.

Brown, J., Fatehi, L., & Kuzma, J. (2015). Altruism and skepticism in public attitudes toward food nanotechnologies. *Journal of Nanoparticle Research, 17*(3), 1–31.

Colquitt, J. A., Greenberg, J., & Zapata-Phelan, C. P. (2005). What is organizational justice? A historical overview. *Handbook of Organizational Justice, 1*, 3–58.

Davies, J. C. (2006). *Managing the effects of nanotechnology*. Washington, DC: Project on Emerging Nanotechnologies, Woodrow Wilson International Center for Scholars.

Douglas, M., & Wildavsky, A. (1983). *Risk and culture: An essay on the selection of technological and environmental dangers*. Berkeley, CA: University of California Press.

Fischhoff, B., Slovic, P., Lichtenstein, S., Read, S., & Combs, B. (1978). How safe is safe enough? A psychometric study of attitudes towards technological risks and benefits. *Policy Sciences, 9*(2), 127–152.

Helmut Kaiser Consultancy. (2015). *Nanofood 2040*. http://www.hkc22.com/nanofood2040.html

ICTA. (2012). *Principles for the oversight of nanotechnologies and nanomaterials*. In Nanoaction: A project of the International Center for Technology Assessment. http://www.icta.org/files/2012/04/080112_ICTA_rev1.pdf

Kahan, D. M. (2012). Cultural cognition as a conception of the cultural theory of risk. In *Handbook of risk theory* (pp. 725–759). New York, NY: Springer.

Kahan, D. M., Braman, D., Gastil, J., Slovic, P., & Mertz, C. (2007). Culture and identity-protective cognition: Explaining the white-male effect in risk perception. *Journal of Empirical Legal Studies, 4*(3), 465–505.

Kasperson, R. E., Renn, O., Slovic, P., Brown, H. S., Emel, J., Goble, R., Kasperson, J. X., & Ratick, S. (1988). The social amplification of risk: A conceptual framework. *Risk Analysis, 8*(2), 177–187.

Kuzma, J. (2006). Nanotechnology oversight and regulation-just do it. *Environmental Law Reporter News and Analysis, 36*(12), 10913.

Kuzma, J. (2014). Properly paced or problematic?: Examining governance of GMOs. In G. Marchant, K. Abbott, & B. Allenby (Eds.), *Innovative governance models for emerging technologies*. Cheltenham: Edward Elgar Publishing.

Kuzma, J., & Besley, J. C. (2008). Ethics of risk analysis and regulatory review: From bio- to nanotechnology. *NanoEthics, 2*(2), 149–162.

Kuzma, J., Najmaie, P., & Larson, J. (2009). Evaluating oversight systems for emerging technologies: A case study of genetically engineered organisms. *The Journal of Law, Medicine and Ethics, 37*(4), 546–586.

Linkov, I., Satterstrom, F. K., Steevens, J., Ferguson, E., & PLEUS, R. C. (2007). Multi-criteria decision analysis and environmental risk assessment for nanomaterials. *Journal of Nanoparticle Research, 9*(4), 543–554.

Myers, N., Rabe, A., & Silberman, K. (2005). Louisville charter for safer chemicals: Background paper for reform No. 4.

Ogus, A. (2002). Regulatory institutions and structures. *Annals of Public and Cooperative Economics, 73*(4), 627–648.

Owen, R., Macnaghten, P., & Stilgoe, J. (2012). Responsible research and innovation: From science in society to science for society, with society. *Science and Public Policy, 39*(6), 751–760.

Pickens, J. (2005). *Attitudes and perceptions. Organizational behavior in health care* (pp. 43–75). Sudbury, MA: Jones and Bartlett Publishers.

Rohrmann, B., & Renn, O. (2000). Risk perception research. In *Cross-cultural risk perception* (pp. 11–53). Boston, MA: Springer.

Rowe, G., & Frewer, L. J. (2000). Public participation methods: A framework for evaluation. *Science, Technology and Human Values, 25*(1), 3–29.

Stilgoe, J., Owen, R., & Macnaghten, P. (2013). Developing a framework for responsible innovation. *Research Policy, 42*(9), 1568–1580.

Thompson, P. B., Kassem, M., & Werner, W. G. (2007). *Food biotechnology in ethical perspective*. Dordrecht: Springer.

White House. (2011). *Executive order 13563—Improving regulation and regulatory review.* Executive Order edn. https://www.whitehouse.gov/the-press-office/2011/01/18/executive-order-13563-improving-regulation-and-regulatory-review

White House ETIPC. (2011). *Principles for the regulation and oversight of emerging technologies.* https://www.whitehouse.gov/sites/default/files/omb/inforeg/for-agencies/Principles-for-Regulation-and-Oversight-of-Emerging-Technologies-new.pdf

Whitfield, S. C., Rosa, E. A., Dan, A., & Dietz, T. (2009). The future of nuclear power: Value orientations and risk perception. *Risk Analysis, 29*(3), 425–437.

Yue, C., Zhao, S., Cummings, C., & Kuzma, J. (2015a). Investigating factors influencing consumer willingness to buy GM food and nano-food. *Journal of Nanoparticle Research, 17*(7), 1–19.

Yue, C., Zhao, S., & Kuzma, J. (2015b). Heterogeneous consumer preferences for nanotechnology and genetic-modification technology in food products. *Journal of Agricultural Economics, 66*(2), 308–328.

Consumer Perceptions of Responsibility

Sue L.T. McGregor

1 Introduction

It is 2013. The scene is the Rana Plaza in Dhaka, Bangladesh, which housed five clothing production factories for US, Canadian and European clothing retailers, including Benetton, Joe Fresh, Walmart, and Primark. Eighty percent (80%) of the workers were women aged 18–20, working a 100-h week, earning less than $10.00US per week. On a fateful day in April, all 3639 workers refused to enter the building that morning because of visible cracks in the factory walls. The owner of the building paid gang members to beat the workers, to force them to work. The factory managers then insisted that refusing to work meant they would not be able to pay them. Faced with this possibility, people went to work, but with dire consequences. That day, the Plaza collapsed, killing upwards of 1200 people (one third of the workers in the building), and injuring an additional 2515. Müller et al. (2014) remarked that although "little is known about whether or how consumers reacted to this event," everyone, including consumers, has to "take on their share of responsibility" (p. 892).

The notion of consumers being responsible for their marketplace decisions is gaining global momentum. Recently, over two thirds (65%) of consumers said they feel a sense of responsibility to society when they consume (6000 consumers in six countries) (Bemporad et al. 2013). Cone Communications (2013) stated that the consumers' role in the responsibility equation continues to evolve, with 88% indicating they feel a responsibility to purchase products *they think* are socially and environmentally responsible (10,287 consumers in 10 countries). Over one quarter (27%) also said that responsible consumers can have a significant, positive impact in the world. The Neilsen Company (2014) found that significant

S.L.T. McGregor (✉)
Mount Saint Vincent University, 11565 Peggy's Cove Road, Seabright, NS B3Z 2Y1, Canada
e-mail: Sue.mcgregor@msvu.ca

© Springer International Publishing AG 2017
G. Emilien et al. (eds.), *Consumer Perception of Product Risks and Benefits*,
DOI 10.1007/978-3-319-50530-5_30

percentages of consumers (more than half) are stating their willingness to participate in socially responsible actions (30,000 internet consumers in 60 countries).
Havas Worldwide (2014) found that when asked which factors determine a good
citizen, being a responsible consumer ranked higher than voting (10,574 consumers
in 60 countries).

Yet, despite this worldwide surge in a consumer-articulated sense of responsibility, consumer perceptions of responsibility is an under-research topic (Devinney
et al. 2006; Luchs and Miller 2015; Middlemiss 2010; Wells et al. 2011). "There is a
startling absence of academic work that directly addresses the question of how
consumers actually think about their responsibilities" (Henry 2010, p. 671). This
contribution is an inaugural attempt to develop the idea of *consumer perceptions of
responsibility*. As a caveat, rather than providing primary empirical evidence, this
contribution conceptualizes this emergent consumer phenomenon so that others can
begin to empirically explore and validate it.

Two other caveats informed this undertaking. First, this contribution is about the
new concept of *consumer perceptions* of responsibility rather than 'consumer
responsibility' or 'perceptions of consumer responsibility.' For clarification, the
concept of consumer responsibility has several aliases, including consumer citizenship, ethical consumerism, sustainable consumption, voluntary simplicity, and
political consumerism. Although distinguishable, they are all based on four premises. People (a) can translate their social concerns into marketplace behavior,
(b) use their dollar votes to exercise their sovereignty and to achieve political goals,
(c) are part of an identifiable market segment of responsible consumers that can be
targeted and acted upon by corporations, and (d) possess responsibility as an
identifiable quality (Caruana and Crane 2008). This contribution is about people's
perceptions of responsibility while in their consumer role.

Indeed, different roles demand different responsibilities (Bemporad et al. 2013;
Williams, no date). The responsibilities of a parent are different from a teacher, a
lawyer, or a politician. As a second caveat, this contribution focuses on how people
perceive responsibility when in their *consumer role*. It is concerned with the noun
consumer, defined as anyone who purchases, uses, and disposes of goods and
services from the marketplace; the focus is *consumer* perceptions of responsibilities. Caruana and Crane (2008) asserted that consumer responsibility is distinct
from citizen responsibility, implying that how *humans* perceive responsibility may
change when they assume their consumer role.

As a general comment, studies have explored what predisposes consumers to be
responsible. Stancu's (2013) literature review revealed that certain demographic
variables predispose consumers to be more or less responsible, including education,
income and socioeconomic status, occupation, gender, the presence of children,
rural or urban, tenancy, political affiliation, age, language, access to transportation,
and membership in community groups. An array of consumer-specific variables
also influence people's propensity to consume more or less responsibly. These
factors include involvement in the community and philanthropic activities, religi-
osity, political interest, cosmopolitanism, tolerance and understanding, trust, self-
actualization, power perceptions, liberalism, environmental and sustainability

concerns, egocentrism versus altruism, and perceived consumer effectiveness. Note that none of the 16 studies in Stancu's (2013) literature review engaged with how consumers *perceive* responsibility, the focus of this contribution.

The contribution begins with an overview of responsibility as a philosophical construct, followed with a synopsis of consumer perception theory. This is followed with an attempt to draw conceptual links between consumer perception theory and the construct of responsibility. The contribution then profiles the exiguous, nascent literature on the topic of consumer perceptions of responsibility. It concludes with a discussion of the role culture plays in consumer perceptions of responsibility.

2 Responsibility as a Concept

Personal or individual responsibility is the idea that human beings choose, instigate, or otherwise cause their own actions. A corollary idea is that because people cause their actions, they can be held morally accountable or legally liable. Responsible is Latin for *re* (back) and *spondere* (to pledge). Latin *respondere* means to answer to, to promise in return, to be obliged. Accountable stems from Latin *accomptare*, meaning to calculate, reckon or estimate. For clarification, responsible means being able to respond (take actions and make choices) while accountable means being answerable for one's actions. People are responsible for their choices (able to live with the consequences), but are accountable if they can neutrally and accurately report on the sequence of those choices leading to the consequences. People *take* responsibility but are *held* accountable (by themselves or others) (Planned Success Institute 2002). This contribution focuses on responsibility as a concept, appreciating that it is intricately linked with accountability (see McGregor 2010).

2.1 Responsibility Defined

In the seventeenth century, responsibility originated as a political concept pursuant to the actions and principles of representative government (an institution), with the modern institution being corporate social responsibility. Today, the more common understanding is the moral responsibility of individuals and of the collective. In particular, individual responsibility revolves around determinism and free will (Smiley 2010; Williams, no date). The principle of determinism holds that any event is completely determined by previous events (linear cause and effect); that is, reality follows a predetermined path, and could not happen any other way than it did. This principle rids people of any agency or free will (i.e., purposeful actions or conscious participation) (Turchin 1991). Determinism is reflected in phrases like 'I had no choice. It was fate or happenchance. It was just a coincidence.'

On the other hand, free will is the crux of human agency because people have the ultimate freedom of choice, ideally a *conscious* choice (Turchin 1991). People with free will have the capacity to choose their own course of action *and* to control their actions. To say people acted freely is to say they successfully carried out a choice of their own volition; that is, they used their will. Free will is necessary for the performance of free actions. People are *free* if some external obstacle is not preventing them from taking a chosen course of action. Furthermore, if people do not have free will, they are not morally responsible for their actions; free will is required for moral responsibility (Timpe, no date).

For clarification, free will is a contentious topic. One strand of philosophy believes in free will (compatible with determinism) and another does not (incompatible with determinism); that is, people either have free will and are morally responsible for their actions or they do not. Respectively, compatibilists believe that addressing moral responsibility requires establishing guidelines for holding people accountable. Noncompatibilists believe that people are not truly free; hence, they are not morally responsible for their actions (Timpe, no date). This contribution embraces the idea that people are moral agents with the free will to engage in free actions of their own volition; hence, they are responsible for their actions. Figure 1 summarizes the dimensions of responsibility that are discussed in the following text.

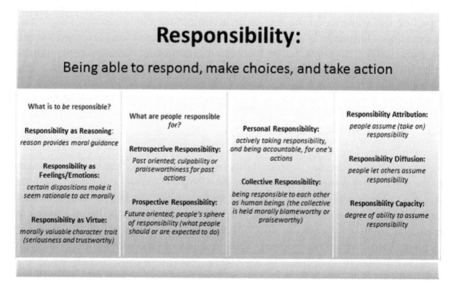

Fig. 1 Dimensions of responsibility

2.2   Perspectives on Responsibility (Reasoning, Feelings or Virtue)

Williams (no date) astutely asked two central questions, "What is it to *be* responsible?" and "What is a person responsible *for*?" The first question pertains to moral agency and is explained by drawing on Kant, Humes, and Aristotle. The second deals with holding people accountable for their actions, and is concerned with past and future-oriented notions of responsibility (i.e., retrospective and prospective). Regarding the former, any discussion of responsibility must respect that it can be viewed from three different perspectives, with each taking a very different slant. Immanuel Kant assumed responsibility stems from moral reasoning. David Humes assumed it stems from feelings and emotions, and Aristotle felt it stems from character (a virtue) (Williams, no date); these three approaches pertain to "What is it to *be* responsible?"

First is responsibility as reasoning. Kant proposed that reason can provide moral guidance and the motivation to act morally. This reason-based understanding of responsibility presumes that people choose to act in light of their principles. This principled choice is possible because people deliberate among reasons to act or not to act. Even if someone feels no inclination to take account of others, *reason* dictates that they should and thus motivates them to do so. Free will also comes into play. People can choose to act or not on the basis of reasons; they are the authors of their own choices. This approach respects people's capacities for rational choice but does not give a proper account of the role of feelings and emotions in their moral life (Williams, no date).

Second is responsibility as feelings and emotions. Humes denied reason as moral guidance proposing instead that, as moral agents, people are equipped with certain dispositions that make it *seem rationale* to act and think morally. This is an emotion/feeling-based approach to responsibility. Humans have tendencies to *feel* sympathy for others, approve of actions that benefit society overall, feel guilt and shame, and be concerned with how others see their actions and character. Humean responsibility questions whether moral reasoning has any validity for people who do not *feel* concern for others. This approach wonders what is it about human interactions that leads people to hold one another responsible (leading to socially, mutually beneficial conduct) but it does not give any account of the validity of reasoning (Williams, no date).

There are similarities between Kantian and Humean notions of responsibilities. The Kantian approach to responsibility is rational while the Humean is emotional. Regardless, "[b]oth positions highlight a series of factors important to responsibility and mutual accountability. These factors include: general responsiveness to others (for instance, via moral reasoning or feelings such as sympathy); a sense of responsibility for our actions (for instance, so that we may offer reasons for our actions or feel emotions of shame or guilt); and tendencies to regard others as responsible (for instance, to respect persons as the authors of their deeds and to feel resentful or grateful to them). In each case, note that the first example in brackets has a typically Kantian (reason-based) cast, the second a Humean (feeling/emotion-related) cast" (Williams, no date, p. 4).

Third is responsibility as a virtue. Aristotle viewed responsibility as a morally valuable character trait. Williams explained that "responsibility represents a virtue that people (and organizations) may exhibit in one area of their conduct, or perhaps exemplify in their entire lives" (2005, p. 8). From the virtue lens, the notions of irresponsibility, seriousness, and trust come into play. Irresponsible people do not take their responsibilities seriously, meaning they cannot be trusted with morally demanding roles. Conversely, a responsible person is both capable of judging what should be done and willing to act accordingly. That same person assesses previous actions and omissions and is prepared to take responsibility for any failings. Responsible people can be relied upon to judge and act in certain morally desirable ways, and when things go wrong, they can be counted on to deal with things.

2.3   Retrospective and Prospective Responsibility

Two approaches to responsibility relate to the question, "What are people responsible *for*?" Retrospective responsibility is concerned with an outcome of the past. Prospective responsibility is concerned with an outcome in the future; people take action in the present to prevent humans and/or nature from being actively harmed or to realize desirable future conditions. In plain language, retrospective responsibility is past-oriented, concerned with after the fact. Given the consequences of an action, what went wrong or what went right? Who is to blame or to be praised? The assumption is that people will learn from analyzing their past actions. Prospective responsibility is future-oriented, concerned with what people are duty bound to perform (what they should do or attend to). What is the sphere of their responsibility? Retrospective and prospective are linked. Different views of someone's sphere of responsibility (what they should do in the future) will lead to very different views of how blame or praise should be assigned after the fact (Williams, no date). More detail follows.

Retrospective responsibility entails a moral judgment of the person deemed responsible for a set of outcomes. It is based on the assumptions that people can be held to blame or be praised, feel remorse or pride, and make amends or receive gratitude. This approach to responsibility holds that if something lies beyond one's control, it also lies beyond the scope of one's responsibility. It deals with causation and accountability of past actions. Although humans may not be the cause of what went wrong (e.g., a storm caused a tree to fall on the highway), when they *are* the cause of harm (moral implications), retrospective responsibility kicks in and people want to hold someone accountable. A key related concept is *just deserts* (i.e., praise and rewards and blame and punishment); that is, what do people deserve given what they have done in the past? When something goes wrong, people want to know why and who was at fault (meriting reproach, remorse, and punishment). Likewise for when something goes right—who was involved and acted well (meriting approval, praise, and gratitude) (Williams, no date).

Rather than looking at the situation after the fact (what went wrong or right), prospective responsibility is future-oriented, concerned with what someone is expected to do. This approach to responsibility assumes that duties emerge by virtue of the roles people hold. For example, corporations have a duty to their employees and stockholders, but from a social responsibility perspective (CSR), they also have a duty to off-shore laborers and the environment. Prospective responsibility also respects that (a) there are degrees of responsibility and (b) people vary in their capacities to act and judge responsibly. Also, people may not be ready for certain duties, or they cannot be expected to understand the implications of their actions. It would not be appropriate to hold someone (fully) responsible for their actions if they are faced with duties that are unrealistic or over demanding (Williams, no date).

2.4 Personal Versus Collective Responsibility

Personal responsibility refers to each person taking accountability for their decisions and actions; people are the authors of their own life. This concept is known philosophically as moral responsibility. Linley and Maltby (2009) explained that personal responsibility is actively *taking* responsibility rather than passively *being* responsible. It aligns with prospective responsibility in that it is future-focused (what ought to be done) instead of concerned with culpability for past transgressions. Having a sense of personal responsibility is a requirement of living in a civilized world, in that the quality of life for all citizens and the whole community is enhanced as a result of people *taking* responsibility for their actions. The opposite of personal responsibility is entitlement and irresponsibility (Linley and Maltby 2009; see also McGregor 2010, Chap. 11).

Social responsibility is concerned with people's collective responsibilities to each other as human beings. While personal responsibility is at the individual level, social responsibility is at the collective level (Linley and Maltby 2009). Responsibilities can be ascribed to the collective *if* the latter is conceived as an agent capable of purposive action (intention); hence, answerable for its (in) actions (e.g., corporations, universities, governments, nations) (Kaufmann 2015). There is no agreement yet about whether particular groups can legitimately be considered morally responsible for the suffering that group *members* have brought about through their faulty actions (Smiley 2010). Resolving this philosophical controversy would greatly contribute to our understanding of whether consumers as a collective (billions of people comprising the consumer society) can be held responsible for the actions of individual consumers and the fallout on society and the ecosystem at large.

Those who deny this culpability claim that, unlike individuals, groups cannot form intentions; hence, they cannot be understood to act or to cause harm. As well, groups cannot be understood as morally blameworthy or praiseworthy in the sense required by moral responsibility. The basic premises are that genuinely collective actions are not possible, and that it would be unfair to consider individual agents morally blameworthy for harm that they did not purposively bring about. Counter-arguments propose that properties and actions of the collective, such as their intentions, beliefs, and desires, supervene those of the individual, meaning collective actions occur later than an individual action, typically in such a way as to change the situation; consequently, collective moral agency emerges (Smiley 2010). This argument paves the way for holding the consumer collective morally responsible for its actions (see McGregor 2010).

That being said, there is still a concern over the problem of attributing responsibilities to a collective for the cumulative actions of many individual agents. Lenk (2006) suggested that everyone who takes part in unsustainable actions contributes to the damage, but any individual contribution is not in itself the final damning act. "Many different little harms well below a threshold accumulate to create a total damage which as such cannot be accounted to each individual. Moral guilt seems to presuppose not only causality but also conscious intention, or at least negligence" (p. 3). The increasing awareness of the damage to the environment due to unsustainable development and consumption has given the idea of collective responsibility keen contemporary relevance (Williams, no date).

If social responsibility is concerned with people's collective responsibilities to each other as human beings (involving intent and blameworthiness) (Linley and Maltby 2009), it is important that people not lose sight of the ongoing philosophical discussion of whether holding collectives accountable is even possible. Can collectives have intention (Williams, no date)? That being said, consumers collectively account for over 75% of most developed nations' Gross Domestic Product (GDP). With such power, they should be held accountable (McGregor 2010). Yet, "having something within one's power is not the same thing as causing it" (Kaufmann 2015, p. 7). The issue remains, can individuals be held morally responsible for the actions of a group with which they are affiliated if they have not actively *collaborated* in these actions (Kaufmann 2015; Smiley 2010; Williams, no date)?

2.5 Responsibility Attribution and Diffusion

The discussion of personal versus collective responsibilities introduced the ideas of responsibility attribution (assigning something to oneself), and responsibility diffusion (spreading the blame around to others). Regarding the former, Portilho (2010) found that self-attribution of consumer responsibilities happens when there is a lack of other social agents who will take on these moral responsibilities. She defined a responsible consumer as someone with "(1) a deep involvement with social and environmental issues; (2) a definition of the consumer as an important social actor; and (3) a self-attribution of duties and responsibilities" (p. 550). Self-attribution means people assign something to themselves, in this case being responsible in their consumer role. With this self-attribution, people see themselves as a responsible consumer, someone "who truly dedicates himself [sic] to activities conceived by him to be environmentally and socially responsible and one who has the intention of changing social life through these activities" (p. 550). Middlemiss (2010) observed that self-attribution for responsibility for sustainable consumption is common in the literature, relative to attribution for collective responsibility.

Middlemiss (2010) also asserted that "a type of consumer exists that attributes responsibility to herself/himself rather than to others" (p. 151). Portilho (2010) agreed, concluding that consumers that self-attribute responsibilities tend to trust in the importance and effectiveness of their own marketplace actions, while mistrusting other social agents. She also proposed that through self-attribution of responsibilities, consumers expand authority over their life, increase their feelings of citizenship, and view their private life as an active political sphere. They believe strongly in their responsibilities, and in the role consumers can play to ensure a sustainable future. They are active consumers who do not feel excessively alienated and manipulated by governments or businesses, thereby enabling them as consumers to become important and decisive social actors.

From a contrary perspective, Middlemiss (2010) found that while sustainable consumers feel the need to take on responsibility, they do not always have a clear view of the boundaries of their own responsibility, and they rarely link responsibility for sustainable consumption to governments or business. Caruana and Crane (2008) also wrestled with "how the process of constructing consumer responsibility draws boundaries around what is to be regarded as within the purview of responsibility" (p. 1512). They tentatively concluded that a responsible consumer is not an absolutely independent and freethinking person, imbued with their own self-knowledge of responsibility; rather, a responsible consumers identity is at least, in part, ethical whereby they approach consumption through their own lens of core values and vision. This process helps them determine the boundaries of their responsibilities.

Contrary to responsibility attribution is diffusion of responsibility to others. Middlemiss (2010) theorized that people's discomfort with not taking responsibility as a consumer could lead them to attribute responsibility for sustainable consumption to other parties (see also McGregor 2010, Chap. 5). Indeed, many who *could* assume responsibility for their consumer decisions may think it is someone else's prerogative, or obligation, to do so. This tendency is called *diffusion of responsibility*; that is, the more people present, the less likely each person feels for being responsible (note that self-attribution happens when few people are present). Diffusion (i.e., spread over a large area) of responsibility happens when responsibility has not been assigned, others are present, and people feel a sense of anonymity (e.g., in a crowd). Absolving themselves of responsibility rarely happens when people are alone. When diffusion does occur, people assume others should be the ones to take action or have already done so. Non-consumer examples include (a) bystanders not intervening in a public assault or (b) subordinates claiming they were following orders with their superiors claiming they merely issued the order (Ciccarelli and White 2009).

Bottom line, diffusion theory holds that not assisting or caring for others in dire situations is not simply a matter of apathy or indifference; rather; it is because *others are present* (to whom the responsibility can be spread around). Considering there are billions of individual consumers in the world, it is not a stretch to suggest they might look to others to take responsibility (McGregor 2010). In fact, aside from people actually being present, the *mere notion* of a group leads to a diminished sense of consumer responsibility. In the real and perceived presence of others, consumers no longer feel solely responsible for their consumer behavior because the crowd can absorb the fallout (Müller et al. 2014).

Müller et al. (2014) also found that when consumers perceive barriers to consuming responsibly and sustainably, they tend to assign responsibility to various stakeholders beyond themselves [e.g., producers, governments, and non-government organizations (NGOs)]; that is, they diffuse responsibility. In light of this finding, Müller et al. (2014) suggested that those concerned with responsible consumption should reflect on "the usefulness of scattering the responsibility for sustainable consumption among various stakeholders" (p. 901). They argued that even if consumers believe they *should* take on the responsibility of the consequences of their purchase behavior, they may not be able to do so, given the complexity of today's supply chains. Bemporad et al. (2013) found that 74% of consumers feel that responsibility for the future should be shared by governments, businesses, and consumers. Müller et al. (2014) recommended "a shared but actor-specific responsibility" (p. 895). Although "there is little research attempting to apply a broader, multi-stakeholder perspective to responsibility" (Wells et al. 2011, p. 814), various stakeholders consider responsibility for the future to be shared (Luchs and Miller 2015).

2.6   Capacity for Responsibility

The basic premise of the capacity concept is that fulfilling responsibilities depends on people's abilities, and people have different abilities to fulfil their obligations (Williams, no date). This concept appreciates that some people will have more capacity than others to fulfil their responsibilities because they have different abilities, and because of different contexts (Middlemiss 2010). She asserted that "the responsibility of an individual depends on the capacity of that individual, afforded by a specific context, to take on sustainable [consumption] practices" (pp. 153–154). In summary "individuals act [responsibly] because they are capable of acting, because they know how to act [responsibly] and because they are taking an opportunity to act that is offered to them by their context" (p. 153). If empowering structures and contexts are not available, the responsibility of the consumer is diminished; that is, their individual agency is compromised.

Portilho (2010) agreed, claiming that the phenomenon of responsible consumption is situated within the context of great global transformation, including deregulation and globalization of markets, the transnationalization of social actors, and the centrality of consumption. These megastructures and ideologies are affecting people's ability to assume responsibility for their consumer behavior. People can take more responsibility in contexts that ensure provisions for conscious living. And, the morality of obligations to sustainability falls on those with the capacity to act (Middlemiss 2010).

3   Consumer Perception Theory

Because this contribution is about consumer *perceptions* of responsibility, this section elaborates on the basic tenets of consumer perception theory. All consumer behavior textbooks contain a chapter on consumer perception theory, intended to ascertain how consumers' insights about a product or service can influence their purchase behavior. Business enterprises and marketers use the theory to determine how consumers perceive them and their offerings, leading to strategic marketing and advertising (i.e., perception manipulation).

Perception is Latin *perceptionem*, for receiving or collecting. The daily life (reality) of consumers is richly complex and diverse. People strive to make sense of their consuming reality so they can cope with, adapt to, and change it. "Perception is the process of selecting, organizing and interpreting sensations into a meaningful whole" (Hanna et al. 2013, p. 75). Put simply, perception is a complex process by which people take input from their five senses (i.e., sight, hearing, smell, taste and touch) and turn these sensations into something that has *meaning* for them. If something is meaningful, it has a useful quality or purpose because it is deemed valid, relevant and significant.

3.1   Sensation, Exposure, and Attention

The process of perception entails three concepts: sensation, exposure, and attention. In more detail, sensation refers to the responses of person's sensory receptors (eyes, ears, nose, mouth and touch) to stimuli from the environment, and the resultant transmission of that response to the brain. A stimulus is something that evokes a reaction by arousing the mind, body, and/or spirit. When people come into contact with stimuli in their environment (either accidentally or on purpose), they experience exposure; however, people do not notice everything they are exposed to in the world. In order for perception to occur, people have to become aware of the stimuli to which they are being exposed. With this awareness, they can pay attention to the stimuli. This attention can be involuntary (forced on them), spontaneous, or planned. A fire alarm would prompt involuntary attention. Actively looking for a birthday present with an open mind would be spontaneous attention. And, intentionally seeking a particular birthday present would be planned attention (Hanna et al. 2013).

3.2 Thresholds

Each of the five human senses has three different thresholds (defined as the point at which something would start or cease to happen or come into effect). The absolute threshold is the lowest level at which a sense can be experienced. Below this level, humans cannot detect it. A differential threshold is the smallest increment in intensity that can still be detected as an increase or decrease. This just-noticeable-difference is the amount something must be changed in order for the change to be noticeable. For example, the absolute threshold for sound would be the lowest volume level that a person could detect. The just-noticeable-difference would be the smallest change in volume that a person could sense. A terminal threshold is the point beyond which further increments in intensity produce no greater sensation (Hanna et al. 2013). Thresholds matter in the theory of perception because they help gauge what degree of change has to happen in order for the change to be detected.

3.3 Perception Overload, Vigilance, and Selectivity

Pragmatically, people cannot pay attention to everything to which they are exposed. Their inability to do so at any given moment results in *perception overload*. Conversely, to accommodate this limited capacity to process all stimuli in their surroundings, people learn to discard much of what they receive through their five senses, a process called *perceptual vigilance*. This vigilance protects people from sensory overload because it involves selectively paying attention to external stimuli. *Perceptual selectivity* entails screening out certain stimuli while allowing others to reach one's consciousness. This screening can encompass selective exposure as well as selective attention. The former means ignoring stimuli and the latter means actively choosing them and giving them credence and consideration. These two processes constitute filters, with *perceptual defences* helping people block or tune out stimuli (Hanna et al. 2013).

3.4 Interpretation of Sensations

In addition to using their five senses to comprehend their near environment, people's interpretation of a sensation plays a critical role, making perceptions both objective and subjective, and easily distorted (Hanna et al. 2013). Interpretation means discerning or explaining the meaning of something. In order to interpret (make sense of) stimuli, people scan their memory from prior experiences and learnings, combine these cues with their expectations (beliefs about future happenings) and/or intentions, and derive meaning from the stimuli. Selective interpretation represents people consciously processing stimuli to which they have paid attention. In some instances, it refers to people reducing dissonance by interpreting ambiguous information so that is seems consistent with their beliefs, thoughts or actions (Hanna et al. 2013).

Other factors can affect people's interpretation of stimuli, including their frame of reference. This is a complex set of assumptions and attitudes that people use to filter perceptions to create meaning. The *frame* can include beliefs, schemas, preferences, values, culture and other ways that bias people's understanding and judgment (Straker 2015). People tend to 'see things' (perceive them) based on their particular frame of reference. This selective perception reflects any number of biases. In addition to frames of reference, expectations can affect how sensations are interpreted and evaluated; that is, expectations help people assign meaning to their perceptions. Expectations are beliefs that something will happen in the future; expectations can lead to misperceptions (Hanna et al. 2013).

Third, people may interpret a sensation differently at various times or in different circumstances. Their conscious perception of the world, though relatively stable, is not static. Being human means seeing the world through one's own constantly shifting lens. Finally, personal qualities of people influence their interpretation of stimuli. These individual factors include "needs, interests, beliefs, goals, experiences, feelings, memories, personality, self-perception, lifestyle, roles, risk tolerance, attention span, and mental sets" (Hanna et al. 2013, p. 87).

3.5 Sensation Pathways

There are two pathways by which a sensation can be registered by people. One is the features of the stimulus itself, and the other is the person's aforementioned individual factors. The former is known as bottom-up processing, and is a sort of automatic response. Imagine a woman in a shopping mall who passes a jewellery shop. Upon seeing a diamond bracelet in the window, she enters the shop without hesitation and buys the bracelet. The bracelet itself was stimulus enough to prompt a positive interpretation (meaningful purchase). On the other hand, top-down processing is dependent upon people's prior knowledge or schemata. In the same scenario, seeing the diamond bracelet triggers a more dynamic process of searching for the best meaning given the individual factors of the person. If she had preconceived notions about blood diamonds for instance, she may opt to not buy the bracelet because she is unsure of the source of the diamonds. Her interpretation of the stimulus (and what it would *mean* if she bought the diamond bracelet) was informed by her existing knowledge about features of the product (Hanna et al. 2013).

3.6   Perceptual Situation and Context

Another variable that determines people's perceptions of things is the situation or context within which the stimuli are being experienced. There are five classes of situational (contextual) variables: physical surroundings, social surroundings, time perspective, task definition, and antecedent states. The first three are self-explanatory. Task definition relates to roles and reasons for engaging in something. Antecedent state is the momentary, temporary physical or psychological state of the person immediately preceding their state when she or he experienced the stimulus (i.e., moods or conditions/circumstances). How people feel, and what is going on in their environment, contributes to how they perceive and interpret stimuli (Hanna et al. 2013).

3.7   Gestalten Principles

Hanna et al. (2013) explained that when people encounter stimuli, they strive to perceive cohesive wholes and find meaningful patterns rather than look for discrete parts. Drawing on Gestalt psychology (*Gestalt* meaning whole or total impression), they proposed that people perceive environmental stimuli through a combination of closure, grouping, proximity, context, and figure and ground. Respectively, when people experience an incomplete stimulus, they tend to see it as a complete object even though parts are missing. People tend to integrate bits of information into organized wholes by grouping small units into chunks. Objects close together seem to belong together (i.e., close proximity intimates association). Contexts and sur-roundings affect the way people perceive things. Finally, people tend to distinguish prominent stimulus (a figure) from less prominent stimuli (figures in the background).

3.8   Perceptual Categories and Classes

Humans also have the tendency to place stimuli into perceptual categories or logical classes so they can simplify information processing and decision making. As an illustration, Hanna et al. (2013) described a consumer deducing that an unknown food item in a supermarket is a pasta product, based on cues from its placement in the store, and its packaging. It was in the pasta section so it must be a form of pasta. This perceptual categorization streamlines people's judgments about stimuli, better enabling them to interpret the experience and make sense of it. People can also engage in perceptual inference whereby they form beliefs based on previous experiences with the stimuli. When they experience the stimulus anew, they can infer a perception of its meaning by associating it with previously held beliefs.

Perceptual inferences can manifest (a) in the form of the halo effect, (b) by linking unfamiliar with familiar stimuli, or (c) by drawing conclusions from general to specific (correlational inferences) (Hanna et al. 2013).

3.9 Schema and Scripts

Finally, perceptions can be affected by stored memories. People's perceptions of stimuli in their environment may be shaped by their personal schema (i.e., inner representation of the world) or inner script. "A schema is an organizing framework, a set of expectations that provide a structure for understanding and interpreting new information" (Hanna et al. 2013, p. 99). When a new stimulus is encountered, the schema kicks in and affords efficient processing of information and interpretations. Scripts amount to personal knowledge and expectations about how to behave and respond to recurring events that people may encounter, or situations that may arise. Scripts organize people's knowledge about what to do in familiar situations (i.e., routines), and let them know what outcome to anticipate from that behavior. Falling back on a script means people do not have to make deliberate, conscious decisions when faced with a familiar situation.

4 Linking Consumer Perception Theory with the Responsibility Concept

This section links the tenets of consumer perception theory with the concept of responsibility. None of these ideas have been empirically tested, so they are presented as a conceptual teaser. To start, what people perceive is shaped by what they are exposed to and what they pay attention to. If they have only been exposed to their consumer rights and not to their attendant responsibilities, there is little chance they will perceive they have *any* responsibilities. How people perceive what it means to *be* responsible will affect their consumer actions. If they perceive it to mean moral reasoning, they will assume they are capable of making conscious choices in the marketplace. This perception is akin to personal moral responsibility. Conversely, if they perceive being responsible to mean how they *feel* about the impact of their decisions on others, their inclination to act responsibly will depend on whether they care about others. This is akin to collective responsibility. If they are not concerned with everyone engaging in socially beneficial conduct, they may not bring this issue to the marketplace.

If people perceive responsibility to be a virtue, a behavior showing high moral standards, they should take their consumer responsibilities seriously. However, it is possible that people may see moral behavior as central to their general life, but not germane to consumer decisions. Shopping is not good or bad, it just is. In this situation, it is likely that consumers will not self-attribute responsibility. The latter would require them to change their self-perception to one of a responsible consumer whereby they believe strongly in their responsibilities for a sustainable future, and that their consumer transactions are paramount to that future.

Perceptions of what it means to *be* responsible definitely affect people's behavior before, during and after marketplace transactions. The notion of thresholds is also central to consumer perceptions of responsibility. It is easy for people to argue that their individual actions are too small to have any overall effect; hence, they have no responsibility. But the notion of a threshold challenges this assumption. Tipping points also play a crucial role in this scenario. They are little changes that have big effects when critical mass occurs. Billions of consumers engaging in unsustainable and morally risky consumption behavior leads to tipping points where thresholds are crossed (knowingly or not), leading to more and wider harm. Diffusion theory posits that if people perceive others are present, they are more likely to shift the responsibility to them, assuming others can absorb the fallout. This transference amounts to billions of blame-shifting consumers setting up an unsustainable dynamic, culminating in the current state of global unsustainability.

Perceptions of when responsible behavior should be sanctioned are also important, and can be associated with sensation pathways. Bottom-up pathways refer to people's automatic responses to things. Many people are not concerned with consumers' responsibilities until after the fact (retrospective responsibility), at which point they automatically assign blame or praise when they perceive a situation (e.g., someone driving a vehicle that is polluting the air). On the other hand, top-down pathways are linked to people's prior knowledge or mental schema. Regarding prospective responsibility, people would enter consumer transactions drawing on their existing knowledge base and make decisions about what should be done to have a positive impact on the future. Bottom-up pathways focus on past transgressions (laying blame or praise) and top-down pathways focus on what is expected or likely to happen given a particular action. The former notion of responsibility is evaluative and the latter is preventative.

It is a given that sensory overload plays a central role in consumer perceptions of responsibility. It is difficult to discern the scope and degree of feasible consumer responsibility if people's senses are overloaded. Excessive packaging and pervasive advertising, massive product offerings, and distant sourcing and production can easily overwhelm even the best intentioned consumer. People will automatically strive to select which stimuli they respond to, but without adequate education about the import of (ir)responsible decisions, they may default to self-satisfaction and self-interest. Given the onslaught of information in a juggernaut consumer culture, people may eschew responsibility by erecting perceptual defenses so they can tune out the cacophony. Given all of the perceived barriers to consuming sustainably and responsibly, people may also be more inclined to diffuse responsibility to others. This individual diffusion leaves no room for collective responsibility because it is so difficult to make a case for moral causality.

To avoid this situation, people may have to learn to respect the power of perceptual vigilance by paying attention to the stimuli required to assess the implications of their consumer choices on others and the environment. They would filter out the manipulative advertising and marketing messages, and related discourse from corporations and like-minded state actors, and focus instead on reasoned critiques of the consumer society and the neoliberal global economy. This critical reflection should better enable them to discern the boundaries of their own responsibility relative to other stakeholders. Responsible consumption could be perceived as within the purview of being a responsible citizen. Indeed, people may come to see themselves as capable of being responsible in the marketplace, and with this perception they can take advantage of opportunities to be responsible.

People's perception of responsibility when consuming can also be explained by the situation and the context. Many things other than personal factors can shape people's interpretations of their responsibilities as consumers. Their physical surroundings when consuming can either facilitate or thwart intentions to consume responsibly. Perhaps a Mom intended to buy an ethically produced toy but was seduced by the packaging of another toy. Time orientations also play a role, shaping if people are past, present or future-oriented. A concern for the future should lead to more sustainable decisions. Even people's moods can affect how they interpret stimuli when shopping. If they are sad and need a boost, they may eschew their normal responsible purchases and buy to feel good. Context keenly matters vis–àvis consumer perceptions of responsibility. In fact, empowering contexts are necessary or else consumers' sense of responsibility is diminished.

Especially intriguing is the potential role of Gestalten principles. People automatically strive to perceive wholes and find meaningful patterns, filling in the blanks and paying attention to the foreground rather than the background. Today's global marketplace does not present a whole picture to consumers. There are many holes in their view of the consumer world and their part in it. If they do not receive sufficient stimuli to convince them to be responsible, they may fill in the blanks and create a scenario the lets them off the hook. If all they see in the foreground that is spend, spend, spend, they can easily miss the background message of spend responsibly, spend consciously, spend sustainably. Their human inclination to perceive wholes may lead them down the path of irresponsible behavior.

Finally, people also tend to infer meaning from previous experiences. If all people have experienced is immediate self-gratification, and been satisfied with that, they may take that perception into all marketplace transactions. This mind trick streamlines people's judgments about marketplace stimuli, leading to unsustainable, irresponsible consumer decisions. People's inclination to simplify information processing by creating perceptual categories needs to be challenged if consumers' perception of responsibility is to change.

Aligned with this is the need to clarify and change (if necessary) people's mental schema about their role as consumer. The grand narrative about consumers is that their role is to make money to spend money, and keep the capitalistic machine forging ahead (McGregor 2010). If people unconsciously fall back on this mental script each time they consume something, they will fail to make deliberate, conscious decisions in the marketplace, thereby acting irresponsibly. Their perceptions of what it means to *be* responsible and *for* what are affected by mental scripts, and their natural predilection to categorize similar activities into meaningful wholes.

5 Nascent Literature on Consumer Perceptions of Responsibility

The discussion will now turn to the few attempts found in the literature that tried to conceptualize *consumer perceptions of responsibility* (gleaned by using proxy terms such as sense of responsibility, conceptions of responsibility, and perceptions of responsibility).

5.1 Consumer Felt Responsibility

Luchs and Miller (2015) tendered the concept of *consumer 'felt responsibility'*. They developed this new concept, and a scale to measure it, using Schwartz's (1977) personal norm activation model. His model views behavior as driven by personal norms (i.e., standards people have about their own actions). Norms are shaped by consumer perceptions of the consequences of behavior and their feelings of personal responsibility for those consequences. A personal norm kicks in when people perceive another's needs, thereby activating an internalized value structure, leading to feelings of moral obligation. Personal norms motivate people to act in ways that are consistent with their own values. The effect of a personal norm on behavior is moderated by what Schwartz (1977) called *ascription of responsibility*. Once people gain a sense of responsibility, they will differ on their propensity to deny personal responsibility for their actions and any negative consequences; that is, the norm (the *felt* obligation) will either be activated or not.

Luchs and Miller (2015) used ascription of responsibility as a way to account for people developing a sense of *consumer* responsibility, a felt obligation. They found that consumers' perceptions of their responsibilities were higher when they knew exactly what *behaviors* were involved in being responsible. Conversely, their self-ascription was lower when the *outcomes* were general in nature (e.g., lower environmental damage). Also, people's perceptions of relative responsibility (consumers relative to business and government) can depend significantly on how the issues are framed (i.e., as specific desirable *behaviors* or general *outcomes*). Participants in their study ascribed equal responsibility to consumers, companies and governments (33% each) for general *outcomes*, but ascription of responsibility was not consistent across specific *behaviors*.

5.2   Sense of Consumer Responsibility

Luchs et al. (2015) extended Luchs and Miller's (2015) consumer felt responsibility concept to include more dimensions. Luchs et al. claimed that consumption behaviors are affected by a heightened sense of personal responsibility, and their 2015 study determined that consumer responsibility *is* a predictor of consumer behavior. They proposed that focusing on a *sense of consumer responsibility* has a greater potential for positively affecting consumer behaviors than does focusing on consumer attitudes.

To develop this idea, Luchs et al. (2015) reconceptualized responsibility from four perspectives, saying these must be taken into account when conceptualizing consumer perceptions of responsibility: cognition, emotion, moral imperative, and sociocultural. Consumer responsibility conceived as a self-oriented cognitive process assumes decisions are rational and intended to enhance personal gains. Emotion-oriented definitions of consumer responsibility hold that consumer decisions are predicated on things like guilt and pride, with the latter sustaining a sense of responsibility.

The other-oriented moral perspective posits that consumer decisions are not as rational and justifiable as cognitive ones, with personal norms activated by an ascription of responsibility. Under pressure from this sense of moral obligation, some consumers may offload responsibility to others, engage in one action thinking it discharges them from their responsibility, or consign responsibility to governments or other consumers. Finally, the socio-cultural perspective suggests that consumers become responsible through the external organized efforts of other actors who convince people "to reflect upon and transform their [consumer] behaviors so they now see themselves as having a sense of moral imperative to act responsibly and conscientiously" (Luchs et al. 2015, p. 13).

5.3   Consumers' Responsibility Orientation

Wells et al. (2011) actually included the phrase *consumer perceptions of responsibility* in the title of their study. They were interested in whether or not consumer behavior is affected by "the responsibility orientation of a consumer" (p. 815); that is, whether or not the consumer feels responsible for the situation or thinks someone else is responsible. In their study on climate change, Wells et al. concluded that the influence of a *sense of responsibility* is significant (statistically and in general), although weak compared to other factors.

A sense of responsibility means people are aware of or appreciate the need to be responsible; however, people with a sense of responsibility (a sense of feeling obligated) do not always follow through (Wells et al. 2011). They further proposed that a sense of responsibility matures over time, with consumers being more or less inclined to ascribe or diffuse responsibility. Indeed, people exhibit a tendency to ascribe responsibility to government or an abstract notion of 'consumers' rather than to themselves (see also Luchs et al. 2015). Wells et al. (2011) used the phrase "consumer perceptions of their *own sphere of influence* and responsibility" (2011, p. 829, emphasis added), alluding to the phenomena of both consumer ascription and diffusion of marketplace responsibility.

Consumers can take responsibility for their actions (self-ascription) or place responsibility onto others (diffusion) (Wells et al. 2011). Either of these two practices may arise depending on what consumers perceive they can actually influence with their behavior; that is, their perceived consumer effectiveness (PCE). PCE refers to the extent to which people perceive their actions will make a difference. In particular, people who feel they are not responsible for something, and that they cannot alleviate the situation, take less responsibility for their decisions. Conversely, people can think they are guilty of contributing to a problem (e.g., they are responsible for unsustainable consumption) without thinking they have the power to solve it. Without this sense of effectiveness, it is easier to diffuse responsibility to others (Ellen et al. 1991).

5.4   Consumer Responsibility Discourse

Caruana and Crane (2008) discovered that a consumer's particular self-conception of what it means to be a responsible consumer is contingent upon prevailing discourses *about* consumer responsibility, especially discourse generated by corporations. Caruana and Crane learned that corporations believe concerned citizens need help transitioning towards being a responsible consumer. To that end, corporations see themselves as not merely stimulating and facilitating responsible choices; they also *construct* consumer responsibility as a meaningful social identity, and then lead concerned citizens to embrace this consumer identity by purchasing *their* product or service. Passive yet concerned *citizens* are then turned into active and responsible *consumers* (something that would not have happened if the corporations had not intervened).

Caruana and Crane's (2008) discourse analysis revealed that the notion of what constitutes a responsible consumer is intentionally constructed by corporations. The latter "provide a coherent myth of responsibility . . . thereby creating a plausible and attractive responsible consumer category" (p. 1513). When consumers are drawn in by this marketing strategy, they tend to avoid considering the impact of their decisions because the corporation has said 'if you by this particular item or service, you fit into the responsible consumer category.' This discourse is gaining momentum in the marketplace, and is corrupting consumers' real sense of responsibility. They abdicate their task of assessing their responsibility to the corporations. Corporations become complicit in allowing consumers to forget about the moral issues and enable them to not engage in moral choices.

6   Culture and Consumer Perceptions of Responsibility

On a final note, this section broaches the topic of how culture informs consumer perceptions of responsibility. One consumer's perception of what constitutes responsibility may differ from another's (Caruana and Crane 2008; Middlemiss 2010). This difference is further complicated by the role of culture. Individual perceptions of responsibility depend on cultural background (Maddux and Yuki 2006); yet, responsibility is one of the hardest words to translate and interpret across cultures. Due to cultural perspectives, responsibility is not conceived and practiced in the same way everywhere, nor do different cultures prioritize the key dimensions of responsibility the same way, although they do agree on them [i.e., (a) being charged with a duty (carrying a charge), and (b) having an account]. It seems that the meaning of responsibility cannot be understood without a cultural context (Sizoo 2010).

6.1   Overview of Western and Eastern Notions of Responsibility

The following discussion shares a profile of the main differences between how Western and Eastern cultures understand responsibility (see Fig. 2). Interestingly, the literature is scarce about African cultures' notions of responsibility relative to the West and the East. Sizoo (2010) commented on the unchanging nature of responsibility in Africa over time. It has always had a sacred nature. Each person is seen as part of the community, and the latter includes those who have passed away. Ancestors are seen as vital forces overseeing and protecting the living, meaning the living are responsible for the ancestors as well. Furthermore, in most African cultures, an individual bears dual responsibility for himself and his extended family (Gyekye 1992).

Also, in African cultures, the notion of *personhood* is central to responsibility. Personhood is not given but has to be achieved by a person being incorporated into a community. Once people are seen to *have* personhood, members of the community view them as having responsibility toward others. The pursuit or practice of moral virtues is intrinsic to the African conception of a person. The human person should promote the welfare of others, and conversely be treated as a morally responsible agent. A lack of recognition and responsibility for others diminishes personhood, which is anchored in community (Gyekye 1992; Menkiti 1984).

Sizoo (2010) focused on country-generated conceptualizations of responsibility. Sizoo edited a collection from 11 countries, each tasked with profiling their culture's understanding of responsibility. All continents were included, represented by the following countries: United States, New Zealand, China, India, the Congo (Africa), Eastern and Western Europe, Egypt, the Philippines, and South America (Brazil). To summarize, non-western cultures often find the word *charge*

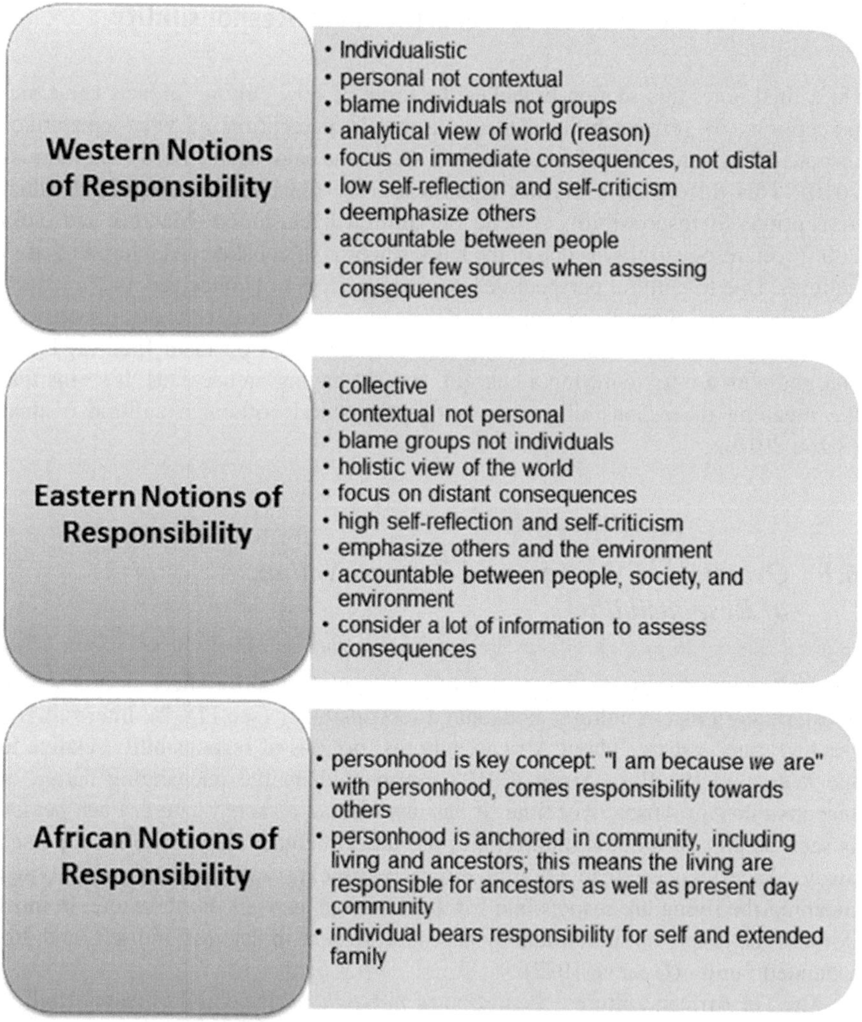

Western Notions of Responsibility	• Individualistic • personal not contextual • blame individuals not groups • analytical view of world (reason) • focus on immediate consequences, not distal • low self-reflection and self-criticism • deemphasize others • accountable between people • consider few sources when assessing consequences
Eastern Notions of Responsibility	• collective • contextual not personal • blame groups not individuals • holistic view of the world • focus on distant consequences • high self-reflection and self-criticism • emphasize others and the environment • accountable between people, society, and environment • consider a lot of information to assess consequences
African Notions of Responsibility	• personhood is key concept: "I am because we are" • with personhood, comes responsibility towards others • personhood is anchored in community, including living and ancestors; this means the living are responsible for ancestors as well as present day community • individual bears responsibility for self and extended family

Fig. 2 Western and Eastern cultural notions of responsibility

synonymous with burden, but not so in Western cultures. In the West, accountability is a matter between people while non-Western cultures see it as a matter between people *and* an environment that is broader than the social. In most cultures, responsibility is aligned with taking action, but in the Chinese culture (where roughly a quarter of the world lives), responsibility means refraining from action. The notion of individualism in America's colonial days makes it hard to be responsible to others and society. On the other hand, Germany is struggling to rid itself of responsibility as a duty to obey and is striving instead for a new consciousness of personal and collective responsibility for society, humankind and the planet (Sizoo 2010).

Maddux and Yuki (2006) focused on cultural understandings of consequences, especially the differences between Western and East Asian cultures (United States, Canada, Australia, Japan, China, Korea, Taiwan). Maddux and Yuki were interested in how the West and the East differ on their inclination to be concerned with the immediate (proximate) versus the long term (distal) effects of actions and events (and attendant responsibilities). This focus directly impacts people's perceptions of responsibility. A compelling profile emerged.

Western cultures feel responsible for their themselves (individualistic). They assess responsibility based on personal factors (not contextual), and take into account minimal information when determining responsibility. They place blame on individuals, not groups, and explain their and other's behaviors in terms of personal characteristics (rather than the context). Western cultures see themselves as independent, separate, autonomous entities that exist apart from social norms and expectations. They take an analytical view of the world (reason) and see things as detached and not connected. This view means they are not responsible for others or for long term consequences. This means they are not able to envision a complex chain of subsequent consequences from an immediate action; they focus on only the immediately evident and visible (Maddux and Yuki 2006).

Eastern cultures are more farsighted and inclusive. They assess responsibility based on the situation and context, and they hold many people accountable rather than just one person. Eastern cultures take into account a lot of information when assessing responsibility, and are constantly aware of other people and how reciprocal actions affect them. They are inclined to explain behavior and consequences in terms of situational factors that influenced the actors (rather than the person's personality traits). Also, they see themselves within a web of social relationships, with everything connected. This leads to a holistic perception of the world and of their responsibilities. Eastern cultures not only take into account possible consequences on oneself but also others who are directly and indirectly affected. This distal sense of responsibility means they are very cognizant of the downstream effects of actions after an event, even long into the future. This means they are able to envision a complex chain of subsequent consequences from an immediate action. Finally, they are inclined to hold an entire group responsible, more so than one particular person (Maddux and Yuki 2006).

Maddux and Yuki's (2006) results can easily be applied to consumer perceptions of responsibilities. Western consumers see themselves as distant from others and the future, focused instead on themselves and immediate concerns. This stance means it is easy to dismiss both those who make consumer goods and services, and the environment. These are all separate, unconnected entities. Because context is not an issue, consuming can happen in a vacuum (meaning no attendant responsibilities). On the other hand, Eastern consumers value the collective web of social relationships from a holistic perspective. This sense of interconnectedness means that consumers would perceive their responsibilities to include others, now and into the future (in anticipated and unexpected ways). Context is paramount, meaning mindful responsibility could be a key factor in consumer behavior.

Cultural can also have impact on an array of factors pursuant to responsibility. Kastanakis and Voyer (2013) shared a very comprehensive discussion of how culture effects people's perceptions of others, emotions, the environment, sensations, self-esteem, self versus others, and information processing (but not responsibilities, per se). Many of their insights are echoed above in Maddux and Yuki's (2006) work, which will not be repeated, but additional illustrative examples are now shared. Kastanakis and Voyer (2013) noted that Eastern, collective cultures need contextual information in order to evaluate responsibility, while Western individualistic cultures rely on inner attributes (needs, goals, desires). People in the West place a high value on their freedom to express their true self (authenticity) compared to Eastern cultures, which evaluate their freedom in light of the costs and benefits to the group. Western cultures de-emphasize others while Eastern cultures see themselves as interconnected to others, and the social context. Their responsibilities align with the well-being of others and the collective, unlike Western cultures where self-responsibility reigns.

People's ability to adopt the perspective of others varies cross-culturally, a behavior at the core of consumer responsibility. Eastern cultures are "better *perspective takers* than Westerners" (Kastanakis and Voyer 2013, p. 428). Western cultures are more inclined to see 'others as like them' than 'themselves as like others' (again making it harder to appreciate the impact of their decisions on different others). Eastern cultures are less likely to make errors when reasoning about others and interpreting their reactions and actions. Conversely, Westerners are prone to egocentric errors; that is, they are unable to differentiate between self and others. This in turn affects their perception of their responsibilities (e.g., if the self is not harmed, others must not be harmed either).

Eastern cultures are more inclined to engage in self criticism so as to avoid future (distal) undesired behavior and consequences. Westerners score lower on self-review and self-criticism measures, intimating they may not reflect on their responsibilities. As well, Western consumers shy away from processing contradictory pieces of information, preferring one view. Easterners are more comfortable with contradictory statements and opinions (Kastanakis and Voyer 2013). Receptiveness to contradictory viewpoints greatly shapes people's perception of responsibilities; a closed view means no chance to hear alternatives to the unsustainable status quo.

6.2 Hofstede's Cultural Dimensions and Consumer Perceptions of Responsibility

Appreciating that different cultures orient people to the world in different ways, Hofstede and his colleagues developed a model of cultural dimensions (Hofstede et al. 2010). The various dimensions represent national preferences for one state of affairs over another, and these preferences distinguish countries and their cultures from each other. Cultures change slowly, so the 70-plus national cultural profiles

Power distance	Uncertainity avoidance	Individualism/ collectivisim	Masculinity/ femininity	Long/short-term orientation	Indulgence/ restraint
• how society handles power inequalities; low distance means society expects a very small gap between ruling power and rest of society (i.e., an even distribution of power)	• society's ability to handle risk and anxiety in the face of uncertainity; its propensity for unorthodox ideas and behavior; its need for rules and structures	• tight or lose knit society; former is individualistic (take care of self and immediate family); latter is collective (take care of each other)	• masculine society means competitive and materialistic; feminine means cooperative and equal opportunities	• society's orientation towards time; long term favors the future (adapt) and short term favors the past and traditions	• society's inclination to suppress (regulate) or express human drives (fun, joy, learn, bond, acquire)

Fig. 3 Hofstede et al.'s (2010) model of cultural dimensions

developed by Hofstede and his colleagues are up to date. The model now comprises six dimensions: power distance, uncertainty avoidance, individualism/collectivism, masculinity/femininity, long/short-term orientation, and indulgence/restraint (see Fig. 3).

The power dimension concerns how a society handles power inequalities among people. If people are comfortable pushing for more equality, the nation has a low power distance; that is, it does not tolerate a large gap between those in authority positions and the rest of society. A nation with higher power distance means the people in that culture accept and expect power to be unequally distributed. A culture high in individualism expects people to take care of only themselves and their immediate family (loosely knit social fabric). Conversely, collectivism means people can expect others to take care of each other (tight knit society). A culture shaped by masculinity is very competitive, informed by achievement, assertiveness, material gains and success. A feminine-oriented society prefers consensus as well as cooperation, caring and quality of life. It also favors equal opportunity for everyone, eschewing rigid role behavior (Hofstede et al. 2010).

Appreciating that the future can never be known, the uncertainty avoidance dimension focuses on whether people should try to control the future or just let things happen. Nations exhibiting high uncertainty avoidance do not tolerate unorthodox behavior and ideas; to this end, they maintain rigid codes of behavior and beliefs. They cannot deal well with vagueness, and need rules and structures. Societies with low uncertainty avoidance are more relaxed in practice, opting instead for a principle-based approach to the future. They are better able to handle anxiety in the face of uncertainty. They are comfortable with changing things. The time perspective dimension pertains to how cultures view time and the importance of past, present and future. A long term perspective focuses on the future, valuing perseverance and adaptability. A short term perspective values the past and traditions, and strives for immediate gratification in the present. Finally, an indulgent culture allows for fun and enjoying life, while restraint stands for a society that suppresses gratification of human drives, opting instead to regulate them (Hofstede et al. 2010).

Notions of responsibility may well be informed by these cultural dimensions. An unequal, individualized, masculine, short-term oriented society that avoids uncertainty and restrains human activities might generate restricted, exclusive ideas of responsibility. Responsibilities would be constrained to the individual in the past/ present, shaped by competition, restraint, societal inequalities, and a low tolerance for uncertainty. Conversely, people living in an equal, collective, consensus-oriented society, which is future oriented, risk tolerant, and indulgent of enjoying life, might have a more inclusive concept of responsibility.

The following discussion applies Hofstede et al.'s (2010) cultural model to consumer perceptions of corporate social responsibility (CSR). This proxy approach is employed because the literature is thin on the topic of how culture influences *consumer* perceptions of responsibility or even consumer responsibility as a distinct concept (Bae and Kim 2013). This is an interesting lacuna, given that culture has a conditioning effect on perception that can help explain consumer behavior (Kastanakis and Voyer 2013).

Regarding socially responsible consumers and CSR, if consumers are socially responsible, they are said to engage in *"conscious and deliberate choice to make certain consumption choices based on personal and moral beliefs"* (Devinney et al. 2006, p. 32). From a totally different stance, Wells et al. (2011) cited scholars who believed that consumers would be socially responsible *if* they held corporations responsible; that is, if consumers can influence corporations' behavior, consumers *must* bear some responsibility for corporations' behavior. Respecting these totally divergent points of view, this section reports on recent work designed especially to link Hofstede's model with how consumer's cultural characteristics affect their interpretation of CSR activities (Bae and Kim 2013). It is used as a proxy to illustrate the usefulness of Hofstede's cultural model to understand consumer perceptions of responsibilities.

Bae and Kim's (2013) comprehensive literature reviewed revealed the following insights. People who naturally accept unequal power distributions (i.e., small consumer versus big corporation) tend to sacrifice their ethical and social responsibility. Also, people who are less likely to accept unequally distributed power place great importance on a corporation's philanthropic responsibility (and are more inclined to buy their products). People who are comfortable with risk (low uncertainty avoidance) tend to privilege their own self-interest and sacrifice social responsibility, leading to unethical consumer decisions (i.e., they risked someone else instead). People with high uncertainty avoidance (cannot cope with unclear situations) expect corporations to engage in socially responsible activities so that consumers *know* they are buying low risk, ethical products. They can then exercise their social responsibility. People with a long-term time perspective (future-oriented) are inclined to support social and ethical responsibilities of everyone, including corporations, relative to those who are short-term past-oriented. The latter lean more towards instant gratification.

Individualistic people favor their own self-interest. For these individuals, CSR activities may be deemed unnecessary because these people privilege self-interest over public interest. Conversely, collectivistic people will call for CSR activities so as to better ensure a protected public interest. In this case, acting responsibly in the marketplace would be predicated on people's expectation of companies engaging in socially desirables actions. Also, the higher the collectivistic propensity, the more likely people are to buy products from socially responsible companies, if price and quality are equal. Finally, high femininity cultures are benevolent and consider it everyone's duty to help society, including corporations. They would place more importance on social responsibility than would those who are masculine (who prefer competition, achievement, and economic success in corporations). Masculine people would perceive themselves as acting responsibly if they supported a successful corporation, regardless of its CSR activities (Bae and Kim 2013).

6.3 Impact of the Consumer Culture on Consumer Perceptions of Responsibility

Culture has a significant impact on the way individuals think about and perceive the world and their responsibilities (Maddux and Yuki 2006). Of paramount concern to this discussion is the fact that we *live in a consumer culture*, and it *too* has a significant impact on how people perceive the world and their responsibilities. A consumer culture is characterized by alienation, dissatisfaction, disenchantment, misplaced self-identity, and false relationships (McGregor 2010).

In more detail, the consumer culture reflects a highly individualized order that is devoid of communal values and is driven by self-interests and material pursuits such that it has intensified people's sense of loss and alienation. Alienation makes it easier to see other human beings as the other; hence, not within one's realm of responsibility. The consumer culture *promises* everything, but never fully delivers. People are permanently disappointed. Dissatisfaction is always one step ahead of satisfaction, with the cycle perpetuating itself. People end up feeling responsible for just themselves (McGregor 2010).

A consumer culture co-opts people's humanity and spirituality. Instead of being socialized to be caring, loving and compassionate, people learn that purchasing things brings a sense of belonging. People end up disenchanted and disillusioned, longing for a sense of identity. In a consumer culture, people create a sense of identity (self) through consuming more, and accumulating different, material objects. This behavior generates a misplaced identity and narrow connotations of responsibility for who and what. In a consumer culture, people relentlessly seek self-fulfillment and self-identity through what they consume instead of through relationships with others. But this misguided behavior creates false relationships because a consumer culture rejects the relationships between the individual and the collective, meaning people end up paying little attention to others' working conditions or the environment. They are responsible only to themselves (McGregor 2010).

Henry (2010) affirmed that the emergence of consumer affluence, and a shift from the collective to individual thinking, along with the ideas of the free market, consumer choice, and consumer sovereignty, are "tightly enmeshed with contemporary consumerism" (p. 670). In today's society, the logic of the market (focused on transactions) prevails over the logic of community (focused on caring and sharing). Consequently, the role of and need for moral responsibility in a disconnected market is questionable. People become characterized as "disconnected mainstream consumers" and a "disinterested body of mainstream consumers" (p. 671). Henry noted that consumers have become distrustful, cynical, apathetic, and are seen as part of the problem because they "shirk their duty to curb irresponsible consumption" (p. 171). Consumers' inaction and disengagement leads others to conclude that they "are endorsing and propagating a wasteful and unethical consumer culture" (p. 671). In light of this critique, his study focused on how mainstream consumers think about their responsibilities, concluding that the individualistic consumer lives on in the twenty-first century. Henry surmised that understanding the ideology of consumerism helps isolate the mechanisms that mute or amplify a consumer's sense of responsibility.

7 Conclusion

This contribution was an inaugural attempt to conceptualize *consumer perceptions of responsibility*. The introduction made the case for this emergent but under researched phenomenon of consumers' self-ascribed sense of social responsibility. After teasing out the philosophical concept of responsibility and the basic tenets of consumer perception theory, they were linked together for new insights into how this theory can inform understandings of consumer perceptions of responsibility. The scarce but growing body of literature on consumer perceptions of responsibilities was summarized, ending with a discussion of how culture informs consumer perceptions of responsibilities.

The immense, pervasive power of the consumer culture makes it necessary that we better understand how people perceive responsibility in their consumer role. Their seeming lack of responsibility, in concert with that of other stakeholders, is threatening the very existence of the human species, which is the steward and guardian of all other species and the earth itself. Scholars and practitioners are challenged to champion the evolution of the concept of *consumer perceptions of responsibilities*, with this contribution a sincere and genuine attempt to scaffold and jump start this political, philosophical, theoretical, and practical exercise.

References

Bae, J., & Kim, S. (2013). The influence of cultural aspects on public perception of the importance of CSR activity and purchase intention in Korea. *Asian Journal of Communication, 23*(1), 68–85.

Bemporad, R., Hebard, A., & Bressler, D. (2013). *Rethinking consumption: Consumers and the future of sustainability*. Toronto, ON: Global Scan. Retrieved from http://www.globescan.com/component/edocman/?task=document.viewdoc&id=51&Itemid=0

Caruana, R., & Crane, A. (2008). Constructing consumer responsibility: Exploring the role of corporate communications. *Organization Studies, 29*(12), 1495–1519.

Ciccarelli, S. K., & White, J. N. (2009). *Psychology* (2nd ed.). Essex: Pearson Education.

Cone Communications. (2013). *Cone communications/echo global CSR study*. Boston, MA: Author.

Devinney, T. M., Auger, P., Eckhardt, G., & Birtchnell, T. (2006). The other CSR: Consumer social responsibility. *Stanford Social Innovation Review, 4*(3), 30–37.

Ellen, P. S., Weiner, J. L., & Cobb-Walgren, C. (1991). The role of perceived consumer expectations in motivating environmentally conscious behaviors. *Journal of Public Policy and Marketing, 10*(2), 102–117.

Gyekye, K. (1992). Person and community in African thought. In K. Wiredu & K. Gyekye (Eds.), *Person and community: Ghanaian philosophical studies*. Washington, DC: Council for Research in Values and Philosophy.

Hanna, H., Wozniak, R., & Hanna, M. (2013). *Consumer behaviour*. Dubuque, IA: Kendall Hunt.

Henry, P. C. (2010). How mainstream consumers think about consumer rights and responsibilities. *Journal of Consumer Research, 37*(4), 670–687.

Hofstede, G., Hofstede, G. J., & Minkov, M. (2010). *Cultures and organizations: Software of the mind* (3rd ed.). New York, NY: McGraw-Hill.

Kastanakis, M. N., & Voyer, B. G. (2013). The effect of culture on perception and cognition: A conceptual framework. *Journal of Business Research, 67*(4), 425–433.

Kaufmann, F. (2015). Responsibility. In F. Kaufmann (Ed.), *Online new world encyclopedia*. St. Paul, MN: Paragon House Publishers. Accessed December 30, 2015, retrieved from http://www.newworldencyclopedia.org/entry/Responsibility

Lenk, H. (2006). What is responsibility? *Philosophy Now, 56*. Accessed December 30, 2015, from https://philosophynow.org/issues/56/What_is_Responsibility

Linley, P. A., & Maltby, J. (2009). Personal responsibility. In S. J. Lopez (Ed.), *The encyclopedia of positive psychology* (pp. 685–689). Hoboken, NJ: Blackwell.

Luchs, M. G., & Miller, R. A. (2015). Consumer responsibility for sustainable consumption. In L. Reisch & J. Thøgersen (Eds.), *Handbook on research for sustainable consumption* (pp. 254–267). Northampton, MA: Edward Elgar.

Luchs, M. G., Phipps, M., & Hill, T. (2015). Exploring consumer responsibility for sustainable consumption. *Journal of Marketing Management, 31*(13–14), 1441–1479.

Maddux, W. W., & Yuki, M. (2006). The 'ripple effect': Cultural differences in perceptions of consequences of events. *Personality and Social Psychology Bulletin, 32*(5), 669–683.

McGregor, S. L. T. (2010). *Consumer moral leadership*. Dordrecht: Sense Publishers.

Menkiti, I. A. (1984). Person and community in African traditional thought. In R. Wright (Ed.), *African philosophy: An introduction* (pp. 171–182). Lanham, MD: University Press of America.

Middlemiss, L. (2010). Reframing individual responsibility for sustainable consumption. *Environmental Values, 19*(2), 147–167.

Müller, T., Gwozdz, W., & Reisch, L. A. (2014, July). Responsibility attribution and consumer behaviour in light of the Bangladesh factory collapse. In *Proceedings of the 39th annual macromarketing conference* (pp. 892–903). Berlin: The Macromarketing Society.

Neilsen Company. (2014, June). *Doing well by doing good*. New York, NY: Author.

Planned Success Institute. (2002). *Accountability vs. responsibility*. Borrego Springs, CA: Author.

Portilho, F. (2010). Self-attribution of responsibility: Consumers of organic foods in a certified street market in Rio de Janeiro, Brazil. *Etnográfica, 14*(3), 549–565.

Schwartz, S. H. (1977). Normative explanations of altruism. In L. Berkowitz (Ed.), *Advances in experimental psychology* (pp. 222–275). New York, NY: Academic Press.

Sizoo, E. (Ed.). (2010). *Responsibility and cultures of the world* (C. L. Mayer, Trans.). Brussels: Peter Lang.

Smiley, M. (2010). Collective responsibility. In E. N. Zalta (Ed.), *Stanford encyclopedia of philosophy*. Stanford, CA: Stanford University. Accessed December 30, 2015, retrieved from http://plato.stanford.edu/entries/collective-responsibility/

Stancu, C. (2013). *Meaning and practices regarding the concept of 'responsible consumer' in the view of Romanian consumers* (Master's thesis, Aarhus University, Romania). Accessed December 30, 2015, retrieved from http://pure.au.dk/portal-asb-student/files/39694363/ Meaning_and_practices_regarding_the_concept_of_responsible_consumer_in_the_view_of_ the_Romanian_consumers.pdf

Straker, D. (2015). *Frame of reference*. Accessed December 30, 2015, retrieved from the Changing Minds website http://changingminds.org/explanations/models/frame_of_reference.htm

Timpe, K. (ca. 2004). Free will. In J. Fieser & B. Dowden (Eds.), *The internet encyclopedia of philosophy*. Martin, TN: University of Tennessee at Martin. Accessed December 30, 2015, retrieved from http://www.iep.utm.edu/freewill/#H3

Turchin, V. (1991). Determinism vs. freedom. In F. Heylighen, C. Joslyn, & V. Turchin (Eds.), *Principia cybernetica web*. Brussels: Principia Cybernetica. Accessed December 30, 2015, retrieved from http://pespmc1.vub.ac.be/FREEDOM.html

Wells, V. K., Ponting, C., & Peattie, K. (2011). Behaviour and climate change: Consumer perceptions of responsibility. *Journal of Marketing Management, 27*(7–8), 808–833.

Williams, G. D. (ca. 2005). Responsibility. In J. Fieser & B. Dowden (Eds.), *The internet encyclopedia of philosophy*. Martin, TN: University of Tennessee at Martin. Accessed December 30, 2015, retrieved from http://www.iep.utm.edu/responsi/

Worldwide, H. (2014). *The new consumer and the sharing economy*. New York, NY: Author.

Printed by Printforce, the Netherlands